TENNESSEE TRAGEDIES

TENNESSEE TRAGEDIES

Natural, Technological, and Societal Disasters in the Volunteer State

Allen R. Coggins

THE UNIVERSITY OF TENNESSEE PRESS

KNOXVILLE

The paper in this book meets the requirements of American National Standards Institute / National Information Standards Organization specification Z39.48–1992 (Permanence of Paper). It contains 30 percent post-consumer waste and is certified by the Forest Stewardship Council.

Library of Congress Cataloging-in-Publication Data

Coggins, Allen R.
Tennessee tragedies: natural, technological, and societal disasters in the Volunteer State / Allen R. Coggins. — 1st ed.
    p. cm.
Includes bibliographical references and index.
ISBN-13: 978-1-57233-841-8 (pbk.)
ISBN-10: 1-57233-841-5 (pbk.)
 1. Tennessee—History—Miscellanea.
 2. Disasters—Tennessee
 I. Title.

F436.6.C64 2011
976.8—dc23
2011033170

This book is lovingly dedicated to my wife, Barbara, the library and sometimes road-trip widow who has been supportive, patient, and actively involved in its development. She has also stood by me through a few personal life crises. She is my rock.

Contents

Part 3. Societal Disasters

ILLUSTRATIONS

Figures

Maps

ACKNOWLEDGMENTS

As a natural hazards planner with the Tennessee Emergency Management Agency (TEMA) in the mid-1980s, I was tasked with developing a history of state disasters for the Tennessee Emergency Management Plan. I quickly realized that no single source of such data existed. There was not even a list of major events, let alone the lesser-known but still poignant tragedies that I have since chronicled in this work. That laborious task grew into an obsession that has now spanned over two and a half decades of days off, weekends, and weeknights spent in libraries, archives, government offices, living rooms, and front porches, from Reelfoot Lake to Copper Hill, from Memphis to Bristol. First came a list, a chronological tabulation of every disaster and tragic account that I could find. Then came the gathering and the interpretation of the details of each event. Obviously, the development of such a database is a never-ending process. New disasters occur, and each foray into some obscure document, photo, or conversation can uncover still another forgotten or as yet undocumented tragedy. I take no small degree of pride in knowing that in writing this book I have contributed to the preservation of historical data that might otherwise have passed into obscurity.

Many individuals and institutions have assisted in the compilation of this material. The Tennessee State Library and Archives and the Tennessee Emergency Management Agency in Nashville; the McClung Special Collections and the University of Tennessee Library in Knoxville; the Memphis, Chattanooga, Nashville, and Knoxville public libraries; and many other town and county libraries and historical societies were all treasuries of information and opportunity. My biggest barrier was time: there was never enough of it. And, it seemed that the final announcement that "the library will be closing in fifteen minutes" was always heard just as I was discovering a new gem of information that sent me scurrying to the copy machine or checkout desk.

I am grateful to my friend and colleague Linda Murawski, a fellow emergency management specialist and technical consultant. I am greatly indebted to Nina Lovel, a research and information coordinator at Georgia Northwestern Technical College who knows the *Chicago Manual of Style* and the art and science of copyediting so much better than I. And I am especially grateful to my editor, Thomas Wells, and others at the University of Tennessee Press for their magic in bringing it all together.

Finally, there are the following individuals who assisted to greater or lesser extents with my journey to completion of this work: Bobby Alford, Ashley Amezcua, Andy and Jo Ann Anderson, Eddie Archer, David Babelay, Owen Bailey, Lyle Bentley, Ellen Bradbury, Bill Brimm, Mike Browning, Don Bruce, Ralph Burris, Tolly Carter, James Castro, Joe Clayton, Christy Carter, Steve Cotham, Tom Durham, Bob Duncan, Albert Dunn, Arthur Echternacht, Jane Ferrel, Nick Fielder, Craig Fischer, Elaine Foust, Todd Groce, Charles Green, Edwin Frank, Pat Guffey, Wayne Hamberger, Dianne Hansler, Mary Helms, Cherel Henderson, Jerry Herndon, Frank Johnson, James Jones, David Logsdon, Anne Lovell, Ned Luther, Amy Maclin, Ann Metzger, Linda Monk, Avagene Moore, Jimmy Moore, Jeffrey Munsey, Gail Palmer, Jeff Piatt, Sally Polhemus, Donald Porter, Nancy Proctor, George Plumlee, Suzette Rainey, Jim Reese, Shane Rhyme, Gail Rindler, Angela Self, Donna Sharp, Lou Sidell, Nancy Sidell, Pam Smith, Ray Smith, Jeanette Stevens, Lacy Suiter, Marianne Wanamaker, and Linda Waters.

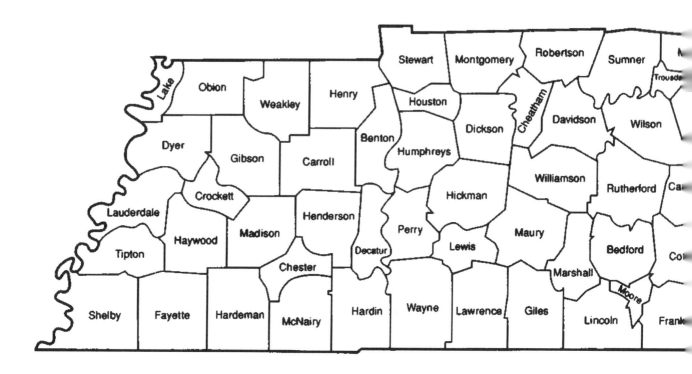

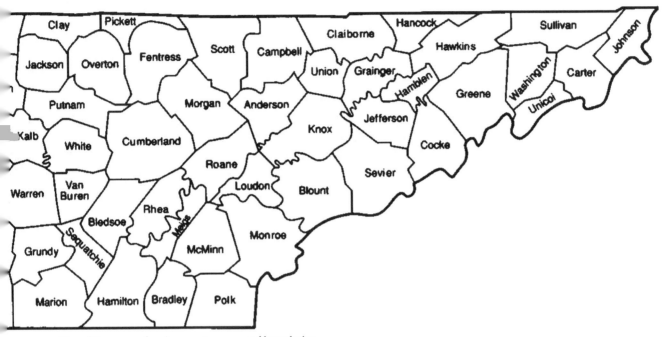

Map of Tennessee showing county names and boundaries.

INTRODUCTION

We are shut up in the head of the entry with a little of air and the bad air is closing in on us fast and it is now about 12: o'clock. Dear Ellen, I have to leave you in bad condition. But dear wife set your trust in the Lord to help you raise my little children. Ellen take care of my little darling Lily. Ellen, little Elbert said that he has trusted in the Lord. Chas. Wood says that he was [saved] if he never lives to see the out[side] again he would meet his mother in heaven. If we never live to get out we are not hurt but only perished for air. There is but a few of us here and I don't know where the other men is. Elbert said for you all to meet him in heaven. All the children meet with us both.

—Jacob L. Vowell to his family, written during the Fraterville Mine disaster of December 9, 1911

Our Fascination with Tragedies

There is something of the macabre in nearly all of us, something that compels us to slow down and gawk as we approach the scene of a traffic accident or other such incident. Or perhaps it is that newspaper account that catches our attention and arouses our imagination. Sometimes a breaking news story on television or a phone call, text message, or email from a relative or co-worker will entice us to stop and turn our attention to a tragedy or disaster that is unfolding.

Some psychologists suggest that our fascination with disasters or tragedies is a need for excitement that may be gained vicariously, and hence safely, through the misfortunes of others. Perhaps it is a celebration of "save by the grace of God, there go I." Then again, according to Frances Kennett, "It is possible that people are drawn to and often obsessed with disaster in the way that they can be drawn to pornography. Sex and death are taboos in our society, and death is perhaps the greater unmentionable. There is a deep-seated fear of death in most people, and disasters are among the only respectable ways that people can indulge their curiosity."[1]

The usual immediate human reactions to disasters and violence are shock, fear, sorrow, rage, and denial. The denial may be immediate in situations in which we are personally involved, or it may manifest itself long after the event has taken place. Examples of violence and tragedy in the human experience can be found throughout history. For historic-era Native American tribes it was constant tension with European settlers. The Old World epidemic diseases they unleashed, along with the settlers' obsession with possessing and monopolizing land, drove the Indians farther and farther west. There they came into contact and conflict with other tribes, resulting in fighting, fleeing, and also a great deal of assimilation. As the old adage goes, when two cultures meet, they will generally bleed and breed.

The Tennessee frontier was the wilderness beyond the pioneer farmstead. As settlements expanded, built environments began to be damaged and destroyed by acts of nature, accidents, and the overt and covert acts of mankind. Nonetheless, the Tennessee pioneers kept building, rebuilding, subduing the wilderness, and attempting to one-up Mother Nature.

Violence, in forms of riots and mob lynchings as well as individual acts of brutality, were much more common in frontier times, when lawmen could not—or would not—control the offenders. In those times, good men often rose to the occasion in the name of justice. Violence was also in the psyche of many whites from the Civil War–Reconstruction era forward. It persisted, albeit to a lesser extent, into the mid-1900s. America has a tradition of vigilantism: this unbridled behavior that was often rampant in our seedy past will become very clear through the events in this book. We will look at the many natural, technological, and societal horrors that have shaped our destiny and written our history, often in blood.

Whatever it is that draws our attention to disasters and tragedies and sometimes even invites our participation, it is a primeval emotion. It beckons for our attention and stirs our passion. Newspaper headlines, supermarket tabloid covers, movie promotional posters, and television programming guides all demonstrate what we've known for years: violence captures the imagination. It is also a strong motivator that can be used literally and subliminally to manipulate our minds, and as an economic incentive to market and vend products and services.

Today, violence has found new forms of expression in terrorist bombings, airline assaults, drug deals gone bad, and children shooting children in our schools. As we enter the end of the first decade of the twenty-first century, we face new challenges, including an uncertain economy. Where we will go from here we can but guess, because history can only be judged from afar, and we are not yet far enough removed from current events.

Definitions, Responses, and Reactions

Disasters, by definition, are events that overwhelm the response capabilities of individuals or local, county, or state governments. However, the term "disaster" can also be quite subjective. In this book it will be used to define events that have caused great destruction and/or resulted in single or multiple deaths and/or injuries. The reason for this broad definition is that not all disasters kill or maim and not all cause wide-scale destruction. Slow-rise floods and severe winter storms have impacted broad areas and caused devastating effects through the years; however, unlike flash floods and structure fires, they occur slowly enough that actions can be taken to avoid or lessen their impact. Hence, they may cause few, if any, deaths or injuries.

Emergencies are events of lesser magnitude than disasters. They may be devastating to the individual or individuals involved, but they do not affect large areas or whole populations in the same way as do major tornadoes, conflagrations, or epidemics. The term "tragedy" is simply a more descriptive term that may be applied to many types of events; however, the word suggests more of an element of grief or sorrow. For example, events that involve death or injury are more tragic than are structure failures or damaging floods that only result in property damage. Accidents are unintentional events that may result in bodily injury, death, and destruction of property and/or cause environmental impacts.

Conversely, epidemic diseases have resulted in hundreds of thousands of deaths with little or no impact on property, infrastructure, or even the natural environment. Dr. J. S. Chambers writes, "Epidemics have ever been one of the greatest tragedies of the human race. Terror has preceded, horror has accompanied and sorrow and want have followed in their wake. Civilizations have fallen into decay; man's very existence has been threatened. Not even war has equaled pestilence as a destroyer of human life. Man has survived by his wits and his excess fertility."[2] Between slow-rise flooding and epidemics, Tennesseans have endured countless natural, technological, and societal disasters that have resulted in varying degrees of carnage, destruction, or both.

Today, when an emergency strikes, we dial 911 to request immediate assistance from a local fire department, law enforcement agency, or ambulance service. The dispatcher contacts the applicable agency, and they respond to the scene. We are fortunate to have emergency response personnel employed to handle many types of tragedies and disasters. Most of them now embrace the "Incident Command System," which enables first responders to provide coordinated, critical, and time-sensitive actions during major life-and-death situations. These dedicated individuals, whether paid or volunteer, are generally well trained, well equipped, and willing to put their lives on the line for the greater good.

When a disaster strikes, all bets are off. In the past, individuals, families, neighbors, or even strangers responded to emergencies or disasters with whatever meager resources were at hand. People within communities, neighborhoods, churches, or social and fraternal organizations supported one another. Such reciprocity was insurance for a time in the future when others might need help. Over time, individuals and groups developed better skills, stamina, and willingness and ability to respond, but there was still a lack of physical resources with which to do so. As communities grew, eventually a local constable or sheriff was hired and deputies and posses were assembled when warranted. There were volunteer and paid firefighters and law enforcement officers. The state militia (later called the National Guard) could be activated in times of crisis. The Red Cross, Salvation Army, and other such quasi-government or private organizations could be present at the site of a disaster within hours. As the American Red Cross has so aptly stated, "Help Can't Wait." However, as is too often the case, the first responders to disasters are usually the victims themselves.

Classifying Disasters and Tragedies

Disasters and tragedies may be divided into three broad categories as well as combinations thereof. Some are natural events, so-called acts of nature or acts of God, and include floods, tornadoes, droughts and heat waves, severe winters, wildland fires, and epidemics. Others are technological, which include explosions, structure fires, structure failures, and industrial and transportation accidents. The third category encompasses societal incidents, including riots, strikes, lynchings, feuds, and hate crimes. The latter include the activities of the Ku Klux Klan, Night Riders, Whitecaps, and warring political factions, as well as spontaneous mob violence. The massacre of native peoples, assassinations, and mass murders also fall within this grouping.

However, these three basic categories are rudimentary at best. A disaster can be a combination of these categories by compounding events leading up to it. For example, a cloudburst or sudden and extreme rainstorm over the upper reaches of a small watershed (the geographic area drained by a stream and its tributaries) could lead to the breach of a downstream dam. The synergistic effects of heavier than normal rain at a time when a reservoir was already filled to capacity could cause more damage than a comparable flood or a dam break could produce independently. Hence we have a flood plus a structure failure: a combined natural and technological disaster.

The chronology in this book provides a brief description of over nine hundred disasters, tragedies, and other events that have occurred across the state over the past two and a half centuries. The more significant events, shown in boldface, list the pages where they are discussed in detail in the book. Readers interested in an event described in the chronology but not detailed in a separate article may obtain more information by using the date and place of the occurrence to search for more details. This expanded information may be found in books, other historical documents, or in past issues of local and regional newspapers preserved on microfilm and stored in libraries. Because many news agencies have been around since the early 1800s, such data is readily available in city, university, state, and historical society libraries and archives.

Reference librarians and historians can assist readers in finding accounts of incidents, particularly if provided with a date, topic, and location. Additional references also appear at the end of each article. Most of the information compiled in this book was gleaned from original documents, state and local histories, government records, and personal interviews. Some of the informants actually experienced the disasters or tragedies, while others related secondhand accounts from relatives or acquaintances.

Perspective on Emergencies, Disasters, and Tragedies

Most of these events occurred between the early 1800s and the present, but a few of them predate statehood (1796). The earliest historic event recorded in this book is a great flood that is said to have occurred on the Mississippi River in the spring of 1543. However, reference has also been made to three scientifically confirmed catastrophes—meteor-impact events—that occurred even earlier than that, in the territory that was to become Tennessee. Because they predate human existence on our planet by tens to hundreds of millions of years, one might question whether they should be classified as disasters.

Not all of the events chronicled here are on the scale of disasters. As already pointed out, they might better be described as tragedies or emergencies, but they are of interest nonetheless. These events garnered much attention at the time they occurred and remained strongly in the collective memories of those who experienced them. However, with the passage of time, they are now long forgotten save by a few. Two examples illustrate this point.

The first is the Great Epizootic of 1872. Called simply a "horse disease," this epizootic erupted in the fall of that year. We now know that it was a form of equine influenza that affected almost 100 percent of horses and mules exposed to it. After several weeks, it would subside in one area and arise again in another. Its mortality rate was fairly low, averaging 1 to 2 percent of infected animals, but it rendered the animals useless until it had run its course. Because it occurred at a time when horse transportation was a necessity, it virtually paralyzed both the state and the national economy. The outbreak was even blamed for contributing to the onset of the great nationwide economic panic of 1873–75.

The second example, an ecological disaster, was the demise of the American chestnut (*Castanea dentata*). The loss of this valuable tree was caused by a fungus, *Cryphonectria parasitica* (formerly called *Endothia parasitica*), which was accidentally introduced into the United States on Oriental chestnut stock in the early 1900s. It quickly spread into the eastern forests, past the Mississippi River to the edge of the Great Plains, north to Canada, and south to the Atlantic and Gulf coasts. It is estimated that this destructive blight killed some 3.5 billion chestnut trees in the Eastern United States. This is equivalent to a 9 million acre stand of trees. The extirpation of this species had wide-ranging consequences for wildlife dependent upon hard mast crops such as chestnuts, acorns, beech nuts, pecans, and hickory nuts. The animals most affected included bears, turkeys, squirrels, and even domestic stock such as hogs. Chestnuts were likewise a significant cash crop to many in the Appalachian states. The nuts were gathered by mega-bushels in Tennessee and then sold or traded locally in country stores and city markets from Mountain City to Memphis. Many Tennessee farmers, especially in the eastern end of the state, depended upon the fall crop of chestnuts to fatten their hogs before harvest. The value of chestnut timber, used for a great variety of purposes from furniture to the construction of homes and factories, was incalculable. Within three decades of the close of the nineteenth century, the chestnut was virtually extinct. At present, we are also losing our native dogwoods and hemlocks to exotic diseases.

Would a twenty-first-century individual consider these events disasters? Granted they lack the flare of twenty-four-hour news coverage and a contemporary time frame, but their impact on the landscape and people of the late-eighteenth and early-twentieth centuries is undeniable. These two examples well illustrate the wide range of events that are termed disasters and tragedies. Tennessee's history is littered with curious and devastating incidents of the macabre, and readers will quickly come to the conclusion that the modernization of Tennessee as the frontiers of the 1800s turned into the industrial cities of the twenty-first century did not always lessen the impact of a sudden disaster.

Causes of Injuries and Deaths in Disasters

Natural, technological, and societal disasters have caused deaths, injuries, and suffering as well as economic and ecological impacts. Natural disasters affect people and their built environments through extremes of heat and cold, ice and snow, lightning, strong winds, landslides, earthquakes, heavy precipitation, floods, fires, epidemics, and pandemics. Technological disasters—that is, transportation, mining, and industrial accidents—are the result of road, rail, and waterway obstructions; equipment defects; operating negligence; explosions, fires, and hazardous materials incidents; structure failures (a consequence of poor engineering, construction, and maintenance); and many still-undetermined phenomena. Societal disasters can generally be blamed on racial conflicts, hate crimes, mob violence, malicious acts, hazardous working conditions, inadequate compensation and benefits leading to labor conflicts, political power struggles, and poor economic conditions. Specific examples of these factors that caused death, injury, property damage and environmental problems are discussed in greater detail under individual disaster headings.

According to the Centers for Disease Control and Prevention (CDC), accidents often occur during, or as the result of, disasters and are the fifth leading cause of death in the United States. The other four are heart disease, cancer, stroke, and chronic lower respiratory diseases, in that order.[3] The major causes of deaths have changed through the years as life expectancy has increased and infant death rates have decreased. In earlier times, fewer people lived long enough to contract chronic heart diseases and cancer, suffer strokes, and develop respiratory maladies. Of course, there were respiratory ailments such as black lung disease, brown lung disease, and other illnesses caused by acute and chronic

occupational exposures to hazardous materials. Conversely, factors that contribute to earlier death such as obesity, sedimentary lifestyles, and chemical food additives and preservatives were not yet the chronic health problems that they are today. Deaths in the 1700s, 1800s, and even the early 1900s were more likely to be caused by common infections, trauma (such as industrial and other occupational injuries), and diseases for which we now have preventative measures and cures.

Death has often been instantaneous, or nearly so, for victims of explosions, tornadoes, and transportation accidents. This was indeed merciful in cases where there was no hope of recovery and no chance for a decent quality of life should the victim survive. Unfortunately, death has been agonizingly slow and painful for others. This was certainly the case for victims of severe burns and other traumas in the days before pain-killing drugs and sophisticated medical treatments. The actual cause of death would vary, depending on the type of hazard or disaster. For those who have lingered at the edge of death for minutes, hours, or days, it would have seemed like an eternity. There were the victims of poisoning, wounds that resulted in gas gangrene, or diseases such as smallpox, cholera, or yellow fever. For some, such as victims of lynching or mob violence who were tortured beyond any hope of recovery and had no possible means of escaping their tormentors, death surely could not have come quickly enough.

Have you ever wondered how you will die? And have you ever wondered which would be the most and least painful ways of dying? (These questions do not refer to suicide, of course, but to accidental death or disease.) As already mentioned, a violent and sudden death is merciful and can be nearly painless. One could also slip into an unconscious state from which he or she would never awake—often referred to as dying in one's sleep. Some individuals are now placed in barbiturate-induced comas while on medical life-support systems. They eventually waste away or have the proverbial plug pulled. Freezing to death and exsanguination (i.e., bleeding to death) are said to be less painful ways of passing away. Drowning, too, is reputed to be rather euphoric, at least after one stops struggling and gives up.

Another less painful way to die, perhaps, is through asphyxiation, one of the major causes of death in coal mine accidents in which victims were not so close to the explosion as to be blown to bits, burned, or had their lungs seared by a flash fire. These were miners who attempted to escape the toxic atmospheres after an explosion by moving farther into the mine, away from the bad air, and barricading themselves in a room or passage to await possible rescue. A deadly gas called afterdamp or firedamp can accumulate rapidly in the confined passages of a mine, burning off oxygen and building up carbon monoxide, carbon dioxide, hydrogen sulfide, nitrogen, and other toxic trace gases. The slow breathing of afterdamp does not cause gagging or convulsions; rather, it induces a drowsy, euphoric sensation. As the brain is deprived of oxygen, the victim will simply fall asleep, slip into a coma, and never regain consciousness.

The condition just described is suggested by notes found on the bodies of East Tennessee mine disaster victims in 1902 and 1911. The men who survived initial mine explosions perished because they were too far from the entrance and were prevented by deadly gases from escaping or being rescued. The physiological effects of asphyxiation explain why the letters of the dying men were free of expressions of fear, panic, and anxiety during the last hours and minutes of their ordeals. Most of the miners were also fundamentalist and fatalistic in their religious beliefs and just accepted the inevitable, writing wills and goodbyes to their loved ones. Finally, they drifted into a death sleep. The tone and wording of some of the written messages seem to suggest that the miners may also have experienced spiritual revelations or consoling hallucinations in their final hours and minutes.

Mitigation and Legislation: Avoiding or Lessening the Effects of Disasters

The impact of disasters on humankind has been staggering in terms of deaths, injuries, suffering, and economic losses. Although some hazards such as tornadoes, earthquakes, droughts, and other severe weather events may never be prevented, there are actions that may be taken to prepare for or lessen their effects. Mitigation is a far superior and a less costly long-term strategy. Unfortunately, many factors have slowed our efforts to mitigate hazards, chief among which are lack of appropriate legislation and capital funding.

Through the years there have been laws, codes, regulations, and standards enacted to protect us from various hazards and threats. Unfortunately, they have not always been properly and impartially enforced. It is also regrettable that it usually takes a disaster to draw our attention to a critical vulnerability. Even then, we have a narrow window of opportunity in which to capitalize on learning from the problem and to fund and implement solutions. Public concern and political action may be strong in the wake of a crisis, but in time sentiments wane and attention turns elsewhere. Unfortunately, there are also situations that individuals may not want mitigated for personal or economic motives. One would think that the effects of hurricanes on the populations and infrastructure of the Atlantic and Gulf coasts would discourage rebuilding along beach fronts. (The same is true of rebuilding within floodplains.) What's more, one would think it prudent that the state or federal government forbid such actions for which taxpayers are responsible time and time again. In spite of this, the allure of sun, sand, and surf along coastal areas seems to far outweigh the potentially deadly and disastrous alternatives. In short, people are willing to accept some degree of risk, often in part because they have convinced themselves that disasters cannot happen where they live, they cannot happen to them, or they won't happen again.

Better examples of prevention legislation specifically concern technological or industrial disasters. Almost a thousand steamboats built between 1811 and 1856 were destroyed by explosions, fires, collisions, snags, and other miscellaneous channel obstructions on the western waters, which at that time referred to the Ohio, Cumberland, Tennessee, and lower Mississippi rivers. As early as 1824 Congress passed an "Act to Improve Navigation on the Ohio and Mississippi Rivers." In 1830 Congress considered a resolution to collect information concerning steamboat accidents and soon passed laws requiring the licensing of boats. This included a requirement that each boat's official name and home port be painted on its starboard and port sides. Owners or companies were also assessed a monthly fee of twenty cents for each crewman on commercial vessels for a general hospital fund.[4] An Interstate Steamboat Commerce Commission was likewise established in 1838 to regulate riverboat traffic; however, the activities of this commission were inadequate, and it wasn't until the passage of the *Steamboat Act of 1852* that the destruction and carnage of riverboat accidents finally began to diminish. In the latter 1800s, government regulations, inspections, and dredging made travel much safer on commercially navigable rivers.[5]

Another well-known example of prevention legislation involved the coal mining industry. The conditions under which Tennessee coal miners toiled varied significantly among companies and mines in the early 1800s. Men were employed to ensure proper ventilation, test for and eliminate toxic or explosive gases, spray to reduce coal dust, and maintain equipment; however, personal safety was the obligation of the individual. Each miner was responsible for installing wooden supports to prevent roof falls in the area where he was working. Unfortunately, because miners were paid for the volume of coal delivered to the surface rather than by the hours

worked, they sometimes waited too long before installing the support timbers. Such hesitation often resulted in cave-ins causing injuries and frequently death. Moreover, production quotas, set by tyrannical mine bosses, were such that safety was usually the last thing on anyone's mind. On December 20, 1859, the state's first major mine disaster occurred in the Nelson Mine in Rhea County. According to state mine inspectors, the mine owners had been warned about excessive methane gas in this mine but failed to take proper precautions to eliminate it. As a result, twenty-eight men and sixteen mules died in the mine that day. The state mine inspector's report of the incident again called for legislation that was vitally needed to regulate the operation of gaseous coal mines in Tennessee.[6] However, a formal mine inspection act was not passed until 1881, and by that time a number of mining disasters had struck Tennessee and the eastern United States.[7]

In our time, many federal, state, and local government agencies have established safety policies designed to prevent death, injury, and destruction and to provide for environmental protection. These include regulations for railroads, highways, waterways, airlines, mines, and industrial operations. Government also regulates fire safety, floodplain management, building codes, zoning ordinances, public health and welfare, law enforcement, and hazardous materials handling, as well as oversees financial operations and commerce. The National Weather Service (NWS) monitors severe weather conditions and issues advisories, alerts, and "watches and warnings" when needed. In many ways, we now live in a safer and more comfortable world. Despite all diligent preparedness, however, disasters continue to occur and require ongoing readiness, response, and recovery.

The Impact of Disasters

Because large numbers of people have died in all manner of disasters and tragedies, oftentimes instantly, the pages of history tend to record the casualties rather sensationally.

However, the relative impact of disasters as major destroyers of life is deceptive. Everyday accidents and chronic diseases such as dysentery, malaria, pneumonia, and influenza are much more prevalent and persistent as causes of death, injury, and suffering. Airline, railroad, and even bus accidents are treated differently by the news media than are most automobile accidents—this in spite of the fact that death rates per million passenger miles is much higher for automobiles and motorcycles than for any other method of transportation. It is the relatively large number of people simultaneously killed in a single airline crash, as opposed to the much larger number of people who die annually in car crashes, that garners the attention of the media and the public.

Similarly, while mining disasters that resulted in the deaths of many were widely recorded and reported over decades, most miners have actually died one or two at a time from roof falls, injuries from heavy equipment, electrocution, and health-related factors. After working for years in dank and dusty mines with poor air circulation, many of them perished from black lung disease, pneumoconiosis, emphysema, or other such chronic respiratory ailments.

Likewise, more deaths from non-epidemic diseases, such as malaria and pneumonia, or infections resulting from everyday injuries cause more deaths and suffering than epidemics, pandemics, and all forms of disasters on an annual basis. This was particularly true before the development of antibiotics and the advent of more stringent public-health strategies. It is well documented that far more people died from diseases and infections than from bullets and bayonets on our country's battlefields, especially between 1775 and 1918.[8] Moreover, until the passage of effective federal, state, and local health and safety regulations and more stringent enforcement, most day laborers died one or two at a time from injuries or chronic ailments.

In the presence of this overall perspective, it appears that disasters are simply tragic anomalies. Neverthe-less, reports of epidemics, tornadoes, mine explosions, hazardous material incidents, and airline crashes have and always will overwhelm our senses and capture our imaginations. Because of their more immediate shock and awe, they will continue to be headline news.

Disasters and the Modern Built Environment

It is important to note that disasters are relatively recent occurrences, at least in respect to geologic time, and they are termed disasters because they now occur within our built environments. Until humans began living in floodplains and establishing permanent structures thousands of years ago there were no flood disasters or structure fires. When rivers flooded, vast quantities of earth, rock, and vegetation were merely washed downstream. Lightning ignited woodland and grassland fires, initiating a natural serial stages of succession that would eventually culminate in a new forest. Such were the dynamics and balances of our living planet. However, with the rise of more densely populated areas, disasters became a reality in very human terms.

A perfect example of this is the 1811 and 1812 earthquakes that occurred along the New Madrid fault lines, which run parallel to the Mississippi River Valley, with a branch extending into northwest Tennessee. These seismic events created dramatic yet only temporary changes in the natural landscape. In fact, now, nearly two centuries later, the untrained eye can hardly discern any evidence of the quakes. While some boatmen on western waters lost their keelboats, their cargos, and their lives, there simply wasn't enough of a population on which the disaster could feed. Native Americans, traders, and settlers were self-sufficient and resilient. Such a hardy lot could accept their fate, recognize the event as an act of God, and continue going about the important business of taming the wilderness and peopling a new nation. Today, a quake of even lesser magnitude along the New Madrid fault line could be truly catastrophic. It might serve one well to remember the words long attributed to the historian Will Durant: "Civilization exists by geological consent, subject to change without notice."

Tennessee's Greatest Disaster?

What is the worst disaster ever to occur in Tennessee? That is a challenging question since the terms "worst" and "disaster" are both quite subjective. In regard to loss of life, the aforementioned devastation of Native American populations by epidemic diseases, among other things, beginning with first European contact, surely ranks among the worst tragedies in Tennessee's history. Whole Cherokee villages were ravaged by smallpox, measles, mumps, and other communicable diseases beginning in the early 1700s. As is discussed later under "Epidemics and Pandemics," the causes of some disease outbreaks have been attributed to early "biological warfare" against Native Americans. Having no natural immunity to nonindigenous diseases, the otherwise healthy Indians perished by the thousands.

A particular technological disaster could also be ranked among Tennessee's worst. At the conclusion of the American Civil War, the riverboat *Sultana* exploded and burned to the water line on the Mississippi River north of Memphis. This disaster killed an estimated 1,800 people, over 300 more than died five decades later on the ill-fated *Titanic*.

Natural disasters are often some of the most egregious events despite comparatively few lost lives. The floods of 1927 produced both incredible economic and social impacts along the Mississippi, Tennessee, and Cumberland rivers and their many larger tributaries. But, by some accounts, the floods of 1937 were twice as destructive. Even more recently, the droughts of the 1980s and the tornadoes and winter storms of the 1990s have caused economic losses unparalleled in the state's history.

As our population has exploded and our built environments have increased, so have the economic costs of disasters, particularly from floods and tornadoes. Even more recently, the coal ash spill at the Tennessee Valley Authority (TVA) Kingston steam plant will certainly be recorded as the most costly and long-term environmental disaster (relative to cleanup and other mitigation efforts) in our state's history. Clearly, one may make a case for several worst disasters. However, a more logical conclusion might be to state that the worst disaster in Tennessee is yet to come.

Emotional Tragedies and Unusual Events

Besides the obvious effects of killer tornadoes and damaging floods, there have been events that have had great emotional impact upon both their victims and those who simply witnessed or heard about the tragedies. One such incident occurred on July 23, 1913. At the time, it garnered little notice, but if it happened today, it would certainly attract national attention. Near the community of Townsend (Blount County), Mrs. John Cooper, a mother of four, was engaged in her weekly laundry duty on the bank of a stream near her home. According to one account, she sent her three older children to gather chicken eggs while she continued her washing. When they failed to return after a time, she left her fourth child, one and a half years old, sleeping on a blanket as she searched for the others. She found them dead or dying from bites suffered in an apparent encounter with a den of rattlesnakes. And while she was gone, it was reported, the fourth child fell into the stream and drowned.[9]

Another deeply disturbing tragedy took place near Newport, Tennessee, on October 13, 1906, at the home of Chalbern Mantooth, a fifty-year-old father of five who was revered by his neighbors as one of the most productive farmers in Cocke County. After receiving word from their doctor that his pregnant wife might die and they would lose their unborn child, he sank into a deep depression. He knew that losing this child and possibly his wife would tear the family apart. Suddenly, on that fateful morning in October, in a fit of insanity, he decided to end the misery for everyone. In an act of unimaginable rage, he picked up an axe and slaughtered four of his children with blows to their heads. After hacking at his wife and fifth child, he is said to have grabbed a straight razor and slit his own throat from ear to ear. His wife and fifth child, although badly mutilated by axe blows to their heads, miraculously escaped death, and the wife even went on to give birth to a healthy baby. Although insanity was the only logical verdict of a coroner's inquest, one will never know what triggered such fervent and depraved emotions within a man otherwise described as normal.[10] Events such as these can hardly be termed disasters of epic proportions as we commonly know them, but their dire nature no doubt stirs our curiosity and warrants inclusion as a Tennessee tragedy.

Likewise, whenever a mine disaster occurred in the coal fields of Tennessee, hundreds or even thousands of people traditionally gathered at the site out of concern, a sense of obligation or solidarity, or sometimes just curiosity. At a time when news spread slowly, and significant distractions rarely occurred in the routine lives of the working poor, these events had strong social significance. Crowds of people were as equally attracted to the drama of a mine disaster as they were to a state fair. The people who gathered at the entrances of the Fraterville and Cross Mountain mines during the great disasters of 1902 and 1911 consisted of distraught family members, their friends and neighbors, miners from neighboring communities, volunteer rescuers, government officials, politicians, clergymen, members of the press, and an assortment of other curious bystanders. These vigils generally continued around the clock until the last miner was rescued or the last body was carried from the mine. Food was often brought in by relatives, friends, and neighbors or, for a price, made available by vendors. In many ways, the event was not unlike a traditional (albeit rather large) Appalachian wake. Emotions waxed and waned as any news from the mine or any rumor from some seemingly credible source resounded through the crowd, raising new hopes or fears.

An examination of notes and letters found on the bodies of the Fraterville and Cross Mountain mine disaster victims of 1902 and 1911, respectively, provide further insight into the emotional state of hopelessly trapped miners.[11]

Jacob Vowell addressed notes of this nature to his wife before eventually suffocating in the Fraterville Coal Mines:

> Elen, darling Good Bye for us both. Elbert said the Lord has saved him. Do the best you can with the children. We are all praying for air to support us but it is getting so bad without any air. Horace, Elbert said for you to wear his shoes and clothing. It is now ½ past 1.
>
> Powell Harmon's watch is in Andy Wood's hand. Ellen I want you to live right and come to heaven. Raise the children the best you can. Oh! How I wish to be with you. Good bye all of you Good Bye. Bury me and Elbert in the same grave by Little Eddy. Good bye Elen Good Bye Lily, Good Bye Jimmie Good Bye Horace. We are together It is 25 minute's after Two. There is a few of us alive yet. JAKE and ALBERT. Oh God for one more breath. Elen remember me as long as you live. Good Bye Darling.

Likewise, Powell Harmon himself scratched a final note to his wife—and a staunch warning to his sons: "it is now 10 minutes til 10 and we are all almost smothered. Don't know how long we will live but it is our time to go. I hope to meet you all in heaven . . . My boys, Never work in the coal mines."

A final example of perhaps Tennessee's most unusual tragic stories relates to Mary, the so-called murderous circus elephant. She was legally executed by being hanged from a railroad derrick for trampling one of her handlers to death. The event took place in Erwin, Unicoi County, in September 1916 (see chronology). The story has been told, retold, and embellished so many times that exact details are now uncertain, but according to a historical eyewitness, when her handler used a long-handled hook to jerk her back into the line of other elephants, she turned and "throwed him against the side of [a] drink stand . . . and when he hit the ground she just walked over and set her foot on his head . . . and blood and brains and stuff just squirted all over the street." The first attempt to hang her was unsuccessful. The chain broke and she fell to the ground, cruelly immobilized by the pain of a broken hip. With another chain around her neck, she was hoisted into the air and after several agonizing minutes, she strangled to death. Meanwhile, a grave was dug near the scene, and she was dropped in and covered over.[12] This final example clearly illustrates a quick reaction based on an outraged response to a tragedy. Today, Mary would likely receive more humane treatment despite what she had done. Perhaps she would be given refuge at Tennessee's own elephant sanctuary in Hohenwald, Lewis County, instead of death by a crane.

Handling and Interment of the Dead

Before the 1900s, when a death occurred within a community, certain traditional responses were anticipated from neighbors and were usually accomplished in a ritualistic manner. These acts were more common in remote, close-knit, rural areas, but even within urban neighborhoods, similar death customs may have been practiced. Relatives and neighbors understood the needs and responded without formal request when a death occurred. Some built or otherwise acquired a casket and others prepared the grave. Unless the person died of a contagious disease, they bathed the body and sometimes applied camphor or another substance to the face and hands in an effort to delay decomposition. They placed

nickels on top of eyelids to keep the eyes closed. (Pennies were never used because the copper content might leave a green mark.) Someone might go to the beehives to "tell the bees" that someone in the family had died and tie a black ribbon around the hives in the belief that, otherwise, the bees might leave.[13] Among more well-to-do white families in the South prior to the Civil War, slaves might have performed these tasks.[14] Neighbors provided for the bereaved families, and the many guests would attend the wake. In the early days, wakes were held in the homes of the deceased or of their extended families. Church funerals came later, primarily after the advent of embalming.

A wake or deathwatch meant a night of sitting up with the family in the presence of the body. In some mountain communities, those present might sit outside on the porch, or in the yard if weather permitted, singing hymns, while one or more individuals stayed with or checked on the body every few minutes. Traditionally, clocks were stopped in the room where the deceased resided to prevent bad luck. Mirrors were shrouded or turned toward the wall. Also, when the body was finally removed from the house to be taken to the "corps yard" (another name for a graveyard or cemetery), it was carried through the door feet first and sometimes blindfolded. The belief was that if it were removed head first, it would beckon others to follow in death.[15] Wakes served three primary purposes. First, they were a show of respect for the deceased. Second, they helped console the family in a time of bereavement. And finally, they served a practical function—the presence of mourners helped protect the body from vermin until it could be interred.

Obviously, weather permitting, it was best to bury the body as soon as possible, especially if it had not been embalmed—a process that was not usually practiced until after the Civil War. In some of the more isolated communities, embalming was uncommon until the early 1900s. Because of this, individuals who died while in communities other than their own were often buried there rather than taken back to their home communities for interment.[16] In the depths of winter, if the ground was frozen, the body was sometimes stored in a secure and cool place to await the spring thaw.

In times of disaster or during epidemics, traditional burial rituals were often forgone. In major floods, conflagrations, and mass riverboat or railroad accidents, bodies might never be recovered. Many were lost to the strong currents of rivers or entombed within or beneath debris piles. Some were burned to ashes in fires, or nearly vaporized in explosions. In some violent coal mine, industrial, or airplane disasters, only unidentifiable body parts might be recovered. If retrieved, bodies could be kept at least for a while, awaiting the arrival of a relative or friend who could transfer them elsewhere for burial or bury them locally. Otherwise they might end up in a mass grave or a pauper's grave at a city or community cemetery, which was often called a potter's field. The term "potter's field" is traditionally linked to the Gospel of Matthew, in which a remorseful Judas returns the thirty pieces of silver he had received for betraying Christ. The priests in turn use this money to purchase a burial place for strangers—a "potter's field" that was unfit for growing crops but rich in clay used by local pot makers. Thus the term potter's field has long been used to designate a cemetery or a section of a cemetery reserved for the burial of impoverished or unidentified individuals.[17] Many 1800s cemeteries in the Old West were referred to as "boot hill" graveyards. They contained pauper's graves or those occupied by gunfighters and outlaws who had died literally "with their boots on."

Individual graves might be provided for disaster victims, and if the identity was known, grave markers of some type might be erected. Accurate and permanent cemetery records were rare, at least before the 1900s. However, during the great epidemics of cholera and yellow fever of the 1800s and the Spanish influenza pandemic of 1918–19, death tolls were enormous. This was especially true in urban areas and larger towns in the days before modern public-health practices. During these times, burial in mass graves was often necessary, especially when the undertakers and the grave diggers could not keep pace with the number of dead, which was often so great that bodies might be taken from homes and stacked like cordwood along city streets. There they would await the death wagons that would haul them to existing city cemeteries or burial grounds often established outside the town limits.

Mass graves were usually set off from the rest of the cemetery when there were large numbers of dead and the identities of the bodies were unknown. The Elmwood Cemetery in Memphis held such burial grounds for the yellow fever victims of 1878. Many of the doctors, nurses, clergy, and others who tended the victims likewise were buried in those plots at Elmwood.

Many victims of the *Sultana* riverboat explosion of 1865 are buried in the National Cemetery in Memphis and elsewhere across the state. Several were laid to rest in the Mt. Olive Cemetery in South Knoxville. There is a commemorative stone marker there and also on the lawn of the Blount County Courthouse. The victims of the *Sultana* disaster were mostly Union soldiers who were being transported home from prisoner of war camps in Georgia and Alabama at the end of the Civil War.

A monument was erected to the memory of the miners who died in the Fraterville mine disaster of 1902. It is located in the Leach Cemetery near Lake City (Anderson County). This great stone monolith bears the names of eighty-nine of the miners who are buried there, laid to rest within what is called the "Miners' Circle," two concentric circles of graves around the monument.[18]

Many cholera victims are buried in the New Bethel Grave Yard, the Mount Ararat Church Cemetery, the Fort Zollicoffer Cemetery, and the Bosley's Grave Yard in Davidson County. Cholera often struck rapidly and always without regard to race and social or economic status.

Of 14,000 Cherokees who were forced to march westward during the infamous Trail of Tears of 1838–39,

4,000 are estimated to have died en route.[19] In their haste to drive the Native Americans as rapidly as possible through the cold and snows of that winter, U.S. soldiers gave them little time in which to bury their dead. Deaths occurred almost daily from exposure, exhaustion, disease, and starvation. The dead were interred in shallow and unmarked graves. There was no time for ceremony and little time for mourning. When daylight came, the men, women, and children were expected to begin moving again. Historical markers in Tennessee and other states have been erected along the various routes of the Trail of Tears to commemorate those who died in this tragic episode.

A stroll through older cemeteries is likely to reveal common dates associated with disasters or tragedies. Many of those who died in 1918 or 1919, for example, were likely victims of the Spanish flu pandemic. Other common dates relate to like disasters, especially epidemics, super-tornado outbreaks, mine explosions, and multifatality accidents.

Authenticity of Disaster Data

Accounts in this book are based on primary documents, original sources, and the recollections of individuals who were part of and, rarely but occasionally, actual witnesses to an event. These accounts can be found in letters, diaries, personal journals, and newspaper articles written at the time of the event. Primary accounts have likewise been taken from photographs and their captions and, as previously mentioned, the messages of farewells and wills scribbled to loved ones on scraps of paper later found on the bodies of trapped miners. Sources also include official government and research records compiled at the time of the incidents. Some trade journals, such as the *Railroad Gazette,* published accounts of deaths and injuries and their causes long before doing so became a requirement of railroad companies under the Accident Reports Act of 1910. Unfortunately, due to a lack of standardization, such data published in the 1870s through the end of the century is unreliable and sometimes contradictory. Moreover, some of the statistics applied only to railroad workers, not to passengers, and the distinction was not always apparent.[20]

Secondary and tertiary sources have been gleaned from later newspaper accounts, history and reference books, magazines, pamphlets, published journals and reports, and other documentation based on primary or secondary data sources. Even when facts appear to be indisputable, amateur and professional historians have sometimes bickered over their interpretations. Likewise, accounts have a way of becoming embellished or distorted through time, whether purposely or by accident. Politics, mores, traditions, prejudices, and religious convictions, or lack thereof, have all influenced how history has been recorded and interpreted. This becomes even more applicable when one works with secondary and tertiary sources or from rumor or speculation. Amateur and, one might suspect, even professional historians sometimes arrive at conclusions in a backward manner. Rather than starting with verifiable facts and developing theories based on them, or extrapolating credible data, they may sometimes begin with preconceived notions and work diligently to manipulate facts in a manner that supports their views.

Even before current ratings wars raged within the print and broadcast media, writers and editors often made assumptions, embellished facts, or interpreted them in a manipulative manner. Putting a spin on an incident or event is a technique perfected by politicians, officials, and experts to provide an interpretation of an action or event in a way designed to sway public opinion, create opposition, or garner support. Librarians and archivists tell horror stories of whole pages being removed from record books or historical data being altered, because someone either did not want the truth known or did not believe what was written and felt compelled to silence it. Additionally, writers of fiction love to embellish as well.

With innovative tools and techniques unavailable until now, today's researchers are unraveling complicated mysteries and refuting many previously held assumptions of past events, including disasters. As a result, conclusions once thought to be indisputable may now be reanalyzed and verified or rejected with greater confidence. For instance, in 1999 official National Weather Service records indicated that three F5 intensity tornadoes had occurred in Tennessee. As shown in the Fujita-Pearson tornado scale (see table 7 in appendix), F5 events are the most extreme tornadoes. They may produce rotational wind speeds exceeding 300 miles per hour and are capable of unimaginable destruction. According to records obtained from the Storm Prediction Center, an F5 tornado occurred in Fayette County on March 21–22, 1952, and two others during the super outbreak of April 3, 1974. However, based upon a reevaluation of the evidence by a Dr. Schaeffer and a group of his students, it appears that all three of these alleged F5 events were actually in the F4 range.

In 1977 Dr. Otto Nuttli presented a scientific paper in which he postulated that the three, possibly four, great New Madrid earthquakes of 1811 and 1812 would have registered between 8.4 and 8.8 on the Richter scale (see table 2 in appendix). Based on more recent scientific evidence, these magnitudes appear to have been overestimated and were probably more in the lower to upper 7.0 Richter range. Naturally, the debate continues.

Accurate Accounting of Losses

There are disasters for which we feel certain that we have a precise accounting of the dead and injured and some for which we do not. A case in point was a 1940s airplane crash in which twenty people were recorded to have been onboard. There should have been no doubt as to the casualty figures, even though the plane and body parts were scattered over a quarter-mile debris field. However, in the case of this military transport plane there was a debate over the number killed. The manifest read twenty onboard, but a doctor on the scene believed that there were twenty-one bodies. He later recanted, saying that the bodies were so mangled that perhaps there were only twenty victims after all. This was, of course, prior to the advent of modern forensic and DNA methods of analysis. A report arose, however, of a missing soldier who may have hitched a ride on the plane; this was a common practice for military personnel on furloughs traveling between bases. In this case, it turned out that the doctor was correct and the manifest was wrong. A twenty-first person had indeed died in the crash.

There are many other disasters for which exact casualty figures will never be known. The number of people who succumbed to cholera, yellow fever, and other such epidemics cannot possibly be determined. Estimates that mention figures in the thousands or tens of thousands relative to smallpox epidemics among the Cherokee and other tribes in the early to mid-eighteenth century are meaningless, except to emphasize that the scope of these epidemics was truly appalling. During the worst of the early smallpox, yellow fever, cholera, and influenza epidemics, many of the dead were buried in mass graves. Traditional ritualistic burial was neither practical nor feasible at those times. The bodies, in various states of decay, needed to be placed beneath the sod, and the sooner the better, for reasons of utility and public health. Sadly, there are even accounts of bodies being hoisted onto death wagons and making their way to city cemeteries, some still faintly showing signs of life.

Professional and amateur historians have long debated the number of people who perished in various disasters. This was especially true in cases where reliable evidence was lacking or questionable. Simply believing something strongly enough or making suppositions based upon incomplete evidence is not proof. Interestingly, however, there are some situations where circumstantial evidence may support guesstimated death tolls. A case in point is the Fraterville Coal Mine disaster of

1902. For years, the number of men and boys killed in that tragedy has been listed as 184. There are 184 known graves in Anderson and surrounding counties with tombstones bearing the date May 19, 1902, and all of them correspond to names on the mining company's payroll records. That should be proof positive, but it is not. There were additional unidentified casualties at Fraterville whose bodies were never claimed. Perhaps some were temporary workers whose names were not listed on the payroll records. Six are represented by headstones bearing no inscriptions in a little-known itinerant cemetery. This small cemetery is located beside the old Fraterville Mine railroad trestle, in the backyard of the Owen Bailey family of Briceville, Anderson County. Adding these graves to the 184 known dead, the count of victims increases to 190. Furthermore, if one asks some of the local residents, including Mr. Bailey, how many actually died in the incident, many of them will estimate between 200 and 214. Where are the others? According to Bailey, there are additional unmarked graves in his backyard. These plots are discerned only by slightly sunken, rectangular depressions in the soil. They are arranged in rows and are of approximately of the same dimensions as those of the marked graves. In short, as the wooden coffins have rotted away through the years and the disturbed soil has settled, the tell-tale signs have emerged. Although neither Bailey nor anyone else knows exactly how many are buried on his property, this evidence does challenge the number of men originally purported to have perished in that early disaster.[21]

Exact cemetery records were difficult to maintain and were rarely kept, especially in the throes of major epidemics and other disasters. Some burials also extended beyond the present boundaries of even well-tended cemeteries. Family and church graveyards often lack even the names, much less the dates of birth and death or causes of death for each of their burials. In some cases, sections of cemeteries, especially where there was a need for mass graves, may have a record of the year

of burial, but no further details. For example, approximately 2,500, or roughly half of the Memphis victims of the great 1870s yellow fever epidemics are buried in four public lots at the Elmwood Cemetery. There are descriptions of bodies being heaped along Memphis streets like so much refuse in the midst of the epidemic: "the remains of an old woman were found so far gone that they were gathered—putrid water and festering flesh—into the carpet on which they were lying, and so lifted into a box, in which she was buried."[22] In many cases, when everyone in the household became ill and died within hours or days of one another, there was no one left to record the names or even the numbers of victims involved, and no one to mourn for the dead.

There is yet another problem concerning the reliability of disaster fatality figures. Not all victims of disasters have died at the scene. Some have passed away hours, days, or even months later from injuries sustained in an incident. A similar case may be made for deaths related to epidemics. For example, cholera, influenza, and smallpox are very contagious and were certainly spread by people escaping areas where those diseases were epidemic. Hence their deaths and those of others they infected may not have been associated with a known outbreak and were therefore uncounted. Even in the case of noncontagious diseases like yellow fever, victims may have left the place in which they contracted the disease before becoming symptomatic. A case in point is the official count of the dead in Memphis as a result of the yellow fever epidemic of 1878. Officially 5,150 died in the city; however, it is known that many of those who fled the city to avoid the plague passed away in other locations. There is no way to know whether those individuals were ever correctly diagnosed or counted as victims of the infamous 1878 Memphis outbreak. Perhaps they died elsewhere, far from home, alone and unsung. It is also possible that they may have inadvertently transported the vectors of the disease (in this case the mosquito) in open containers of water or other rainwater catchments, further spreading the plague and resulting in even more deaths.

There have been other incidents in which accurate death tolls were allegedly censored for purposes of national security. During the 1918–19 Spanish flu pandemic near the end of World War I, Spain was one of the few nations to publish accurate influenza mortality figures. Being a neutral country, it had nothing to gain or lose by revealing its actual number of flu deaths. In contrast, other nations are believed to have purposely deflated their morbidity and mortality rates. This is one possible reason why the disease was called the Spanish flu. Because Spain's statistics were factual, their per capita death rate appeared greater in comparison to other countries. This led many to assume that the disease originated there, which it did not. The death toll from influenza in 1918–19 has been estimated at somewhere between 50 million and 100 million worldwide. A conservative estimate of the number who died of the disease in the United States is half a million. A. W. Crosby, in his book *America's Forgotten Pandemic,* states that the number of dead from this disease exceeded the casualties of World War I, World War II, the Korean War, and the Vietnam War combined.[23]

All of this begs another question: when should a person be counted among the fatalities of a disaster? Although there is no definitive or legal answer to this question relative to disaster deaths, at one time there was a judicial precedent relative to murder. The "year and a day rule" is a principle of English law stating that a death could not conclusively be presumed to be murder if the victim died more than a year and one day after a shooting, stabbing, poisoning, etc. The application of this rule was used so often that it became enshrined in common law. However, the rule was abolished by the Law Reform (Year and a Day) Act of 1996.[24] The concept was abandoned because of advances in modern medicine (such as life support systems). People could now be kept alive for longer and longer periods of time. Therefore, application of this principle seemed no longer prudent. However, if

the spirit of the "a year and a day" law can be applied to disasters, one can make a good case for including those deaths in the mortality figures of a particular disaster. This would be true regardless of the time lapse. A brief example of this occurred in the Owen Graham Salvage & Sundry Store in Memphis in 1965. Two firemen were overcome by carbon monoxide poisoning. One died at the scene. The second went into a coma from which he never recovered and died fifteen years later in a nursing home.

Racial Bias and Disaster Data

As in the case of the itinerant workers at the Fraterville mine disaster, some individuals may be listed separately or parenthetically, almost as if to imply that their deaths were not as noteworthy or significant as those of other victims. This was fairly common among black and other ethnic workers. Table 8, for example, illustrates a partial list of the individuals who died in tornadoes that struck West and Middle Tennessee in 1900. The full names of several white casualties are given, but five others are referred to simply as negroes or blacks.

All too often, in fact, the tragic conditions under which minorities died in any sort of calamity were acknowledged—but not their names. For example, in his 1879 book on the yellow fever epidemic of the previous year and its catastrophic effects on the city of Memphis, J. M. Keating included these grim details about stricken members of the black community:

> A colored man was prostrated, September 2d, on the corner of Fifth and Suffarans Streets, in Chelsea. He was seen to fall by Captain A. T. Lacey, who went to him and found him insensible. Captain Lacey reported the case to the health office, and an ambulance was sent for him, but he was dead when it got there.[25]

> The dead body of a negro woman was found at No. 13 Commerce Street, September 3d, her living baby trying to nurse from her putrid breast.[26]

> The body of a negro woman, name unknown, was found in an out-house, defaced beyond recognition, and half the body eaten by rats, hundreds of which were lying dead near by.[27]

It is altogether likely that no attempt was even made to determine the identities of these anonymous victims.[28]

The Media and Disasters

Throughout history, the media have provided news in a predictable fashion and often with their own unique spin, playing up the sensationalism of events. Because violence sells, reporters often aggressively seek out controversial aspects of news stories; hence, media outlets compete to acquire exclusive coverage and to be the first to break a story.

Given the sensationalistic tendencies of the media, an irony at disaster scenes in modern times is that some of the best information about what is actually occurring often comes from the media's onsite coverage. Emergency operation centers (EOCs) utilize media monitors whose mission it is to watch television and listen to voice feeds from inside an event so as to better understand what is actually occurring. Emergency responders may feed data to the EOCs, but the media have cameras and microphones embedded at the scene, often recording events as they unfold. They also interview victims and eyewitnesses. Tracking rumors, erroneous facts, or misinformation recorded by the media enables emergency public information officers to address inaccuracies during live media briefings or in written news releases.

Unlike today's instantaneous news feeds and constant updates, written accounts of disasters and tragedies that occurred decades or centuries ago are often fraught with inaccuracies. Erroneous information is commonly perpetuated in the telling and retelling of stories. Early newspaper and magazine writers used flowery language and much hyperbole in describing and interpreting disasters. They needed to paint vivid pictures in the minds of their readers for lack of the photos and video footage we have today. These sensationalized accounts were generally published a few days or even a few hours after the event. More accurate details are often found in newspaper accounts written a week, a month, or even years later, by which time a more precise accounting of dead and injured has been determined. Unfortunately, the media's (and even the public's) interest in events wanes after a certain amount of time. At this point, the best data may be accessible only through government records or eyewitness accounts. It is unfortunate that standardized data on historic incidents has been long in coming.

Occurrence, Recurrence, and the Historic Record

A close examination of the chronology might suggest that weather-related incidents such as tornadoes, extreme straight-line winds, floods, and droughts have increased significantly in number and severity in recent years. Global warming aside, there is no reason to believe such incidents are any more numerous or potentially destructive today than in the past, although some events may be cyclic in nature. However, most scientists and emergency management specialists agree that if a hazard has affected an area before, it will do so again. This has been called the "Theory of Recurrence." For example, it is a misconception that lightning never strikes the same place twice. The Empire State Building in New York is struck by lightning an average of 100 times per year. That being said, determining the exact time between the occurrences of various types of disasters is problematic. Tornadoes presently recur on average about a dozen times a year in Tennessee, which ranks sixteenth in average number of tornadoes per year in the United States.[29] But even this number has been calculated based on relatively short-term data and cannot be extrapolated with much accuracy.

Much research has been conducted on the recurrence intervals of floods as well as earthquakes, volcanoes, tsunamis, and hurricanes. Many scientists presently believe that large meteors may visit our planet at a rate of one per century. Unfortunately, estimates of exactly when such events will occur are still far, far beyond our predictive capabilities. The last major meteor impacts, as evidenced by craters in Middle Tennessee, occurred tens of millions of years ago. What we can predict with assurance is that low-intensity (less damaging) events will recur more often than high-intensity (more damaging) events. That is to say that barely felt microquakes occur more frequently than highly destructive mega-quakes.

For years the NWS, its predecessor organizations, military and other government agencies, and trained volunteer observers used fixed recording stations to monitor weather and climate. Some of those records have been maintained, albeit sporadically, for 150 years or more. In fact, the NWS has only maintained consistent weather records since the 1950s. For that reason, entries within the chronology in this book may appear skewed. The TVA and the United States Army Corps of Engineers (USACOE) have compiled data concerning early floods by gathering information from old newspaper accounts, interviews with eyewitnesses, and earlier miscellaneous government documentation. They also established stream-gauging stations throughout the Tennessee and Cumberland river basins as early as the mid-1800s for the USACOE and the 1930s for TVA.

Accurate scientific records of earthquake activity extend back an even shorter period of time. However, the use of early descriptions of earthquake effects has allowed seismologists to approximate the magnitude of some past earthquakes. This information is discussed in greater detail in the section on earthquakes. Early disaster accounts hold scant data; yet most scientists would probably agree that the incidence of natural disasters has neither increased nor decreased substantially. Records have merely been more accurate and better maintained in recent years.

In the past only the most spectacular and destructive natural and technological disasters (as well as civil disturbances) were documented. They were recorded in various government reports, magazines, newspapers, letters, and personal diaries. A good example is an account of the Mississippi River flood of 1543 recorded in the *Chronicles of Hernando de Soto*. Accounts of significant disasters have also been passed down by word of mouth and sometimes transcribed by historians or other writers. Such accounts may be mere conjecture or hearsay and subject to embellishment; however, if they give some indication of time and place, they may often guide researchers to more accurate written documentation and hence verification of an event and associated facts.

Public health departments in a number of cities and counties have maintained records concerning diseases, including epidemics and pandemics, since the mid-1800s or earlier. However, reliable and standardized records only go back into the early 1900s. Data on wildland fires and their effects have been maintained for only the past few decades. The Department of Labor began keeping mining and some industrial accident statistics and other such information in the late 1800s. Although the record is incomplete, some data on transportation accidents have been recorded since the early railroad and steamboat days. Official reliable aviation accident data also extends back only a few decades. The National Transportation Safety Board (NTSB) was established in 1967 to investigate and maintain records relative to marine, railroad, aviation, highway, pipeline, and hazardous materials accidents. In short, record keeping has been poor at best until the last few decades.

With today's technology, disaster data is much more accurate because more people are reporting incidents; additional follow-up studies are being conducted; more accurate real-time data from which to work is available; and more precise meteorological and seismological data-gathering technologies are being used, including Doppler weather radar, well-trained meteorologists and storm spotters, and strategically spaced seismographs and weather observation stations. The National Oceanic and Atmospheric Administration (NOAA) also uses satellites and permanent fixed global recording stations. The modern broadcast and print media record events as they occur and provide periodic summaries. Today, there are more people on earth, they are more widely dispersed, and there are more built environments as targets for natural and technological hazards. On the other hand, there are also better methods of alerting and warning people of impending danger, better emergency-response capabilities, and facilities and infrastructure that are more disaster resistant as a result of enhanced building codes.

It is worth mentioning that some of Tennessee's most appalling disasters and tragedies are not included in this book. These are events that occurred during, or as the result of, military conflicts. They include very early assaults and skirmishes between settlers and Native Americans, battles between various Indian tribal groups, and clashes between foreign (French, Spanish, and British) troops and American frontiersmen. Conflicts between foreign troops and Native Americans, as well as military actions during the American Revolution and the Civil War, are also excluded. These types of hostilities have been omitted because they would fill volumes and are beyond the intended scope of this work.

An exhaustive authoritative record of Tennessee's historic disasters and other tragedies will never be complete. Many events were never documented, and countless records have been lost. Untold accounts, in the form of written, graphic, and photo documentation have been accidentally or thoughtlessly discarded. Some materials have been burned as garbage or have deteriorated in dank basements, storerooms, and warehouses. Much data have been lost to fires, floods, and even tornadoes in homes, libraries, museums, and courthouses. This disaster data itself is ironically lost to the elements and sometimes to disasters themselves. Other records have been discarded by well-meaning individuals who failed to realize the value of such historical materials. A number of years ago, I contacted the Tennessee Department of Labor in Nashville to inquire about records relative to East Tennessee coal mine disasters. I was informed that the Caryville Regional Office of Mines in Anderson County had closed and that their records were no longer of benefit and consequently were "surplused." I suspect this was a polite way of saying tossed in the garbage or burned.

The Aftereffects of Disasters and Studying Them

The aftereffects of disasters often extended far beyond the events themselves. For example, coal mine explosions, which resulted in heavy fatalities, usually had devastating and long-lasting effects upon the families and the communities of the miners. Southern Appalachian coal miners were poorly compensated until fairly recently, and the economic and social conditions of most mining towns were deplorable. Life and accident insurance was either nonexistent or beyond the financial means of the average miner's family. There was no Social Security system; wives often had many children to support, and as a rule they had little formal education or marketable skills with which to support their families after their husbands died.

The effect of the Fraterville Mine disaster on its small company town demonstrates an extreme case of both broken homes and a broken community. Only three adult male residents remained in Fraterville after the disaster of 1902. Many women lost every male member of their families, including young sons, as there were no child-labor laws at the time. Because their families needed the income, boys as young as twelve worked and died in the Appalachian coal mines. The widows and families of the miners killed in the Fraterville disaster settled out of court for a mere $320 for each confirmed death. Adjusted for inflation to 2007, that would amount to only a little over $7,500. Unless they had an extended family network to sustain them, these 150 widows and their children, who numbered between 800 and 1,000, had to depend upon the benevolence of their friends and neighbors, most of whom had few surplus resources to offer.[30] As author Jack London is said to have observed, "A bone to the dog is not charity. Charity is the bone shared with the dog, when you are just as hungry as the dog."

This book is not intended to simply dramatize or sensationalize incidents of doom, mayhem, and destruction, although these are the usual consequences of disasters. Rather, its purpose is to provide an accurate chronicle of the natural catastrophes, exploits of man, and other events that have devastated Tennessee and Tennesseans throughout the state's history. Emotionally speaking, this book has not been easy to compile. Gathering the details of many of the events has been physically and emotionally draining to many of my informants, as well as to me personally. The informants' distress came from reliving the events through their stories. My own was not unlike that of the medical student who, while studying a disease in detail, begins to physically experience its symptoms. There were nights when I could not sleep as I pondered many incidents that could have been prevented—and would have been in this day and time. Often it was just some graphic details of an accident or the suffering and death of an individual or group. Regardless of how stoic one tries to be in chronicling tragic events, something will eventually strike a nerve, forcing the writer to either put aside the work for a while or to focus on the writing and not the emotion. The natural disasters have made me sad; the technological disasters have made me angry. Those labeled "civil insurrections," particularly the lynchings and other hate crimes or racially motivated atrocities, have made me weep. But the end result is, I hope, an important work that tells the history of a state through its trying times and ultimately showcases the triumph of a hearty people over adversity in the face of Tennessee's tragedies.

Notes

1. Frances Kennett, *The Greatest Disasters of the 20th Century* (London: Marshall Cavendish, 1975), 152.

2. J. S. Chambers, MD, *The Conquest of Cholera: America's Greatest Scourge* (New York: Macmillan, 1938), 17.

3. Lewis R. Aiken, *Dying, Death, and Bereavement* (Mahwah, NJ: Lawrence Erlbaum Associates, Publishers. 2001), 19.

4. J. Haden Alldredge, Mildred Burnham Spottswood, Vera Victoria Anderson, John H. Goff, and Robert Mallory La Forge, *A History of Navigation on the Tennessee River System*, Tennessee Valley Authority (Washington, DC: Government Printing Office, 1937), 64.

5. James T. Lloyd, foreword, *Lloyd's Steamboat Directory and Disasters on the Western Waters* (Cincinnati: J. T. Lloyd & Co., 1856).

6. State of Tennessee, *Fifth Annual Report, Bureau of Labor, Statistics and Mines* (Washington, DC: Government Printing Office, 1896), 16.

7. H. B. Humphrey, *Historical Summary of Coal-Mine Explosions in the United States 1810–1958* (Washington, DC: U.S. Dept. of Labor, Mine Safety and Health Administrations, National Mine Health and Safety Academy, 1998), 15.

8. Vincent J. Cirillo, "Two Faces of Death: Fatalities from Disease and Combat in America's Wars, 1775 to Present," *Perspectives in Biology and Medicine* 51, no. 1 (Winter 2008): 121.

9. James B. Jones, *Every Day in Tennessee History* (Winston-Salem, NC, 1966), 145.

10. *Nashville Banner*, Oct. 13, 1906, and *Knoxville Journal and Tribune*, Oct. 14–15, 1906.

11. Copies of the text of these letters were provided by Charles Green, director, Mines Division, Tennessee Dept. of Labor, Jacksboro, May 1994.

12. Joan V. Schroeder, "The Day They Hanged an Elephant in East Tennessee," *Blue Ridge Country*, Feb. 13, 2009, 1–7, http://www.blueridgecountry.com/archive/mary-the-elephant.html.

13. Dr. Gale Palmer, Univ. of Tennessee College of Communications, personal correspondence with author, Nov. 29, 2009.

14. Meg Greene, *Rest in Peace: A History of American Cemeteries* (Minneapolis: Twenty-First Century Books, 2008), 31.

15. Aiken, *Dying, Death, and Bereavement*, 138.

16. Palmer, personal correspondence with author.

17. Aiken, *Dying, Death, and Bereavement*, 24.

18. David Rogers, *Reflections in the Water, Cove Creek to Lake City: A History of Lake City, Tennessee* (Clinton, TN: Courier-News, 1976), 68.

19. Ben Harris McClary, "Trail of Tears, or *NUNNA-DA-UL-TSUN-YI*," in *Tennessee Encyclopedia of History and Culture*, ed. Carroll Van West, 985 (Nashville: Tennessee Historical Society and Rutledge Hill Press, 1998).

20. Charles W. McDonald, *The Federal Railroad Safety Program: 100 Years of Safer Railroads*, booklet (N.p., 1993), 3–5.

21. Owen Bailey, Briceville, TN, personal correspondence with the author, May 26, 2001.

22. J. M. Keating, *History of the Yellow Fever: The Yellow Fever Epidemic of 1878, in Memphis, Tenn.* (Memphis: Howards Association, 1879), 154.

23. A. W. Crosby, *America's Forgotten Pandemic* (Cambridge, UK: Cambridge Univ. Press, 1989).

24. A copy of the reform bill can be found in Rollin M. Perkins and Ronald N. Boyce, *Perkins and Boyce's Cases and Materials on Criminal Law and Procedure*, 3rd ed., University Textbook Series (Mineola, NY: Foundation Press, 1982), 47–48.

25. Keating, *History of the Yellow Fever*, 153.

26. Ibid., 152.

27. Ibid., 156.

28. Interestingly, as I note in the article on the 1878 epidemic, African American victims of yellow fever, such as those described here, were actually rare in comparison to whites: blacks who remained in Memphis during the plague suffered only a 7-percent death rate as opposed to a 70-percent death rate for whites. This was because blacks possessed a greater immunity to yellow fever, a disease indigenous to Africa, than did whites, Asians, and especially Native Americans.

29. Based on National Oceanic and Atmospheric Administration, National Weather Service Laboratory data collected between 1950 and 1991. See http://www.srh.noaa.gov.

30. *Clinton Courier-News*, Nov. 5, 1987. My adjusted-for-inflation figures are based on the latest reliable data, which precedes the economic crash in early 2008.

PART 1
NATURAL DISASTERS

Droughts and Severe Heat Waves

Droughts are unique disasters. If less rainfall than normal falls during the wet months of the year, it is unlikely there will be a surplus during the dry ones. One year of this cycle does not make much difference, but repeat the formula a second, third, or fourth year and it is a disaster in the making.

The Palmer Drought Severity Index developed by meteorologist Wayne C. Palmer in 1965 uses temperature and rainfall information in a formula to determine dryness. The Palmer Index is used in determining long-term drought, or a lack of precipitation over a period of several months. It is not as accurate with short-term forecasts over a period of weeks. On the scale, 0 is normal, and drought is shown in terms of negative numbers; for example, –1 is a mild drought, –2 is a moderate drought, and so forth. Conversely, positive numbers indicate wet conditions. (See table 1 in appendix.)

There are many definitions for drought, but three are most commonly used. A meteorological drought is a long period of precipitation deficiency. A hydrologic drought is a period of water supply shortage. An agricultural drought is a period of dryness adversely affecting crops, livestock, landscapes, forests, wildlife, and reservoir levels, which often includes major fish kills and harm to other aquatic life as stream, pond, and spring levels drop. An agricultural drought may not occur during a meteorological or hydrologic drought if even minor precipitation occurs at the right times during the growing season. This happened during Tennessee's most severe extended drought of the mid- to late 1980s. Farmers suffered greatly in 1986 and 1988, but 1985 and 1987 yielded near bumper crops in spite of otherwise dry conditions. Hence, the frequency and timing of precipitation appears to be more important than the total volume in a given year.

Drought and extreme heat waves can lead to a greater number of wildland fires, more damaging fires, and more acres burned within each fire. This is especially true when fires have not occurred in an area for several years and the forest litter (fallen trees, limbs, branches, and dead leaves) has accumulated in greater quantities. As these fuels build up, they dry out even more, producing a greater potential for a disastrous wildland fire season.

Because the frequency of precipitation is more important than the total amount over a period of time, the years of deficit precipitation are not necessarily the years of droughts. However, if one pairs periods of deficit precipitation with years of poor crop yields, a pattern of drought materializes. In fact, when NWS annual precipitation records are compared with Tennessee Department of Agriculture crop yield records, a distinct model emerges. This pattern for Tennessee shows that at least sixteen severe drought periods have occurred over the past 200 years in Tennessee. Other extreme droughts occurred in 1980–81, 1969–71, 1966–67, 1913–14, 1877–78, and 1853–54. Some individual years (e.g., 1887, 1830, 1819, and 1797) were recorded in diaries and newspaper articles as extremely dry and were accompanied by crop failures, heavy wildland fires, water shortages, massive fish kills, and, one would suspect, a greater incidence of waterborne epidemic diseases. The state's earliest recorded drought occurred in 1797. It was particularly severe in the mid-state area, where it was said that springs believed to be everlasting dried up, as they also did in the drought of 1853–54.

Oftentimes severe heat waves coincide with droughts. The state's highest recorded temperature of 113 degrees at Perryville, in Decatur County, in 1930 was associated with the extreme drought of 1930–31. Conversely, the state's worst heat wave is believed to have occurred in 1980. It resulted in 150 heat-related deaths, most of them in the western end of the state. Thirty-eight heat-related deaths also occurred in 1952. This was the result of temperatures over one hundred degrees on three occasions during the year. Each period had three to eight consecutive days of extreme temperatures.

Heat has been described as a silent killer. When your body temperature rises to between 104 and 106 degrees or higher, your brain begins to swell and your thinking becomes extremely fuzzy. Dehydration and loss of vital electrolytes means that your body can no longer cool itself. Your blood flow becomes sluggish, your kidneys and other organs begin to shut down, and you slip into a deep coma. At this point, you are subject to death, most likely via cardiac arrest. This process occurs most rapidly in the elderly, infirm, and those with compromised immune systems.

Drought of 1930–31

STATEWIDE

> The Mississippi Valley flood of 1927, while more spectacular, and calling for relief of a costlier type because homes and possessions were swept away, affected hardly one-fourth of the number of people who suffered because of the drought [of 1930–31].
>
> —**Red Cross relief worker**

The greatest drought the United States has ever experienced as a whole was the infamous Dust Bowl of the 1930s. Surprisingly, however, in terms of overall deficit precipitation, this one ranks as only the fourth worst drought in Tennessee history. In terms of total adverse effects, though, it was still probably the worst. This drought occurred in conjunction with a whole series of natural and economic disasters, including the boll weevil's devastating attack on southern cotton crops, the subsequent collapse of the cotton market, and high wartime prices. Worst of all, it took place during the Great Depression, a time of worldwide economic panic.

This dry period affected 1,057 counties in twenty-three states, including Tennessee. It brought about hunger and deprivation that had never been experienced by most Americans, and it was a national crisis. From 1930 through 1931 many agencies joined to support the American Red Cross as they delivered humanitarian aid. During this time some Tennesseans filed trespassing charges against neighbors stealing water from their wells. One lady vindictively filled a neighbor's well with kerosene when denied use of water. Memphis police even blamed a rash of robberies on unemployment brought on by the drought and heat.

The drought was most devastating to the agricultural counties of West Tennessee: as the land dried up, so did the work. Hungry sharecroppers and their families inundated Memphis in search of employment and humanitarian assistance. City welfare agencies rendered aid to some 45,000 needy persons, most of them direct drought sufferers. Farmers bore some of the worst of the effects. The poor economy meant severely depressed markets, and the drought meant that they could not raise adequate crops. It was not only a shortage of water that made the drought so severe; it was also its lengthy duration. In short dry periods, irrigation can save crops, but when the wells and streams dry up, so do the field crops, pastures, orchards, and people's spirits. In 1930 and 1931 much livestock was slaughtered early to keep the animals from starving to death.

Tennesseans could do nothing but wait as ruin spread across their land, intensifying daily. Clouds would gather but then dissipate without giving a drop of water to the parched land. Crops wilted in the fields, topsoil dried out and blew away, pasture land changed from green to brittle brown, and wells, springs, streams, and springs ceased to flow. Farm ponds evaporated and winds blew their stench of dead fish and stagnant water across the land. Then came the chilling winter's cold. Barns and root cellars were empty, cupboards were bare, and credit soon became almost impossible to obtain. Without credit, many farmers were forced to give up. As they lost their homes, many migrated westward only to face even more bitter harvests. This ominous period in American history is brilliantly chronicled in John Steinbeck's *The Grapes of Wrath*.

SOURCES: American National Red Cross, *Relief Work in the Drought of 1930–31*, Official Report of Operations of the American National Red Cross, ARC-901 (Washington, DC: American National Red Cross, 1931); Lee Keck, Tennessee Dept. of Health and Environment, Nashville, personal correspondence with author, May 2, 1987; Nan Elizabeth Woodruff, *As Rare as Rain: Federal Relief in the Great Southern Drought of 1930–31* (Urbana: Univ. of Illinois Press, 1985).

Drought of 1984–88

STATEWIDE

The 1980s were the driest on record since the founding of the nation. Rainfall in Tennessee between 1984 and 1988 declined at a rate of some fifteen to twenty inches per year, resulting in a historical drought. According to the National Weather Service, this deficit amounted to fifty to seventy inches less rainfall in Tennessee and other southeastern states for that time period. Actually, some believe the drought began to develop as early as 1980–81. Ironically, in the midst of the drought (1985), many farmers grew bumper crops because the small amount of rain that came fell at just the right time in the growing cycle.

The eastern and middle sections of the state were particularly hard hit by this drought. The TVA reported

the lakes were running fifteen to forty-five feet below normal pool level. Even with these deficits, thanks to TVA and U.S. Army Corps of Engineers dams, the Tennessee and Cumberland rivers managed to supply as much as 50 percent of the water flowing down the lower Ohio and Mississippi rivers during the period. Several springs, supplying about twenty utility districts in East Tennessee, were down by half their normal flow volume by 1988. Because of low-water levels in TVA reservoirs, the dams could not produce enough hydroelectricity. As a result, TVA was forced to purchase electricity outside the area at a cost of $100 million.

The drought resulted in a deficit of groundwater, depleting the water table. Once this happened, some springs ceased to flow and well water dropped below the level of the wells' intake pipes. These problems led many municipal water suppliers to ask for voluntary (later implementing mandatory) water rationing in some areas.

Farmers, nurserymen, barge transportation companies, and the forest products industries were hit hard as the drought persisted. Farm crops and fruit shriveled in the field and on the trees and vines. Lawns dried up and weeds (stalwart drought resisters) retreated into the last remnants of shade, seeking the last remaining ground moisture. As lake and river levels dropped, snags created navigational hazards, causing an increase in boat and water sports accidents. In the surface water that remained, algae and bacteria growth increased prodigiously, as did the relative amounts of iron, magnesium, and other chemicals dissolved from bottom sediments. This resulted in challenges and increased expense in treating municipal water supplies; although the water was made safe for drinking, bad tastes and odors became increasingly difficult to eliminate.

It has been said that the answer to pollution is dilution. However, at this time some manufacturing facilities and municipalities were dumping more biological and industrial wastes into shallow streams adversely affected by the drought, resulting in greatly increased water pollution. Although mosquitoes continued to find stagnant, standing water in which to flourish, quick and decisive actions by local and state health officials prevented major disease outbreaks. Higher overall water temperatures and increasing stagnation lowered the percentage of dissolved oxygen in stream and lake waters, resulting in a number of massive fish kills during the period. The Tennessee, Cumberland, and Mississippi rivers and their tributaries fell to record low levels. At Memphis, the Mississippi River dropped to almost eleven feet below its base level, the lowest point since the founding of the nation. This halted almost all barge traffic on the river, resulting in spoilage of vast amounts of perishable commodities and the loss of countless millions of dollars in revenue. During this period, wildland fires (many believed to be the result of arson) resulted in millions of dollars in lost forest resources, wildlife, structures, and infrastructure. During the worst periods of the drought, the State Division of Forestry was forced to recruit additional firefighters from outside the state to control forest and brushfires, especially those along the so-called wildland-urban interface.

The drought was finally broken by the return of heavy rainfall in the winter, spring, and fall of 1989. Ironically, this rain was so plentiful that it caused the wettest fall in the Tennessee Valley in many years and resulted in considerable area flooding.

SOURCES: Allen R. Coggins, "Strangers in a Dry Land," *Tennessee Conservationist* 15, no. 3 (May/June 1989): 6–8; Lee Keck, Tennessee Dept. of Health and Environment, Nashville, personal correspondence with author, May 2, 1987; *Knoxville Journal,* May 23, June 6, and July 1, 1988; *Knoxville News Sentinel,* Feb. 22, May 1, 2, 31, Aug. 25, Sept. 23, and Oct. 3, 1989.

Severe Heat Wave of 1980

STATEWIDE

Technically, a period of extreme heat occurs when temperatures hover ten degrees or more above the av-

erage high temperature for the region and last for several weeks. Such prolonged periods of extreme heat are rare in Tennessee, but they do occur. Consecutive days of temperatures over 100 degrees have occurred in East Tennessee but are more likely to occur in the more westerly counties. According to the National Weather Service, the highest temperature ever recorded in Tennessee was 113 degrees, in West Tennessee at Perryville, Decatur County, on July 29 and August 9, 1930.

The summer of 1980 brought a heat wave blamed for 156 heat-related deaths; 88 of these (roughly 56 percent of the fatalities) occurred in Memphis. Chattanooga reported sixteen heat-related fatalities, Nashville registered ten, and the other forty-two were scattered elsewhere across the state. According to the Tennessee Department of Public Health in a February 1982 report, about 72 percent of the deaths occurred in West Tennessee between the Tennessee River and the Mississippi River. Memphis recorded thirty-three days in which the thermometer was at or above 100 degrees; fifteen of these days were consecutive, and on July 13 the temperature reached 108, which was only five degrees less than the record high temperature for the state.

According to the Centers for Disease Control and Prevention (CDC), the people most affected by the 1980 heat wave were urban, nonwhite, and lower economic class elderly citizens. The death rate for women was greater than for men. Accessibility to air conditioning in working and living environments was identified by CDC as the single most important factor that could have prevented heat stroke and other deadly heat-related conditions. Sadly, it was reported that many of those deaths could have been prevented with fans and air conditioners. It seems that some people (most of them elderly) living in Memphis slums chose dying of heatstroke in their homes rather than opening their windows and risking home invasions, burglaries, or worse.

This heat wave, which did not end until September, extended far beyond Tennessee, from Texas to the Dako-

Memphis firefighters extinguish brushfire during the statewide heat wave of 1980. Courtesy of Special Collections, University of Memphis Libraries.

tas and from Florida up the East Coast to New England. The long-term high temperatures dried up reservoirs, withered crops, killed livestock, ignited wildland fires, burned out machinery, overloaded urban water and electric utility systems, turned homes and businesses into furnaces, and even buckled up miles of asphalt roadways. In terms of loss of life and property damage, this period of severe heat is considered among the most devastating disasters ever to occur in the United States in recorded history. It is estimated to have claimed as many as 1,700 lives across the United States and caused property damage amounting to some $20 billion (or over $50 billion when adjusted for inflation to the year 2007).

Meteorologists believe that this extended period of extreme heat was caused by an abnormal jet stream pattern. As it moved far to the north in the United States, three giant high pressure centers formed to the south. One was centered over Hawaii and the other two over the Mid-Atlantic and the south-central states respectively. As the high pressure centers stagnated, the weather grew progressively hotter and drier each day. Ironically, while the Americas suffered from stifling heat, those on the opposite side of the Atlantic Ocean suffered a miserable, unusually cold and rainy summer.

SOURCES: *Chattanooga Times,* July 11–15, 1980; NOAA Satellite and Information Service, *Billion Dollar U.S. Weather Disasters, 1980–1999* (Asheville, NC: National Climatic Data Center, 2000); Tennessee Dept. of Public Health [TDPH], *Deaths of Tennessee Residents from Extreme Heat and from Extreme Cold, 1949–1980* (Nashville: Tennessee Dept. of Health and Environment, 1982); TDPH, *Heat Related Deaths of July, 1980* (Nashville: State Center for Health Statistics, 1982).

EARTHQUAKES

"A bad earthquake," wrote Charles Darwin in *The Voyage of the Beagle* (1839), "at once destroys our oldest associations; the earth, the very emblem of solidity, has moved beneath our feet like a thin crust over a liquid; one second of time has created in the mind a strange idea of insecurity, which hours of reflection would not have produced."

Few major earthquakes have occurred in Tennessee over the past 200 years, although felt quakes are not uncommon, especially in West Tennessee. The most significant events, called the New Madrid quakes of 1811 and 1812, occurred over a period of only two months, but many strong aftershocks accompanied them for months, and still lesser events for years.

Two additional temblors of relatively high magnitude also shook West Tennessee on January 4, 1834, and August 17, 1865. Fortunately, they caused much less damage in Tennessee than those of 1811 and 1812. A strong quake, whose epicenter was in Giles County, Virginia, caused damage to structures in upper East Tennessee in 1897, and major quakes on August 31, 1886, in Charleston, South Carolina, also caused damage to structures in East Tennessee as well as adjacent states.

The effects of major earthquakes could be devastating and widespread along the Central Mississippi River Valley, including all of West Tennessee, due to the nature of the area's geology. The greatest areas of risk are obviously along the west coast of California, Washington State, and northward along the Pacific boundary of Alaska. Hawaii, particularly the largest island, is also prone to quakes and volcanism. In Tennessee, however, the greatest potential for damaging earthquakes is from the Tennessee River west to the Mississippi River. Although East Tennessee is also considered earthquake country, its potential for damaging quakes is less than in the western third of the state. The Highland Rim, Central Basin, and Cumberland Plateau regions have a very low probability for destructive quakes; however, they could certainly be affected by large earthquakes originating in the New Madrid or East Tennessee seismic zones.

The areas of California with the greatest risk for earthquakes are in hard rock, along the San Andreas Fault Zone. The effects of quakes are quite severe in that region, but the area of impact is relatively small. This is because earthquake waves, measured as peak ground acceleration, cannot extend as far outward in solid rock as they can in less dense materials, such as soil or water. Conversely, the Mississippi Embayment—which essentially includes all of Tennessee west of the Tennessee River—is underlain by unconsolidated sediments. There are no hard rocks at the surface; instead, the surface materials are soft and in many areas prone to liquefaction. Liquefaction is a process by which soils behave more like a viscous fluid than a solid medium when subjected to earthquakes. Because of liquefaction, built structures lose stability, sink, and overturn during a strong quake. Infrastructure with the highest risk are highways, railways, solid walls, bridge abutments, buildings, towers, and so forth. Buildings of various heights can fail and pancake (floors dropping, or telescoping, simultaneously), depending upon the magnitude of the quakes. Utility lines could be broken, causing massive power and communication outages. Cellular, radio, and television towers could topple or become misaligned,

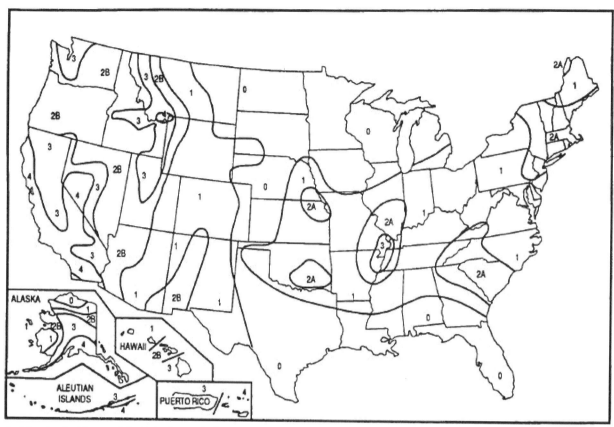

As this seismic risk map of the United States indicates, much of Tennessee (particularly the western and eastern portions of the state) falls in zones 2A and 3, which means that at least moderate damage from earthquakes is predicted. See Richard G. Stearns and Robert A. Miller, *Earthquake Hazards in Tennessee,* Environmental Geology Series No. 4 (Nashville: State of Tennessee Dept. of Conservation, Div. of Geology, 1977).

interrupting cellular phone, commercial broadcasting, and vital emergency radio communications. Pipelines that supply water and natural gas to, and carry sewage away from, homes and commercial establishments could be severed. In addition, the major natural gas pipelines running through West Tennessee into the eastern and northeastern states could be jeopardized. These are but a few of the catastrophes that strong earthquakes could cause as they crumble buildings and infrastructure, ignite fires, set off explosions, and otherwise wreak havoc. It is these multiple and simultaneous damages that make earthquakes so potentially devastating and terrifying.

The damaging effects of earthquakes cited in this book are listed in terms of either their magnitude or intensity. The Richter scale is a measure of the magnitude or total amount of energy released by earthquakes (see table 2 in the appendix). It is a ten-point scale expressed in Arabic numerals. Each step in the scale indicates a thirtyfold increase in the amount of energy generated by an earthquake. In other words, a 6.0 earthquake is thirty times more destructive than a 5.0 earthquake, sixty times more destructive than a 4.0 quake, and so on. The energy or maximum impact of a quake occurs at its focus, or point of origin. This occurs along a fault line beneath the surface of the earth. The epicenter of an earthquake is the point on the surface of the earth directly above the focus. This is generally, but not always, the area of greatest impact or destruction.

Another scale, the Modified Mercalli (MM), describes an earthquake's severity, or intensity, in terms of the amount of actual destruction caused (the damage to people and their built environments). The steps on this scale, as shown in table 3, are represented by Roman numerals (I–XII). Those in the I range (known as micro quakes) are only detectable using seismographs. XII represents the most powerful effects conceivable. Although there is no direct correlation between the magnitude of an earthquake and its intensity, the two may be compared in general or relative terms. Furthermore, if one has a description of the effects of an earthquake that occurred in, say, 1907, that description (e.g., "the quake caused small cracks in the brick walls of the county jailhouse") allows geologists to assign it a value on the MM scale. In this way, seismologists can use newspaper accounts, diaries, and other historical records to assess the intensity ratings of past earthquakes and estimate the magnitude and location of quakes for which there are no seismographic records.

Table 4 is a generalized comparison of the MM and Richter scales in terms of actual or predictable impact. Hence, through written historical accounts of earthquake effects recorded at the time of the occurrence, one may predict the approximate locations of past quakes and to some extent their approximate magnitudes.

New Madrid Earthquakes
PRIMARILY WEST TENNESSEE, 1811–12

In the winter of 1811 Napoleon was fighting his way across Europe, a future president named Harrison was fighting Indians on the Tippecanoe River, and the riverboat *New Orleans* was plying the currents of the Mississippi River on its maiden voyage. Then, suddenly, on the bitter cold morning of December 16, the first in a series of catastrophic earthquakes struck West Tennessee and the entire Central Mississippi River Valley. Two more would follow in the weeks ahead. "With respect to their large region of damage and widespread area of perceptibility, as well as the physiographic changes caused by them," seismologist Otto Nuttli of St. Louis University wrote in the 1970s, "the Mississippi Valley earthquakes of 1811 and 1812 rank as the largest to have occurred in North America since its settlement by Europeans."

The estimated strength of each of the three great New Madrid earthquakes is still a matter of controversy. Nuttli estimated the magnitudes of these quakes in the 8.0-plus Richter range. However, other scientists now believe them to have been in the 7.0-plus range. The first of these violent quakes, and the second greatest in severity, occurred in the St. Francis River area of northeast Arkansas. From written descriptions and eyewitness accounts of this and the other quakes, Nuttli estimated its magnitude at 8.6 on the Richter scale and XI–XII on the Modified Mercalli scale (MM XI–XII). Revised estimates place it in the mid- to lower 7.0 range. The second struck five weeks later and several miles to the northeast. It was the mildest of the three quakes, which Nuttli estimated at a magnitude of 8.4, or MM X–XII. Others now place it at or just under 7.0 on the Richter scale. Finally, on February 7, 1812, the most severe of the quakes, with a Nuttli magnitude 8.8, or MM XI–XII, struck the river hamlet of New Madrid, Missouri. It is now believed that this temblor was on the upper end of the 7.0 range. It was felt over most of the continental United States and parts of Canada and Mexico.

Geologists attribute the quakes to an ill-defined series of deeply buried faults that run roughly parallel to the Mississippi River Valley. This so-called New Madrid or Central United States seismic zone runs roughly from Cairo, Illinois, south through Missouri to Marked Tree, Arkansas. A side branch extends into the Reelfoot Lake region of northwest Tennessee.

Left: Tree with a double set of roots formed in the aftermath of the New Madrid earthquakes of 1811 and 1812. The ground sank by several feet, creating low areas flooded by the Mississippi River. Courtesy of U.S. Geological Survey. Right: Trees twisted by the New Madrid earthquake on the Chickasaw bluffs, east side of Reelfoot Lake. Courtesy of U.S. Geological Survey.

According to a few personal diaries and eyewitness accounts quoted in local newspapers, the endless days and nights of aftershocks were dreadful to experience. Besides the three great quakes, there were dozens of events in the 5.0 to upper 6.0 range and literally thousands of even smaller aftershocks. These mighty temblors occurred in an area where few people had ever even heard of earthquakes, let alone experienced them. The small number of primitive roads into the area were made impassible by downed trees and cracks and fissures in the earth. There was great destruction along the Mississippi River from southern Ohio and Indiana south to Memphis and northwestern Mississippi. Great cracks and fissures opened up to spew out sand and water. These "sand blows," as they are called, still plague the cotton and soy bean farmers of the area since they are not nearly as fertile and productive as the surrounding soils. Gaping crevices formed, some twelve feet wide and deep and twenty feet long. Two temporary waterfalls developed on the Mississippi River, one formed upstream and the other downstream of New Madrid, Missouri. Although both were audible from that hamlet, they were short lived in the soft sediments of the river valley. All along the Mississippi, islands, sandbars, and other familiar riverine features changed: seasoned river pilots had a whole new stream with which to contend. The quakes caused waves to rush over river banks, and return currents washed limbs, whole trees, and other debris into the main channel. Massive logjams also formed, making navigation even more perilous. Many boats were capsized or crushed in logjams, and their crews and cargo were never seen again. Massive landslides occurred all along the high Mississippi River bluffs. Some areas rose or fell twenty feet relative to their surrounding elevations. A twenty-acre area near Piney River in Tennessee sank so low that the tops of its trees were at the same level as the surrounding ground. This area quickly filled with water to become a swamp. Tennessee's only large natural lake, Reelfoot, was either formed or enlarged by the quakes, and the Mississippi River was said to have flowed backward, for a time, to fill and flood the natural reservoir. Other large areas of lakes and swamps were also elevated above their previous levels, and in time the water drained away and they evolved into upland forests and prairies. Today these areas support Tennessee cotton and soybeans. As devastating as these early quakes were, destruction in human terms was relatively light. There were few people and not many built environments to be affected.

The late Ralph Burris, former superintendent of Reelfoot Lake State Park, once told the author a story about the first quake and the first voyage of the steamboat *New Orleans.* On the morning of December 16, 1811, that great riverboat, first to ply the waters between Cincinnati and New Orleans, was just rounding the bend from the Ohio into the Mississippi River. Word of the great vessel passed quickly among the local Native Americans, and many began gathering on the banks to scrutinize it. Suddenly, as they watched the boat and the smoke billowing from its stacks, it blew its mighty steam whistle. It was at that moment that the first of the New Madrid quakes coincidentally occurred. According to Ralph, many of the Native Americans, assuming a cause-and-effect relationship, stayed well clear of riverboats thereafter.

SOURCES: Ralph Burris, superintendent, Reelfoot Lake State Park, personal correspondence with author, Jan. 31, 1983; Allen R. Coggins, "Earthquakes 1811–1812," in *The Tennessee Encyclopedia of History and Culture,* ed. Carroll Van West, 271–72 (Nashville: Tennessee Historical Society and Rutledge Hill Press, 1998); James Cornell, *The Great International Disaster Book* (New York: Scribner, 1976); Myron L. Fuller, *The New Madrid Earthquake,* Dept. of Interior, U.S. Geological Survey, Bulletin 494 (Washington, DC: Government Printing Office, 1912); Webb Garrison, *Disasters That Made History* (Nashville: Abingdon Press, 1973); David R. Logsdon, Nashville, "'I Was There!' In the New Madrid Earthquakes of 1811–12," MS, 1990; Jeffrey Munsey, Tennessee Valley Authority seismologist, Knoxville, personal correspondence with author, Sept. 15, 2009; Otto W. Nuttli, "The Mississippi Valley Earthquakes of 1811 and 1812: Intensities, Ground Motion and Magnitudes," *Bulletin of the Seismological Society of America* 63, no. 1 (Feb. 1973): 227–48; James Lal Penick Jr., *The New Madrid Earthquakes* (Columbia: Univ. of Missouri Press, 1981).

EPIDEMICS AND PANDEMICS

Epidemics are rapidly spreading diseases affecting a collective population of people simultaneously. Pandemics are large-scale epidemics that may cover a nation, a continent, or the entire planet. Diseases, in the form of pandemics, epidemics, or individual outbreaks, have been ever present and persistent in causing human suffering and death. Four great epidemic, and sometimes pandemic, diseases have ravaged Tennessee, beginning with smallpox, which was recorded among the Cherokee and other native tribes as early as 1738. This disease was the great slayer of Native Americans. Yellow fever and cholera entered Tennessee in the early 1820s and early 1830s respectively. They had devastating effects within cities and towns lacking, at that time, even rudimentary sanitation practices and health regulations. Finally, a great pandemic of influenza killed thousands of Tennesseans in 1918 and 1919. Lesser epidemics of influenza likewise occurred as late as 1957 and 1968. The Centers for Disease Control and Prevention Pandemic Severity Index shows the relative virulence of these three major disease outbreaks in comparison to that of the normal seasonal flu (see table 5 in the appendix). Yellow fever is an example of one of the terrifying early epidemic diseases that killed many Tennesseans. It was said of this disease that

> the pain worsened, crippling movement and burning the skin. The fever rose to 104, maybe 105 degrees, and bones felt as though they had been cracked. The kidneys stopped functioning, poisoning the body. Abdominal cramps began in the final days of illness as the patient vomited black blood brought on by internal hemorrhaging. The victim became a palette of hideous color: Red blood ran from the gums, eyes and nose. The tongue swelled, turning purple. Black vomit roiled. And the skin grew deep gold, the whites of the eyes turning brilliant yellow. (Crosby, 2)

Of all the disasters that affected the aboriginal peoples of the New World, epidemics had the greatest impact. For want of natural immunity, Native Americans were highly susceptible to Old World diseases that moved inland from the Atlantic coastal settlements, Canada, and Mexico beginning in the sixteenth century. In fact, the toll inflicted upon American Indians from both contagious and noncontagious diseases has been greater than that caused by all European weapons and other military actions combined. Many historians and anthropologists also believe that the effects of epidemics on Native Americans in the Southeast (including Tennessee) in the seventeenth and eighteenth centuries may have been greater than at any other place and time in the New World.

Determining the numbers of deaths from specific diseases, including epidemics, is problematic. Although some reliable records (as cited by John Duffy in *Epidemics in Colonial America*) indicate that epidemic fatality figures may have ranged from 55 to over 90 percent, exact statistics are impossible to ascertain because many outbreaks were not clearly defined, were not accurately accounted for, or were within isolated areas and never recorded. With some exceptions, there are also discrepancies in records that do exist. Early diaries, letters, and even newspaper accounts mention epidemics, but rarely list the number of ill or dead. Accounts of such incidents in the chronicles of Hernando DeSoto, those of other European explorers, and even early research papers are ambiguous and hence suspect.

The same diseases that decimated Native Americans also affected European settlers on ships bound for the New World and within early settlements. On some so-called coffin ships as many as half of the immigrants were reported to have died in close quarters. Furthermore, contrary to myth, most epidemics did not affect large populations over broad geographical areas. It has been suggested that they tended to follow specific corridors such as trade routes, advancing, dying out, and then flaring up again in new locations. As mentioned, the epidemic most devastating to Native Americans was smallpox. Fortunately, inoculations against the disease, a concept first introduced by Dr. Edward Jenner in the spring of 1796, eventually curbed incidents, even among Native Americans.

By 1802 the War Department instructed the Army to begin enacting measures that would curtail contagious diseases among Native Americans near military posts. In 1832 Congress authorized the first large-scale smallpox vaccination programs for Native Americans. However, it is believed that this was done not so much for the benefit of the Native Americans as it was to protect U.S. soldiers. Whites suffered less from smallpox than from chronic diseases such as dysentery and malaria. Cholera and yellow fever became problems in the early to late 1800s, with influenza arriving later.

Although fatalities from epidemics were high in the early years, survivors developed immunity and were not as likely to contract (at least that strain of) the disease again. Commonsense care, including bed rest, nourishing food, and cold compresses to bring down fever were somewhat effective in treating these diseases. Unfortu-

nately, when everyone in a household or a village came down with the disease simultaneously, they could not care for each other. In these cases, those who might otherwise have been strong enough to survive died from starvation or neglect. This was particularly true in Native American settlements.

Throughout the 1800s, many towns, cities, and counties established so-called pest houses (short for pestilence houses), which were hospitals of sorts where the ill were literally incarcerated or forced into quarantine until they either got well or died. Food and water were passed through portals to the patients. Contrary to what one might think, being sent to a pest house was not tantamount to a death sentence. There is some evidence (as cited below) that the survival rate for those in pest houses was greater than for those who were simply abandoned or treated at home, where the entire family might come down with the disease and perish. At least those in pest houses had advantages, such as daily food, fresh water, and some (albeit meager) medical care.

Until fairly recently the causes of many diseases and their vectors (carriers such as mosquitoes and fleas) were unknown. Although unsanitary conditions were suspected of causing disease, even physicians did not understand how. The very idea that tiny organisms like mosquitoes might carry and spread diseases would have been considered preposterous at the time. Through much of the 1800s and early 1900s, Tennessee's larger towns and cities were perfect environments for outbreaks of cholera, yellow fever, and other dread diseases.

> Garbage, ashes, and kitchen slop were piled in back alleys and yards or, too often, thrown into the streets until they were picked up by an overworked scavenger hired by the city. The scavenger hauled the refuse by wagon to the river, loaded it on "bump boats" and threw it into the Cumberland [River]. Horses and mules, the main source of transportation, produced enormous quantities of

manure, and with their hooves and wagon wheels pounded it into the brick and crushed stone pavement, where it was then soaked with thousands of gallons of urine each day. This, joined by the garbage, privy fumes, and the contributions of assorted dogs, chickens, and hogs, created an abominable stench on hot summer days. Dead animals were left in the streets for days before being dragged by the city scavenger to the river to be dumped. (Doyle, 83–84)

In the early years, there were no public health officials, newspaper reports were unreliable, and there was little communication and coordination even among doctors. Reports of mysterious diseases, even those reaching epidemic proportions, were rarely recorded or reported, often for fear of public panic. For example, a dreadful disease simply called "fever" at the time struck Knoxville in 1800, and hardly a family, including the William Blount family, escaped it. At that time, William Blount, the former governor of the Territory South of the River Ohio, was speaker of the Tennessee state senate. Mrs. Blount's mother was the first victim in the household, followed by one of William's sons. Finally, the governor himself contracted the disease and died at the age of fifty-three.

Another devastating epidemic struck in 1829, in Fulton, a small port in Lauderdale County on the Mississippi River, just above the mouth of the Hatchie River. Two hundred or so of its citizens were believed to have died from the disease. By 1832 Fulton was a ghost town, but three years later it was settled again.

A disease called cold plague occurred in 1816. At the time, this mysterious illness was thought by some to have arisen in the aftermath of the great earthquakes of 1811 and 1812. It was also called ague, malarial fever, marsh fever, or periodic fever and was characterized by convulsions, contortions, and "dancing." This dis-

ease was described in the diary of Raccoon John Smith. Born in Sullivan County, Tennessee, Smith moved his family to Madison County, Alabama, by 1815. According to an excerpt from his diary, appearing in the *Challens Monthly* in March 1858, "At that time a disease called the 'cold plague' prevailed in that country [Alabama]. On the 17th of April [1815] my wife died; and about the 20th I was attacked with that awful complaint. This is all the death-life spell of sickness I have ever had."

Before the causes of diseases had been scientifically established, many theories were suggested to explain how they evolved and spread. According to one notion, cholera and other such diseases were caused by immorality. Another hypothesis held that there were poison gases in the night air called "miasma." We know now that these vapors were actually methane, sewer gas, or swamp gas caused by putrefying organic matter. Many millponds that dried up around Knoxville in 1838 were said to give off this toxic "miasma." Some believed that simply breathing such vapors could cause a disease (hence the myth about night air being dangerous to one's health). It would be decades before science proved that the actual carrier of the dreaded illness was the mosquito. In fact, it was not until the 1880s and 1890s that the causes of some of the world's worst infectious diseases, including tuberculosis, typhoid fever, diphtheria, cholera, and tetanus, were discovered.

SOURCES: Abraham B. Bergman, et al., "A Political History of the Indian Health Service," *Milbank Quarterly* 77, no. 4. (1999): 571–604; Betsey B. Creekmore, *Knoxville* (Knoxville: Univ. of Tennessee Press, 1958); Molly Caldwell Crosby, *The American Plague: The Untold Story of Yellow Fever: The Epidemic That Shaped Our History* (New York: Berkley Books, 2006); Don Harrison Doyle, *Nashville in the New South, 1850–1970* (Knoxville: Univ. of Tennessee Press, 1985); John Duffy, *Epidemics in Colonial America* (Baton Rouge: Louisiana State Univ. Press, 1953); G. R. Milner, "Epidemic Disease in the Post Contact Southeast: An Appraisal," *Mid-Continental Journal of Archaeology* 5, no. 37 (1980): 56; Southern Historical Press, *History of Tennessee: From the Earliest Times to the Present, 1886* (Greenville, SC: Southern Historical Press, 1997).

Cholera

STATEWIDE, 1832–73

Perhaps the most famous cholera victim in the epidemic of 1849 was President James K. Polk. En route to Nashville shortly after leaving the White House, he contracted the disease and died within two weeks. On the day of his funeral, 34 other cholera victims were buried in the same [Old Gray] city cemetery. In 1850, the number of cholera deaths was even higher. Officially 91, or one in every 12.6 citizens, remaining in the city, died from the disease.

—**Byrd Douglas,**
Steamboatin' on the Cumberland

Cholera is a highly contagious disease that thrives in filthy environments. Throughout its history, it is believed to have wiped out as much as a third of the earth's population. It was to the nineteenth century what the bubonic plague was to the fourteenth century, and it was second only to influenza in its rapid and sweeping coverage of the globe. When the disease struck, death often occurred within days or even hours of the first onset of symptoms. Some people were reported to have gone to bed at night feeling fit and by morning they were dead. One victim was quoted as saying that he felt no symptoms of the disease until he pitched forward into the street, "as if knocked in the head by an axe" (Davis, *Nashville Tales,* 118).

Cholera is a bacterial infection that attacks the body quickly, causing severe diarrhea, acute spasmodic vomiting, excruciating muscle cramps, and extreme dehydration. As the body loses moisture, the blood literally begins to congeal like tar. The face and body turn purplish-blue, and in death, the hands, feet, and skin are drawn and wrinkled. When cholera struck, "it was like turning on a faucet and letting all the fluids rush out of the body. The patient's skin turned blue and clammy, and sank in shriveled, puckered folds. When he died, his body was dry as parchment" (Davis, *Nashville Tales,* 118).

The causative organism of cholera, first isolated and identified by Robert Koch in 1883, is a comma-shaped bacterium (*Vibrio comma*) that infects and quickly multiplies within the human digestive tract. It enters the body through food or water contaminated by other victims. This contamination generally spreads through polluted water or by flies that have been in contact with the fecal material or the bodies of victims. There are treatments for the disease, but there is no cure. The victim either survives the disease or dies.

Cholera was restricted to parts of Asia for 2,000 years, but it suddenly spread westward through Europe and eventually to the New World in the early 1830s. The first case in North America was reported in June 1832, in Quebec City, Canada. It is believed that the disease was transported from Dublin, Ireland, via an immigrant ship that was initially refused entry into the port of New York. From Canada it spread quickly into the United States along major transportation corridors. Half of all untreated cholera victims died as the disease grew to epidemic intensity seven times between 1833 and its final eradication from the United States in 1892.

The disease was first reported in Tennessee in December 1832. It became epidemic in 1832–33, 1838, 1849–50, 1866, and 1873, with some isolated outbreaks in between. It spread rapidly along navigable streams and roadways in 1832–33 and is believed to have entered West Tennessee from the Mississippi River, but in middle and East Tennessee it traveled more directly along highway routes. Most cholera deaths occurred in the larger cities of Memphis, Knoxville, Chattanooga, and Nashville. However, many smaller towns and villages

Tomb of President James K. Polk, who died of cholera shortly after leaving the White House in 1849, on the Tennessee State Capitol grounds. He died in Knoxville. Photograph by Brent Moore.

probably suffered proportionally greater effects since they had even less awareness of proper sanitation practices. Zane's Trace, a highway from Zanesville, Kentucky, to Florence, Alabama, served as a major route for the spread of the pestilence through Middle Tennessee. Four towns and cities along this route were particularly hard hit. Gallatin was struck during the winter and spring of 1832, and Nashville in December. Contradictory reports cite between 158 and 173 deaths in Nashville during the period. Of that total, about 70 died in June 1833 alone. Thirty-four out of a population of 1,000 died in Pulaski in only six days. In Shelbyville 70 contracted the disease and 55 died.

As cholera came calling, victims fled, further contributing to its spread. In fact 5,500 of Nashville's 6,000 residents fled the city to avoid the epidemic. Knoxville was only slightly affected by the disease in 1832–33, but was said to have suffered severely five years later. In July 1847 a pandemic moved westward out of the Ganges Valley of India, and by December it had spread to the New World, entering New York via immigrant ships. Over the next couple of years it spread across the continent, arising periodically throughout the rest of the century.

The busy river port of Memphis suffered relatively few cases in 1849, owing in part to the city's abundant pure water, supplied by deep artesian wells. However, as the pestilence moved up the Tennessee, Ohio, and Cumberland rivers into Middle Tennessee, the death toll was much greater. Nashville was hit hard, and Clarksville, Gallatin, Columbia, and Lebanon had so many cholera victims that there were few persons left to tend the sick and bury the dead. As conditions worsened, public meetings, including court sessions and school classes, were canceled. Even political candidates canceled speaking engagements.

In the wake of the Civil War (1866), as Tennesseans were struggling for economic recovery, they suffered yet another large cholera epidemic. Spreading primarily via infected troops as they moved south and west through Nashville to other towns and cities (including Memphis), this wave paralyzed commerce. Nashville lost 659 and Memphis some 900 people. This time, even the deep, pure artesian wells of Memphis did not prevent the epidemic.

The state's worst, and mercifully its last, great outbreak occurred in 1873. In fact, that year's epidemic was probably more widespread and devastating for Tennessee than for any other state. Although it occurred throughout Memphis, some areas were affected more than others.

> [In 1873] the streets of Memphis were unclean, the alleys reeking with filth; the back yards . . . were full of slops and garbage. Vessels filled with the refuse of kitchens and laundries were emptied in the streets, to decay or be devoured by the swine, the only scavenger carts of the city. Privies had remained unemptied for years, and were in many places running over with the foul accumulations. In many parts of the city, ponds of water were undrained and stagnant, evaporating the filth [of] the streets and lots which poured into them. The place was rife with the elements of a great plague, and only needed the specific germ to diffuse it widely

A Mississippi River steamer crowded with men, women, and children infected with cholera. *John Maynard Woodworth, Cholera Epidemic of 1873 in the United States* (Washington, DC: Government Printing Office, 1875), 192.

> and fatally amid a people who had forgotten that such things existed as the laws of health and disease. (Chambers, 301)

In one neighborhood, eighty persons died within a few days of one another; some families lost every member of their household. Over a thousand cases occurred from May through mid-August, and a quarter of the victims died. The disease also broke out among prisoners working on the Paducah to Memphis railroad. Some fled into the swamps and others were transported by rail back to the state prison in Nashville. By the time they reached the city, most of the seventy-five convicts and their four women cooks had contracted the disease.

While the epidemic was severe in Memphis, it was even worse in Nashville, where half of those stricken perished. As in Memphis, Nashville's public health laws and basic sanitation practices were practically nonexistent, making the city ripe for disaster from the spreading plague. One physician, Dr. J. Berrien Lindsley, described Nashville as the "filthiest city on the continent" (quoted in Davis, *Nashville Tales*, 121).

Even Nashville's topography worked against it, as open privies drained into creeks and sinkholes in an area of shallow soils and limestone beds honeycombed with cracks, fissures, and caves. This allowed sewage to seep into the groundwater that then emerged in springs and wells in low-lying areas. It was not coincidental that the first civilian casualty died on Lick Branch, just opposite the prison's sewer outlet, since the epidemic had arrived in Nashville via infected prison inmates. From here the pestilence spread over the city and out into the countryside. The first victim died in May, and the epidemic peaked on June 20, thereafter referred to as Black Friday, when 72 died. Although half of Nashville's citizens had abandoned the city by the end of June, around 1,500 cases had been reported, and half of those eventually died.

The community of New Bethel (in Nashville) was called a great slaughterhouse. As in the case of smallpox and Native Americans, whole families suffered and perished when no one was strong enough to care for the others. Forty-nine were buried in the New Bethel graveyard, fifty-three at Mount Ararat Church, forty at Bosley's graveyard, thirty-eight at Fort Zollicoffer cemetery, and twenty-eight at Mill Creek Cemetery. According to Dr. William K. Bowling, "They [the African American citizens of New Bethel] marched uncomplaining through their gardens to their graves."

By 1873 Nashville had sustained six epidemics of cholera and lost 3,000 of its citizens. About a third of those deaths occurred during the 1873 event. While attending an industrial trade fair in Nashville in May, many people from across the state became infected with cholera. When they left the city, many carried the disease back to their communities, causing hundreds of additional deaths. Jonesboro was devastated by the disease, and at one point only about seventy-five of its citizens remained. One man on the cemetery crew, digging graves ahead of schedule, died and ironically was buried in one of the graves he had dug the day before.

Jonesboro, according to Charlotte Crutcher, "wore a deserted and melancholy aspect. At night the howling of the dogs and the screams of the dying and bereaved added to the general gloom. How can one describe the scenes of that terrible period? What pen can accurately portray the agony of the sick and dying and the anguish and distress of the bereaved? Who can depict the gloom and horror that prevailed?" (77) An awareness of the connection between disease and poor sanitation eventually brought about more stringent public health strategies and the eradication of cholera from the United States and other civilized nations.

SOURCES: William King Bowling, *An Account of the Cholera, as It Appeared in Nashville in the Year 1873* (Nashville, Univ. Book & Job Office, Medical College, 1873); J. S. Chambers, MD, *The Conquest of Cholera: America's Greatest Scourge* (New York: Macmillan, 1938); Charlotte Crutcher, "Asiatic Cholera in Jonesboro, 1873," *Tennessee Historical Quarterly* 31 (Spring 1972): 74–79; Louise Littleton Davis, *Frontier Tales of Tennessee* (Gretna, LA: Pelican Publishing Co., 1976); Davis, *Nashville Tales,* (Gretna, LA: Pelican Publishing Co., 1981); Byrd Douglas, *Steamboatin' on the Cumberland* (Nashville: Tennessee Book Co., 1961); Federal Writers Project, *Tennessee: A Guide to the State* (New York: Viking, 1939); *Knoxville Chronicle,* Aug. 2, 1873; Dixon Merritt, ed. *The History of Wilson County: Its Land and Its Life* ([Lebanon, TN]: County Court of Wilson County, 1961); Charles E. Rosenberg, *The Cholera Years: The United States in 1832, 1849, and 1866* (Chicago: Univ. of Chicago Press, 1962); Tennessee Dept. of Public Health, *A Century of Progress: A Challenge for the Future* (Nashville: State of Tennessee, 1977).

Influenza

STATEWIDE, 1872–1968

As their lungs filled . . . the patients became short of breath and increasingly cyanotic. After gasping for several hours they became delirious and incontinent, and many died struggling to clear their airways of a blood-tinged froth that sometimes gushed from their nose and mouth. It was a dreadful business.

—Isaac Starr, Univ. of Pennsylvania medical student, 1918

To place influenza in perspective as a disease, one must realize that it has the dubious distinction of having killed more people in a year's time in the pandemic of 1918–19 than any other event in human history. Additionally, two factors have made it unique in the annals of epidemic disease.

First, epidemics generally target the very young, the very old, the weak, and the infirm. Influenza, especially in the epidemic of 1918–19, struck healthy young men, many living in close quarters within World War I military camps. Hence a humorous, yet insightful statement by an anonymous woman who described the effects of the disease: "People been dying 'round here, ain't never died before." The close proximity of so many people gave opportunity to a disease that spreads from person to person via airborne droplets from coughing and sneezing.

Second, no other disease has ever spread as far and as rapidly as influenza did during that pandemic. Even isolated South Pacific islands were affected, and some native Alaskan settlements were wiped out. How this occurred, as well as the plague's point of origin, are still mysteries, but it is certain that World War I troops, both in America and abroad, helped spread the disease. This pandemic is known to have been a variety of avian influenza (bird flu), which might explain its rapid spread, by wild birds, to all corners of the earth.

A highly contagious and acute viral respiratory disease, influenza is characterized by high fever, profuse perspiration, coughing, headache, general aches and pains, weakness, and inflamed respiratory mucus membranes. It routinely occurs during the winter months of most years, but in some years it has become epidemic or pandemic in other seasons. When properly treated, most people's symptoms subside within two to five days, followed by several days or weeks of convalescence. However, some individuals are more susceptible and may develop secondary complications, such as pneumonia or a respiratory infection, which sometimes leads to death. History has shown that fatalities are most likely to occur during epidemics and pandemics, as new mutant strains of the viruses evolve.

Tennesseans have suffered many greater and lesser bouts of influenza. Of the former, the most recent have been the London flu (1972–73), Hong Kong flu (1968), Asian flu (1957), type A1 flu (1947), and type AO flu (1934). Many previous outbreaks were undoubtedly misdiagnosed as nonspecific respiratory diseases or pneumonia. Vital statistics including morbidity (illness) and mortality (death) records were not officially or broadly maintained in Tennessee until a Bureau of Vital Statistics was established by the state in 1913. Consequently, even some widespread epidemics may not have been detected and publicized prior to this.

A severe flu outbreak in 1928 resulted in 2,752 known deaths in the state. Epidemics of influenza and pneumonia also swept the United States during the bitter winter of 1936–37 as a result of unprecedented floods within the Mississippi and Ohio River valleys. The exposure of refugees to the elements, along with overcrowded camps, added significantly to the spread of the disease and subsequent cases of pneumonia. The State of Tennessee also recorded 180,164 cases of influenza in 1957. The death rate that year was about nine persons for every one thousand that contracted the disease.

These outbreaks were trivial, however, in comparison to what took place during the pandemic of 1918–19. Two great waves of influenza occurred during this period. The first was relatively mild, but the second literally covered the globe within a period of two months. This second wave, called Spanish flu, appeared in the United States in August 1918. As mentioned in the introduction, the term "Spanish flu" was a misnomer since there was no definitive evidence that the disease either arose in Spain or was any worse there than in other parts of the world. It could have been called Spanish flu because the first influenza epidemic in the Americas came from Valencia, Spain, in 1647. It is now believed that the disease was initially carried by sailors into the port of Boston. From there it quickly spread to population centers along the East Coast. By the fall of 1918, it reached burgeoning military training camps and other densely populated sites throughout the country.

Wherever the disease occurred, it would strike hard, spread for a week or two, linger for a month or two, causing much suffering and death, and then quickly subside. Worldwide, deaths from influenza probably exceeded those from the bubonic plague (Black Death) of Europe between 1347 and 1350. There were about 20 million cases of flu reported in the United States, and 548,452 of them were fatal. In Tennessee the official death toll was 7,721. In Nashville the disease affected one in every four citizens, killing nearly 600 in a three-month period.

Small towns were affected as severely as larger cities, but of all the communities in Tennessee, Old Hickory, near Nashville, was hardest hit. On September 28, 1918, the disease erupted among workers at its E. I. DuPont Munitions Plant. That plant was particularly vulnerable due to its large labor force (over 7,500 employees) and their close proximity during working hours. Since flu was easily transmitted via sneezing and coughing, it spread swiftly through the plant and out into the community. As in earlier epidemics, as one in every four citizens contracted the flu, public gatherings, including religious services, civic events, movies, school classes, and court sessions were canceled. Temporary hospitals were established wherever space could be found, and doctors and nurses were recruited from nearby Nashville and surrounding areas. Nashville, including Old Hickory, recorded 1,300 fatalities in 1918. So many people died in such a short period of time that the basement of the Nashville YMCA was converted to a temporary morgue. Unfortunately, it too quickly overflowed with bodies.

SOURCES: John M. Barry, *The Great Influenza: The Story of the Deadliest Pandemic in History,* (New York: Penguin Books, 2004); Allen R. Coggins, "Influenza Pandemic of 1818–1819," in *The Tennessee Encyclopedia of History and Culture,* ed. Carroll Van West, 461–62 (Nashville: Tennessee Historical Society and Rutledge Hill Press, 1998); John Egerton, *Nashville: The Faces of Two Centuries, 1780–1980* (Nashville: PlusMedia, 1979); Gina Kolata, *Flu: The Story of the Great Influenza Pandemic of 1918 and the Search for the Virus That Caused It* (New York: Simon and Schuster, 1999); C. W. Potter, "A History of Influenza," *Journal of Applied Microbiology* 91, no. 4 (Oct. 2001): 572–79; Tennessee Dept. of Public Health, *Influenza Statistical Data for the State* (Nashville: Tennessee Dept. of Public Health, 1977).

Smallpox

STATEWIDE, 1738–1935

Smallpox was by far the most devastating disease ever experienced by the southeastern Native Americans. Although not as virulent as in the native population, it was also a great killer of whites in the early Tennessee country. This acute, highly contagious viral disease (for which there is still no cure) has long been a scourge of humankind, surpassing even cholera, yellow fever, and bubonic plague in its persistent impact and global diffusion. As early as 1520, long before white men entered what is now Tennessee, periodic epidemics of smallpox occurred among Native Americans along the Atlantic Coast. It spread from person to person and settlement to settlement by body fluid contact and by droplet infection. As victims sneezed or coughed, others breathing the spray of infected droplets became ill. People also became infected by coming into contact with the corpses of victims, on which the virus could remain active for up to three weeks. Clothing and blankets, especially in a moist environment, could theoretically remain infectious for up to a year.

At onset, smallpox produced high fever, intense headaches, vomiting, and excruciating muscular and joint pains in the legs and back. By the end of the second week, red spots appeared on the face, hands, and feet, eventually spreading over the entire body. Those spots soon became raised lesions filled with pus. In time, crusty scabs developed over the lesions forming pustules. The next phase of the disease was critical. If the scabs dried up and fell off, the victim could recover. Some victims became blind, and most were permanently scarred with dime-sized pockmarks. If the disease progressed, the lesions would begin fusing, forming hemorrhaging sores that eventually spread to the mouth and throat. The flesh sloughed off the body, leaving raw exposed muscles and bone. From this point, a slow agonizing death was virtually assured.

Smallpox became epidemic only in cities, towns, and villages where people lived in close proximity. As it spread outward from higher to lower density populations, its frequency diminished. When it could find no new bodies on which to feed, it ceased to be an epidemic. However, if an infected person traveled to a new area, it would arise again. And arise it did, countless times, eventually becoming the deadliest epidemic disease ever to infect the American Indians. Oftentimes, outbreaks of smallpox would spread from Native Americans back into white populations with even greater virulence. On June 10, 1894, James Perry, an African American, was taken from the Knox County Jail and lynched for introducing smallpox into the community.

The worst episodes of smallpox throughout the Americas occurred in 1665–67, 1696–99, 1729, 1738–39, 1753, 1755–60, 1762–66, and 1779–83. By 1801, after the practice of vaccination was proven effective in stopping the spread of the disease, President Thomas Jefferson launched an unprecedented smallpox vaccination program, which included Native Americans.

The smallpox epidemic of 1738–39 is believed to have killed half of the Overhill Cherokees in East Tennessee. The British claimed that the disease was innocently transported to Indian country on trade items (e.g., blankets and such) that had been unknowingly contaminated via contact with a shipment of "Guinea-men" (African slaves) at Charleston, South Carolina. Some French agents speculated that the trade items had been purposely contaminated as a means of further eradicating Indians. It has been suggested that pustules or scabs, containing the smallpox virus, were ground up and smeared on blankets and clothing; however, this and other accounts

of such early "biological warfare," even in the Jamestown colonies, continues to be a matter of contention among historians. Nonetheless, by whatever means, the disease continued to spread relentlessly among native tribes and white settlements for generations.

Another severe smallpox epidemic erupted among the Chickamauga Indians near Chattanooga in February and March 1780. Middle Tennessee was settled initially by two groups of whites that traveled from Ft. Patrick Henry in upper East Tennessee to what would become Nashville. An advance party, headed by James Robinson, was sent over land to the settlement. A second, the Donelson party, traveled via a flotilla of flatboats down the Holston (Tennessee) River and up the Ohio and Cumberland rivers to the early Cumberland settlement at Fort Nashborough (Nashboro). Along one of the most perilous stretches of the Tennessee River, through a deep gorge in the Cumberland Plateau just west of Chattanooga, members of the Stuart family and others were found to be ill with smallpox. They were not abandoned but made to lag behind the rest of the flotilla to keep from infecting others. This lone boat proved to be a vulnerable target for the hostile Chickamauga Indians whose villages lay along that section of the river. The solitary boat was attacked and its twenty-eight passengers massacred or taken prisoner. In *Early Times in Middle Tennessee,* John Carr wrote, "though but a small boy at the time, I recollect very well the reports of the great and terrible mortality which prevailed in the Cherokee Nation after the capture of Stuart's boat. Without doubt, the wenches paid dearly for their booty. It was said that, when they were attacked with the smallpox, and the fever was upon them, they took a heavy sweat in their houses for that purpose, and then leaped into the river and died by the scores."

Although we will never know how many perished in the months that followed, it was undoubtedly one of the worst smallpox outbreaks in the state's (possibly the nation's) history. This epidemic also spread to neighboring tribes of Cherokees and Creeks. Three years later, another great smallpox scourge ravaged the Cherokee and other Indian nations. Isolated outbreaks of the disease continued to affect the state into the 1920s, the most notable occurring statewide during the Civil War years, among the Cherokee (1866), in Madison County (1877), Morristown (1882), Chattanooga (1882–83), Cleveland (1883), Putnam County (1900 and 1904), and Anderson County (1924).

During the Civil War, as food supplies fell to famine levels, smallpox, typhoid fever, and pneumonia were often rampant. "Ghastly stories are recorded of children whose bodies were covered with scabies and putrid sores. For clothing there were only rags for men, women, and children. But worst of all in the bitter cold came the pestilence of smallpox . . . So scarce was labor and so many were the victims that women often scooped out shallow graves and many dead bodies were wrapped in rags for interment. But often so destitute were the living that the corpses were stripped of every vestige of clothing for interment" (Riednour, 66). Over a hundred Cherokees and other Native Americans died in 1866 after attending the funeral of a fellow Indian who had just returned from service in the Civil War.

During a smallpox epidemic in Chattanooga in 1882–83, 103 out of a population of 21,000 died in just one month. The city of Cleveland, however, had fewer cases because it took precautions to prevent and contain the disease. Quarantines were enforced, funeral and burial procedures were closely monitored, victims' belongings and furnishings were gathered or burned, and each house with a case of smallpox was made to fly a yellow flag in the yard.

SOURCES: John Carr, *Early Times in Middle Tennessee* (Nashville: E. Stevenson and F. A. Owens, 1857; Mary Jean DeLozier, *Putnam County, Tennessee, 1850–1970,* ([Cookeville, TN]: The County, 1979); John Duffy, "Smallpox and the Indians in the American Colonies," *Bulletin of the History of Medicine* 25 (1951): 324–41; Hamblen County Tennessee Historical Program Committee, *Historic Hamblen, 1870–1970* (Morristown, TN: Hamblen County Tennessee Historical Program, 1970); Philip M. Hamer, ed., *The Centennial History of the Tennessee State Medical Association, 1830–1913* (Nashville: Tennessee State Medical Association, 1930); Donald R. Hopkins, *Princes and Peasants: Smallpox in History* (Chicago: Univ. of Chicago Press, 1983); Roy G. Lillard, *Bradley County,* Tennessee County History Series (Memphis: Memphis State Univ. Press, 1980); G. L. Ridenour, *The Land of the Lake: A History of Campbell County, Tennessee* (La Follette, TN: La Follette Publishing Co., 1941); Edward Steers Jr., "The Good Samaritan," *North and South* 3, no. 7 (Sept. 2000): 2; W. W. Stearn and A. E. Stearn, *The Effect of Smallpox on the Destiny of the Amerindian* (Boston: Bruce Humphries, 1945); Tennessee Dept. of Public Health, *Health Briefs* 1, no. 4 (Apr. 1924): 2; Emma Inman Williams, *Historic Madison: The Story of Jackson and Madison County, Tennessee* (Jackson, TN: Madison County Historical Society, 1946).

Yellow Fever

STATEWIDE, 1800–1879

Many said you could smell [yellow] fever, on bodies and in the places they had suffered and died. It was the odor of rotting hay, old rats' nests, and decaying flesh.

—**Shields McIlwaine,**
Memphis Down in Dixie

For almost a hundred years, yellow fever, the "scourge of the South," brought death and suffering to densely populated cities and towns lacking even rudimentary sanitation practices. This acute viral illness came to the New World via infected slaves from West Africa. Known by several names (e.g., strangers fever, yellow jack, yellow jacket, saffron scourge, and plague) it was one of the great medical puzzles of the eighteenth and nineteenth centuries. Not until 1901 was the cause of the disease and its vector, a mosquito (*Aedes aegypti*), discovered by U.S. physician and medical researcher Dr. Walter Reed.

The first symptoms of yellow fever usually occurred within a few hours to a week of the bite of an infected mosquito. This induced chills and fever followed by vomiting, constipation, severe headache, and muscular pains, particularly in the back and limbs. The victims' temperature soared, sometimes as high as 105 degrees. This stage lasted from a few hours to several days. After this, the temperature subsided and the victims began to feel somewhat better. At this point they would either recover or advance into the second, often terminal, phase of the disease, in which extreme exhaustion would set in, the patients' temperature would soar upward again, and the skin would turn yellow, giving rise to the term "yellow fever." Bleeding occurred from various parts of the body, and vomiting was persistent. A black vomit consisting of partially digested blood, resembling coffee grounds in texture, was a principal diagnostic characteristic of the disease. Victims often became irritable, restless, delirious, and convulsive. Although recovery was still possible at this stage, many slipped into a coma and died from organ or circulatory system failure.

Tennessee's eight major episodes of yellow fever occurred between 1828 and 1878 and were well documented. Lesser epidemics also took place. Memphis was ravaged by this disease far more than any other U.S. city, and it first showed its cruel presence in 1828, when 150 of its 650 cases proved fatal.

In 1836–37, a severe and mysterious epidemic struck Knoxville, at the other end of the state. Called the "Black Death," its mortality rate was very high. At the time, its presence was only whispered about by local physicians, but some historians now believe it was yellow fever.

On August 14, 1855, two cases of the fever were reported in Memphis. It spread rapidly throughout the city, eventually resulting in 1,250 official deaths out of a population of 12,000. Two hundred and twenty died before the first frost brought relief. This was the city's first

realization that a great epidemic could occur in Memphis, as it had in New Orleans in 1853 and 1854. Unfortunately, such warnings by doctors, health officials, prominent citizens, and even the press went unheeded by the politicians and businessmen who controlled the city. The next significant epidemic occurred in 1867. It lasted about seventy days and affected some 2,500 residents, a quarter of whom died.

In the spring and summer of 1873, after an unusually harsh winter, Memphis and other sections of the state suffered epidemics of cholera, smallpox, and yellow fever. During this episode, 2,000 of 5,000 victims of yellow fever died in Memphis. The fatality rate had climbed to 40 percent!

Finally, in 1878 the worst yellow fever epidemic, and one of the worst disasters in U.S. history, struck the lower Mississippi Valley and other parts of the southern United States. The death toll ranged between 14,000 and 20,000. The effects of the disease were greatest in the western and southern portions of the state as far east as Chattanooga, Decatur, and other Tennessee River towns. Up to that time, eastern communities, which were cooler and believed healthier, were thought to be "yellow fever proof." Not only was Chattanooga not quarantined during the period, but its officials also failed to examine persons arriving from known infected areas for signs of the plague. As a result of this complacency, the illness became epidemic, especially in lower swampy areas along streams. Hundreds contracted the fever and almost 200 died.

A strict quarantine in Jackson, Tennessee, demonstrated that such outbreaks could be abated, even though town merchants and other businessmen called the action too stringent. Eventually, after hearing and reading about the effects of the fever on adjacent towns and communities, the skeptics were quite thankful for the actions of their headstrong sheriff and other town officials. Unfortunately, other cities and towns, especially those along navigable streams, railroads, and highways were not as lucky and suffered great losses.

Although Memphis had been ravaged by five of the state's seven major yellow fever epidemics, nothing could prepare it for what was to occur in 1878. At that time, Memphis was anything but the all-American city we know today, and it contained about 15 percent of the state's population. In spite of being a center of trade and commerce for the mid-South, it was still reeling from the effects of the Civil War and was also bankrupt, with a municipal debt of some $5 million. Its population had doubled in the previous two decades, and vile elements, including rough and raucous river boatmen, prostitutes, and thugs, prowled its streets. The stifling air reeked of filth and human excrement. Such poor sanitation resulted in heavy infant mortality and waves of infectious diseases.

> There was no organized scavenger system, no means by which the ashes and garbage could, as it should be, carted away. The accumulations of fifty years were decaying upon the surface of a bayou [Bayou Gayoso] dividing the city, and which was the receptacle of the contents of privies and water closets, was sluggish and without current owing to the want of water, and the fact that there had scarcely been any rain for it, and the pools that had formed at the abutments of several bridges were stagnant and covered with a scum of putridity, emitting a deadly effluvia. The cellars of the houses in the leading thoroughfares were also alembics in which were manufactured noxious gases which stole out and at times made every affliction that could aggravate a disease so cruel seemed to have been purposely prepared for it by the criminal neglect of the government, who turned a deaf ear to the persistent appeals of the process and the few who took an interest in sanitary science. (Keating, 651–52)

Grave diggers in Memphis's Elmwood Cemetery during the yellow fever epidemic of 1878. Courtesy of Memphis and Shelby County Room, Memphis Public Library and Information Center.

A Mrs. Bionda, whose family operated a rather unsanitary restaurant on Front Street, has often (but probably erroneously) been credited with being the first yellow fever fatality in the city in 1878. She allegedly became ill in her kitchen on the morning of August 13; by afternoon, she was dead. Although the official announcement of her death by yellow fever may have alarmed some citizens, it was the twenty-two new cases reported the next day that panicked them. As could be expected, businesses closed and everyone with the financial means

Memphis under quarantine rule. The Sisters of Charity administer to sick and dying victims of yellow fever. Courtesy of Memphis and Shelby County Room, Memphis Public Library and Information Center.

Some surrounding communities even established "shotgun" quarantines to prevent the spread of the plague. Unfortunately, an estimated 25,000 citizens had already left the city. Local newspapers and public officials pleaded with those exiting the city to go to one of seven refugee camps set up nearby, but most went elsewhere. Naturally, many carried the disease with them, thus igniting new epidemics even as far east as Chattanooga.

Eventually, three quarters of the city's population, including 6,000 whites and 14,000 blacks fled, leaving only the destitute, the ill, dedicated medical and public officials, and other merciful caregivers. Both black and white police officers and militiamen patrolled empty streets as the Memphis Board of Health began isolating the worst affected areas. Men and mule teams also began disinfection operations, sanitizing privies and houses where death had occurred. They spread lime and copperas solution and saturated the dead bodies in zinc sulfate in hopes of preventing further spread of the disease.

According to Shields McIlwaine, life in the city was

> almost suspended; the awful stillness was punctuated by few sounds of the living: the rattling of a buggy and the clatter of hooves as someone rushed to a deathbed . . . the heavy tread of a policeman on his beat . . . the shrieks of someone in feverish delirium . . . the knocking axles and wheels of the coffin wagons until they rumbled by . . . the tolling of the bell at Elmwood Cemetery as the next load of bodies passed through the gate. Day and night over the city, dogs howled for their dead masters, and cattle lowed for those who would never come to feed them. (168–69)

to do so began to flee the city. Panic-stricken citizens forced their way onto boats and into overcrowded railroad cars, sometimes entering via windows and climbing over others to do so. According to the *Memphis Commercial Appeal* on September 9, 1878, "Parents have deserted children and children parents, husbands their wives, but not one wife a husband."

As the death toll rose in Memphis, cities as far away as New Orleans, Norfolk, Galveston, and Cairo began enacting quarantines against anyone arriving from there.

Caskets, stacked like cordwood on many street corners, went unattended for days. Still others were piled high at the city cemeteries, awaiting interment in single or mass graves.

One unfortunate woman "was found on Main Street near the Louisville Depot, in a miserable hut, sitting stiff. Stark dead in a chair, with a dead child hanging by the nipple of her left breast on which it had closed its little gums as it breathed its last. Another child was lying in a pallet just breathing, and died a few moments after [being found]." The person finding the bodies remarked that "the walls, floor, and everything in the room was covered with black vomit and excreta, the sight as well as the smells being sickening to the extreme. Mother and children were buried in the same box" (Keating, 152).

Not all the victims perished from the disease. Some, under extreme mental and physical stress, literally worked themselves to death. They cared for the ill, buried the dead, or otherwise continued their daily labors under deplorable conditions. Undertakers complained that it was getting harder and harder to get materials for coffins, carpenters to build them, and laborers to dig graves. By September 7, only two people remained at the *Memphis Commercial Appeal* office: the editor and a pressman. Although the newspaper was reduced to a single page at one point, not an edition was missed throughout the entire epidemic.

Many cared for the victims during the epidemic, including appointed health officials, police officers, firemen, undertakers, physicians, and nurses. There were also clergymen and others with faith-based organizations and fraternal and civic groups such as the Freemasons, Odd Fellows, temperance lodges, Knights of Pythias, Knights of Honor, and Protestant, Catholic, and Jewish organizations. Hundreds of these relief workers, including over sixty physicians, gave their lives in the effort.

An organization known as the Howard Association, or simply "the Howards," also provided volunteers, money, and other resources for relief efforts. These were mostly ordinary men of varying ages and occupations with an extraordinary mission. Named for John Howard (1726–90), a British philanthropist and social reformer, they were dedicated to the reduction of crime, prison reform, and public health, especially the scourge of yellow fever. When the great yellow fever epidemic struck Memphis in 1878, the Howards took action. They raised money for relief efforts targeted at the sick, the destitute, and others who had nowhere to turn when the epidemic struck. After dividing Memphis into districts, they went house to house and shanty to shanty, seeking out the needy and distributing food, clothing, and medicine. They helped establish refugee camps, solicited professional medical care, personally ministered to the ill, and helped bury the dead. Although a number of Howards had died in earlier yellow fever epidemics, there always seemed to be new courageous volunteers willing to put their lives on the line in the name of humanitarian service. As conditions worsened during the 1878 plague, the Howards appealed to their fellow associations and other charities for additional money, doctors, nurses, and other such resources.

Another unlikely heroine in this epidemic was "Madame Annie" Cook. She was no ordinary nurse and certainly not the kind of person one would normally associate with humanitarian service. She operated a well-known, fashionable, and legally licensed house of prostitution (Mansion House) on Gayoso Street in Memphis. Yet, during the yellow fever epidemics of 1873 and 1878, she dismissed her ladies of the evening and turned her brothel into a hospital where she personally cared for, or supervised the care of, yellow fever victims. Prior to the Civil War, this attractive German-born woman (whose real name was unknown) had ministered to smallpox victims in Kentucky. In a letter penned by a group of prominent women in Louisville, Kentucky, Annie Cook was recognized for her noble and selfless efforts in the face of the 1878 yellow fever epidemic in Memphis.

On September 11, 1878, she, too, fell victim to the disease and died. Her obituary in the *Memphis Commercial Appeal* read in part: "Annie Cook, the woman who after a long life of shame, ventured all she had of life and property for the sick, died September 11, of yellow fever, which she contracted while nursing her patients. If there was virtue in the faith of the woman who but touched the hem of the garment of the Divine Redeemer, surely the sins of this woman must have been forgiven her . . . Out of sin, the woman in all the tenderness and true fullness of her womanhood, emerged transfigured and purified, to become the healer . . . She is at peace." Her remains rest today in an unmarked grave in the Howard Association lot of the Elmwood Cemetery in Memphis. Unfortunately, when some bodies were moved in the cemetery some years ago, the site of Annie's grave was lost.

The great epidemic, which Memphis author and historian Colonel J. M. Keating called "the horror of the century, the most soul-harrowing episode in the history of the English-speaking people in America," finally ended with the coming of frost at the end of October. Of the 17,000 infected that year, over a quarter, or 5,150, were officially listed as fatalities. Others, known to have died after leaving the city, were either included in the casualty figures of other locations or otherwise were not counted.

It is interesting to note that there was an extremely disproportionate number of white to black deaths in this epidemic. Of the population remaining in Memphis in 1878, some 90 percent of the whites contracted the disease and 70 percent of them died. The death rate among blacks was only 7 percent. Since yellow fever was a disease indigenous to Africa, most of the blacks transported to the New World as slaves had greater immunity than whites, Asians, and especially Native Americans. African slaves also showed a greater immunity to smallpox and malaria allegedly for the same reason. In fact, the resistance that African Americans had to yellow fever and other diseases prevalent in the South actually made them more desirable as slaves. Thus, their immunity was both a curse and a blessing. A number of black men became police officers for the first time in the history of Memphis, owing, in large part, to this immunity factor. It is also interesting to note that many of the Memphis citi-zens who survived the epidemic of 1878 did so because they had previously contracted the disease and lived through it, thereby developing immunity.

Old Memphis is said to have never recovered from its plague of 1878. Many of those who had fled the city, including some of its wealthiest citizens, found greener, or at least less hazardous, pastures in Atlanta, New York, and St. Louis. Because of the deplorable physical and worsening economic conditions of Memphis, it was forced to surrender its municipal charter the following year. The city became a Taxing District of Shelby County. The legislature provided a council to govern the municipality, and department heads were elected by the public. This continued until the city was chartered anew in 1891. Meanwhile, in 1878 Memphis began a massive cleanup campaign stressing both sanitation and quarantine. Yellow fever returned in 1879, but the epidemic was not nearly as severe. Some twenty-two years before Dr. Walter Reed identified the mosquito as the vector of the disease, Memphis had been transformed.

The rebirth of the city was well described by a Tulane University professor, Gerald M. Capers, in his *Biography of a River Town: Memphis, Its Heroic Age:* "there have been two cities on the fourth Chickasaw Bluff: the old river town existing prior to 1878, and the new city that has grown up since 1880." He goes on to state that "the accountant's diagnosis of its fatal disease was bankruptcy. But a careful post-mortem examination of historical remains shows clearly that the primary cause of (its) death was yellow fever" (quoted in Ellis, 89).

SOURCES: Christopher Caplinger, "Yellow Fever Epidemics," in *The Tennessee Encyclopedia of History and Culture,* ed. Carroll Van West, 1089–90 (Nashville: Tennessee Historical Society and Rutledge Hill Press, 1998); Paul R. Coppock, *Memphis Sketches* (Memphis: Friends of Memphis and Shelby County Libraries, 1976); James Cornell, *The Great International Disaster Book* (New York Scribner, 1976); John Duffy, *Epidemics in Colonial America* (Baton

Rouge: Louisiana State Univ. Press, 1953); John H. Ellis, "Disease and the Destiny of a City: The 1878 Yellow Fever Epidemic in Memphis," *West Tennessee Historical Society Papers,* no. 27 (1974): 75–89; Phillip M. Hamer, *The Centennial History of the Tennessee State Medical Association, 1830–1930* (Nashville: Tennessee State Medical Association, 1930); J. M. Keating, *A History of the Yellow Fever: The Yellow Fever Epidemic of 1878, in Memphis, Tenn.* (Memphis: Howards Association, 1879); Shields McIlwaine, *Memphis Down in Dixie* (New York: E. P. Dutton and Co., 1948); *Memphis Commercial Appeal,* Sept. 9, 12, 1878.

WILDLAND FIRES

The Tennessee Division of Forestry has only maintained official wildland fire statistics since 1960. Their records include number of fires per year, acres burned per year, and the average acreage per fire. The latter record is obtained by dividing the number of acres burned by the number of fire incidents. During that time the worst fire season was from 1986 to 1988, when some 1,500 individual fires burned almost a quarter million acres statewide. The period from 1976 to 1978 sustained more individual fires (1,700), but the total acreage burned was only 180,000. Other severe fire seasons during the past half century occurred in 1980–81 and 1999–2001. The fires of the 1980s started during severe droughts and some of the highest temperatures ever recorded in the state.

Even though official records only extend back to 1960, data does exist relative to particularly significant fires and fire seasons. For example, one of the most severe wildland fire seasons occurred in 1925–26. During that period 207,000 acres of fields and forests were ablaze, including sections of the Great Smoky Mountains, until then believed to be unburnable. This is based on the fact that the higher elevations of the Smokies receive annual precipitation in excess of eighty-five inches, keeping them very moist and fairly fire resistant. However, during that time the Smoky Mountains were being timbered and the slash (combustible materials left over from logging operations), along with unusually hot summer temperatures and a drought, created a perfect condition for extreme wildland fires. Ironically, heavy precipitation during the following two years created severe erosion and flooding within the Smokies and elsewhere across the state.

One can only assume that other drought years produced costly wildland fire years as well. For example, such fires were severe in 1952–53, and they also occurred during the drought of 1952–54. According to the Tennessee State Forester, the worst fire season to that date, since the establishment of the Division of Forestry, occurred in 1930–31. And then there was the drought of 1819, when the woods were uncommonly dry. For two weeks, the woods burned and the whole atmosphere was so darkened by smoke that a person could not see for 200 yards.

SLOW-RISE AND FLASH FLOODS

Floods are unpredictable. They can occur along any stream at almost any time. Yet history has shown some patterns. The worst slow-rise flood season is in winter and early spring, roughly from December through April. This is a time of general migratory storms, which spawn high intensity thunderstorms that often stall out in the eastern highlands of the state. Both widespread flooding and flash flooding occur during this period. In the summer months, from June to September, heavy convection thunderstorms frequently result in intense rain, causing severe, local flash floods. In the eastern half of the state, July rainfall exceeds the precipitation of any other month. In the fall, flood-producing rains are rare because of slow moving, rain suppressing, high pressure systems. However, Gulf and Atlantic hurricanes occasionally carry flood potential inland over Tennessee and other southern states.

Historically, flooding has been one of the most common natural disasters in Tennessee; floods generally occur somewhere in the state even during periods of drought. These floods are caused by either a cloudburst (very heavy rainfall over a short period of time within a relatively small stream basin) or from prolonged soaking rains over much larger areas. Snowmelt, even in the higher elevations of the eastern mountains, can play a minor role in flooding. (After all, eight inches of snow only melts down to 0.8 inch of water.) However, there have been exceptions, such as the great Tennessee River flood of 1867. It was said to have arisen quickly after heavy snowmelt in the Appalachian Mountains. This flood quickly inundated Chattanooga and other towns along the stream.

Tennessee has sustained hundreds of relatively severe floods since Europeans began wandering into the state in the 1700s. Normally, as storm clouds gather and rain begins to fall, thirsty soils and vegetation soak up the water like a sponge. Under normal conditions the rainfall is released slowly via springs, seeps, and rivulets. There comes a point, however, at which the soils become saturated and vegetation can no longer absorb the excess moisture. Puddles begin to form and water starts running off the surface. Tiny rivulets begin feeding into brooks, creeks, and, finally, rivers and lakes. Ever increasing in size and capacity, major flood waves then move more and more rapidly down tributaries to the main streams, the Tennessee, the Cumberland, and finally the Ohio and the Mississippi rivers. These ancient courses eventually reach the Louisiana Delta and ultimately flow into the Gulf of Mexico. In fact, all of the water that falls in Tennessee ends up in the gulf. During periods of heavy precipitation, the streams, ponds, lakes, and other bodies of water overfill, spilling back onto the land, and thus floods are born. Unless caused by dam or levee failures, severe floods in Tennessee have always been preceded by greater than usual periods of precipitation. When multiple storms carry ever-increasing precipitation over one or more of the state's watersheds, each storm adds to the burden. Soils often freeze in cold weather, which diverts even more water from land to stream and adds to the fury of the flood. Such sizable events are known to have occurred in about a third of the past 150 years in Tennessee.

As will be discussed later, slow-rise floods are not uncommon in our state's major streams, but their present-day effects are negligible in comparison to historic data. Nearly fifty major flood events have been recorded since before the founding of the state. These events have resulted in casualties, numerous injuries, and extreme economic losses, sometimes in the millions of dollars when adjusted for inflation. The state's most recent severe slow-rise flood occurred on May 1–3, 2010. Nashville was the area hardest hit, as flood waters rose almost twelve inches higher than in any previously known flood. Described as the worst disaster in Middle Tennessee since the Civil War, economic losses exceeded $2 billion.

Slow-rise floods affect broad areas and hence cause extreme economic repercussions. But when those intense, rapid, and violent storms occur and produce heavy rainfall in short periods of time, the results can be sudden and often destructive flash floods (or "freshets," in the vernacular of the old-timers). These are often more deadly than slow-rise floods. Flash floods, which can arise within hours or even minutes following a severe thunderstorm, are more common in the mountainous East but have also occurred statewide.

Five major, and a number of lesser, flash floods have occurred through the years and have been quite costly in terms of injury, loss of life, and property damage. In order of severity, they are the Cardens Bluff flood of 1924, the Whites Creek flood of 1929, the Pittman Center flood of 1938, the Doe River flood of 1998, and, finally, the Clinchmore flood of 1969.

Fortunately, with the exception of an occasional flash flood, flooding has been relatively low on the blood and gore scale. Floods do, however, cause other, often intangible losses. Besides direct economic costs relative to destruction, repair, and replacement of homes, businesses, bridges, roads and utilities, as well as agriculture land, these floods sometimes destroy irreplaceable historic features, artifacts, government records, and family treasures.

Slow-rise and flash floods are still the most widespread and costliest natural disasters in the United States, but thanks to the taming of the Tennessee and Cumberland rivers and other flood control actions in the upper, middle, and lower sections of these streams, major floods that once plagued Tennessee and other states within the Tennessee Valley no longer present a major flood threat. Some troublesome streams still overflow, but for the most part, slow-rise flooding is no longer a significant problem on the Tennessee and Cumberland rivers. The Mississippi River is another matter, however. According to Mark Twain, "One who knows the Mississippi will promptly aver—not aloud, but to himself—that ten thousand River Commissions, with the mines of the world at their back, cannot tame that lawless stream." He went on to write, "Why, they could buy ground and build a new Mississippi cheaper (than trying to control the present stream)."

When TVA dammed the midsection of the Tennessee River west of Chattanooga, some of the worst navigation hazards on that stream were eliminated. A few miles downstream of Chattanooga, however, the Tennessee River enters the Narrows. Here the river breaches the Cumberland Plateau before beginning its long, gentle crescent course south and west across Alabama and then barely touching the northeastern corner of Mississippi. From there it flows due north back across Tennessee, where it joins the Ohio River. The Tennessee and Cumberland empty into the Ohio near its confluence with the Mississippi River. Before the Tennessee River was dammed to create a lake in the narrow gorge west of Chattanooga, its flow was swift, turbulent, and extremely hazardous. It was said that craft appeared as if they were being pushed through this section of river by a tornado. In fact, early boatmen gave descriptive names to certain navigational hazards along this treacherous stretch of stream. They were called "boils," "the boiling pot," "sucks," "the skillet," "the frying pan," and "tumbling shoals," to name a few. The scenery along this narrow valley, called the Grand Canyon of Tennessee, was majestic, but the water was so treacherous that few noticed the scenery. Prior to the days of TVA, many boats and crews met their maker in these dark and swift waters.

SOURCES: S. A. Weakley, "Cumberland River Floods since the Settlement of the Basin, with Special Reference to Nashville, Tennessee" (master's thesis, Vanderbilt Univ., 1935); Mark Twain, *Life on the Mississippi* (Boston: James R. Osgood and Co., 1883).

Floods of 1867

TENNESSEE RIVER AND TRIBUTARIES, MARCH 1–13

> We have no heart this morning to dwell at length upon the terrible calamity which has befallen the citizens of Chattanooga and surrounding country. For miles and miles the land is hidden, only a few of the higher points of hills being above the water. In Chattanooga tonight [Saturday, March 9, 1867] there is from 4 to 8 feet of water on all the streets. The losses of our merchants, businessmen, and citizens cannot be estimated. Such a flood has never been known or heard of by anyone in this section.
>
> —*Knoxville Commercial,* **Mar. 10, 1867**

Although this event and the storms that spawned it occurred before reliable meteorological records were kept, it was no doubt the worst known flood to that date on the Tennessee, Holston, French Broad, and Little Tennessee rivers. The Watauga, Doe, and Duck rivers were also effected, as were other tributaries, all the way downstream to the Ohio River. Details of this flood are sketchy, but the main points have been compiled by piecing together information from various sources.

Heavy precipitation over the Tennessee Valley from Virginia to Alabama contributed to this unprecedented flood event. To the old-timers it was known simply as "The Flood." Sixteen inches of rain falling over a large part of the region in a seven-day period sent the streams out of their banks. The Tennessee River spread to half a mile wide at Rogersville and to ten miles wide near the mouth of the Duck River. Tributaries in the upper reaches of the Holston and French Broad rivers flooded first, sending more and more floodwater southward into Knoxville and then to Chattanooga. Among the many structures washed away in the flood was a pontoon bridge constructed during the Civil War at the site of Knoxville's present Gay Street bridge. It was replaced by another bridge that later blew down in a windstorm in 1875. That structure was then replaced by a new bridge in 1880 before construction of the present iron and concrete Gay Street bridge, which spans Knoxville's Fort Loudon Lake today.

This was the most severe flood ever to occur on the Upper Tennessee River above Muscle Shoals, Alabama, with the possible exception of the flood of 1791, for which no comparison data is available. In terms of property damage and loss of life, it was unprecedented in the Tennessee Valley at the time. According to the *Knoxville Commercial,* "the destruction and loss of property [was] even greater than was caused by the last four years of the Civil War."

The property damage, suffering, and loss of life were unparalleled in the Tennessee Valley. Practically every farm, home, barn, and outbuilding near the banks of the Tennessee River and its tributaries was demolished or damaged in some way. Chattanooga riverfront warehouses, stores, factories and other businesses were inundated or washed away along with their merchandise, furnishings, tools, machinery, and other equipment. Witnesses reported twenty-five log cabins and houses floating down the river past Chattanooga on March 8. All manner of debris, from parts of broken buildings and rafts to fences and hog pens, boxes and barrels, and bushels of grain, were swept down the Great Valley by surging currents. This included some 100,000 bushels of

From Point Park, Chattanooga is seen in the top image during the flood of 1867. The bottom image, taken from the same vantage point at Point Park, illustrates 100 years of urban development and the level of devastation Chattanooga could expect if a flood of the same magnitude struck the city again. Courtesy of Paul A. Hiener Collection, Chattanooga–Hamilton County Bicentennial Library.

corn washed from just a few adjacent warehouses in one community.

Hay mounds, millions of board feet of new lumber, and whole trees of all sizes floated upon the great tide. Along with the water flowed precious topsoil and the bloated carcasses of cows, horses, sheep, hogs, and every imaginable species of wildlife, all destined to contribute fertility to riverside farms along the lower Tennessee, Ohio, and Mississippi rivers. Even live chickens were seen perched upon floating debris, clucking and crowing from dawn to dusk. The railroads and highways were severely damaged as wagons, locomotives, boxcars, freight, tracks, trestles and bridges were inundated, buried by mud, or washed away.

Each tributary along the Tennessee River added to the fury until it reached Chattanooga, where the water began rising fast as it piled up against the narrow Tennessee River Gorge south and west of the city. Even farther downstream, floodwater in the city of Johnsonville covered every street in town to a depth of ten to fifteen feet. Chattanooga bore the brunt of the deluge, however, with 8,900 acres, including the heart of the city, under water. In fact, most of the flat ground in Chattanooga between Lookout Mountain and Missionary Ridge was inundated by four to eight feet of murky water. Only the highest hills and knobs remained above the waves as currents churned through the city of 5,000 citizens. Local newspaper accounts stated that the backwater extended up Lookout Valley to a point some forty miles from the river.

This flood was said to have arisen quickly after a heavy snow melt in the Appalachian Mountains; the effects of the flood were exacerbated by the bitter cold weather. Downstream from Chattanooga, the water in the Tennessee River gorge was as much as 100 feet above its normal level. As severe as this flood was, according to TVA engineers, there was a Cherokee legend that spoke of an even greater flood (one source said at least ten feet higher) occurring on the Tennessee River in the years before white man entered the area. This information has never been confirmed, however.

At Knoxville the river was over 50 feet deep, rising 12 feet above the previous high water mark of the great flood of 1847. At Chattanooga, it was even higher, cresting at 58.6 feet and 15.5 feet above the 1847 submergence. At one point during the flood, the steamboat *Cherokee* maneuvered up Chattanooga's Market Street to Fifth Street before the mayor put a stop to the action. He and others feared that the waves from this and other boats would further damage the buildings. Many people were seen

along the river standing on their roofs, waving handkerchiefs, hoping to be sighted and rescued. Although there was no official accounting of the total dead and injured, Kingsport reported six drowned, Chattanooga newspapers announced ten dead, and one man said he counted fifteen bodies of men, women, and children floating down the Tennessee River past the Lookout Mountain Road.

SOURCES: *Chattanooga News Free Press,* Feb. 25, 1990; Lucile Deaderick, ed., *Heart of the Valley: A History of Knoxville, Tennessee* (Knoxville: East Tennessee Historical Society, 1976); David E. Donley, "The Flood of March, 1867, in the Tennessee River," *East Tennessee Historical Society's Publications,* no 8. (1936): 74–81; *Knoxville Commercial,* Mar. 13, 1867; *Knoxville News-Sentinel,* Mar. 9, 1967; J. W. Livingood, *History of Hamilton County* (Memphis: Memphis State Univ. Press. 1981); *Nashville Banner,* Mar. 9, 1967; Franklin D. Roosevelt, *The Chattanooga Flood Control Problem: Message from the President of the United States* (Washington, DC: Government Printing Office, 1939); Tennessee Valley Authority, *Floods and Flood Control.* Report No. 26 (Knoxville: TVA, 1961); TVA, *Floods of Nolichucky River,* Report No. 0.6589 (Knoxville: TVA, 1967).

Floods of 1882

STATEWIDE, JANUARY–MARCH

Flooding was prevalent along the Mississippi, Tennessee, and Cumberland rivers in 1882. A heavy snowfall (eighteen inches at Chattanooga), followed by a rainfall of up to ten inches, created a general overflowing of the state's rivers. The Mississippi River was twenty miles wide at places and an average of ten feet deep from bank to bank from Cairo, Illinois, to the Gulf of Mexico. Hundreds of people were rescued from rooftops and treetops during this flood, and many new levees were constructed as a result.

The flood was significant both for the amount of time the high water lasted and for the heavy property damage and widespread destruction it caused. Continuous rains fell in some areas from January through March. According to the Mississippi River Commission, an estimated 235 billion cubic yards of water fell over the Mississippi River Valley during this event. The flood came in swells, and high winds generated by the storms created strong waves that further threatened the levees. It has been estimated that 138 people died, and damages have been calculated at $15 million for the entire area. Stock, crops, structures, and infrastructure were washed away along many streams. Specific details of the flood were not widely known at the time for lack of adequate communications. Furthermore, follow-up studies were never conducted. However, through the River and Harbor Act of 1882, the Mississippi River Commission was appropriated $5.4 million, $1,315,000 of which was used to construct and repair levees along the Mississippi.

The Cumberland River at Nashville crested at 15.3 feet above flood stage. The Tennessee River at Chattanooga rose 31.3 feet, from 8.9 to 40.2 feet!

SOURCES: *Memphis Commercial Appeal,* Jan.–Mar. 1882; Jay Robert Nash, *Darkest Hours* (Chicago: Nelson-Hall, 1976); *Nashville Tennessean,* Jan.–Mar. 1882; Smithsonian Institution. *Smithsonian Institution Annual Report, 1938* (Washington, DC: Government Printing Office, 1939).

Floods of 1901

EAST TENNESSEE, MAY–AUGUST

> Eight inches of rain fell in a 24-hour period on ground already saturated by heavy rains. On the Nolichucky River, the old timers called this flood the "May Tide."
>
> **—Tennessee Valley Authority report**

The storms of May 18 through 23, 1901, spawned death, injury, and some of the most destructive floods yet known. The hardest hit counties were Carter, Johnson, Greene, Sullivan, Unicoi, and Washington in upper East Tennessee. High winds, severe rain, damaging hail, and

deadly lightning also played havoc with sections of middle and West Tennessee during the same period. Clarksville, Columbia, Dyersburg, Humboldt, Jackson, Lewisburg, Milan, and Ripley were particularly hard hit.

The first three days of this period brought particularly violent storms to East Tennessee, setting the stage for further flooding. Eight inches of rain or more fell in a twenty-four-hour period on already saturated soils. As most of the streams overflowed their banks, high-water records were set on the South Fork of the Holston rivers at Kingsport in Sullivan County and on the Doe, Watauga, and Nolichucky rivers around Elizabethton in Carter County, as well as Erwin in Unicoi County. Even Knoxville, well downriver from the other towns, suffered some flood damages.

Newspapers bore vivid accounts of many water spouts (small tornadoes) and landslides resulting from heavy precipitation in the mountains and valleys. It also described the rapid rise and excessive quantities of floodwater in the upper reaches of the Watauga, Doe, and Nolichucky rivers and the lower portions of the French Broad and South Holston rivers. This was one of the greatest floods ever on Coal Creek, at what is now Lake City in Anderson County. The stream rose two feet higher than ever before, washing out seven railroad trestles and over a thousand feet of track. Many homes and other buildings in the community were damaged or destroyed, and the Black Diamond Coal Company mines were partially inundated.

A substantial debris dam from 50 to 100 acres in size and up to thirty feet deep formed on the east side of a railroad embankment and threatened the town of Coal Creek for a time. Had it broken, it would have washed away much of the town. Fortunately, the rains subsided, the water level dropped, and the debris causing the impoundment was cleared before a breach occurred. Elizabethton, in Unicoi County, was one of the hardest hit areas, especially along the Doe and Watauga rivers. There seventy-five homes, a dozen small manufacturing plants, and other buildings and infrastructure were severely damaged or demolished. Along a one-mile stretch of river through this community, eighteen houses, large trees, huge boulders, and other debris washed downstream and accumulated in one heap. The Doe River literally rerouted itself along a whole new channel. At least half a dozen people, including three small children, drowned; some families lost everything, and faced total destitution for the first time in their lives. Seven railroad bridges and some fifteen miles of track were washed away along the East Tennessee & North Carolina Railroad between Mountain City in Johnson County and Elizabethton in Carter County. The railroad along the Nolichucky River in Unicoi County was a total loss as trestles and tracks were washed away. Two bridges were lost along the railroad tracks above Erwin, and the Southern Railway lost its bridge at Embreeville. This Washington County community also lost a foot bridge, a railroad bridge, a ferry boat, and two wagon bridges to this flood.

About a hundred homes, along with numerous mills and four substantial steel bridges, were damaged or demolished along the Doe River between Roan Mountain and Elizabethton, both in Carter County. The estimated value of these bridges exceeded $100,000. One major bridge was left standing, but even horses had trouble maneuvering most of the area's roads.

Thousands of acres of crops, some newly planted, along the floodplains of streams throughout the state were devastated by high water, and rich topsoil was washed away. Sand, river rocks, and everything from railroad ties to baby cradles formed twenty- and thirty-foot-high debris piles along the streams. The General Wilder Dam, a log crib structure fourteen feet high, was breached by the flood just southwest of Erwin, which resulted in the loss of a large sawmill operation and practically every log in its inventory.

SOURCES: David Rogers, *Reflections in the Water Coal Creek to Lake City: A History of Lake City, Tennessee* (Clinton,

TN: Courier-News, 1976); Tennessee Valley Authority, *Floods and Flood Control,* Technical Report No. 26 (Knoxville: TVA, 1961); TVA, *Floods on Nolichucky River and North and South Indian Creeks in Vicinity of Erwin, Tennessee,* Report No. 0.6589 (Knoxville: TVA, 1967); TVA, *Floods on Streams in the Vicinity of New Port, Tennessee,* Report No. 0.6665 (Knoxville, TN: TVA, 1968).

Floods of 1902
EAST AND MIDDLE TENNESSEE, FEBRUARY–JULY

Storms and flooding were sporadic yet intense at times throughout the Tennessee and Cumberland river valleys from late February into July 1902. The storm that produced some of the worst flooding on the Tennessee and Upper Cumberland rivers dropped eleven inches of rain at McMinnville in Warren County on March 26 and 27. A foot of rain fell in only 114 hours over some other areas during this period.

At Nashville, the river rose from 10.8 feet to 33.5 feet in one day, and near the Tennessee and Kentucky line it rose from 4.7 feet to 54.7 feet during the same period. The Duck River at Pulaski, the Elk at Prospect, and Richland Creek, all in Giles County, reached their highest known crests. Barren Fork, in Warren County, also reached its record flood level during this period. According to the *Knoxville Sentinel* on March 5, 1902, the flood was caused when heavy rain fell on ground already saturated by melting snow. At first, the storm did not alarm the citizens of Newport in Cocke County. They went to bed as usual that evening. Shortly after midnight, the waters began to creep into homes closest to the river. The local telephone exchange began to warn citizens. According to a TVA report in March 1968, "About 3:00 in the morning a house came tearing down the river and smashed into the county bridge between Newport and Old Town. The shock knocked down one of the pillars throwing the two spans of the bridge on the Old Town end into the river. The bridge over the French Broad [River] between Old Town and Parrottsville was swept away sometime during the night, nothing but the pillars now remaining."

Eleven bodies were reported to have been recovered at Pulaski, Giles County, and five were drowned in a factory in McMinnville. There were undoubtedly other fatalities and injuries throughout the area, as associated hail, windstorms, and even tornadoes devastated area farms and crops.

According to the *Chattanooga Times,* many individuals were forced to flee in the middle of the night, and homes were washed away. Neighbor helped neighbor call the alarm and then helped others to evacuate lower lying areas. A large backwater lake formed in Chattanooga as the Tennessee overflowed its banks, and from a county bridge and the riverbanks thousands of Knoxvillians watched as industrious men attempted to capture very large logs and haul them ashore. Those that succeeded reaped sizable rewards at local sawmills.

Additional flooding occurred throughout the Tennessee River Valley in and around July 5, with economic losses for that one event estimated at $6 million. The accompanying table shows the effects of the February and March flood of 1902 relative to a number of cities and towns along the Tennessee and Cumberland rivers and their tributaries.

SOURCES: Jay R. Nash, *Darkest Hours* (Chicago: Nelson-Hall, 1976); R. E. Reams, "Several Drowned, Houses and Manufacturing Plants are Washed Away," *Southern Standard,* Apr. 2, 1902; Tennessee Valley Authority, *Floods and Flood Control,* Technical Report No. 26 (Knoxville: TVA, 1961); TVA, *Floods on Streams in the Vicinity of New Port, Tennessee,* Report No. 0.6665 (Knoxville: TVA, 1968); TVA, *Floods on the West Fork Little Pigeon River: Gatlinburg Tennessee,* Technical Report No. 0–5830 (Knoxville: TVA, 1958).

Locale	Stream	Flood ranking (at the time)
Buffalo Valley (Putnam County)	Caney Fork	Possibly greatest on record
Columbia (Maury County)	Duck River	Flood of record
Various communities	Upper Cumberland River	Severe
Various communities	Barren Fork	Greatest on record
Various communities	French Broad River	Third highest flood
Various communities	Holston River	Fourth highest flood
Erwin (Unicoi County)	Nolichucky River	Second highest flood
Iron City (Lawrence County)	Shoal Creek	Flood of record
Knoxville	Tennessee River	Third highest flood
Manchester (Coffee County)	Duck River	Flood of record
Nashville	Cumberland River	Severe
Newport (Cock County)	Pigeon River	Second highest flood
Prospect (Giles County)	Elk River	Flood of record
Pulaski (Giles County)	Richland Creek	Flood of record
Shelbyville (Bedford County)	Duck River	Flood of record
Smyrna (Rutherford County)	Stones River	Severe

Cardens Bluff Flash Flood

CARTER COUNTY, JUNE 13, 1924

> Swarms of green flies made it easy to locate pig, cow, or horse [carcasses] beneath the stacks of driftwood [piled behind the Horseshoe Dam]. The smell of death was intermingled with the unique smell of flood.
>
> —Dan Crowe, *The Horseshoe People*

On this date, an intense localized storm caused a severe flash flood in the vicinity of Cardens Bluff, Siam, Hunter, Horseshoe, and Blue Springs, just east of Elizabethton in Carter County. A 150-square-mile area was affected, with the greatest concentration being over a fifty-square-mile area of the Watauga and Doe River watersheds. A violent hailstorm struck the area around 6:30 PM, with some hail alleged to be the size of quart jars. Changing to torrential rain, the tempest lasted until around 10:00 PM, then slacked off to a moderate drizzle until just after midnight. At that point, the sky right over Cardens Bluff opened up again and it rained heavily until 2:30 the next morning.

According to witnesses, continuous lightning and the deafening sound of thunder seemed to be everywhere. At Cardens Bluff, fifteen inches of rain fell in an eight-hour period and one foot in just three and a half hours. The Horseshoe community received over eleven inches of rain during the first part of the storm. At the center of intensity, the rain fell as whirling masses of solid water. In fact, one victim said that a number of waterspouts (described as small tornadoes) appeared to literally attack his house and blow it apart, tossing himself, and two of his sons, into the woods. Eyewitnesses said that the rainfall was so intense at times that one could not stand in it without strangling. Gashes four-feet deep and thirty to sixty feet wide on Iron Mountain today seem to bear this out. Some of the scars look as if they were made by hydraulic jets.

An eight- to ten-foot high wall of water plummeted down one narrow valley, crushing two homes and kill-

ing nine people as they slept. In all, twelve lives were lost and a number of people were seriously injured during this event. Around 2,000 people combed the debris piles and vegetation along area streams searching for victims. The bodies of three victims were found eighteen miles downstream from Elizabethton. Some of the bodies were never recovered. The most severe damage occurred within an area twelve miles long and eight miles wide. Car-sized rocks were washed down slopes, and what were usually six-inch-deep streams were now gullies large enough to swallow houses. In *The Horseshoe People,* author Dan Crowe wrote, "A thirty inch long copperhead, scared out of its venomous character by the stormy pandemonium, meekly sought safety by wrapping itself meekly around the leg of . . . a fisherman" (121).

Many sections of roads and a number of bridges were washed away. Over a dozen homes were demolished and others damaged by the deluge. Hundreds of acres of good farmland was either scoured from the valley or covered by rock and other debris washed down by the torrential rains. Chickens, hogs, cows, and horses were drowned and buried beneath mud and boulders. Several trestles were washed out, and tracks were covered by mudslides along a twenty-mile stretch of the Southern Railroad. The Watauga Power Company Horseshoe (Wilbur) Dam was damaged as it was overtopped by six and a quarter feet of water at 9:45 PM on June 13. Two men laboring to keep the power generator racks free of brush and other debris watched horses, cows, railroad ties, parts of houses, and all other manner of wreckage plunge over the spillway of the dam. Economic losses from the flood were estimated at over a million dollars.

SOURCES: Dan Crowe, "Floods on the Watauga," *Tennessee Conservationist* 40, no. 12 (Dec. 1974): 21–23; Crowe, *The Horseshoe People* (Johnson City, TN: Sabre Printing, 1981); Warren R. King, *Surface Waters of Tennessee,* Bulletin No. 40 (Nashville: Tennessee Div. of Geology, 1931); *Knoxville Journal and Tribune,* July 15, 1924; Donald W. Newton,

Tennessee Valley Authority hydrologist, personal correspondence with author, Feb. 18, 1987; Tennessee Valley Authority, *Floods in the Vicinity of Newport,* Report No. 0.6665 (Knoxville: TVA, 1968).

Floods of 1926–27

STATEWIDE

> From Cairo to the Gulf, about one thousand miles, the flood rolled on, sometimes spreading out to nearly one hundred miles across. In essence, the Mississippi River had reclaimed its [former natural] alluvial plain, and only a few levee tops, telephone poles, housetops, Indian mounds, and trees protruded above the flood.
>
> —**Pete Daniel,** *Deep'n As It Come*

This epic flood, the second worst in U.S. history, affected parts of seven states, inundating 26,000 square miles of land along the Ohio, Mississippi, Cumberland (and to a lesser extent the Tennessee) rivers and their tributaries. Even though the National Weather Service predicted heavier than normal precipitation and flooding, the U.S. Army Corps of Engineers and others believed their multimillion dollar levee systems would hold back the mighty Mississippi—this time. However, the levees did begin to fail in late March, and the crest of the flood wave, rampaging down the river, did not enter the Gulf of Mexico until June.

During the flood, levees along the Mississippi broke in 145 places, and Tennessee was among the seven states most affected by levee breaks and flooding. It was a national catastrophe, and at the time perhaps the greatest domestic disaster since the Civil War.

The abnormally high rainfall that gave rise to this flood began in August 1926 and continued through the fall, winter, and on into the spring of 1927. An average of 9.5 inches of rain occurred throughout the region in

Floodwaters cover the street and inundate homes in Memphis during the great Mississippi River Valley flood of 1927. Courtesy of Special Collections, University of Memphis Libraries.

March and April, but some areas received in excess of twenty-four inches. This is probably the greatest amount of rain ever to fall over so wide an area in Tennessee in a nine-day period. The rainfall and subsequent floods had no chance to dissipate before a new round occurred. This heavy precipitation, repeatedly landing on already saturated soils, was the primary cause of this great flood.

The manmade levees were another factor contributing to the severity of the flood. These levees were constructed to constrict and channelize the Mississippi so that it would not overflow into its natural floodplain, which had been reclaimed for cropland. Unfortunately, many of the levees failed, creating even greater economic damages.

Along the western border of Tennessee, the Mississippi River delta looked like a vast inland sea. It was estimated that 162,017 homes were damaged and 41,487 structures demolished, leaving some 650,000 people homeless. Previous severe floods in 1858, 1862, 1867, 1882, 1884, 1890, 1897, 1903, 1912, 1913, and 1922 had produced little if any loss of life. In this flood, however, the death toll was conservatively estimated at over 300 throughout the entire Mississippi and Ohio valleys. Total economic destruction probably exceeded $300 million.

Since the worst of the rainfall and flooding occurred during the winter of 1926 and spring of 1927, both winter and new spring crops were destroyed. In fact, agricultural losses were proportionately higher than in other industries and estimated at almost $125 million. Wildlife also suffered and died in the flood, resulting in economic impacts in areas where trapping and hunting were practiced commercially as well as for sport.

Nashville was one of the cities most affected by what became known as the Christmas Day flood. As the Cumberland River gauge reached 56.2 feet, the stream overflowed its banks, driving over 5,000 Nashvillians from their homes. The water was three miles wide in places, and damages were extensive. Rainfall in the Nashville area December 20–26 measured 11.38 inches. The flood-water extended thirty-one blocks into East Nashville at one point. It spread to beyond the Capitol in the central section of town and from the Cleveland Street viaduct on the east to Twelfth and Pearl streets on the west side. High water reached nearly to the top of the first floor of the businesses along First Avenue and lower Broadway. It was several feet deep along Second Avenue and reached as far west as Third Avenue.

Twelve streetcar lines were under water, and only the Woodland Street bridge provided access across the Cumberland River. Had utility poles and lines not been there, a portion of lower Broadway would have been navigable to steamboats. Tennessee state highways suffered over $50,000 in damages, and Nashville and other cities were partially to totally isolated during the flood episodes. All major roads out of Nashville were blocked, with the exception of the ones to Springfield and Murfreesboro. Long detours were required to reach communities normally only thirty minutes or so from the city.

Refugee camps were setup throughout the Mississippi and Ohio river valleys to serve people and livestock rescued along the rivers. They consisted of wooden platforms and tents, sanitation facilities, electric lights, and large group feeding facilities. People came to the camps by train, boat, automobile, and on foot. Since Memphis was situated on high bluffs overlooking the Mississippi River, most of the city was spared direct flood damage. The Memphis Fairgrounds became the center of relief and rescue activities and the location of the largest refugee camp. All city employees who could be spared were put to work on regional rescue and relief projects. The U.S. Army Corps of Engineers coordinated the federal share of the relief and rescue efforts working with the Army, Navy, Coast Guard, Veterans Bureau, Public Health Service, and Commerce Department. Civilian flood relief efforts were coordinated by the American Red Cross. In all, about 33,000 people worked the floods.

The railroads and the Rockefeller Foundation also provided assistance. The newspapers and the people of

Memphis and the surrounding region likewise assisted by raising some $17 million and collecting and distributing food, clothing, and other necessities. Relief and rescue efforts were often hampered by heavy precipitation and high winds that sometimes intensified and prolonged the deluge.

Federal relief agencies established a four-phase strategy in response to the 1926–27 floods. This included search and rescue operations; immediate sustenance and health care; reconstruction of homes and reestablishment of land, crops, and jobs; and, finally, long-term reconstruction and relief efforts, including repair and replacement of infrastructure.

Because public health officials were concerned about potential epidemics such as smallpox, typhoid, and malaria in the wake of the flood, they developed mandatory vaccination and inoculation programs, established mosquito and rodent control, tested and treated drinking water, and expanded their rural and home nutrition education programs. As a result of these proactive public health efforts, the overall health of the people in the lower Mississippi Valley actually improved in 1927, in spite of the floods. So successful were their efforts that Public Health Service physician Dr. L. L. Lumsden said, "We are going to have that country so healthy they'll have to shoot people on judgment day" (quoted in Tilly, 52).

SOURCES: American National Red Cross, *The Mississippi Valley Flood Disaster of 1927: Official Report of Flood Operations* (Washington, DC: American National Red Cross, 1927); James Corness, *The Great International Disaster Book* (New York: Scribner, 1976); Pete Daniel, *Deep'n As It Come: The 1927 Mississippi River Flood* (New York: Oxford Univ. Press, 1977); John Egerton, *Nashville: The Faces of Two Centuries 1780–1980* (Nashville: Plus Media, 1979); Jay Robert Nash, *Darkest Hours* (Chicago: Nelson-Hall, 1976); Tennessee Div. of Geology, *Surface Waters of Tennessee,* Bulletin No. 40 (Nashville: State of Tennessee, 1931); Bette Baird Tilly, "Memphis and the Mississippi Valley Flood of 1927" (master's thesis, Univ. of Mississippi, 1968); U.S. Army Corps of Engineers, *Flood Records of Nashville Gage from May 4, 1840–May 1984* (Nashville: USACOE), Nashville District general files.

Floods of 1929
Middle and East Tennessee, March 21–23

According to the National Weather Service, the flood of March 23, 1929, resulted from the last in a series of four intense storms that swept the Southeast between February 26 and March 23. It produced the most devastating floods recorded to that date in Tennessee. This fourth storm dropped between seven and eleven inches of precipitation in a twelve- to fifteen-hour period. Half of that, described as a cloudburst, lasted from midnight until 2:00 AM on March 23. It moved northwesterly from Florence, Alabama, to Middlesboro, Kentucky, with its greatest force being felt on either side and at the base of the Cumberland Plateau. Among the cities, towns, and communities affected were Buffalo Valley, Carthage, Caryville, Celina, Cove Creek (now Lake City), Crab Orchard, Crossville, Dayton, Fayetteville, Glen Mary, Harriman, Huntsville, Jellico, LaFollette, McMinnville, Nashville, New River, Oakdale, Oliver Springs, Oneida, Petros, Rock Island, Rockwood, Shelbyville, Spencer, Spring City, Sunbright, and Wartburg. All of these cities and towns are in middle and East Tennessee.

Every stream in the region flooded, and some reached record levels. The rain fell on already saturated soils so that almost all of it ran off rapidly into tributaries of the Cumberland and Tennessee Rivers, including the South Fork of the Cumberland, Caney Fork, Collins, New River, Barren Fork, Clinch, Emory, Elk, and Duck rivers.

Forty to fifty lives were known lost, and property damage exceeded $10 million. Bodies were found all along the Emory River amid piles of debris or buried in

A

B

Scenes from the flood on Barren Fork at McMinnville, March 23, 1929. Tennessee Division of Geology, Surface Waters of Tennessee Bulletin 40 (1931): plate 8.

silt and sandbars. Half of the dead were never recovered, and the body of one man was found forty miles downstream. Fifty percent of the reported damage from this regional flood occurred at Harriman, Oakdale, and other points along the Emory River. In fact, every town along this river was partially or wholly flooded. An intact house was reported to be floating down the Caney Fork River, lamps still burning inside, and a cat on the roof.

In Lake City, practically every house and business was affected by three- to four-foot-high water. Fifty homes were washed away at Harriman, in Roane County, leaving over 200 people homeless and killing twenty. Many businesses and industries were severely damaged or destroyed, and several were never rebuilt. The Emory River bridge at Harriman, a substantial structure, collapsed when it was struck by several railroad boxcars, entire trees, and large pieces of houses washed down from Oakdale.

A great debris dam also accumulated behind the U.S. Highway 57 bridge on Whites Creek, in Roane County. This resulted in the death of eight Boy Scouts and their scoutmaster (see "Whites Creek Flash Flood"). The flood on the Emory River crested at 61.1 feet, 12.5 feet above the next highest flood of March 1902. During the same period, at Burnside, Kentucky, the Cumberland River was said to have risen from 10 feet to 69 feet in just forty-eight hours.

The State of Tennessee appropriated $20,000 to assist victims of this devastation through the American Red Cross chapter in Nashville. The money was used to feed, clothe, and temporarily house almost 1,500 people in the flood-stricken areas of East and Middle Tennessee. In addition, over 100 sanitary privies were constructed (with Public Health Department assistance) to replace those destroyed during the flood.

SOURCES: *Harriman Record,* Oct. 24, 1957; Owen Meredith, *History of the American Red Cross in Nashville* (Washington, DC: American Red Cross, 1982); Walter T. Pulliam, *Harriman the Town the Temperance Built* (Maryville, TN: Marion R. Mangrum Brazos Press, 1978); David Rogers, *Reflections in the Water: Coal Creek to Lake City* (Clinton, TN: Courier-News, 1976); Smith County Homecoming '86 Committee, *History of Smith County,* vol. 1 (Dallas: Curtis Media Corp., 1987); Tennessee Dept. of Public Health, *Health Briefs* 6, no. 5 (1929); Tennessee Div. of Geology, *Surface Waters of Tennessee,* Bulletin No. 40 (Nashville: Tennessee Div. of Geology, 1931); Tennessee Valley Authority, *Floods and Flood Control* Technical Report No. 26 (Knoxville: TVA, 1961); S. A. Weakley, "Cumberland River Floods since the Settlement of the Basin, with Special Reference to Nashville, Tennessee" (master's thesis, Vanderbilt Univ., 1935).

Whites Creek Flash Flood
ROANE COUNTY, MARCH 22, 1929

Although separated by 81 years and 525 miles, one of Roane County's worst tragedies shares a haunting parallel to the pain and suffering now being felt in Caddo Gap, Ark. [after flash floods killed twenty people in the Ouachita National Forest] . . . On March 22, 1929, a similar horror was visited upon members of Rockwood's Boy Scout Troop 45. What began as a long-anticipated spring outing abruptly turned into a nightmare that claimed the lives of seven youngsters and their leader.
—*Knoxville News-Sentinel,* June 14, 2010

Around 4:00 AM on March 22, twenty-one Boy Scouts and their scoutmaster, James Tarwater Wright, were sleeping in their cabin, the Tarwater Bungalow, near Whites Creek just south of Rockwood. Suddenly they were awakened by the crescendo of rising water on the normally tranquil stream. Although the cabin was eight feet above the stream, water quickly rose over the first floor. The scoutmaster ordered them to grab their gear and head out the door. Unfortunately, the rampaging torrent had surrounded the cabin, and there seemed to be no escape route. Their options limited, he told the boys to climb the iron bars over the windows to the roof. Everyone climbed onto the roof and waited, watching the water as it continued to rise around them. At one point they saw lights on the railroad trestle that crossed Whites Creek. They tried to send a distress signal using Morse code, but the three men on the bridge could not read the signal.

Just upstream of the cabin, a debris dam consisting of logs, brush, planks, and other material was beginning to form behind the U.S. Highway 27 bridge. The scouts had no way of knowing it at the time, but this bridge and the debris piling up behind it was holding back the floodwaters. At around 6:00 AM the crushing force of the rising water caused the bridge to give way, releasing the full fury of the flash flood.

Within seconds, the tangled mass of iron, wood, and other debris collided with the cabin, breaking it in two and turning it around. Several boys fell into the water. A couple of the scouts fell between the two halves of the building as it came back together; they were likely crushed to death.

At this point, the scoutmaster grabbed two of the smaller scouts and yelled "Jump!" to the others. With this, all but two of the remaining boys leaped into the murky, debris-laden stream. As the remaining portion of the cabin floated midstream and the scoutmaster hit the water, the two small scouts were swept from his arms. As Wright swam to the safety of a tree, he saw another scout struggling against the current. Without hesitation, he jumped into the water and started swimming toward the youth. Both perished.

By dawn, the sounds of the Rockwood Volunteer Fire Department whistle and church bells had alerted the community that something was wrong. Word spread quickly, and literally thousands of people spread out along the creek banks in search of the boys. The normally 60-foot-wide stream had spread to 600 feet in places

Whites Creek flood monument on the U.S. Highway 27 bridge, south of Rockwood, commemorating the deaths of the Boy Scouts and their scoutmaster who perished in the flash flood of March 23, 1929. Photograph by the author.

along its flood plane. The cries of the youth and sight of them was at first blocked by the roar of the stream and the massive entangled debris piles along the banks. By 10:00 AM the flood had peaked and began to subside. All along the banks, the surviving scouts climbed one tree after another as the current washed them loose from the bank.

By 2:30 PM, the fourteen surviving scouts were rescued. One had a broken hip and another a broken leg. Ironically, his leg was crushed as it was struck by a floating log, just as he was pulled to safety by the other boys. Forty-eight hours after the ordeal began, the last body was recovered downstream. A rock monument commemorating the loss of the Boy Scouts and their heroic scoutmaster can be seen today on the east side of the new U.S. Highway 27 bridge. It was erected in 1957, not far from the cabin in which eight scouts from Troop 45 spent their last terrifying night on earth.

SOURCES: Else Staples Burkett, ed. *Historical Review: Rockwood Centennial Year 1868–1968* (Rockwood, TN: Rockwood Times, 1968); Roane County Heritage Book Committee, *The Heritage of Roane County, Tennessee 1801–1999* (Waynesville, NC: County Heritage, 1999); "This Week Notes 37th Anniversary of Whites Creek Boy Scout Tragedy," *Rockwood Times,* Mar. 24, 1966.

Floods of 1936–37
STATEWIDE, DECEMBER–JANUARY

> Down at the Fairgrounds on my knees,
> Prayin' to the Lord to give me ease—
> Lord, Lord, I got them high-water blues!
> **—Song of a refugee at Memphis Fairgrounds**

The moderate to heavy rainfall in December 1936 seemed to be no harbinger of disaster. However, rain, snow, and sleet, exceeding twenty-one inches, continued falling through most of January 1937, and soils became saturated. Soon the Mississippi, Cumberland, and Tennessee rivers, along with their tributaries, began overflowing into some of the most industrialized and populated sections of Tennessee and twenty-one other states. It was to be a record flood year for these river systems and the worst seasonal flooding in the state's history. These rampaging waters affected areas that had never known such destruction.

Almost a million and a half people were affected by this flood. Socially and economically, it is believed to have been the worst single flood disaster in U.S. history.

Ironically, it occurred just as the nation's economy was beginning to boom again after the Great Depression. By all accounts this event was twice as severe as the previous record floods of 1926–27. Economically it rivaled the combined effects of the 1926–27 floods and the devastating Dust Bowl drought of 1930–31. Losses were estimated at between $300 and $400 million. This was the most expensive non–war related disaster in U. S. history. Adjusted for inflation to the year 2007, the cost of the flood was between $4.4 billion and $6.0 billion.

According to the National Weather Service, 21.24 inches (156 trillion tons) of rain fell over the Mississippi, Tennessee, and Cumberland river valleys in January alone to fuel this great disaster. January 24 was dubbed Black Sunday as rivers overflowed in Tennessee and eleven other states, inundating 12,700 square miles and affecting 75,000 homes. Few if any cities, towns, or rural communities on these great rivers or their tributaries escaped unscathed. The state's record for a monthly rainfall, 23.90 inches, occurred at McKenzie, in Carroll County, during this period. Fourteen Tennessee counties were most severely affected. The highest flood level ever recorded on the Mississippi River at Memphis (48.7 feet on their gauge) occurred during this period. Estimates of the dead and injured in the flood vary widely. Some sources claim that as many as 900 people may have perished as a direct or indirect result of the flood; however, this number is probably inflated. Other sources cite the number of dead at around 250. Another 850 are believed to have been seriously injured in the floods. Most deaths were not from drowning but from fires and explosions, many of which resulted from broken gas lines and ruptured gasoline tanks. At times, these fires spread over the surface of rivers and lakes, igniting homes, factories, businesses, and wildland areas.

On January 23, 1937, President Roosevelt issued a proclamation stating that the "disastrous floods in [the] Ohio and Mississippi River Valleys already have driven 270,000 from their homes." The proclamation went on

Memphis homes almost completely submerged beneath floodwaters during the great Mississippi River Valley flood of 1936–37. Courtesy of Memphis and Shelby County Room, Memphis Public Library and Information Center.

to state that the number would probably increase until the floodwaters crested, and that the "snow, sleet, and freezing weather added to the suffering and made more hazardous the work of the rescue." It also stated that the "victims of this grave disaster [would be] dependent upon the American Red Cross for food, shelter, fuel, medical care, and warm clothing," and that various agencies of the federal government were to cooperate to the fullest extent possible.

The Memphis District U.S. Army Corps of Engineers was heavily involved in rescue work along the Missis-

sippi River from Cairo, Illinois, to Memphis. Because there was fear that the new levees, established upstream along the Mississippi as a result of the floods of 1926–27, would fail, the Red Cross Regional Office at Memphis was assigned additional rescue responsibilities. In Tennessee, rescue parties were established from Tiptonville to Memphis to evacuate those already affected by the flooding and those who would be affected if and when the northern levees should fail. Some agricultural areas were sacrificed (levees breached purposely) to save more populated areas. In fact, the U.S. government ac-

Stranded Memphians being rescued during the 1937 flooding. Courtesy of Memphis and Shelby County Room, Memphis Public Library and Information Center.

quired flowage rights (easements to land) just for that purpose.

As the flood wave along the Ohio reached the Mississippi, it caused the water level in Lake County to rise to the point of threatening the Bessie and Hickman levees and the town of Tiptonville. Thousands of highway patrolmen, National Guardsmen, and volunteers fought in vain to reinforce levees until the Corps of Engineers finally advised those downstream to evacuate. Many refused to leave the rooftops of their houses or the tops of trees where they had built platforms, reasoning that the floods would soon subside as they always had before.

Refugee centers, or tent camps, were established throughout the flooded areas with the help of the Red Cross, civic and social agencies, and Army and National Guard units. Fourteen Tennessee schools were also used as shelters. For days destitute people made their way to the camps by train, truck, boat, and on foot. These people were suffering from hunger and exposure, causing the incidence of illness to skyrocket. In these camps, every attempt was made to make the refugees comfortable and restore some semblance of order to their lives. Supply warehouses were established at Memphis, Nashville, and Knoxville. The Memphis Fairgrounds boasted the largest refugee camp, where up to 60,000 people were fed, sheltered, and given medical assistance. The Nashville Fairgrounds also served as a refugee camp.

A majority of the flood victims were sharecroppers and river-town people, referred to at the time as "riverees." Because so many were hungry, suffering from exposure, and in need of medical attention, additional emergency hospitals were established. Pneumonia and influenza were widespread, and the potential for other epidemics was increasing. Fortunately, proactive public health efforts kept disease and suffering in check. Around 8,000 were eventually hospitalized in the Memphis area, 10 percent of them with pneumonia. (Also see the "Influenza" section.)

In middle and East Tennessee, the rivers sustained record floods, prompting Governor Gordon Browning to activate the National Guard. They worked in concert with the Red Cross and other relief agencies to provide temporary housing, food, and clothing for thousands of additional refugees. The Red Cross raised over a million dollars in cash, along with large quantities of clothing and food to assist in the effort.

SOURCES: American Red Cross, *Ohio-Mississippi Valley Flood Disaster of 1937* (Washington, DC: American Red Cross, 1937); Allen R. Coggins, "Floods of 1937," in *The Tennessee Encyclopedia of History and Culture,* ed. Carroll Van West, 312–13 (Nashville: Tennessee Historical Society and Rutledge Hill Press, 1998); James Cornell, *The Great International Disaster Book* (New York: Scribner, 1976); Federal Writers Project, *Tennessee: A Guide to the State* (New York: Viking, 1939); Jay Robert Nash, *Darkest Hours* (Chicago: Nelson-Hall, 1976); Smithsonian Institution, *Annual Report of the Board of Regents of the Smithsonian Institution,* Publication 349 (Washington, DC: Government Printing Office, 1939); Tennessee Valley Authority, *Services Rendered by the TVA during the January 1937 Flood Disasters on the Ohio and Mississippi Rivers* (Knoxville: TVA, 1937).

Pittman Center Flash Flood
SEVIER COUNTY, AUGUST 4–5, 1938

So saturated were the soils along Webb Mountain as a result of an intense cloudburst on August 4, 1938, that waters literally exploded or blew out along springs, seeps, and small tributaries. According to TVA engineers, between eleven and fifteen inches of rain fell over a twenty-seven-square-mile area of southeast-central Sevier County in a three- to four-hour period. As the water plummeted from the slopes of the mountain, it created erosion scars, many of which are still visible today. The flood arose suddenly in the middle of the night as people slept, unprepared for such total devastation.

Some of the most severe precipitation was in Shults Hollow, where the swollen creek uprooted trees fifty feet high and three feet in diameter, striking and splintering buildings along the banks. Rock, brush, and other debris was piled fifteen feet high in places, as crops, stock, and human bodies were spread for miles downstream. Many people barely escaped with their lives by jumping from their porches or climbing through windows as an estimated ten- to twelve-foot-high wave of floodwater plummeted down Webb Creek to its confluence with the middle prong of the Little Pigeon River near Gatlinburg in Sevier County.

Sometime after 2:00 AM, six members of the Alfred Ball family and two of their friends were drowned when the Ball home was crushed and washed away in the wake of the flood. After voting at Pittman Center, the two friends, Mr. and Mrs. Evans, decided to spend the night at the Ball house rather than walk an additional mile upstream to their own home. One child was discovered lodged in a stream-side debris pile three miles from where it was washed from its crib by the flood. The body of Alfred Ball, the head of the family, was found in a tree seven miles downstream. All six members of this family were eventually located and buried together in a single seven-by-nine foot grave. In 1988, the Smoky Mountain Historical Society voted to erect commemorative markers to these victims.

Several vehicles, including an ambulance and a school bus, were washed downstream, along with homes, bridges, barns, garages, a store, a power plant flume, and other infrastructure. Mud was knee deep along a section of roadway paralleling Webb Creek. Over fifty people were left homeless, and economic damages were estimated at a quarter million dollars.

Although Pittman Center sustained the worst damage, nearby Gatlinburg was also affected, as was the Calderwood watershed on the Little Tennessee River by what many locals called the Election Day Flood of 1938.

SOURCES: Cherel Henderson, "Pitman Center Flood 1938," *Smoky Mountain Historical Society Newsletter* 13, no. 1 (Spring 1987): 15–19; *Knoxville Journal,* Aug. 6, 7, and 8, 1938; *Knoxville News Sentinel,* Aug. 6, 1938; Donald W. Newton, supervisor, Hydrology Section, Tennessee Valley Authority, letter to author, Feb. 18, 1987; Tennessee Valley Authority, *Flood Report 0.5751* (Knoxville: TVA, 1969); TVA, *Floods on Streams in the Vicinity of Newport* (Knoxville: TVA, 1968).

Floods of 1963

EAST TENNESSEE, MARCH 4–19

Three great storms bombarded the western slopes of the Appalachians from Alabama to West Virginia in March 1963, causing widespread flooding, particularly in East Tennessee and portions of the Cumberland Plateau.

The first storm, on March 4–6, dumped two to six inches of rain over East Tennessee, saturating the soil and causing several streams to overflow their banks. The storm was especially severe on the western slopes of the Smokies. The second storm dropped an average of 4.2 inches of rain throughout the Tennessee Valley on March 11–13. A band of rainfall twenty-five miles wide, from Athens, Alabama, to Maryville, Tennessee, produced an average of six inches, with some areas receiving over eight inches of precipitation in the three-day period. This produced record-breaking floods in the eastern end of the state, as well as a number of tornadoes. The storm resulted in five deaths in East and Middle Tennessee and caused severe destruction to businesses, homes, roadways, bridges, and other infrastructure. Roads and railroads were inundated throughout portions of the af-

fected area, and practically every highway into Knoxville was flooded or washed out. The third storm, on March 16–19, further aggravated an already disastrous situation. It produced prolonged flooding in upper East Tennessee, as well as sections of Kentucky and Virginia, and it took at least twenty-two lives. Damage was particularly bad along the Clinch and Powell rivers. Thirty thousand people had to evacuate their homes, and damage to private, commercial, and government property, including highways, railroads, and other infrastructure, exceeded $50 million.

Floods along the upper Nolichucky River affected the town of Embreeville in Washington County. The Clinchfield Railroad sustained damage estimated at over $60,000. Roads, bridges, stock, and crops were heavily damaged along the Nolichucky bottoms between Erwin and Douglas Lake. The Lowland community, near Morristown, suffered wide-scale flooding, stranding families in their homes and causing significant damage to farmlands, roads, and bridges in the vicinity of Erwin.

Shortly after midnight on March 12, Oostanaula Creek at Athens began overflowing its banks. By 3:00 AM it began inundating portions of the heavily developed downtown business district. The local rescue squad said the water rose a foot and a half in only forty minutes in the Chilhowie section of the city. Eventually rising ten feet above flood level, the water damaged fourteen homes, twenty-five businesses, two industrial properties, the railroad station, and the Tennessee Highway Patrol station. It was the worst flood in the history of Athens.

On March 12, the Little River at Maryville, in Blount County, exceeded all flood depths recorded since 1875. It drove 100 families from their homes, flooded the city's wastewater treatment plant to a depth of three feet, disrupted the municipal water supply, and destroyed the Tennessee Avenue bridge.

The city of Sevierville (Sevier County) looked like a broad lake by March 12, flooding up to one and

Vehicle swept into the Little River during a flood in Blount County, 1963. Courtesy of Knoxville Journal Collection, McClung Historical Collection, Knox County Public Library.

three-quarter miles wide in places. It was said that the water in the streets along rows of homes was reminiscent of the canals of Venice. Businesses, homes, and outbuildings up to a quarter of a mile from the Little Pigeon and the West Fork of the Little Pigeon rivers were inundated. Water was five feet deep in places, and motorboats were used to evacuate some 200 families to safety on higher ground. The Little Pigeon River rose to even greater heights than it did during the record floods of 1875 and 1890. Economic damages in Sevier County, where over 100 bridges were washed away, were the heaviest in the state, estimated at half a million dollars.

According to the Tennessee Division of Water Resources, some 3,000 homes were damaged or destroyed, 1,500 head of livestock lost, 100,000 acres of winter crops damaged, one half million acres of cropland flooded, and 1,000 bridges damaged or demolished in fifty counties of the multistate area. Estimated economic losses were $10 million.

The Sequatchie River normally overflowed its banks in the winter, but this year the flood was unprecedented as it scoured the valley, damaging roads and bridges. The flood crested at 32,700 cubic feet per second as it swept through the Little Sequatchie River Valley above Alum

Cove, Marion County, where it claimed the lives of four people and caused major destruction.

Other East Tennessee cities and towns affected by flooding included Cleveland, Elizabethton, Greeneville, Harriman, Jasper, Kingsport, Newport, Oliver Springs, South Pittsburg, and Sweetwater. Areas along the Cumberland River of Middle Tennessee were affected to a lesser degree.

Engineers carefully routed wave after wave of floodwaters down through the reservoirs along the Tennessee River, thus avoiding the kinds of devastating floods that had occurred on the stream prior to the TVA. In fact, the TVA estimated that through its flood control strategies it had prevented over $103 million in damages in Chattanooga alone.

SOURCES: Harry H. Barnes Jr., *Floods of March 1963: Alabama to West Virginia,* Open-File Report (Atlanta: U.S. Dept. of Interior, Geological Survey, 1964); Tennessee Valley Authority. *Floods of March 1963 in Tennessee River Basin,* vol. 1, Report No. 0-6425 (Knoxville: TVA, 1964); TVA, *Precipitation in Tennessee River Basin,* Report No. 0-243-336, Div. of Water Control Planning, Hydraulic Data Branch (Knoxville: TVA, 1963); TVA, *Precipitation in Tennessee River Basin,* Report No. 0-243-337, Div. of Water Control Planning, Hydraulic Data Branch (Knoxville: TVA, 1963).

Clinchmore Flash Flood

CAMPBELL COUNTY, JULY 24, 1965

I remember standing there at the grave side and it was like [*emotional pause*] it seemed so sad because I knew [*emotional pause*] the young girl who had died, you know I always thought I always wanted my hair to be like hers [*emotional pause*]. And I just remember [*emotional pause*] I remember being very sad . . . just standing there watching [*emotional pause*], and that she was just buried . . . and I have always remembered her name . . . and I

didn't know until just recently that they had found her [body] so close to our home.

—**Donna Sharp, Clinchmore flood survivor**

Just after 4:00 AM on July 24, 1965, the normally tranquil Stony Fork Branch and its tributaries were struck by a rampaging torrent of water that literally swept away the communities of Clinchmore and Gennett Camp. The flood swelled to 300 yards wide in places along the narrow valley, literally from mountain to mountain. The height of the wall of water in advance of the flood may have been as high as forty feet through narrower parts of the valley, and from eight to ten feet where the hollow spread out. By any account, it was the worst flood ever to occur in this usually placid vale.

A number of people were injured and six died, one in Jefferson County and a family of five in southeast Campbell County, whose home was demolished. Local resident Early Byrge, after being awakened by the storm, telephoned his father, the Reverend Jim Byrge, who lived about a mile upstream. He talked with his father for about a minute before the phone went dead. The younger Byrge believes that it was at that moment that the flood carried the Reverend Byrge's home downstream, killing its five occupants. Their bodies were found scattered several miles downstream, lodged in fences and debris piles. "The youngest child . . . was discovered entangled in a barbed wire fence [about six miles downstream]," the *Clinton Courier News* reported. "Two children looking out the back window of Phillips Store told their father, 'There's a big doll with long hair stuck in the fence.' He went out and found the little girl's body."

Many of the 250 or so people living in the poor mining towns in this area were awakened in the early hours to the sound of barking dogs, intense thunder and lightning, and neighbors pounding on doors or otherwise calling an alarm to one another. Seven homes were demolished, along with a church. Several other homes, stores, churches, and outbuildings were damaged to varying

A bridge washed out during the Clinchmore flash flood in 1965. Courtesy of Knoxville Journal Collection, McClung Historical Collection, Knox County Public Library.

degrees. Nine bridges were washed out as portions of gravel roads were submerged to become stream ways. Sections of railroad track and other infrastructures were inundated. Large trees, tons of topsoil, and huge boulders shifted downslope with the flood, stripping gardens from the valley floor and drowning livestock. As many as twelve cars and trucks were washed away, some never found under huge debris piles. Heavy mining equipment and railroad cars were literally flattened by the force of the water, and steel railroad rails were bent U-shaped around trees.

A number of families spent the night within and at the mercy of the flood. They were helped to safety the next morning by the Anderson County Rescue Squad.

The American Red Cross rushed to the area to assist the families in distress, about twenty-five of which applied for meals, household goods, temporary housing, and other assistance.

This flash flood occurred as the result of a severe thunderstorm and heavy precipitation along the eastern escarpment of the Cumberland Plateau, just upstream of the communities six miles southwest of Lake City. The rains began around 7:00 PM on the evening of the twenty-third and continued until about 8:00 AM the next morning. The National Weather Service officially recorded 4.9 inches of rain during the thirteen-hour event in the vicinity of nearby LaFollette. However, according to TVA engineers, 12 inches of rain fell along the Tennessee Valley Divide, partially within the watershed of Stony Fork Creek during an eight-hour period. Most of that fell in just three hours.

According to the *Knoxville News Sentinel,* the presence of so much water in such a small watershed and in such a short period of time can best be explained by evidence found after the flood. It was theorized that logs, limbs, and brush cut from a strip-mine and timbering operation upstream of the Clinchmore and Gennett Camp may have washed into the stream and lodged behind an upper railroad bridge, creating a debris dam. As the water stacked up behind the dam from natural runoff and strip-mine seeps, the pressure became so great that the temporary dam blew out, sending a towering wall of water plummeting down the narrow valley of Stony Fork Creek and inundating its communities. A similar phenomenon may also have occurred on other smaller tributaries above and below the railroad bridge.

SOURCES: *Clinton Courier News,* July 29, 1965; Allen R. Coggins, "Folklore Study of a Flash Flood Disaster at Clinchmore and Gennett Camp, Campbell County, Tennessee, July 24, 1965" (paper for Anthropology 412, Univ. of Tennessee, Knoxville, fall 1993); *Knoxville Journal,* July 26, 1965; *Knoxville News Sentinel,* July 25, 26, 1965; Donna Sharp, flash flood survivor, Clinchmore, personal correspondence with author, Oct. 24, 1993; Tennessee Valley Authority, *Storms and Flood of July 24, 1965, in Vicinity of Clinchmore, Tennessee* (Knoxville: TVA, Div. of Water Control Planning, July 1965).

Red Boiling Springs Flash Flood
MACON COUNTY, JUNE 23, 1969

> The body of Renah [Renee] Louise Bilbrey, 8, was found around 2:00 PM that afternoon. The body of her younger sister, Jennifer Rae, 2, wasn't discovered until around 11:00 AM that Friday, about four miles downstream.
>
> —*Macon County Times,* **July 3, 1969**

Three people, including two children, were killed in a flash flood that inundated Red Boiling Springs, a former mineral bath health spa resort, in the early morning hours of June 23, 1969. Officially, almost eight inches of rain was recorded at Red Boiling Springs in a period of just five hours. Unofficial readings of ten inches were reported from various sources. A wall of floodwater, estimated at eight feet high, surged along Salt Fork Creek, the stream that runs through the center of the community.

Within hours, the town was literally cut in half by the flood, with the downtown area under as much as ten feet of water. Two men who stopped for gasoline at a local station were said to have climbed atop the gas pumps as the flash flood washed their cars away. Every business in town was either damaged or destroyed. Roads were washed away, and forty to fifty residences, including mobile homes, were damaged or demolished. Over 100 vehicles, including a Trailways bus, were swept down tributary streams throughout the county. The bus finally came to rest against a steel reinforced concrete bridge. Half of the community's approximately 900 residents were affected by the flood. Crops, stock, and farm equipment was also swept downstream by the swift currents of the flood. Damages to roads, bridges, and other infrastructure in the amount of thousands of dollars also occurred throughout Macon County. Other areas of Middle Tennessee and south-central Kentucky also suffered from the effects of the storms and flooding. Economic losses from the storm were estimated at $2 million in the Macon County area alone. According to the National Weather Service, the lack of an emergency warning system meant that the citizens of Red Boiling Springs and surrounding communities had virtually no notification of the impending disaster.

SOURCES: *Knoxville Journal,* June 24, 1969; *Knoxville News-Sentinel,* June 23, 24, 1969; *Macon County Times,* June 3, 26, 1969.

Red Boiling Springs was virtually destroyed by a flash flood after a cloudburst sent Salt Fork Creek over its banks and straight through the center of town in 1969. Courtesy of Special Collections, University of Memphis Libraries.

Floods of May 1–3, 2010

West and Middle Tennessee

A controlled release . . . of water from Old Hickory Dam during the flooding actually prevented further flooding and loss of the dam. Water had reached a level of 451.4 feet behind the 452-foot-high dam. If we had allowed the lake to go to 452 and overtop Old Hickory Dam, the loss of that dam would have added another four feet of water to the flood levels in downtown Nashville.

—Lt. Col. Anthony Mitchell, USACE

The floods that inundated middle and West Tennessee, as well as portions of north Mississippi and south-central Kentucky, on May 1–3, 2010, were caused by severe thunderstorms and torrential rainfall during the first two days of the month. As much as nineteen inches of rain fell over some areas from Memphis to Nashville. Numerous all-time-high forty-eight-hour precipitation records were broken, especially on May 1 and 2. Although not as widespread as during the great Mississippi and Ohio Valley floods of 1937, the devastation was as great or worse in some areas within the Cumberland and Tennessee river watersheds. In fact, this event has been described by some as the worst disaster in West and Middle Tennessee since the Civil War. In addition to the thunderstorms and flooding, a number of tornadoes touched down, with one death attributed to a twister in Hardeman County.

Described by the U.S. Army Corps of Engineers as a "thousand-year" category flood, it killed twenty-four people in Tennessee alone. There may have been additional casualties, since at least three other individuals were reported missing. Economic losses were estimated at over $2 billion, making this the most costly flood disaster in Tennessee history in terms of economic losses. It was also one of the most costly non-hurricane weather-related events in U.S. history. It should be noted that this figure does not take into consideration lost wages or lost revenue from businesses forced to close down as a result of flood and storm damage.

Nashville received its highest recorded precipitation prior to this event: 13.0 inches of rainfall in a two-day period. This was almost double the previous record of 6.68 inches delivered by Hurricane Fredrick in 1979. Much of the damage in Middle Tennessee occurred within karst terrain—that is, topography characterized by subterranean drainage via caves and sinkholes. In this case the swollen streams and a rapid rise in groundwater backed up onto the land, often surging from underground cavities, sinkholes, and springs some distance from streams. This explains why areas not considered to lie within the immediate flood zones of major streams were so severely affected, especially in Nashville and surrounding counties.

The water rose so quickly in some places that many victims had little time to react. Homes and other build-

Aerial view of downtown Nashville inundated by floodwaters, May 1–3, 2010. Photograph by Anne Lovell.

ings were literally lifted from their foundations and floated away with occupants still inside. Some died in vehicles while sitting in traffic or attempting to cross flooded roadways. Still other individuals were quickly and unexpectedly overcome by torrential currents and swept downstream. Most of the structural damage, however, was caused simply by the slow and steady rise of the floodwaters.

New records were set on the Cumberland River at Nashville, which crested at 51.86 feet, nearly 11 inches above its normal 40-foot flood stage—its highest level since the Great Mississippi and Ohio Valley floods of

Businesses on Charlotte Avenue in Nashville are nearly submerged beneath floodwaters. Photograph by Anne Lovell.

1937 and the worst in recorded history to that date (see "Floods of 1936–37").

At Clarkesville, in Montgomery County, the Cumberland crested at twelve inches above its normal flood level, and on the Red River at Port Royal, on the Montgomery and Robertson county line, it crested at nineteen inches above normal flood level.

High water records were also broken along the Duck River at Hurricane Mills and Centerville, in Humphreys and Hickman counties respectively; on the Buffalo River at Lobelville, in Perry County; and the Harpeth River at Bellevue and Kingston Springs, in Davidson and Cheatham counties respectively.

Thousands of automobiles, homes, other structures and infrastructure were inundated in Nashville and surrounding communities. Antioch and Bellevue in Davidson County were the two hardest hit communities. Whole neighborhoods were partially or totally submerged, and hundreds of individuals had to be evacuated to public shelters. Fifteen hundred guests at the Gaylord Opryland Resort and Convention Center were temporarily housed at Nashville's McGavock High School as floodwaters in portions of that resort rose to ten feet or more. The American Red Cross set up dozens of mass care shelters in the mid-state area, providing food, water, and other creature comforts for both refugees and disaster workers. One of Nashville's two water treatment plants was damaged by the flood, prompting the mayor to call for a voluntary water-rationing program. Unfortunately, to a large extent that request went unheeded.

Hundreds of bridges and roads were closed throughout West and Middle Tennessee because they were submerged, weakened, or otherwise damaged by the floods. Power and communication outages were also reported throughout the affected area. Nashville's historic riverfront warehouse district, which dates to the 1800s, was flooded along First and Second avenues, which parallel the Cumberland River. In recent years this area of Nashville had become a popular tourist destination, with bars, restaurants, retail shops, and residential lofts. Popular Riverfront Park, at the lower end of Broadway, was completely submerged. Schermerhorn Symphony Center, Metro Center, Opry Mills Mall, Bridgestone Arena (home of the NHL team Nashville Predators), and LP Field (home of the NFL team Tennessee Titans) likewise sustained extensive flood damage. Even the new command center for the Tennessee Emergency Management Agency in south Nashville was partially flooded.

SOURCES: "Epic Flood Event of May 2010," *National Weather Service,* May 4, 2010, http://www.srh.noaa.gov/

ohx/?n=may2010epicfloodevent; *Knoxnews.com,* May 3,
6, 2010; *Nashville Tennessean,* May 2, 3, 6, 11, 2010; *New
York Times,* May 6, 2010; WBIR TV Knoxville (Associated
Press), May 7, 2010; WSMV-TV Nashville, May 1, 3.

Floods of April–May 2011

West Tennessee

> It's too much precipitation in too short a time
> and in the wrong places. It is the confluence of
> vast amounts of precipitation in terms of melt-
> ing snowfall and rain, and then also the rain-
> swollen Ohio River flowing into the already
> swollen Mississippi.
>
> —**Chris Vaccaro, Natural Weather Service**

As this book was in the late stages of production, some of
the most devastating flooding in the state's history was
taking place along the Mississippi River, with its greatest impact on Tennessee's western-most tier of counties.
According to the National Weather Service, heavy snow
melt to the north and an extremely wet early spring in
the southern states had caused unprecedented flooding
all along the mighty stream. As the rapidly intensifying
tide moved southward, it was joined by still more floodwaters out of the Ohio River. The combination of these
two events, a "hydrological perfect storm," brought disastrous flooding.

Law enforcement, fire, and other emergency management officials, preparing for the worst, went door to
door in downtown Memphis and in other at-risk cities
and communities to urge residents and business owners to move to higher ground. Enormous tracts of agricultural land to the north of the city were inundated by
the massive surge of floodwaters. Some southern states
had received as much as 600 percent more precipitation
than normal during the winter and early spring of 2011.
That amounted to one third of their annual rain- and
snowfall for the entire year.

Although destruction was severe in places, the
levees, floodwalls, and reservoirs that had been con-

structed after earlier Mississippi River floods seemed to
be holding their own against the latest episode of rampaging waters. Some levees were being reinforced with
sandbags and the U.S. Army Corps of Engineers was
forced to breach others, diverting floodwaters onto vast
agricultural land so as to protect more densely populated
areas and critical infrastructure downstream. Barge traffic was halted for a time out of fear that wakes from the
barges could further jeopardize the integrity of the levees. This action alone had a great economic impact on
the nation as a whole. Another problem was that smaller
rivers were unable to drain into the already inundated
Mississippi. Hence, these smaller tributaries were overflowing their banks, unable to absorb or rid themselves
of their own runoff. Such backwaters had inundated
areas as far east of the Mississippi as Dyersburg (Dyer
County), as well as sections of the Cumberland River in
Stewart County.

Floodwaters eventually inundated thousands of
acres in Tennessee and other states along the middle
and lower Mississippi and Ohio river valleys. The Mississippi River rose to nearly forty-eight feet on the Memphis flood gauge, mere inches from the all-time record
set in 1937. However, even after the streams reached
their maximum flood levels, authorities said it would
take weeks for them to return to normal. Complete recovery could take months or even years. At the request
of the governors of the affected states, President Obama
declared the areas most effected by the floods as eligible for federal disaster assistance in the form of private,
state, and local grants and low-interest loans.

Economic losses were expected to be in the billions
and included damages to non-public properties, industries, businesses, agricultural lands, and infrastructure. At least 2,500 structures were either damaged or
destroyed by the floodwater in the Memphis/Shelby
County area alone.

Because warm air holds more water vapor than cold
air and because of global warming, scientists are pre-
dicting even more precipitation in the future. In fact,

meteorologists have said that we have already experienced an increase in precipitation in the second half of the twentieth century. Thus, this threat will likely continue.

SOURCES: *Christian Science Monitor,* http://csmonitor.com; CBS News, http://www.cbsnews.com; *Huffington Post,* http://www.huffingtonpost.com; personal correspondence with Cecil Whaley, director of plans and mitigation, Tennessee Emergency Management Agency; Reuters website, http://www.reutersreprits.com; Tennessee Emergency Management Agency website, http://www.tnema.org/; *Memphis Commercial Appeal,* http://www.commercialappeal.com; *Washington Post,* http://washingtonpost.com.

TORNADOES AND STRAIGHT-LINE WINDS

The most frequent and devastating natural disasters in Tennessee involve tornadoes. Tennessee averages about fifteen tornadoes per year, six of which usually involve fatalities. This number is based on National Weather Service records. Reports of some tornado events go back to 1916, but official standardized records were not initiated until 1950. Some of the most severe tornadoes prior to 1916 have also been documented in county and state histories, old newspaper articles, and oral tradition. Tennessee ranks very high in per capita number of tornado deaths in the United States.

Although Tennessee is too far from the Atlantic Ocean or Gulf of Mexico to be directly affected by hurricanes, remnants of those great storms often move inland, across the Southeast and through Tennessee, spawning heavy rains, thunderstorms, and individual tornadoes or supercells.

The word "tornado" is from the Spanish term *tronada,* which means "thunderstorm." This term is altogether fitting since tornadoes are the progeny of thunderclouds, dropping down from storm fronts to release their fury as loners or even more destructive families of funnel clouds. This latter phenomenon is also referred to as a super outbreak. Tornadoes vary greatly in their size, shape, intensity, behavior, and potential for destruction. From late winter to early summer, warm, moisture-laden air masses move up from the Atlantic or Gulf coasts to converge with cold fronts coming from the north or, more often, the west. When these two powerful air masses collide, they often set up rotational forces that evolve into tornadoes. The most severe such storms are likely to occur in Tennessee from March to May. Tornado season begins earlier in the southern states and lingers longer to the north. Tennessee also lies within a region called "Dixie alley," which is separate from the tornadic region of the southern to central Midwest called "tornado alley." Dixie alley lies within the lower Mississippi and Upper Tennessee valleys, including portions of the state of Tennessee. Here the tornadoes occur from October through December.

The high number of fatalities, injuries, and economic damages from tornadoes in this region relate to several factors. For one thing, Dixie alley storms do not occur in the more nationally publicized May-to-June tornado season. Additionally, many of the twisters occur at night, while people are sleeping and unaware of approaching danger. The area also contains a high concentration of manufactured (mobile) homes that are more vulnerable to tornado damage. Some 63 percent of tornado deaths are associated with such structures. And, lastly, much of this area is heavily forested and hilly, which makes it quite difficult to visualize tornado funnel clouds, especially during heavy rainfall and thunderstorm activity.

It is estimated that over 500 twisters have tracked across the state since 1916. Most meteorologists believe that the average number of tornadoes in Tennessee and across the rest of the nation has remained fairly constant through the years. Damages have grown because of expanding populations and the greater dispersal of people and their built environments have essentially created more targets for tornadoes. On the other hand, more accurate and timely severe weather forecasts, real time advisories, and public education have reduced the numbers of tornadic deaths in recent years. According to studies at NOAA's Geophysical Fluid Dynamics Laboratory, global warming may increase the number and severity of hurricanes over the next century. This could also mean an increase in tornadic activity in Tennessee. Some scientists predict that we will experience stronger and more frequent tornadoes as well as massive thunderstorms. Others are just as certain that we will have fewer tornadoes and perhaps more droughts. Still others state with equal enthusiasm that there will be little overall increase or decrease, but the storms we do have will be stronger than the present ones. And, finally, there are those who suggest that we simply cannot predict future tornadic activity either way. With the limited knowledge we currently have about individual tornadoes and the conditions under which they form, how can we calculate future occurrences? Tornadoes form and dissipate within hours or even minutes, often as supercells. All things considered, it is probably too early for us to understand the far-reaching implications of global warming as it relates to tornadoes, floods, thunderstorms, lightning, hail, or even the probability that it will raise ocean levels appreciably. Some refer to this correlation as "the weather factor," a mysterious unknown dynamic that cannot (yet) be quantified. Perhaps all we can ever hope to do is simply accept what may come, a sentiment well expressed in the following lines, penned by an anonymous poet who has abandoned all hope of actually doing anything about the weather.

Whether the weather be mild or whether the weather
     be not,
Whether the weather be cold or whether the weather
     be hot,
We'll weather the weather, whatever the weather,
Whether we like it or not.

Twisters have wrought destruction in every county in the state, but destruction has been more prevalent in flat country, below 2,000-foot elevation mostly in West and Middle Tennessee. About 60 percent of all tornadoes move from the southwest to the northeast, and 97 percent come from some westerly direction. Although they can skip along a narrow or broad path at up to seventy miles per hour, they generally average a forward speed of twenty-five to forty miles per hour. However, it is the rotational forces near the base of the tornado that creates the destruction. Its cone or tubular shape is usually accompanied at its base by a bush, a rounded mass of whirling wind that may contain dust and all manner of debris (including an occasional cow or tractor trailer truck). It is within this field of flying projectiles that most injuries, deaths, and damage occur. The severity of tornadoes is measured on the Fujita-Pearson tornado scale (see table 7). This scale is a measure of the tornado's rotational velocity with intensities from F0 to F5, with F5 being the most severe. At least one F5 event was believed to have occurred in the 1974 super outbreak. However, as previously discussed, some suspected F5 events were actually in the F4 range, especially in 1998, 1952, and 1923.

The most severe super outbreak in the state's history occurred in March 1952. On this date thirty-one twisters ravaged Tennessee and five other states. At least sixty-seven deaths and over 280 injuries occurred in ten Tennessee counties. This event caused more deaths than any previous super outbreak, and some of the individual tornadoes were the most severe ever to occur in the state.

Another super outbreak took place in April 1974 and affected fourteen counties. This was the deadliest and most destructive series of tornadoes in U.S. history, as 148 twisters struck thirteen states, killing 330 people and injuring almost 5,500. Forty-four of the deaths and over 600 of the injures occurred in Tennessee. However, in terms of loss of life, it was only our second worst super outbreak. Most of the state's tornado deaths and injuries occurred in 1933, 1900, 1909, and 1925, and the greatest economic losses were felt in 1952, 1933, 1909, and 1974. Severe thunderstorms, straight-line winds, and hail have also been prevalent across the state. Table 9 is the Beaufort scale of wind speed effects. Table 6 lists some of the most intense rainstorms ever recorded in the state.

Tennessee's earliest officially recorded tornado, which occurred on May 24, 1808, caused fish to rain down on Knoxville. It touched down in Roane County and moved almost due east for 150 miles through sections of Knox, Sevier, Jefferson, and Cocke counties, finally dissipating at Hot Springs (Madison County), North Carolina. Its path was reported to be one-half to one mile wide in places. It damaged or destroyed many of the houses and barns along its path and may have killed eight or possibly more people. It was also said to have carried large trees up to eight miles from the area of greatest impact.

It should be noted that straight-line winds (or extreme wind gusts) can be as damaging as tornadoes—and sometimes more so. These convective wind currents, also known as outflows and downbursts, develop out of thunderstorms. Such winds meeting or exceeding 58 miles per hour are classified as severe by the National Weather Service. They are produced by the downward momentum in the downdraft region of a thunderstorm. An environment conducive to strong straight-line wind is one in which the updrafts (and thus downdrafts) are strong, the air is dry in the middle troposphere, and the storm has a fast forward motion. One particularly notable example of a straight-line wind occurred in Hamilton County on July 4, 1997; though unconfirmed, its velocity was said to have been 230 miles per hour.

SOURCES: "Service Assessment: Super Tuesday Tornado Outbreak of Feb. 5–6, 2008," *National Weather Service,* http://www.nws.noaa.gov/om/assessments/pdfs/super_tuesday.pdf; John V. Vaiksnoras, *Tornadoes in Tennessee (1916–1970), with Reference to Notable Tornado Disasters in the United States (1880–1970)* (Knoxville: Univ. of Tennessee Institute for Public Service, Civil Defense Univ. Extension Program, 1972).

Tornadoes of 1900

MIDDLE AND WEST TENNESSEE, NOVEMBER 20

A very sad case is that of a good old negro "aunty" who is rendered totally blind. She has had but one eye since the close of the civil war. The storm destroyed her home and blew her quite a distance. She regained consciousness in a world of utter darkness, for a splinter of wood had punctured the ball of her good eye. She sustained no other injuries.
—*Nashville Banner,* Nov. 23, 1900

The most destructive tornadic storms ever known to strike Tennessee prior to this date arose in northwest Mississippi, pushed south, east, and then north, entering Tennessee at LaGrange, Fayette County, in the early evening hours. Considerable damage occurred within the Tennessee and Mississippi border counties. From LaGrange, the storm activity tracked to the northeast in an erratic path through Columbia, Thompsons Station, Franklin, Nolensville, LaVergne, and Gallatin before dissipating. The path of the twisters varied from fifty feet to a quarter of a mile in width, as they leveled homes, businesses, and other structures. They ripped up large trees by their roots, pushed rail cars from the tracks, and otherwise created severe havoc. Although accounts vary, this series of tornadoes appeared to have killed over 50, injured more than 100, and resulted in tens of thousands of dollars in direct losses. However, when the effects of severe rainfall, hail, and flooding are added in, economic losses surely ran into the hundreds of thousands of dollars. Although isolated impacts occurred throughout East and Middle Tennessee and north Mississippi, the most affected areas were in Davidson, Fayette, Giles, Maury, Robertson, Rutherford, and Williamson counties. According to the National Weather Service, the most destructive of the tornadoes reached category F4 intensity.

The greatest loss of life, injuries, and economic damages occurred in Columbia, Maury County, where between twenty-five and twenty-seven died and seventy-five were injured. There a twister touched down around 9:30 PM and moved northeast along the Mount Pleasant Pike for some five terrifying minutes. It was particularly destructive in the black hamlet of Macedonia, where it killed twenty, injured dozens more, and damaged or demolished scores of homes and other structures. Most of the impoverished residents of Macedonia were left destitute by the storm, but the citizens of Columbia quickly came to their aid, providing food, clothing, money, and assistance in rebuilding their homes. There were also estimates of up to 125 structures damaged or destroyed in the Columbia area. Whole stretches of railroads and roadways, as well as bridges, power, and communication lines were devastated throughout Maury County.

To the north, an incredibly destructive twister, estimated to be of F4 intensity, touched down at LaVergne in Rutherford County. Although it lasted only about fifteen to twenty seconds, it cut a swath 200 yards wide through the heart of the town, leaving over two-thirds of the citizens homeless and destitute. As the storm ripped through the community, its deafening sound was punctuated by the shrieking of the injured and dying. Scores of homes, along with the town's only high school and railroad depot, were demolished. According to a large clock that once graced the depot, the storm struck at 6:41 PM Five of the community's stores were also demolished, along with all of their contents. Another was badly damaged, and one was left untouched. So fierce was the storm that a number of citizens were said to have literally had their clothes blown off their bodies. Some structures were demolished, and in some cases their foundations were wiped clean of every splinter of wood.

Most of the approximately 100 business and residential structures in LaGrange (Fayette County) were also severely damaged or destroyed by a tornado that touched down around 4:50 PM. In addition to the eco-nomic losses, at least three people were killed and others injured.

A deluge of rain and hail that accompanied the tornadoes continued well after the twisters passed through the central and western portions of the state. This precipitation resulted in severe flooding, particularly in the communities of LaGrange, Nashville, Nolensville, Clarksville, Big Sandy, and Huntingdon. Roads, bridges, and other infrastructure were severely damaged or demolished by slow rise and flash flooding. In addition, hundreds of stock animals and countless acres of crops were also damaged or destroyed there and in other counties. Flooding also caused several rafts of lumber, anchored at the mouth of the Wolf River, to break loose. As a result, an estimated quarter million dollars in wood products drifted into and were lost to the mighty Mississippi River. On this date a severe precipitation record was set at Nashville, where a torrential one inch of rain fell in a ten-minute period.

According to the November 22 *Nashville Banner,* "Mrs. M. I. Viles, who kept the [Mt. Pleasant Pike toll] gate was killed and buried under the ruins of the chimney. Her four little grandchildren were blown out against a barb-wire fence and, barring a few slight scratches, escaped injury. When first found, the little tots were engaged in a pathetic attempt to take the bricks off grandma."

SOURCES: *Memphis Commercial Appeal,* Nov. 21–24, 1900; *Nashville Banner,* Nov. 21–24, 1900; National Oceanic and Atmospheric Administration, online database, http://www.srh.noaa.gov.

Tornadoes of 1909
MIDDLE AND WEST TENNESSEE, APRIL 29–30

Details of the calamity indicate that the loss of life and property is far greater than at first supposed. In many sections whole families perished among the ruins of their storm-wrecked homes. Snow and intense cold add[ed] to the sufferings of the victims whose homes were destroyed in the mountainous sections.

—*Nashville Tennessean*, **May 2, 1909**

Reports of the number of people who died in the tornadoes of 1909 vary greatly, and the exact number will never be known. Shortly after the incident, the National Weather Service reported 125 deaths and hundreds injured in Tennessee and five other southern states. However, the May 1, 1909, edition of the *Nashville Banner* listed the names of 123 people known to have died in Tennessee and several others who were expected to die. Furthermore, these were confirmed deaths and injuries compiled the day after the event. At that point, reports of additional deaths and injuries had not yet arrived from outlying areas, where communication lines had been severed. The *Nashville Tennessean* reported some 57 additional deaths on May 2, with the headline "List of Those Perishing in Recent Hurricane [*sic*] May Yet Reach 100." Of those listed as injured, more deaths surely occurred. Although the exact number of dead and injured will never be known, based solely on the number of confirmed dead listed in the *Nashville Tennessean* and the *Banner* this tornadic incident ranks as the most severe in the state's history in terms of lives lost.

At least six major tornadoes touched down and plowed paths of destruction over twenty-seven cities and towns within ten Tennessee counties between 9:00 PM and midnight on Thursday, April 29. The counties affected were Dickson, Franklin, Giles, Hickman, Lincoln, Maury, Montgomery, Rutherford, Williamson, and Wilson. Much of the damage was blamed on the fact that the storms struck without warning. Thursday morning was bright and balmy, and there was no indication of the severity of the weather to come. Besides the tornadoes, reports seem to indicate some extreme straight-line winds followed by torrential rains and in some cases fires ignited by lightning. The following excerpt from the May 2, 1909, *Nashville Tennessean* described the conditions prior to the arrival of the rampaging tornadoes on April 29 and 30:

The sun shone bright and warm, and there was a breath of coming summer in the air. Dull rain-clouds dotted the horizon during the late afternoon, and by nightfall the weather was threatening. There was not, however, any indication that a tornado was brewing. Owing to this fact, none gave a thought to the increasing velocity of the wind until it suddenly descended upon the doomed section, shrieking and yelling like an army of daemons. There was no time to escape. In many instances houses sheltering entire families were torn to pieces in an instant, all those whom it sheltered meeting death before they realized their danger.

The worst of the damage occurred in West and Middle Tennessee, where tornadoes reached category F2 to F4 intensity. But heavy winds, rain, and even snow showers occurred as far east as Knoxville and Chattanooga. Besides the structural damage to homes, businesses, and outbuildings, power and communication lines were ripped from poles, and trees were uprooted. Heavy precipitation made gullies out of many spring gardens and fields. Countless stock animals also perished in the storms and tornadoes. On May 2, 1909, the *Nashville Tennessean* described the tornadic activity, stating that "all indications point toward the certainty that this was the most terrific hurricane [*sic*] that ever spread death and disaster through the state." It went on to report that "it is, of course, impossible to make any estimate as yet as to the awful loss of life and property, but it is safe to say that never before have the destroying elements wrought such damage or taken such pitiless toil as they have on this occasion."

Within the areas of greatest destruction there were grisly scenes awaiting searchers at first light. Two fifteen-year-old twin brothers torn from their beds as they slept were hurled several hundred feet, and their bodies were found mangled in a pile of timbers. And, as in other such storms, there were strange events that defy explanation. For example, in East Centerville, Mr. and Mrs. Carey Deason were standing in their home when a tornado struck, lifted up their house and furnishings and carried everything away. Well, almost everything. Mr. and Mrs. Deason were left standing on the bare floor, unharmed but in a dazed condition.

SOURCES: *Nashville Banner,* Apr. 30 and May 1, 1909; *Nashville Tennessean,* May 1–3, 1909; National Oceanic and Atmospheric Administration, online database, http://www.srh.noaa.gov/bna/tornado/alltor.htm.

Tornadoes of 1923

CHESTER, MADISON, AND MONTGOMERY COUNTIES, MARCH 11

> Here and there the remains of a bed or other household articles hung to a tree top, while in the middle of a field, by a queer freak, the storm deposited a dressing table with its woodwork smashed, but the mirror intact.
>
> —*Memphis Commercial Appeal,* **Mar. 14, 1923**

As victims crawled out of the wreckage and ruin at Pinson in Madison County, where the first tornado had touched down, they observed a scene of absolute desolation. It was the outlying community rather than the town center that bore the brunt of this storm. The final count of the dead was twenty; over seventy were injured, and damages amounted to some $1 million. A total of seventy-five miles of tornado tracks were associated with this storm

event, which destroyed homes, churches, and businesses within a three-county area.

At Pinson, a number of railroad cars were blown off a side track by the intense winds, and a large number of barns and other farm buildings were damaged or destroyed. Literally hundreds of cattle and other stock animals killed in the storm had to be buried. Heavy rains that accompanied the tornadoes destroyed much tobacco that had been stored in barns.

Two other towns most affected by the tornadoes were Deanburg, in Chester County, and Clarksville, in Montgomery County. Even areas as far east as Chattanooga sustained some serious wind damage. The storm, accompanied by severe and widespread lightning, ignited fires in Clarksville, causing over $200,000 in losses. Although there was no loss of life or serious injury in Jackson, there was wind damage, which caused utility wires to fall across roads, interrupting traffic flow and relief efforts to the south. Medical aid was rushed to Pinson and further on to Deanburg. Many of the injured were then returned to Jackson hospitals, where local volunteers assisted overburdened medical staffs.

These Tennessee tornadoes were part of a larger storm event that ravaged many sections of the country between the Rockies and the Appalachian Mountains on March 10–11, 1923. Death, injury, and destruction also occurred in Arkansas, Illinois, Kentucky, Mississippi, Ohio, and Wisconsin. The American Red Cross was heavily involved in relief efforts in the aftermath of these tornadic storms. They conducted damage assessments within the disaster areas, distributed food and clothing, and even provided cots, blankets, and tents to those whose homes were damaged or demolished. Friends, neighbors, and churches also raised money for and gave assistance to several hundred people who had been affected by the storms.

Henry Kline, a Pinson youth, was recognized for his heroic efforts in garnering assistance for the people of his community. With communications lines down and roads blocked by fallen trees and other debris, Kline walked ten miles to Jackson to deliver news of the disaster and request help.

SOURCES: *Memphis Commercial Appeal,* Mar. 13, 14, 1923.

Tornadoes of 1925

BEDFORD, RUTHERFORD, SUMNER, AND WILLIAMSON COUNTIES, MARCH 18

Singularly calm, with death-like stillness hanging over it is the narrow strip of countryside that was traversed by the tornado Wednesday afternoon in Sumner County, leaving death and destruction in its path. Scattered pieces of timber, all that remains of what were once dwellings that housed family circles; fallen trees, thousands of them, for the most part lying towards the east, with a few gaunt and limbless tree trunks, standing like markers pointed the way of the destroyer, indicated the course of the destructive wind demon.

—*Nashville Banner,* Mar. 20, 1925

A category F4 intensity tornado touched down at Buck Lodge, eight miles north of Gallatin, in Sumner County, around 5:00 PM, killing thirty-nine and injuring another ninety-five. At least five additional weather-related casualties occurred during this period. Two died from a tornado at Selmer, in McNairy County; a man died in a tornado at Kirkland, in Rutherford County; and in Wartrace, in Bedford County, one man was struck by lightning and another electrocuted when he encountered a live downed power line. From its impact point, the Sumner County storm tracked to the northeast through Keytown, Angle, Oak Grove, and Liberty before passing into Kentucky. Sumner was by far the most severely affected county in the state, and most of the property damage occurred there. However, tornadoes, severe straight-line winds, hail, and torrential rainfall affected other portions of Tennessee as well.

A section of Maury County received an unprecedented 1.3 inches of rain in just a few minutes at the height of the storm. Besides the F4 intensity storm in Maury County, Rutherford, Bedford, and Williamson counties also sustained two F3 intensity twisters. Nine people died in one household near Sulphur, in Sumner County, when the tornado struck. The house was blown apart and its human contents deposited a hundred yards away, all in a thirty-square-foot area of woods. Their bodies were mangled, with two children literally torn in two and their mother decapitated by the force of the wind. Many body parts here and in other areas, which were unrecognizable, were simply buried where found with little formality of interment. No portion of a building was left standing along the direct corridor of this powerful tornado. Its path was erratic and in places a quarter mile wide. In fact, even the concrete and rock foundations of many structures were ripped up and the ground swept clean, indicative of the power of an F4 intensity storm. Some structures were blown 200–300 yards from their foundations. According to a Sumner County judge, the death toll was out of proportion with that of the injured along the main course of the storm, with practically every person within that path killed directly or mortally injured. This fact alone would indicate the intensity of the storm.

Other towns that sustained severe damage or destruction included Bethpage, Sumner County; Kingston and Rockwood, Roane County; Walterhill, Fosterville, and Florence, Rutherford County; Chapel Hill, Maury County; Bellbuckle and Wartrace, Bedford County; Erwin, Unicoi County; and some additional isolated areas of East Tennessee. The National Weather Service identified about ninety-two miles of combined tornadic

The ruins of a home where all occupants were killed in a tornado, March 18, 1925. Courtesy of the Tennessee State Library and Archives.

tracks relative to this storm event. High winds and severe hail were also recorded at Jackson, Madison County; Cottage Grove, Williamson County; and Humboldt, Gibson County. Some hailstones were said to be the size of hen's eggs and caused considerable damage. Freak incidents are not uncommon in tornadoes, and a case in point occurred near the hamlet of Vannatta in Bedford County. A woman sleeping on a cot there was hurled several hundred feet to her death as she and the cot were wrapped snugly around a tree. Other states that also sustained deaths, injuries, and heavy destruction from tornadic activity included Missouri, Illinois, Indiana, and Kentucky.

The *Nashville Banner* reported a grimly humorous observation relative to the people in the area affected by the tornadic storms in Benton, Illinois. Some women were dressed like men or wore a mixture of apparel.

Some men were wrapped in nothing but women's coats. It was also hard to tell the sexes of some of the younger children. Small boys were wearing dainty little dresses, and small girls were running around the tumbled ruins in trousers and caps. Occasionally a little group assembled and innocently traded garments.

SOURCES: *Knoxville Journal,* Mar. 19–21, 1925; *Nashville Banner,* Mar. 18–20, 22, 1925; National Oceanic and Atmospheric Administration, online database, http://www.srh.noaa.gov/bna/tornado/alltor.htm.

East Nashville Tornado, 1933
DAVIDSON COUNTY, MARCH 14

I opened the front door [of my East Nashville home]. The sight witnessed is beyond description. Houses were blown flat. Light wires were in the middle of the street. Houses were on fire. People were yelling . . . That morning . . . revealed the stage of catastrophe. As far as the human eye could see, destruction had taken its toll. A church was blown completely down. Where houses had been, there was not even a foundation.

—Dr. L. A. Cardell, *A History of the American Red Cross in Nashville*

The lightning that struck power lines along the Woodland Street bridge looked like fireworks as it sent a spray of sparks into the Cumberland River. Then the power failed, and the city was plunged into an eerie darkness. Sheets and buckets of rain and hail the size of baseballs struck the city with a fury, further exacerbating the dire situation. The turbulent winds, rain, and hail were unrelenting in their great sound and fury; then a momentary quiet fell over the city. After that, the sounds of howling dogs, the moaning and crying of the injured, and the squeal of fire trucks and ambulances filled the night air. Fires had been ignited in some structures in isolated pockets of wreckage.

The single most destructive tornado in the city's history had struck the public square around 7:30 PM and then skipped rapidly across the Cumberland River into East Nashville. On the square it blew out windows, removed bricks and roofs from several structures, and sent projectiles, from produce to wagons whirling skyward. Miraculously, only a dozen lives were lost and 175 were injured in the wake of a tornado that damaged or destroyed over 1,600 homes, businesses, and other structures. Most of the destruction lay along a half-mile-wide path between the downtown L&N Railway Station on the west and Woodland Avenue on the east. From there it traveled to Porter Road, Shelby Park, and Inglewood.

People emerged from hiding; some stunned, others pumped with adrenaline and ready for action. Whole city blocks were in ruin as rumors ran rampant. Frantic searches, some organized and some helter-skelter, were

launched for loved ones by relatives, friends, city workers, and strangers. What started as terror soon turned to compassion and then to morbid curiosity as the bodies of the living and dead were pulled from bloodstained rubble. The injured were transported to makeshift first-aid stations and to the hospital by ambulances and private vehicles. Rescue work continued through the night by candle and lantern light. General Hospital called in all reserve staff and worked around the clock while clergymen ministered to the living and the dead.

Looting was light, but nevertheless merchants armed themselves to protect what the storm had not taken. Every policeman, fireman, and emergency worker in the city was called to duty, some working twenty-four to thirty-six hours straight until they collapsed from exhaustion. The National Guard also patrolled the worst hit areas, assisted the victims, and helped prevent looting. As search and rescue transitioned into recovery operations, work began to be hampered by curiosity seekers. They came by car and by foot into the disaster area from other parts of the city. Fallen limbs and whole trees, along with shrubs, fences, vehicles, utility lines, poles, cables, and even human bodies lay on, in, and between demolished structures. Belongings were strewn along roadways and across lawns, some hundreds of yards from their original locations. Clothing, furniture, and all other sorts of odds and ends clung to tree branches and blew or rocked in the wind. In the days that followed, city trucks hauled belongings and debris from the area in long and exhaustive clean-up efforts. The steadfast American Red Cross and Salvation Army were on the scene almost from the beginning, providing organized assistance, easing suffering, and feeding, clothing, and housing the victims.

After leaving Nashville, the tornado tracked eastward for a total distance of some forty-five miles across Davidson, Wilson, and Smith counties. By 8:15 PM it dissipated against the Cumberland Escarpment. Other areas hard hit by tornadoes on this date were Campbell County (1 dead and 64 injured), Claiborne County (12 dead and 102 injured), Hancock County (8 dead and 11 injured), and Sullivan County (11 dead and 200 injured).

As the final tallies were completed, the people learned that this outbreak of tornadoes had claimed the lives of 52, injured over 550, and caused economic losses exceeding $3 million. In terms of lives lost, this was the third most severe tornadic incident in the state's history. In terms of injuries, it was the second worst.

SOURCES: American Red Cross, *Tornadoes of March and May, 1933 in Kentucky and Tennessee: Official Report of Relief Operations of the American Red Cross,* ARC 930 (Washington, DC: American Red Cross, 1933); Henry McRaven, *Nashville: Athens of the New South* (Chapel Hill, NC: Scheer and Jarvis/Tennessee Book Co., 1949); Owen Meredith, *History of the American Red Cross in Nashville* (Washington, DC: American Red Cross, 1982); John V. Vaiksnoras, *Tornadoes in Tennessee 1916–1970* (Knoxville: Univ. of Tennessee Institute of Public Service, 1971).

Tornado Super Outbreak of 1952
WEST TENNESSEE, MARCH 21–22

In cumulative effect this is the worst natural disaster to strike the Lower Mississippi Valley since the devastating, life-destroying flood of 1927 (and 1937–38). Children have been orphaned. Wives have lost breadwinners. In some instances entire families have been wiped out and small towns leveled. For many, the material possessions of a lifetime of work, including homes, were dissipated in a few tornadic seconds. Grief, misery and shock are indescribable.

—*Memphis Commercial Appeal,* **Mar. 23, 1952**

Although the tornado outbreak of April 3–4, 1974, produced more twisters over a broader area of states and counties, along with more injuries, the super outbreak of 1952 caused more deaths. Furthermore, the super outbreak of 1909 probably caused more deaths than the other two combined. Both the 1974 and 1952 episodes were believed, at the time, to have spawned at least one category F5 tornado, although recent reanalysis of the tornadoes of those periods tend to dispute that claim. Nonetheless, there is no doubt that both years produced severe category F4, if not borderline F5, twisters.

The 1952 Tennessee tornadoes were part of some thirty-one storms that also ravaged five other states (Alabama, Arkansas, Kentucky, Mississippi, and Missouri), killing 343 and injuring around 1,400. This was the ninth deadliest tornado in U.S. history. Sixty-seven of the known deaths and 282 of the injuries occurred in Tennessee. The economic losses for the six states were estimated at $15 million; $5,662,000 of that was in Tennessee. About 730 structures were either demolished or severely damaged by the rampaging storms, leaving thousands homeless and destitute.

Some of the refugees were taken in by relatives, friends, or neighbors; many others stayed in American Red Cross mass care shelters that were established in churches, schools, and other buildings to feed, clothe, lodge, and provide medical assistance to the victims. Red Cross volunteers also fed the relief workers; conducted damage assessments in coordination with federal, state, and local officials; and kept records of the dead, the injured, and those temporarily housed in public shelters.

Almost textbook tornadic weather conditions set the stage for these disastrous storms that tore through six states on the evening of March 21 and the next morning. A cold front moving in from the northwest encountered a stationary mass of warm, moist air over the mid-south. Dark and ominous storm clouds began to gather, defining a squall line. Along this foreboding frontal boundary, the atmospheric pressure plunged downward. Lightning, rainfall, and hail began to develop and move toward the northwest. It was along this frontal line that the tornadoes began dropping down from the sky, striking with deadly rotational speeds of up to 300 miles per hour.

Ten separate tornadoes ripped through as many Tennessee counties in a night of terror. Three twisters struck Dyer County, destroying sixty homes and damaging seventy others. The first funnel cloud touched down shortly before dark at Bonicord, killing at least two before moving through Roellen, LaPlatt, and Edgewood. Around 8:30 PM the second tornado skirted the edge of Dyersburg, demolishing twenty homes and ten automobiles. It is ironic that most of the cars were swept from the highway into surrounding fields as they were en route to Roellen to view the storm damage there. Those thousands of vehicles traveling through the area not only put themselves at risk, but also tied up highways and hampered search, rescue, and medical evacuation operations. A few minutes later the third storm struck Broadmoor and Miston, both in Dyer County, killing and injuring several more.

Hangars and small private planes were also damaged at the Dyer County Airport. Henderson, in Chester County, was the most affected single town, although Moscow, Fayette County, was struck by the most powerful of the tornadoes, a category F4 or borderline F5 twister. It took five lives. At least nine people were killed and over 100 injured in Henderson. Some buildings were swept from their foundations; others burned. Power poles were snapped off at the base, and trees were torn up by their roots. Damage was estimated at over a half million dollars in that area alone.

People were also killed and injured at Lexington and Chesterfield, in Henderson County; Leach, in Carroll County; and Medina, in Gibson County. In fact, several were killed at Medina, dozens were injured, and forty houses were either damaged or destroyed by fire and wind. Other counties affected by the storm included Decatur, Hardeman, Hickman, and Humphreys.

Family members, neighbors, and friends, as well as emergency workers and volunteers, searched around the clock in the wake of the storms, sifting through wreckage for both the living and dead. Scores of victims, left homeless by the storms, wandered aimlessly about the wreckage or sat dazed in shelters or hospital lobbies not knowing where to turn. The hospitals were scenes of terror and confusion as frantic relatives milled about seeking information about loved ones or neighbors. According to the March 22, 1952, *Memphis Commercial Appeal,* a woman at the Dyersburg Hospital, wet and bleeding, was screaming, "Oh God, they have all been killed--they have all been killed." Still others ran into the building pleading, "Someone please go help them." Some rapid mass burials were held in many communities before family members, neighbors, and disaster workers resumed the grim tasks that still faced them.

SOURCES: *Memphis Commercial Appeal,* March 22–25, 1952; National Oceanic and Atmospheric Administration, online databases, http://www.awc- kc.noaa.gov/wxfact/farch. htm, http://www.spc.noaa.gov/archive/tornadoes/f5torns. htm, http://www.srh.noaa.gov/bna/bornado/alltor.htm.

Tornado Super Outbreak of 1974
EAST AND MIDDLE TENNESSEE, APRIL 3–4

In terms of total number, path length, and the total damage, the massive tornado occurrence of April 3–4, 1974, was more extensive than all previously known outbreaks. (The incident affected areas from the Gulf of Mexico through the Southeast and Midwest to the Canadian border.)

—NOAA, *Natural Disaster Survey Report 74-1*

During a sixteen-hour period between April 3 and 4, 1974, 148 twisters struck thirteen southeastern and midwestern states, killing over 330, injuring an estimated 5,484, and causing some $600 million in economic losses. In terms of the number of tornadoes sighted and total damages, this so-called super outbreak was the worst in U.S. history.

Tennessee was one of the states most affected by the rampaging tornadic storms, as forty-four twisters wrought death, injury, and economic destruction across nineteen eastern and midstate counties. At least 47 people lost their lives, around 774 were injured, some seriously, and economic losses amounted to an estimated $30.6 million. These deadly tornadoes were spawned by a large and intense low-pressure cell that traveled rapidly east from the Rockies in a matter of a few hours. As the storm front moved eastward it encountered warm, moist air moving north from the Gulf of Mexico. This created a very unstable and volatile atmospheric condition that caught weather forecasters totally off-guard.

The first of the Tennessee tornadoes caused considerable property damage when it touched down around 3:00 PM in Bradley County, southeast of Cleveland, and moved northeast. Within two hours, another twister struck Cleveland, causing more destruction as it moved northeast to the town of Etowah, where it played havoc with the downtown area. Fifty-eight structures were demolished and another 330 damaged by these two twisters. Two deaths and fifty injuries were recorded. Smaller, yet still damaging tornadoes also occurred later in the afternoon of April 3, in Blount, Loudon, and Monroe counties.

Within the next hour, three tornadoes were reported in Middle Tennessee, one near Lebanon, Wilson County; one near Murfreesboro, Rutherford County; and a third in Nashville and Davidson County. The former two caused some injuries and property damage, and the third resulted in one death, a number of injuries, and an estimated half million dollars in damages. Just after dark, eighteen more twisters touched down along the eastern Highland Rim and western Cumberland Plateau. These occurred at Lincoln and Franklin counties on the Alabama state line and moved northeastward to Scott and Pickett counties and then north into Kentucky. These cyclonic storms killed eleven in Franklin and Lincoln counties; ten in Putnam County, around Cookeville; seven in Fentress County, near Jamestown; and five in

Pickett County, near Moodyville and Caney Creek. Well over 100 were injured in these incidents, and property damage was substantial along each tornadic path. Just before midnight, three were killed and 140 injured in storms in Overton and Scott counties. A little later, two more twisters killed two, injured fifty, and caused heavy property damage in Cumberland, Putnam, White, and Knox counties.

The highest death toll from the tornadoes occurred in the Bingham, Mount Herman, and Rocky Point communities of Putnam County. The county sheriff estimated one and a half million dollars in damages to houses, mobile homes, commercial property, and infrastructure such as power lines. Other counties with high death tolls included Fentress, Franklin, Lincoln, and Pickett. The area of Fentress County between Jamestown and Allardt sustained seven deaths and 150 injuries. About 200 homes, businesses, and other structures were also damaged or demolished in this area. Cleveland and Etowah were the hardest hit communities in southeast Tennessee. Some victims lost their homes and everything they owned to these storms. A tornado and several severe thunderstorms killed three-and-a-half-year-old twins, injured another twenty people, and caused over $1 million in damages in Knox County.

A number of Red Cross shelters were established throughout the affected areas to assist the hundreds of families left homeless by the storms. According to TVA officials, the storm damage throughout the valley was the highest ever inflicted upon their facilities, power lines, and substations. They estimated damages in the millions of dollars. Power was out at times throughout the affected counties, but local power crews and TVA acted quickly and decisively to restore service.

In the wake of the storms, National Guard troops and state highway patrol officers were dispatched to the hardest hit areas around the state to assist professional and volunteer emergency workers in search, rescue, and recovery operations. They also helped local law enforcement agencies curtail looting and vandalism and otherwise protect property. President Nixon quickly declared several states, including Tennessee, as eligible for federal disaster assistance. This included direct federal dollars and other services, such as low interest loans, through the Farmers Home Administration and the Small Business Administration.

SOURCES: *Knoxville Journal,* Apr. 4, 5, 1974; *Knoxville News-Sentinel,* Apr. 4, 5, 1974; *Nashville Banner,* Apr. 4, 5, 1974; *Nashville Tennessean,* Apr. 4, 5, 1974; National Oceanic and Atmospheric Administration (NOAA), online databases: http://www.ezl.com/~fireball/Disaster15.htm; http://www.publicaffairs.noaa.gov/storms, http://www.publicaffairs.noaa.gov/storms/description.html, http://www.publicaffairs.noaa.gov/storms/tennessee.html, http://www.srh.noaa.gov/bna/tornado/alltor.htm, http://www.weather.com/weather_center/special_report/sotc/storm2.

Tornadoes of 2002

WEST, MIDDLE, AND EAST TENNESSEE, NOVEMBER 9–10

> Before his dumbfounded eyes, the winds ripped the flames from garbage burning in a 55-gallon barrel and then blew his golden retriever out of its pen and across a field. Clay, 40, dropped to the ground between his house and a carport supported by 4×6 wood posts. "All I heard was the sound of twisting metal," Clay said. "The tornado sounded like sticking the nozzle of a leaf blower right next to your ear." Fortunately, neither Clay nor his dog was seriously injured.
>
> —*Knoxville News-Sentinel,*
> **Nov. 12, 2002**

Storms and swarms of twisters ravaged the South and Midwest from Louisiana to Pennsylvania during this period, with Tennessee and Alabama bearing the brunt of the effects. At least 35 people were killed and over 100 injured. Tennessee's death toll stood at 17, with 80 plus injuries. Economic losses were estimated at $160 million from some thirteen separate tornadoes.

Across the state, more than 100 residences, including single homes, mobile homes, and apartments, were destroyed and many others damaged. Although this was not the usual time of year for severe "tornado alley" tornadoes, the atmospheric conditions were perfect for the formation of loner and multiple tornadoes of the "Dixie alley" type. As cold high-altitude air moved to the east across the Midwest, it overtook a broad, warm, and moist air mass hugging the ground and moving north from the Gulf. As the two met, tornadoes began forming along the storm front, some with rotational winds approaching 200 miles per hour (category F3 twisters).

Two waves of storms pummeled the state, the first late Saturday night and early Sunday morning, and the second on Sunday night. The first tornadoes touched down in West Tennessee. The Mossy Grove community in Morgan County was one of the most severely affected areas. It lost seven of its citizens as a twister touched down and cut a five-mile swath around 8:30 PM on Sunday. Winds as high as 140 miles per hour and golf ball–sized hail accosted the sleepy little community in what is considered one of the poorest counties in the state. After visiting Mossy Grove, the tornado veered east into Petros and Joyner, not far from Brushy Mountain State Prison. Things quieted down a bit after the twister passed through Mossy Grove. However, heavy rain continued in the darkness, punctuated by bright flashes of lightning.

As one witness recalls, the screaming began and the praying continued. After crawling out of his basement, one survivor of the tornado was quoted as saying, "Everything was just instantly gone. You wouldn't believe the power of that thing (the tornado). It was a horrible noise, then silence and then the rain. When you come out here and look at the damage, it's a wonder anybody survived it."

Tornadoes also killed four in Crossville, Cumberland County, and two each in Fredonia, Coffee County; Leach, Carroll County; and Port Royal, Montgomery

Deadly tornadoes ripped through the Mossy Grove, Morgan County, community in November of 2002. President Bush declared sixteen counties in Tennessee disaster areas. Photograph by Jason Pack, FEMA News Photo, Nov. 12, 2002.

County. A firefighter at Briceville, in Anderson County, also suffered a fatal heart attack while on duty.

Responding to the tornadoes, emergency workers simply followed the path of debris to find the dead and injured. According to one emergency worker, bodies perform the same way as other debris in a tornado. Workers must search through all the rubbish and wreckage and cannot depend on search dogs during the first hours of a disaster. During this period the bodies are still fresh and cannot always be detected by cadaver dogs trained to find decaying flesh.

The *Knoxville News-Sentinel* summed up the incident well in a single paragraph: "It might be days or weeks before the assessment of damage, both in human and dollar terms, is complete. It will be much longer before the area returns to anything resembling normal. And it will be beyond the lifetimes of the survivors before the memory of that terrible night is forgotten."

SOURCES: Associated Press, Nov. 11, 2002; *Knoxville News-Sentinel,* Nov. 14, 2002; *Nashville Tennessean,* Nov. 11, 2002; National Oceanic and Atmospheric Administration (NOAA), online database: http://www4.ncdc.noaa.gov.

Tornadoes of 2003

MIDDLE AND WEST TENNESSEE, MAY 4

Tornadoes are neither evil nor righteous . . . they're something that happens.

—**Rev. Martin Field, St. Luke's Episcopal Church, Jackson, TN**

Aerial view of Mossy Grove's tornado devastation. Photo by Liz Roll, FEMA News Photo, Nov. 13, 2002.

Eleven people lost their lives in a category F4 tornado that touched down at 10:35 PM southwest of Jackson in the Denmark community. The twister, with winds exceeding 205 mile per hour, plowed a path of destruction 880 yards wide and twenty-six miles long through Madison County. Three others were killed by flooding related to the deadly storm. This occurred in Cannon County when two vehicles were swept from Tennessee State Highway 145 by a swollen stream. In addition to the fifteen deaths, over 100 were injured and 4,800 structures were damaged or destroyed in twenty-nine Tennessee counties. The most severely affected counties were Dyer, Madison, Montgomery, and Weakly.

This deadly storm system that spawned twisters in northeast Oklahoma also caused death and destruction in Arkansas and Missouri. The F4 category tornado that devastated Denmark, Madison County, traveled through Jackson and finally dissipated northeast of Beech Bluff, in Henderson County. Nine of the deaths occurred between Jackson and Denmark, but most of the economic damage occurred in downtown Jackson and surrounding suburbs. Sadly, an infant in East Jackson died when it was literally snatched from the arms of its mother by the tornadic winds.

One of the oldest churches in Tennessee, St. Luke's Episcopal Church (constructed in 1844) was also destroyed by the storm. The National Guard Armory, the Carl Perkins Civic Center, the Tennessee Supreme Court Building, the downtown post office, and several businesses and industrial facilities were also severely

Historic commercial buildings in Jackson's business district reduced to rubble by a tornado. Photograph by George Armstrong, FEMA News Photo, May 18, 2003.

damaged or destroyed. According to the *Memphis Commercial Appeal,* "Police authorities finally permitted access to the heaviest-damaged residential areas of Jackson on Wednesday to reveal what an F4 [intensity] tornado can do to 150-year-old oaks, fragrant cedars and long established neighborhoods."

Ironically, a memorial commemorating eight victims of a January 17, 1999, Jackson tornado was also damaged in the 2003 storm. Infrastructure, including communications, electrical power, and water treatment facilities, were also severely damaged by the event.

Most of the counties damaged by the severe weather were declared federal disaster areas by President Bush, making residents, businesses, and even local and state government departments eligible for federal grants and loans.

In addition to the tornadoes, torrential rain, hail (up to baseball size), and severe straight-line winds also caused considerable damage. Chattanooga, for example, experienced its worst flooding in thirty years, and, as already mentioned, three were drowned by flooding in Cannon County.

SOURCES: *Knoxville News-Sentinel,* May 6, 2003; *Memphis Commercial Appeal,* May 5–11, 2003; National Oceanic and Atmospheric Administration (NOAA), "Event Record Details, May 2003," online database, http://www.srh.noaa.gov.

The Historic Mother Liberty CME Church takes serious damage from an F-4 tornado that swung through West Tennessee. Photograph by Mark Wolfe, FEMA News Photo, May 7, 2003.

Tornadoes of 2008

WEST AND MIDDLE TENNESSEE, FEBRUARY 5–6

> Elsewhere in the area, a mother was found dead in a creek bed about 50 yards from where her house stood. Her baby was found alive 250 yards away. The child was taken to a local hospital.
>
> **—Jay Austin, Sumner County primary death investigator**

The deadliest tornado outbreak in two decades occurred in West and Middle Tennessee on February 5–6, 2008. Dozens of twisters touched down, killing twenty in Ar-kansas and Kentucky. Thirty-three died and dozens were injured in Tennessee. There were fourteen deaths in Jackson and Macon County alone. The first tornado arose in Mississippi and tracked across southeastern Memphis. It damaged both commercial and residential areas, including portions of Pleasant Ridge and Germantown in Shelby County. It caused damage to the Memphis International Airport and to adjacent FedEx facilities. At least four died in Shelby and Fayette counties, but Jackson and Madison counties bore the brunt of the death and destruction, as two F4 and one F3 category twisters struck that area. They were called long-track tornadoes because they touched down and hugged the ground for some distance rather than skipping up and down along their paths.

Union University, a Christian college in Jackson, sustains major damage from a tornado. Photograph by Jocelyn Augustino, FEMA News Photo, Feb. 7, 2008.

Many students and staff were trapped in collapsed buildings at Union University in Jackson. Nine were hospitalized but none suffered life-threatening injuries.

Two firemen, searching for survivors in a field littered with dolls, had an unexpected surprise. The first trip to the field turned up nothing. On the second trip, one of the firefighters saw a figure lying ahead. It was thought to be a toy but looked very lifelike. As he turned to the other firemen to comment on the doll, it moved. When he went to the child, it was lying face down in the mud amid tall grass and debris. When he turned it over it took a deep breath of air and started crying. The rescuer said that the baby had been hurled the length of a football field from its home but was alive.

A lone home was left standing after a tornado merely shifted the structure off its foundation but razed the homes surrounding it. Lafayette, Macon County. Photograph by George Armstrong, FEMA News Photo, Feb. 8, 2008.

WINTER STORMS: SNOW, ICE, AND EXTREME COLD

The western and central portions of Tennessee, as well as the Tennessee Valley, have a relatively mild and humid subtropical climate. The eastern portion, especially the Appalachian Mountain region, is classified as having a maritime temperate climate. On the other hand, because of its variable topography, weather within specific areas, such as on the Cumberland Plateau, can be extreme, sporadic, and difficult to predict. Most of the state's fifty-plus inches of annual precipitation come from the Gulf of Mexico as warm moist air moves north to encounter cooler air or extremely cold air masses moving southward and eastward. This latter factor is most responsible for our winter snow, ice, and freezing rain. Since the majority of the state's precipitation falls in the winter and early spring, a cold air mix can quickly turn rain to freezing rain, sleet, and snow. Consequently, even though Tennessee has a fairly mild overall climate, freak winter storms and periods of extended cold, snow, and ice occur regularly. Blizzards are characterized by sustained winds and wind gusts in excess of thirty-five miles per hour and are accompanied by falling and blowing snow for three hours or more. Such events are rare, but they have occurred in Tennessee.

The Appalachian Mountains, especially the highest and most rugged portions within the Great Smoky Mountains, have their own unique weather extremes. In the Rocky Mountains, snowmelt accounts for a large volume of the stream flow in the spring, but this is not the case for the Southern Appalachians. The higher elevations of the Smokies can receive over 100 inches of snowfall in a given year; however, eight inches of snow equals less than one inch of rain. Therefore, as previously mentioned, snowfall does not contribute significantly to the amount of water flowing out of the mountains. On the other hand, cloudbursts have produced destructive local flash floods, and when they occur during the colder months, the snow and ice melt adds to the deluge.

The snowiest year on record for the Great Smoky Mountains National Park was 1993—the year of the so-called Super-Storm, with the overall average snowfall for five weather stations being almost seventy-five inches. Oddly, just two years prior to that, only twenty inches, the least amount ever officially recorded, fell in the park.

The most notable and destructive severe winters have occurred fairly recently in the decade of the 1990s. The longest and costliest winter storm in Tennessee history occurred in early to mid-February 1994. It was more severe than the infamous Blizzard of 1951 that killed 200 people and resulted in $60 million in economic losses. It was also colder and costlier than the extreme winter of 1835. This latter incident was called the outstanding winter event of the nineteenth century, and so severe was its impact that many hogs, cattle, and other stock animals literally froze to death in its icy grip. Equally damaging in many ways was the "Appalachian Storm" of late November 1950. It dropped very deep snow across the state and all along the western slopes of the Appalachian Mountain chain. The winter of December 1876 and January 1877 was so cold that legend had it that whiskey froze solid in warehouses (an obvious exaggeration), and ice floes on the Mississippi River damaged docks, wharves, and boats along the western tier of counties, especially in Memphis.

The severe winter of February and March 1960 has been described as having produced the most damaging ice storms in U.S. history. These events affected a dozen states, including Tennessee. At one point during March, a period of freezing rain lasted some thirty-six hours. An average of 22 inches of snow fell across the state and all-time snowfall depths were exceeded in many places. Mountain City, in Johnson County, holds the record of 75.5 inches for the state's greatest overall snowfall season in 1960.

Harsh winter weather plagued the state from 1917 through 1919 and especially from January to March 1917. An account of that severe event appears below under the "Winter Storms of 1917–18" heading.

Early February 1835 was heralded as the outstanding winter event of the century in respect to overall severity of cold, human suffering, and economic hardship. The worst part of the storm moved over East Tennessee on February 6, and for many years 1841 was called the "year of the big snow." On March 26, four feet of snow fell in White and surrounding counties and lingered for six weeks. And, finally, a blizzard on January 22, 1873, was so severe that three score years later the old-timers were said to shiver at the memory of it.

Other record cold years, determined by averaging the temperatures for two or more months, included 1884–86, 1894–95, 1898–99, 1901–2, 1904–5, 1935–36, 1940, and 1993.

SOURCES: David Hotz, "Technical Attachment: Great Smoky Mountain National Park Snowfall Analysis," Dec. 2006; *National Weather Service, Southern Regional Headquarters,* http://www.srh.noaa.gov/topaics/attach/pdf/ssd06-04.pdf; David M. Ludlum, *Early American Winters II: 1821–1870* (Boston: American Meteorological Society, 1968); Monroe Seals, *History of White County, Tennessee* (Spartanburg, SC: Reprint Co. Publishers, 1974); H. Clay Smith, *Dusty Bits of the Forgotten Past: A History of Scott County* (Huntsville, TN: Scott County Historical Society, 1985); Dixon Merritt, ed., *The History of Wilson County: Its Land and Its Life* ([Lebanon, TN]: County Court of Wilson County, 1961).

The Year without Summer, 1816

STATEWIDE

The summer of 1816 was a season of unusually low temperatures across North America and the rest of the Northern Hemisphere. It would eventually become known as "the year without summer." Freak snowstorms and freezing temperatures occurred in the northern states, and it was said that birds that had flown to New England for the summer were found frozen in their nests.

The effects were even felt into the Deep South. For example, Savannah, Georgia, reached a high of only forty-six degrees on the afternoon of the Fourth of July. August had daytime temperatures in the thirties and forties, and nights often fell into the freezing range in Tennessee. It was particularly cold in the mountains of East Tennessee. Crops failed during the summer, and the poor, destitute, and chronically ill suffered greatly from diseases and frigid conditions usually only prevalent during the colder months.

It is now believed that this inclement weather phenomenon, which affected many parts of the earth, was the result of three major volcanic eruptions nowhere near the United States. The first was Soufriere on St. Vincent Island in 1812; the second, Mayon and Luzon in the Philippines in 1814; and the third and greatest of all, Mount Tambora on the island of Sumbawa, in the Indonesian archipelago (then the Dutch East Indies) on April 10, 1815. This last eruption was the world's worst volcanic disaster in recorded history. As 13,000-foot Mount Tambora exploded, it was reduced in elevation by some 4,200 feet and spewed ninety-three cubic miles of very fine volcanic dust and ash into the atmosphere. The eruption caused global climate anomalies because of the volume of volcanic ash it produced, ash that extended far up into the earth's stratosphere. Days turned to night as the great cloud of volcanic dust began circling the globe at a height of about twenty-five miles. After a few months, the volcanic cloud literally began to shade the earth. Less sunlight, and therefore heat, was able to pass through this cloud, and much of it was reflected back into space. It took over a year for the atmospheric dust to settle back to earth. Adding to the cooling problem was the fact that 1816 was also a year of reduced solar flare activity. This phenomenon, known as the "Dalton Minimum," is a period of low magnetic activity on the sun that reduces the number of bright spots, making the sun a little dimmer. When this occurs, there is less radiant heat from the sun and hence a cooler earth.

It is estimated that some 10,000 people in the vicinity of the volcano died almost instantly from the pyroclastic blast, heat, deadly fumes, and suffocating ash. Some 82,000 additional people died in the months that followed. Most perished from famine, disease, and exposure. To add to the misery, a great drought also occurred during this period of extreme cold. Crop prices went up, and it was said that some farmers in North Carolina began selling their farmland and moving south and west to avoid potential worsening conditions where they lived.

SOURCES: James Cornell, *The Great International Disaster Book* (New York: Scribner, 1976); "Historical Winter Storms? 1800s," *Weather Channel,* http://www.weather.com/encyclopedia/winter/1800s.html; C. Edward Skeen, "'The Year without a Summer': A Historical View," *Journal of the Early Republic* 1, no. 1 (Spring 1981): 51–67.

Severe Winter Storms of 1899

STATEWIDE, FEBRUARY

The winter of 1898–99 was so severe that almost all the bluebirds in the county were killed. It has been during only the past few years that they have been seen in any consid-

erable numbers, but they are rapidly regaining prominence. It was so cold that winter that horses and cattle froze to death, and houses "popped."

—**Auburn Powers,** *History of Henderson County*

February 1899 probably holds the record for the coldest period in the state's history. Nineteen all-time-low temperatures were recorded at various Tennessee weather stations as a result of a gigantic frigid air mass moving into the southeastern United States from Canada.

Two-thirds of the nation, between the Rockies and the Atlantic seaboard, suffered the greatest winter storm of the nineteenth century and one of the most devastating winter weather events in our nation's history. Severe cold weather lingered from late 1898 through February 1899. Blizzard conditions occurred even in the Deep South during the first two weeks of February 1899. Even Florida suffered an unprecedented blizzard on February 12, making it the first time temperatures in that state fell below zero. Tallahassee saw two degrees below zero.

Southerly winds pushing north off the Gulf of Mexico encountered frigid temperatures moving south to create a rare phenomena called "Gulf effect snow." As cold air moved southward from Canada during the second week in February, many Tennessee towns and cities experienced record all-time low temperatures. A number of them have never been equaled or surpassed to this day. The lowest average mean monthly temperature, based on weather data from forty-three stations occurred January 1940. However, the lowest temperature in the winter of 1899 was thirty degrees below zero at Crossville. That was only two degrees higher than the lowest temperature ever recorded in the state (at Mountain City, Johnson County, in December 1917). The accompanying table lists some all-time-low temperatures for the state in February 1899.

There was a heavy ice tide (gigantic chunks of floating ice from shore to shore) on the Mississippi River during this winter, some of which eventually flowed out into the Gulf of Mexico. Smaller yet still damaging ice jams also formed on sections of the Tennessee and Cumberland rivers and some of their tributaries. Snowfall was also heavy across the state, and it lingered for days as a result of the severe cold. Unknown numbers of people, livestock, and wildlife suffered and perished in this unforgiving frigid weather.

According to an article in the *Nashville Banner* on February 11, 1899, "February was ushered in with zero weather, and it looks as if it would go out under the same conditions. The ground hog failed to see his shadow, and as the fable has it, is now wandering about in the cold. A little fellow said to his papa this morning that he 'hoped the nasty thing would freeze to death.'"

SOURCES: *Chattanooga Times,* Dec. 4, 1960; "Historical Winter Storms? 1800s," *Weather Channel,* http://www.weather.com/encyclopedia/winter/1800s.html; *Knoxville*

Journal and Tribune, Jan. 31, 1899; *Memphis Commercial Appeal,* Feb. 10–15, 1899; *Nashville Banner,* Feb. 1, 9–11, 13–15, 1899; Auburn Powers, *History of Henderson County* (N.p.: n.p., 1930); R. M. Williamson, "Severe Winters in Tennessee," *Journal of the Tennessee Academy of Science* 15 (July 1940): 282–87.

Severe Winter Storms of 1917–18
STATEWIDE

Ice gorges along the Mississippi River developed rapidly and rose to twenty-five feet at Bessie and Richardson Landing in Tipton County. According to old river men, these ice floes in West Tennessee in the early part of 1918 were the worst ever in the history of river traffic on the Mississippi River. The ice tore steamboats and barges from their docks and moorings and sank several commercial and government vessels. During the same period, ice jams and dams formed on the Tennessee from

Temperature Extreme (°F)	Location
–30	Crossville (Cumberland County)
–29	Trenton (Gibson County)
–26	McMinnville (Warren County)
–23	Johnsonville (Humphreys County)
–22	Cedar Hill (Robertson County)
–20	Sparta (White County)
–20	Dickson (Dickson County)
–18	Dover (Stewart County)
–18	Wilder (Henderson County
–17	Byrdstown (Pickett County)
–16	Union City (Obion County)
–15	Franklin (Williamson County)
–14	Clarksville (Montgomery County)
–13	Nashville
–13	Bolivar (Hardeman County)
–12	Loudon (Loudon County)
–11	Sewanee (Franklin County)
–10	Chattanooga
–9	Memphis

Chattanooga northward to Knoxville and even up the French Broad and Holston rivers.

An eight-inch snowfall in West Tennessee on December 8, 1917, was only a harbinger of worse times ahead. The ground was frozen for days as temperatures remained below zero. A record fifteen degrees below zero was reached on January 11, 1918. By the twelfth, the Mississippi River was frozen so solid at Randolph, Tipton County, that people walked across it into Arkansas. According to Don Porter, a TVA hydrologist/ historian, teams of mules were driven across the frozen Mississippi River at Cottonwood Point near Dyersburg, in Dyer County.

A mid-January 1918 snowfall closed mines, businesses, highways, and railroads statewide. When trains could run, they were sometimes eighteen hours behind schedule. That year a so-called coal famine closed schools and businesses throughout the region. In fact, the coal shortage was so grave in Tennessee that Washington gave the State Fuel Administrator the most far-reaching authority ever granted under such circumstances to deal with the situation.

From December 1917 until mid-March 1918, snow clung to the ground in Middle Tennessee. At times the area endured rare blizzard conditions with heavy snow and blinding winds. Much of that time the thermometer hovered slightly above or below zero during the evening hours. Ponds and streams were frozen solid for weeks. In fact, they were so deeply frozen that no one worried about the ice breaking while ice skating.

All-time low temperatures were recorded across the state. December 1917 through January 1918 was the coldest overall period in recorded Tennessee history. Tazewell registered –29°F; Johnson City –25°F; Springville –22°F; Jackson –21°F; and Rogersville, Dover, and Kenton all dropped to –18°F. The mercury also fell to –20°F in Trenton and –19°F in Johnsonville, but these were not record lows. The lowest temperature ever recorded in Tennessee occurred on December 30, 1917, when the mercury dropped to –32°F in Mountain City, Johnson County.

According to the February 17, 1993, *Chattanooga Times,* "The city [of Chattanooga] remained in the deep freeze through most of the rest of the month, and yet another cold wave was predicted on January 29. But rain came instead, causing the most sudden rise of the Tennessee River in history. The river rose 13 feet in 12 hours."

From January to March 1918, Scott County endured very freakish weather, including a very rare sand-and-ice storm that originated out of the Southwest and was followed by an eight-inch snowfall. Gale-force winds exceeding twenty miles per hour placed two inches of sand and ice on top of the eight inches of snow already on the ground. This was followed by an additional four inches of snow and one inch of ice. This snow-sand-ice pack was as sharp as razor blades and severely injured the legs of wild and domestic animals walking on it. Trails had to be broken through the ice and snow to get cattle, horses, and other domestic livestock to feed and water. Rabbits were stranded and became vulnerable prey to man and predators alike. This perilous and frigid weather did not break until March.

SOURCES: Beasley, Gaylon Neil. *True Tales of Tipton* (Covington, TN: Tipton County Historical Society, 1981); *Chattanooga Times,* Feb. 17, 1993; *Knoxville Journal and Tribune,* Jan. 20–24, 1918; Don Porter, Tennessee Valley Authority hydrologist and historian, personal correspondence, Jan. 28, 1988; H. Clay Smith, *Dusty Bits of the Forgotten Past: Scott Country Tennessee* (Nashville: Williams Printing Co. [for the Scott County Historical Society], 1985; Jonathan T. Smith, *Benton County Tennessee Heritage Notes* (Memphis: Rich Harris Printer, 1975); Seth S. Stuart, "A Brief History of Burns, Tennessee from Early Pioneer Days to 1975" (unpublished MS, 1975); R. M. Williamson, "Severe Winters in Tennessee," *Journal of the Tennessee Academy of Science* 15 (July 1940): 282–87.

Severe Winter Storms of 1940

STATEWIDE, LATE JANUARY

According to TVA records, January 1940 was the overall coldest month in the history of the state. Low temperatures in many locations rivaled or exceeded those that occurred in 1889. In fact, snow storms reached almost to the Gulf Coast during this period. The Cumberland River also froze over in Middle Tennessee. The accompanying table shows some of the record low temperatures for several cities and towns during the winter of 1940.

Conditions were so severe during this period that many believed that 1940 would surely go down as the coldest year in Tennessee history, though, ultimately, this was not the case. The heavy snow, ice, and intense cold made highways treacherous, and frozen rivers halted barge and other boat traffic on Tennessee waterways. Some people suffered greatly, especially the poor, the homeless, and the chronically ill. Some died of exposure and other factors related to the prolonged frigid temperatures. The economy also felt the brunt of the severe weather. However, as bad as the first month of the year was, the rest of 1940 was fairly moderate, weather-wise.

SOURCES: *Chattanooga Daily Times,* Jan. 4–9, 19–31, 1940; *Chattanooga News Free Press,* Mar. 30, 1980; *Knoxville Journal,* Jan. 24–31, 1940; *Memphis Commercial Appeal,* Jan. 19, 21–31, 1940; State of Tennessee. *The Resources of Tennessee,* vols. 7 and 8 (Nashville: State Geological Survey, 1918); R. M. Williamson, "Severe Winters in Tennessee," *Journal of the Tennessee Academy of Science* 15 (July 1940): 282–87.

Blizzard of 1951

STATEWIDE, JANUARY 28–FEBRUARY 4

The Blizzard of 1951 will long be remembered as one of Tennessee's most severe winter storm events. During this period ice and snow, spawned by freezing Canadian air moved south and east to collide with warm, moist air moving up from the Gulf of Mexico. Economic effects of this prolonged and ruthless weather were felt as far south as Florida and other southern Gulf states. Citrus and other crops in Florida were damaged or ruined. Losses were estimated in the hundreds of millions of dollars throughout the region.

Middle and West Tennessee, from Memphis to Nashville, were hardest hit, with Nashville being one of the most severely affected areas. On January 30 the temperature at Nashville dropped to eighteen degrees. However, the air mass about 5,000 feet above the city and the surrounding area was around forty-eight degrees, well above freezing. As rain from the upper atmosphere fell through the lower, more frigid air mass, it changed to sleet and snow. The city became shrouded by a thick

Temperature Extreme (°F)	Location
–29	Crossville (Cumberland County)
–28	Oneida (Scott County)
–22	Coldwater (Lincoln County)
–21	Waynesboro (Wayne County)
–20	Marshall County
–20	Rugby (Morgan County)
–20	Palmetto (Bedford County)
–19	Florence (Rutherford County)
–19	Decatur (Meigs County)
–19	McMinnville (Warren County)
–18	Byrdstown (Pickett County)

A riverboat on the frozen Mississippi River during a severe ice storm in the winter of 1940. Courtesy of Memphis and Shelby County Room, Memphis Public Library and Information Center.

layer of ice that covered roadways, bridges, utility lines, and vegetation. Snow and ice continued to accumulate as Nashville temperatures plummeted from one below zero on February 1 to thirteen below on the second and third. The power grid was knocked out across the region, and roads became even more treacherous; many were impossible to traverse. Traffic and airline accidents, and fires and frigid conditions resulted in eight deaths and countless injuries across the state. Schools, government offices, stores, and businesses closed for days. Temperatures warmed slightly between February 5–8 but then plummeted again, bringing more ice that lingered for almost two more weeks.

The American Red Cross set up mass-care shelters throughout Middle Tennessee, with the Army supplying blankets and cots. Nashville suffered food shortages as a result of poor road conditions and a national rail strike that occurred simultaneously. To ensure an adequate supply of natural gas to private homes and institutions, Memphis and other cities throughout the eastern United States cut off their supply to large industries.

Because of snow and icy conditions, a five-mile line of cars, buses, and trucks were stalled on the Rockwood Mountain along a section of U.S. Highway 70 in Roane County on January 30. This was but a harbinger of worse conditions to come. East Tennessee was affected less than the rest of the state, but by February 1 several streams, especially around Knoxville, began flooding. As temperatures dropped, much of the water on streets and sidewalks turned to ice. By February 2, the floods had subsided, but the ice continued to plague the city as the temperatures plummeted once again. Middle and West Tennessee were also immobilized under eight inches of snow and ice and subzero temperatures. Bus, train, and airline service into middle and West Tennessee were discontinued for a time. This storm, which affected crops, stock, forests and wildlife, cost an estimated $100 million in economic damages, twenty-five lives, and several hundred injuries across the South. It would be another four decades before weather this severe would again paralyze the state.

SOURCES: James A. Crutchfield, *Yesteryear in Nashville,* WSM-TV, Channel 4, Dec. 24, 1979–Dec. 31, 1980; *Knoxville News-Sentinel,* Jan. 30–Feb. 4, 1951; Jay Robert Nash, *Darkest Hours* (Chicago: Nelson-Hall, 1976.)

Ice Storm of 1960

STATEWIDE, FEBRUARY–MARCH

A cold, cruel storm swept away the comforts of modern living for thousands of people and pointed sharply at the narrow margin upon which men exist.

—**Govan and Livingood,**
The Chattanooga Country

The most damaging ice storm in U.S. history, including a thirty-six-hour period of freezing rain, occurred in March 1960. The accumulation of ice twisted and contorted trees, snapped limbs and power lines, and broke down power poles as though they were matchsticks. The snapping sound of utility wires, poles, and vegetation was almost continuous for days. Thick layers of ice on roads and sidewalks made driving and even walking treacher-

ous. Heavy winds during the period, sometimes gusting in excess of thirty miles per hour, added to the misery and the wind chill factor. It would take decades for the forests, especially those in southeastern Tennessee, to recover from the damages. Just after this ice storm Bowater Paper Corporation offered fourteen dollars per cord of fallen trees for pulpwood, an unprecedented low price.

Some of the hardest hit areas were along the eastern escarpment of the Cumberland Plateau, especially the residential neighborhoods around Chattanooga. This area alone suffered an estimated $5 million in economic losses. The costs of snow, ice, and debris removal and repair of roads and other infrastructure were high all across the state. Businesses and industries were also heavily affected. This was the worst winter storm on record, based on comparison figures as far back as March 1872. Below-normal temperature readings (in some cases thirty degrees below normal) persisted from March 1 through March 26. Twenty-two inches of snow fell at Morristown on March 9, which was the state's record for a twenty-four-hour period. The state's single snowstorm record of 28 inches occurred at Westbourne (Campbell County) between February 19 and February 21. A week earlier, Knoxville received 18.8 inches of snow. The state record for the greatest snow accumulation in a one-month period, 39 inches, occurred during this winter at Mountain City, in Johnson County. Mountain City also holds the record, 75.5 inches, for the greatest overall snowfall season in the state's history. The average snowfall over the Tennessee Valley region between November 1959 and March 1960 was 34.8 inches. Tens of thousands of homes in Tennessee were without power, heat, and communications during the period. A state of emergency was declared in parts of the icebound Chattanooga areas, and the National Guard was activated to provide assistance in coping with the disaster. Heavy snow accumulations of 150 inches or more were reported in the Great Smoky Mountains during the period. Ultimately, this winter storm is estimated to have killed more than 150 people across the country.

An ice storm on Walden's Ridge, Signal Mountain, Hamilton County, downed power lines as a pair of automobiles brave the conditions, March 3, 1960. Photograph by Jim Mooney. Courtesy of Chattanooga News-Free Press Collection, Chattanooga–Hamilton County Bicentennial Library.

SOURCES: *Chattanooga News Free Press,* Mar. 3, 1960; Feb. 25, 1990; *Chattanooga Times,* Mar. 2, 5, 23, 1960; Dec. 4, 1960; Mar. 3, 1970; Gilbert Eaton Govan and James W. Livingood, *The Chattanooga Country, 1540–1976: From Tomahawks to TVA* (Knoxville: Univ. of Tennessee Press, 1977); Lucinda Elizabeth Welch Hardy, *An Album of Historical Memories: Chatata-Tasso, Bradley County, TN, 1830–1961* (N.p.: n.p., 1962); *Knoxville News-Sentinel,* Mar. 3–5, 21, 1993; Tennessee Valley Authority. *Snow and Ice Storms of 1959–1960 in Tennessee River Basin,* Report No. 0-243-300A, Supplement to Precipitation in the Tennessee River Basin (Knoxville: TVA, 1960).

Severe Winter Storms of 1993
STATEWIDE, MARCH 12–18

It was a record-breaker in more ways than one. For the first time anyone can remember, *The Knoxville News-Sentinel* did not deliver a newspaper on Sunday morning. However, there's good news. Today, you are getting a Sunday and Monday newspaper rolled into one. It's a commemorative edition with special coverage on the snow storm.

—*Knoxville News-Sentinel,* **Mar. 14–15, 1993**

Although exceeded in severity by the winter storm of 1994, the Blizzard of '93, at the time, was considered "the storm of the century" and one of the all-time worst natural disasters to affect the eastern United States. It struck East and Middle Tennessee with harsh winds, extreme cold, and blinding ice and snow. There were also rare winter thunderstorms and eerie lightning. The storm produced two-foot-thick snowfalls in many areas of the Tennessee Valley and twice that in higher elevations of the Cumberland Plateau and the Appalachian Mountains. Five feet of snow covered the top of Mt. LeConte and other peaks within the Great Smoky Mountains National Park. Chattanooga surpassed its former snowfall record of 14.5 inches set in December 1886 by an estimated 5.5 inches. Record low temperatures exacerbated the misery and suffering and caused additional property damage. Four- to eight-foot-deep snow drifts were present on some roads and fields. Fifty counties (over half of those in Tennessee) applied for federal disaster assistance from the Federal Emergency Management Agency.

Highway traffic came to a halt, stranding both commuters and through traffic on Tennessee roads. Hikers and campers were marooned on trails and in shelters in the Smokies, the Cherokee National Forest, and elsewhere. People vacationing in cabins and motels within the higher elevations of the mountains were also stranded. Hundreds of rescue squad, National Guard, and national park personnel and volunteers searched for hikers and other stranded victims. Helicopters dropped 400 bags of food to those stranded in buildings in the mountains around the resort city of Gatlinburg. Schools, government offices, airports, businesses, and industries closed down, and many events were postponed or canceled during the worst part of the storm. In spite of its famous pledge—"Neither snow, nor rain, nor heat, nor gloom of night stays these couriers from the swift completion of their appointed rounds"—even the U.S. Postal Service gave up on mail delivery during this time.

Snow was so heavy that it collapsed many roofs in East and Middle Tennessee. Power and communications lines broke under the weight of ice that formed on them, and limbs, heavy-laden with ice and snow, snapped, landing on and breaking additional lines. Over 200 people were stranded for over twelve hours on the interstate highways in the Chattanooga area on March 15. Hundreds of motorists were also stalled on I-75 at Jellico Mountain and I-40 at Crab Orchard. Emergency 911 services were disrupted for a time in the Knoxville area, and tens of thousands of homes lost power and phone service, some for up to a week.

There were numerous deaths and injuries associated with the storm in Tennessee, and economic losses were estimated at $22 million. This storm pushed cold, ice, and snow clear to the Gulf Coast. Three inches of snow accumulated in Mobile, Alabama, and five inches in the panhandle of Florida. The Northeast also foundered under record snowfalls, ice, and bone-chilling cold. Ultimately, this storm took 270 lives, with economic costs estimated between $3 billion and $6 billion.

SOURCES: *Chattanooga News Free Press,* Mar. 13, 14, 1993; *Chattanooga Times,* Mar. 15, 16, 1993; *Knoxville News-Sentinel,* Mar. 14–21, 1993.

Severe Winter Storms of 1994

STATEWIDE, MID-FEBRUARY

Nashville shivered through a night punctuated by the sounds of crashing trees and exploding transformers. "You could hear trees crashing all night long," according to one citizen, "one about every 30 seconds." What some residents thought were lightning flashes during the night were the sharp blue explosions of electrical transformers blowing out.

—Nashville Banner, Feb. 11, 1994

According to Cecil Whaley, supervisor of planning with the Tennessee Emergency Management Agency, "Last year we thought the blizzard of 1993 was the worst natural disaster. We spent $22 million to clean up from that. Everything that we've seen so far indicates that last week's winter storm [cost] will be worse."

What has been termed the longest and costliest winter storm in the state's history occurred in mid-February 1994. Cold temperatures, snow, and ice closed schools, businesses, and government offices. Church services, court sessions, and many other community activities were also postponed or canceled. Many of those without power were sheltered in schools and shopping malls. Economic losses were estimated in the tens of millions of dollars.

As rain fell through a very cold blanket of air hugging the ground throughout the state on February 11, it began to change to ice. In portions of Middle and West Tennessee more than an inch of ice accumulated and snapped power and communications lines. Many trees and shrubs were likewise damaged or killed. Ice caused the malfunction of electrical equipment such as transformers that exploded as the result of ice or tree limbs falling on them. Half a million people across the state were without power, some for weeks.

East and southern Middle Tennessee suffered severe flooding as a result of rain and melting ice and snow. Portions of roadways and even bridges were washed away, and homes and other buildings flooded in some areas. To make matters worse, utility crews and emergency workers had to deal with icy roadways, bridges, overpasses, and traffic signal and street lighting outages. They also had to contend with vegetation so weighted down with ice that large limbs and whole trees fell across and blocked roadways. The gravity of the situation was apparent in some areas where ice toppled trees as large as four feet in diameter.

Fortunately, unlike the Blizzard of 1951, temperatures quickly began to moderate rather than plunging into the negative figures. This helped curtail further disruption of power and communications, but it did little to alleviate the previous devastation.

As in the case of most disasters, those without power and heat toughed it out in their own homes, sought commercial lodging, or stayed with relatives, friends, or neighbors. Others, particularly the elderly, stayed in public shelters provided by the American Red Cross in seventeen counties across the state. To assist state and local governments and private citizens in meeting the crisis, the governor activated about 500 National Guardsmen. They ran emergency errands, assisted utility crews, and transported people and materials, especially in remote areas or under emergency conditions. An additional 600 troops were placed on standby to assist troops already in the field to maintain law and order.

Electric companies followed their standard operating procedures for restoring power. Hospitals and nursing homes came first, followed by special needs households with terminally ill patients on life support systems or otherwise under critical care. The next priority was to areas where the largest numbers of customers without power were concentrated. This meant that many thousands of customers had to wait several days and hundreds of them for two weeks or more before power and phone service could be restored. In Nashville even the homes of the governor, the mayor, and the chief of the Nashville Electric Service were without power in the early stages of the outage.

Utility companies worked sixteen-hour shifts, around the clock, with extra personnel brought in from East Tennessee and surrounding states to speed the process. State and local emergency management personnel had one of the busiest couple of weeks in decades as they responded to the hundreds of problems that arose as a result of the severe winter weather.

Although many roads remained impassible and commercial planes were grounded, those who could get out of their homes inundated businesses that managed to remain open, especially grocery and hardware stores. Malls were bustling in the metro area since they provided warm places to dine, shop, or otherwise ride out the winter storm. There was the usual run on milk, bread, eggs, beer, batteries, candles, lamps, and fuel oil. The demand for chainsaws and portable generators also increased exponentially. Businesses were delighted at their sales figures, which some said were as great as revenues during the Christmas season.

Fortunately, there were few major injuries or fires, and only about half a dozen lives were lost as a result of the severe weather. Thanks to moderating temperatures shortly after the ice storm, conditions soon became more inconvenient than life threatening. Nonetheless, in terms of the disruption of life and loss of property and productivity, the severe winter of 1994 surpassed that of 1993, which was formally dubbed the "winter storm of the century."

SOURCES: *Nashville Banner,* Feb. 10, 11, 14–15, 1994; *Nashville Tennessean,* Feb. 11–15, 1994.

PART 2
TECHNOLOGICAL DISASTERS

EXPLOSIONS

An explosion is a sudden release of mechanical or chemical energy, usually in a violent manner, accompanied by the generation of high temperatures and the release of gases. It can also be a violent and instantaneous bursting of a large storage vessel, as the result of a buildup of internal pressure in a boiler, or as the result of a puncture, rupture, or hazardous chemical reaction. The first major explosion in Tennessee not related to war occurred in 1847 at the Sycamore Powder Mill in Cheatham County. Another explosion took place at the same plant in 1898.

Around twenty significant explosions—that is, events that either killed or injured a number of individuals or resulted in significant damage to structures or infrastructures—are recorded in the chronology, along with some lesser incidents involving heavy economic losses but no loss of life. Events that have involved gunpowder manufacturing mills, railroad yards and tank cars, service stations, natural gas lines, and fireworks factories, as well as explosions related to or resulting from disasters in mines, quarries, airlines, railroads, riverboats, and structure fires are discussed herein under those topics.

Sycamore Powder Mill Explosion
Cheatham County, October 12, 1847

A horrendous explosion occurred at the Sycamore Powder Mill in Cheatham County about twenty-five miles northwest of Nashville on October 12, 1847. The blast, involving in excess of 500 kegs of black powder, occurred during a violent thunderstorm and was thought to have been caused by lightning striking a storage building at the mill. Virtually nothing remained of that storage building or any other nearby structure. The explosion erupted between four and five in the evening and was said to have been heard sixty miles away. The shockwaves were so severe that many people in nearby Springfield, in Robertson County, and Hopkinsville, Kentucky, thought it was an earthquake.

Four mill employees were killed and twenty injured in the incident. Fifty homes and other structures were demolished, rock fences were leveled, and trees up to two feet in diameter were either sheared off or uprooted by the blast. Nearly every building in the town of Sycamore was damaged to some degree, and there was not a single structure without some or all of its windows broken. One large rock was hurled 200 yards by the blast. It struck a log house and passed through both of its walls. From there it sheared off two cedar logs and then continued for 200 more yards before plowing a deep furrow into the ground. Another rock, estimated to weigh 100 pounds, became airborne and crashed through the roof of the nearby Nashville Inn, coming to rest in its basement. Still other pieces of debris from the blast were reported to have been found three miles away.

SOURCES: *Nashville Banner,* Mar. 29, 1898; *Nashville Daily Union,* Oct. 13, 14, 1847.

Hartsville Threshing Machine Explosion
Hartsville, Trousdale County, July 6, 1897

The heads of two of the Allen boys were blown from their shoulders and cannot be found. The Negro Barksdale weighed 200 pounds and his mangled body was found more than 100 yards from the engine.

—*Nashville Banner,* **July 7, 1897**

Nine men were killed and seven were severely injured when a threshing machine boiler exploded just after 1:00 PM on this date. Eight died instantly in the blast and the ninth the next morning. It was believed at the time that five more would die from their injuries. However, later details of this incident could not be found. Twenty-five men had been working around the machine and had just completed their morning work. Many were just sitting down under a tree to eat lunch when the machine's boiler blew up without warning. The incident occurred on the William A. Allen farm just across the Cumberland River from Hartsville in Trousdale County. Two doctors from nearby Dickson Springs were on the scene shortly after the explosion. Neighbors, hearing the blast, also came quickly to assist in any way they could. Eventually hundreds of curious onlookers had gathered at the scene. Some of the victims were severely mangled in the explosion. Parts of the machine were blown over seven hundred yards away. It was believed that the accident occurred because the machine contained too little water when additional cold water was added too quickly.

SOURCES: *Knoxville Tribune,* July 7, 1897; *Nashville Banner,* July 7, 8, 1897.

Jellico Railroad Yard Explosion

CAMPBELL COUNTY, SEPTEMBER 21, 1906

> Early Saturday morning, the head of Joe Seller, the Proctor engineer, was found a distance up the mountain of a quarter of a mile from the scene of the explosion.
>
> —*Knoxville Journal and Tribune,*
> **Sept. 24, 1906**

September 21, 1906, began like most other mornings in Jellico, a small town on the Campbell County, Tennessee–Kentucky border. Suddenly, at 7:47 AM, all that changed as 450 cases (approximately eleven tons) of dynamite detonated in a horrendous fireball in the town's railroad yard. This explosion killed a dozen people and injured around 200. Some of the seriously injured died later as a result of the trauma. Another 500 (approximately one-quarter of the community's population) were left homeless on both sides of the Tennessee-Kentucky state line. The massive blast occurred in a freight car temporarily parked on a rail siding about a hundred yards from the Jellico Union Railway Station.

Practically every structure within a one-mile radius was demolished or damaged by either the blast or by the heavy debris raining down seconds later. Parts of buildings, rail cars, pieces of rails and ties from the tracks, and even body parts were scattered over a broad area. Three men standing near the explosion were literally blown to bits. Curiously, the pocket watch of an engineer killed in the incident was found on the ground with a knife blade driven through it. A mile away from the blast, a young boy had his knee cap torn off by a piece of falling pig iron. His leg was later amputated.

Many stores, businesses, and homes were twisted out of shape by the force of the blast and shifted from their foundations. Roofs were blown away, chimneys crumbled, and doors blasted out. Windows, mirrors, dishes, and glass containers were shattered in practically every building in town. With doors, windows, and roofs missing, the cold and rainy weather that followed caused even more damage to the furnishings and other contents of the buildings not already damaged by the blast.

The blast created a crater seventy-five feet in diameter and thirty feet deep. The explosion was audible some forty miles away at High Cliff, in Campbell County, and in Barbourville, Kentucky. The impact caused many local water wells to cave in or drain dry. The economic losses at the time were estimated at a million dollars on both sides of the state line.

What caused the dynamite to explode will never be known for sure. There were a number of theories, but during a coroner's inquest, two were considered the most feasible. According to the first, a number of eyewit-

A crater 30 feet deep and 100 feet in diameter created by an explosion at the Jellico railroad yard in 1906. Courtesy of George Eddie Archer.

nesses claimed that an agent of the local Jung Brewing Company was standing in the rail yard with two other men target shooting with some special steel bullets. These were the three men blown to bits in the explosion. Witnesses claimed that one of the bullets could have penetrated the explosives-laden rail car and caused the detonation. According to the second theory, other witnesses insisted that a train was being made up (cars assembled) and that a car load of pig iron could have slammed against the car containing the dynamite with enough force to cause the explosion. If nitroglycerin were present with the dynamite, as it was rumored, this explanation would have been even more plausible.

SOURCES: *Knoxville Journal,* Sept. 21, 1956; *Knoxville Journal and Tribune,* Sept. 22–26, 1906; Miller McDonald, *Campbell County Tennessee USA: A History of Places, Faces, Happenings, Traditions, and Things,* vol. 2 (LaFollette, TN: County Services Syndicate, 1993); *Nashville Banner,* Sept. 22, 1906.

Colyar Reese Oil Plant Explosion
MEMPHIS, JANUARY 24, 1921

Andrew McKinley, Negro workman, who was perched near the bowl of the tank car cap, was thrown to the ground. He then ran to the opposite side of Front Street to his

home, where he fell to the pavement unconscious. It was found at the General Hospital
that his chest, head and face were horribly
seared, so that the flesh hung only by the aid
of bandages which were wrapped tightly
around his form. He died at 6 o'clock that
night.

—*Memphis Commercial Appeal*, **Jan. 25, 1921**

Around 7:45 AM on January 24, 1921, a spectacular explosion rocked the city of Memphis. It occurred when an
8,000-gallon railroad tank car loaded with casing head
gas exploded at the Colyar Reese Company. This was a
Sinclair Oil Company plant located on Front Street and
Mill Avenue in North Memphis. Casing head gasoline is
very light and volatile. It is made by an absorption process where the vapors leaking from the casing head of an
oil well are mixed with two equal parts of naphtha, also
a volatile substance distilled from crude oil. It is highly
explosive, spreads rapidly, and is easily ignited. It is used
primarily as an automobile fuel. Ten people died in this
accident, some instantly from the explosion and others
from burns or related trauma. Scores were injured, some
seriously.

The plant sustained considerable damage from the
explosion, but the most appalling effects occurred just
across the street. There, a dozen or so block and frame
tenant houses were damaged or demolished in the catastrophe. As the explosion occurred, gasoline literally
rained down, forming pools around and upon the structures. In the process they were blown to splinters and instantly ignited. Several deaths occurred in these shanties
as they caught fire and collapsed. Some occupants were
even blown into the streets. A number of victims were
killed instantly, their bodies terribly mangled, while others were fatally burned and died later at local hospitals.
The blast shattered windows in stores and residences
for three blocks in all directions and was felt a half mile
away. The plant was heavily damaged, and the storage

Curious spectators fill the Jellico railroad yard the day after the
explosion. Courtesy of George Eddie Archer.

warehouses, office, pump house, and oil stocks were demolished. Economic losses were estimated at $200,000.

It was first believed that a workman had caused the
explosion and subsequent fire using a chisel and hammer
to loosen the cap of the railroad tank car in preparation
for offloading its contents. This would have generated
sparks that might have ignited the pressurized vapor as
it escaped from the tanker. However, after a thorough investigation, officials from the U.S. Interstate Commerce
Commission Bureau of Explosives placed the blame on
a defective valve. The tank car's spring-loaded safety
valve, designed to release built-up pressure, failed on the
tanker, but the workman used a short wooden two-by-
four, not a hammer and chisel, to open the cap. As the
worker removed the cap from the dome of the tanker
car, a vapor-pressure explosion occurred, blowing the
cap upward along with a gigantic stream of liquid and
a pall of black smoke the diameter of an old-fashioned
washtub. Rising to a height of some fifty feet and then
spreading out, the liquid fell back to earth and pooled on
surfaces, making it vulnerable to ignition. The investigators believed that the sources were most likely the open
flames of stoves in the residences across the street from
the plant. The explosions blew off the corrugated roofs
of two big sheds within the plant, causing everything
within seventy-five feet of the source of the explosion

to burst into flames. Witnesses reported two explosions: the initial tanker vapor eruption and the explosion from scattered pools of ignited gasoline. What the blasts did not destroy, the flames did. Only the chimneys and fireplaces of the shanties remained standing.

The Memphis Fire Department sent every available piece of firefighting equipment and personnel to the scene. They worked for hours spraying water on leaking grease and oil drums that continued to explode under the two corrugated roof storage sheds. They also continued to spray water on a dozen nearby 11,000–12,500 gallon gasoline storage tanks. This helped cool them down to prevent additional explosions. Fortunately, an adjacent tanker of the same type and with the same contents was unaffected by the explosion and fire, and its valve was found to be in working order.

SOURCES: *Knoxville Journal and Tribune,* Jan. 25, 26, 1921; *Memphis Commercial Appeal,* Jan. 25, 26, 1921; *New York Times,* Jan. 25, 1921.

Bristol Service Station Explosion
SULLIVAN COUNTY, FEBRUARY 27, 1947

Frank Robinette, Sr., 51, was dead when pulled from the wreckage . . . His head was crushed, other bones of the body were broken, and his face singed by the fire which followed the detonation. Apparently he had been instantly killed.

—*Knoxville Journal,* **Feb. 28, 1947**

A deadly explosion occurred around 11:00 AM on February 27, 1947, at the Robinette Service Station on the corner of State Street and Pennsylvania Avenue in Bristol, Sullivan County. Five people were killed instantly, and several others were injured in the incident. A sixth victim died later from injuries sustained in the explosion.

Three of the victims, a man and two young children, could be seen in the rubble, but emergency workers could not reach them for over two hours due to the intense heat produced by the inferno. Within minutes of the accident, Frank Robinette, owner of the service station, was found dead in the wreckage. He was killed instantly by the trauma. His son's body was recovered two hours later, along with the bodies of two other men. About a dozen people were injured in the incident, one of which was extricated from the wreckage and taken to Kings Mountain Memorial Hospital in Bristol. He was treated for lacerations, broken bones, a concussion, severe shock, and third-degree burns. He later died.

The explosion occurred as the result of three 1,000-gallon-capacity underground gasoline storage tanks bursting into flames. One erupted into a fireball, followed closely by the other two. The triple blast was heard over a mile away, and immense walls of flame shot into the air, hurling huge chunks of concrete hundreds of feet in all directions. As the blast wave expanded and debris rained down, windows in many nearby structures were shattered. One particularly expensive stained-glass window at nearby First Baptist Church was demolished. Several stores, homes, and other structures within the blast zone sustained additional substantial damage, as did five cars and a pickup truck parked at, or near, the station. Economic losses were estimated at $100,000. Two Tennessee deputy fire marshals investigated the incident, but the exact cause of the explosion was never determined.

SOURCES: *Knoxville Journal,* Feb. 28, Mar. 1, 1947; *Knoxville News-Sentinel,* Feb. 27, 28, 1947.

Texaco River Terminal Gasoline Explosion
CHATTANOOGA, JUNE 25, 1955

The explosion, accompanied by a fearsome "whoosh," sent a wall of searing flame high into the air. The concussion rocked the boat violently. In a fraction of a second, the fire spread over the surface of the water, licking dangerously at the loaded barges and three other [barges] moored at the terminal.

—**Alex Corliss,** *Chattanooga Sunday Times*

Six people were killed and another seven injured in a gasoline explosion and fire on the Tennessee River at Chattanooga on June 25, 1955. The accident occurred around noon at the Texaco Waterfront Terminal gasoline storage tank farm just off Manufacturers Road. The accident occurred after an eight-inch fuel supply hose became uncoupled or ruptured while gasoline was being pumped from a two-and-a-half-million-gallon capacity barge into a massive Texaco storage tank onshore. Between one thousand and several thousand gallons of fuel were spilled into the river before the pump was stopped onshore. The fumes were ignited by either a kitchen stove on the 135-ton towboat *Donna Lee* or sparks from its engine. Fortunately, neither the barges nor the gasoline storage tanks at the terminal caught fire or exploded. One of the barges had been off-loading its fuel for about an hour, and the other for about half an hour, when the incident occurred. As soon as the spill was detected and word relayed to the captain, he immediately suspended onboard smoking and ordered that the galley stove be turned off. As he did so, he started to maneuver his boat away from the area of danger. Unfortunately, it was too late. The flames immediately spread across the water, instantly engulfing the towboat, the barge, and the dock area.

After the *Donna Lee* was beached by a Chattanooga power barge and the fire brought under control, the charred body of one of its crewmen was found on its starboard side. He appeared to have died instantly in the explosion or the fire. The boat's cook and relief cook, both women in their mid-forties, jumped overboard into the river but were fatally burned. They died of their injuries at Chattanooga's Newell Hospital within hours of the incident. Three other crewmen were seen swimming from the scene. Their badly burned bodies were later retrieved from the river by the Chattanooga Red Cross Rescue Squad and Coast Guardsmen. Seven crewmen survived the fire, but only one did so with no serious injuries.

SOURCES: *Chattanooga Daily Times,* June 27, 1955; *Chattanooga Sunday Times,* June 26, 1955.

Tennessee Eastman Chemical Plant Explosion

KINGSPORT, SULLIVAN COUNTY, OCTOBER 4, 1960

John D. Looney, 18, was knocked from his feet. "I got up and started running and passed a man with his leg cut off," he said. "I saw another man lying on the ground. I guess he was dead."

—*Knoxville News-Sentinel,* **Oct. 5, 1960**

Fifteen people died and an estimated 200 were injured in an explosion and fire that erupted around 4:45 PM on October 4, 1960, at Kingsport's Tennessee Eastman Chemical Plant. Eleven are believed to have died instantly in the tragic accident. Others died later as a result of injuries or were finally found within the debris. Most of the injuries were caused by the direct impact of the blast and lacerations resulting from flying glass. It literally rained down debris in the form of glass, metal, bricks, and other materials from the blast. The initial explosion is believed to have been caused by the detonation of a toxic mixture of nitrobenzene, nitric acid, and water. Several smaller blasts also occurred within the plant. Firefighters and other responders battled blazes for nearly three hours before the devastating event was brought under control.

The injured were transported to other area hospitals as the nearest one, Holston Valley Hospital, became overwhelmed. Because of the threat of an additional large explosion, relatives and curious onlookers were pushed back from the plant. Offers of assistance came from throughout the region, and at one point twenty-five ambulances were lined up near the scene to take the injured to medical facilities. The worst of the damage was confined to a city-block area within the so-called aniline facilities, where chemical dyes are made. This section of the plant's acid division is operated completely by remote control, so there were no employees within the facilities where the blast actually occurred. Hundreds of thousands of windows were shattered in the 160 some odd buildings within the plant. The blast also broke windows in downtown Kingsport and was audible some twenty miles away in Johnson City. Economic losses were estimated at $4.5 million within the 400-acre plant.

SOURCES: *Kingsport Times,* Oct. 10, 1960; *Knoxville News-Sentinel,* Oct. 5, 6, 1960; *New York Times,* Oct. 5, 22, Nov. 12, 1960.

Waverly Liquid Propane Gas Explosion
WAVERLY, HUMPHREYS COUNTY, FEBRUARY 24, 1978

It was just big rolls of flame and black smoke . . . There were people in the air, landing on fire, people with their clothes burning. It was just a ball of fire.

—**W. E. Bishop, local police dispatcher**

On February 22, 1978, twenty-three cars of Louisville & Nashville Freight Train No. 584 hauling two 30,000 gallon liquefied petroleum gas (propane) tanks derailed just after 10:30 PM at the town of Waverly in Humphreys County. The cars were located near the intersection of Railroad Avenue and Richland Avenue. Residents of the area were evacuated in preparation for transferring the dangerous propane to other tanks, and the evacuation was complete by morning. On Friday, February 24, as cleanup proceeded on the wreck, people began returning to their homes and businesses. They were told that they could return temporarily, until the railroad began

Waverly disaster historical marker in Humphreys County. Photograph by the author.

transferring the gas. Everything seemed to be normal. By 2:00 PM, people were again informed to leave the area in advance of the transfer. About 3:00 PM, before the transfer could begin, one of the tanks ruptured, and its heavier-than-air contents began leaking and moving along the ground surface. Seconds later it found an ignition source and burst into a gigantic fireball. This explosion, technically called a BLEVE (boiling liquid expanding vapor explosion), generated 1,700 degrees of heat almost instantaneously and covered an area of about three city blocks.

The blast killed sixteen people and injured ninety-seven others. Half of the victims were critically or seriously burned. Fifteen nearby businesses were destroyed, along with six homes, three police cars, two fire trucks, and several other government and privately owned vehicles. Five of the casualties died instantly, while others suffered for hours and some even for weeks before dying. Most of the dead were railroaders, emergency workers, and town officials. In fact, this marked the first time in Tennessee history that the state had to take over operation of a municipality due to the large number of government officials killed or severely injured. The dead included the mayor, police chief, and fire chief. Those with the gravest injuries were transported to Nashville hospitals, including Vanderbilt Medical Center, and to burn centers at Birmingham, Alabama; Cincinnati, Ohio; Louisville, Kentucky; and Durham, North Carolina. The American Red Cross temporarily housed 275 evacuees as a result of the disaster. Overall damages from the incident were estimated at $1.8 million.

SOURCES: Humphreys County Historical Society, *Humphreys County, Waverly, Tennessee: Humphreys County Heritage* (Waverly, TN: Humphreys County Historical Society, 1979); *Kingsport Times,* Feb. 27, 1978; National Transportation Safety Board, *Derailment of Louisville and Nashville Railroad Company's Train No. 584 and Subsequent Rupture of Tank Car Containing Liquid Petroleum Gas, Waverly, Tennessee, February 22, 1978,* National Transportation Safety Board Railroad Accident Report No. NTSB-RAR-79-1 (Washington, DC: National Technical Information Service); *Tennessee Fireman,* May–June, 1978; *The World Almanac and Book of Facts* (Cincinnati: Scripps Howard Co., 1987).

West Haven Home Explosion
KNOXVILLE, JULY 2, 1978

A horrendous explosion just before noon on July 2, 1978, demolished a home at 3112 Silverwood Road in Knoxville's West Haven neighborhood. Three were killed instantly and two others injured. The explosion is believed to have occurred as Donald M. Rankin was reloading ammunition with gunpowder in his basement. Rankin and his three-year-old and five-year-old daughters died in the blast. His wife was literally thrown out of the house by the force of the explosion. A next-door neighbor was injured by flying debris as he was mowing his lawn. There was an initial explosion, followed by four additional blasts. The multiple detonations were believed to have been caused by a large store of black powder, reloaded ammunition, an acetylene gas tank (used in welding), and a container of portable camp-stove fuel. The house where the victims died was leveled to its foundation by the blast, and surrounding combustibles were ignited. The house next door sustained damage from the blast, and litter rained down on lawns up to 200 feet away. The shockwave from the blast rattled windows and was audible for over a mile.

SOURCES: *Knoxville News-Sentinel,* July 3, 4, 1978.

Benton Fireworks Factory Explosion
POLK COUNTY, MAY 28, 1983

The cause of the May 1983 explosion was never determined, but it triggered a federal investigation that uncovered a nine-state illegal fireworks ring and sent more than a dozen people, including factory owner Dan Lee Webb, to prison.
—*Knoxville News-Sentinel,* **June 6, 1997**

Just after 9:00 AM on May 28, 1983, a series of explosions rattled the town of Benton, in western Polk County. These explosions resulted from the accidental detonation of large quantities of gunpowder and fireworks at an illegal fireworks factory on the Webb bait farm just off U.S. Highway 64, three miles south of the town.

The blasts, heard and felt fifteen miles away in Chattanooga, Cleveland, and Parksville, sent billows of coal black smoke mushrooming 600 feet into the cool morning air. Windows were broken and pictures knocked off mantels and walls several miles away. The windows and doors of a nearby house were also blown out, as the structure was shifted off its foundation. Miraculously, the elderly residents inside escaped injury. Smaller explosions followed the initial blast, with individual firecrackers still popping off half an hour later.

Six men and five women were killed in the incident. Three of the bodies were found intact, but the others were literally blown apart and spread over several hundred square yards of woods and fields. The partial limbs of some victims were found more than a hundred yards from the forty-by-seventy-foot metal building that housed the illicit operation. The body of one man crashed through the roof and landed in the attic of a nearby home. Disaster workers used white sheets and red markers to keep track of the widely scattered body parts as each was bagged and placed in a refrigerated truck. This allowed officials to reconstruct the scene of the terrible blast during subsequent investigations. The bodies and body parts were taken to a temporary morgue behind the Polk County Jail for sorting and identification.

First responders arrived at the grisly scene to find a lone, dazed, badly burned survivor wandering aimlessly. This sole survivor was Dan Lee Webb, owner of the operation. He was taken to a Chattanooga hospital, where he was treated for second- and third-degree burns over 30 percent of his body.

SOURCES: *Knoxville News-Sentinel,* May 27, 28, 1983, June 6, 1997.

Liquid Propane Gas Tanker Truck Explosion

MEMPHIS, DECEMBER 23, 1988

> When I came out of the car, I was one solid fireball. I knew I was dead. (I felt my glasses melt off my face). Everyone was on fire. Everything was on fire—houses all over the place. One man was completely burned up but was still running around . . .
>
> —**Mary Carr, survivor**

It was 10:20 on Christmas Eve morning in 1988. A truck carrying a huge tank of liquid propane (LP) gas suddenly skidded off an exit ramp and struck a concrete overpass near the intersection of Interstates 40 and 240 in midtown Memphis. The truck's 10,000 gallon capacity tank ruptured upon impact, spreading a gigantic fire ball, some 700 feet in diameter, along the interstate before becoming airborne and crashing into a nearby duplex apartment.

Before firefighters arrived on the scene to contain the blaze, several buildings to the east of the crash site were ignited and gutted by the explosion. As the fireball spread westward, it engulfed six vehicles, reducing them quickly to bare metal. Some victims were burned to death as they tried to escape their flaming vehicles; three others perished in the adjacent house fires. A ninth man, a truck driver, was also killed in the ensuing traffic pileup. At least a dozen additional people were injured in the incident; six of them were admitted to the burn unit at the Memphis Regional Medical Center.

This disaster attracted hundreds of spectators who lined the overpass, viewing the gruesome scene in horror. According to one witness, "We saw people just burning up. There were four people walking down the street just burning and screaming. We saw one person in flames, rolling out of his car and another body lying still, smoking." Cars and trucks were strewn all along the interstate, some still ablaze. Broken concrete from the overpass littered the roadway, grass was blackened for several hundred feet in both directions, and several adjacent houses were on fire.

Traffic was backed up for miles as a result of the accident, and it took emergency workers hours to bring the situation under control.

SOURCES: *Memphis Commercial Appeal,* Dec. 24, 1988; *Nashville Banner,* Dec. 24, 1988.

Pyro Shows Inc. Explosion
LaFollette, Campbell County, June 5, 1997

The blast created a minefield of fireworks shells, which littered a broad swath of ground around the blast site. Some of them were still live.

—**Jack Widener, LaFollette police chief**

An explosion occurred just before noon on June 5, 1997, at a fireworks production factory, Pyro Shows Inc., located on Old Jacksboro Pike in western LaFollette. The blast, possibly caused by friction or some other ignition source, occurred as workers were loading explosive charges into cannon (canisters) for use in a Fourth of July multimedia fireworks show.

Four people were killed and fourteen others injured in the blast. The four killed in the incident were inside one of four steel reinforced shipping containers when the blast occurred. Three were killed instantly. The fourth died from severe burns and other injuries en route via helicopter to Knoxville's University of Tennessee Medical Center. The explosion was reported to have been heard some thirteen miles away. As flaming debris rained down hundreds of feet from the site of the blast, the shockwave rocked the community, shattered windows, and caused other damage to nearby businesses and homes. Much of the damage was spread along U.S. Highway 25W, which runs through the town.

In a nearby church, one man was thrown against a wall with such force as to fracture his shoulder. The explosion also ignited a church parsonage as well as a number of nearby vehicles. Some individuals were found on the ground outside their residences. They were not seriously injured but had been knocked down from the concussion of the blast. Local residents said that they first thought they heard thunder, soon followed by firecracker blasts, and then even louder multiple explosions. This was followed by the appearance of a mushroom cloud of dark smoke rising above the site as though an atom bomb had been detonated.

Firefighters and paramedics, along with officials from the state fire marshal's office, state and local police, and the Federal Bureau of Alcohol, Tobacco, and Firearms were soon on the scene. Their first mission was to contain and clean up more than 200 pounds of unexploded fireworks shells still littering a 270-acre area surrounding the scene of the disaster. These live pyrotechnic devices were taken to a local rock quarry and detonated.

After that, a seventeen-member federal response team began a comprehensive investigation of the incident. They interviewed eyewitnesses and combed the site for clues to what had caused the catastrophe. This team included specialists who had also investigated incidents, including the bombings of the World Trade Center in New York, the Federal Building in Oklahoma City, and the Atlanta Olympics. Their investigation quickly ruled out negligence on the part of the company and termed the incident accidental. They could not pinpoint the exact triggering mechanism and said it might never be known. However, when the first fireworks exploded, others followed almost simultaneously. Once started, there was no stopping the deadly chain reaction.

Two of the victims were high school sweethearts working for the company for the summer to earn enough money for college tuition and to get married. The third victim was a twenty-year-old female who had been with the company only a few days. The fourth was a forty-nine-year-old veteran part-time employee of the company who was also a state mine safety instructor. He had served as vice mayor and as a longtime councilman for nearby Caryville. The carnage could have been much worse, since the explosion occurred shortly after ten other company employees had left for lunch. There were other storage magazines containing explosives, located near the four steel reinforced shipping containers in which the blast occurred. Fortunately they did not ignite.

Pyro Shows Inc. is internationally renowned for its multimedia fireworks displays that often incorporate music and laser lights in its performances. Until this incident, it had an excellent safety record. There had never been a complaint filed against the company through any state or federal agency. In fact, a company spokesperson said that they had recently received an exemplary rating after being inspected by the U.S. Bureau of Alcohol, Tobacco and Firearms. Two insurance companies had also conducted inspections and gave the company a high rating.

SOURCES: *Knoxville News-Sentinel,* June 6–8, 10, 11, 1997; *LaFollette Press,* June 12, 1997.

STRUCTURE FIRES

Structure fires are the most common technological disasters to occur on an annual basis, and every city, town, and community in the state has suffered numerous fire losses. Capturing information on all of them would be impossible. However, the major ones that have occurred in Chattanooga, Knoxville, Memphis, and Nashville, have been fairly well documented. Not only individual structures but multiple urban blocks have been destroyed in many conflagrations. The fires described in this book are those that have taken human lives or resulted in over $1 million in economic losses, adjusted for inflation to the year 2007.

In the early days when fires broke out, men and women formed bucket brigades. Containers of various shapes and sizes were filled at some water source and rapidly passed to the scene of the fire. This rarely saved a major structure but often helped contain the flames to protect adjacent buildings by wetting them down. Even when a fire was discovered quickly, there was little hope of extinguishing the flames, as they spread rapidly though early nineteenth-century buildings and infrastructure, especially standard frame structures. Volunteer fire departments eventually evolved with primitive equipment that was hauled to the scene of an inferno by men or horses. Streams of water were pumped via human power to quench the blazes. James B. Jones, a public historian with the Tennessee Historical Commission, has researched and written extensively on the exploits of early Tennessee firefighting volunteers both in Nashville and Memphis. In the latter 1800s, volunteer fire brigades were composed of burly men who quickly rushed to the scenes of urban fires. They served a noble public cause, but if two brigades arrived at the same fire at the same time, they often started fistfights over who would be allowed to extinguish the fire rather than jointly addressing the crisis. One of the most notorious such incidents occurred in Memphis in 1858 when Independent Company #1 and Washington Company # 6 rioted with guns, knives, and fists shortly after the two engines collided in the dark at the corner of Main and Poplar streets. The melee was finally broken up by Memphis police after an appeal from the mayor.

Eventually, such volunteers became full-time, paid, and well-trained professionals who could respond to structure fires, hazardous materials incidents, and other such emergencies within minutes. Many volunteer fire departments continue to serve Tennessee communities, and in fact there are almost 400 of them in the state. This is ten times the number of full-time, paid, city, town, and county departments. Volunteer firefighters are also professionally trained, certified, and dedicated individuals.

SOURCES: James B. Jones, "Mose the Bowery B'hoy and the Nashville Volunteer Fire Department, 1849–1860," *Tennessee Historical Quarterly* 40, no. 2 (1981): 170–81; Jones, "The Social Aspects of the Memphis Volunteer Fire Department," *West Tennessee Historical Society Papers* 37 (1983): 62–73.

Specht Bakery Fire
MEMPHIS, DECEMBER 24, 1864

This was the worst known fire of record for Memphis in terms of the number of lives lost.

—**Memphis Division of Fire Services**

Sixteen lives were lost when a rooming house located above the Joseph Specht's Confectionery and Bakery was set afire sometime before 3:00 AM on Christmas Eve 1864. The fire is believed to have started from a pile of burning charcoal behind the four-story building. This well-known confectionary and bakery was located on Madison Street, between Second and Main.

When the fire department arrived, the entire building, including its fourth-floor rooming-house section, was filled with smoke. Several victims jumped to their deaths from windows, while others succumbed to smoke (particularly carbon monoxide) inhalation in their beds or while trying to flee. Nine of the dead, employees of the establishment, were burned to death. The flames were extinguished fairly rapidly by the fire department; ironically, there was little damage to the building as a whole.

SOURCES: *Specht Bakery Fire,* Memphis Fire Dept. Video Documentary; *Titusville (PA) Morning Herald,* Dec. 21, 1866.

Memphis Navy Yard Fire
NOVEMBER 17, 1887

> The entire heavens above the city wore a lurid tinge, which rendered the location of the fiend's frightful work almost impossible . . . At last the whole northwestern part of the city seemed ablaze and in that direction the crowds surged. "IT IS THE NAVY YARD!"
>
> —*Memphis Appeal,* Nov. 18, 1887

The first fire at the MCP&S Company Cotton Warehouse was believed to have erupted in Compression No. 1 (a cotton baling facility), to the east of the railroad tracks. This fire was reported around 6:30 PM by an employee named Walter Mendenhall. He indicated that the fire spread from a single bale of cotton to others surrounding it. The workers at the Navy Yard were able to suppress this initial blaze after about half an hour. They immediately went back to work baling and preparing cotton for shipment. Within minutes, Mendenhall came back shouting that another fire had broken out in cotton compressing facility No. 4. The laborers moved quickly to that new fire and began fighting it. It was in a more isolated section across the railroad tracks on the northwest corner of the yard. This fire proved much more difficult to attack from any angle, as it was surrounded by many bales of cotton that could not be moved out of the way for the workers to get close enough with their hoses to extinguish it. Within minutes the sheds above the fire were involved, and the flames spread quickly, rising fifty feet into the air. The fierce heat caused the workers to move back behind nearby railroad cars. They continued to pour water on the flames from there and from the roof of unit No. 1.

Soon units No. 4 and No. 5 were ablaze. Within twenty minutes of the alarm being sounded, the fire had spread between the railroad tracks and the Mississippi River. By about 7:30 PM, emergency responders were en route to the Memphis Navy Yard, where bales of cotton were ablaze. Every piece of firefighting equipment, every foot of hose, and every firefighter in the city eventually attacked the inferno; however, the intense heat and flames kept them from being effective. Because the fire was not approachable from all angles, one responder commented that had they had three times the firefighting capability, their efforts would still have been futile.

Various fire companies approached the fire from the most accessible locations. One set up at the corner of Winchester and Front streets on the east, another at the south end of the plant, and others along Promenade Street. Such widely spaced engines required more hose than the Memphis Fire Department had, so they had to acquire additional hoses from the cotton compression company itself. About one hundred men were eventually involved in battling this inferno.

An estimated 13,222 bales of cotton were burned in these two sheds, along with others already loaded in railroad cars awaiting shipment. The bales that did not burn were ruined by being scorched. Eventually, most of the rail cars in the Navy Yard, some fifty in all, were burned to the rails. Most were loaded with cotton, staves, salt, coal, and other materials. Twenty other box and flatcars were hooked to a locomotive and successfully moved from harm's way. Although it could not be confirmed at the time, it is believed that at least two people died in this conflagration. Economic losses included the 13,222 bales of cotton ($661,100); fifty railroad boxcars and flatcars ($35,000); two large cotton compressors ($55,000); the sheds ($20,000); and other miscellaneous engines, boilers, and running gear ($30,000). This equaled about $800,000. Walter Mendenhall, who reported both fires, was arrested for suspicion of arson, based on circumstantial evidence. It is not known whether he was ever convicted of the crime.

SOURCES: *Memphis Appeal,* Nov. 18, 1887; *Memphis Daily Appeal,* Nov. 19, 20, 1887.

Nashville Insane Asylum Fire
MARCH 14, 1891

> This morning [a portion of] the Central Insane Asylum . . . is almost a mass of ruins, and beneath it are the charred bodies of half a dozen of the unfortunate inmates.
> —*New York Times,* **Mar. 15, 1891**

About 10:15 PM on this date, a night watchman discovered a fire erupting from the west wing of the main facility of what was then called the Nashville Insane Asylum. This hospital for the mentally and criminally ill was located on the south side of Murfreesboro Road, about seven miles east of the city. The fire spread rapidly upward from the first story, into the second and third stories, cutting off several rooms and trapping the patients within. Sadly, these unfortunate few, all males, had no means of escape. After the staff was alerted, they quickly began evacuating the approximately 400 patients, and panic and mayhem set in.

Twenty-two of the twenty-eight men in the burning section of the building were quickly led to safety; the others had no chance of escape and were asphyxiated or burned to death. When the city fire department was contacted by phone, they refused to respond until they could locate their chief. Meanwhile the fire consumed the west wing of the facility and continued to spread. The staff and some patients formed a bucket brigade to slow the progression of the fire until the chief was found, some two hours later. Two fire engines finally arrived at the scene about four hours after the fire had begun. They began battling the flames with streams of water and eventually extinguished the fire, but by this time the entire west portion of the facility and half of the main building lay in almost complete ruins. With the staff busy fighting the fire, mass confusion ensued. The facility guard tried but was unable to maintain complete control of the inmates. By 3:15 AM most of the patients were returned to the unburned east wing of the asylum. Unfortunately, some confused and terrified patients began running about helter-skelter. About twenty-five of them, mostly harmless, escaped into the countryside. All but one was recovered and returned to safety. Later, a single female patient was found drowned in a lake on the grounds of the asylum. To the author's knowledge, no one ever determined how the fire started.

SOURCES: *New York Times,* Mar. 15, 1891; *Waterloo (IA) Daily Courier,* Mar. 16, 1891; wire dispatches from Nashville, Mar. 14, 16, 1891, Tennessee State Library and Archives.

Knoxville's Million Dollar Fire
APRIL 8, 1897

In the spring of 1897, Knoxville sustained a severe conflagration that destroyed the largest and finest businesses in its downtown commercial district. It is said that Knoxvillians referred to this event as their "Million Dollar Fire," as if bragging over the fact that their fair city had a million dollars, worth of something to burn. One of the South's most devastating fires, it destroyed every structure in a two-block stretch on the east side of the Gay Street business and warehouse district. This included the Hotel Knox, along with the Sterchi Brothers Furniture store, W. W. Woodruff Wholesale Hardware Company, S. B. Newman Printing Co., and fourteen other significant structures. The heat and flames also damaged other buildings along the west side of Gay Street along these two blocks. The fire is believed to have started in the basement of the Old Knox Hotel and spread north and south from Commerce to Union Avenues, eventually demolishing the eighteen buildings. The alarm was received by the nearby Market Square Fire Hall around 3:45 AM and eventually involved every firefighter and every piece of firefighting equipment in the city.

As the fire chief realized that his crews were going to be unable to control the fire, he and the mayor sent an urgent telegram to the Chattanooga Fire Department, 111 miles to the south. They pleaded for rapid assistance. Loading their equipment and firemen on railroad flatcars, the Chattanooga Fire Department responded immediately, arriving at Knoxville in 106 minutes. At that time, this was a record run for the railroad. Meanwhile, the Knoxville fire raged on. It was described as being so hot in places that window panes melted, ran down the sides of the buildings, and literally puddled against their foundations. At one point, gunpowder stored in the old W. W. Woodruff Warehouse exploded, blowing that building apart and damaging nearby structures. The state militia was called in and used a large cannon in hopes of knocking down a wall to create a firebreak.

Eventually the fire was brought under control. The exact number of deaths from the fire could not be

The ruins along Gay Street following Knoxville's Million Dollar Fire, April 8, 1897. Courtesy of Thompson Photograph Collection, McClung Historical Collection, Knox County Public Library.

ascertained since the register at the Knox Hotel was destroyed in the inferno. Most sources indicate that five or more people were lost, either in the flames or while attempting to jump to safety from upper stories of the hotel. A number were also seriously injured. Even after the flames were extinguished, some of the ruins smoldered for a week.

Eventually all but one of the businesses were rebuilt. This still ranks as the worst fire in the history of Knoxville, with economic losses estimated at somewhere between $1.1 and $1.5 million.

SOURCES: *Knoxville Daily Journal,* Apr. 9, 10, 1897; Knoxville Fire Dept. records, State Library and Archives, Nashville; *Knoxville Journal,* Apr. 22, 1934; *Knoxville News-Sentinel,* Apr. 2, 1922, Oct. 6, 1963.

Memphis Front Street Fire
MEMPHIS, SEPTEMBER 3, 1904

> A stiff wind from the northwest, fanned the flames that fed upon the combustibles and sheets of fire leaped from roofs and windows, lighting the heavens and throwing a lurid glare far across the Mississippi [River].
> —*Memphis Commercial Appeal,* **Sept. 3, 1904**

Around one in the morning a fire erupted in the rear of the sixth floor of the Oliver-Finnie Grocery Company. At eight stories, this was one of the tallest buildings in Memphis's downtown business districts. The fire burned so intensely that its glow could be seen ten miles away, and it lit up the Memphis skyline like no other fire in the city's history.

By the time a night watchman discovered the fire, it was already well engaged and growing rapidly. When the flames reached the area where fireworks were stored, the fire took on a whole different nature. The explosions were deafening within the crumbling walls of the store, and sparks rained down on other structures within a half-mile radius. As flames spread to every

portion of the Oliver-Finnie store, its iron-reinforced masonry structure began to collapse on the north and south, crushing, igniting, and consuming the adjoining buildings on either side. The next building to the north along Front Street was destroyed, while the adjacent building to the south on Front was damaged, though not a complete loss. It seemed for a time, however, that all of the city's major wholesale businesses along the western side of Front Street (from Gayoso and Union) would be ignited and destroyed. As word spread of the conflagration, hundreds of spectators began gathering to view the drama. Every piece of equipment and nearly every fireman in Memphis was eventually engaged in bringing the fire under control. After some eight hours, the flames began to die down, leaving only smoke and flying cinders.

Fortunately, only one person, a fireman, was seriously injured during the event. Damages from the fire were estimated at $1 million. The Oliver-Finnie Grocery Company was the largest employer of all the wholesale houses along Front Street, leaving many workers with the prospect of unemployment. Excitement exploded, however, when the employees learned that the company had struck a deal the very next morning to purchase the nearby A. W. Newsom and Son building and resume business immediately.

SOURCES: *Memphis Commercial Appeal,* Sept. 3, 4, 1904.

East Nashville Fire
MARCH 22, 1916

> Thousands of helpless people stood by and watched as the inferno drove rapidly and mercilessly forward until its course was spent. The fear and anxiety in the hearts of every man, woman, and child were reflected in their faces as they watched the flames coming toward them.
>
> —**Henry McRaven,**
> *Nashville: Athens of the New South*

This, the state's worst ever urban conflagration, occurred in East Nashville and was said to be the most awe-inspiring sight ever witnessed there. The fire was alleged to have been ignited just before noon by a child playing with a ball of yarn. When the yarn got too close to a fireplace grate, it caught fire and the boy threw it outside, where it ignited dry leaves and grasses. The fire spread to a pile of wood shavings in the nearby Seagroves and Company Planing Mill and then continued to feed upon limbs, brush, and other dry debris that made excellent tinder. Pushed by sustained winds of fifty miles per hour that gusted to nearly sixty-eight miles per hour, the fire quickly spread to other yards and buildings directly and via airborne sparks. Most of the homes and buildings were constructed of wood and most also had wood-shingled roofs that were highly flammable. The fire spread relentlessly for nearly five hours. It was estimated to have moved forward at about forty-two feet per minute, consuming two or more structures simultaneously. Utility lines and poles, as well as fire trucks, hoses, and other equipment, were destroyed in the flames. Unable to stop the inferno, Nashville fire chief Rozetta ordered his men to try to contain it in any way possible.

An abandoned fire engine in the vicinity of Russell and Fatherland streets in East Nashville, March 22, 1916. Courtesy of Tennessee State Library and Archives.

The fire had started near the Cumberland River, at the corner of First Street and Oldham, and spread southeastward initially along a path four blocks wide. Firemen were eventually successful in narrowing it to a two-block corridor, all the way to Lenore Street. Additional firefighters and their equipment were rushed to Nashville via railroad flatcars from as far away as Chattanooga, Louisville, Kentucky, and Evansville, Indiana. Interestingly, not every house or every block was destroyed, since the inferno was spread from area to area by flying embers. Although it had proven impossible to stop, firefighters did manage to contain it to within an area thirty-two blocks long. When the wind and flames finally died down, about 700 homes and other structures, valued at some $2 million, lay in ruin. A small frame house across Lenore Street was the last structure to burn down.

Most sources state that only one person died in the flames, but many others were injured, some mortally. About 3,000 people were left homeless by the incident. The American Red Cross worked tirelessly to collect food and clothing and raise money to feed and clothe those who had lost their homes and to find temporary and then permanent lodging for them.

SOURCES: James A. Crutchfield, *Yesteryear in Nashville: An Almanac of Nashville History* (N.p.: n.p., 1981); Gordon Hall and Martha Hall, *Fire on the Scene in Nashville.* (Johnson City, TN: Overmountain Press, 1991); Henry McRaven, *Nashville: Athens of the New South* (Chapel Hill, NC: Chapel Hill Press, 1949); *Nashville Banner,* Dec. 7, 1959; *Nashville Tennessean,* Mar. 22, 1966, July 11, 18, 21, 1975.

Old Hickory Powder Plant Fire

DAVIDSON COUNTY, AUGUST 10, 1924

A devastating fire broke out at Old Hickory, twelve miles from Nashville, around 5:20 AM on August 10, 1924. It was believed to have erupted within a solvent recovery facility in the northeast section of a forty-acre tract owned by the Nashville Industrial Corporation, formerly called the Old Hickory Powder Plant. Only about half of the facility was involved in the conflagration. From there the fire spread to other buildings within the powder and munitions storage areas. An estimated 22,500 tons of smokeless powder (some estimates are higher) and about fifty buildings were destroyed in the fire. The damaged and destroyed buildings included solvent recovery facilities, powder mixing houses, a garage, powder press houses, a refrigerating plant, and offices containing surveillance and inventory records. Much machinery used in the production of gun powder and ammunition as well as a number of vehicles were also damaged or destroyed. Although there were no major explosions involved in the incident, thousands of rounds of small arms ammunition were set off by the heat of the inferno. Fortunately, this was contained within the brick storage facilities in which they were kept.

Miraculously, no one was seriously injured in the fire, and only about half of the storage capacity of the facility was affected. The powder, which had been valued at $28 million during the war, had a peacetime estimated cost of only $2 million. It was owned by the U.S. government and stored within the Old Hickory facility as military reserve. As word of the fire spread, thousands of vehicles of curious spectators lined the highways into the area. However, the fact that the event occurred during daylight hours and that no dramatic explosions were to be seen or heard made the trip anticlimactic for most. Owing to the lack of brisk winds, the heavy construction and separation of the facilities housing the powder, and the heroic efforts of firefighters, the flames were suppressed before the fire reached the main storage building and other facilities within the plant site. Plant firefighters as well as those from Nashville and surrounding communities were involved in these efforts. The fire was under control by 12:30 that afternoon, some seven hours after it had erupted. This fire was said to have caused the greatest economic military loss since World War I and was one of the most devastating incidents in the history of U.S. military munitions facilities. Fortunately, the buildings, the powder, and all the machinery used to produce it were totally covered by insurance.

SOURCES: *Nashville Tennessean,* Aug. 11–13, 1924; *Old Hickory News,* Mar. 29, 1929; *Washington Post,* Aug. 11, 1924.

Memphis Industrial Settlement Home Fire
AUGUST 29, 1929

> The bathroom in which the bodies were found was right in the center of all the flames. The door had been burned off. There was only one window, high up, and those children didn't have a chance to get out. The fire didn't enter the room, but it was just like they had been put in an oven.
>
> —*Memphis Commercial Appeal,* Sept. 2, 1929

Just before 6:00 AM on this date, a fire broke out in the Memphis Settlement Home, an African American orphanage at 366 Driver Street. Eighty of the children and staff members escaped, but eight children became trapped and died in an upstairs bathroom. The oldest of these children was only six. It is not known for sure how the eight ended up in the bathroom, but they probably panicked and ran there to escape the raging flames. Unfortunately, their bodies were not discovered until the fire had been extinguished. One of the matrons of the home, who was sleeping downstairs, awoke to the smell of smoke and quickly woke up another matron. They found the fire and tried to extinguish it with a bucket of water. When their efforts failed, they screamed for the director of the home, who was sleeping upstairs. The director went to the fire gong, started clanging it, and yelled to the older girls upstairs to grab the babies and get out. The director and her matrons said they made another run upstairs before leaving the burning building and believed that all the children had gotten out safely.

The alarm arrived at the fire department at 5:51 AM and a second alarm was sounded at 5:56, sending another fire company to the scene. By the time they arrived, the fire had spread quickly up the back wall of the large dormitory type structure. Soon the entire back of the building was in flames. Initially, the fire was believed to have started at two places in the basement at the same time. However, subsequent investigations proved otherwise.

Shortly after the fire, a fifteen-year-old girl confessed to police and fire officials that she was responsible for the fire. She said she started it because she was angry about being whipped for some infraction. She said she decided to burn down the Settlement Home, and after finding matches in the kitchen, she ignited a downstairs storage closet. After doing so, she slipped back upstairs and got into bed. As it turned out, she had been implicated in setting arson fires on two other occasions: the first at a detention facility in Okolona, Mississippi, and another in Memphis, shortly after arriving at the present Settlement Home. After the interrogation in which she admitted to the crime, she was sent to the matron's quarters of the city jail to await further action.

Humanitarian assistance was provided very quickly by the citizens of Memphis after the fire. The children were provided food, clothing, and housing at various locations around Memphis in hopes of eventually being brought back together in another, safer facility. The burial cost for the eight victims was also provided. The city commissioner, Sam Jackson, met with officials, citizens, and members of various black community organizations who provided the necessary relief and services. The Settlement Home had been known as a potential firetrap for some time. It had been cited several times by city fire inspectors for fire code violations. These officials insisted that more exits and a fire escape from the second floor be added, but managers of the home had asked for extensions, citing lack of funds. Ironically, the city fire marshal had just given them a final warning to improve the conditions of the home or move out within the week. The director of the home assured him that they planned to vacate the facility immediately and move the children to another location, outside of the city. Unfortunately, it was too late for the eight children who died in the fire.

SOURCES: *Memphis Commercial Appeal,* Sept. 2, 3, 1929; *New York Times,* Sept. 2, 4, 1929.

Southern Hotel Fire
CHATTANOOGA, FEBRUARY 7, 1942

> Mr. and Mrs. Arone [a newly married couple] were found in a bathroom, their arms locked in a dying embrace. They are believed to have darted into the bathroom in a frantic search for a fire escape.
> —*Chattanooga Times,* Feb. 8, 1942

Five people died of asphyxiation or burned to death on February 7, 1942, when a tragic fire erupted in Chattanooga's Southern Hotel on Market Street. Some thirty people were registered in the hotel at the time of the incident, but fortunately many had left for the day. The department received its first report of the fire at 9:19 AM and responded rapidly to the scene. Almost every fireman in the city, along with nearby volunteer departments and eight men from the Fort Oglethorpe, Georgia, Fire Department, battled the flames and the billowing smoke from the old wood-frame structure for nearly three hours. Despite being hampered by thick smoke, flames, and hot tar raining down from the roof, firefighters were able to rescue eight people. Unfortunately, they could not reach the other five victims in time. Other residents made it out on their own.

Through rapid and persistent efforts, the firefighters were able to save four adjacent buildings along the same side of Market Street. Thousands of spectators gathered to view the spectacle from the vicinity of Terminal Station, just across the street. The fire was believed to have started around nine in the morning in a second-floor room used to store luggage and trunks. Damages to the structure were estimated at $40,000.

SOURCE: *Chattanooga Times,* Feb. 8, 1942.

State Fairgrounds Fire
NASHVILLE, SEPTEMBER 20, 1965

The largest single structure fire in Nashville history erupted at the State Fair Grounds on September 20, 1965. The flames of the immense inferno were visible throughout the city, and heavy smoke engulfed much of South Nashville.

Eighteen of the injured were taken to Nashville General Hospital, where most were treated for burns. Ten of the injured were firefighters who suffered from smoke inhalation. Emergency workers combed the ruins throughout the night and the next morning. Fortunately, they found no additional casualties.

Faulty electrical wiring was believed to have caused the fire, which broke out around 10:15 PM in the women's building. Luckily most of the fair visitors had left the main buildings and grandstands by the time the fire ignited and began to spread. The half-century-old, three-story-high women's building, and the adjacent three-story merchants and administration buildings were all framed structures; these and the grandstands were heavily damaged by the conflagration. Concession stands and vendor booths were likewise engulfed in flames, along with their contents. Many of the vehicles and trailers belonging to the fair workers were also destroyed, because they were parked in the main area of the fire. The main livestock area was spared, but many smaller animals like rabbits and chickens were burned, along with some wildlife species displayed by the Tennessee Wildlife Resources Agency.

The flames spread quickly, causing small explosions, and with electrical lines dropping to the ground, most people began running away to escape the heat and flames. Unfortunately, those in the Midway and in other areas of the fairgrounds began running toward the fire to get a better look. Both groups clashed in the confusion, greatly complicating response actions. Wide-scale looting occurred in stands near the fire line. While a few violators were caught, many fairgoers escaped the Midway area with food and other booty. Eventually, the police were able to move the workers and spectators back a couple of blocks to secure the area.

Many of the fairground facilities, such as the midway and the Coliseum were not affected. Nonetheless, economic losses in this fire were estimated at $10,000–$12,000.

SOURCES: *Knoxville News-Sentinel,* Sept. 21, 1965; *Nashville Tennessean,* Sept. 21, 1965.

Maury County Jail Fire
COLUMBIA, JUNE 26, 1977

> I've had time to think about this. If we'd had electric doors, if we'd had a button to push, I would have pushed that button and let them all run. We could catch them later rather than lose a life.
>
> **—Bob Farmer, former chief deputy,**
> **Maury County Jail**

Deputy Sheriff James Duke stands in the once padded cell where the Maury County jail fire was ignited, June 26, 1977. Courtesy of Special Collections, University of Memphis Libraries.

The day after the devastating Maury County Jail fire, a deputy noticed a faint white figure on a bunk in an otherwise soot-blackened cell. Closer examination revealed that it was the outline of a human body, that of a prisoner who had died there the day before. The soot had rained down over the room, covering everything except the part of the bunk where the victim had laid. This was a lesson learned. It wasn't the fire in the concrete and steel structure that had killed, it was the smoke. To be more exact, it was the toxic cyanide and carbon monoxide fumes from the burning polyvinyl chloride mattresses in a nearby padded cell.

Fifty-six inmates and forty visitors were in the jail at the time of the incident. Forty-two people died and an additional thirty-three were injured. Thirty-three of the dead were prisoners and, because Sunday was a visitation day, nine were not.

Among the survivors was Andy Zinmer, the sixteen-year-old emotionally disturbed runaway from Wisconsin who was responsible for the incident. Being a juvenile, he had been placed in an isolated cell away from the adult inmates, awaiting extradition back to Wisconsin. Bored by the whole matter, he decided to attract some attention by plugging up the commode in his cell so it would overflow. This prank led to his being moved to a smaller nearby room that had plastic polyurethane mattresses, or pads, on the walls. It was a room normally reserved for mentally disturbed prisoners who might injure themselves. Even more disturbed by this smaller, isolated space, he asked a passerby for a match to light a cigarette and then used the match to ignite the polyurethane mattresses in his cell. Within seconds, the lethal black smoke filled the room and shortly thereafter someone yelled, "Smoke! Fire!"

Because the juvenile's cell was only a few feet from the dispatch room, he was the first person pulled to safety. His clothes were on fire, and he was pink all over and choking, but he was dragged from his cell alive. A bulldozer, a wrecker, and sledgehammers were used to breach the concrete and steel walls at the back of the jail, but these efforts were futile. The toxic smoke spread too rapidly through the jail, in part through air-conditioning and ventilation ducts.

Deputies were able to rescue only three others. Those three had stopped breathing and had to be resuscitated. However, twenty-three (possibly more) were able to make it out on their own. The rest were trapped and dead within minutes. There was probably no way, under the circumstances, that those in the interior of the jail could have been saved. The vapors were too toxic and there just was not enough time.

The youth responsible for the deaths and injuries was later convicted of arson and forty-two counts of involuntary manslaughter. Today he lives near his mother in Wisconsin. Although no longer in jail, he will never be free. The tragedy will surely haunt him for the rest of his life.

SOURCES: *Kingsport News,* June 28, 1977; *Nashville Banner,* June 22, 1987; *The World Almanac and Book of Facts* (Cincinnati: Scripps Howard Co., 1987).

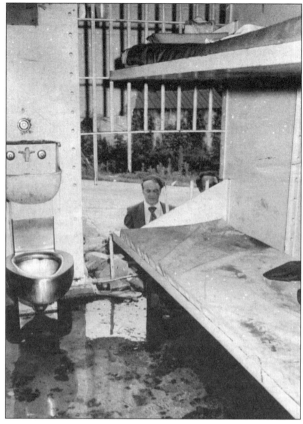

Authorities at the Maury County jail used bulldozers to free inmates and visitors that were trapped in the fire, June 26, 1977. Courtesy of Special Collections, University of Memphis Libraries.

Johnson City Retirement Home Fire
JOHNSON COUNTY, DECEMBER 24, 1989

> Up to 250 firefighters were eventually involved in fighting the fire. Since the worst fire damage was on the first and second floors, the deaths on the upper floors were probably caused by the smoke.
>
> —*Knoxville News-Sentinel,* Dec. 26, 1989

The worst structure fire in Johnson City history erupted just after 5:00 PM on Christmas Eve in 1989. The tragedy occurred in the ten-story John Sevier Retirement Center at the corner of Roan and Market streets. In terms of lives lost, this was the second worst structure fire in Tennessee history.

The fire began on the first floor of the 1920s vintage brick structure and spread rapidly to the second and third stories. The fire and smoke eventually killed 16, injured 51, and left 145 homeless. The incident is believed to have been caused by either a cigarette being dropped on a couch or a kitchen grease fire in an apartment.

Most of the elderly occupants were rescued from the upper stories of the structure where they had fled to escape the heat and smoke of the rapidly spreading flames. Nearby Munsey Memorial United Methodist Church was used as a staging area for triage and for providing food and comfort to the injured, their families, the displaced, and the emergency workers. The injured were taken to three area hospitals and the dead to a temporary morgue in the Downtown Center Courthouse.

Many firefighters and other emergency responders were injured or suffered frostbite as they battled the blazes and searched for victims in icy eight-degree weather. It took six and a half hours to extinguish the inferno. This was the second fire in two months at the center, which local firefighters later described as a tragedy just waiting to happen. The first fire had taken the life of one elderly resident and caused the evacuation of 150.

SOURCES: *Bristol Herald Courier,* Dec. 26, 27, 1989; *Knoxville News-Sentinel,* Dec. 26, 1989.

Nashville Healthcare Center Fire
SEPTEMBER 25, 2003

> When you opened the doors to their rooms, you could see their silhouettes . . . You had so many to get out. You would go into a room and there would be two people in there, and you had to get one and tell the other, I'll be back in a minute.
>
> —**Capt. Michael Wilkerson, Nashville Fire Department**

Around 10:15 PM on this date, a fire broke out in the privately operated Nashville Healthcare Center (NHC) Nursing Home. Within minutes, smoke began entering rooms, and the more lucid elderly and terrified helpless patients within the nursing home began screaming for help. The four-story facility is located at 2215 Patterson Street in Nashville. According to the Nashville Fire Department, the fire erupted in a patient room on the east side of the second floor of the facility. About 116 residents were in the facility at the time of the incident. Sixteen individuals died, eight at the scene and another eight in local hospitals as a result of burns or smoke inhalation. In all, some eighty elderly patients were hospitalized as a result of the incident, some in very serious conditions.

The six-alarm fire brought thirteen Metro Fire Department ambulances and several private ones for use in transporting the frail, elderly patients to local hospitals. The victims were carried out by firefighters or otherwise evacuated by facility staff. The sixteen who perished in the fire were all women. Other patients and staff suffered from smoke inhalation and other traumas related to the incident. The residents of the nursing home were taken temporarily to a terrace outside the facility, triaged, and those with injuries were transported to three area hospitals. It took forty pieces of equipment and scores of firefighters over two hours to knock down the fire and evacuate all the residents. This was one of the worst nursing home fires in the state's history. The second floor was the most affected by flames, but it was the smoke on the second, third, and fourth floors that caused the greatest problem for patients, staff, and even firefighters.

Unfortunately, because of its age the nursing home was exempt from having a fire sprinkler system. According to fire officials, such a system might have saved at least some of those who died in the disaster. As a result of this incident, the governor and the Tennessee legislature eventually passed regulations requiring that every nursing home in the state be constructed with or retrofitted with fire sprinkler systems.

A charred bed located in the room where the fire allegedly began was removed and sent to the U.S. Consumer Product Safety Commission in New York, where it was inspected to determine if it played a role in causing the fire. A charred aerosol can was found in the bed. Despite these findings, no definitive cause of the fire has ever been determined, and fire officials believe it never will be.

SOURCES: Associated Press, Aug. 4, 2004; *Knoxville News-Sentinel,* Sept. 27, 2003; *Nashville Tennessean,* Sept. 26–30, 2003; WSMV Television News Channel 4, Nashville, Dec. 20, 2006.

MINE AND QUARRY DISASTERS

Eleven major coal mine explosions, one copper mine explosion, and one quarry accident have occurred in Tennessee since the first such disaster in 1895. All of the coal mine disasters took place in East Tennessee and involved eight or more deaths each. They occurred within the Cumberland Plateau, which contains the state's rich Pennsylvanian geologic age coal strata. These were drift mines, which follow relatively shallow coal seams entered laterally rather than via deep vertical shafts, as was the case of the single Tennessee copper mine disaster. Three of the coal mine explosions occurred in Rhea County in 1901, 1902, and 1985. The two most severe incidents occurred in Anderson County in 1902 and 1911. Two also occurred in Roane County in 1925 and 1926. And one each involved mines in Campbell County (1943), Cumberland County (1917), Marion County (1981), and Scott County (1959). The single copper mine incident took place in Polk County in 1943 and the quarry explosion in Jefferson County in 1922.

In the eighty-nine years between the first and the most recent mine and quarry disasters, 470 men and boys have died. About 63 percent of the deaths occurred in only two mines, the Fraterville Mine in 1902 (200 killed) and the Cross Mountain Mine in 1911 (98 killed). Even though state and/or federal mine inspectors conducted investigations of each of the state's mine disasters, details concerning some are sketchy. This applies to the description of the first one that took twenty-eight lives in the Nelson Mine in Rhea County. The state's most recent coal mine explosion took place in Grundy County Mining Company Mine No. 21 at Whitwell in Marion County on December 8, 1981; this incident received the most intense inspection of all.

The fatalities in these mine and quarry disasters resulted from trauma (impact from the explosions or roof-falls), burns (from external flames and/or internal flame inhalation), or suffocation (from lack of oxygen or from breathing deadly afterdamp or sulfurous gases). Some of the explosions have been horrendous, and many miners have been killed by the sheer impact of the blasts. In the case of the Roane Iron Company Mine disaster in 1926, some of the men were literally blown to bits by the impact of the explosion. The bodies of miners were mingled with the carcasses of the mules that were used to move coal cars within commercial mines (possibly as late as the 1930s).

The Burra Burra Copper Mine disaster of 1943 was the only major mining accident ever to occur in the Tennessee (Polk County) Copper Basin. It was also the only major non–coal mine disaster in Tennessee history, with more than nine fatalities. The Strawberry Plains (Jefferson County) quarry disaster was also the only known quarry accident to kill more than nine individuals in one incident.

Nelson Mine Disaster, 1895

DAYTON, RHEA COUNTY, DECEMBER 20

> Hundreds of women and children soon gathered [at the mouth of the mine] and the picture of their grief and despair [was] heart rendering. Mothers, wringing their hands, weeping daughters and little children,

sweethearts and gray headed grandparents all in the greatest distress . . . hysterical faces were blanched with horror as . . . they [were] told that there is no hope. It was . . . a spectacle from which one turns sick at heart.

—*Knoxville Journal*, **Dec. 21, 1895**

Tennessee's first major mine disaster occurred just after 7:00 AM on this date in Dayton Coal Company's Nelson Mine No. 10. This mine was located about three miles from Dayton in south Rhea County. An explosion is believed to have occurred about two miles inside the mine when workers encountered deadly and volatile methane gas. According to state mine inspectors, the owners of the mine had been warned about the gas but apparently failed to take necessary precautions to stay away from the so-called marked-out rooms of the mine. These rooms had been inspected by the mine fire boss earlier in the morning. The open flame lamps of the miners most likely ignited the methane gas, which, when combined with coal dust, initiated the explosion. Another account blames the catastrophe on the fire boss, Tom Hawkins, who ignited the gas found during his morning rounds, burning it off in small pockets. This was a routine and customary procedure for a fire boss. The latter account went on to conclude that the flames may have drifted into other areas of the mine to mix with coal dust suspended in the mine atmosphere and trigger the horrific explosion. Twenty-eight of the 113 men and sixteen of twenty mules working in the mine that day were killed. Some died from the trauma of the explosion, some in roof falls, and the others suffocated from the deadly afterdamp gases produced by the blast. The fire boss was rescued from the mine but later died.

Within hours, rescuers began bringing the blackened corpses of the dead miners to the surface for identification and release to the next of kin. The youngest of the miners was fourteen. A major roof fall, producing some 5,000 tons of slate and coal, was encountered in the section of the mine where the explosion occurred. This prevented the escape of the victims and later hampered recovery efforts. The rescuers who first entered the mine were turned back by foul air but returned after the mine ventilation fans had removed enough of it to resume work. Digging, which continued day and night, was accomplished in short shifts, one miner spelling another as they tunneled through the rubble, which had fallen on and crushed several of the victims. Some of the dead miners were also removed through an adjoining abandoned mine that joined the Nelson mine under Richland Creek. The January 5, 1895, issue of the *Chattanooga Times* reported that two of the bodies were still entombed in the mine but were expected to be recovered in a few weeks. Since most of the twelve-year-old Nelson Mine was unaffected by the explosion and cave-in, production resumed there within a few days.

A state mine inspector's report on the incident stated that the accident was due to miners' carelessness and that legislation was vitally needed to regulate the operation of gaseous mines in Tennessee.

SOURCES: Bettye J. Broyles, *History of Rhea County, Tennessee* (Collegedale, TN: Rhea County Historical and Genealogical Society and College Press, 1991); Hiram B. Humphrey, *Historical Summary of Coal-Mine Explosions in the United States, 1810–1958,* Bulletin 586 (Washington, DC: U.S. Bureau of Mines, 1960); *Knoxville Journal,* Dec. 21, 1895; Jay Robert Nash, *Darkest Hours* (Chicago: Nelson-Hall, 1976).

Richland Mine Disaster
DAYTON, RHEA COUNTY, MAY 27, 1901

At approximately 4:30 PM on May 27, 1901, two almost simultaneous explosions killed twenty-one men and severely or fatally injured another nine in the Richland Mine, which lies about three miles north of Dayton. According to state mining officials, the disaster was the result of the use of excessive black powder charges, or shots.

Instead of blasting loose the coal as intended, they blew outward in a long flame. This fire ignited fine coal dust particles suspended in the mine atmosphere, resulting in an instantaneous flash fire through the entire length of the mine. In fact, it was so severe that it even scorched tree leaves a hundred feet outside the entrance. This blast also resulted in the explosion of a keg of black powder stored in the mine, thus further intensifying its effect.

The explosions caused massive sections of coal and slate to fall from the roof throughout the mine, some crushing and burying the miners. The violent nature of the explosions was evidenced by the disfigured and blackened bodies, which were retrieved one at a time from beneath debris and slate falls caused by the blasts. Burned pieces of clothing, as well as battered and even flattened miners' lamps and dinner pails, also evidenced the force of the blasts.

Examination of the areas where the miners had been working before the explosions revealed that excessively heavy black powder charges had been detonated. The investigation by mine inspectors following the disaster found that windy and blown-out shots were actually of frequent occurrence in the mine. There were no rules limiting the number of shots in each workplace or the quantity of powder that could be used to charge each hole. This served as further evidence that the disaster was attributed to reckless and extravagant use of powder charges by the miners in close proximity in a relatively small area.

SOURCES: Bettye J. Broyles, *History of Rhea County, Tennessee* (Collegedale, TN: Rhea County Historical and Genealogical Society and College Press, 1991); Hiram B. Humphrey, *Historical Summary of Coal-Mine Explosions in the United States, 1810–1958,* Bulletin 586 (Washington, DC: U.S. Bureau of Mines, 1960); *Knoxville Journal and Tribune,* May 28, 1901; R. A. Shifflett, *Fourteenth Annual Report of the Mining Department* (Nashville: Foster, Webb and Parker, 1905).

Fraterville Mine Disaster
COAL CREEK (NOW LAKE CITY), ANDERSON COUNTY, MAY 19, 1902

Probably the longest any lived was from seven to eight hours, while most of the men died within a much shorter time. The presence of unbearable heat and or afterdamp in the mine prevented the escape and caused the death of all who were not injured in the explosion.

—**Memorial program for**
Fraterville mine disaster victims

The worst mine disaster in the South and the eighth worst in U.S. history occurred on May 19, 1902. It happened in the oldest mine in the Coal Creek District, which had been in operation since 1870. Between 200 and 214 men and boys entered the mine around 7:30 AM, and minutes later a horrendous methane and coal dust explosion erupted, sending debris and smoke belching from the ventilation shaft and the mouth of the mine.

Many were killed instantly by the heat and the concussion of the blast. Along the main entry, the force of the explosion splintered mine cars and timbers and dismembered the bodies of the miners. Some victims found in side passages off the main entry showed no signs of trauma. They likely lived for a short time before suffocating from the buildup of toxic gases and from lack of oxygen. These toxic gases, called "afterdamp" are a mixture of carbon monoxide, carbolic acid, nitrogen, and other by-products of methane gas explosions. The other miners, who were alive but unable to escape toward the entrance, moved still deeper into the mine. There they constructed barricades in a futile attempt to close out the afterdamp and the stifling heat. Twenty-six men were found barricaded in one side passage. Some were still alive as late as 2:30 in the afternoon, as evidenced by notes found with their bodies. Many of these poignant notes, including letters to loved ones, wills, and such, have been reprinted in newspapers, magazines, and books.

Rescue efforts commenced immediately, but the first party had to turn back about 200 feet into the mine after encountering a dead miner and bad air. By late afternoon, toxic gases had been vented to the point that rescue efforts could continue farther into the mine. Shift after shift of volunteers began inching their way along the partially caved-in main entry and side passages. To do this, they had to construct a ventilation system of bratticing (that is, a conduit made of cloth fabric impregnated with creosote) to provide fresh air and dilute the toxic air. As they moved farther and farther into the mine, they searched one side passage after another, slowly retrieving bodies. Some of the bodies were torn apart and mutilated beyond recognition. At that time, mules were still used in the mine to pull coal cars to the surface. According to Miller McDonald's 1993 *Campbell County, Tennessee, USA,* there is a legend about the Fraterville disaster "that a mule's body was [found] pinned to the mine roof by a plank driven through the mule and into the slate roof, by the explosion." The last of the miners' bodies were not carried from the mine until four days after the explosion.

At the mine entrance a crowd of around 2,000 relatives, friends, neighbors, fellow miners, and spectators anxiously awaited word of the fate of the still-unaccounted-for victims. A temporary morgue was established at the Farmers Supply Company in Coal Creek (now Lake City).

The precise cause of the explosion was never determined or never disclosed. However, it was known that the mine's ventilation furnace had been shut down all weekend, which could account for the accumulation of toxic and explosive methane gas. When this gas exploded (probably ignited by the open flames of the miners' lamps), coal dust was blown into the air, precipitating an almost simultaneous secondary explosion.

The effects of this mine disaster on the small town of Fraterville demonstrate an extreme case of both broken homes and a broken community. Only three adult male residents remained in Fraterville after the disaster.

Fraterville miners' monument in the Leech Cemetery, Briceville, Campbell County. Eighty-seven of the miners were buried in a circle around the monument. Photograph by the author.

Many women lost every male member of their families, including their husbands, fathers, grandfathers, brothers, uncles, and sons. Social networks, particularly area churches, helped support those women in the months and years ahead. Some remarried locally or remarried and moved away, but others stayed, even after the mines were closed. At the Leach Cemetery in Anderson County, eighty-seven of the Fraterville miners are buried in a circle around a large monument that honors them. Still others are buried in family, church, and community cemeteries throughout the surrounding counties. In the backyard of the Owen Bailey family in Briceville, Anderson County, there is a cemetery where some itinerant miners (those whose bodies were unclaimed) are buried.

SOURCES: Owen Bailey, personal correspondence with author, May 19, 2001; Coal Creek Watershed Foundation, Knoxville, 2000–2009, http://www.coalcreekaml.com; Allen R. Coggins, "Fraterville Mine Disaster," in *The Tennessee Encyclopedia of History and Culture,* ed. Carroll Van West, 339 (Nashville: Tennessee Historical Society and Rutledge Hill Press, 1998); Hiram B. Humphrey, *Historical Summary of Coal-Mine Explosions in the United States, 1810–1958,* Bulletin 586 (Washington, DC: U.S. Bureau of Mines, 1960); Miller McDonald, *Campbell County, Tennessee, USA: A History of Places, Faces, Happenings, Traditions, and Things,* vol. 2 (LaFollette, TN: County Services Syndicate, 1993); *Memorial Services in Memory of Those Who Lost Their Lives in Fraterville Mine Explosion Coal Creek, Tennessee on Monday, May 19th, 1902* (memorial program).

Nelson Mine Disaster, 1902

DAYTON, RHEA COUNTY, MARCH 31

[The blast] literally tore . . . bodies to pieces, as the force of the explosion hurled the bodies of the miners violently against the walls and beams of the mine. Nothing more horrible could be pictured than the bodies of the men [and the mules used to haul coal within the mine] that were . . . literally a mass of flesh, torn to pieces, bones broken, skulls fractured in dozens of places and the skin burned until it shriveled around the horrible remains of the bodies.

—*Chattanooga Times,* **Apr. 2, 1902**

Around 4:35 PM on March 31, 1902, a horrendous explosion erupted in the Nelson Mine, located on the east side of Waldens Ridge, two and one-half miles northwest of Dayton. Twenty-five men and eighteen mules were killed in the disaster. Eleven men were also badly injured. The force of the explosion was so great that flames shot out of the entrance. In fact, the blast killed and injured men and damaged or destroyed objects, including outbuildings, up to fifty feet from the entrance. Somehow, forty miners survived the disaster, and some were not even injured.

The Nelson Mine was considered by many as one of the most dangerous in the state. Since 1889, it had killed fifty-seven people and injured scores in three separate explosions. According to local news accounts, this was the most violent of the three.

On a typical day in the Nelson Mine, the men would remove and load the coal blasted loose with black powder charges, called shots, placed in holes drilled in the coal seams the day before. Charges were set by 4:30 PM each day. All but two of the miners, known as the firemen, were then allowed thirty minutes to get out of the mine. At 5:00 PM the firemen would set off the shot inside the mine and then head for the surface. According to mine inspectors, for some reason on this day the charges were fired fifteen minutes ahead of schedule, and one of them was believed to have been overcharged, possibly with an inferior grade of blasting powder, and improperly positioned. Therefore, rather than exploding and breaking the coal loose as intended, it blew outward, igniting coal dust already in the air and additional dust instantaneously placed in suspension by the blast.

Although Dayton Coal and Iron Company owners admitted that the Nelson Mine was prone to producing high levels of methane (coal mine gas) they claimed that records showed no appreciable methane in the mine that day. On the other hand, some of the miners suggested otherwise. Following the 1895 explosion in the Nelson Mine, a branch of this large and complex mine had been sealed off with stone and mortar walls. It was theorized that present mining operations were dangerously close to those old passages, in which methane gas may have built up. The present explosion could have broken into one or more of the sealed-off shafts, releasing methane and adding to the fury of the recent explosion.

In either case, the blast caused a roof-fall a half mile back from the entrance of the mine. This coal and overburden rock debris had to be removed by rescuers before the bodies of their comrades could be retrieved. To make matters worse, a number of fires had been ignited by the heat of the explosion, and much of the mine was filled with deadly afterdamp. Mine timbers (roof braces), pumps, coal cars, and tracks were also damaged or demolished in portions of the mine, greatly impeding rescue efforts. All fires had to be suppressed and the shafts ventilated before search and recovery efforts could be resumed.

The extraordinary intensity of the blast was evident from mine inspectors' reports that lumps of coal weighing as much as 50 pounds had been blown over eighty feet from the site of the explosion. One block weighing 200 pounds had also been thrown over fifty feet down the tunnel. It isn't hard to imagine what such a blast did to men and the mules that worked this mine. At least the relatives of the dead could rest assured that their loved ones had died almost instantaneously, mercifully never knowing what struck them.

SOURCES: Bettye J. Broyles, *History of Rhea County, Tennessee* (Collegedale, TN: Rhea County Historical and Genealogical Society and College Press, 1991); *Chattanooga Daily Times,* Apr. 1, 2, 3, 1902; *Knoxville Journal and Tribune,* Apr. 1, 2, 3, 1902; State of Tennessee, *Fourteenth Annual Report, 1902: Nelson Mine* (Nashville: State of Tennessee Mining Dept); Hiram B. Humphrey, *Historical Summary of Coal Mine Explosions in the United States, 1810–1958* Bulletin 586 (Washington, DC: U.S. Bureau of Mines, 1960).

Cross Mountain Mine Disaster

BRICEVILLE, ANDERSON COUNTY, DECEMBER 9, 1911

Rescue workers brought bodies to the surface over a period of 10 days. The five survivors found two days after the explosion, learned later that graves had already been dug for them. The disaster left 53 widows and 146 orphans.

—*Knoxville Journal,* Feb. 20, 1949

Because of a shortage of coal cars at Briceville, only 89 men and boys, instead of the usual 150, entered the Cross Mountain Mine #1 at 6:30 AM on the rainy morning of December 9, 1911. Less than an hour later, the ground shook above the mine (also called Slatestone Mine), and a blast wave erupted from the entrance, knocking down workers outside. The second worst coal mine disaster in Tennessee history had just occurred.

Rescue efforts were launched immediately. As was the custom, the advance search team carried a caged canary with them. Being much more susceptible to low levels of oxygen and high levels of carbon monoxide, these small birds were used to detect bad air in the mines. Only a short distance from the entrance, their bird fell dead. Retreating to the surface, they learned that the giant ventilation fan that had kept air circulating in the mine had been badly damaged by the blast. After a while, they entered the mine again, some wearing self-contained breathing apparatuses, and some constructing brattices or ventilation conduits made of creosote-permeated cloth.

As rescue efforts continued past dusk, a crowd estimated at 5,000 gathered at the mouth of the mine. These were the wives, children, and other relatives of the miners, as well as neighbors and miners from surrounding communities. They were also the press and mere curiosity seekers, all waiting, and some praying, for word of survivors—for any word at all.

Some of the miners were killed instantly by the impact of the blast. Others were overcome and suffocated by toxic gases, including carbon monoxide, called "afterdamp" or "blackdamp" and generated as a result of the explosion. Among those not killed instantly by the blast, some suffocated within minutes, while still others held out for hours in the far reaches of the mine, fighting for their final breaths.

For five of the miners, the fight and the wait paid off. Those five had walled themselves off in a small room, away from the rest of the mine. For around sixty hours, they burned only one lamp at a time and kept their movement to a minimum to conserve precious oxygen. They also shared what coffee and food they had among them.

Rescue crews worked in shifts searching for survivors and hauling bodies of dead miners to the surface. Some used newly developed devices called oxygen helmets. There were small fires to put out, and there was the ever-present smoke and afterdamp. The giant fan that had been used to ventilate the mine was also a casualty of the explosion, so a temporary fan, borrowed from a nearby mine, was quickly installed to take its place. Fires were built at the top of upper shafts to help pull bad air out of the mine.

The last of the victims were carried to the surface ten days after the explosion. Many of these men, along with those of the Fraterville Mine Disaster of 1902, were buried in the Leach Cemetery at Briceville. They were laid to rest in two circles of graves surrounding a marble monolith erected in their honor.

An extensive investigation of the cause of the mine explosion was conducted by the state's chief mine inspector. The conclusions were somewhat vague due to a lack of definitive evidence gathered during the investigation. However, the explosion was believed to have resulted from either an open flame from a miners lamp or perhaps from a blown-out shot (that is, a blasting powder charge) that ignited quantities of coal dust great enough to have caused such an explosion. The inspector also indicated that "there may [also] have been a small amount of [methane] gas present in the air which rendered the dust more sensitive, causing it to propagate more readily." The intensity of the blast was so great that it moved a three-ton electric motor several feet from its original position.

Monument in a Briceville church cemetery commemorating the miners who died in the 1911 Cross Mountain mine disaster. Photograph by the author.

SOURCES: *Coal Creek/Lake City Visions of the Past: A History of Lake City, Tennessee and the People and Communities of Coal Creek Valley* (Lake City, TN: Lake City Home Coming Committee, 1986); K. B. Hoskins, *Anderson County History* (Memphis, TN: Memphis State Univ. Press, 1979); Hiram B. Humphrey, *Historical Summary of Coal-Mine Explosions in the United States, 1810–1958,* Bulletin 586 (Washington, DC: U.S. Bureau of Mines, 1960); *Knoxville Journal,* Feb. 20, 1949; *Knoxville News-Sentinel,* Sept. 25, 1966; *New York Times,* Dec. 10, 1911; David Rogers, *Reflections on the Water: Coal Creek to Lake City: A History of Lake City, Tennessee* (Clinton, TN: Courier-News, 1976); State of Tennessee, *Twenty-First Annual Report of the Mining Department, 1911,* prepared by George E. Sylvester, chief of mine inspection (Nashville: Williams Printing Co., 1912).

Flat Rock Mine Disaster
CATOOSA, MORGAN COUNTY, DECEMBER 19, 1917

Twenty men were working in the Flat Rock Mine, northwest of the town of Catoosa, in Morgan County, around 4:00 PM on December 19, 1917, when a devastating explosion and flash fire killed eleven of them. Although badly burned and severely mutilated, all of the bodies were recovered.

The nine survivors, working in other sections of the mine, were shaken but otherwise escaped unharmed.

According to mine inspectors, the accident occurred near the main and a side entrance to the mine when a blown-out shot (improperly placed powder charge) ignited coal dust. In turn, that touched off about twenty-five pounds of black powder stored in kegs at two other locations inside the mine. The chain reaction explosion produced intense heat and a blast wave that blew coal, dust, and soot several hundred yards out of the mine entrance. This broke and uprooted trees up to 400 feet away. The presence of coke (partially burned coal) and soot in the section of the mine where the explosion occurred, along with the mutilated condition of the bodies, led inspectors to believe that the victims were probably killed instantly. Unlike many other coal mine disasters, methane gas was not believed to be a contributing factor in this explosion. In fact, the mine was well ventilated and considered to be free of gas.

SOURCES: Hiram B. Humphrey, *Historical Summary of Coal-Mine Explosions in the United States,* 1810–1958, Bulletin 586 (Washington, DC: U.S. Bureau of Mines, 1960); *Knoxville Journal and Tribune,* Dec. 21, 1917.

Strawberry Plains Quarry Explosion

STRAWBERRY PLAINS, JEFFERSON
COUNTY, JUNE 27, 1922

> I never knew what happened. I was standing up right in the wagon when suddenly the earth trembled. When [I] regained consciousness, I was fully 40 feet from where I had been standing.
>
> —Quarry explosion survivor

Two broken watches fix the time of a Holston Quarry Company explosion at twenty-eight minutes past noon on June 27, 1922. The accidental detonation occurred as workers were setting charges for routine blasting in the quarry. Eight were killed instantly, one was mortally wounded, two were seriously injured, and seven others received minor bruises. Three of the dead were literally blown to smithereens, with no trace ever found of them. Body parts of the other six were hurled up to 300 feet from the scene of the tragedy.

Some of the dynamite had already been loaded into holes, and the rest was being loaded into a hole fifteen feet deep when the blast occurred. Windows were broken a mile away in Strawberry Plains, and the blast, made up of twenty-four cases (fifty pounds) of dynamite, was heard and felt even farther away. Items on the shelves of the nearby commissary littered the floor, and the company bookkeeper said he was thrown from his chair by the force of the detonation.

The exact cause of the explosion was never determined. C. C. Smyre, general superintendent at the quarry, was the only man close enough to the blast to have seen what occurred. Unfortunately, he died within an hour of the accident without regaining consciousness. Smoking was ruled out, as it was prohibited, and as far as anyone knew, no one had ever smoked on the site while explosives were being handled. Heat from the sun on that hot summer day, and/or the possibility that one of the cases of dynamite was dropped or jarred with sufficient force to detonate it, were the only other plausible explanations.

SOURCES: John Hyvarinen, Leland H. Johnson, and D. O. Kennedy, *Major Disasters at Metal and Nonmetal Mines and Quarries in the United States (Excluding Coal Mines),* information circular (Washington, DC: U.S. Bureau of Mines, Dept. of Interior, Apr. 1949); *Knoxville Journal and Tribune,* June 28, 1922.

Roane Iron Company Mine Disaster, 1925

ROCKWOOD, JULY 23

A crew of ten men died from a double explosion around 5:10 AM on July 23, 1925, while attempting to extinguish a coal mine fire, approximately two miles inside the Roane Iron Company Mine. The only survivor was the fire boss, who had been surveying another section of the mine for the presence of methane (deadly coal mine gas) and was on his way back to where the crew of ten was working. When he was within about 2,000 feet of the crew, an explosion occurred, followed by another, more violent one.

The mining crew was attempting to extinguish a coal mine fire when the two blasts occurred almost simultaneously. The fire had been discovered in a side passage in a distant portion of the mine three months earlier. At that time, it had simply been sealed in hopes that it would burn itself out. When the passage was reopened, however, a portion of it was still burning. The miners were dumping buckets of water on the fire in an attempt to put it out so the section could again be mined. During the next four hours, the smoke grew heavier, and deadly methane gas accumulated on both ends of the passage where they were working.

The second explosion was powerful enough to cause cave-ins along sections of several passages. It also knocked the fire boss off his feet, tossing him about a hundred feet down the passage. He was bruised, suffered two broken ribs, and was stunned by the impact. His safety light had been extinguished and was lost. At this point, he began crawling away from the point of the explosion, with his face against the bottom of the passage to take advantage of the only good air. He was in total darkness and an estimated two and a half miles from the entrance. As he felt his way along the passage, he encountered a mule hitched to a haulage wagon. The mule, half crazed by the trauma of the explosion, had become entangled (probably in its harness ropes) and could not move. After crawling on for a while, the fire boss encountered good air. After a short rest, he returned to the mule, freed it, and crawled into the haulage wagon. The mule pulled him toward the entrance, where he eventually met the morning crew of miners coming into the mine. He told them what had happened, and they all headed toward the surface. Had he not made it out, some of them could have died before realizing that the air was bad.

By the time he reached the outside, a rescue crew was assembled and immediately entered the mine. They were hoping that at least some of the miners had survived. As they reached a point 800 to 1,000 feet from the source of the explosions, they found two victims whose bodies were blown to pieces by the blasts. One was identified only by the initials on his belt, and the other by his ring. It was later determined that these bodies had been hurled some 800 feet from the source of the explosions.

All attempts to recover the additional eight bodies failed as the rescue crews were repeatedly turned back by the thick smoke and deadly afterdamp resulting from the explosions. It took the rescuers two hours to recover the initial two bodies and transport them to the surface, where a host of friends, neighbors, coworkers, relatives, and curious bystanders were assembled.

The fire in this area of the mine, known as the Rogers Run, continued to smolder, and it was increasingly difficult to get anywhere near the remaining bodies. There was no logic in risking the lives of other miners to recover the bodies. Furthermore, there was no hope that anyone could have survived the powerful explosions. Therefore, after two days of unsuccessful efforts, state and federal mine officials, along with the mine owner, decided to cease recovery operations and seal off that section of the mine until the fire burned itself out.

The area of the mine containing the eight dead miners was reopened on October 22, and the fire was found to be extinguished. Ventilation was provided to that section of the mine, and all eight bodies were recovered by volunteer mine rescue workers led by the chief of the West Virginia Department of Mines. Some of the bodies were well preserved because of a lack of oxygen. Others, lying where some oxygen was present, had deteriorated and were identifiable only by their clothes. The positions of the bodies showed that just before or after the explosion some of the miners had attempted to escape to the surface; lack of oxygen and the toxic atmosphere had made it impossible. By the next day, all the bodies had been placed in metal caskets and returned to their relatives for proper burial.

The first explosion was believed to have been caused by methane gas. The second was precipitated by coal dust, most of which was blown into the air by the first explosion and spontaneously ignited. Subsequent investigations of the mine brought to light still other safety violations capable of causing other serious accidents. These included heavy levels of coal dust, excessive methane gas build up, inadequate ventilation, open miners' lights, open-type electrical equipment, gasoline locomotives, and overcharged blasting holes.

SOURCES: Hiram B. Humphrey, *Historical Summary of Coal-Mine Explosions in the United States, 1810–1958,* Bulletin 586 (Washington, DC: U.S. Bureau of Mines, 1960); *Knoxville Journal,* July 24, 25; Oct. 22, 24, 1925; *Knoxville News-Sentinel,* July 24, 25, 1925; Roane County Heritage Book Committee. *The Heritage of Roane County, Tennessee 1801–1999.* (Waynesville, NC: Heritage Books, 1999).

Roane Iron Company Mine Disaster, 1926

ROCKWOOD, OCTOBER 4

Twenty-eight men were killed in a devastating methane gas and coal dust explosion around 9:30 AM on October 4, 1926. It happened three miles inside the Roger's Entry No. 2 Roane Iron Company coal mine near Rockwood, Roane County, and it took ten days to recover all the bodies of the dead miners. Newspaper accounts at the time reported that some of the bodies were literally blown to pieces by the force of the explosion, with body parts burned and intermingled with those of others and with mules used to pull coal cars in the mine. Official reports stated that the bodies, although burned and in bad condition, were not badly mingled. In any case, all the bodies were eventually identified.

Some of the victims died from suffocation as a result of breathing deadly fumes, called "afterdamp," following the explosion. One body was recovered about a thousand feet from the source of the explosion. Despite escaping the blast, this miner succumbed to the afterdamp fumes. Out of a crew of thirty-three working in the section of the mine where the explosion occurred, only five survived.

Rescue workers realized the full fury of the blast when they found a shovel that had been driven into a railroad crosstie with such force that it could not be pulled out. The tremendous heat generated near the source of the explosion was said to have turned a carload of coal into coke.

The explosion may have been generated by a spark from a miner's tool or from an open light. It could also have been touched off by a smoldering coal fire in an adjacent mine. In any event, the explosion occurred near the same spot where ten miners had died in April of the previous year. This mine, because it produced a considerable amount of methane, a natural coal mine gas, was considered by many to be one of the most potentially dangerous in the state at the time. Since opening in 1866, it had taken the lives of thirty-seven men.

SOURCES: Hiram B. Humphrey, *Historical Summary of Coal-Mine Explosions in the United States, 1810–1958,* Bulletin 586 (Washington, DC: U.S. Bureau of Mines, 1960); *Knoxville News-Sentinel,* Oct. 4, 5, 7, 1926; *Roane County News,* May 26, June 23, 1982; Tennessee Dept. of Labor, Div. of Mines, *Thirty-second Annual Report of the Mineral Resources of Tennessee* (Nashville: Service Publishing Co., 1926).

Burra Burra Copper Mine Disaster

DUCKTOWN, POLK COUNTY, JANUARY 5, 1943

Nine men died and seventeen were hospitalized as the result of a mid-afternoon sulfide-dust explosion on January 5, 1943, in one of the old Tennessee Copper Company mines at Ducktown. Eight died, probably within minutes, from suffocation, and a ninth died later as a result of injuries sustained in the mine on that ill-fated day. The other seventeen men were hospitalized at Ducktown and Copperhill, with burning, irritated eyes and varying degrees of respiratory asphyxiation from sulfur-filled lungs.

According to the mine superintendent, the explosion occurred 2,000 feet below the surface, at the tenth level, as the men were changing shifts. The normal 3:00 PM placement and detonation of dynamite in the mine, done to blast loose the ore, somehow went afoul. Thirty-five holes were drilled and each filled with dynamite. When the first one blew, it stirred up a great amount of sulfur dust, which exploded and set off the other events. This chain reaction of near simultaneous explosions shut down the main ventilating fan on the surface, which reversed the air currents in the mine. The remaining sixteen men working in the mine at the time of the explosion were unaffected by the explosion and escaped without injury. The seventeen surviving victims were able to save themselves by shutting down a power fan and opening a compressed air line until rescuers could get to them. This provided enough fresh air to dilute the deadly sulfide dust. The eight dead miners, along with the injured ones, were retrieved from the mine within two and a half hours of the explosion.

The Burra Burra mine is named for a famous Australian copper mine and is listed on the National Register of Historic Places. The 1943 explosion was the worst mining accident ever to occur in the history of the Copper Basin mines.

SOURCES: *Chattanooga News Free Press,* Jan. 6, 1943; Patricia Bernard Ezzell, "Burra Burra Copper Company," in *The Tennessee Encyclopedia of History and Culture,* ed. Carroll Van West, 104–5 (Nashville: Tennessee Historical Society and Rutledge Hill Press, 1998); John Hyvarinen, Leland H. Johnson, and D. O. Kennedy, *Major Disasters and Non-Metallic Mines and Quarries in the United States (Excluding Coal Mines),* I.C. 7493 (Washington, DC: U.S. Dept. of the Interior, Bureau of Mines, Apr. 1949); *Knoxville Journal,* Jan. 6, 1943; *Knoxville News-Sentinel,* Jan. 6, 1943.

Nu Rex Mine Disaster

LaFollette, Campbell County, May 5, 1943

> As some went down the entry,
> They didn't even dream,
> Working, toiling and sweating,
> Their last daylight they'd seen.
>
> **—Joseph A. Riggs,**
> **"The Blast of the Etna Mine"**

A little after 1:00 PM on May 5, 1943, dust and flames erupted from one of the entrances of the Nu Rex Coal Mine, five miles north of LaFollette, in Campbell County. This was also known as the Etna Mine. Shortly thereafter, two men fled the mine with severe burns on their hands and faces. Farther into the mine, ten men were killed. Some died instantly from the explosion, while others were overcome and suffocated by deadly afterdamp, a mixture of carbon monoxide and other gases caused by the explosion.

Eighteen other workers near the explosion site moved deeper into the mine, knowing that the deadly gases were drifting toward them. Their only chance was to barricade themselves in and the gases out. They quickly constructed a board wall and sealed it with strips of vent tubing and brattice cloth (a material impregnated with creosote). For the next seven hours they waited, talked, and prayed. About half an hour before they walked safely out of the mine, they heard the rescue workers moving down the shaft toward them and pecked out a signal indicating that they were still alive. The rescue team was only about 2,000 feet from the entrance when they located the trapped miners, but their progress had been slow as they stopped to extinguish fires and carry out the dead found along the way.

The area of the mine where the explosion occurred was near a mined-out and abandoned tunnel where methane gas had accumulated. A dynamite charge used to break up coal in the vein apparently opened up the old abandoned shaft, allowing the potentially explosive methane gas to bleed into the new tunnel. There it was ignited either by the dynamite charge itself or by a spark from a piece of mining machinery.

SOURCES: Hiram B. Humphrey, *Historical Summary of Coal-Mine Explosions in the United States, 1810–1958,* Bulletin 586 (Washington, DC: U.S. Bureau of Mines, 1960); *Knoxville News-Sentinel,* May 6, 1943; Miller McDonald, *Campbell County, Tennessee, USA: A History of Places, Faces, Happenings, Traditions, and Things,* vol. 2 (LaFollette, TN: County Services Syndicate, 1993).

Phillips and West Mine Disaster

ROBBINS, SCOTT COUNTY,
    MARCH 23, 1959

> When the [mine ventilation] fan was started, [the methane] gas migrated through the brattice cloth stoppings and/or open crosscuts to the haulage road where it was ignited by arcing when the trolley wheel of the locomotive left the wire or by workers smoking. All nine men underground died of burns or noxious gas fumes resulting from the gas and dust explosion.
>
> **—Bureau of Mines summary**

Nine men were killed when an explosion ripped through the Phillips and West Coal Company Mine on March 23, 1959. This small coal mine is located on Brimstone Creek, ten miles east of Robbins, in Western Scott County. The men entered the mine around 7:30 AM, and shortly thereafter the muffled sound of an explosion was heard at the entrance. Four of the dead were recovered immediately. Intense heat, pungent gas fumes, and fallen debris hampered further rescue efforts. Nonetheless, local miners were able to bring out the other five bodies by 2:30 in the afternoon, shortly before state and federal mine inspectors arrived on the scene. Three of the four owners of the mine died in the explosion.

Officials who investigated the incident believe it was caused by a methane gas explosion. The methane gas apparently had accumulated in the mine slowly throughout the night, was not sufficiently removed by the mine ventilation fan, and was ignited by sparks from mine machinery the next morning. It could also have been ignited by one or more workers smoking in the mine.

A crowd of about a hundred family members, neighbors, friends, and fellow miners gathered at the entrance of the mine in a solemn vigil, anxiously awaiting the arrival of each victim from the dank mine. The bodies of the miners were so badly burned that identification was difficult. In fact, only one body could be identified for certain. All of the dead, who lived in and around Oneida, were related to each other by blood or marriage. This was the county's worst mine disaster and was followed by its largest funeral.

SOURCES: *Knoxville News Sentinel,* Mar. 23, 24, 1959; H. Clay Smith, *Dusty Bits of the Forgotten Past—A History of Scott County* (Nashville: Williams Printing Co., 1985); U.S. Dept. of Interior, Bureau of Mines, *Historical Summary of Coal Mine Explosions in the United States, 1959–81,* I.C. 8909 (Washington, DC: Government Printing Office, 1983).

Whitwell Mine Disaster

MARION COUNTY, DECEMBER 8, 1981

> Inspectors from the federal Mine Safety and Health Administration said the mine's atmosphere contained an explosive concentration—at least 5 percent—of methane gas, which issued from an inactive area of the mine into which the men cut from the working area. The explosion occurred when one of the miners lit his cigarette lighter, inspectors said.
>
> **—*Chattanooga Times,* Dec. 8, 1981**

The state's worst coal mine disaster in seventy years struck Grundy County Mining Company's Mine No. 21 at a little after noon on December 8, 1981. The mine is located just off State Highway 108 in the Griffith Creek Community, near Whitwell, in Marion County. A sign in large black letters at the Whitwell High School summed up the feelings of the community for the lost miners and their families. It read, "We offer our hands, heart and prayers in sympathy."

Thirteen men, including eleven miners and two supervisors, were killed almost instantly by a violent explosion and flash fire. One rescuer was quoted as saying the men could not have lived more than a second or two. It occurred just after noon as they were digging a four-by-seven-foot ventilation shaft into a long-abandoned adjacent mine. At this point, one of the miners decided to have a smoke, and when he lit his lighter it set off the deadly explosion. The blast was of such magnitude as to blow out headlights in trucks parked a hundred feet from the mine entrance; however, thirty other miners working in another section of the mine were unhurt.

The first indication that something had gone wrong within the mine occurred shortly after noon, when telephone service to the affected area was interrupted. Per standard procedure, rescue operations were begun immediately. Rescuers reached the dead miners within five hours, but the last body was not recovered until thirteen hours later. The charred bodies of the dead were placed in flat coal cars and transported to the surface.

One rescue worker interviewed by the *Chattanooga Times* said that the explosion occurred about three miles inside the mine and that the affected area "looked like a hurricane had hit it." He went on to say that "the men had been burned [and] their clothes were brittle. I could recognize most all of them only by their features."

According to the rescuers, there was clear evidence that a horrific explosion had occurred within the area where the dead miners were found. Telephone and power cables were burned to bare wire in the tunnel, which measured about twenty feet wide and three feet tall. Both state and federal mine inspectors, as well as officials from the Tennessee Consolidated Coal Company (the owner of the Grundy County mines), investigated the cause of the incident and filed requisite reports. Their final conclusion was that the incident resulted from the failure of management to provide adequate ventilation inside the mine and to enforce the no-smoking provision of the federal law. Although an individual miner had caused the explosion, the mining company had allowed it to happen. In January 1985 a final judgment was handed down, and the Grundy County Mining Company pleaded guilty to violations leading to the death of the thirteen miners. They agreed to pay $105,000 in fines. They also settled lawsuits with the families of the victims in the amount of millions of dollars each.

SOURCES: *Chattanooga News-Free Press,* Dec. 9, 1981; *Chattanooga Times,* Dec. 9–11, 1981, Feb. 25, 1982, Jan. 15, Dec. 8, 1985; *Nashville Free Press,* May 4, 1982.

STRUCTURE FAILURES

The most recent disaster relative to built environments occurred in December 2008, when a waste reservoir facility failed at TVA's Kingston Steam Plant at Harriman, in Roane County. This released 5.4 million cubic yards of potentially toxic fly ash, or coal sludge, into the Clinch and Emory rivers and from there into the Tennessee River. The spill is said to have been 100 times greater in volume than that of the *Exxon Valdez* oil spill in Alaska's Prince William Sound in March 1989. Although the Tennessee event is touted as one of the worst environmental accidents in our nation's history, its actual effects must be put into perspective. It did not produce the immediate pollution so destructive of marine life and devastating to a fisheries industry as did the *Exxon Valdez* oil freighter disaster. It did not kill or injure a single individual, as did the 1950s toxic effluents at Love Canal near Niagara Falls, New York. It did not evoke the immediate terror that erupted from the 1979 partial core melt down of the Three Mile Island Nuclear Power Facility near Harrisburg, Pennsylvania. Some fish and other aquatic life did die as a consequence of the spill; however, the Tennessee Valley Authority is in the process of mitigating the hazard, and only time will tell if significant long-term impacts result from this spill.

Two structure failures have involved dams, one of which was a multiple dam failure along Barren Creek in Claiborne County in August 1916. This incident occurred as the result of severe rainfall in the upper watershed of this stream. It was the second most costly structure failure in Tennessee history in terms of lives lost. Twenty-four people were drowned and others injured by the raging torrent of water that caused the failure of Barren Creek Dam and four other smaller ones farther downstream. The state's second most severe dam failure occurred in June 1928. Heavy rainfall across the Falling Water River watershed resulted in a breach of a portion of the Cookeville Power Dam at Burgess Falls. This incident, in DeKalb County near Cookeville, destroyed a downstream hydropower production facility and damaged or demolished a number of other structures. Astonishingly, no lives were lost and no major injuries were sustained in the mishap.

Four incidents of bridge collapse have occurred, two of which resulted in fatalities. In April 1989, the U.S. Highway 51 bridge across the Hatchie River near the Lauderdale and Tipton county line failed. Five automobiles, including a tractor trailer truck, plunged into the water, killing eight. In March 1977, the Owl Creek bridge on State Highway 142 in McNairy County collapsed, killing three. Four vehicles were involved, with one driver surviving to flag down others who might have otherwise become victims. In September 1928, the Harahan River bridge across the Mississippi River at Memphis caught fire and was destroyed. It was a combination railroad and automobile bridge and, at the time, was the only vehicular crossing of the Mississippi River south of St. Louis. This resulted in a major transportation impasse: automobiles had to be ferried across the river, and trains were rerouted over hundreds of miles.

A pontoon bridge constructed across the Tennessee River at Knoxville during the Civil War was washed away in the great flood of 1867. It connected downtown Knoxville with South Knoxville on the opposite side of the river and was located at the site of the present Gay

Street bridge. Without it, people started referring to South Knoxville as South America, because without the bridge it was practically as inaccessible. A bridge that replaced it failed in a very violent windstorm in May 1875. A new Gay Street bridge was built in 1880 and was replaced eighteen years later by the present iron and concrete structure. No casualties seem to have been associated with any of these latter structure failures, but the economic costs and inconveniences were great.

The most costly structure failure in terms of fatalities occurred in Nashville's Maxwell House Hotel during the Civil War. At the time, the luxury hotel, which was still under construction, was being used to house Confederate war prisoners. On the morning of September 29, 1863, as the soldiers were descending a temporary wooden stairway for breakfast, the structure collapsed, trapping, injuring, and killing many men. The number who died in the collapse, or later of injuries, was rumored to be somewhere between twenty and fifty individuals. The exact number was never determined, nor was it ever released by Union army officials. Although this incident occurred during wartime, it was not related to military action.

A sixty-five-foot high iron mine tipple collapsed at the McLanahan Pinkney Mine in Lawrence County in May 1897. Thirteen men were killed instantly in the fall, and several others were mortally injured. The failure of the tipple, a high railroad trestle used to dump iron ore into a processing area, was blamed on poor engineering and shoddy construction.

Finally, in November 1912, a wall twenty-two feet thick of Nashville's Eighth Avenue water reservoir failed, sending some 25 million gallons plummeting downslope. Economic losses to structures and streets were severe, but fortunately no one was killed or even injured in the incident.

Maxwell House Stairway Collapse
Nashville, September 29, 1863

The steps leading from the fourth to the fifth story gave way and fell with the men on them to the floor immediately underneath which also gave way as did also the floor next in succession and together with two flights of steps the whole falling in mass on the second floor ... The screams of the dying men and the rush of the ambulance wagons alerted the citizens of Nashville.

—*Nashville Daily Union,* Sept. 30, 1863

At 8:00 AM on September 29, 1863, the signal was given for breakfast at the Maxwell House Hotel in Nashville. Confederate prisoners of war incarcerated there hurriedly lined up and began descending a wooden stairway to get their meals. It was a temporary stairway, intended only for workers, in a hotel still under construction. For some reason, a guard at the bottom of the stairway temporally halted the hungry soldiers, allowing more and more to crowd upper and middle flights. Suddenly, the heavily laden stairway collapsed accordion style from the fifth floor downward.

The screams and moans of the maimed and crushed prisoners, pancaked under the splintered mass of timbers, soon became audible in the streets. Of 400 prisoners confined to the facility, over a hundred were said to have been involved in the incident. Somewhere between twenty-one and fifty men were believed killed instantly or to have died of their injuries a short time later. Many Nashville women trying to come to the aid of the wounded and dying were literally held back at bayonet point as armed federal officers, their troops, and other prisoners worked frantically to regain control and respond to the catastrophe.

The injured were taken to military hospitals, some outside the city. Accounts vary as to exactly what happened and how many were killed and injured. No doubt some details were suppressed by Federal authorities, who controlled the local media. According to the *Nashville Dispatch,* the day after the tragedy, "[Only] two men were killed instantly . . . Four died within 20 minutes, and 92 are in the hospital, 15 of whom will probably die from the effects of their wounds."

"The sight," the article continued, "was one of the most appalling ever witnessed, except on the battlefield, one man having his head mashed flat as a board, others frightfully bruised or mutilated, and all more or less injured." As the Union medical director dispatched physicians and ambulances to the scene, "the Provost Marshall took possession of the barracks and kept it entirely clear for those employed in cleaning up the wreckage and removing the dead and wounded."

After the fall of two Confederate forts, Donelson and Henry, in the early days of the Civil War, Nashville came under Union control. After the Battle of Chickamauga, the city's Maxwell House Hotel, still under construction, was used to house Confederate prisoners of war. It was called the Zollicoffer Barracks. The stairway collapse was the worst incident ever to occur in the famous hotel, which finally burned to the ground Christmas Day 1961. Some say the hotel was haunted and that the agonizing cries of the wounded and dying Confederate prisoners could often be heard in the dead of night from the rooms and hallways near the site of the tragedy.

SOURCES: James A. Crutchfield, *Yesteryear in Nashville: An Almanac of Nashville History* (N.p.: n.p., 1981); Walter T. Durham, *Nashville the Occupied City: The First Seventeen Months—February 16, 1862, to June 30, 1863* (Nashville: Tennessee Historical Society, 1985); Valary J. Marks, "Maxwell House Saw Much Life before Death," *Nashville Banner,* Apr. 6, 1976; Henry McRaven, *Nashville: Athens of the South* (Chapel Hill, NC: Tennessee Book Co., 1949); *Nashville Daily Union,* Sept. 30, 1863; *Nashville Dispatch,* Sept. 30, 1863; *Nashville Tennessean,* undated news clipping in vertical files, Tennessee State Library and Archives.

Pinkney Mine Tipple Collapse
LAWRENCE COUNTY, MAY 13, 1897

When Dr. Turner had pronounced a victim of the disaster dead, a sheet was spread over the body to await arrival of family members. It was a terrible scene as relatives searched for their loved ones among the injured first. Then, some of them had to turn to the sheet covered bodies.

—Pauline Garretson,
"Disaster at the Pinckney Mines"

In 1897 a new sixty-five-foot-high tipple was constructed near the Wright Mine, at the community of Pinkney (also spelled "Pinckney"), in Lawrence County. Situated at the end of a three-mile-long track that hauled ore from the Lawrence Iron Company mines, the tipple was to serve a new ore dump site near a stone water reservoir. The mine workers had misgivings concerning the soundness of the tipple as they watched it being constructed. They were especially leery of its lack of adequate reinforcement. Their gut feelings about the safety of the tipple intensified as the structure was built higher and higher with even less lateral bracing employed. But mining company management made light of such concerns, and the structure was completed as designed.

The finished tipple was tested to see if it could bear the weight of twenty empty ore cars and finally twenty full ones. Even then, some of the men who were to work atop the tipple still had doubts about its structural integrity. Around 2:30 on the afternoon of May 13, 1897, the worst fears of the miners were realized. As James Crow, the engineer and his son Charley, the fireman, started out over the tipple with several loaded ore cars, the structure suddenly shuddered and broke apart. It seemed to some watching from below that the rails, ore cars, and people standing atop the structure were momentarily suspended in midair before the structure disintegrated and dropped sixty-five feet into the valley below. According to one very poignant account, as the father and son (engineer and fireman) dropped downward, they were locked in a final embrace. The son died instantly. The father, after tenderly kissing his son's brow, died two minutes later. Accounts vary, but at least thirteen men standing atop the tipple at the time of its collapse, fell to their death. Others were injured, some severely. Two of those on top of the tipple jumped to safety as the collapse occurred. One jumped twenty feet into a tree and shimmied down with a broken jaw and a piece of limb impaled in his chin. Another jumped to the ground on the side of the valley, tumbled a few times, and survived the fall with only a sprained ankle. A special train carrying doctors was dispatched from Florence, Alabama, when word reached them of the seriousness of the accident. Unfortunately, it took that train about six hours to reach the scene.

In the meantime, a local doctor by the name of Turner was summoned and provided as much medical assistance to the victims as any solitary physician could. The exact cause of the tipple collapse was not immediately known; however, poor design and construction was alleged to be the root cause. The families of the dead and the surviving victims of the accident received some financial compensation, but no individual or family received more than $500. Those injured were also paid their regular salary of about eighty cents a day until they were able to return to work.

SOURCES: Bobby Alford, Lawrence County historian, personal correspondence with author, Jan. 13, 2011; Pauline Garretson, "Disaster at the Pinckney Mines," in *History of SW Lawrence County* (Lawrenceburg, TN: self-published, 1988); *Huntsville (AL) Special,* May 14, 1897; Lawrence County Historical Society, *Lawrence County, Tennessee: Pictorial History* (Paducah, KY: Turner Publishing Co., 1994; *New York Times,* May 14, 1897.

Nashville Reservoir Failure
NOVEMBER 5, 1912

When the Eighth Avenue reservoir ruptured in 1912, spilling twenty-five million gallons of water over a wide area, morning-after photographs gave the structure the appearance of a Roman ruin.

—**John Egerton,** *Nashville: The Faces of Two Centuries 1780–1980*

Just after midnight on November 5, 1912, a section of Nashville's Eighth Avenue Reservoir suddenly collapsed along its southeast wall, releasing 25 million gallons of water. This sent an estimated nine-foot-high wave of water plummeting down Kirkpatrick Hill, across Eighth Avenue and other streets, in the direction of the fairgrounds. Although no one was killed or seriously injured in the incident, property damage was extensive as homes and other structures were flooded or washed away. The circular structure, which is 1,746 feet in circumference and holds 51 million gallons of water, is constructed of limestone blocks and is 22 feet thick at the base. Fortunately, a center dividing wall that held during this failure prevented the water in the west side of the reservoir from being lost. The damage was repaired and the structure still functions today.

SOURCES: James A. Crutchfield, *Yesteryear in Nashville: An Almanac of Nashville History* (Nashville: n.p., 1981); John Egerton, *Nashville: The Faces of Two Centuries 1780–1980* (Nashville: Plus Media, 1979).

Barren Creek Dam Failures
CLAIBORNE COUNTY, AUGUST 1–2, 1916

But all of this is naught compared with the sacrifice of human life, to say nothing of the wreckage and ruin in the path of the flood. From the head waters of this wreck to Clinch river the [hand] of death and

The Nashville reservoir after it ruptured on November 5, 1912. Courtesy of Tennessee State Library and Archives.

devastation was laid heavily on every foot of the valley. The worst was from Thompson's mill on down. The big dam there gave way and a wall of water 25 feet or more high went sweeping down the winding valley.

—*Hancock County News,* **Jan. 14, 1944**

Officially only nine inches of rain fell along Barren Creek, southwest of Tazewell in Claiborne County, on August 1 and 2, 1916. Unofficially, the total may have been as high as twelve to fifteen inches in some areas of the watershed. The rains began around 8:00 PM, but between midnight and 2:00 AM they reached cloudburst proportions. They literally turned a normally docile creek into a rampaging river. As the rains diminished, the millions of gallons of water and tons of debris that plummeted down the pristine valley caused five mill dams to fail in succession. The greatest impact was within an area one mile wide and about six miles long, in the headwaters of Big Barren Creek, a tributary of the Clinch River.

John Thompson Dam, the largest of the five structures, was the first to fail, releasing a 25-foot-high wall of water that rapidly demolished the smaller Meyer, Keck, Chumley, and Heath (or Johnson) dams below it. It is believed that even if this 30-foot-high, 100-foot-wide rock dam had not failed, the water that overtopped it would have breached the others downstream. There was little or no warning for those living along the narrow stream valley, where the water was said to have risen thirty to forty feet above its normal bed level. Unaware and unable to escape, twenty-four people perished in the deluge, most as they slept. The last positively identified victim was recovered some fourteen miles downstream. Another body of a young boy was reported to have been spotted twenty miles downstream, but it disappeared before anyone could reach or identify it. Eighteen of the dead were children, and eight were members of the same (Porter) family.

Many others were left homeless and destitute in the wake of the flood, which literally swept the valley clean for six to eight miles below the Thompson Dam. The torrent washed away mill houses, stores, homes, barns, outbuildings, farm equipment, vehicles, crops, stock, and furnishings. Roads, bridges, and other infrastructure were also damaged or demolished, further isolating the tiny, secluded community. Economic impact was estimated at three-quarters of a million dollars, with a third of that in the Barren Creek Community alone.

Stories abound of deeds of heroism as men gave their lives in valiant efforts to save their wives, mothers, and children. One man, Crockett Edmondson, survived after being washed five miles downstream among piles of floating driftwood and other debris. His wife and three children died, but two other children were found alive, clinging to floating timbers three miles downstream.

SOURCES: *Claiborne Progress*, Aug. 9, 1916; *Hancock County News*, Jan. 14, 1944; *Knoxville Sentinel*, Aug. 3, 5, 1916.

Cookeville Power Dam Failure
BURGESS FALLS NEAR COOKEVILLE, PUTNAM COUNTY, JULY 29, 1928

The Cookeville Municipal power dam, just above Burgess Falls, is located on the White and Putnam County line, just southwest of Cookeville. Heavy rains in late July 1928 sent the Falling Water River well above its flood stage and threatened the dam. Around fifty local firefighters and community volunteers tried to reinforce the dam with bags of sand and concrete, but to no avail. Around 5:30 PM on July 29, 1928, the north (right) wing of the dam suddenly gave way to the massive force of the water flowing over it. The roar of the water passing through the gaping breach in the structure could be heard for miles as a thirty-foot-high wall of water surged down the Falling Water gorge and the hydroelectric power plant about a mile downstream.

Mercifully, no one was killed or injured in this flood. This was due in part to the fact that messengers were dispatched from the dam shortly before the failure. They rode down each bank of the stream on mules, spreading the alarm of the impending disaster. Unfortunately, this would not be true for all portions of the nine-county area affected by the storm. In fact, several people were killed, many injured, and scores of homes and other buildings were damaged or destroyed by heavy flooding throughout portions of Middle Tennessee. Overall economic losses at the time were estimated at around $1 million.

When it was constructed in the early 1920s, this dam provided the only major municipal hydropower in the state. In fact, it was said to be the first such municipally operated facility of its kind constructed in the United States. The power plant building, associated structures, and a concrete bridge were located about a mile downstream, at the base of scenic Burgess Falls. Each of these structures was severely damaged or destroyed by the flood. A wooden flume line that had carried water from the dam to the hydroplant building was also demolished.

Economic losses to this operation alone probably exceeded half a million dollars, and the damage left the city of Cookeville and the surrounding community without electricity. The city was also without telephone communications for some time. The reservoir behind the 225-foot-long earthen and concrete core dam extended over 20 miles upstream and controlled a 128-square-mile watershed. On the day preceding and the day of the flood, seven to ten inches of rain had fallen over portions of the Cumberland Plateau, including the Cookeville area. In spite of the fact that its floodgates were wide open, six feet of water was overtopping the spillway and dam when the breach occurred.

Within a year of the failure of this dam, a new and better-engineered structure and powerhouse were constructed on the same sites by the City of Cookeville. Operation of the power facility ceased in the mid-1940s with the coming of cheaper Tennessee Valley Authority power. Today, the falls and the deteriorating powerhouse structure form the centerpiece of Burgess Falls State Park and Natural Area.

SOURCES: Warren R. King, *Surface Waters of Tennessee,* Bulletin 40 (Nashville: Tennessee Div. of Geology, 1931); *Nashville Tennessean,* July 30, 1928; Tennessee Dept. of Environment and Conservation, State Parks Div., *Burgess Falls State Natural Area,* brochure, n.d.

Owl Creek Bridge Collapse
SELMER, McNAIRY COUNTY, MARCH 5, 1977

As far as I can tell they probably didn't even see the bridge was out and use their brakes. In the dark it probably looked like water on the road.

—**Charles Richardson,**
Tennessee Highway Patrol officer

Sometime between 1:00 and 2:00 AM on March 5, 1977, heavy floodwaters scoured out bridge supports, causing

a fifty-foot section of the Owl Creek bridge on Tennessee Highway 142 near Selmer, McNairy County, to collapse. A car driven by a Selmer resident, Junior Sweat, said that he had crossed the bridge at about 1:00 AM. By 2:00 AM the center section of the old asphalt and wooden bridge had failed and collapsed. At that point, a Chevy Nova, driven by Janie Miller, plunged into Owl Creek. Normally between three to four feet deep, the stream had swollen to some twenty feet in depth as a result of recent heavy rains. Shortly before 5:00 AM a second vehicle, a 1977 Plymouth station wagon, also plummeted off the bridge and into the murky water, killing a man and his son. Highway patrolmen stated that the occupants of both vehicles may have died upon impact or drowned in the rapid currents of the stream.

Not long after the station wagon dropped into the water, a late-model Volkswagen followed. Fortunately, its occupant, Roger McClain of Michie, also in McNairy County, escaped his vehicle and swam to safety. Once out of the water, he was able to climb back onto the road to flag down other vehicles. By 6:00 AM the Highway Patrol had arrived, and McClain, suffering from shock, was taken to Hardin County Hospital. The patrolmen said they closed the road but had to wait until the next morning for the flood to subside before they could begin recovery efforts. The last car was pulled from the stream around 2:30 PM by a heavy-duty crane being used to construct a new bridge adjacent to the old one. It was used to recover all three vehicles and the dead occupants of two.

SOURCE: *Memphis Commercial Appeal,* Mar. 5, 1977.

Hatchie River Bridge Collapse
LAUDERDALE–TIPTON COUNTY LINE, APRIL 1, 1989

COVINGTON, Tenn.—About 8:15 Saturday night, the three Haynie brothers were doing about 55 miles an hour behind an 18-wheeler. Seconds later, they weren't behind anybody. About 20 feet ahead on U.S. 51, the truck's lights had wobbled, and the big rig—along with two cars beside it—had disappeared. When their van finally stopped, the brothers were staring through the windshield at the muddy Hatchie River instead of a concrete bridge. Below them, at least seven people were lost.

—*Memphis Commercial Appeal,* **Apr. 4, 1989**

A tractor-trailer truck and four automobiles plunged into the Hatchie River about 8:15 PM on April 1, 1989, when the 84-foot-long northbound lane of the U.S. Highway 51 bridge collapsed. The final death toll was eight. According to Tennessee Department of Transportation (TDOT) officials and the National Transportation Safety Board, the muck and sandy soil around the pilings (piers) supporting the bridge had been scoured away by slow-rise floods and changing currents since the bridge was constructed in 1933. On the night of the accident, surging floodwater from spring rains finally caused a concrete-and-steel slab of the northbound bridge section to give way and drop 25 feet into the river. As the truck and the other vehicles plunged into the water, they are believed to have broken the supporting pilings under another 30-foot section of bridge, causing it to also give way and fall into the river. Although the rains had stopped, the stream was about 2.7 feet above flood stage that night and had swollen to 500 feet, or three times its normal width, beneath the bridge.

The 4,000-foot-long U.S. Highway 51 twin bridges are located about six miles north of Covington and forty-six miles north of Memphis on the Lauderdale-Tipton County line. The collapse took place on the northbound bridge, but the southbound lane was also closed for several days pending inspection by TDOT engineers. It also served for a time as a staging area for recovery efforts following the accident. The cold, oily, murky, and debris-laden stream, with its swift currents, made search and rescue efforts difficult. A severe thunderstorm on Sunday night also suspended recovery efforts for a time.

Divers said they literally had to feel their way along the bottom of the riverbed, fighting the current and searching for vehicles and bodies. All or parts of the ill-fated vehicles were buried beneath the collapsed slabs of concrete and steel that weighted some 75,000 pounds each. The last vehicle, and its victim, was not recovered by divers until the fourth day of the recovery efforts.

The failed bridge had been inspected by TDOT engineers two years prior to the accident and was due for reinspection in six months. At the time of inspection, its condition was rated as poor, due to overall deterioration and misalignment. In spite of this, it was not considered, at the time, as being among the state's top priority projects. In fact, according to one federal inspector, "[one] cannot predict what will happen to an older bridge hit by fast-moving flood waters. If my preliminary information is correct, you could have inspected it [the bridge] the day before [the accident] and not found anything." As is often the case, after a high-profile disaster, this incident brought about a review of, and changes in, the state's highway bridge inspection program, starting in 1989.

SOURCES: *Knoxville News-Sentinel,* Apr. 3, 1989; *Memphis Commercial Appeal,* Apr. 2–5, 1989.

Kingston Coal Ash Reservoir Failure
ROANE COUNTY, DECEMBER 22, 2008

Even as the authority played down the risks, the spill reignited a debate over whether the federal government should regulate coal ash as a hazardous material. Similar ponds and mounds of ash exist at hundreds of coal plants around the nation.

—*New York Times,* **Dec. 29, 2008**

What has been described as the worst environmental disaster of its kind in U.S. history occurred at the Tennessee Valley Authority (TVA) Kingston Fossil Plant in Harriman, Roane County. It was an early December morning when a breach occurred in that facility's eighty-four-acre coal ash settling pond. A 60-foot section of the earthen retaining wall of this structure gave way, releasing an estimated 5.4 million cubic feet of potentially toxic sludge. This is enough material to fill 1,660 Olympic-size swimming pools. TVA and others continue to study the incident and believe that heavy rains and freezing temperatures were significant factors in the structure failure. Although no one was killed or even injured as a result of the incident, its long-term effects upon the environment are yet to be determined.

The economic impact relative to property damage and cleanup has been estimated at over $1 billion; however, this figure will undoubtedly increase as a result of litigation, fines, and forced mitigation against TVA, the nation's largest privately owned utility. The material released in the accident was composed of fly ash, the particulate matter left over from the combustion of coal in the production of electricity. It is captured, mixed with water, and stored, rather than being released into the atmosphere. Once the ash is dewatered, it is transferred into other dry storage reservoirs. A portion of this material is recycled for commercial use, but at present there is no market for all of it. The water and fly ash mixture, also called slurry, is about the consistency of face power and contains varying amounts of potentially toxic chemicals. These include arsenic, mercury, lead, chromium, manganese, barium, benzene, and even trace radioactive metals.

If released into the atmosphere or ground water, these substances are alleged to have the potential to cause cancer, liver damage, and neurological health effects.

When the accident occurred, the material spread out over an area of some 300 acres to a depth of six feet in places. It damaged or destroyed fifteen homes and over forty residential properties. It knocked down trees and utility poles and covered a stretch of road and a section of railroad track used to bring coal into the plant. It also ruptured a major natural gas pipeline and broke a water main.

Some of the sludge flowed into the Emory and Clinch rivers, both tributaries of the Tennessee River, where it caused the death of fish and other aquatic life. This stretch of the Tennessee River is impounded as Watts Bar Reservoir by a downstream TVA dam; thus, the natural flushing effects of the Emory and Clinch rivers are slowed as they enter the reservoir. Additional environmental damage is expected as TVA continues cleanup operations. Although the situations differ in many ways, the quantity of sludge released in this accident was 100 times greater than that of the *Exxon Valdez* petroleum spill into Prince Edward Sound, Alaska, in March 1989.

SOURCES: Associated Press, Dec. 24, 2008; CNN, Dec. 24, 2008; *Chattanooga Times Free Press,* Dec. 25, 29, 2008; Fox News, Dec. 29, 2008; *Knoxville News-Sentinel,* Dec. 26, 2008; *New York Times,* Dec. 29, 2008.

AIRPLANE CRASHES

On September 17, 1908, a plane piloted by Orville Wright crashed. Orville sustained a broken leg, but his passenger, Lt. Thomas C. Selfridge, became the first airplane passenger fatality in U.S. history. Air travel remains the safest form of transportation relative to miles traveled in comparison to watercraft, trains, and automobiles. Of the many scores of airplane accidents that have occurred in Tennessee (between 1930 and 1996), only twenty-eight have involved five or more fatalities. These crashes have included private, commercial, and military aircraft, the latter on search and rescue missions, training maneuvers, or otherwise transporting troops under noncombat conditions. Most of the crashes have been attributed to pilot error, severe weather, or mechanical failures. However, in some cases the exact cause will never be known.

Tennessee's first major airplane crash occurred near Oliver Springs, Anderson County, on March 27, 1943. The plane exploded in midair, killing eleven soldiers and spreading bodies and wreckage over a square-mile area. Although the incident occurred near the then-secret atomic bomb production plants at Oak Ridge, any suspicion of espionage was quickly ruled out.

The state's worst air disaster occurred on July 9, 1964. It involved a United Airlines Viscount 745D commercial flight that burst into flames and crashed in a remote area near Parrottsville, Cocke County, killing thirty-nine. This incident left aircraft and body parts spread over several acres of rugged terrain, and it is believed to have been caused by mechanical problems. The second worst accident also involved a commercial plane, an American Airlines twin engine DC-3. It crashed into the Mississippi River on its final approach to the Memphis Airport in February 1944. At the time, this was the second worst airline tragedy in U.S. history. All twenty-four passengers and crew onboard were killed. The cause of the crash was never determined, but the plane apparently exploded as it plunged into the river. The wreckage and bodies were quickly carried downstream by the strong Mississippi River currents.

The third and fourth deadliest air disasters involved military transports. The first occurred on December 11, 1947, near the Memphis airport. Unlike the 1944 crash, this one occurred on land, rather than in the Mississippi River. It was a C-48 military cargo plane carrying twenty-one officers and enlisted men, all of whom were killed instantly upon impact. In June 1946, another military transport, a B-29 bomber, crashed into Clingmans Dome within the Great Smoky Mountains National Park, killing a dozen men. The accident was caused by the pilot's failure to adjust the altitude of his plane to 8,000 feet in order to clear the mountains.

One of the most unusual incidents took place during an air show in April 1930. It occurred in Fayetteville, Lincoln County, when a pilot, carrying two passengers, lost control of his craft and crashed into a crowd of people, killing eight and injuring over twenty.

Fayetteville Flying Circus Airplane Crash

FAYETTEVILLE, LINCOLN COUNTY, APRIL 27, 1930

An American Legion–sponsored air show, called a flying circus, occurred on April 27, 1930. During the event, a single-engine airplane encountered a sudden downdraft, or wind shear, and dropped some eighty feet, crashing into a crowd of spectators standing on an elevated railroad embankment. The accident occurred on an airfield adjacent to the Lincoln County Fairgrounds, just outside of Fayetteville. Several thousand individuals were attending the show. They had been warned several times by sponsors of the event not to climb onto or stand too close to the rail embankment. However, a few dozen did so to get a better view of the aerobatics. Coming in for a landing, the sightseeing plane, carrying a pilot and two passengers, suddenly careened into a crowd of spectators, resulting in mass carnage. Eight people were killed—four of them decapitated by the plane's propeller—and twenty injured. Ironically, neither the pilot nor his passengers sustained more than superficial bruises and cuts, and the pilot was able to land the plane.

As the pilot set the plane down, an angry mob of spectators started to close in on him. Fearing a riot, the local sheriff and his deputies took the pilot into protective custody and quickly transported him to a jail in a nearby county to await a hearing the next day on technical charges of murder or involuntary manslaughter. The pilot later stated that he was aware of a brisk and variable southerly wind that day and had taken his plane up three times to get a feeling for the atmospheric conditions before taking on passengers. The pilot later indicated that the incident happened so quickly that he was not certain what had occurred to cause his plane to go out of control.

A local resident, whose wife and child had been injured in the accident, said the pilot was flying much too low. He believed the plane clipped a telephone wire, which might have caused it to drop down into the crowd. In fact, investigators later found a piece of the phone line attached to the plane. In the mass frenzy that followed the accident, members of the American Legion Post took charge and assisted law enforcement officers in getting the injured to the Lincoln County Hospital and transporting the dead to a local funeral home.

SOURCES: Associated Press, Apr. 27, 28, 1930; *Connellsville (PA) Daily Courier,* Apr. 28, 1930; *Memphis Commercial Appeal,* Apr. 27, 1930.

Oliver Springs Airplane Crash
OLIVER SPRINGS, ROANE, AND MORGAN COUNTIES, MARCH 27, 1943

I saw it [the Army plane that crashed at Oliver Springs] sailing over a hill. Then the sky was full of metal. It looked just like a flock of birds scattering for all they were worth.
—**Fred Snider, eyewitness**

A U.S. Army plane crashed about a mile west of Oliver Springs, on the Roane County and Morgan County line around 12:35 PM on March 27, 1943. All eleven soldiers and crewmen onboard were killed. It was the worst airplane crash, in terms of lives lost, in the state's history up to that time. It now ranks fifth in number of fatalities. The twin-engine cargo plane was en route from Pope Field, Fort Bragg, North Carolina, to Tulsa, Oklahoma, when it suddenly blew up in midair. Bodies, cargo, and plane parts rained down over a square-mile area between the Harriman Highway and State Highway 61.

As the large military bomber crossed over the city of Oliver Springs, almost at rooftop level, many said they heard what they described as a peculiar motor racket. Moments later, the plane nosed down toward the ground just before exploding.

The owner of the farm where the crash occurred said that the wreckage was spread along a path between his store and his home, which are about thirty yards apart. Some debris landed on these two structures and other outbuildings.

The bodies of some of the victims, both Army officers and enlisted men, were badly broken but not burned in the crash. It had been raining for some time before the crash, and the ground was wet and soft in places. One eyewitness reported seeing a victim buried so deep in mud that only his head was visible. Others were also partially buried in the muddy field, as were plane parts, cargo, and the personal items of the men who died in the crash. The bodies were secured in place until after the initial investigation. Later they were taken by ambulances to two funeral homes in Oliver Springs. Early reports listed a dozen bodies, but the final tally accounted for only eleven.

The plane was on a navigation mission at the time of the crash and was scheduled to return to its home base in North Carolina the next day. Initially, the military police from nearby Oak Ridge (a top-secret military facility at that time) took control of the scene and all operations. The next evening, they relinquished operations to investigators from an Army Air Force base at Berry Field in Nashville. Over the next few days, investigators searched the wreckage very thoroughly and took statements from local people who witnessed the explosion and the crash. Their final analysis indicated that the explosion and crash was most likely caused by a structural flaw in the aircraft. The explosion was believed to have been caused by the accumulation of gasoline fumes in the forward cabin of the plane.

SOURCES: *Knoxville Journal*, Mar. 28, 29, Apr. 2, 1943; *Knoxville News-Sentinel*, Mar. 27, 28, 1943.

Wrigley Airplane Crash
HICKMAN COUNTY, OCTOBER 15, 1943

> Soldiers from the Nashville Municipal Airport toiled on a rugged hillside this morning to remove 10 bodies from an American Airlines Memphis-bound plane which crashed head-on in a heavily wooded section of Hickman County near Wrigley last night.
> —*Nashville Banner,* Oct. 16, 1943

An American Airlines passenger plane crashed around 11:17 PM on this date, killing six passengers and four crew members. The crash occurred about forty-seven miles south of Nashville, in a heavily wooded section of Hickman County, near Wrigley. The flight, which was scheduled to arrive at the Memphis airport at one minute past midnight, departed Nashville around 10:48 PM and was last heard of a little after 11:00 PM This corresponded to the time on a broken wristwatch torn from the arm of one of the victims and found at the scene. The last radio contact from the ill-fated craft was unintelligible, but is believed to have been a distress call. It must have been shortly after this last radio contact that the plane crashed into a small heavily wooded hollow.

Both the Army and Civil Air Patrol began searching for the aircraft shortly after it failed to arrive in Memphis. The search continued into the next morning, when a twelve-year-old boy told his father he smelled gasoline in the air. The father investigated, found the wreckage, and reported it to the Hickman County Sheriff's Department. Search and rescue crews did not reach the crash scene until about ten the next morning. Only the tail section and part of one wing of the aircraft were still intact. However, from the twisted pile of wreckage it was determined that the plane had nosedived straight down into a scrub oak hollow without igniting and burning.

The bodies of the victims were so mangled that their identification was difficult or impossible to determine at the scene. The bodies had to be carried some 250 yards up a steep grade to the four ambulances that transported them to Nashville. Governor Prentice Cooper was among the officials who visited the site out of concern for one of the victims, Blan R. Maxwell, the Speaker of the Tennessee Senate. Maxwell would have been next in command should something have happened to the governor.

SOURCES: *Nashville Banner,* Oct. 15, 16, 1943.

Memphis Airplane Crash, 1944
FEBRUARY 10
The second worst civilian airline tragedy in Tennessee occurred around 11:30 PM on February 10, 1944, when

an American Airlines twin-engine DC-3 transport plane crashed into the Mississippi River, just south of Memphis. Twenty-one passengers and three crew members died in the crash. At the time, it was also the second worst civilian airline tragedy in American history. The plane went down near Cow Island, fifteen miles below the city.

One of three witnesses known to have seen and heard the crash was a watchman on a Mississippi River barge near the impact site. He heard the plane and saw it descending about 200 or 300 feet above the ground. As it came down, he saw its flashing red and green signal lights and heard a sort of swishing sound. Suddenly it struck the water with a loud roar, and a ball of flames seemed to roll out and then dissipate as the plane glided smoothly beneath the surface. Aviation officials said later that the fire probably came from one of the engines that broke off in the crash. The river man went on to say that it did not plunge or nose dive, but rather glided into the water at an angle. Since the craft should have been at about 2,000 feet in elevation at this point in its approach to the airport, it was probably out of control and falling fast. Soon after the crash the river man and another barge worker took a small powerboat out to where the plane had disappeared. Strangely enough, they found no debris, fuel, or oil, nothing on the surface. Shortly thereafter, they returned to shore and reported the crash.

This large Douglas airliner, nicknamed the "Sun Country Special," was en route from Dallas, Texas, to New York City and was due to land at the Memphis Airport at 11:38 PM It was stopping to put off one passenger and take on another, of higher priority, which was a common practice during the war years. As it approached Memphis from the Arkansas side of the Mississippi River, it made its last radio contact with the airport. That was at 11:31 PM, perhaps only seconds before it crashed, and nothing was said to indicate a mechanical or any other kind of problem at that time.

The plane was believed to have crashed into an area near the center of the great crescent channel that curves around Cow Island. Submerged in about twenty-five feet of water, the wreckage was quickly carried downstream by the Mississippi's strong current. Attempts to locate and raise the wreckage from the riverbed began at daybreak. Unfortunately, by that time the winter weather had turned nasty. It was a most miserable condition under which to carry out a search operation.

The plane was believed to have been traveling about 200 miles per hour when it hit the water. The speed of impact, and the fact that the twisted pieces of wreckage included a broken and shattered engine, indicated that the plane literally exploded and disintegrated upon impact. Or, as one U.S. Army Corps of Engineers official put it, the plane had probably "burst like a water-filled paper bag hurled against a concrete wall," when it plummeted into the river. Those onboard were most likely killed instantly. Inspectors doubted that the passengers ever knew what happened. The crew was probably so busy trying to remedy the problem that during the last minutes or seconds before the crash they had no time to either alert the airport tower or instruct the passengers to prepare for a crash. At the time of the collision, the current of the river where the plane went down was about five miles per hour. Mail bags, pieces of seat cushions, luggage, clothing, and other associated debris was quickly swept many miles downstream. In the hours and days that followed, much of it was found on the surface and on the banks of the river.

Sightseers watched as U.S. Army Corps of Engineer barges and a number of other boats underwent the grim task of searching the surface and dragging the riverbed near the crash site. Very slowly did the river yield up pieces of the plane and definitive clues as to why it crashed. Only six bodies, or parts of bodies, were found within four days of the air disaster. All but one was mutilated by the trauma of the crash. Fortunately, all six were identified by papers found on their bodies or by their features. Since the fuselage had exploded and broken apart on impact, there was little hope of ever recovering the remaining bodies. Small and large pieces of twisted wreckage and other debris were slowly brought up from the riverbed as the dredging barge and other boats criss-crossed the plane's potential crash debris field downstream of the impact site.

Officials from the Federal Bureau of Investigation, American Airlines, U.S. Army Corps of Engineers, a U.S. Senate Committee on Safety in the Air, Civil Aeronautics Board, and others investigated the crash. Weather—partly cloudy with light winds—was not believed to have been a factor in the crash. Visibility was also good. At the time of the investigation, there was little hope of finding out exactly what caused the crash of the plane; more has never been learned.

This crash occurred just a few miles below the point where the steamboat *M. E. Norman* capsized and sank in 1925, killing twenty-three.

SOURCES: *Memphis Commercial Appeal,* Feb. 12–15, 1944; *Memphis Press Scimitar,* Feb. 11, 12, 1944; Jay Robert Nash, *Darkest Hours* (Chicago: Nelson-Hall, 1976).

Whigs Mountain Airplane Crash
CHEROKEE NATIONAL FOREST, MONROE COUNTY, APRIL 8, 1945

> We'd been at work fighting the blaze and raking fire-break-lines for quite a spell before we began coming on metal pieces of the airship. That's the first inkling we had of a plane crash. Finally . . . we worked our way to the bodies. We played water around them with the pack-pumps on our backs, and were able to keep them from burning further.
> —*Knoxville News-Sentinel,* Apr. 10, 1945

Around 11:30 PM on April 8, 1945, a U.S. Forest Service fire spotter reported seeing a small blaze from his lookout tower within Cherokee National Forest. His tower was situated about twenty-two miles southeast of Tellico Plains. When a Forest Service fire crew arrived at the scene and started fighting the fire, they began finding

pieces of metal and then body parts. It was soon learned that the fire was caused by a four-engine (B-17) military aircraft known as a Flying Fortress that had crashed into the western slope of Whigs Mountain. The accident occurred one and a half miles south of Johns Knob Mountain, within the national forest.

Initially, only seven bodies were found at the crash site, but as daylight approached, three more were discovered. All were badly burned and believed to have died instantly upon impact. The ten soldiers were on a routine training mission out of Keesler Field in Biloxi, Mississippi.

According to the official U.S. Air Force report of the incident, the crash was caused by the aircraft flying too low to miss the summit of the mountain. However, some believe the aircraft was in trouble and was attempting to land in a small but rocky clearing on the side of the mountain. If so, it overshot the clearing and clipped the tops of a number of large trees before crashing into a craggy cliff. The wreckage, including the charred bodies of the victims, was spread over an acre of ground at an elevation of around 4,600 feet. This was just 400 feet beneath the summit. The only large piece of the plane was a ten-foot-long section of the fuselage. Three of the bomber's motors were scattered within the debris field. However, the fourth motor and a tire were catapulted over the mountain, landing a quarter of a mile away.

SOURCES: *Chattanooga Times,* Apr. 10, 1945; *Knoxville Journal,* Apr. 10, 11, 1945; *Knoxville News-Sentinel,* Apr. 9–10, 1945.

Clingmans Dome Airplane Crash
GREAT SMOKY MOUNTAINS NATIONAL PARK, JUNE 12, 1946

A B-29 Superfortress bomber, carrying a crew of twelve, crashed in the Great Smoky Mountains National Park about 2:30 AM on June 12, 1946. Everyone onboard was killed. The plane was en route from Chicago to MacDill Air Force Base in Tampa, Florida, on a routine night navigational flight when the accident occurred. The crash site of the plane was located at about 8:15 the next morning when one of its giant engines was found blocking the National Park's Clingmans Dome Road.

The four-engine bomber struck the Tennessee side of Clingmans Dome near Collins Gap and plowed up over the peak, finally coming to rest three quarters of a mile below the Clingmans Dome parking area, on the North Carolina side of the mountain. As it did so, it cut a fifty-foot-wide swath through the trees before its giant wings were sheared off. Then, after striking a two-ton boulder, the fuselage became airborne again before bursting into flames and completely breaking apart. The crash debris field, on the western side of the mountain, was a quarter mile long, with the charred remains of the airmen scattered along the final 300 yards.

The plane was ripped into thousands of pieces in the violent crash. Its giant engines were the only large pieces left intact. The bodies of the crash victims were badly crushed and mutilated; five were found at one spot within what had been the fuselage, and the seven others were scattered elsewhere about the scene. Most of the bodies were badly burned, five beyond recognition. There was no doubt that they had all died almost instantaneously in the fiery explosion and impact.

It was believed that the plane was cruising between 210 and 220 miles per hour, at an elevation of 5,500 feet, on a course to Knoxville from Chicago when it made a routine radio check with the Knoxville Airport about 2:15 AM When radio contact was attempted again fifteen minutes later, there was no answer. The pilot should have changed elevation to 8,000 feet, since that course would have taken the plane across the Smokies. He must have not made this elevation change, explaining the plane's crash into the 6,642-foot-high Clingmans Dome. Conditions were believed to have been cloudy to partly cloudy in the Smokies, and the pilot may have only seen the mountains at the last moment. At that point, he would have tried to bring up the nose of his aircraft as rapidly as

possible to climb over them. This action would explain why the plane hit the eastern side of Clingmans Dome at such an angle as to skip up and over the peak and finally come to rest on the western side of the summit, some twenty-five yards from the Clingmans Dome Road.

SOURCES: *Knoxville Journal,* June 13, 14, 1946; *Knoxville News-Sentinel,* June 13, 1946.

Memphis Airplane Crash, 1947
DECEMBER 11

> The first thing I did was to summon help over my radio transmitter. Then when I got out of the truck I noticed seven or eight men grimly bending over burning bodies beating out the flames . . . There wasn't a sound except crackling flames.
>
> —*Knoxville News-Sentinel,* Dec. 12, 1947

A C-47 twin engine-military transport plane crashed on a wooded hillside near the Memphis airport about 6:00 PM on December 11, 1947. All twenty-one Army officers and enlisted men onboard were killed instantly. The fiery crash occurred as the plane dropped too low and collided with a grove of pine trees about a thousand feet inside the state from the Tennessee and Mississippi state line. The crash occurred about two miles short, and directly south, of the airport runway.

There was some question at first about the number of passengers onboard, but the plane's manifest recorded only twenty. Many of those onboard were homeward bound for a Christmas furlough, according to papers found within the wreckage. The crash literally tore some of the bodies apart, but a doctor at the scene felt certain that there was one additional passenger, probably a soldier who had hitched a ride on the transport at the last minute. This is not uncommon on military flights and was later proven to be the case. There were twenty-one soldiers killed.

The flight was en route from Biggs Field in El Paso, Texas, to Memphis and possibly on to its home base at Aberdeen, Maryland. The cause of the crash was not immediately known, but bad weather was ruled out as a contributing factor. A guard from the County Penal Camp was the first person on the scene of the crash, and he extinguished flames on the burning bodies that were scattered among the wreckage.

After the plane touched down, it continued to slide about 300 yards through a pine forest, ripping the craft apart as it went. The plane disintegrated before coming to rest, and most of its bodies and debris were spread over an area roughly 100 feet wide and 200 feet long. There were few recognizable pieces of the plane left, and since everyone onboard was killed, there was little hope of ever determining the exact cause of the crash.

SOURCES: *Knoxville Journal,* Dec. 12, 1947; *Knoxville News-Sentinel,* Dec. 12, 14, 1947.

Tri-Cities Airplane Crash

Near Shady Valley, Sullivan County, January 8, 1959

A strange, mocking light—never explained—helped lead to the discovery of the Southeast Airlines plane wreckage Friday. The beacon of light, first sighted by lifesaving crew members at approximately 5:00 AM started an intensive search for the lost plane. "As we'd wave our light horizontally back and forth, the beacon would do likewise . . . " On the scene parties [later] ruled out the possibility of the light coming from the plane.

—*Knoxville News-Sentinel,* **Jan. 10, 1959**

Southeast Airlines Flight 308 crashed just after 8:30 PM on January 8, 1959, killing all ten people onboard. The pilot of the twin-engine DC-3 passenger plane had just contacted the air traffic control tower at Tri-Cities Airport.

He advised that he was starting an instrument procedure turn in preparation for his final approach when the radio went dead. That was the last word from the crew. Shortly thereafter it crashed into the rugged Holston Mountains. It went down near Shady Valley, about twenty miles east of Kingsport and eight miles east of the Tennessee Valley Authority Holston Dam, in Sullivan County.

Search operations were launched immediately, and a Tennessee National Guard plane spotted the wreckage about 11:50 the next morning. The area where the crash occurred was quite rugged and remote, as evidenced by the fact that a Navy plane that had crashed in the same general area about a year before was not found for three weeks. The Southeast Airlines plane crashed just northeast of where it should have been when it made the turn for a final approach to the airport.

A search and rescue team consisting of about fifty military and civilian personnel reached the wreckage on foot within three hours. All seven passengers and three crew members were dead on impact. Three of the bodies were badly burned, but all were easily identified. Low hanging clouds and periodic snow showers over the area prevented the use of helicopters in recovery of the bodies. The bodies were finally carried out of the area to jeeps that transported them to the airport, where they were identified and claimed by relatives.

The plane split into three large pieces—the fuselage, the tail assembly, and one wing—and burst into flames upon impact. The rest of the plane and the bodies of the victims were scattered at random. The plane had nose-dived into the side of Iron Mountain at an elevation of 3,800 feet, near the junction of Sullivan, Johnson, and Carter counties, literally spreading the crash site over a three-county area. The air traffic controller said that the sky was hazy with about five miles visibility. However, snow had been falling in the area at the time of the crash and may have been a contributing factor in the accident.

Flight 308 originated in Memphis and stopped at Nashville and Knoxville before continuing on to the

Tri-Cities Regional Airport, which serves Kingsport, Bristol, and Johnson City.

SOURCES: *Knoxville News-Sentinel,* Jan. 9, 10, 1959; *Newport Times,* Jan. 9, 1959.

Parrottsville Airplane Crash

Cocke County, July 9, 1964

> It was an eerie, hellish scene at the site of the crash. The smell of kerosene and burned flesh, the thick smoke, the smoldering wreckage, and the odd stillness of the night made the site and the situation seem unreal. A rescue worker said, "Bodies were spread over an acre or more. Strips of flesh hung from trees," he said. "It was horrible."
>
> —*Knoxville News-Sentinel,* **July 10, 1964**

About 6:15 on the evening of July 9, 1964, United Airlines Viscount 745D Turboprop Airliner (Flight 823) caught fire and crashed into a heavily wooded and vine entangled hillside two and one-half miles northeast of Parrottsville in Cocke County. All thirty-five passengers and four crew members onboard the ill-fated flight perished in the state's worst ever airline disaster.

During its last radio contact with the Knoxville McGhee Tyson Airport, the captain reported nothing wrong. There were scattered thunderstorms in the area, but in the parlance of the air traffic controllers, there was a 4,000 foot ceiling, thirty-mile visibility, and scattered clouds. Minutes later the four-engine plane disappeared from the radar screen. The flight had originated in Philadelphia, and after stopping in Washington, D.C., it was en route to Knoxville.

Apparently the plane experienced trouble just prior to crashing, as some eyewitnesses were quoted as saying that they saw smoke and flames coming from the plane and heard a lot of noise shortly before it collided with the ground. Some indicated that it exploded in the air and again when it hit the hillside. Others said there was only one crash, and that was on impact. There were also rumors that objects, possibly bodies, were seen falling from the aircraft while it was still in the air. These observations were never officially confirmed. One witness stated that the plane was terribly disintegrated. A part of one engine was about 1,000 feet from the rest of the wreckage. There were no seats, just small pieces of metal. Another witness said that the plane hit three trees before it exploded.

The crash site, spread over a two-mile-long area, was on a southwest slope of a hill about 300 yards from Trentham Hollow Road in rural Cocke County. The scene was so heavily wooded and isolated that a crude road had to be bulldozed along the contour of the hill to get the recovery workers and their equipment in and the bodies out. Floodlights were set up at the scene to aid in the overnight cleanup. As the bodies and body parts were recovered, their locations were marked with pieces of colored cloth to help in subsequent investigations. Human remains were placed in airtight plastic bags, with matching pieces of colored cloth, and transported by military trucks and jeeps to awaiting ambulances. One rescue worker said he found the body of a woman. When he turned her over to pick her up, he found she was clutching a child in her arms. Small fires flared up within scorched trees and brush, but these were quickly extinguished by rescue workers. A temporary morgue was established in the Memorial Building in nearby Newport. There, the remains of the victims were laid out on library tables for sorting and identification.

Some papers found in the wreckage were associated with the Atomic Energy Operations at Oak Ridge, Tennessee. They were in the possession of four scientists en route to Oak Ridge for a conference at Oak Ridge National Laboratories. FBI agents, brought in to investigate the crash and help in identification of the victims, confiscated those papers.

Several hundred spectators flocked to the scene of this disaster, creating a huge traffic jam. It was only after the National Guard arrived that recovery operations could continue in earnest.

Rescue workers at the scene of the Parrottsville, Cocke County, crash of United Airlines Flight 832, July 9, 1964. Courtesy of Knoxville Journal Collection, McClung Historical Collection, Knox County Public Library.

SOURCES: *Kingsport News,* July 10, 1964; *Knoxville News-Sentinel,* July 10, 1964; Jay Robert Nash, *Darkest Hours* (Chicago: Nelson-Hall, 1976).

Parsons Bald Double Airplane Crash
GREAT SMOKY MOUNTAINS NATIONAL PARK, JANUARY 3–4, 1978

A twin-engine Cessna 421 crashed about 8:30 PM on January 3, 1978, as it was making an approach to the McGhee Tyson Airport in Knoxville. All five persons onboard were found dead when the rescuers reached the wreck about midmorning. The next morning an Army helicopter carrying a rescue party also crashed nearby while searching for the downed Cessna. Four were killed and four others injured.

A Knoxville airport air traffic controller was in the process of giving landing instructions to the pilot of the Cessna when he lost voice and radar contact with the craft. This was about 8:25 PM. Five minutes later the Cessna plowed into the southwest flank of Parsons Bald, about ten miles south of Cades Cove, within the Great Smokies National Park.

On the morning of January 4, about an hour into the search, an Army rescue helicopter sent from Fort Campbell to assist in the search and rescue operation crashed just minutes after it radioed the search and rescue command post in Cades Cove. The last words from this chopper crew were that they had spotted the wreckage of the Cessna. The rescue helicopter was believed to have experienced engine problems. The crew of a companion search chopper said that the ill-fated craft seemed to be operating normally. Suddenly its engine stalled and it dropped, hitting the treetops, flipping over, and disappearing into the dense forest canopy. From there it fell around 85 to 100 feet to the ground. According to those onboard who survived the crash, the pilot tried to ease the chopper down into the trees as the engine failed. Unfortunately, the rotor caught on the trees and flipped, causing the craft to fall and come to a rest on the mountainside. However, it never burst into flames.

The fixed-wing Cessna aircraft was en route from Ft. Lauderdale, Florida, to Knoxville for an overnight stop before continuing on to Chicago. It was carrying four members of the same family and the pilot's girlfriend. All were from Illinois. It had an emergency signal device onboard that began broadcasting at the moment of the crash. It was this radio signal that finally enabled the search choppers to locate the Cessna. Recovery crews had to hike through extremely remote and rugged mountain terrain to reach the wreckage. Debris from the crash was spread over a wide area along both sides of the Tennessee and North Carolina state line.

Because both crashes occurred in a very remote section of the park, and because of the steepness of the terrain, ground rescue forces had to climb down a mountain and through thick, almost impenetrable undergrowth to reach both planes. The four killed in the chopper included the pilot, a division surgeon, the crew chief, and a well-known Knoxville Civil Air Patrolmen, Lt. Col. Ray Maynard. The survivors included two park

rangers, an Army paramedic, and an Air Force officer. They were airlifted from the side of the mountain and taken to Cades Cove. There a waiting Knoxville rescue chopper took them to the University of Tennessee Hospital, about twenty-five air miles to the north. The most severely injured of the four suffered multiple fractures and a back injury.

SOURCES: *Knoxville Journal,* Jan. 4, 5, 1978; *Knoxville News-Sentinel,* Jan. 4, 5, 1978.

Cherokee National Forest Airplane Crash

MONROE COUNTY, AUGUST 31, 1982

A giant C141B (Starlifter) cargo jet crashed into the craggy flanks of Johns Knob, in the Cherokee National Forest, around 2:27 PM on August 31, 1982. Nine men from the 437 Military Airlift Wing, stationed out of the Charleston Air Force Base, died instantly in the crash. The plane was about an hour and a half into its flight out of Charleston, South Carolina. It was traveling at an estimated speed of 260 miles per hour, and the impact against the solid rock flank of the mountainside was so great that it simply disintegrated. None of the bodies of the victims were found intact. Bodies and body parts were spread all along the crash site, trees were snapped off like matchsticks, and everything was charred by flames within the half-mile-long debris field. Only the tail section of the military transport remained intact after the crash.

The wreckage was located mostly on the Tennessee side of the Tennessee and North Carolina state line, but debris and body parts were spread over both sides within an area locally called Hoopers Bald Mountain. The incident occurred under rainy, cloudy, and foggy conditions while the plane was on a low-level training flight. It is believed that the crash was caused by the aircraft flying too low to miss the range of 5,000-foot-high mountains over which it was attempting to fly. Had it been flying a few hundred feet higher, it would have missed the mountain peak. Inclement weather hampered recovery efforts at the crash site within a fog-shrouded area of Cherokee National Forest, situated about twenty miles east of Tellico Plains. The crash occurred about forty minutes after the crew's last radio contact with Atlanta air traffic controllers.

SOURCES: *Indiana (PA) Gazette,* Sept. 3, 1982; *Knoxville Journal,* Sept. 3, 1982; *Knoxville News-Sentinel,* Sept. 2, 3, 4, 1982.

Highway Accidents

Literally thousands of highway accidents have occurred in Tennessee through the years. Many have injured and killed drivers, passengers, and pedestrians. And, in fact, automobiles account for the vast majority of transportation accidents each year. The Tennessee Highway Patrol (THP) was established in 1929, and although it patrolled state and federal highways, and investigated many traffic accidents, it did not maintain official records of such incidents in the early years.

THP has no historian, and only sporadic records on highway accidents, injuries, and deaths have been maintained during the last few decades by the Tennessee Department of Safety. The department did not begin compiling official crash records until the 1970s. It started reporting fatal crash incidents to the Federal Fatality Analysis Reporting System database beginning in 1975. Since 1978 it has maintained an electronic database of its motor vehicle incidents, particularly those involving injuries and fatalities. In correspondence with the author on November 6, 2009, Mike Browning, director of Public Affairs at the Tennessee Department of Safety, wrote that even though crash data existed in an electronic format, the earliest electronic database to which the department now has access only goes back to the 1990s. Hence, until the last two decades there has been no accounting for the total number of accidents, fatalities, injuries, or economic losses. Some records of particularly severe crashes involving multiple fatalities are also lacking.

Some of the more prominent accidents (those involving multiple deaths and injuries) have been chronicled in newspaper and magazine articles through the years. With no database from which to work, it would be extremely difficult to ferret out these incidents without the slow and laborious process of scanning copious media records. Fortunately, articles frequently compare current accidents to similar wrecks in the past, thus providing some additional data.

The worst traffic accident in Tennessee in terms of lives lost is believed to have occurred on June 5, 1943. On this date an Army truck plunged off a bridge in Nashville, dropped thirty feet headlong onto the Nashville, Chattanooga & St. Louis railroad tracks, and then turned upside down, trapping most of the victims. Sixteen died at the scene, and three others died at, or en route to, the hospital.

Harrison Pike Train and Wagon Wreck
Chattanooga, February 24, 1897

> The wagon was struck a second later, when squarely across the tracks and instantly the air was filled with the bodies of the ill-fated family; and the splinters of the shivered wagon. Shrieks rent the air and mangled bodies were strewn along both sides of the track . . . The body of Mrs. Montgomery was found on the front of the pilot, with her dead infant held in her arms in the rigid clasp of death, the motherly instinct controlling to the last.
>
> —*Knoxville Journal,* **Mar. 3, 1897**

About 12:30 PM on February 24, 1897, Southern Railway train No. 7 struck a horse-drawn farm wagon carrying ten passengers at the Harrison Pike Crossing, about three and a half miles north of Chattanooga. The engineer saw the wagon and sounded his whistle, but it was too late to stop. The wagon driver apparently panicked when he spotted the train and started whipping the horses. Unfortunately, the animals became spooked and refused to move, leaving the wagon positioned squarely across the tracks. Seconds later, the train, traveling at about thirty-five miles per hour, struck the wagon broadside. The horrific impact shattered the wagon and threw its occupants in all directions. Nine people were killed: a mother and eight of her children. A ninth child miraculously survived the impact unscathed. The collision forced her underneath the extension on the front of the locomotive.

The train had just emerged from a cut when the engineer saw the wagon at the Harrison Crossing, about 300 yards ahead. He applied his brakes as rapidly as he could, but saw that the wagon was not moving across the track. After the impact, the train traveled another two hundred yards before coming to a stop. Seven of the victims were killed instantly, but two of the daughters, ages ten and eighteen, were mortally injured and died later. One of the horses was killed, and the other ran away. The mother, her youngest child, and another daughter were caught on the cow catcher on the front of the locomotive. One witness to the accident said, "After the crash, I saw the people hurled through the air. It looked to me as if they went as high as the telegraph wires. I saw five of them in space at one time and all appeared to be falling head downward."

Two of the girls were leaving home, and their mother was taking all of her children into Chattanooga for a family photo that fateful day. They stopped at a

Sketch of the Harrison Pike train and wagon wreck. *Chattanooga Daily Times,* February 24, 1897.

neighbor's house for lunch and to pick up another family member. However, it was a beautiful day, and because of some financial business in Chattanooga, the father and his oldest son decided to walk ahead and meet the others later. They were still walking some distance ahead of the family wagon when the accident occurred. Hence the father, his eldest son, and the one baby that had been in the wagon survived that day. It was feared for a while that Abe Laird, the engineer, would lose his mind, but the incident was ruled an unavoidable accident by railroad and local law enforcement officials. The railroad sent a special train to retrieve the bodies and take them to a funeral home in Chattanooga. There they were met by a huge crowd of spectators, along with the father of the family and his eldest son. The railroad paid for all the caskets and other burial expenses.

SOURCES: *Chattanooga Times,* Feb. 25–27, Apr. 22, 1897; Nov. 16, 1898; *Knoxville Journal,* Mar. 3, 1897.

Eads Train–School Bus Wreck
Shelby County, October 10, 1941

> "Every child on the bus was screaming for the driver to stop." Frank Jones, ambulance driver for Hinton Funeral Home, also told reporters that the bus driver was clutching a sack of "roll your own" tobacco in his hand when he was extracted from the wreckage.
>
> —*Memphis Commercial Appeal,* **Oct. 11, 1941**

A Shelby County school bus was struck by a Memphis-bound North Carolina & St. Louis passenger train around 2:55 PM on October 10, 1941. Six students and the driver died at the crash scene, and another died later from fatal injuries. The wreck occurred near the Shelby and Fayette county line, twenty miles from Memphis. Eight others were injured, all pupils of the George R. James Grammar School. The train was moving about forty to fifty miles per hour and the bus was traveling down a parallel country road on the south side of the tracks.

Without slowing down or looking in both directions, the bus driver, Benjamin Priddy, suddenly turned across the tracks and directly into the path of the oncoming train. It all happened so quickly that it was impossible for the engineer to stop or even apply his brakes. This impact nearly ripped the bus in two. Both the bus driver and the engineer were experienced and had excellent safety records with their individual employers. Priddy had been driving the same route for fifteen years. One of the passengers on the train was able to force open the front door of the bus and crimp off or disconnect the bus's gas line to prevent a fire or explosion.

All of the children were tangled within bent and smashed bus seats, shattered glass, and a mass of twisted metal. To make matters worse, the impact threw the bus into a briar patch about thirty yards from the point of impact, slowing progress in extricating the students. Ambulance drivers and deputies described this as the most gruesome scene they had ever encountered. Four children were thrown out of the bus and died instantly; a little girl was crushed under the bus. One child was actually thrown through the floorboard of the bus and two or three were decapitated. Parents of the victims moved through the halls of the hospital, praying that their child was not one of the dead. The grim task of identification took hours, since some of the children's bodies were so mangled as to be almost unrecognizable. One little girl was identified only by a plaster cast on her arm. Although the train sustained some damage, no one onboard was injured. Initially some passengers did not even realize that a wreck had occurred. This was reported to be the worst tragedy in the history of Shelby County schools.

SOURCES: *Memphis Commercial Appeal,* Oct. 11–13, 1941; *Memphis Press-Scimitar,* Oct. 11, 1941.

Nashville Army Truck Wreck
June 5, 1943

> Captain Painter said [that after the wreck] the lieutenant picked himself up and stag-

gered nearly 400 yards to a nearby home where he placed an emergency call for help to Nashville city police.

—Nashville Tennessean, **June 7, 1943**

Nineteen army troops died and seven were injured when their truck crashed through the guardrails of the Woodycrest Road bridge. This bridge spans the Nashville, Chattanooga & St. Louis Railway tracks between Murfreesboro and Nolensville roads. The two-and-a-half-ton truck plunged thirty feet down an embankment onto the double railroad tracks below shortly before midnight on June 5, 1943. Sixteen of the victims were killed instantly as the truck nosed straight down, struck the ground, and flipped upside down. Two more soldiers died of injuries in the Nashville Army Air Center Hospital the next morning. One additional victim died still later. In terms of the number of fatalities, this is believed to have been the worst single vehicle automobile accident in Tennessee's history.

The truck was severely crushed and twisted into a shapeless mass by the collision, and some of the victims were impaled and mangled within the wreckage. In fact, it took military, state, city, and county emergency responders over three hours to extricate the bodies of the dead and injured from the wreck. To make matters worse, a northbound train approaching the site of the accident almost hit it. Fortunately, a train that was southbound on the two-way tracks had just passed the scene and stopped to flag down the northbound train. The northbound engineer hit his brakes hard and came to rest only 100 feet from the scene of the accident. Had he not been flagged down, he would surely have struck the wreckage, causing additional casualties.

One of the survivors said he felt the truck go over the foot-high curb of the bridge after tearing through the railing. The next thing he remembered was the truck landing nose down in the railroad cut. He was ejected from the vehicle. Although injured and dazed, he was able to stagger nearly 400 yards to a house, where he notified local officials of the wreck.

The soldiers, members of the Second Army's Field Artillery Unit Headquarters Company, were on maneuvers at the time of the accident. The truck driver had taken a wrong turn, and it is believed he was attempting to take a shortcut to rejoin his convoy on Murfreesboro Road. By the time he realized how narrow the one-lane bridge was, it was too late. The accident occurred near Nashville's Woodbine and Glencliff communities.

SOURCES: *Knoxville Journal,* Aug. 8, 1966; *Nashville Banner,* June 7, 1943; *Nashville Tennessean,* June 6, 7, 1943.

Spring City Train–School Bus Wreck
RHEA COUNTY, AUGUST 22, 1955

According to one witness, "The diesel freight hit toward the rear of the bus, ripping it apart and scattering children. One body was found under a rail hand car that was overturned by the ricocheting bus. Three bodies were unidentifiable except by clothes. One of the most pitiful things was a father and mother carrying a little brown oxford, searching through the ambulances where the bodies were stored, trying to identify their son."

—Knoxville News-Sentinel, **Aug. 23, 1955**

Eleven students were killed and thirty injured when a Southern Railway freight train struck a school bus at the Main Street crossing in Spring City on August 22, 1955. The Southern Railway tracks run north and south through town, paralleling U.S. Highway 27 on one side and Main Street on the other. Ten of the victims died on impact and one other died two days later at Rockwood Hospital. The children ranged in ages from six to twelve years old.

The wreck occurred only two blocks from Spring City Elementary School, minutes after forty-three students boarded the ill-fated bus, bound for their homes in rural Rhea County. The school bus had just entered the tracks when the collision occurred. Freight Train

No. 51 was pulling about 140 cars and traveling southbound about forty-five miles per hour when it struck the bus broadside near the rear end and knocked it between forty and fifty feet toward the city side of the tracks. The impact scattered some of the young bodies for a hundred yards along the tracks and trapped others in the mangled wreckage of the bus itself. Witnesses said the dead seemed to be spread about ten feet apart along one stretch of the track. Some of the bodies were badly mangled and unrecognizable, even by some of the children's teachers who were brought to the scene for the gruesome task of body identification. One little girl was recognized by one of her classmates only by the dress she was wearing. Writing tablets and textbooks were scattered over a wide area, all torn apart and splattered with blood.

Some parents became alarmed when the bus carrying their children did not show up on time. Because it was late in the day, others were still at work and did not even know about the accident until contacted by authorities, many of whom bore grim news. The crash was said to be surprisingly quiet, but it was heard by people of the town, who quickly descended on the scene to find children—some screaming in agony, some only moaning, and others forever quiet. They began separating the dead from the injured and the seriously injured, helping to comfort each child in any way they could. Some brought pans of water and towels to wash away the blood that was everywhere. The scene was pandemonium as anxious and panic-stricken parents searched frantically for their children. They looked first under white sheets by the side of the tracks, next in ambulances, and then in the hospitals at Rockwood, Dayton, Crossville, and even as far away as Chattanooga. Some children were transported to the medical facilities in private vehicles and others by ambulances.

The Rhea County school bus driver said that he had stopped at the crossing, but a number of railroad cars obstructed his view of the tracks. He said that by the time he saw the train, and heard the whistle blowing, it was too late. He also said that the automatic crossing signal was not working at the time. One student on the bus disputed the fact that the driver stopped before going across the tracks, and other bystanders testified that the automatic signal was working both before and after the crash. The driver had only been driving the bus for a short time. He was charged with manslaughter in the incident and placed into protective custody outside Spring City to protect him from distraught parents.

This was the worst train–school bus accident in the state's history. Governor Frank Clement visited the funeral homes where the initial ten victims were taken. He also visited all thirty-one children injured in the incident and gave each a silver dollar. He also placed a highway patrol car and patrolmen at the disposal of each of the ten families who had lost children in the wreck for some time before and after the funerals. In addition, he charged the State Highway Patrol, the Tennessee Bureau of Identification, and the State Education Commission with investigating the exact cause of the accident.

A plaque and fountain were erected in 1956 at the Spring City Elementary School in memory of the eleven children killed in the incident. After construction was completed on an expansion of the school around 2002–2003, $5,000 was raised to establish a new memorial at the site of the crash, which was placed in 2005.

SOURCES: *Kingsport News,* Aug. 23, 1955; *Knoxville Journal,* Aug. 23–25, 1955; *Knoxville News-Sentinel,* Aug. 23, 24, 1955.

National Guard Truck Wreck
CHUCKY, GREENE COUNTY, AUGUST 7, 1966

The [State] Trooper said he heard several of the men screaming in pain. "There was a lot of moaning under the truck bed," he said. "We couldn't get the truck off them without a wrecker. We got a shovel and dug a hole so they could get air under the bed."

—*Knoxville News-Sentinel,* Aug. 8, 1966

Eight were killed and twelve injured around 7:20 AM on August 7, 1966, when the brakes failed on an Army National Guard truck near the community of Chucky (Greene County). The truck was traveling about forty to forty-five miles per hour when it struck a passenger car, slid off the road, rolled down a twenty-foot embankment, and flipped over on its top. Most of the dead and injured were pinned beneath the five-ton truck for several hours before local wreckers were finally able to pull the monster vehicle into an upright position. The surviving soldiers suffered broken limbs, backs, and other severe injuries and were transported to Johnson City Memorial and the Johnson City Veterans' hospitals.

The wreck occurred near Chucky High School, on a curve of U.S. Highway 11E, about eight miles east of Greeneville. It had been raining, and according to State Troopers the road surface was treacherous in places. This was one of the worst motor vehicle accidents in Tennessee history.

The soldiers, members of Greeneville and Johnson City's Company A, 1st Battalion, 117th Infantry, 1st Brigade, were on weekend maneuvers. They were en route, along with two other five-ton personnel carriers, to Johnson City when the wreck occurred. According to the driver of the passenger vehicle involved in the crash, the truck veered out of control across the highway and sideswiped the car. The driver of the car tried to swerve to avoid the impact, but the truck struck the car, skidded back across the highway, and lunged over the embankment before flipping over. The driver of the automobile suffered multiple injuries, and his three passengers were treated for minor cuts and abrasions, which is amazing considering the fact that the top of the car was literally sheared off level with the hood.

SOURCES: *Knoxville Journal,* Aug. 8, 1966; *Knoxville News-Sentinel,* Aug. 8, 1966, May 14, 1972.

U.S. Highway 11W Bus-Truck Wreck
Bean Station, Grainger County, May 13, 1972

Tennessee's second worst multiple vehicle highway traffic accident, in terms of lives lost, occurred on U.S. Highway 11W when a double-decker Greyhound bus veered six feet over the center line and collided with a tractor-trailer truck. The accident occurred around 5:45 AM on May 13, 1972. Fourteen people, including both drivers and twelve bus passengers, died in the incident. An additional twelve bus passengers were injured, some seriously, and treated at hospitals in Morristown, Kingsport, and Knoxville. Fifteen ambulances responded to the scene, but some of the injured were taken to medical facilities before the ambulances arrived. The accident occurred about eleven miles north of Rutledge near Bean Station in Grainger County.

The bus had originated in Memphis, passed through Knoxville, and was en route to Roanoke, Virginia, and New York when the accident occurred. The wreck happened in the predawn hours, so most of the passengers were asleep. For this reason, no one could say exactly what caused the accident. It occurred on a relatively flat and straight stretch of highway, and although heavy rainfall began after the collision and hampered response efforts, it was dry when the wreck occurred. A Morristown ambulance, responding to the incident, also collided with another vehicle, injuring its driver.

Upon arriving at the scene, Grainger County Rescue Squad members found another victim in the bus that the state troopers had missed. Most of the seats had been knocked out of the bus, but some victims were trapped in the back section. Others, including some babies, were sprawled over the road. A young girl was found in the front of the bus in a standing position, encased in metal; she was eventually extricated. The truck, which belonged to Malone Freight Lines in Birmingham, Alabama, was carrying vinyl flooring and flammable adhesive pastes. It burst into flames upon impact, as its saddle fuel tanks ruptured and ignited the truck's cargo. It burned for several hours. Some of the bodies of the dead proved difficult to identify.

The National Transportation Safety Board investigated the incident, which occurred on what was at the time one of the state's most dangerous two-lane roads: the stretch of U.S. Highway 11 West between Interstate 81 at Bristol and Interstate 75 at Knoxville. Shortly after this accident, the highway was widened and improved.

SOURCES: *Knoxville Journal,* May 15, 1972, Jan. 31, 1973; *Knoxville News-Sentinel,* May 13, 14, 15, 1972.

Silliman Evans Bridge Auto Wreck
NASHVILLE, JULY 27, 1973

Around 5:45 AM on the foggy morning of July 27, 1973, a 1971 Mercury sedan crashed through a guardrail on Nashville's Silliman Evans Memorial bridge and plunged ninety feet to the ground on the bank of the Cumberland River. Eight people were killed, seven instantly, and the eighth died about an hour after the wreck was discovered. Some were thrown from the car; others were trapped inside. One Metro police officer was quoted in the *Nashville Banner* as saying, "it was a horrible scene . . . bodies were scattered everywhere." The eighth victim lingered for some time in the mangled wreck. The only survivor was a five-year-old boy who suffered a broken arm and a smashed pelvis. The nine passengers were traveling to Flint, Michigan, from Pine Bluff, Arkansas, to visit relatives. Police believe that a combination of high speed and heavy fog led to the fatal crash. They also suspected that the driver (the grandmother of the family) may have fallen asleep at the wheel.

The vehicle landed on its top on the grounds of the Mid-State Steel Company, and a wrecker had to turn it over before the bodies could be removed. Many of the responders were critical of the Metro Police Department for not having extrication equipment readily available. In fact, it was over an hour before the Tennessee Highway Patrol could get a metal power saw to the scene, and the eighth victim died just as the top was being cut away from the vehicle.

According to officers, more wrecks have occurred on the Silliman Evans Memorial bridge, a stretch of I-65 and I-24, than any other place in Nashville, and this was the worst single car accident in the city's history.

SOURCE: *Nashville Banner,* July 27, 1973.

I-75 Multivehicle Wreck
McMINN COUNTY, DECEMBER 11, 1990

> It was an accident from hell. God wouldn't
> do something like this.
>
> **—Emergency responder**

On this cool winter morning, numerous cars and trucks were traveling along a half-mile stretch of Interstate 75 near the Hiwassee River bridge, in McMinn County. Abruptly and without warning, they entered a dense fog bank. Someone later told the McMinn County Emergency Management Agency director, "The fog arose suddenly like someone throwing a blanket over your windshield." Some drivers said that visibility was reduced to only ten to fifteen feet. Within moments, vehicles in both the north- and southbound lanes began colliding with one another. Before the fog lifted, twenty-seven separate crashes involving ninety-nine vehicles had occurred. The interstate was closed for eight miles in both direction for hours.

The first call concerning the incident reached the Bradley County Sheriff's Department at 9:14 AM. By 9:17 a deputy radioed from the scene to the sheriff's dispatcher that he could "still hear them [the vehicles] hitting one another." He further advised them to, "Close down the interstate and send all available assistance."

The incident was believed to have begun in the southbound lane, where the majority of the crashes occurred. Some said the crashes continued for up to thirty minutes, but this was not confirmed. Many of the vehicles burst into flames upon impact, and only a few of the drivers had the forethought to get out of their cars and trucks and flee the crash zone. A large truck carrying a toxic and explosive substance, dicumyl peroxide, blew up, hampering initial rescue efforts. Another truck carrying liquid propane gas, which is much more flammable, mercifully remained intact. Some of the wreckage was compacted and fused to the point that it was initially impossible to determine what had hit what and how many vehicles were involved. A Chevy Blazer was so tightly sandwiched between two tractor-trailer rigs that it could have fit into a telephone booth with room to spare. The driver of the Blazer miraculously escaped; others were not so lucky.

A dozen people died and fifty-six others were injured in this devastating traffic accident, to which more than 200 emergency workers responded. It was the state's worst ever transportation accident in terms of the number of injuries and vehicles involved. In the initial hours of the mishap, firefighters, rescue workers, emergency medical technicians, state emergency management officials, and local and state law enforcement officers moved quickly from vehicle to vehicle extinguishing fires and searching for survivors. Some of the victims were able to escape on their own and just in time. Some were pulled out and placed on stretchers, and a few had to be extricated from the tangled masses of twisted metal and broken glass. During initial triage, the locations of fatalities were merely noted. They could wait; the injured could not. Some of the victims themselves rendered aid to those less fortunate. Others stood by in shock or wandered about, dazed and disoriented.

Most of the injured were transported by ambulances to hospitals in nearby Athens and Cleveland. Some of the more seriously injured were airlifted to Chattanooga and Knoxville trauma centers. Bodies were initially assembled in a makeshift morgue on the median of the highway and were later transported in a refrigerated truck to an Athens Funeral home, where identities were confirmed and bodies claimed.

It was soon realized that the fog that triggered the tragic accident had been caused by water vapor from cooling ponds at a nearby pulp and paper mill. This mill was operated by the Bowater Southern Paper Corporation. Similar accidents had occurred in the same general area on at least three other occasions (see March 9, 1974; December 16, 1977; and November 5, 1978 in the chronology). Following the incident of 1990, the Tennessee Department of Transportation installed a multimillion-dollar fog detection and warning system along this stretch of interstate. It includes a number of fog detection devices, warning signals, signs, and barricades. These automatically close down the interstate, routing traffic off at exit ramps and closing down entry ramps until the fog dissipates. Since that time, there have been no fog-related traffic accidents in the area. The Bowater Southern Paper Corporation eventually settled forty-four separate lawsuits at a cost of approximately $10 million.

SOURCES: *Knoxville Journal,* Dec. 12, 14, 1990; *Knoxville News-Sentinel,* Dec. 12, 1990, Jan. 22, 1994.

RAILROAD ACCIDENTS

Although railroad construction began in Tennessee in the late 1830s, regular railway service did not commence until the mid-1850s. Expansion and civilian operations were slowed during the Civil War, and many of the established rail lines, bridges, and other infrastructure, as well as the rolling stock (engines, freight, and passenger cars), were damaged or demolished during that period. When the economy picked up after the war years, more tracks were constructed, and rail service expanded across the state and across the nation. Unfortunately, too rapid an expansion of the nation's railway system was also a contributing factor to the economic panic of 1893. As more tracks and more and faster trains evolved, the potential for railroad accidents involving deaths, serious injuries, and heavy economic losses also increased. Of the numerous railroad accidents in Tennessee between 1865 and 1944, only fifteen have involved five or more fatalities along with multiple injuries. Those that occurred during the Civil War (with the exception of one non–war related incident) are not discussed in this book for reasons stated earlier. Seven of the wrecks, including the worst two, involved head-on collisions between trains due to misinterpreted orders or failure to receive proper orders. Other causes of wrecks included excessive speed, runaway rail cars, faulty or obstructed rails, failed signals, and bridge or trestle collapses.

The worst passenger rail accident in U.S. history occurred in Belle Meade, just west of Nashville in July 1918. It killed over a hundred people and was reported to have injured as many as 300. Some of those injuries were undoubtedly fatal; hence, the death toll is probably much, much higher (see the introduction for a discussion of accurately accounting for losses of life). In spite of its severity, this horrific incident received scant attention in newspapers at the time. There are several reasons for this: it was a civilian wreck during a time of war and might have seemed almost insignificant in comparison; it had to compete for newspaper column space with the great Spanish influenza pandemic that was raging across the state and the globe; and many of the wreck victims were black—at a time of nationwide racial unrest—and therefore may not have received the attention it deserved from a predominantly white press. At any other time in history, this event would have been one of the lead media events across the nation and around the world.

The Reynolds Station train wreck in Giles County was the earliest serious railroad tragedy in Tennessee and occurred when a Chattanooga & Alabama Railroad trestle collapsed into Richland Creek, killing over thirty-five and injuring another thirty. Little is known of the incident except that it occurred during the Civil War, though it was not believed to have been war related. According to the August 26, 1865, *New York Times,* a boxcar containing about thirty black convicts was submerged in the stream, and they all drowned before anyone could free them.

Reynolds Station Train Wreck
GILES COUNTY, AUGUST 25, 1865

Until the wreck is cleared away, the extent of this dreadful catastrophe cannot be ascertained. It is one of the most direful ever known in Tennessee. A heavy gang of workmen is employed removing the debris, and in repairing the damage to the [rail]road.

—*Nashville Daily Press and Times,*
Aug. 29, 1865

Around noon on August 25, 1865, a locomotive hauling nine rail cars crashed into Richland Creek when a defective trestle gave way. The wreck occurred at Richland Neck, on the Chattanooga & Alabama Railroad, about three-quarters of a mile south of Reynolds, or Reynolds Station, in Giles County. This town was once located at the point where U.S. Highway 31 crosses over the railroad tracks north of Pulaski, but it no longer exists.

The train departed Nashville at 7:30 AM and was en route to Huntsville, Alabama. It consisted of a locomotive, a passenger coach, four express cars, and four boxcars. The latter were loaded with prisoners, mostly blacks. The official death toll in the incident was eventually recorded as thirty-five. Most died at the scene or later of injuries sustained in the wreck. The identities of most were unknown. Thirty others were reported injured, some severely. The injured and dying were taken to local homes, where they received such basic doctoring as was available in rural communities of the time. A large number of the dead were the black prisoners trapped in boxcars submerged in the creek and covered by tons of debris. More than five days after the incident, the wreck was still being cleared and bodies retrieved. Besides the two boxcars that lay partially submerged in the water, two others stood upended. During this time of war it was vital to get trains rolling again, but the Richland Creek trestle and the tracks torn up by the wreck took much time and effort to repair.

SOURCES: Tolly Carter, Giles County Library, personal correspondence with author, Aug. 6, 2009; *Nashville Daily Press and Times,* Aug. 27–29, 1865; *New York Times,* Aug. 26, 1865; *Macon (GA) Daily Telegraph,* Aug. 31, 1865; Robert B. Shaw, *A History of Railroad Accidents, Safety Precautions and Operating Practices* (Potsdam, NY: Clarkson College of Technology, 1978).

Flat Creek Train Wreck
NEAR CORRYTON, GRAINGER COUNTY, AUGUST 22, 1889

The headlines in the *Knoxville Journal* on August 22, 1889, read, "THE FIRST TRAIN, ON THE NEW KNOXVILLE, CUMBERLAND GAP AND LOUISVILLE, WILL LEAVE THE CITY EARLY THIS MORNING." The article went on to state that the train "will be a special leaving this city at 8 o'clock this morning, carrying officials of the road, members of the city council, the board of public works, representatives of the press and a few invited guests." The train was scheduled to visit Cumberland Gap by noon and return the same day.

However, about midmorning things went terribly wrong. The engine and the first car of the train crossed the New Flat Creek trestle without incident, but its second car hit an obstruction or broken rail and bumped along the ties for several yards before turning over and plunging into the streambed twenty-three feet below. The engine and second car were undamaged and came to a stop just beyond the trestle.

The wreck occurred near Corryton, in Grainger County, about twenty-two miles north of Knoxville. At first, the scene of the crash was total chaos. Since the engine and second car were not damaged, they were sent north to bring back medical assistance and a railroad section crew. The only physician on the train, Dr. T. A. West, had sustained internal injuries and could not help the others.

The ill-fated car was resting on its top with the sides crushed and broken away. Cries and agonizing moans came from the injured that lay with the dead between overturned seats, splintered planks, and broken glass. Everywhere there were gaping wounds and crushed and broken limbs. Blood pooled to the center of the car, and, to make matters worse, a hard summer rain began falling. Those with less serious or no injuries crawled from the wreck and attempted to aid the others. In time, they were joined by people from the community who brought what medical supplies they had and offered their homes as temporary shelters.

Three men—Col. S. T. Powers, a prominent merchant; Judge George Andrews; and attorney Alex Reeder—died at the scene or en route back to Knoxville. Three others—Col. Isham G. Young, chairman of the Knoxville Board of Public Works; F. Hockenjos, city alderman; and businessman Edward E. Barker—died later of injuries sustained in the crash. Of the remaining forty-eight passengers, over half suffered various fractures, concussions, internal injuries, impalements, lacerations, and bruises, but recovered.

Several of the victims were taken to nearby homes until they could be transported back to the city. When the train returned, a number of physicians began working with the injured. The track was quickly repaired and the dead and injured were loaded onto the train for the long and jarring ride homeward. Meanwhile, news of the terrible wreck reached Knoxville. This time the *Knoxville Journal* headlines read, "HORRIBLE! OH: THE PITY OF IT. CRASH OF TIMBERS—WRECK OF LIVES. DEAD, DYING AND WOUNDED. The Flower of Our Citizenry In an Awful Railroad Wreck."

Hundreds flocked to the depot in shock and disbelief to await the arrival of the train. Throughout the city almost every store, office, and business closed for the day out of respect for the dead and concern for the injured. This was, at the time, the worst disaster to strike the city since the Civil War.

SOURCES: *Knoxville Daily Journal,* Aug. 23, 1889; *Knoxville Journal,* Aug. 22, 23, 24, 1889.

New Market Train Wreck
HODGES, JEFFERSON COUNTY, SEPTEMBER 24, 1904

I saw a woman pinioned by a piece of split timber which had gone completely through her body. A little child, quivering in death's agony, lay beneath the woman. I saw the child die, and within a few feet of her lay a woman's head, while the decapitated body was several feet away.

—**John W. Brown,**
editor of the *Rogersville Star*

At 10:18 AM on September 24, 1904, two Southern Railway passenger trains collided head-on in the vicinity of Hodges, between Strawberry Plains and New Market. The state's second greatest railroad catastrophe took the lives of somewhere between 63 and 114 people (possibly including 8 Italian citizens) and injured an estimated 150 to 160. Still others most likely died later, as a result of serious injuries sustained in the crash.

The larger of the two trains, southbound No. 15, en route to Knoxville, was given orders at Morristown to pull onto a side track at New Market and give the right-of-way to the northbound train, No. 12. The latter train, the *Carolina Special* was coming out of Knoxville en route to Bristol. Unfortunately, the engineer of train No. 15 either misread or ignored his orders and sped on toward Knoxville. Both trains were traveling at around thirty-five miles per hour, the equivalent of striking each other at seventy miles per hour. Some say the sound of the wreck was heard fifteen miles away at the Sevier County and Jefferson County line.

When on schedule the trains generally met at the Hodges Station; otherwise, they met a few stations in either direction. On this day, No. 12 was on time but No. 15 was behind schedule. Nonetheless, the orders were not ambiguous, both train crews were seasoned and trusted professionals, the tracks and equipment were in top-notch condition, and bad weather was not a factor. Although several theories have been advanced to explain why or how Engineer William Kane on No. 15 misinterpreted or ignored his order to pull off the main track, we will never know. Perhaps the most plausible answer was that since No. 15 was behind schedule, the engineer thought he could pull off at the Hodges Station to make up some time. It has also been suggested that Kane was in a hurry to get to Knoxville because he had a horse running in a harness race later that day and did not want to miss it.

There were more than 300 passengers on the two trains, but only the engineer and crew were killed on No. 15. All the other casualties were on No. 12. It was a smaller train, with a heavy engine on the front and sturdy, metal Pullman cars on the rear. Sandwiched between these two stronger and heavier units were a couple of flimsy wooden passenger coaches. When the impact occurred, these cars collapsed like egg shells, telescoping into one another, crushing precious human cargo within a critical mass of splintered wooden planks and smatterings of window glass. These were the death traps in which most of the fatalities and serious injuries occurred.

About a hundred railway workers arrived just after noon to begin the grisly task of removing bodies and body parts, assisting the injured, and clearing the tracks. Hundreds of local citizens soon joined the effort, some wandering aimlessly around the wreck not knowing what to

Spectators gather around the site of the New Market train wreck in Hodges, Jefferson County, September 24, 1904. Courtesy of Frank Johnson Collection, McClung Historical Collection, Knox County Public Library.

do and others doing anything they could to aid and lend comfort to the victims. The whole scene was horrendous and surreal. The dead and injured lay on, under, and intermingled within the wreckage. A New York newspaper reporter was quoted in the *Knoxville News-Sentinel* as stating that "five of the cars are smashed and the engines are bent and twisted. The trains are all afire and the steam coming from the boilers is curling around the bodies that are piled atop them. These bodies are held fast by the twisted iron."

Every available physician in Knoxville and the surrounding area was summoned to the scene of the wreck. The injured were taken by rail to the Old Knoxville General Hospital, which overflowed with victims. About fifty victims are believed to have died at the scene, others while en route to the hospital, and still others while in the hospital or after being discharged.

Soon after the wreck, Sanford Jack, a claims agent, was dispatched to the scene of the accident with $30,000 in cash to settle as many claims on the spot as possible.

SOURCES: *Atlanta Constitution,* Sept. 26, 1904; Jim Claborn, "Back When: 96-Year-Old Recalls Famous Train Wreck," *Morristown (TN) Citizen Tribune,* Sept. 5, 1991; Federal Writers' Project, *Tennessee: A Guide to the State* (New York: Viking, 1939); Edgar A. Haine, *Railroad Wrecks* (New York: Cornwall Books, 1993); *Jefferson County Standard Banner,* Sept. 20, 1979; *Knoxville Journal,* Sept. 24, 1983; *Knoxville News-Sentinel*. Sept. 12, 1954, Sept. 16, 1979; Robert B. Shaw, *A History of Railroad Accidents, Safety Precautions and Operating Practices* (Potsdam, NY: Clarkson College of Technology, 1978); *Washington Post,* Sept. 25, 1904.

Chattanooga Streetcar Wreck
OCTOBER 18, 1907

John Brown [also known as John Cleveland], a fifteen-year-old Negro boy, residing with his father, James Cleveland, in Churchville was killed instantly. Both of his legs were mashed off while he had a deep hole cut in the side of his head. He was caught under the car when the floor went in.

—*Chattanooga Daily Times,* Oct. 19, 1907

Chattanooga's worst electric streetcar accident occurred around 6:45 AM on October 18, 1907, near the city limits. Six people were killed and as many as eighty were injured, some critically, as two streetcars collided head-on. The wreck occurred along a steep dip on Harrison Avenue. Five died at the scene, and the sixth died hours later in Erlanger Hospital. The wreck occurred in a dense early morning fog on the Chattanooga Railway Company's Boyce or Sherman Heights line, about halfway between the Queen and Crescent crossing and East End Avenue. The cars were believed to have been traveling at full speed, or about twelve miles per hour, when the collision occurred. Both of the streetcar motormen died instantly at the scene and an inquiry put the blame for the incident on the conductor and motormen of outgoing (eastbound) car No. 49. It was not as heavily loaded as the incoming, or westbound, car No. 200. The latter coach was carrying early morning commuters into town.

The cause of the accident was believed to be the result of a confusion of signals, with the fog as a contributing factor. There was also a loss of electricity from the powerhouse that interrupted communications, at least for a short time. Visibility was said to be about twenty feet, so there was no way that the motormen could have seen each other and even slowed down their vehicles in time to avoid the deadly crash. Several passengers jumped from their respective cars or were thrown off when the collision occurred. Some riders sustained severe injuries, while others had only minor cuts and scratches.

SOURCES: *Daily Times Chattanooga,* Oct. 19, 20, 1907.

Runaway Mine Cars–Train Wreck
RICHLAND GULF, RHEA COUNTY, MAY 27, 1909

> When the engineer realized the danger, he hit the throttle and the train moved forward with a bound just a few seconds before the impact. This undoubtedly saved many lives!
> —*Chattanooga News,* **May 27, 1909**

In the early morning hours on May 27, 1909, a locomotive climbed the steep incline near the Richland Gulf North Pole Drift Mine and unhitched a couple of cars. The rear car was loaded with slate and the forward one with mule feed. Several men then maneuvered the two incline cars into position so that they could offload the mule feed. This was a standard operation. Suddenly and without warning, the brakes on the cars somehow disengaged and both started plummeting downslope, picking up speed as they went. There was no way of stopping them, no way of knowing how far they would travel, and no way of knowing where they would end up. Worst of all, there was no way of warning anyone down the tracks of the runaways.

Meanwhile, the locomotive that had delivered them to the mine had moved down to the Nelson Mine to pick up 250 men and take them home to Morgantown, in Rhea County. The miners were loaded into four coke cars and were unaware of the catastrophe that they were about to face. The carloads of men were just two miles ahead as the slate and mule feed cars sped downslope, still gaining speed. Partway down the steep incline, a "monkey," or safety switch, should have derailed the runaways; unfortunately, it had not been pulled and the cars sped on.

Just then, some of the coal miners in the rear car of the target train saw the incline cars speeding toward them. However, instead of telling the engineer to move forward rapidly to avoid a collision, they yelled for him to stop so they could jump off. This was a fatal error. Finally seeing what was behind him, the engineer hit his throttle, causing the coke cars to lunge forward just before the collision. This helped lessen the impact to some degree and probably saved several lives. However, when the runaway cars collided, at an estimated speed of fifty to sixty miles per hour, six men were killed instantly. Three more died later from injuries sustained in the accident, and about twenty were injured, some severely.

The impact was lessened to some extent by the mule feed car being in the front of the slate car. Nonetheless, the rear coke car, still filled with some fifty passengers, was torn to pieces; the second car derailed; and the third car was severely damaged. The front car and the engine were unscathed by the impact. The two incline cars derailed, tumbled off the tracks, and finally came to rest at the base of an embankment.

SOURCES: Bettye J. Broyles, *History of Rhea County, Tennessee* (Collegedale, TN: Rhea County Historical and Genealogical Society and College Press, 1991); *Chattanooga Times,* May 27, 1909.

Sherwood Train Wreck
FRANKLIN COUNTY, DECEMBER 23, 1915

> Most of those killed in the wreck are said to have been horribly mangled and broken, and of those injured, it is thought that six or eight have no chance of recovery.
> —*Chattanooga Daily Times,*
> **December 24, 1915**

At 4:17 PM on December 23, 1915, a passenger train collided head-on with a freight train between Rockledge, south of Cowen, and Sherwood. The wreck occurred about two miles south of Rockledge and two miles north of the tunnel, on the Nashville, Chattanooga & St. Louis Railroad in southeastern Franklin County. Fifteen people, mostly black laborers, were killed in the incident, and another twenty-two were injured. Some bodies were trapped under the wreckage for hours. As many as eight of the injured probably died later as a result of injuries sustained in the wreck. Unfortunately, a final death toll was probably never published.

The freight train (No. 55) was hauling forty-five cars. The other, a local passenger train (No. 2) was pulling four coaches. The latter train, which made regular runs between Nashville and Chattanooga, was hauling black laborers home to Nashville for the Christmas holidays. The root cause of the wreck was some sort of signal failure. Both engineers had green lights indicating that they had the right-of-way and could proceed. Unfortunately, within minutes their trains were on a deadly collision course with one another. The locomotives hit head-on within the deep and rocky, half-mile-long Hominy Hill cut. Excessive speed was not a factor, even though both engines were demolished. The freight locomotive never left the tracks. The passenger engine derailed but remained upright. Because the collision occurred on a fairly sharp curve, neither engineer saw the other until they were only yards apart.

Unfortunately, the tender (coal car) of the lighter passenger train No. 2 telescoped, or crashed through, the interior of the two cars behind it. Both of these coaches were carrying a number of laborers. The freight was headed downhill and the passenger train uphill when the wreck occurred. Doctors were rushed to the scene of the accident from Cowen and from Chattanooga to attend to the more seriously wounded. Some of the injured were taken back to Sherwood, where they were treated, mostly for non–life threatening injuries. Wrecking crews were sent to the scene very quickly, and by 2:30 the next morning, the tracks were clear for normal traffic.

SOURCES: *Chattanooga Daily Times,* Dec. 24, 1915; *Knoxville Journal and Tribune,* Dec. 24, 25, 1915; Robert B. Shaw, *A History of Railroad Accidents, Safety Precautions and Operating Practices* (Potsdam, NY: Clarkson College of Technology, 1978).

Dutchman's Grade Train Wreck
NASHVILLE, JULY 9, 1918

The baggage car behind her was crushed. When it was finally jacked up by the wrecking crew, thirty persons, only one of them alive, were taken from underneath. The next three cars were gouged out, shattered and tossed aside in a terrible fashion, while the last four cars remained on the rails.

—**E. B. Heineman,**
America's Greatest Rail Disaster

The worst passenger rail accident in U.S. history occurred on this date at the Dutchman's Grade, in Belle Meade, five miles west of Nashville. This event would normally have been in headlines around the world, but it was overshadowed by other world events, including the close of World War I and the nation's worst influenza pandemic.

This head-on collision, between the southbound Memphis to Atlanta Passenger Express No. 1 and a westbound local, Train No. 4, took place on a curved section of track. The curve, plus a slight grade, wooded terrain, and an overhead bridge made it virtually impossible for the engineers to see each other's train until it was too late.

The No. 1 Express normally arrived in Nashville at 7:10 AM and Train No. 4 usually left Nashville at 7:00 AM. As a general rule, they met on a double track between the Nashville Union Station and the Harding Railroad Shops, two and a half miles west of town. By written orders, the No. 1 Express always had the right-of-way; whenever it was late, No. 4 was supposed to wait on the side track until it passed. On this occasion, the Nashville bound No. 1 was about thirty minutes late and No. 4 was about seven minutes late. Coincidentally, about this same time a third train, a switch engine pulling ten freight cars, entered the picture, passing No. 4 on the double tracks, inbound for Nashville. What happened next is anybody's guess.

The Dutchmans Grade train wreck, considered the nation's worst passenger rail accident, occurred just west of Nashville on July 9, 1918. Courtesy of Tennessee State Library and Archives.

The engineer of No. 4 may have misread his orders, thinking that the smaller switch engine was the one he was supposed to wait for; or he might have become distracted and mistaken it for train No. 1. Whatever the reason, he immediately pulled his engine out onto the main track and began increasing his speed to fifty miles per hour. Meanwhile, the No. 1 Express was unknowingly racing toward him, also at fifty miles per hour.

The resulting collision demolished both locomotives and many of the other rail cars. Some coaches tele-scoped, bending, splintering, and squashing everything in their path, including passengers. No. 1 derailed to the west side of the track and No. 4 to the east side. Behind No. 1, the baggage car and the next three wooden passenger coaches were crushed and scattered around the scene. Thirty casualties were found under the baggage car alone. The last four cars of No. 1 sustained only minor damage. Five wooden passenger coaches behind No. 4 were ripped apart and derailed. The last three cars of this train were not derailed and were only slightly damaged. Fires broke out at several locations within the wreck, hampering rescue efforts and causing additional casualties and injuries.

The collision was heard for miles around, and there were a number of eyewitnesses to the event. The number of dead and injured was variously reported, but the official Interstate Commerce Commission figures were 101 killed and another 300 injured. Some of the injured undoubtedly died later, but no records to that effect have been found. Interestingly, there were even rumors that the true casualty figures were suppressed by the military since our nation was at war and most of the victims were soldiers and laborers (from as far away as Texas) en route to the munitions plant at Old Hickory, in Davidson County.

SOURCES: Allen R. Coggins, "Dutchmans Grade Railway Accident," in *The Tennessee Encyclopedia of History and Culture,* ed. Carroll Van West, 268 (Nashville: Tennessee Historical Society and Rutledge Hill Press, 1998); John Egerton, *Two Faces of Nashville 1780–1980* (Nashville: Plus Media, 1979); Webb Garrison, *Disasters That Made History* (Nashville: Abingdon Press, 1973); Edgar A. Haine, *Railroad Wrecks* (Cornwall Books, New York. 1993); Interstate Commerce Commission. *Report of the Chief of the Bureau of Safety Covering the Investigation of an Accident Which Occurred on the Nashville, Chattanooga & St. Louis Railway at Nashville, Tenn., on July 9, 1918* (Washington, DC: Interstate Commerce Commission, 1918); Owen Meredith, *History of the American Red Cross in Nashville* (Washington, DC: American Red Cross, 1982); Jay Robert Nash, *Darkest Hours* (Chicago: Nelson-Hall, 1976); *Washington Post,* July 10, 1918.

Glen Mary Train Wreck

SCOTT COUNTY, NOVEMBER 11, 1929

The track and ties were torn up for several hundred yards. Phone poles were broken off like match stems and the hundreds of tons of steel and human freight were thrown into a tangled mass.

—*Knoxville News-Sentinel,* **Nov. 11, 1929**

Five people were killed and seventy-five injured when the Ponce de Leon, a so-called Crack Southern Train derailed at 1:20 am on November 11, 1929. It was en route from Jacksonville, Florida, to Cincinnati, Ohio, and was only slightly behind schedule. The wreck occurred about a mile south of Glen Mary (Glenmary), right at the Morgan County and Scott County line and about twenty-five miles south of the Kentucky border. The train consisted of an engine, baggage car, express car, a mail car, three Pullmans (sleeper cars), and five coaches. It was said to have been moving about forty miles an hour as it sped down a steep grade and around a sharp curve in a very rugged section of southwest Scott County. After leaving the track, the engine plowed some six feet into the rocky and muddy terrain and was bent at a near perfect ninety-degree angle from the impact. It came to rest some 500 feet from the point at which it left the tracks.

Both the engineer and fireman were killed instantly. The other cars, except for three rear Pullmans, piled up behind the engine parallel to the tracks. The engine and nine cars derailed and were scattered along the edge of a muddy field. Three of the coaches ended up in a triangle, situated end to end, with each crushed into the next. Cars were on their sides or upside down. The mail car and one other were crammed into an almost unrecognizable mass. Three of the cars remained on the track, leading investigators to believe that excess speed was not a factor in the crash. Several hundred yards of track was damaged or demolished, and some passengers were thrown from one end of their cars to the other. Many victims suffered severe injuries, while others sustained only minor cuts and bruises. Several hundred workers labored for hours with torches, wrecking bars, and brute force to clear the debris and recover the dead and severely injured. The accident occurred on a double track, and normal traffic was resumed on the other track by 4:00 AM. A special train with doctors and nurses was rushed 120 miles north from Chattanooga to the scene of the accident. Another was sent south from Somerset, Kentucky, and both transported the dead and injured back to their respective cities. A Michigan man with a broken ankle miraculously saved other lives by using a flashlight to flag down two other trains as they approached the site of the accident. One was behind the Ponce de Leon wreckage, on the northbound track, and the second was heading south on the other track.

According to Southern Railroad officials, the wreck was not caused by faulty tracks, rain, or speed. It was most likely caused by an obstacle falling from or hanging off of one of the coaches.

SOURCES: *Knoxville Journal,* Nov. 12, 13, 1929; *Knoxville News-Sentinel,* Nov. 11, 12, 1929; Jan. 25, 1931.

Helenwood Train Wreck
SCOTT COUNTY, JANUARY 24, 1931

Two of the victims, both women, were thrown through a window, and ended up beneath the wreck. Their bodies were mangled beyond recognition and they were identified only by the length of their hair and their jewelry.
—*Knoxville Journal,* Jan. 25, 1931

Just before 1:00 PM on January 24, 1931, passenger train No. 5, the *Suwanee Special,* derailed, killing three passengers and two crewmen. Another forty were injured, some seriously. The wreck occurred along the famous Chicago-to-Florida Queen and Crescent Route of the Southern Railway, just south of Helenwood in central Scott County.

According to an Interstate Commerce Commission investigation team, the train was traveling at about sixty miles per hour, an excessive speed along this stretch of tracks, and derailed as it came out of an S-curve. The engineer was behind schedule and was most likely trying to make up the time between Cincinnati and Chattanooga. However, one of the railroad inspectors indicated that he thought the wreck could have been caused by some sort of mechanical failure, since trains run fast along that stretch of track all the time, and the rails seemed to have been in excellent condition.

The engine and tender left the tracks, plunged into, and slid along a rock embankment to the right. It was severely crushed and partially buried in mud. The other nine cars also derailed but remained more or less on the roadbed, almost in a straight line. The second and third cars came to rest about a thousand feet beyond the engine, one upright and the other on its side. The dining car and four Pullman cars were overturned and damaged; a few cars also slid some distance down the railroad bed. The rail cars constructed of wood were torn up worse than the metal ones. Some passengers were also trapped in their seats in the seventh car, which had struck the engine and was damaged on its right side. The last two cars remained upright and were only slightly damaged. The rails were damaged and were later replaced or reset for a distance of some 500 yards along the line of wrecked cars.

The crash was said to have been heard about a mile and a quarter away at Helenwood. Crowds of curious people began gathering at the scene, where they heard the cries and agonizing pleas of the injured. Some provided what aid they could, while others simply watched the drama as it unfolded. Local Red Cross volunteers responded to the scene fairly quickly, as did practically every doctor in Scott County.

The engineer was killed when his forehead was struck by or impaled on the throttle and the fireman was scalded to death and badly mangled. Both were trapped in the engine and covered by coal from the tender. The engineer was still alive when other victims of the wreck discovered him. Unfortunately, he died before they could dig him out. The fireman had most likely died on impact or shortly thereafter.

The *Knoxville News-Sentinel* stated that twenty-one of the injured were taken to hospitals in Chattanooga by a special train that had brought doctors and nurses to the area. Those with lesser injuries were taken to Rockwood, Tennessee, and Somerset, Kentucky, hospitals.

SOURCES: Interstate Commerce Commission, Bureau of Safety, *Summary of Accident Investigation Reports, No. 47. January, February, and March 1931* (Washington, DC: U.S. Government Printing Office, 1931); *Knoxville Journal,* Jan. 25, 1931; *Knoxville News-Sentinel,* Jan. 25, 26, 1931; H. Clay. Smith, *Dusty Bits of the Forgotten Past—A History of Scott County* (Nashville: Williams Printing Co., 1985).

Waverly Train Wreck

HUMPHREYS COUNTY, MARCH 15, 1942

A westbound freight train crashed head-on with an eastbound passenger train at 4:25 AM on March 15, 1942, near Denver, about eight miles southwest of Waverly and seventy-four miles west of Nashville. Miraculously, only five crewmen were killed and one other critically injured in the collision. The wreck occurred on the North Carolina and St. Louis Railroad. The trains collided near the middle of a two-mile-long curve, beside a fifty-foot-high bluff of the mile-long Denver Hill. At the top of the bluff, U.S. Highway 70 parallels the tracks, and below is a deep gulf into which some of the wrecked cars tumbled.

The freight train, hauling thirty cars, left Nashville at 12:40 AM en route to Memphis. The express passenger train, pulling nine passenger and mail cars plus the locomotive and tender, left Memphis at 11:30 PM and was bound for Nashville. The accident occurred as a result of the passenger train failing to receive its operational orders. Had they been received and obeyed, the passenger train would have reached Denver first and pulled to a side track, yielding to the freight train, which had orders to proceed.

Ironically, a father and son, A. C. Hargrove Sr. and Jr., were killed in the crash. One was the fireman on the freight and the other a fireman on the passenger train. The engineer on the freight train, A. H. Loudermilk, and an apprentice fireman on the passenger train, Henderson Edmondson were also killed. The engineer of the passenger train, W. C. Ferguson, suffered multiple injuries and had to have a leg amputated. The other injured crewman, S. W. Patterson, a brakeman, was badly scalded over his entire body. Robert Hargrove, father and grandfather to the two firemen who died in the crash, came to the scene just as his grandson was pulled from the wreckage, but it took hours for his son to be extricated.

The trains were moving about fifty miles an hour when they collided, and according to witnesses, they hit their brakes only in the last few seconds before the collision. If either engineer saw the lights of the other train, he probably thought they were automobile lights along U.S. Highway 70, which parallels the tracks at this point. Both locomotives reared upward, exploded, and fused in a gnarled and tangled mass of steel before tumbling over into the Trace Creek Gulf. The sound of the collision was audible five miles away and was described as a thunderous roar. Some of the cars behind the engines, including the tender, mail, freight, and passenger cars, crisscrossed the tracks behind them. Fortunately, in crushing together, these cars shielded the passenger cars that were still farther back, and they never left the tracks. The two steel mail cars left the tracks and slid down on top of the other derailed cars already in the gorge. Fortunately, they did not turn over. Two men, sorting mail in these cars, were shaken up but not injured.

Not a single one of the regular sixty paying passengers on the eastbound train was hurt. Some minor injuries were sustained by several railroad employees returning from, ironically, a Saturday night safety-first rally in Bruceton. These veteran trainmen said that it was a miracle that no one else died, or was even seriously

Head-on collision of two trains near Denver, Humphreys County, March 15, 1942. Courtesy of Tennessee State Library and Archives.

injured in the wreck. Had it occurred some 100 yards farther down the track, some of the cars would surely have fallen into the then-flooded Trace Creek, and many casualties would have occurred.

When the trains collided and heaved high above the tracks, they knocked out telephone and telegraph service to stations east and west. However, some of the railroaders set out flares on both ends of the wreck to stop any additional oncoming trains, and others flagged down vehicles on Highway 70 and asked them to report the accident via the first telephone they came to. By midday, a Greyhound bus had arrived to take the remaining passengers back to Union Station in Nashville.

SOURCES: *Memphis Commercial Appeal,* Mar. 16, 1942; *Nashville Banner,* Mar. 16, 1942; *Nashville Tennessean,* Mar. 15, 16, 1942.

High Cliff Train Wreck
NEAR JELLICO (CAMPBELL COUNTY), JULY 6, 1944

Me and my buddy tossed a coin to see who got the top bunk. My buddy was killed. He got pipes run through him. A train wreck wraps those pipes and things around you like a piece of string.

—**High Cliff train wreck survivor**

A southbound Louisville-Nashville passenger train designated as "Troop Train Number 47" derailed at around 9:00 PM on July 6, 1944. This incident killed thirty-four and injured at least another hundred. The wreck occurred near the mountain community of High Cliff, about three miles east of Jellico and south of the Tennessee-Kentucky state line. The exact location of the derailment was at the northern entrance to a mountain pass known as the "Jellico Narrows." After emerging from that gorge and a long straight stretch of track, the train entered a curve where the locomotive and four cars plunged into the deep gorge of Clear Fork Creek, some fifty feet below. Four additional cars derailed but did not fall into the stream.

Fortunately, the stream in which cars landed was shallow: only two to four feet deep at the time. Also, because a fifty-yard section of track was torn up by the derailment, the forward motion of the remaining coaches was stopped. The locomotive and cars that had fallen into the boulder-strewn gorge were piled atop, beside, and beneath one another. The engine telescoped into the first Pullman (passenger) coach, splitting it in two. The second crushed or buckled behind it, and a third lay crosswise of the wreckage. The engine exploded upon impact, crushing or scalding many of the victims in some of the forward coaches, as well as the engineer, who was trapped and killed instantly beneath the wreck. The engine was lying on its side in four feet of water. One of

Steam engine of Troop Train 47 and four passenger cars in Clear Fork Creek near High Cliff, Campbell County, July 7, 1944. Photograph by Homer W. Anderson Sr. Courtesy of McClung Historical Collection, Historical Photograph Copy Project, Knox County Public Library.

the two coaches still situated on the track, closest to the one hanging off the cliff, was standing on end. It, along with the kitchen-baggage car in front of it, had caught fire. They burned and smoldered for hours, shedding an eerie light over the scene of the disaster.

This has been described as one of the nation's major troop train accidents, and as one of the top twenty-five U.S. railway accidents of all times. However, the train was not transporting troops but rather recent military inductees en route from Virginia to Camp Croft, South Carolina.

The first doctors, nurses, and ambulances arrived at the scene within two hours. Rescue and firefighting crews, along with other medical responders, continued to arrive through the night. They came from Jellico and LaFollette and then from Knoxville, Oak Ridge, and even Corbin and Middlesboro, Kentucky. However, the officers and young men in the train cars that did not derail, as well as those who survived the plunge into the gorge, had already climbed down the steep bluff to assist the injured and remove the dead and dying from the wreckage. The screams, groans, and cries of agony of the injured echoed through the gorge that night. Orders were barked by officers and others who took change. Everywhere was the sound of hammering, the prying of metal, and shouts for assistance. At first, only hand tools such as automobile jacks and crowbars were available to remove the wood and twisted steel that held so many of

Opposite view of Troop Train 47. Photograph by Ed Westcott. Courtesy of David Ray Smith.

the victims captive. Later, torches were brought in to cut the cars apart. By the third day, railroad cranes began pulling the remaining wreckage from the gorge.

Locals also helped to extricate those still trapped in the coaches. They brought what medical supplies they had, took victims into their homes, fed them, and allowed them to bathe and sleep after their horrible ordeals. Because of the steepness of the gorge, the injured had to be hoisted up to the tracks by improvised pulleys. From there they were carried to awaiting cars and later ambulances for transport to medical facilities in Jellico, La-Follette, Corbin, and other nearby cities and towns.

Many were pinned in the cars and several bodies were burned beyond recognition. Some were crushed and broken, bleeding, and severely scarred from the wreck. Mangled steel held some of the injured in horribly awkward positions, a number survived for hours and died after being freed. One victim was said to be trapped in a sixteen-inch space unable to move anything but one arm. Near him were several dead and dying victims that could not be removed until the steel cables and rods encasing their bodies could be cut away with hacksaws or torches. Another victim that survived the trauma said that one of his buddies was hanging in the air, pinned by his head, left arm, and left foot and that they could not get him loose.

Local Red Cross chapters set up feeding stations to serve both victims and emergency workers. Local Boy Scout groups launched a door-to-door campaign to gather clothes and other necessities for the victims who had lost most or all their belongings. Since the wreck occurred at night, many of the men had retired for the evening and were in their underwear when the wreck occurred.

As the fireman on the ill-fated train crew lay dying in the Jellico Hospital, a friend asked him what happened. He replied, "She jumped the tracks." The exact cause of the wreck was never confirmed, but there has been much speculation. It was suggested that the train was

behind schedule and was simply moving too fast to make the turn. The curve on which the wreck occurred was only an eleven-degree arc, yet it was said to be the worst curve on the entire L&N track. There were rumors that the engineer was drunk. Some suggested that excessive speed, along with a damaged axle, had caused instability leading to the derailment. And, of course, there was the espionage theory.

Because the wreck occurred near the top secret wartime Oak Ridge area, there was immediate suspicion of espionage, so military officials soon arrived to take command of the scene. There was a news blackout, and the press and photographers were held at bay. No one was allowed to stop on the highway above the wreck, and everyone entering the area was scrutinized. Railroad, military, and FBI officials quickly ruled out espionage, blaming the crash on excessive speed.

In his book *She Jumped the Tracks,* John P. Ascher suggested that all the facts surrounding the incident were never revealed. He also wrote that not all the dead were accounted for, and there may have been as many as forty-four additional casualties. An official report by the Interstate Commerce Commission, after a thorough investigation, stated that the accident was caused by excessive speed on an off-gauge track.

A monument at Jellico lists the names of the thirty-four victims of this tragedy. Only twenty-five of the dead could be identified, the others mangled or burned beyond recognition. Some victims suffered minor injuries, while about ninety were taken to area hospitals. A few of the recruits were dismissed from military service, having paid a price even before attending boot camp. The able-bodied eventually reached their induction center in South Carolina.

SOURCES: John P. Ascher, *She Jumped the Tracks: America's Tragic Stateside 20th Century Military Disaster* (Farragut, TN: M.J.A., Inc., 1994); *Clinton Courier News,* Mar. 26, 1981; Edgar A. Haine, *Railroad Wrecks* (New York: Cornwall Books, 1993); *Knoxville Journal,* July 7, 8, 1944; *Knoxville News-Sentinel,* July 5, 1994; *LaFollette Press,* July 4, 1985; *New York Times,* July 7–9, 1944; *Press Enterprise,* July 6, 1994; David Ray Smith, "1944 Troop Train Wreck," reprinted in "Historically Speaking" column, *Oak Ridger* (Oak Ridge, TN), May 22–Sept. 24, 2007.

RIVERBOAT ACCIDENTS

Most of the serious transportation accidents in Tennessee between the 1830s and 1860s involved steam-powered riverboats. Both side-wheelers and stern-wheelers plied the waters of the Mississippi, Tennessee, and Cumberland rivers and their major tributaries. Navigability and access to some ports changed with the seasons. In the dryer months it was limited, and even stretches of the major rivers were perilous and impassable due to shallow water or obstructions. In times of high water, during spring and fall floods, riverboats were able to gain access to upstream towns and smaller river ports and conduct commerce, albeit quickly, before water levels dropped, leaving boats stranded until the next flood. Sometimes, when streams were flooded, riverboats could not get under bridges. At other times, the floods were so severe that bridges presented no obstacles. For instance, in March 1847, the Cumberland River rose fifteen feet above its normal stage at Nashville. This high water allowed a steamboat to avoid the Gallatin Pike bridge in East Nashville by simply floating around it. During the flood of 1867, the steamboat *Cherokee* maneuvered up Chattanooga's Market Street to Fifth Street before the mayor put an end to such antics. Many feared that the wakes of big boats would further damage the already inundated buildings. Although such floods caused much damage, they were often of economic advantage to the riverboat companies.

Tennessee streams could be treacherous, with swift currents, hidden sandbars, and rocky shoals, and large sunken logs or stumps called snags could puncture or shatter the hull of a boat. Other submerged and floating debris and additional navigational perils were also pres-

ent during times of low, normal, and even high stream levels. The steam engines, especially the boilers, were often poorly designed, crudely constructed, shoddily maintained, and stressed beyond their capacity, hauling too much cargo and too many passengers against relentless currents.

During these rough and tumble times, there were often impromptu steamboat races along the Mississippi, Tennessee, and Cumberland rivers. When two boats found themselves traveling the same stretch of river in the same direction, the captains of the vessels often found it difficult to resist a good race, for fun and profit. This was great sport, usually to the delight of the passengers and crews of both boats, and the reputation of the boats and their skippers were at stake. Unfortunately, these infamous and competitive events sometimes ended in tragedy as a result of boiler explosions, fires, and other catastrophes. Considering these races and other hazardous conditions, it is not surprising that the average life expectancy of a riverboat in the mid-1800s was, according to James T. Lloyd's *Steamboat Directory and Disasters on Western Waters* (1856), between three and five years. Even so, steamboat companies profited greatly from the commerce along Tennessee's river systems.

Besides the disasters caused by stressing boilers to the point of explosions during races, many riverboats have been torn apart by exploding boilers and/or engulfed by flames while attempting to move excessive freight and human cargo against extreme currents. Because the early riverboats were constructed of wood and often carried great quantities of combustible cargo on their decks or in their bays, the potential for fire was always present. These early boats were also fueled by wood, which was usually stacked near the boilers. In such an environment, onboard fires were common and usually devastating. Once the fires ignited, there was little the crews could do but push the burning material overboard or head for shore to unload passengers and watch the boat and cargo go up in flames.

Between 1831 and 1833, of 234 riverboats operating on the Mississippi, Tennessee, and Cumberland rivers and their major tributaries, most were destroyed by explosions and/or fires. Twenty-four were sunk after hitting snags that ripped through their hulls. Five were sunk as the result of collisions with other boats, bridges, or miscellaneous obstructions along swift or narrow channels. Seven were lost to ice floes, and others were wrecked in storms or capsized. One was even reported to be sunk by a tornado. Sometimes passengers and crews survived the wrecks and only cargo was lost, but death and serious injuries were nonetheless common.

SOURCES: James T. Lloyd, *Lloyd's Steamboat Directory and Disasters on Western Waters* (Cincinnati: J. T. Lloyd & Co., 1856); Tennessee Valley Authority, *A History of Navigation on the Tennessee River System* (Washington, DC: U.S. Government Printing Office, 1937).

Helen McGregor Riverboat Disaster
MISSISSIPPI RIVER, MEMPHIS, FEBRUARY 24, 1830

Amid the smoke and dust were to be seen, at the same moment, the death struggle and spouting blood of those who had received their wounds; while the shrieks of the wounded and the dying were mingled with the general confusion.

—*Memphis Advocate,* **Feb. 26, 1830**

About thirty minutes after arriving at the port of Memphis on the cold winter morning of February 24, 1830,

one or more of the steamer *Helen McGregor*'s boilers exploded suddenly, killing and injuring many people on the decks, gangplank, and adjacent wharf. One of the boilers was thrown overboard, the smoke stacks collapsed, and the other boilers were dislodged. The boiler deck, engineer's room, and adjacent offices were literally ripped apart by the blast. Although the steamer sank, those within the cabins were believed to have been uninjured. Local citizens, as well as doctors and nurses, quickly rushed to the scene to render assistance to the injured and dying.

At the time of its occurrence, this was believed to be the worst Mississippi riverboat accident ever to occur. Although there were an estimated 410 passengers onboard or in the vicinity of the boat, no accurate accounting of the number of casualties was determined because the accident happened at a time when many people were boarding or going ashore. Even an accurate passenger list would not have helped ascertain the number of people affected by the disaster. Some were blown into the water, their bodies never recovered. Rough estimates of the number killed ranged between thirty and sixty.

The number injured probably exceeded twenty-five. Among the injured were the skipper (Captain Tyson), a pilot, an engineer, and at least one crewman. It is believed that some of the injured later died of burns or other wounds sustained in the explosion or from the scalding water that erupted from the boilers. The *Helen McGregor* (aka *Macgregor*) was a 400-ton paddle steamer constructed in 1823.

SOURCES: Louis C. Hunter, *Steamboats on the Western Rivers: An Economic and Technological History* (Cambridge, MA: Harvard Univ. Press, 1949); James T. Lloyd, *Lloyd's Steamboat Directory and Disasters on Western Waters* (Cincinnati: J. T. Lloyd & Co., 1856); *Memphis Advocate,* Feb. 26, 1830; Jay Robert Nash, *Darkest Hours* (Chicago: Nelson-Hall, 1976).

Brandywine Riverboat Disaster

MISSISSIPPI RIVER, NORTH OF MEMPHIS, APRIL 9, 1832

It appears, too, that the *Brandywine* was racing with the steamboat *Hudson* at the time the fire broke out; and that, for the purpose of producing more intense heat, and thus accelerating the boat's speed, a large quantity of rosin had been thrown into the furnaces. This fatal ruse was resorted to because the *Brandywine* had been compelled to stop and make some repairs, and the *Hudson* in the meantime, had gained considerable headway.

—**James T. Lloyd,**
Lloyd's Steamboat Directory

About 7:00 PM on this date, the riverboat *Brandywine* was plying the waters of the Mississippi, about thirty miles north of Memphis near Randolph, in Shelby County. A 483-ton stern-wheeler riverboat constructed in 1829, the boat was en route to Louisville, Kentucky, and, it is believed, in a race with another riverboat, the *Hudson*. The *Brandywine* had fallen back to make repairs earlier, and the skipper, Captain Hamilton, was probably pushing the boat to make up time. It was common practice in those days to throw pitch, or pine rosin, into a ship's firebox to increase heat, thereby producing more steam and hence a faster speed. The captain was probably anxious to catch up with and pass the *Hudson,* for in those days rivalries were in vogue, reputations were at stake, and large wagers were often made on impromptu yet extremely hazardous riverboat races.

The *Brandywine* carried an estimated 230-plus passengers and crew and was heavily laden with cargo. Included in the cargo were a number of carriage wheels that had been wrapped in straw for protection and stored on the boiler deck, under the hurricane roof near the officers' quarters. The wind was brisk that night and soon some glowing cinders, believed to be from the smoke stack, found their way into the straw casings and started a fire.

By the time the pilot and crew noticed the fire and spread the alarm, the straw around the wheels was burning fiercely. The crew quickly swung into action, trying to extinguish the flames and throw the straw and wheels overboard. As they did, however, the wind spread sparks back into the other bales, which began to ignite other flammable items. Within five minutes nearly the entire ship was in flames.

As the crew tried to launch the only lifeboat (a yawl) onboard, it turned over and sank. Although the yawl could have saved some of the passengers, it was very small and would have had to make many trips to the shore and back to save them all. Since the shore lay some distance away, it would have taken considerable time to reach it; time was not an option at that point.

As the smoke and flames intensified, panicky passengers began jumping overboard in desperation. It was said the crew stayed until the last minute, trying to help the passengers. Some swam toward shore or sandbars, and others grasped for anything buoyant enough to keep them afloat. The captain also attempted to run the *Brandywine* ashore but ran onto a sandbar. There the steamer burned to the waterline, about a quarter mile from the riverbank on the Tennessee side.

If a passenger list existed, it did not survive, so no one knows for sure how many passengers and crew members were onboard. However, the death toll was high. Estimates of the number drowned or burned to death in the initial accident range between 135 and 175. Most of the estimated 75 initial survivors were seriously burned or otherwise injured, and many of them probably perished later as a result of trauma.

SOURCES: Louis C. Hunter, *Steamboats on the Western Rivers: An Economic and Technological History* (Cambridge, MA: Harvard Univ. Press, 1949); James T. Lloyd, *Lloyd's Steamboat Directory and Disasters on Western Waters* (Cincinnati: J. T. Lloyd & Co., 1856); Jay Robert Nash, *Darkest Hours* (Chicago: Nelson-Hall, 1976).

Belle of Clarksville Riverboat Disaster
MISSISSIPPI RIVER, MEMPHIS, DECEMBER 14, 1844

Mr. J. H. French, one of the passengers, had with him three negro slaves, and three valuable horses, among them the celebrated Ann Hayes; these slaves and horses were all drowned. The iron safe containing $12,000 was saved.

—James T. Lloyd,
Lloyd's Steamboat Directory

On December 14, 1844, the riverboat *Belle of Clarksville* was moving north up the Mississippi to the Ohio and Cumberland rivers, bound for Nashville. Another boat, the *Louisiana,* was southbound for New Orleans. Both riverboats were heavily overloaded with passengers and cargo. The *Belle* was transporting stores of sugar, salt, coffee, and molasses. Both boats were in their proper (traditional) positions to pass one another (the *Belle,* the ascending boat, was hugging the bar and the *Louisiana,* the descending boat, was running the bend). Unfortunately, the *Belle* hit shallow water and was deflected into the path of the *Louisiana.* The steamers collided near the old river hamlet of Old Town, not far from Memphis. Although the *Belle* was demolished, the cabin somehow stayed intact. The hull separated and sank almost immediately, tossing many of the passengers, crew, and cargo from the deck into the frigid water. The cabin, still afloat, grounded about a half mile downstream, and all the passengers and crewmembers within it miraculously survived. The *Louisiana* was relatively undamaged and immediately turned about to take on survivors from the water and the cabin. Between thirty-three and thirty-six people are believed to have died in the incident, most of them deckhands.

SOURCES: Josephus Conn Guild, *Old Times in Tennessee, with Historical, Personal, and Political Scraps and Sketches* (Nashville: Tavel, Eastman and Howell, 1878); Louis C. Hunter, *Steamboats on the Western Rivers: An Economic and Technological History* (Cambridge, MA: Harvard Univ. Press, 1949); James T. Lloyd, *Lloyd's Steamboat Directory and Disasters on Western Waters* (Cincinnati: J. T. Lloyd & Co., 1856); Jay Robert Nash, *Darkest Hours* (Chicago: Nelson-Hall, 1976); *Nashville Republican Banner,* Dec. 16, 1844.

Sultana Riverboat Disaster
MISSISSIPPI RIVER, NORTH OF MEMPHIS, APRIL 27, 1865

The boat . . . had burst one of her boilers and almost immediately caught fire, for the fragments of the boiler had cut the cabin and the hurricane deck in two and the splintered pieces had fallen, many of them, back upon the burning coal fires that were now exposed. The light, dry wood of the cabins burned like tinder and it was but a short time ere the boat was wrapped in flames.

—Chester D. Berry, *Loss of the* Sultana

At 2:00 AM on April 27, 1865, the trusty side-wheeler riverboat *Sultana* was struggling against the surging current of the Mississippi River eight miles north of Memphis. It was rainy and chilly and the boat was grossly overloaded. Suddenly, one of the leaking boilers exploded, triggering the worst inland marine disaster in U.S. history. The sound of the explosion was said to have been heard in Memphis.

The initial impact ripped the vessel in half, igniting flames, releasing scalding steam, and instantly killing or mortally wounding hundreds of sleeping passengers as well as a number of stock animals. Within seconds, bodies and body parts, along with metal pieces from boilers, splintered wood, and other debris began raining down

Riverboat Sultana on fire, April 27, 1865. Courtesy of Special Collections, University of Memphis Libraries.

onto the boat and into the frigid water. As the flames spread, those who survived the initial explosion began jumping overboard, thinking they were near the shore. Unfortunately, the river was flooded and the *Sultana* was near mid-channel, four and a half miles from either bank. Because there were no lifeboats onboard and little in the way of safety equipment, panicky passengers resorted to ripping wooden planks and any other buoyant objects from the boat before jumping into the dark and icy water. Meanwhile, the flames cast an eerie glow into the night and onto the mass of live and dead humanity thrashing or bobbing about the sinking boat. Both chaos and panic must have ensued as those in the water either tried to help one another or competed for handholds on every available piece of floating debris.

The first rescue craft, the *Bostonia No. 2,* was an hour and a half away when the crew spotted the glow of the *Sultana* pyre in the night sky. As it approached the scene, the crew of the *Bostonia* began throwing bales of hay and anything else that would float to the struggling survivors. As dawn approached, other craft arrived, and more victims were transported to shelters and hospitals in Memphis. The dead were also retrieved from the water, and many were later buried in mass graves in Memphis.

The wooden-hulled, 260-foot-long *Sultana,* valued at $90,000, was licensed to carry only 376 passengers and crew. However, on this occasion the steamer may have been carrying as many as 2,685 people. Exact figures were never established and are still controversial, but it is known that there was an economic reason for such a large number of people on this boat: the federal government was paying five dollars per prisoner for their final passage. Most of those onboard were Union war prisoners from Andersonville, Georgia, and Cahaba,

Alabama, homeward bound after the Civil War. Many of them were East Tennesseans from Blount, Claiborne, Hancock, Knox, Sevier, and Union counties. Estimates of the dead ranged between 1,700 and 2,100, exact figures vary. Ironically, only four battles of the Civil War produced casualty figures higher than the number lost on the *Sultana*. In fact, its death toll may have exceeded by as much as 300 that of the ill-fated *Titanic* ocean liner that sank in the North Atlantic in 1912.

The *Sultana* incident has remained a relatively obscure disaster for several reasons. First of all, the disaster occurred at the end of the Civil War, a very busy news period. Second, it was considered more of a civilian incident and therefore not as noteworthy as some other incidents, including reports of the number of war dead and a looming economic panic. Third, some of the details of the incident were allegedly covered up by the War Department. And, last, it had to compete for press space with the death of President Lincoln and the capture of his assassin John Wilkes Booth. In fact, the *Sultana* was carrying news and details of Lincoln's assassination to New Orleans, Vicksburg, and Memphis on its final voyage.

A monument erected to the memory of the East Tennessee dead by the survivors of the *Sultana* disaster stands in the Mount Olive Cemetery in South Knoxville. The monument has the following inscription: "In memory of the men who were on the Sultana that was destroyed April 27, 1865, by explosion on the Mississippi River near Memphis, Tennessee."

It is a modest tribute to the many brave Tennesseans who suffered the toils of war and almost made it home.

SOURCES: Chester D. Berry, ed., *Loss of the* Sultana *and Reminiscences of Survivors* (1892; repr., Knoxville: Univ. of Tennessee Press, 2005); Fred Brown, "Remember the Sultana," *Knoxville News-Sentinel,* Apr. 21, 1996; Allen R. Coggins, "*Sultana* Disaster of 1865," in *The Tennessee Encyclopedia of History and Culture,* ed. Carroll Van West, 897 (Nashville: Tennessee Historical Society and Rutledge Hill Press, 1998); Sue Marine, "Journey of Death," *Smoky Mountain Historical Society Newsletter* 11, no. 3 (Autumn 1985): 64–75; Gene Eric Salecker, *Disaster on the Mississippi: The* Sultana *Explosion, April 27, 1965* (Annapolis, MD: Naval Institute Press, 1996); Wilson M. Yager, "The *Sultana* Disaster," *Tennessee Historical Quarterly* 35 (Fall 1976): 306–25.

Silver Spray Riverboat Disaster
PACIFIC PLACE, LAUDERDALE COUNTY, AUGUST 1, 1870

> By this time I began to see the scalded . . . Edward Long, my nephew, first came in sight; he was nearly naked and was wild from the pain . . . My clothing was soon saturated from the blood that came from Ed's bear [*sic*] flesh. He suffered terribly, and when the *City of Cairo* came up I, too, was about exhausted. They soon had Ed wrapped in cotton and oil . . . and they put back to Memphis, where Ed died, soon after he got to the hospital.
>
> —**Jos. Legler, steward on the *Silver Spray***

About midnight on August 1, 1870, the stern-wheel riverboat *Silver Spray* was towing a barge up the Mississippi from New Orleans to Cincinnati. The boat was about thirty miles north of Memphis near the old river port of Pacific Place, Lauderdale County, when the boilers exploded. Although the exact cause of the explosion was not determined, the engineer, who survived the disaster, was quoted in the August 6 *New York Times* as stating that "the mud might have clogged a connecting pipe between the boilers, and thus kept out the supply for one boiler. Then, when by some lurch or other cause the mud loosened, the water would rush into the empty boiler and produce an explosion." In any event, the boat was quickly enveloped in flames. A number of passengers and crew were killed or seriously injured in the initial explosion and fire. Some drowned, while others managed to swim some 300 yards to the nearest shore.

Darkness made it impossible to help the more critically injured, and it was two hours before another steamboat happened along.

Meanwhile, the remains of the *Silver Spray* and its barge floated back downstream, lodging on a bar and burning to the water line. The Steamboat *City of Cairo* was headed upstream to St. Louis when the crew encountered the wreck. They stopped to take on the survivors and recover as many bodies as could be found on the river in the darkness. News of the demise of the *Silver Spray* spread through the city of Memphis, and citizens rallied to the aid of the victims. The mayor ordered that those in need of medical care be taken by ambulance to city hospitals. The survivors had lost everything but were provided essentials such as clothing by the crew and officers of the *City of Cairo* and by the citizens of Memphis. The dead were held until their bodies could be claimed. Besides its cargo of some 300 crates of Queensware (tableware), human cargo consisted of the crew and cabin passengers, many of whom died in the accident. Since the vessel's record books were destroyed, the exact number of individuals who perished, or died later of injuries, was impossible to determine. However, the boat's records clerk, a survivor himself, estimated that about twenty-six people were probably lost in the *Silver Spray* disaster.

SOURCES: *New York Times,* Aug. 2, 6, 1870.

Crescent City Towboat Disaster

MISSISSIPPI RIVER, SOUTH OF MEMPHIS, MARCH 24, 1874

> Shortly before the boiler blew up, the first engineers says "He was aft at the time . . . [and was] knocked down by the explosion . . . On regaining his feet he started forward, but was stopped by the steam. A moment afterward he found himself standing in the water,

and, realizing his danger, he ran up stairs, closely followed by the water."

> —*Nashville Union and American,*
> **Mar. 26, 1874**

The towboat *Crescent City* was bound for St. Louis from New Orleans when its boiler exploded at Montezuma Island about ten miles downstream from Memphis. Although the reported numbers vary between five and sixteen, at least a dozen were killed and several injured in the incident. The accident occurred about 8:30 AM, causing the *Crescent City* to literally disintegrate. It caught fire and sank in only three minutes, midstream and in relatively shallow water.

The survivors climbed onto a portion of the roof and huddled there until the riverboat *Phil Allen* arrived only minutes after the explosion and transported them to Memphis. The Mississippi River and its tributaries were well above flood stage when the incident occurred; hence, the currents were swift and the bodies of the dead, with the exception of one, were never recovered. The partial remains of one crew member, believed to be Jno (Jonathan or John) Strauder, were taken with the survivors to St. Louis aboard the Steamer *City of Vicksburg.*

The *Crescent City* was towing five freight barges loaded with 600 tons of sugar, 500 tons of coal, and 200 tons of Queensware (porcelain plates bowls, saucers, cups, etc.) and was assisted by a tailing boat when the explosion occurred. All seven vessels were destroyed and sank with the cargo. The *Crescent City* was owned by the Mississippi Transportation Company and was valued at $70,000. The total economic losses in the incident were estimated at $300,000.

SOURCES: *Atlanta Constitution,* Mar. 25, 1874; *Nashville Union and American,* Mar. 25, 26, 1874; *New York Times,* Mar. 26, 1874.

Golden City **Riverboat Disaster**
MEMPHIS, MARCH 30, 1882

The Coroner's jury, which had been holding an inquest on the body of the woman found floating in the water near the wreck of the steamer *Golden City,* returned a verdict this afternoon to the effect that "the woman came to her death by violent means, to wit, by inhaling flaming fire on the steamer *Golden City* on Monday, March 30."

—*New York Times,* **Apr. 2, 1882**

As the Southern Transportation Company's *Golden City* packet approached the Anchor Line wharf at Memphis, around 4:30 AM on March 30, 1882, the captain (McIntyre) signaled the intent to dock. Suddenly, the fire alarm was sounded.

Walking along the deck of the boat to awaken the deck crew, the captain of the watch was carrying a lantern. Somehow a spark from his lamp is believed to have accidently ignited a pile of very flammable jute rope. The fire spread rapidly to stores of tar, 800 barrels of oil, and other combustibles in the deck room of the boat. It all

Steamer *Golden City* on fire, March 30, 1882. Courtesy of Special Collections, University of Memphis Libraries.

happened so quickly that there was little time to spread the alarm to the forty passengers and sixty crew members onboard.

The vessel was quickly maneuvered ashore at the foot of Beale Street. It reached the dock within four minutes, but on its way it ignited several coal barges, an ice boat, the tugboat *Oriole,* and one other vessel. Several people died as the flames spread and they attempted to escape the burning boats and barges.

The *Golden City* was able to connect to the dock with one rope, but before another could be secured, the first one caught fire, and the vessel broke loose and began drifting downstream. By this point the vessel was totally engulfed in flames, and those still onboard either died of asphyxiation or burned to death. Several passengers and crew were able to jump to one of the coal barges or into the water while the *Golden City* was still near shore. Some successfully made their escape, but others drowned. After the captain lost steerage of the boat, it continued to burn for around thirty minutes as it drifted downstream at the mercy of the Mississippi River's strong currents. The *Golden City* finally sank in deep water just above Presidents Island, three miles below Memphis and about 200 yards offshore.

The boat had left New Orleans bound for Cincinnati on March 25, carrying around 800 tons of cargo plus passengers and crew. Also onboard was the W. H. Stowe Circus, with a menagerie of exotic animals, including birds, monkeys, cats, horses, an elephant, and other beasts. The elephant was said to have been rescued by a local saloon owner who kept the beast as a curiosity for his patrons. As the fire broke out, a bear, buffalo, elephant, and three horses were able to escape by jumping overboard and swimming to shore. The other animals died in the flames or drowned as the boat sank.

Because of the great loss, this incident has also been called one of the most tragic chapters in U.S. circus history. It was said that the incident occurred so quickly and the fire spread so rapidly that all onboard, crew,

passengers, and even the circus animals, seemed paralyzed with terror, unable to scream, shriek, or yell for help as they abandoned ship or were overcome by smoke or flames. Some probably suffocated or burned in their berths, never knowing what happened. Many spectators gathered at the river's edge to watch the drama unfold, and rumors ran rampant as to the number killed, ranging from twenty to a hundred. By final count, thirty-five of the hundred persons onboard perished in the disaster. There were fifteen women and nine children onboard, and a majority of them died.

Having had no time to collect their belongings, the survivors were destitute, and because it was so early in the morning, some passengers and crew were even naked as they jumped from the burning boat. However, the citizens of Memphis came to their aid with clothing, food, lodging, and other necessities until they were able to return home or continue on to their destinations.

A coroner's inquest on April 1, 1882, returned a verdict that the *Golden City* fire had been caused by "Wash Smith, colored, Captain of the Watch." While walking upon the deck of the boat with a lamp, he had accidentally ignited a large volume of jute (rope) stored on the boat. The verdict went on to read that the jute and other flammables had been improperly stored on the boat; therefore, criminal carelessness was involved. U.S. steamboat inspectors also made inquiries into the cause of the tragedy. A grand jury eventually convicted some of the crew of the *Golden City* of criminal negligence and carelessness in the operation of their vessel. Estimates of total economic losses in the incident are unknown, but the *Golden City* itself was valued at $40,000 and insured for $30,000.

SOURCES: *Daily American Nashville,* Mar. 31, Apr. 1, 2, 4, 1882; John D. Kunzog, "Mississippi Disaster Brings Tragic End to Early Circus," *Hobby Bandwagon* 5, nos. 10–11 (Nov.–Dec. 1950): 8–10; *Memphis Daily Appeal,* Mar. 30, 31, 1882; *New York Times,* Mar. 31, Apr. 2, 1882.

M. E. Norman **Riverboat Disaster**
MEMPHIS, MAY 8, 1925

> The sinking of the oil-burning stern-wheel streamer [*M. E. Norman*] probably will go down in history as the most orderly disaster of the century. The tragedy was devoid of all the hysteria, screams, and panic that the average imagination would suggest in the sinking of a river steamer with 72 passengers aboard, a third of whom lost their lives.
>
> **—Maj. Donald H. Connolly,**
> **USACE Commander**

On May 8, 1925, the U.S. steamship *Norman* capsized and sank on the Mississippi at the south end of Josie Harris Island, just fifteen miles below Memphis about 5:00 PM. When the tragedy struck, the steamer was carrying a sightseeing tour of professional engineers, members of the American Society of Civil Engineers, along with their wives, children, and guests.

The boat had been noticeably listing, and when this was called to the attention of the captain, he attempted to bring the vessel about and head for shore. It was riding about three feet higher on one side than the other. He asked that the passengers, most of who were standing on one side of the boat, to be repositioned on the deck to help stabilize his failing vessel. Unfortunately, it was too late. As he encountered a whirlpool in midstream and attempted to turn the wheel, the rudder failed completely, and the vessel dipped deeply starboard and then rolled over. This is believed to have tossed a number of passengers overboard. Others, realizing the gravity of the situation, simply jumped into the cold, murky water. All this probably occurred in a matter of thirty seconds or so. Now, the boat was upside down in the water, and as some passengers pulled themselves back onto the bottom of the boat it continued to take water and it rolled over again, dumping everyone off. It then sank beneath the surface very quickly.

Many government and private boats quickly responded to the scene, and several individuals also walked the banks of the river, searching for survivors and the bodies of the dead at the water's edge. Twenty-three passengers and crew drowned. Some were retrieved from the water, some from shore, and the others were trapped within the boat as it sank in 54 feet of the muddy Mississippi River. The boat drifted some 500 feet downstream of where it sank and about 300 feet offshore. Attempts to raise the vessel the day after it sank were foiled by heavy winds and foul weather.

Life preservers were available, but there was not enough time for most people to put them on. In fact, the entire event, from the moment the captain failed to turn the boat toward shore until it went down, was only about five to eight minutes. Most of the lifeboats, tethered to the mother ship by ropes, could not be launched in time, so they too went under. Life preservers, wooden

Tom Lee was treated as a hero after pulling thirty-two survivors from the water after the sinking of the *M. E. Norman,* Memphis, May 8, 1925. Courtesy of Special Collections, University of Memphis Libraries.

planks, oars, and other such debris were used as flotation devices by some, but others merely swam to keep afloat, awaiting rescue by nearby vessels. Those without the strength to stay afloat eventually gave up and drowned in the strong Mississippi currents.

Survivors picked up from the water were dropped off on the nearby shore and along sandbars so that rescue craft could go back after others. Forty-two-year-old Tom Lee was moving past the *Norman* in a small Tennessee Construction Company boat when he saw it roll over and sink. He became a hero that day as he rescued thirty-two survivors, making at least four or five trips to bring ashore those still afloat. Tom Lee Park, on the Mississippi riverfront, was established in his honor in 1954.

The survivors managed to locate each other, and some, soaked to the bone, were said to have buried themselves in the warm sands along the banks of the river to keep warm. They eventually made it to signal fires along the bank to warm themselves. A two-room hut was made available to shelter the victims and was later turned into a makeshift hospital. The shoreline where the survivors gathered after the accident was about six miles from the nearest accessible roadway, so most survivors were brought back to Memphis via boat. Many military and civilian boats assisted in the search, rescue, and recovery operations.

The passenger list included some of the most prominent professional engineers in the United States, who were attending their annual conference. One of the victims, George W. Foster, was the first man to relay word of the tragedy to local authorities. After coming ashore, he walked about seven or eight miles to call the Memphis police chief, who dispatched and notified the *Commercial Appeal* with word of the incident. Within two hours of the sinking of the *Norman,* thousands of Memphis citizens were lining the docks and milling around Baptist and General Hospitals awaiting word of the passengers' and crew's fate. However, the swiftest currents on the Mississippi River lie between Cairo, Illinois, and Vicksburg, Mississippi, and even the good swimmers of the group found it difficult or impossible to fight the strong currents.

Tom Lee's memorial at his namesake park in Memphis. Photograph by Mary Johnston-Clark.

PART 3
SOCIETAL DISASTERS

LABOR WARS, STRIKES, AND ECONOMIC DISASTERS

Societal disasters are broad in scope and best understood when broken down into subcategories including long-term labor wars, short-term blue-collar workers' strikes, race wars and riots, hate crimes, assassinations, lynchings, political wars, and even bloody family feuds.

Tennessee's violent and bloody labor wars, as elsewhere in the nation, have generally involved grievances between employees and employers. These include such issues as wages and benefits, methods of compensation, hours worked per day and per week, price fixing and monopolies, job security, safety issues, and the rights of workers to organize and form unions. Labor strikes were sporadic but relatively ineffective from the end of the Civil War until the 1890s. By this time national labor unions had begun to accrue greater powers. Conflicts continued to brew between labor and management as a result of growing union activity from the 1890s to the onset of the Great Depression. With more and more people joining unions, the powers of collective bargaining became a formidable tool. The Tennessee coal mine wars of 1891 and 1892 involved the cost (including labor costs) of extracting, hauling, and processing coal. It also involved the employment of free laborers (both black and white), the use of state convicts as laborers, and the desire of miners to form or join unions for the purpose of collective bargaining. As tragic as they were, the Coal Creek Miners Wars of the 1890s eventually brought about both labor reform and prison reform in Tennessee. Under Tennessee's convict lease system, state prisoners were hired out to coal companies, large farms, and other enterprises. These private companies provided food, clothing, medical care, and secure housing for the convicts and paid the state for their services. This relieved the state from the burden of incarcerating and caring for the prisoners. Furthermore, for the first time in its history the state prison system not only became a self-sustaining agency, it actually brought revenue into the state coffers. In fact, between 1870 and 1890, the state took in over $770,000 from private enterprise for the use of convict laborers. That equates to about $16.4 million when adjusted for inflation to the year 2007. On the other hand, the system proved to be cruel, abusive, and corrupt. The use of convict labor also took jobs away from free white and black miners and gave the mine company owners and investors enormous bargaining power when it came to negotiating wages and benefits. It was obvious in that day and time that the mules used to work the mines were more valuable to the mine owners than the convicts or even the free miners. When a mule died, another had to be purchased to replace it. When a free miner died, there might be litigation and perhaps some monetary settlement involved. But when a prisoner died, he was simply replaced at no cost to the mining company or the state.

The Black Patch Wars, which took place between 1904 and 1914, involved price fixing by tobacco "trusts" and the plight of local tobacco farmers to break monopolies by forming so-called planters protective associations. In this case the farmers were not just fighting big business, but also each other, since those who did not join such cooperatives weakened the bargaining capabilities of the united farmers. Bloodshed was inevitable.

Some of the earliest textile workers' strikes occurred in Tennessee and revolved around low wages, heavy workloads, and long and arbitrary work schedules. Additionally, women received lower wages than men who were doing essentially the same tasks. Wage conflicts also arose a few years later in the Aluminum Company of America (ALCOA) strike in 1937. Workers demanded wages equal to those of other aluminum workers elsewhere in the country. ALCOA officials argued that the wage differential was due to the fact that the cost of living was less in East Tennessee than in others areas of the country and that the issue was nonnegotiable. In the end, the employees went back to work with no concessions and in the process lost about half a million dollars in wages during their two-month-long strike.

In 1908 and 1909 a number of men in and around Reelfoot Lake, in northwest Tennessee, were threatened with losing their commercial hunting and fishing rights. This menace came from a corporation that was buying up land around the lake and wanted to turn the area into a private sportsmen's preserve. In retaliation, a vigilante group known as the Night Riders of Reelfoot Lake was formed. They used every tactic at their disposal, including fear, intimidation, and even a lynching, to fight for their livelihood and their traditional way of life.

On Christmas Day in 1927, a gun battle ensued in the streets of South Pittsburg, in Marion County. The fight was between city policemen and the owners of a local stove-manufacturing plant on one side and, on the other, civilian strikers and county deputies who supported them. Although the incident lasted less than five minutes, it resulted in the death of six lawmen and the wounding of several others. In this case, the incident was more about a feud between law enforcement officials than it was about the strike. Sixty National Guardsmen were dispatched to the area by the governor to help restore order.

Early municipal transportation strikes in Tennessee did not result in unionization and improved wages, benefits, and working conditions for employees—at least not initially. The conditions under which Memphis sanitation workers toiled, even into the 1960s, were deplorable. In the words of Dr. Martin Luther King Jr., the Memphis sanitation strike was not so much a matter of equal rights as it was of human rights. However, the strike came to rapid fruition after the assassination of King on April 4, 1968. His death ironically ended that strike and at the same time set the stage for a civil rights revolution across the nation. Following a deadlocked Memphis firefighters strike a decade later, both the city and the firemen received some but not all of the concessions they wanted after giving in to federal mediation. Still, it all came at a very steep price. Within a forty-eight-hour period, an estimated 225 fires were intentionally ignited during the strike by firefighters and their sympathizers. When it was all over, the city, many private property owners, and their insurance companies were left with a bill estimated at between five and six million dollars.

Economic Panic of 1857–58

STATEWIDE AND NATIONWIDE

Tennessee has usually led the South in iron production during the first half of the nineteenth century, but financial difficulties brought about as a result of the conditions that led to the Panic of 1857 and the monumental technological changes that led to the New Age of Steel effectively doomed the charcoal iron industry of the Volunteer State.

—**Michael T. Gavin, "Iron Industry"**

As with other economic panics, the root causes of this event in 1857 are still being debated by economists and scholars. Opinions on the matter have been numerous and varied. The panic probably began as a downturn in the U.S. economy in the wake of speculation and prosperity following the Mexican-American War of 1846–48 as well as discovery of vast deposits of gold in California. This gold quickly and greatly inflated the value of U.S. currency. Coincidentally, the USS *Central America,* carrying 30,000 pounds of gold from California to New York City, was lost along the North Carolina coast in a hurricane. Over 400 passengers died in this shipwreck. The loss of the gold, valued at some $2 million at the time, further shook confidence in the economy as a whole and added to economic fears.

Americans were also concerned over decreasing purchases of domestic farm products. During the Crimean War in Europe, men were away from their farms and were dependent upon the American farmer to supply their needs. After the war, they returned to plant and harvest their own crops; thus their need for American commodities diminished dramatically. With the advent of the telegraph, some news traveled very rapidly across America, so in the fall of 1856, within hours of the failure of the Ohio Life Insurance and Trust Company, word was out that many had been left destitute. Fearing that other financial companies would follow suit, especially in light of decreasing demands for European exports, investors panicked and began selling off their stock and withdrawing their funds from other institutions. Because telecommunications were limited, many people got their news secondhand; hence rumors further fueled the fires of economic uncertainty.

All this eventually drove about 500 companies out of business and put thousands out of work. It also caused the stock market to decline by around 66 percent. As usually happens in economic panics, fear fed upon itself. Other causes, including excessive real estate speculation (especially in the West), frivolous activity in stock purchases, and excess railroad building, have been cited as causing, or further complicating, already out-of-control economic circumstances. Short-sighted banking and other financial polices and widespread business corruption added fuel to the fire. The government's reluctance to issue additional paper money and its refusal to increase foreign tariffs also aggravated the situation, as did extravagant lifestyles and psychological insecurity among the elite. The overturn in the economy was brief, but the return to normalcy was prolonged and more political than economic. This event lasted over a year and a half, especially in the northern states, and in some areas it lasted until the onset of the American Civil War. Its effects also eventually spread to South America, Europe, and Asia.

SOURCES: Eric Foner, *Free Soil, Free Labor, Free Men: The Ideology of the Republican Party before the Civil War* (New York: Oxford Univ. Press, 1995); Michael T. Gavin, "Iron Industry," in *The Tennessee Encyclopedia of History and Culture* online edition, ed. Carroll Van West (Knoxville: Univ. of Tennessee Press, 2002), accessible at http://tennesseeencyclopedia.net/; James Huston, *The Panic of 1857 and the Coming of the Civil War* (Baton Rouge: Louisiana State Univ. Press, 1987); Gary Kinder, *Ship of Gold in the Deep Blue Sea* (New York: Vintage Books, 1998); Kenneth Stampp, *America in 1857: A Nation on the Brink* (New York: Oxford Univ. Press, 1990).

Coal Creek Miners Wars
COAL CREEK (NOW LAKE CITY) AND BRICEVILLE (ANDERSON COUNTY), 1891–92

Many good people abhorred the practices employed in working convicts, especially practices employed by the Tennessee Coal, Iron and Railroad Company. A committee of the Tennessee legislature in the late 1880s condemned the use of convicts in labor camps, some of which were described as "cruel, inhumane and barbarous . . . hell holes of rage, cruelty, despair and vice."

—**Marshall McGhee and Gene White,**
Briceville: The Town That Coal Built

After the Civil War, the crime rate in the South exploded and prison populations grew rapidly. States were nearly bankrupt, and many state agencies filled with corrupt officials. Out of this situation came the radical concept of a convict lease system. Under this initiative, state prisoners were leased to coal companies, large farms, and other enterprises as laborers. In return, the companies paid the state a fee per convict and provided their food, clothing, medical care, and secure housing. Initially the system seemed a win-win for all, and the decades between 1870 and 1890 produced hundreds of thousands of dollars in revenue for the state. However, the cruelty to state prisoners under the lease system was no secret. Some individuals even alleged that more and more men were being imprisoned on trumped-up charges just to increase the labor pool and hence the profits to the leasing companies and the state.

One of the largest coal mining operations in the state was the Tennessee Coal, Iron and Railroad Company (TCIRC), and they soon gained a monopoly over all available convict laborers. The ones they could not use were subleased to other companies. According to the *Second Annual Report of the Commissioner of Labor, 1893*, "The mining conditions were atrocious: defective ventilation; insufficient drainage; horrible sanitation; only one entrance to the mine; and no protective inspection of the mine prior to work. The convicts were inadequately fed and forced to work and sleep in the same clothing."

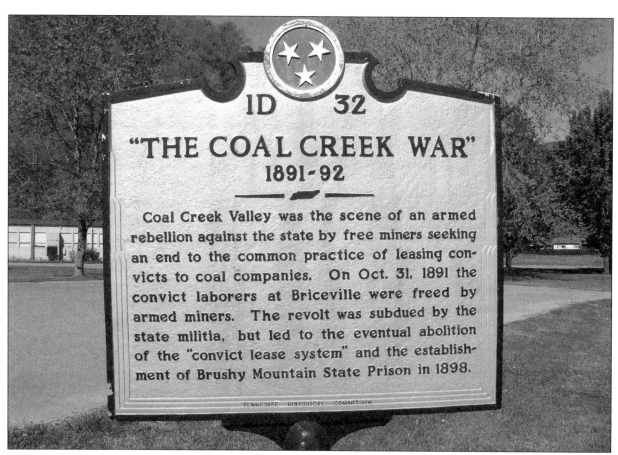

The Coal Creek War historical marker in Briceville, Campbell County. Photograph by the author.

Local miners tried to strike for better working conditions and fairer wages. When they did this, the coal companies either hired or threatened to hire state prisoners to take their place. Hence the convict lease system proved to be a determent to local free white and black miners. Prior to the Civil War, poor white workers competed only with free slave labor. Now they both faced competition with convicts. The prisoners were not only used as bargaining chips by mine operators, but they were actually preferred since they could be worked longer hours and at a much lower cost to the companies.

There were three specific coal company policies that disgruntled the free miners. The first was the practice of paying miners in script (company coupons redeemable only at company owned stores for food and other merchandise, or at other outlets for just 80 percent of their value) rather than cash, which could be used anywhere. Second, the companies refused to allow miners to appoint their own checkweighmen to ensure that the coal companies were not cheating them out of wages. (Miners were not salaried; they were paid by the ton of coal delivered at the surface.) Third, the coal companies insisted that the independent miners sign ironclad contracts that would prohibit them from striking or joining unions.

The free coal miners first struck for higher wages and the abolishment of the convict lease system as early as 1871 in Tracy City (Grundy County). Smaller strikes continued throughout the following decade. The worst of the violence, however, occurred between 1891 and 1892 during a long coal miners' strike at Briceville and Coal Creek (now known as Lake City), along with another one in Grundy County. This latter event, the state's first major labor strike, came to be known as the Coal Creek War.

After enduring several months of a strike at the Briceville mines and others across the state, the TCIRC announced that it intended to bring in prisoners to work its mines. The first convicts arrived in mid-July 1891 and began to raze the shacks formerly leased to the independent miners and their families. After that they constructed a large prison compound (stockade). The miners, local merchants, and other citizens quickly united in protest over the use of convict laborers in their community. After a mass meeting in Briceville, 300 men armed with rifles, sticks, stones, and other improvised weapons descended upon the stockade in what would become known as the first of five insurrections. After overpowering the guards, they forced the prisoners and even some mine officials onto a nearby train bound for Knoxville. The miners then simply went home, without a drop of blood being shed. They also sent a letter to Governor John Buchanan with a plea to intervene on behalf of the miners who were fighting for their livelihood.

After no action was taken by the governor or the state legislature, peaceful negotiations gave way to a second and more violent insurrection as the miners again attacked the stockade and sent prisoners, guards, and company officials packing via the nearest train. The miners attacked yet one more time in late October (the third insurrection), this time releasing prisoners, burning the stockade, and destroying the mining company buildings and infrastructure at Briceville. Two days later they attacked the Cumberland Mine at Oliver Springs.

By January 1892, however, the convicts were brought back to Briceville, by order of the governor and under the protection of the state militia. A fort was constructed on a knoll called Militia Hill, where Gatling guns and cannon were set up for defense. Attacks continued in August in Grundy County. During the fourth insurrection convicts were again put on a train; this time they were sent to Nashville. A number of miners and soldiers were injured, some possibly killed, during the last attack at Briceville. In spite of this, the miners again overtook the stockade, burned it to the ground, and sent the prisoners back to Knoxville via rail. The fifth and last insurrection occurred in Tracy City in April 1893.

Throughout the miners' wars, lawlessness, bloodshed, and destruction were rampant. An unknown number of miners and soldiers were wounded or killed, at least one man was lynched, and over a thousand men, women, and children were jailed. Half of them were incarcerated for months. By 1896 the free miners finally prevailed, and the convict system was repealed by the Tennessee legislature. Conditions continued to improve thanks to the tenacity of the miners, negotiations by organizations like the United Mine Workers of America and the Knights of Labor, and better enforcement of federal and state mining regulations.

SOURCES: Fran Ansley and Brenda Bell, eds., "Miners' Insurrections Convict Labor," *Southern Exposure* 1, nos. 3–4 (Winter 1974): 144–59; *Chattanooga Sunday Times,* Jan. 31, 1937; Coal Creek Watershed Foundation Inc., Knoxville, http://www.coalcreekaml.com/Legacy.htm; Pete Daniel, "The Tennessee Convict War," *Tennessee Historical Quarterly* 34, no. 3 (Fall 1975): 273–93; Federal Writers' Project. *Tennessee: A Guide to the State* (New York: Viking, 1939); A. C. Hutson, "The Overthrow of the Convict Lease System in Tennessee," *East Tennessee Historical Society's Publications,* no. 8 (1936): 82–103; James B. Jones Jr. "Convict Lease Wars," in *The Tennessee Encyclopedia of History and Culture,* ed. Carroll Van West, 204–5 (Nashville: Tennessee Historical Society and Rutledge Hill Press, 1998); *Knoxville News-Sentinel,* May 27, 1993; Marshall McGhee and Gene White, *Briceville: The Town that Coal Built* (Jacksboro, TN: Acting Printing, n.d.); David Rogers, *Reflections on the Water, Coal Creek to Lake City, TN* (Clinton, TN: Courier-News, 1976); Willard Yarbrough, "Miners' Guns Finally Helped End Convict Lease Law," *Knoxville News-Sentinel,* Oct. 30, 1966.

Economic Panic of 1893

STATEWIDE AND NATIONWIDE

It's like a war, a revolution, a strike—like any crisis in human affairs when men have to walk up and face the consequences of their ignorance, folly, or wickedness—the panic of '93 was a period of bad times chiefly for the innocent.

—**Lincoln Steffens, "Bulls and Bears"**

Prior to the economic panic of 1893, in the post–Civil War days, there was a rapid expansion and diversification of manufacturing in the United States. This allowed a growing independence from foreign imports, along with an increase in U.S. exports. Farming as an occupation had declined significantly, except in the South, where it accounted for some 65 percent of the labor force. Agricultural production had expanded greatly as a result of mechanization, development of improved varieties of crops and stock, more innovative cultivation techniques, and broader trade in overseas markets. The volume of virgin timber being harvested from the Southern Appalachian forests, including large sections of East Tennessee, was unprecedented in its scope. Unfortunately, high yields of farm products became a curse as well as a blessing. Agricultural overproduction in the United States and competition from emerging overseas markets created a vast surplus that subsequently led to falling prices and reduced farm wages. In trying to overcome this problem by producing more corn, wheat, cotton, and other such crops, U.S. farmers only exacerbated the problem.

Expansion of railroads greatly increased access to markets for farm products as well as coal, iron, steel, lumber, and all manner of manufactured goods. Unfortunately, overexpansion of the railroads caused many of them, including the Philadelphia & Reading, Union Pacific, Northern Pacific, the Atchison, Topeka & Santa Fe, and some seventy others, to either go bankrupt or go into receivership. This had a ripple effect that led to the failure of hundreds of banks, thousands of businesses, and other interests that were dependent upon the railroads.

In short, the Depression of 1893 has been attributed to deflation following the Civil War, as well as overproduction of goods that upset the laws of supply and demand. As surpluses increased, production was cut back and workers lost their jobs. Additional blame has been placed on the gold standard (as opposed to bimetallism), questionable and unsound economic policies, and governmental wastefulness and overspending. Although its roots can be traced back to the close of the Civil War, this severe downturn in the economy lasted roughly from 1893 to 1897, with a short reprieve between 1894 and 1895. It was also tied to global instability as specie (gold and silver as opposed to paper money) vacillated between Europe and the United States. Recessions in Britain, France, and Germany also produced severe repercussions in America, creating instability in the U.S. stock market, tight money and credit, business failures, and increased job losses. Unemployment rose rapidly during this period and stayed at or near the 12 percent range for five or six years. At its worst, unemployment may have exceeded 20 to 25 percent. In this respect, it was not unlike the Great Depression of the 1930s.

All in all, the panic of 1893 was one of the worst in U.S. history and is believed to have created the end of the Populist and free silver political crusades and the inception of a new political balance. It brought about major changes in U.S. policy and an evolution in its economy. It is believed to have spurred far-reaching social and intellectual consequences. It occurred during a period of often violent labor strikes and bloody riots as employment and the economy ebbed and flowed.

In 1894 there was a loosely organized march of unemployed men, called Coxey's Army, that drew attention to their plight by marching from Ohio and Pennsylvania to Washington, D.C., and there was the infamous Pullman Strike that literally closed down railroad transportation from coast to coast in July 1894. Also, as in the case of the depression of 1857, lack of accurate and immediate communications meant that rumors were rampant, adding to economic uncertainty. The McKinley administration eventually restored confidence in the nation's economy and the Klondike gold rush finally brought about a decade of renewed and rapid economic growth.

SOURCES: Robert Higgs, *The Transformation of the American Economy, 1865–1914* (New York: Wiley, 1971); Charles Hoffmann, *The Depression of the Nineties: An Economic History* (Westport, CT: Greenwood Press, 1970); Charles P. Kindleberger, *Manias, Panics, and Crashes: A History of Financial Crises* (New York: Basic Books, 1989); Howard J. Langer, ed., *America in Quotations: A Kaleidoscopic View of American History* (Westport, CT: Greenwood Press, 2002); Douglas Steeples and David Whitten, *Democracy in Depression: The Depression of 1893* (Westport, CT: Greenwood Press, 1998); Lincoln Steffens, "Bulls and Bears," in *The Autobiography of Lincoln Steffens*, 187–96 (New York: Harcourt, Brace, and Co., 1931); Richard Timberlake, "Panic of 1893," in *Business Cycles and Depressions: An Encyclopedia*, ed. David Glasner, 516–18 (New York: Garland, 1997).

Black Patch War
MONTGOMERY AND ROBERTSON COUNTIES, 1904–14

Invoking what they saw as the spirit of the Boston Tea Party and the Ku Klux Klan, the night riders throughout the Black Patch whipped, and in a few cases killed, hillbillies and trust buyers, scraped plant beds, burned or dynamited tobacco barns and warehouses, and, as they became more sure of themselves and their power, staged spectacular raids that captured entire towns at night.

—Rick Gregory, "Robertson County and the Black Patch War, 1904–1909"

Beginning in the early 1800s a prized heavy-leafed, black burley, or so-called black-fired, tobacco, was cultivated in Robertson and Montgomery counties in Tennessee and nineteen adjoining counties in Kentucky. In time, the area in which this tobacco was cultivated became known simply as the Black Patch.

Eventually, the American Tobacco Company, the Imperial Tobacco Company, and others formed a trust of sorts that began to monopolize and control the price of tobacco in the area. The old auction method of purchasing tobacco (which made for good competition) was abolished in favor of the companies going to individual farmers and offering one price. There was, of course, an agreement among the buyers that they would not try to outbid one another, and, in fact, they probably set prices to which all would adhere.

To counter this scheme, some of the tobacco farmers in the area formed a cooperative called the Dark Tobacco District Planters' Protective Association of Kentucky and Tennessee. This organization became known as the PPA or the "Association." They established their own strategy to break the monopoly of the trust. They intended to reduce the flow of tobacco into the market (reduce production) so as to increase the prices and their profits. Unfortunately, to be effective, all or most of the tobacco growers in the area would have to cooperate. Those who refused to join the PPA (dubbed "hillbillies") were detrimental to the cause of the other tobacco growers. As the PPA saw it, it had two enemies, the trust and the hillbillies. There were also other problems, such

as occasional poor crop years due to inclement weather, and good years in which there was overproduction, which caused prices to fall.

In the fall of 1904, in response to falling tobacco prices and the underhanded tactics of the trust to control crop prices, some of the more radical members of the PPA established a secret and militant society. This fraternal order was known as the "silent brigade," the "inner circle," or simply the "night riders." The members of this paramilitary group pledged allegiance to one another, swearing to employ every means possible, including violence, to control the output of tobacco from the region. They were intent on forcing the hillbillies to join their association and to fight against the trust to loosen its economic hold on them. Each member was required to take a blood oath during a mysterious initiation cer-

Night riders whipping a tobacco farmer, circa 1908. Armed bands of men fighting the monopolistic tobacco companies used intimidation against less cooperative tobacco farmers. Courtesy of Library of Congress.

emony, pledging loyalty to one another and promising not to reveal the secrets of the brotherhood.

The night riders were heroes to some (those wanting to get fair prices for their crops) and villains to others (those associated with the trust). The ten-year battle they waged over the region became known as the Black Patch War.

All the night riders were assumed to be members of the PPA, and even those who did not participate in their tactics were at least sympathetic to the cause. For a time, the PPA printed a newspaper called the *Black Patch Journal*. Its purpose was to promote the cause of the tobacco growers in the region, even to the point of boycotting businesses not sympathetic to the cause of the farmers. They used threats, intimidation, and terrorism, and when those did not work, they allegedly resorted to physical violence and even murder to coerce buyers into purchasing only from association farmers.

The hillbillies were assaulted or discriminated against in the communities. PPA members refused to socialize with them, go to church with them, or even to allow their children to associate with one another. During the most violent phase of the Black Patch War, between 1907 and 1909, the night riders scraped and salted tobacco beds and destroyed the tobacco crops in the fields to decrease supply. They burned and dynamited barns and warehouses filled with tobacco, destroyed machinery, killed livestock, and even raided and terrorized the citizens of a number of towns and communities in the dark of night.

Both the state and federal governments became involved in the battle and eventually passed laws against violent night rider activities and the destruction of tobacco crops and farm and warehouse infrastructure. Even National Guard troops, brought in to restore order, could not completely curtail the activities of the night riders.

In the end, the PPA was successful in raising and stabilizing tobacco prices, but not without some nega-tive effects. According to the *New York Times,* the overall costs were appalling in economic destruction, suffering, and loss of life. C. Vann Woodward, in *Origins of the New South, 1877–1913,* described the period in this way: "the South seems to have been one of the most violent communities of comparable size in all Christendom."

SOURCES: *Acts of the State of Tennessee, 55th General Assembly* (Nashville: Tennessee, Secretary of State, 1907); Rick Gregory, "Beliefs of Their Fathers: Violence, Religion, and the Black Patch War, 1904–1914," *Border States: Journal of the Kentucky-Tennessee American Studies Association* 9 (1993): Border States On-line: http://spider.georgetowncollege.edu/htallant/border/bs9/gregory.htm; Gregory, "Black Patch War," in *The Tennessee Encyclopedia of History and Culture,* ed. Carroll Van West, 68–69 (Nashville: Tennessee Historical Society and Rutledge Hill Press, 1998; Gregory, "Robertson County and the Black Patch War, 1904–1909," *Tennessee Historical Quarterly* 39, no. 3 (1980): 341–58; James O. Nall, *The Tobacco Night Riders of Kentucky and Tennessee.* Louisville, KY: Standard Press, 1939; *New York Times,* May 8, 1908; C. Vann Woodward, *Origins of the New South, 1877–1913,* 2nd ed. (Baton Rouge: Louisiana State Univ. Press, 1971).

Night Riders of Reelfoot Lake
LAKE AND OBION COUNTIES, 1908–9

There is a remedy for the Night Riders. It is a hemp rope justly but speedily noosed. There can be no room for any thought but to hunt down the murderers and strike them with the extremest penalty of the law.
—*Nashville Tennessean,* Oct. 21, 1908

On January 9, 1909, six men were sentenced to hang and two others to serve twenty-five years each for the heinous slaying of Col. Quinton Rankin, a Spanish-American War veteran and one of the state's most prominent attorneys of that time. The eight were ringleaders of the night riders of Reelfoot Lake. Like the Ku Klux Klan, these night riders practiced a form of vigilante justice. They engaged in the burning of the J. C. Burdick fishing docks at Samburg, the whipping of a handicapped Lake County official, the murder of members of a black family near Hickman (Kentucky), and the kidnapping of two Tennessee attorneys, one of which was lynched.

About 100 others were also implicated in the crime, sixty-three of whom were incarcerated for some time in a prison barracks in Obion County. After two years of delays, postponements, hung juries, and some extraordinary legal maneuvering, the eight major players in the night riders episode were released, leaving Colonel Rankin's murder unavenged. Ironically, it is the consensus that no event in the region's history, with the exception of the Civil War, polarized the population of Obion County as did the night rider episodes of 1908 and 1909.

Reelfoot, an 18,000-acre natural lake was formed, or at least enlarged, by earthquakes in the winter of 1811 and 1812 (see "New Madrid Earthquakes"). For years it had been open to commercial hunting and fishing, from which many in the area had made a meager living. In later years there were legal actions to claim the land around and under the lake and thus charge a fee for any fish or game taken there. There were also efforts to harvest the timber within the shallow lake and its environs and to drain it for farmland. In the summer of 1907 the West Tennessee Land Company claimed ownership of the area and launched efforts to turn the lake into a private sportsman's resort. They also planned to lease some of the land for timbering, grazing, and other agricultural uses. Since 1853 many locals, knowing that private ownership would affect their lives and traditional livelihood, had fought all such efforts. They even went to court, but to no avail.

Capt. Quentin Rankin (left) was hanged by night riders on October 9, 1908. Col. R. Z. Taylor (right) escaped the night riders by jumping into a lake. Courtesy of the Tennessee State Library and Archives.

For about seven months between 1908 and 1909 the night riders terrorized many of their neighbors throughout northwestern Tennessee and southwestern Kentucky. In hoods and robes they acted as judge, jury, and sometimes executioner whenever they felt the law could not, or would not, intervene. The core of the night rider group in Lake and Obion counties numbered twenty, but in time others joined their ranks, some in a spirit of solidarity and some out of boredom. Still others were forced into membership, threatened with beatings and hanging if they did not join and support the effort. Calling themselves the "Knights of Fun" and the "Sons of Joy," they reveled in the mysticism and secrecy of their clandestine fellowship. Originally they had arisen in protest to unfair tobacco pricing (see "Black Patch War"). Now they arose to preserve their livelihood as commercial hunters and fishermen in the Reelfoot Lake area. Some of their actions were taken under the guise of protecting the weak, the poor, and the downtrodden from outside influences. Eventually, as with the Ku Klux Klan, a criminal and often sadistic element crept into the group and seized leadership. Also like the Klan, they displayed prejudice against other races and perpetrated a number of atrocities, particularly against blacks.

On October 19, 1908, two lawyers representing the West Tennessee Land Company met at Ward's Hotel in Walnut Log, Obion County, to negotiate a real estate lease agreement with another local attorney, Fred Carpenter. Knowing that this transaction would jeopardize their longtime fishing and hunting rights in the area, the night riders decided to act. About midnight, an armed and hooded group of night riders raided the lodge and kidnapped Colonel Rankin and his associate Col. Robert Z. Taylor. They were taken to a nearby bluff at Bayou Chien. They were questioned by their captors, and Colonel Rankin was subsequently hanged and his body riddled with bullets. In the frenzy, the other captive, Colonel Taylor, made a daring escape by jumping into the lake. The nightriders fired some thirty shots in hopes of kill-

ing him or scaring him into not talking. Taylor miraculously escaped through the murky waters, hiding for a couple days and finally emerging on the west side of the lake near Hickman, Kentucky. He was exhausted, disoriented, and suffering from exposure, but he was alive.

As soon as news of the tragedy reached Nashville, Tennessee Governor Malcolm Patterson offered a $10,000 reward to anyone who could bring the assassins to justice. He also dispatched several companies of Tennessee militiamen from Nashville and Memphis to restore order in the area. Posses organized and within two weeks fifty-four suspected night riders, including their eight ringleaders, were rounded up and jailed at Union City.

Besides the kidnapping of Taylor and Rankin and the murder of the latter, the night riders were implicated in about 120 other criminal incidents in northwest Tennessee and Fulton County, Kentucky. The alleged crimes included assault, arson, and murder. One woman, whose husband was a night rider, was taken from her home and severely whipped for attempting to sue for divorce. Another man was whipped for allegedly neglecting his family. A Lake County squire was whipped and subsequently died from the trauma. They threatened to destroy Union City, the seat of Obion County, and later to kill one of Reelfoot Lake's largest landowners, Judge Harris. They burned the fishing docks at Samburg, in Lake County, and they crossed into Kentucky to burn the home of Dave Walker, described as an arrogant Negro farmer. Walker, his wife, and their two children were shot to death as they ran from the burning cabin. Three other children were wounded but survived.

The initial trial for the death of Rankin and the kidnapping of Taylor lasted for several weeks. Subsequent appeals went on for almost two years, but in the end the indictments against the night riders were dismissed by the state supreme court. No one was ever convicted.

In a way, the legend of the night riders of Reelfoot Lake lives on. It is said that many of the folks living around Lake and Obion County are still suspicious of outsiders, and those in the know are still tight-lipped about the events of 1908 and 1909. In 1914 the State of Tennessee finally attained ownership of the lake and much of its surrounding land through condemnation. Today it is protected as a Tennessee state park and natural area, and as a federal wildlife refuge under the U.S. Fish and Wildlife Service.

SOURCES: *Nashville Tennessean,* Oct. 21, 1908; Hillsman Taylor, "The Night Riders of West Tennessee," *West Tennessee Historical Society Papers* 6 (1952): 77–86; Bill Threlkeld, "Night Riders of Reelfoot Lake," in *The Tennessee Encyclopedia of History and Culture,* ed. Carroll Van West, 690–91 (Nashville: Tennessee Historical Society and Rutledge Hill Press, 1998); Paul J. Vanderwood, *Night Riders of Reelfoot Lake* (Memphis: Memphis State Univ. Press, 1969).

Chattanooga Streetcar Strike
SEPTEMBER 6–24, 1917

Although most Chattanooga businesses and industries were small enterprises in the 1880s, a few workers began joining secret organizations that were the forerunners of labor unions. One such organization, chartered by the American Federation of Labor in 1897, was the Central Labor Union (CLU). This organization made an early attempt to organize labor in Chattanooga that led to a violent streetcar strike in 1916–17. Prior to this (around 1911), there had been a failed attempt to unionize after several motormen were dismissed by the Chattanooga Railway and Light Company for allegations of drunken and reckless behavior.

In another attempt to win union recognition, the first streetcar strike was launched in the summer of 1916. It too was the result of employees being dismissed by the company. There was no particular intention of violence when the streetcar conductors and motormen simply abandoned their cars, one at a time, causing gridlock along Market Street. However, as curious onlookers began to gather, the local police became uneasy. Some streetcar windows were smashed, but damage and injuries were

slight. In anticipation of tensions getting even worse, the fire and police commissioner decided to become proactive and head off any further violence. The commissioner ordered that fire hoses be turned on the crowd. Some arrests were also made by heavily armed police officers.

Eventually the company was forced to recognize the union, but hostilities still persisted over a number of matters. It also appeared as if some citizens were beginning to revel in the disorder that these incidents gave them. Violence broke out again on September 6, as union men stopped and abandoned their streetcars at 6:00 PM. This time they abandoned their cars wherever they happened to be at the time. A number of strikebreakers and company officials attempting to take the cars back to the main garage were attacked and beaten (some severely). There was more damage and threats of burning the streetcars. Violence spread, and four abandoned cars were pushed down St. Elmo Street, where they crashed together, one at a time. By September 11, conditions became so severe that Federal troops (including two cavalry and one machine gun company) were dispatched from Fort Oglethorpe, Georgia, to help restore order.

The incident culminated on September 23–24, when violence broke out along Market and adjoining streets. On September 24, 1917, the *Chattanooga Daily Times* reported that "the clash was between union men, their sympathizers, and idlers on the one side and non-union employees of the company on the other." As bystanders became caught up in the fracas, a mob of some 2,000 began screaming, cursing, attacking strikebreakers, and vandalizing or destroying streetcars. The paper went on to state that a local brewery worker was killed by a shotgun blast, a young boy was shot in the leg, and three streetcar company platform men were beaten almost into unconsciousness. Many others were likewise injured, some seriously. There was also considerable damage to streetcars and other company equipment as well as private and public property during the incident.

Eventually the strike was broken as the streetcar company signed a new contract that included recognition of the union. Unfortunately, by 1919 the Chattanooga Railway and Light Company was in financial ruin and went into receivership.

SOURCES: *Chattanooga Daily Times,* Sept. 24, 1917; G. E. Govan and J. W. Livingood, *The Chattanooga Country, 1540–1976: From Tomahawks to TVA,* 3rd ed. (Knoxville: Univ. of Tennessee Press, 1977); James W. Livingood, *Hamilton County: Tennessee County History Series* (Memphis: Memphis State Univ. Press, 1981).

Knoxville Streetcar Strike

OCTOBER 17–NOVEMBER 5, 1919

Many labor problems gripped the nation in the wake of World War I as lucrative military contracts dried up and the troops returned home to a dwindling job market. Competition was particularly hard for women and blacks as racial problems and threats of strikes by workers exacerbated already tense situations. In Knoxville this was evidenced by racial unrest, fears of a nationwide coal miners strike, and, even closer to home, a streetcar workers strike.

At the stroke of midnight on October 17, 1919, about 250 Knoxville Railway and Light (KRL) Company streetcar motormen, conductors, shop men, and powerhouse employees walked off their jobs. They demanded both higher wage scales and a better system of compensation. They were all members of Local 767 of the Amalgamated Association of Street and Electric Railway Employees of America.

During World War I, a National War Labor Board (NWLB) had been established to control labor strikes and wages. In August 1918 the NWLB set the wages for KRL workers at thirty-six to forty-six cents an hour. By the time that the wartime contract expired, the NWLB had been disbanded and both the company and the workers agreed to extend the terms of the old contract for the time being. Later, as the costs of living increased, the workers began to demand higher wages. As the company and its employees reached an impasse, the strike ensued. Ironically, it became less a question of increased wages and more a question of who had the authority to mitigate the issue.

As the strike progressed, city police officers went on twelve-hour shifts, an electric fence was constructed around the Knoxville powerhouse, electricity was temporarily furnished from the Tennessee Power Company's Ocoee Plant in Polk County, and the governor dispatched the state adjutant general and a number of troops to Knoxville to monitor activities.

Because postwar unemployment was high, KRL was able to hire plenty of strike-breaking, nonunion workers. However, the union was not about to give up that easily. Meanwhile, the local newspaper placed blame on both sides for inconveniencing the public.

On October 26 a union meeting was held outside the Knoxville County Courthouse with 2,500 members and spectators in attendance. Unfortunately, this was also the day that KRL resumed full streetcar service using strikebreakers as conductors and motormen. Sporadic riots broke out that day and continued into early November. Many streetcars were vandalized or otherwise damaged, and several strikebreakers were injured. Some even required hospitalization. In the days that followed, other trolleys were mobbed by workers and sympathizers. Streetcars were shot at and stoned, trolley ropes were cut, rocks were piled on tracks, and car windows broken. The city mayor was threatened, and evidence grew that some police officers (who were union men) either ignored or assisted in some of the violence toward KRL and its strikebreakers. By October 27, both national guardsmen and federal troops had arrived in Knoxville. The next day Governor Roberts also arrived to denounce the local labor unrest, laying blame on the strikers.

By November 5, streetcar and electrical power services were restored throughout the city. Although minor protests and sporadic violence continued, the strike ended with striker demands never being met. KRL also suffered almost $100,000 in economic losses as a result of the strike. This strike, one of several thousand labor disputes that occurred in the wake of World War I, appears to have been only a part of a period of civil unrest that began with the August 30 Knoxville Race Riot and ended with a November 1 nationwide coal miners strike.

SOURCES: James A. Burran, "Labor Conflict in Urban Appalachia: The Knoxville Streetcar Strike of 1919," *Tennessee Historical Quarterly* 38, no. 1 (Spring 1979): 62–78; *Knoxville Journal and Tribune,* Oct. 18, 24, 27, 29, 30, Nov. 2, 3, 6, 1919.

South Pittsburg Gunfight

MARION COUNTY, DECEMBER 25, 1927

> The body of Ewing Smith [South Pittsburg City Marshall] was found riddled with bullets, having apparently taken two heavy shotgun loads at close range. Hennessey [deputy sheriff] was shot in the left breast, a shotgun charge tearing and riddling his flesh and opening a huge wound in his heart. Sheriff Coppinger was shot three times, a bullet entering the heart, another four inches below and another in the leg.
>
> —*Nashville Tennessean,* Dec. 26, 1927

Around 9:30 PM on Christmas Day 1927, ten county and city police officers and an estimated ten civilians engaged in a gun battle in the middle of Third Street in downtown South Pittsburg. The Marion County sheriff, a sheriff's deputy, and three special city police officers died at the scene. The South Pittsburg police chief died the next morning in a Chattanooga hospital. "I got the man who shot me," were said to have been the final words of the police chief. Four others sustained non–life threatening wounds and ten others were unharmed. The incident was the result of a feud between local police, county law officers, and workers over a labor strike that was taking place at the H. Wetter Stove Company Manufacturing Plant. The melee lasted less than five minutes, and when the sidearms of the dead men were taken from their bodies and examined, none had been fired. According to the *Nashville Tennessean,* the violent struggle had been fought exclusively with shotguns except for one pistol shot that ended the life of O. H. Larrowe, a special policeman employed by the plant. Local businessmen contacted the state for assistance almost immediately, since nearly all the peace officers in South Pittsburg and vicinity were dead or wounded in this incident. Then Governor Henry Horton activated about sixty National Guardsmen (from Chattanooga) to patrol the city streets and the plant to prevent further violence. The town was never under martial law, and the troops were sent simply to assist the remaining local police.

The incident occurred so quickly that neither those involved nor other eyewitnesses could say for sure who fired the first shot, who was involved, or the specific cause of the conflict. On the other hand, it was well known that there had been ill feelings for several weeks between both city and county law officers over the local strike and the lack of progress in its resolution. The town mayor and police were trying to protect the plant and its management, while county officers were sympathetic to the strikers.

Deputy Sheriff Thomas Connor, the brother of the city police chief, was believed to have given the only true account of what happened that night. He said that city officers had drawn pistols on him earlier in the evening. When he reported this to the sheriff, the county law officers decided to arrest the city police for brandishing weapons against, and threatening, fellow peace officers. The city police resisted and the gun battle ensued.

SOURCES: *Nashville Tennessean,* Dec. 26, 27, 1927.

Aluminum Company of America Labor Strike

ALCOA, BLOUNT COUNTY, MAY 18–JUNE 8, 1937

Around 2,900 American Federation of Labor workers at the Aluminum Company of America (ALCOA) Fabricating Plant in Blount County walked off their jobs on

May 18, 1937. Their grievance was over the fact that aluminum company employees in some other sections of the country received better pay, and they were demanding higher wages. The company argued that the differential in wage rates was based on costs of living and other regional economic factors, and that the rates were non-negotiable.

After a couple of days, the company closed down its operations and the strikers went home. Everything remained peaceful until the eighth week of the strike. Then it was announced that the plant was going to re-open, allegedly at the request of a majority of its former labor force. Union officials threatened to close down the plant if this happened. Around 12:30 PM on the afternoon of July 7, violence erupted when a truck attempted to cross the picket line and enter the plant. Between 200 and 500 (estimates vary) picketers surrounded the truck, advanced toward the gates, and allegedly started shooting at special police officers hired to protect the company.

As the rioters advanced toward the gates and invaded the plant, the officers moved into the crowd brandishing billy clubs and returning fire. The strikers stood their ground with metal pipes, wrenches, hammers, clubs, knives, and other improvised weapons. Nonetheless, they were soon subdued. Spokesmen for the strikers later claimed that they had no guns and that only the officers fired the estimated 500 rounds during the incident. The officers claimed that the strikers fired first and that the officers didn't have weapons—they had to go to their vehicles to retrieve them. The melee was short lived, lasting perhaps eight minutes or so, but during that time one officer was killed and a striker lay mortally wounded. Somewhere between twenty and forty others were injured, some seriously.

Even though calm was restored very quickly by local authorities, Tennessee Governor Gordon Browning sent around 200 Tennessee National Guardsmen to the area. They set up camps around Maryville and Alcoa and remained there until the plant reopened.

The eight-week strike ended on July 12, with workers returning to their jobs at the same rate of pay and with no other concessions. The incident cost the strikers an estimated half million dollars in wages. According to the *Maryville Enterprise,* the company continued to insist that "differentials in wage rates between different communities, districts, or sections of the country are based on sound and fundamental economic conditions and any changes in such differentials by any industry or large employer would seriously affect every other industry and business."

SOURCES: Hugh D. Graham and Ted R. Gurr, *The History of Violence in America: Historical and Comparative Perspectives* (New York: Praeger, 1969); *Knoxville News-Sentinel,* July 8, 1937; *Maryville Enterprise,* July 8, 1937; Prof. Paula McGhee, Maryville College, personal correspondence with author, Sept. 24, 2009; Russell D. Parker, "Alcoa, Tennessee: The Years of Change 1940–1960," *East Tennessee Historical Society's Publications,* no. 49 (1977): 99–115; Federal Writer's Program, *Tennessee: A Guide to the State* (New York: Viking, 1939).

Memphis Sanitation Workers Strike
FEBRUARY 12–APRIL 16, 1968

> Nor do the statements tell what it was like in Memphis, the texture of that southern spring, warm winds sweeping up from the Gulf with azalea, the freak snow that offered a moment of false respite, the fear which gripped both blacks and whites. The strike did not so much happen in Memphis as engulf it.
>
> —**Joan T. Beifuss, *At the River I Stand***

Following a two-month Memphis sanitation workers strike, unskilled black laborers eventually received fairer compensation, better working conditions, a voice in their labor relations, and finally some long overdue dignity. Unfortunately, their victory was overshadowed by one of the darkest pages of our nation's history, the assassination of civil rights leader Dr. Martin Luther King Jr. King denounced the starvation wages and harsh labor conditions of Memphis sanitation workers at the hands of municipal government officials. Today it is difficult to fathom the inhumane conditions under which black sanitation workers labored up until just some four decades ago. In fact, King described those conditions as being a question of human rights more than civil rights.

It was said that the plight of the black sanitation worker in Memphis was the epitome of the black urban poor. Many men and women of color worked two or more jobs each and still qualified for welfare. Health and safety considerations were practically nonexistent, and few had vacations or any other benefits. The working conditions were deplorable, and at the time there was no questioning these conditions. Those that did were suspended or fired. "The man's" (manager's) word was law. When it rained, blacks were generally sent home without pay, whereas whites stayed and received their regular salaries. There was no pension plan, no sick leave, and not much of anything else of a positive nature.

Every backyard had one or more fifty-gallon garbage cans. The sanitation workers had to empty these cans into leaking tubs that they carried on their shoulders or heads. All manner of filth, including putrid liquids and maggots, spilled over the tubs or through holes onto the garbage men. Besides not having toilets, there were no facilities where the men could wash up before eating lunch or returning home after work. Most simply went home and removed their clothes at the door to keep out the filth.

Under these inhuman conditions, the sanitation workers organized and began attending secret union meetings. Those suspected of being union members could lose their jobs, and often did, since there were snitches all around. Nonetheless, many continued to meet in secret and plan a strategy. After trying and failing many times to bargain with the city relative to wages and working conditions, they were at their wits' end. A strike of sanitation workers in 1966 ended in an injunction that sent everyone back to work.

On February 1, 1968, two black sanitation workers crouched in the back of a garbage truck taking refuge from a severe storm because they were not allowed to go into the lounge. It was reserved for whites only. When lightning hit the truck, it activated the automatic compressor, crushing the men to death. It was this event that finally initiated the strike of February 12, 1968. Thirteen hundred men walked off the job, demanding recognition of their union as a bargaining agent with the city. They wanted higher wages, dues check-off (automatic deduction of union dues from their paychecks), and other concessions, along with a written contract. Memphis mayor Henry Loeb (who also happened to be the former director of the Sanitation Department) refused to bargain with, or even acknowledge, their union. This was the first attempt to unionize a municipal workers' organization in Memphis; others, including the Memphis Park Commission, housing authority, and firefighters, would eventually follow.

Racial-economic oppression, along with rampant police brutality, created a virtual powder keg in Memphis in the 1960s. When black strikers tried to march peacefully to city hall in protest of their treatment under a depressive municipal government, they were assaulted and maced by white police squads. As a result, the Tennessee National Guard was activated to enforce a curfew throughout the city.

One can only imagine the unsanitary conditions and health concerns that began to face the city when the garbage workers went on strike. Rotting and putrefying garbage accumulated, and the stench became unbearable in the backyards, alleys, and urban thoroughfares throughout the city. Conditions deteriorated rapidly from being simply a nuisance to a major public health concern.

The sanitation workers were not without their supporters. King and members of his influential civil rights organization were convinced to come to Memphis. In a speech before 10,000–15,000 Memphis citizens, he denounced starvation wages and the struggle for genuine equality for black people. This brought national media attention to the strike. When he returned in March to lead a mass march, riotous conditions ensued, exacerbated by alleged police violence. A black youth was shot and killed by police and the governor ordered National Guard troops into the city to restore order. Ultimately, 37 were injured, 329 were arrested, and 490 fire calls were made, only 49 of which were false alarms.

Undaunted, King returned again the first week in April, but this time an assassin's bullet took him down. That event set off a wave of violence across the nation, causing death, injury, and destruction—the very acts that King abhorred and worked so faithfully to prevent. It is likely that most citizens of Memphis were behind the sanitation workers, at least in spirit. Black leaders and ministers supported them, and labor unions from across the country gave them financial and moral support. They were provided food, and their rent or mortgages were paid for during the three months of the strike.

Firestone Union Hall, used as a headquarters for the strikers, was bombed the day they walked out of it and marched to Memphis City Hall. Fortunately, no one was in it at the time.

The strike ended on April 16, sixty-four days after it began. The city finally agreed to recognize Local Union 1733 as a bargaining agent for the workers and to provide dues check-off. Although the workers did not get the wage increase they had insisted upon, nor a written contract (at that time), the city agreed to cease all racial discrimination against workers in respect to job status. They agreed to provide access to facilities such as restrooms, lounges, and lunchrooms. They also agreed to rehire all workers and not discipline any for their activities during the strike. The pay increase fell short of what they expected, but it was eventually provided, along with a written contract.

SOURCES: Joan T. Beifuss, *At the River I Stand* (Memphis: St. Luke's Press, 1990); William H. Harris, *The Harder We Run: Black Workers since the Civil War.* New York: Oxford Univ. Press, 1982; Michael Keith Honey, *Black Workers Remember: An Oral History of Segregation, Unionism, and for the Freedom Struggle* (Los Angeles: Univ. of California Press, 1999).

Memphis Firefighters Strike
JUNE–AUGUST, 1978

> You don't have spontaneous combustion just suddenly occur on July 2, 1978, and uninhabited homes all over the city suddenly burst into flames.
>
> **—Memphis Mayor Wyeth Chandler**

In the forty-eight hours following the 7:00 AM shift change of the Memphis Fire Department on July 1, 1978, 225 structure fires erupted in the city. It was either one of the most extraordinary cases of coincidence in history, or the fires were intentionally set. The fact that all of the fires occurred in condemned, abandoned, or otherwise uninhabited buildings, dumpsters, and such, and the fact that the fires occurred during the Memphis firefighters strike leaves little doubt about the cause. Public officials attributed over 95 percent of these incidents to acts of arson by members of the Memphis International Union of Firefighters Local 1784 and their sympathizers. The firefighters stated that they thought most of the fires were set by a few rogue firemen and arsonists who used the strike as an opportunity to make a point or get a thrill.

As the strike progressed, firefighters blocked egress to fire stations and fires. They harassed or otherwise interfered with supervisors and volunteers who attempted to respond to the city's emergencies. Fire equipment and ambulances were affected by the strike, with tires slashed, engines sabotaged, and emergency medical equipment damaged by persons unknown. Vandalism, including broken windows, also occurred at the city's

A littered street during the Memphis Sanitation Workers' Strike, February 1968. Courtesy of Special Collections, University of Memphis Libraries.

fire stations. Some citizens supported the efforts of the striking firefighters, but others did not. One woman was even quoted as saying, "They ought to be shot."

The strike began on June 30 and involved some 1,400 firefighters. Some continued to work, and they did agree to step back in when and if lives were threatened. The rest took turns walking picket lines. The strikers claimed that they deserved higher wages, at least as high as that of police officers, since their work was equally dangerous. They also demanded so-called shift differential pay for night duty. Other city and county employees

received this compensation for all time worked beyond eight hours in any twenty-four-hour period. At issue was also the fact that the firefighters were so underpaid that many were forced to moonlight (work two or more jobs) just to make ends meet. They also asked for better overall working conditions. When the city was not willing to concede on all of these issues, most of the city's firefighters walked off the job.

The mayor soon realized that local authorities would be unable or unwilling to control the strikes and that there were too few volunteers and fire supervisors

Strikers walk a picket line during the Memphis Sanitation Workers' Strike, 1968. Courtesy of Special Collections, University of Memphis Libraries.

to handle the increasing fire load. In fact, as a show of solidarity for the firefighters, some of the city sanitation employees refused to work. Eventually, the mayor called upon the governor to provide assistance through the Tennessee National Guard. The state adjutant general activated 860 guardsmen along with an additional 102 foresters from the State Forest Service. Some 134 Marine and Navy volunteers also served during the incident, as did twenty emergency workers from outside of the Memphis area. Their jobs were to staff the city's fifty-one fire stations, keep order between the active and striking firefighters, patrol the streets, and respond to fire calls. Although they had ammunition readily available, as far as is known the guardsmen were never asked to load their weapons during the incident.

Because of the large numbers of fires breaking out simultaneously around the city, the working firefighters were instructed to cover only the exposure area, especially in the case of fires in vacant buildings. In other words, they were to try to prevent the fires from spreading to adjacent structures rather than extinguishing them. Many of the fires were also located on fire station

Signs are passed out to union members during the 1978 Memphis firefighters strike. Courtesy of Special Collections, University of Memphis Libraries.

district boundaries. This exacerbated the problem and added even more credence to the suspicion that the fires were the calculated work of the strikers, intent upon complicating an already bad situation.

The initial fires came in two waves. The first occurred just after 9:30 PM on June 30, and the second around midnight the next day. A dozen of these fires were major events, involving schools, city libraries, and commercial buildings. One of the worst occurred at the three-story Nutrena Mills Plant on Provine Avenue. It nearly spread to the Memphis Molding Inc. plant and adjacent residences. At one point the flames from this fire rose 250 feet into the Memphis night and were visible throughout the city. The fire was not brought under control until about eleven that evening. Buildings within

a two-block area of the downtown section of Memphis were also damaged or destroyed by fires.

On the second day of the strike, the mayor declared a state of civil emergency and ordered a 10:00 PM to 6:00 AM curfew. This curtailed some arson activities but took its toll on local merchants and the general activities of everyday citizens. Because of the strike, and the fires being purposely set, many of these merchants had to beef up their own security and had mixed emotions about the event. On the one hand, they were losing business; on the other, because of the curfew, they were not as likely to have their stores, factories, warehouses, and other places of business burned down, vandalized, or looted. In spite of the presence of the National Guardsmen, a number of commercial buildings, single and multiple unit houses, and other structures were damaged or destroyed by fires and vandalism. Insurance companies paid dearly for the melee.

On the morning of July 4, the firefighters finally agreed to return to work in a good faith effort, even before negotiations with the city were completed. This action came after Chancery Court Judge Robert Hoffman ordered them to go back to work or face criminal contempt charges. Some of the returning firefighters included those on the union's executive committee who the major had previously fired for insubordination. As the strike neared its end, most of the guardsmen were sent home, and the Memphis curfew was lifted. The remaining National Guardsmen left on the morning of July 15. After the city and the union were unable to come to a compromise, both agreed to allow a federal mediator to come in and negotiate a final settlement. Both sides made concessions and received some of what they wanted, but the big losers were the citizens of Memphis and Shelby County. They were left with a bill amounting to some five to six million dollars, and the insurance companies, also hard hit, were forced to raise rates in light of their losses.

A National Guardsman patrols the smoldering ruins of a feed mill in Memphis. The National Guard was dispatched to Memphis to fight fires that allegedly were set by strikers and their sympathizers during the 1978 Memphis firefighters strike.

SOURCES: James B. Jones Jr., "The Memphis Firefighters Strikes, 1856 and 1860," *East Tennessee Historical Society Publications*, no. 49 (1977): 37–60; *Knoxville News-Sentinel*, July 2, 1978; *Memphis Commercial Appeal*, July 2–6, 9, 1978.

Tennessee Banking Empire Failure
KNOXVILLE AND EAST TENNESSEE, 1982–86

What's the difference between a hog and a bank? You slaughter a hog, you Butcher a bank.

—**Graffiti in restroom,
University of Tennessee**

As de facto apprentices in their father's Union County Bank of Maynardville, Jacob ("Jake") Butcher and his younger brother Cecil Hilque ("C.H.") Jr. had an inclination and an aptitude for all things financial. By 1976, with good business savvy and a lot of other people's money, they had amassed a banking operation in Tennessee and Kentucky valued at around $1 billion. They eventually acquired forty banks between them with assets of approximately $3 billion.

Some bank examiners became suspicious of the Butcher brothers' financial operations as early as 1982, but their banking empire did not begin to fall apart until January 1983. Shortly thereafter, the Federal Deposit Insurance Corporation (FDIC) issued a cease-and-desist order against Jake Butcher's United American Bank (UAB) in Knoxville. That was followed a month later by another one accusing UAB of providing false and misleading data regarding the financial soundness of the bank. On February 14, 1983, UAB was declared insolvent. However, it was quickly sold to the state's largest bank holding company and reopened as the First Tennessee Bank of Knoxville. Nonetheless, this led to suspicion and panic on the part of many depositors and a subsequent run on several of the Butcher banks, resulting in the Southern Industrial Banking Corporation filing for bankruptcy the following month. During the next two months, nine more of the brothers' banks failed and eleven others were either merged or sold.

Further investigations by the FDIC found that the Butcher brothers had been making questionable (if not illegal) loans to one another, other banks, business associates, and their friends without proper collateral. They had accomplished this without ensuring creditworthiness, and with little or no official financial documentation. They were also involved in loan document forgery, pyramid schemes, and other illegal and unethical practices. According to federal records, at one point UAB held almost $58 million in commercial loans guaranteed by the government, and almost a third of those borrowers were delinquent in their payments.

The brothers' bank was also one of the largest lending institutions under the FDIC building and industrial loan programs. They had negotiated some thirty loans in the amount of $28.3 million in Tennessee and nine other states. Of those thirty, thirteen (accounting for 43 percent of the total) were delinquent in payments. Nine of their Knoxville borrowers, representing about 30 percent of their city's loans, were also delinquent in payments. The brothers managed to cover up their unethical and illegal accounting practices by shuffling the loans between their various banks. State and federal bank examiners had long been suspicious of what they perceived as the brothers' $3 billion mostly paper banking empire, but unfortunately there were problems in proving it. The fact that the Butchers' forty banks were located within three Federal Reserve Districts, two FDIC regions, and two states, Tennessee and Kentucky made it difficult to detect or prove irregularities and illegal financial manipulations. Finally, on November 1, 1982, 180 FDIC investigators converged on all of the Butcher banks simultaneously. This strategy prevented the brothers from transferring any funds between banks, which they had previously done to cover their scheme.

The FDIC eventually estimated that the Butcher banking fiasco totaled over $380 million. It was the fourth greatest cumulative bank failure in U.S. history at the time. As a result of ongoing investigations over the next three years, Jake was indicted on numerous criminal charges. In April 1985, he pleaded guilty to twenty of ninety-two counts of bank fraud and four of nine charges of conspiracy. He also pleaded guilty to tax evasion for failing to report $38.5 million in income. This latter charge carried a penalty of up to fourteen years in prison. However, as the result of a plea bargain, he was given only five twenty-year sentences for conspiracy and bank fraud, with the understanding that the terms would run concurrently. Had he been given the maximum penalties under the law, he could have been sentenced to over five hundred years in prison and fined over $435,000. He was paroled in 1992 after serving only seven years of his sentence.

C. H. Butcher was also eventually brought to justice. He was convicted of two counts of conspiracy and four counts each of bank fraud and bankruptcy fraud. He was sentenced to twenty years in prison, of which he served only six. After leaving prison, C.H. managed to pay off fines in the amount of $319,000. Perhaps justice had been done; however, the biggest losers in this financial disaster were local businesses and many Tennessee citizens who lost their life savings, their children's college funds, and their retirement nest eggs.

SOURCES: *American Banker,* Feb. 17, 1983, July 1, 1985; *Business Tennessee,* http://businesstn.com/content/vestige-empire; *Business Week,* May 3, 1976; *Financial Times,* Dec. 20, 1984; *Knoxville News Sentinel,* May 2, 2007; *New York Times,* July 7, 1983; Sept. 1, 1986; Apr. 8, 1987; *Oak Ridger,* May 1, 2002; *Time,* Feb. 28, 1983; *Washington Post,* May 26, 1983.

RACE RIOTS AND RACIAL VIOLENCE

Race riots were not uncommon in Tennessee between the end of the Civil War and the early part of the twentieth century. The feelings and motivations of many have been deeply rooted in hatred and intolerance relative to ethnicity, religion, gender, and other such factors. A so-called racial massacre occurred in Memphis in 1866 while thousands of black troops were garrisoned there awaiting discharge. At the time, bigotry, prejudice, and narrow-mindedness were prevalent between both whites and blacks. Discontent and misbehavior between those troops, urban blacks and whites, and especially Irish laborers soon reached a breaking point, resulting in injury, rapes, deaths, and severe property damage mostly in the black slums of the city. According to a special congressional committee established to investigate the Memphis racial incident, the city lost over $130,000. Short-lived race riots also occurred in Franklin, Williamson County; Knoxville and Columbia, Maury County; and Clinton, Anderson County.

Only within the last couple of decades has the term "hate crime" been coined for racially motivated discrimination in its most blatant form. According to the Federal Bureau of Investigation's Web site (http://www.fbi.gov), a hate crime is "a criminal offense committed against a person, property or society which is motivated, in whole or in part, by the offender's bias against a race, religion, disability, sexual orientation or ethnicity/national origin." The murderous acts of one "Wild Bill" Latura serves as an example of a classic hate crime in its most sinister expression. On December 10, 1908, Latura, a man of ruthless and merciless reputation who fancied himself a sort of folk hero, walked into a black saloon in Memphis, pulled out a gun, shot three men dead, and wounded three others, including a woman. Although he freely admitted to the crime, was arrested, and was tried for it, an all-white jury found him not guilty. A December 12, 1908, editorial in the *Memphis Commercial Appeal* denounced the killings, but unfortunately it also read, "You will find Negros in this community with barely enough clothes on to hide their nakedness, yet on their person will be a pistol of the latest improved pattern. The Negro is an imitative sort of animal and he often gets his inspiration for carrying a gun from the white man." The article went on to imply that a black man with a gun might be equally tempted to use it on a white man.

Another hate crime, the Mormon Massacre, occurred on August 10, 1884. A mob of hooded white men attacked and killed five members of the Church of Jesus Christ of Latter-Day Saints in Lewis County. Mormons had been persecuted for their religious beliefs even before coming to Tennessee and settling in Lewis County. They were eventually driven out of the area as a result of continuing threats of violence.

KKK Insurrection and the Invisible Empire
STATEWIDE, 1866–PRESENT

Although the Ku Klux Klan (KKK) is the nation's first homegrown terrorist organization, its beginnings were allegedly modest and anything but politically or racially motivated. According to some accounts, it was a boring winter evening in the small town of Pulaski, Giles County, in 1866 when six young Confederate veterans conceived of the idea for a secret fraternity whose purpose would be simply to have fun and play innocent pranks. After some deliberation, they even came up with a name for their group. They chose a word from the Greek *kuklos*, meaning "circle" (or group), and after agreeing to the name, someone suggested the word "clan," which they spelled with a *k* to go with *kuklos*. The clan would signify their camaraderie and alliance to one another. And so, it is said, the KKK was born. After debating a purpose for their new club, the six wrapped themselves in sheets and donned pillow cases with eye holes cut out. Then they mounted their horses and began caterwauling about Pulaski, to the amusement of themselves and to the curiosity of all.

Soon others asked to join in their organization, and the six charter members came up with some nonsensical and preposterous rituals to initiate new members. For the initiated, the night-riding escapades were fun and allowed them to blow off steam. However, to local blacks, who soon became the brunt of many of their antics, the situation was a growing threat. Eventually, similar groups (called dens) began to arise in other communities in Tennessee and in other states.

Even if the club was not initially conceived as a subversive alliance with intentions of malice, hostility, or violence toward blacks and other minority groups, it did in time evolve into such. This was a time when many Southerners felt disenfranchised by the federal government and extremely nervous of the fact that blacks were beginning to gain greater political power in the South. The Civil War had not only freed the slaves but also destroyed the South's former social and economic customs and traditions. The old plantation structure was gone, and for the first time blacks were in direct job competition with poor or working-class whites.

The ghostly and ghoulish appearance of the night riders in their white sheets and pillow cases became particularly threatening to many uneducated and supersti-

KKK member Charles Reed during a protest outside an integrated Nashville grammar school. The text on his badge reads "Keep Our White Schools White." Courtesy of Special Collections, University of Memphis Libraries.

tious blacks. At first, blacks were merely intimidated by the KKK antics. As southern hostility continued to rise against the blacks, some KKK members began to realize that their games could be used as a means of controlling, manipulating, and even punishing the latter (keeping them "in their place" in the social order). The Klan saw their tactics as useful in stopping the alleged petty thievery and other offenses that the ex-slaves were committing. In short, it was a way to regain the southern white dominance of pre–Civil War plantation aristocracy. It was also a way of elevating the social status of poor whites above blacks. Wearing their disguises allowed them to suppress and harass the blacks and anti-slavery sympathizers without fear of being recognized, arrested, and prosecuted by local, state, or federal offi-

Klansmen gather at the Silverdale Confederate Cemetery in the summer of 1979. Silverdale was the final resting place of 155 unknown soldiers of General Bragg's army that swept through the Chattanooga area in 1862. Courtesy of Chattanooga News-Free Press Collection, Chattanooga–Hamilton County Bicentennial Library.

cials. By 1867 some Klan dens and imitators began to be infiltrated by irresponsible men of questionable disposition and motives. Many of the atrocities committed may have been at the hands of such riffraff. To many blacks, these night-riding terrorists were reminiscent of prewar days, when similar groups of whites patrolled southern roads at night looking for runaway slaves, enforcing a curfew for blacks, suppressing potential black uprisings, and using the whip (or worse tactics) to punish violators.

As atrocities against blacks and other racial, ethnic, and religious groups increased, the organization was officially disbanded. The federal government also took a solid stance against Kukluxism, meaning any actions designed to intimidate or control blacks, black voting, sympathetic whites, and others considered a potential threat to white supremacy. As a result, two pieces of legislation were passed: the Force Act of 1870 and the Ku Klux Klan Act of 1871. Both were aimed at suppressing terrorist organizations opposed to Radical Reconstruction. Although openly banned, the KKK simply went underground as the Invisible Empire of the South, continuing and in some cases increasing the frequency and severity of white supremacy vigilante tactics.

Violence continued sporadically until the mid-1870s, when the need for KKK tactics, aimed at controlling blacks, diminished. By then, southern states had enacted the Black Codes and Jim Crow laws restricting the civil rights and civil liberties of African Americans and other members of nonwhite groups under the guise of so-called separate but equal strategies.

In the past, Klan activity has been particularly strong in the Middle and West Tennessee counties, including Dyer, Fayette, Gibson, Giles, Hardeman, Hardin, Haywood, Humphreys, Lincoln, Marshall, Maury, McNairy, Obion, Rutherford, Shelby, and, to some extent, Sullivan County in East Tennessee. Throughout the area of Klan influence, blacks and other minority individuals were assaulted, tortured, and murdered, often for the smallest of infractions and without any real provocation. Many of the incidents described in this book, especially lynchings, were the result of KKK activity throughout the state.

Not all secret, white supremacy, and antiblack organizations were KKK. There were similar groups, such as the Yellow Jackets, Red Caps, White Caps, and Night Riders, as well as mere imitators of such groups.

In many cases, blacks did not have to be physically assaulted, murdered, or confronted directly. There were subtle ways of getting the point across, such as pistol shots on election eve near black homes or communities. There were also expensive poll taxes and intimidation at polling places. Kukluxism was most feared for its intangibility. African Americans were expected to "know their place" and to stay there. If they did not, they were put on the straight and narrow. Although some of the activities of the Klan and other such groups may have been blown out of proportion (perhaps on purpose), others were well documented and devastating to entire communities. Certainly not all southerners sided with the Klan or turned their backs on discriminatory actions, but even a silent majority can have devastating effects.

There was a revival of KKK activity in the 1920s that was spurred on by several factors. First, there was a mass migration of millions of Europeans and Asians into the United States following World War I. American involvement in the war made Americans feel that they had helped stamp out the enemy overseas. Now, however, they began to perceive enemies from within. This included foreigners, increasing widespread corruption in local, state, and federal governments, and even

actions that challenged religious fundamentalism. An example of this was the famous Scopes trial that took place in Dayton, in Rhea County. In addition, the labor union movement was threatening to place poor white and black miners, factory, and millworkers in a collective bargaining position. Lastly, World War I saw a change in the attitudes of many blacks, who after fighting and sacrificing in the Great War refused to step back into the role of second-class citizens upon return. They too had a right to a better life.

In the midst of all this, vigilantism arose again with a vengeance, this time focused not just on blacks but also on Catholics, Jews, Mexican immigrants, and others whom they saw as threats to the traditional American way (white supremacy). There was a resurgence of lynchings, beatings, and other cruel actions. In reaction to this, many national newspapers began printing impassioned editorials denouncing lynching and other such actions. In fact, the *Memphis Commercial Appeal* won the 1923 Pulitzer Prize for its editorial cartoons and for its articles attacking the resurgence of the KKK.

SOURCES: Thomas B. Alexander, "Kukluxism in Tennessee, 1865–1869," *Tennessee Historical Quarterly* 8, no. 3 (Sept. 1949): 195–219; Gary R. Blankenship, "The *Commercial Appeal's* Attack on the Ku Klux Klan, 1921–1925," *West Tennessee Historical Society Papers* 31 (Oct. 1977): 44–58; Carson C. Cook Jr., *A Hundred Years of Terror,* a special report from the Southern Poverty Law Center. http://www.csupomna.edu/~diversity/kkk.html; *Nashville Banner,* May 3, 1936; "111 Years of KKKronology," *Southern Exposure* 8, no. 2 (Summer 1980): 58–59; Wyn C. Wade, *The Fiery Cross: The Ku Klux Klan in America.* New York: Simon and Schuster, 1987.

Memphis Racial Massacre
MAY 1–3, 1866

> The whole evidence discloses the killing of men, women, and children—the innocent, unarmed, and defenseless pleading for their

lives and crying for mercy; the wounding, beating, and maltreating of a still greater number; burning, pillaging, and robbing; the consuming of dead bodies in the flames, the burning of dwellings, the attempts to burn up whole families in their houses, and the brutal and revolting ravishings of defenseless and terror stricken women.

—**U.S. House of Representatives report**

During the days of Reconstruction following the American Civil War, there was much animosity between freed slaves and whites. Thousands of blacks living under deplorable conditions crowded into southern cities. In Memphis they lived in slums on the south side, many subsisting on government rations and, by their plight,

depressing the wages of whites, especially (in the case of Memphis) Irish day laborers. Episodes of violence between these two groups were commonplace, and the violence was attributed to both. Thus the social atmosphere of the city was charged for an inevitable confrontation. The underlying causes of the riot revolved around complex political, economic, and social conditions during the post–Civil War period, aggravated by age-old prejudices.

At the conclusion of the Civil War, some 4,000 black soldiers were garrisoned at, and awaiting discharge from, Fort Pickering in Memphis. In his 1888 work, *History of the City of Memphis and Shelby County, Tennessee,* John Keating (568) wrote, "Gangs of them had assaulted white women as well as men, and there was a growing feeling on the part of the best people that unless they were removed bloodshed must ensue." President

The burning of a freedmen's schoolhouse during the Memphis racial massacre of 1866. Courtesy of Memphis and Shelby County Room, Memphis Public Library and Information Center.

Andrew Johnson's administration was petitioned to do so but refused. As a result, the alleged misconduct was said to have continued. In his essay "Memphis Riots," Bobby Lovett suggests that it was not so much black troops as urban blacks in general who were, in the eyes of many whites at the time, behaving inappropriately. Most southern whites, having been defeated by the North, hated the Yankees. However, unable to take out their aggression against Yankees per se, they attacked the freed slaves, whom they believed to be arrogant, lazy, and a drain on an already faltering economy.

Exactly what set off this riot/massacre has been seriously debated. However, on May 1, 1866, verbal abuses were exchanged between some allegedly intoxicated black soldiers from Fort Pickering and Irish police officers who were attempting to make an arrest in South Memphis following a minor traffic accident. Some shots were fired, both sides claiming the other side fired first, and the police retreated. When police reinforcements showed up, a riot ensued, setting off a bloody massacre. Violence and street fighting continued for three days. A congressional investigation at the time concluded that although the black soldiers may have started the trouble, it was the whites who were responsible for aggravating and prolonging it.

According to a congressional report on the incident, what was at the time called a "riot" was in reality a massacre. The report contended that Memphis newspapers had "grossly misrepresented" the circumstances of the event, "while great efforts had been made by the citizens to belittle it into a simple row between some discharged Negro soldiers and the Irish Police." The report concluded that local African Americans "had nothing to do with it after the first day, except to be killed and abused." The altercation between police and soldiers became a pretext "for an organized and bloody massacre of the colored people of Memphis, regardless of age, sex, or condition, inspired by the teachings of the press, and led on by sworn officers of the law composing the city government, and others." What ensued, the report stated,

"can scarcely find a parallel in the history of civilized or barbarous nations, and must inspire the most profound emotions of horror among all civilized people."

When the police reinforcements found no black mob at the scene of the initial confrontation, they initiated a spree of terror and violence against local blacks in general. According to the congressional report, "the riot, as far as the colored people were concerned, was ended by dark on Tuesday evening, at the time the colored soldiers left the ground and went [back to their fort]." Many of the atrocities committed against blacks thereafter are without equal in the South. Forty-eight people (forty-six of them African Americans) died in the incident, and between seventy and eighty were injured. As the melee continued, Memphis's black community bore the vengeance unleashed within the first hours of the first day. Before it was over, four churches and twelve schools were lost. Ninety-one homes were damaged or destroyed by fire and vandalism, one hundred people assaulted and robbed, and five women raped. The economic losses were estimated at about $131,000. The violence ended only after federal troops arrived from Nashville and placed the city under martial law, forbidding the assembly of whites or blacks.

The congressional report contains chilling descriptions of blacks being fired upon indiscriminately. In one such account, a house was set ablaze and the occupants, a woman and her children, were shot as they tried to escape the fire. "It was reported that the arm of a little child was shot off," the congressional investigators noted. In a similar incident, a sixteen-year-old girl named Rachel Hatcher (said to be "intelligent, and of pure and excellent character") fled a burning house after trying to help her neighbors, only to be fired upon by the entire mob. Within moments flames from the burning house partially consumed her bullet-riddled body—"a spectacle horrible to behold."

What the report described as "the crowning acts of atrocity and diabolism" were the rapes of five women "by these fiends in human shape." One such victim was

Frances Thompson, "who had been a slave and was a cripple, using crutches, having a cancer on her foot." The female victims, the report stated, were violated "under circumstances of the most licentious brutality."

Following this orgy of "burglary, robbery, arson, mayhem, rape, assassination, and murder committed under circumstances of the most revolting atrocity," the bodies of many of those killed were left to decompose on the ground for forty-eight hours because their relatives and friends were too afraid to venture outside and claim them. "Authorities permitted them to remain longer than they would have permitted the body of a dead dog to remain on the street," the report said, concluding that the violence "had resulted from the character of the city government, and the bad conduct of the city officials" and that it was further stimulated by the "disloyal press" of Memphis.

The accompanying table summarizes the grim statistics of the massacre.

SOURCES: Jack D. L. Holmes, "The Effects of the Memphis Race Riot of 1866," *West Tennessee Historical Society Papers,* no. 12 (1958): 125–221; John McLeod Keating, *History of the City of Memphis and Shelby County, Tennessee,* 2 vols. (Syracuse, NY: D. Mason & Co., 1888); Bobby L. Lovett, "Memphis Riots: White Reaction to Blacks in Memphis, May 1865–July 1866," *Tennessee Historical Quarterly* 38, no. 1 (Spring 1979): 9–33; U.S. Congress, House, *Report of the Select Committee on the Memphis Riots and Massacres,* 39th Cong., 1st. sess., no. 101 (Washington, DC: Government Printing Office, 1866); J. P. Young, *Standard History of Memphis, Tennessee* (Knoxville: H. W. Crew, 1912).

A Recapitulation

Killed (black)	46
Killed (white)	2
Wounded	75
Raped	5
Maltreated	10
Robberies	100
Houses and cabins burned	91
Churches burned	4
School-houses burned	12
Total estimated economic losses	$130,981.41

Franklin Race Riot
WILLIAMSON COUNTY, JULY 6, 1867

Racial tensions ran high in the South in the years following the Civil War. The slaves had been freed, but the real battle for racial justice and equality for African Americans had just begun. It would be decades before the hostilities subsided, and even today there is prejudice in the hearts and minds of many whites and blacks throughout the country.

So it was in Franklin on July 6, 1867, when a short-term riot of sorts reared its ugly head as a result of divergent political views. Political speeches were made that day by two opposing parties—the colored Loyal League on one side and a group of Conservatives, made up primarily of ex-rebel soldiers and blacks, on the other. John Trimble, a radical Republican candidate for Congress, and W. Y. Elliott, a Republican candidate for the state legislature, spoke at a large political gathering at the Franklin Courthouse Square. Later that afternoon, a black conservative by the name of Joe Williams was passing through town and was requested to speak on behalf of the citizens of the opposite political persuasion. He agreed to do so, and each speaker was respectively allowed their turn on the stump.

Behind the scenes, resentment had been growing, especially by former rebels who were up against former slaves in a political race for superiority. After the speeches were concluded, the black conservatives walked away and assembled at a grove of trees just outside of town. There they discussed a torchlight parade that they had been planning to make back to Franklin Square. Some recommended against it, fearing that it might anger the locals, but others were intent on following through. It was to be simply a peaceful final march into the town in recognition of their political views. After that, they would disband and return to their individual homes. They had two reasons for wanting to conduct the march. First of all, they did not want their opponents to think them cowards by staying away. Second, they had been planning the parade for some time and would have been disappointed to just give up on it.

There are conflicting views as to what happened next. As the two groups faced off from opposite sides of the street, gun shots rang out. The blacks and whites on both sides were armed and had been for some time, fearing violence from one another. Some say a single shot and others say a number of shots were fired from one side or the other. Shortly, however, volleys of fire erupted from both sides. A physician who treated the wounded attested to the fact that the members of the colored Loyal League sustained most of the deaths and injuries and that most had been shot in their backs and the backs of their limbs. This indicated that they were fleeing the scene at the time of the melee.

The exact number killed, mortally wounded, or otherwise injured in the incident was never definitively determined. Most accounts put the casualties in the scores, with severe carnage on both sides. After this brief skirmish, the matter was settled and no additional violence occurred. Army troops were sent from Nashville on the following Sunday, but they were not needed and were soon sent home. In fact, subsequent investigations revealed that, overall, the citizens of Franklin were embarrassed by the incident. Assistance was provided to the wounded on both sides, and reparations were made to the families of the dead. This dark page in the history of Franklin ended as quickly as it had begun. However, Jim Crow laws (measures in state and local courts passed ostensibly to establish separate but equal treatment for blacks and whites) were eventually passed. This legislation was aimed at returning real power to whites, particularly in the South. It would be decades before the courts would begin the long and arduous process of re-

storing true social equality, civil rights, and civil liberties to people of color in both the South and the North.

SOURCES: *Memphis Daily Appeal,* July 9, 1867; *Nashville Daily Press and Times,* July 6, 8–10, 1867; *New York Times,* July 8, 1867; *Republican Banner,* July 9, 11, 1867.

White Capping in Sevier County
1892–96

> I do solemnly swear before God and man that if I reveal anything concerning our organization or anything we may do, the penalty shall be to receive one hundred lashes and leave the county within ten days or be put to death. Now I take this oath freely and voluntarily, and am willing to abide by the obligation in every respect. I further agree and swear before God that if I reveal anything concerning our organization, I will suffer my throat to be cut, my heart to be shot out and my body to be burned; that I will forfeit my life, my property and all that I may have in this world and in the world to come: So help me God.
>
> **—Secret Oath of the White Caps**

As increasing numbers of the citizens of Pigeon Forge and other areas of Sevier County became aware of, and incensed by, certain lewd and immoral activities such as prostitution, pressure was placed on local law enforcement officials to stop it. When this did not happen, a vigilante group known as the White Caps was organized to take matters into their own hands. At first they left notes at the doors of suspected wrongdoers, vowing whippings or worse if they did not leave the area. When such notices went unheeded, thrashings and beatings ensued. The first such incident occurred in nearby Emerts Cove (Sevier County). From there it spread rapidly to other areas around Sevier County, especially Pigeon Forge. Eventually this vigilante justice intensified to an almost nightly affair. All the while, the good citizens and even the law turned a blind eye to what many considered just punishments. The strength and reputation of the White Caps continued to grow as more men joined the illicit band. Like the Ku Klux Klan, which persecuted blacks and other ethnic groups, each member was obliged to take an oath not to reveal the identify of his fellow members or any details of their activities. It was a blood oath punishable by death. However, in time, leadership of the White Caps began to be taken over by irresponsible men and thugs. Many became bent upon personal revenge and other illicit acts under the guise of ridding their community of immorality. As white-capping careened out of control and lost popular support, another organization known as the Blue Bills arose to stop it. Frequent clashes occurred between the two factions.

The reign of the White Caps finally culminated in the cold-blooded murder of Laura and William Whaley, two completely innocent citizens of Pigeon Forge. They had been wrongly accused of an offense based solely on the word of a White Cap member seeking personal revenge. This despicable event finally led the state legislature to pass a law condemning White Capping as a criminal offense. Over the next couple of years the vigilantes responsible for the murders were brought to justice. Some were tried and legally executed, others murdered by parties unknown, and still others simply fled the area, never to be seen again. Within the decade, law and order was restored to Pigeon Forge and surrounding communities. In fact, in 1903 an article in the *Knoxville News Sentinel* reported that "Sevier County is now one of the most orderly counties in Tennessee. The criminal docket of the circuit court is light; and punishment is given swiftly, if necessary, for any murder or outrage. Citizens no longer have the least fear of the midnight assassin."

SOURCES: Allen R. Coggins, *Historic River Hamlet of Pigeon Forge: A Driving Tour* (Pigeon Forge, TN: Pigeon Forge Dept. of Tourism, 2007); Marion Mangrum, *Interment of the White Caps* (Maryville, TN: Brazos Printing, 1963);

Sevier County Heritage Book Committee, *Sevier County, Tennessee and Its Heritage* (Waynesville, NC: County Heritage, 1994); Cas Walker, *White Caps and Blue Bills: A Story of a Feud between the White Caps and the Blue Bills in Sevier County in the Great Smoky Mountains* (Knoxville: Cas Walker, 1974).

White Capping in Marshall County
OCTOBER 5, 1901

> The sheriff is making every effort to apprehend the White Cappers and the best citizens of that section of the county are giving him all assistance possible. The Caney Springs community includes some of the best and most law abiding citizens of Marshall County, who are greatly humiliated over the lawless and bloody act. The act is deplored by the people of the entire county, and if the perpetrators are apprehended they will be severely dealt with.
>
> —*Nashville American,* Oct. 8, 1901

Several versions of this incident were reported by state and national newspapers, and one indicated that it nearly turned into a riot or race war. The exact truth will never be known. Poor race relations between some blacks and some whites had been festering for some time in north central Marshall County. Allegedly, this was the result of a rash of thefts suspected to have been committed by local blacks and possibly some white ringleaders.

On the evening of October 5, a group of some thirty-five blacks were returning from a picnic, a festival, or some other sort of gathering near Caney Springs. They were walking down the road between Caney Springs and Lewisburg when they were stopped by a group of about 100 hooded White Caps stationed at the opposite end of a bridge. When told by the White Caps to halt, they did so and were allowed to continue over the bridge, one at a time. In a sort of inquisition, each was asked to give his name. Supposedly any blacks believed to be of bad character were to be taken into custody by the White Caps. When one of the blacks, a large man by the name of Puckett, started across the bridge, one of the White Caps asked for his name. According to an article in the *Nashville American,* October 8, 1901, the black man roared, "It is none of your d*** business! Who are you?" Puckett is alleged to have pulled a pistol at this point, shooting the white man in the chest. As the wounded man fell, the White Caps started firing pistols and shotguns indiscriminately into the crowd of blacks assembled at the other end of the bridge.

As panic ensued, the whites quickly retreated with their wounded comrade. As the ordeal ended, between twelve and fifteen blacks lay wounded and three or four dead or dying. One woman and one man were blinded by sprays of birdshot in their faces. A similar White Capping incident was said to have occurred in this same general area some years prior to this event. Although the cowardly action of White Capping was strongly denounced by the citizens of Marshall County, it is not known if anyone was ever apprehended or convicted in this matter.

SOURCES: *Nashville American,* Oct. 8, 1901; *Nashville Banner,* Oct. 8, 1901.

Knoxville Race Riot
August 30–31, 1919

> On the night of his execution, Mays said, "I am to die to satisfy a few Republican politicians. Some Republicans told the governor he'd lose 20,000 votes if he helped me."
> —**John Egerton, "A Case of Prejudice"**

A headline in the August 31, 1919, *Sunday Journal and Tribune,* "Bloody Riots Follow Attack on Jail; Five Known Dead; Many Are Wounded," was not unusual for the so-called Red Summer of 1919. However, its occurrence in Knoxville was. Knoxville had never been a town of violent race relations, at least not in comparison with other southern cities of comparable or larger size.

In fact, according to *History of the Knox County Sheriff's Department 1792–1992,* "The riot of 1919, the tragic events of deaths and the plunder, which was credited to the drunken mob during the outbreak, was the most tragic event in the history of Knoxville since the Battle of Fort Sanders, during the war Between the States." However, when the word got out that Maurice F. Mays, a well-known black man of questionable reputation, had allegedly broken into a home and murdered a white woman, Mrs. Bertie Lindsay, a drunken mob of whites soon stormed the Knox County jail. They would have vigilante justice, or at least so it seemed.

Anticipating the worst, the Knoxville sheriff had secretly smuggled Mays down to Chattanooga to await trial in a safer environment. Even after a number of private citizens' delegations had been allowed to inspect the jail to see for themselves that Mays was not there, the mob still broke down the door, smashed windows, and overpowered the guards in a vain attempt to have their way with the alleged murderer. In retrospect, many believe that the actual motive of the mobsters was not so much frontier justice as it was a desire to release some of their buddies from the jail and confiscate a large cache of illicit liquor stored there.

Meanwhile, it was maintained that angry blacks were also rallying in nearby "colored town" for the purpose of ensuring that Mays received protection and a fair trial. Near midnight on August 30, 1919, a group of blacks gathered and marched toward Vine Avenue and Central Avenue. Within moments they were face to face with two National Guard machine gun companies and a mob of angry whites. This included two detachments of National Guardsmen who had just completed maneuvers near Knoxville and an inspection by Governor A. H. Roberts. They were on their way home when they were called back to help subdue the growing racial tension in Knoxville.

The machine guns were ordered positioned at the intersection of Vine Avenue and State Street as a show of force, but told not to fire unless ordered to do so. Unfortunately, in the confusion of the clash and the ongoing riot, one or both of the machine guns were fired into the crowd. One white man died when he stepped into the line of fire. According to witnesses, he was cut in two by the spray of bullets. The exact number of blacks and whites killed or wounded by the machine guns and in the riot as a whole will never be known. According to newspaper accounts, only two people were officially listed as killed in the entire riot; however, eyewitness estimates vary widely. Chief Deputy Carroll Cates stated that twenty-five or thirty were killed. National Guard Major Maurice Robert reported thirty or forty dead. Others estimated casualties in the hundreds, with rumors that many bodies had been dumped into the Tennessee River from the Gay Street bridge or buried in mass graves outside the city. Such claims were never confirmed.

As tensions built, white crowds began looting hardware stores and pawn shops along Gay Street for the purpose of arming themselves against the black community and local authorities. They were said to have stolen every conceivable kind of weapon, from guns and knives to razors and pitchforks. After the arrival of some 1,100 guardsmen, 150 special police, and 100 special deputies, and with the implementation of martial law, the violence was curtailed.

The number of blacks participating in the insurrection, and their actual intentions, may never be known. Many contend that their motive was simply to show support for their brother through peaceful demonstrations, not through militant action or direct confrontation. The violence, on the other hand, seems to have been precipitated by certain individuals in the white community who overreacted to a perceived threat.

During the jail assault, several prisoners occupying outer cells subject to bombardment by bricks were released for their own protection. In the confusion of the siege, several prisoners escaped and others were released by the rioters. However, among those set free were four convicted murderers and a "certified lunatic." Only about thirty whites were eventually charged with

participating in the riots and the siege. It is not surprising, considering the atmosphere of racial tension at the time, that all were acquitted by a jury of their (white) peers.

Eventually, Mays, the alleged murderer, was tried for the murder of Bertie Lindsay. Although the prosecution was unable to establish a motive, failed to show that he was at the scene, and failed to prove that his gun had even been fired, he was convicted of the killing. After another trial and many appeals, Mays was put to death in the electric chair in the state prison at Nashville.

After his execution, thirty-two similar crimes against women occurred in Knoxville. Eight of the victims were murdered, and twelve others were raped and robbed. By that time, it was clear that Mays had been innocent. A private detective who investigated the crimes claimed that a solitary white man had committed all the assaults, including the one for which Mays was accused. Matters became even more confusing in 1927. As John Egerton noted, "Five and a half years after the execution of Maurice Mays, a white woman walked into the police station in Norton, Virginia, and calmly told the officer in charge that she was the murderer of Bertie Lindsay."

SOURCES: John Egerton, "A Case of Prejudice: Maurice Mays and the Knoxville Race Riot of 1919," *Southern Exposure* 11, no. 4 (July/Aug. 1983): 56–65; *History of the Knox County Sheriff's Department 1792–1992 Commemorative Book* (N.p., n.p.); *Knoxville Journal and Tribune,* Aug. 31 and Sept. 1, 1919; Matthew Lakin, "A Dark Night," *Journal of East Tennessee History,* no. 72 (2000): 1–29; Lakin, Knoxville, personal correspondence with author, May 9, 2001; Bill Murrah, "The Knoxville Race Riot: 'To Make People Proud,'" *Southern Exposure* 1, nos. 3–4 (Winter 1974): 105–6; Lee E. Williams and Lee E. Williams Jr., *Anatomy of Four Race Riots* (Hattiesburg: Univ. and College Press of Mississippi, 1972).

Columbia Race Riot

MAURY COUNTY, FEBRUARY 25–28, 1946

> After State Highway Patrolmen and State Guardsmen had finished their job of wrecking, machine-gunning, and terrorizing peaceful [black] citizens who only defended their homes and families, they left their emblem for all to see. That emblem was a bold and proud KKK scrawled across the side of a hacked coffin in the Morton Funeral Home.
>
> —**National Committee for Justice, Columbia**

When Gladys Stephenson and her son James stopped by the Castner-Knott Department Store in Columbia on the morning of February 25, 1946, little did they know that they would launch a civil insurrection that would reverberate throughout the country.

Mrs. Stephenson had stopped to pick up a radio left for repairs but was informed that it had been accidentally sold to another customer. When she demanded retribution, Mrs. Stephenson was verbally abused and then slapped and kicked by a white store clerk, William Fleming. At this point, witnesses say that her nineteen-year old son, a World War II veteran, stepped forward to defend his mother. He fought with Fleming and allegedly pushed him through a plate glass window. His wounds were minor, but some witnesses indicated that the Stephensons were surrounded by a number of whites and assaulted just before officers arrived. The Stephensons were charged with breach of the peace, pleaded guilty, paid a fifty-dollar fine, and went home.

Two days later, an editorial in the *Knoxville Journal* stated that if the three persons involved in the dispute had been either all white or all black, nothing more would have come of the incident. However, Columbia was a southern town, and the concept of what the southern racial structure ought to be was firmly fixed in the minds of many town citizens. At the time, the nation was also on the verge of a civil rights revolution, and this event, along with other southern atrocities, was about to help launch it.

When William Fleming's father heard about the incident, he became enraged and took out a warrant against James Stephenson for attempted murder. Stephenson was again arrested but was soon bailed out by a local black businessman. In this racially charged atmosphere, some of the white citizens of Columbia began to gather at the town square and talk about an old subject: lynching.

In 1925 three black men had been lynched in Maury County, and some in this growing white mob said it might be time for another such demonstration aimed at keeping the black folks in line. Many of them were armed, some drinking, and rumors were running rampant. The mob numbered about seventy-five.

Meanwhile, in the black community of Columbia, and especially in a business district called Mink Slide, there was growing restlessness. As rumors of a lynching reached them, many blacks prepared to defend themselves, their homes, and businesses. They became an armed camp, and allegedly, under the leadership of local black businessmen, all lights were turned off and streetlights were shot out. A number of World War II black veterans were armed and posted about the neighborhood in anticipation of trouble. As night progressed, a number of white citizens were alleged to have shot randomly into the black neighborhood, and there were drive-by shootings. When local authorities heard about the lights being shot out in Mink Slide, four officers, including the chief of police, approached the area in an unmarked vehicle to investigate. Someone from the darkness yelled "Halt!," and soon the officers were being fired upon. All four were wounded; one seriously. The blacks claimed that they did not know that the car contained police officers, and they felt that they were merely protecting themselves and their families.

Later that night, the governor sent Tennessee Highway Patrol officers to Columbia to assist local authorities in restoring order. The Highway Patrol arrived in the early hours of February 26. They surrounded the Mink Slide area and began a sweep. In the process, they fired machine guns and automatic rifles randomly into homes and businesses. Later they searched homes and

Weapons seized in a raid by Maury County constables during the Columbia race riot, February 27, 1946. Courtesy of Special Collections, University of Memphis Libraries.

ransacked stores without warrants. They looted stores, doctors' offices, and a funeral home, chalking KKK on an already vandalized casket. They also took cash and other valuables from homes and confiscated around 300 weapons. They eventually arrested and jailed somewhere between 70 and 100 black men, women, and children and refused them either legal counsel or bail. Meanwhile National Guard Troops also arrived just in time to prevent armed white civilians from entering the Mink Slide area to allegedly assist the Highway Patrolmen. Order was soon restored.

After three days, the Highway Patrol officers and the National Guardsmen were dismissed. On the twenty-eighth, the blacks that were still incarcerated in the Maury County Jail were interrogated to determine who had shot the four local officers. While three suspects were being transported from the jail to the sheriff's office for further questioning, it is alleged that all three grabbed guns and tried to escape. Two were shot dead and another wounded. Some of the other prisoners alleged that the three blacks were actually murdered in retaliation for the earlier wounding of the four officers.

After the Columbia riot ended, the litigation and publicity continued. Many of the whites believed that they had won because they had restored the southern racial structure by keeping the black community in check.

Many blacks, on the other hand, felt victorious for having stood up against the white community and survived. In retrospect, the intense publicity that arose from this incident no doubt helped spur interest in, and set the stage for, the civil rights movement and racial reforms into the 1950s and 1960s.

SOURCES: Dorothy Beeler, "Race Riot in Columbia Tennessee, February 25–27, 1946," *Tennessee Historical Quarterly* 39, no. 1 (Spring 1980): 49–61; John Egerton, *Speak Now Against the Day: The Generation before the Civil Rights Movement in the South* (New York: Knopf, 1994); *Knoxville Journal,* Feb. 27, 1946; *Terror in Tennessee,* pamphlet (New York: National Committee for Justice in Columbia, Tennessee, n.d.).

Clinton Racial Violence

ANDERSON COUNTY, 1956–58

> That night the crowd overturned cars, slashed tires, smashed windows and frightened Negro travelers, some of them servicemen who just happened to be coming through. Youngsters and juvenile-minded [white] adults took over the town threatening to dynamite the mayor's home, the newspaper plant, and even the Courthouse itself.
>
> —**Thomas Wells,** *Clinton Courier-News*

Racial unrest erupted in Clinton, Anderson County, in 1956 as a result of a U.S. Supreme Court order to desegregate its high school. Until then, black students had been bussed to nearby Knoxville High School. Local reaction to the court action was not well received by everyone at first, but in August of that year black students registered for school and began attending classes without incident. In fact, a majority of the white and black students got along well together. Unfortunately, the peace and harmony did not last.

Frederick John Kasper, a racial agitator from New York, and several of his segregationist cronies came to Clinton hell bent on stirring up racial hatred, prejudice, and violence. Turmoil erupted in short order, primarily between whites in opposition to integration and those who felt the court order should be implemented. Most of the blacks stayed home. Horace Wells, owner, publisher, and editor of the *Clinton Courier-News* stated that the controversy was about blacks, but it was between whites. The blacks were on the sidelines, mere observers, as it were. As tensions swelled, acts of violence were launched against local blacks and white sympathizers. Dynamite was set off around the city and crosses were burned, Ku Klux Klan style, on the lawns of both black and white citizens. At the height of the protests, several blacks who just happened to be driving through the town one evening were stopped and assaulted by agitated mobs. A black sailor who had come to Clinton to visit his girlfriend was taken into protective custody by local authorities for fear of what might happen to him.

A local white minister who boldly accompanied black students to and from school was attacked and beaten for his efforts. There were also threats that the local courthouse would be burned down if blacks continued to attend classes. Amid this turmoil, the governor sent State Highway Patrol officers to the troubled town to assist local police in dealing with the situation. As conditions worsened, the National Guard was activated and a curfew initiated.

Investigations into the incident by the FBI and others led to the arrest and prosecution of Kasper and several of his mob leaders by the U.S. Marshall's Office. Seven men were eventually prosecuted, including Kasper. He eventually served prison time for obstructing federal justice. Although racial tensions subsided in the weeks following the initial violence, the homes of the local police chief, the town's newspaper editor, and those of several students were bombed.

Fortunately, no one was hurt in these incidents, and the tension mostly subsided. In 1957 Clinton High became the first white public school in the state of Tennessee to graduate a black student. His name was Bobby

Police (foreground) and rioters amass at the Anderson County courthouse during the desegregation of Clinton High School on September 1, 1956. This photograph was taken seconds before tear gas was used to disperse the crowd. Courtesy of Special Collections, University of Memphis Libraries.

Cain. According to one Clinton High School student, "Before Bobby graduated, word spread that some people were going to try to disrupt the processions and keep him from graduating. Bobby had won the respect of many white children in his class, and they planned to defend him if anyone tried to take him from the graduation line. The students felt Bobby had earned his diploma, and they intended to see that he received it. This was by no means an isolated act of compassion. In retrospect, we know that the majority of the white students, and most of the citizens of Clinton, had supported the black students and held no resentment toward them.

However, in the early morning hours of October 5, 1958, three dynamite blasts erupted and destroyed a large portion of the high school. Although the perpetrators were never brought to justice, this final, vile, and cowardly act ended most of the overt racial violence in the small East Tennessee town.

SOURCES: June N. Adamson, "Few Black Voices Heard: The Black Community and the Desegregation Crisis in Clinton, Tennessee, 1956," *Tennessee Historical Quarterly* 53, no. 1 (Spring 1994): 30–41; Margaret Anderson and Robert Marlowe, eds., *Clinton—An Identity Rediscovered* (Clinton: Clinton Courier-News, 1985); Gilbert E. Govan and James W. Livingood, *The Chattanooga Country 1540–1976,* 3rd ed. (Knoxville: Univ. of Tennessee Press, 1977); K. B. Hoskins, *Anderson County History: Tennessee County History Series* (Memphis: Memphis State Univ. Press, 1979); Jim Stokely and Jeff D. Johnson, eds., "Children's Museum of Oak

Clinton High School after a bombing, October 5, 1958. The school was bombed only one month after federally mandated desegregation occurred. Courtesy of Knoxville Journal Collection, McClung Historical Collection, Knox County Public Library.

Ridge," in *An Encyclopedia of East Tennessee* (Kingsport, TN: Kingsport Press, 1981); Thomas Wells, Editorial, *Clinton Courier-News,* Oct. 4, 1957.

Martin Luther King Jr. Assassination
MEMPHIS, APRIL 4, 1968

> We've got some difficult days ahead. But it really doesn't matter with me now. Because I've been to the mountain top. I don't mind. Like anybody, I would like to live a long life. Longevity has its place. But I'm not concerned about that now. I just want to do God's will. And he's allowed me to go up to the mountain. And I've looked over and I've seen the Promised Land. I may not get there with you. But I want you to know tonight: THAT WE AS A PEOPLE WILL GET TO THE PROMISED LAND.

—**Dr. Martin Luther King Jr., Apr. 3, 1968**

One of the most appalling and controversial incidents in the history of Memphis, the state of Tennessee, and the nation occurred on April 4, 1968. At approximately 6:00 PM civil rights leader Dr. Martin Luther King Jr. was standing on the second floor balcony of the Lorraine Motel in Memphis. He was conversing with Jesse Jackson and musician Ben Branch in the parking lot below. Suddenly a single sniper's bullet (caliber .30–06) struck his right jaw, tore downward through his neck, severed his spinal cord, and lodged in his shoulder blade. Some thought a car had backfired, but it was quickly apparent that King had been shot. He dropped to the floor of the concrete balcony and never regained consciousness. He was pronounced dead about an hour later at Memphis's St. Joseph's Hospital.

King, the nation's foremost apostle of nonviolent protest, had come to the city to participate in a peaceful march in support of black sanitation workers. They had been striking for higher wages and better working conditions since March 12, 1968. It was hoped that King's presence would help end the strike by convincing the city to accept their terms. At the time of his death, he was staying in room 306 of the Loraine Motel on Mulberry Street. King's favorite downtown Memphis lodging establishment, this location now serves as a civil rights museum.

In the wake of King's death, violence erupted nationwide in hundreds of cities and towns. Scores of people died in these riots and hundreds of others were injured or arrested, many for crimes of vandalism or resisting arrest. Damage from arson and fire bombings, along with destruction of vehicles, buildings, and infrastructure, was rampant. Violence escalated during the long hot summer of 1968. The cities of Memphis, Nashville, and Chattanooga in Tennessee were virtual powder kegs ready to explode—and explode they did, time after time.

Coverage of the riots by the print and broadcast media undoubtedly helped fuel the ensuing episodes of nationwide violence. Curfews were imposed, and law enforcement and National Guardsmen used fire hoses, police dogs, tear gas, batons, and brute force to suppress riots in many cities. Blacks boycotted white-owned businesses in a show of solidarity. In the end, King's martyrdom did much to secure the long overdue civil rights of blacks and other minorities in America.

The sanitation workers' controversy, in which King had planned to participate, was quickly resolved by the city of Memphis. As King had so eloquently put it, the plight of the sanitation workers was more about human rights than it was civil rights. (See "Memphis Sanitation Workers Strike.")

President Lyndon Johnson declared April 7, 1968, as a national day of mourning for King. His funeral was attended by individuals from across the country and around the world. Vice President Hubert Humphrey attended the funeral in place of President Johnson for fear that the appearance of the latter might stir further violence. Despite King's nonviolent message of peaceful protest, his death launched further actions by militant civil rights groups under the mantra of "Black Power."

An investigation of King's murder revealed that the assassin's shot was fired from a boardinghouse across the parking lot from the Lorraine Motel. A hunting rifle with a scope, along with a pair of binoculars, was found in a bathroom of the boardinghouse. All three bore the fingerprints of a prison escapee by the name of James Earl Ray. Even today controversy continues to surround the senseless death of King, a preacher and teacher of nonviolent protests. Did Ray act alone in the assassination or in association with others? A number of seemingly credible conspiracy theories have been suggested. Some contend that Ray acted alone, while others say the assassination occurred at the hands of another unknown party. There have been allegations that the Memphis police were involved, that the FBI orchestrated the event, and even that the Mafia was responsible.

Nonetheless, Ray's fingerprints were found on the weapon, abandoned in a restroom of the boardinghouse, and he alone was responsible for pulling the trigger. A man of Ray's description was reportedly seen fleeing the scene after the shot was fired; he had fled the country only to be apprehended two months later at Britain's Heathrow Airport. After robbing a London bank, he allegedly awaited a flight to South Africa. He had hoped to go there, hide out, and serve as a mercenary fighter until the King incident blew over. Until his death on April 23, 1998, in the Tennessee State Prison in Nashville, Ray continued to maintain his innocence, citing a series of often controversial stories about what really happened and the role he played in the assassination of Dr. Martin Luther King Jr.

SOURCES: Joan T. Beifuss, *At the River I Stand* (Memphis: St. Luke's Press, 1990); *Knoxville Journal,* Apr. 5, 6, 8–10, 1968; *Knoxville News-Sentinel,* Apr. 5, 1968.

Civil rights parade in Memphis following the assassination of Martin Luther King Jr. in 1968. Courtesy of Special Collections, University of Memphis Libraries.

Lynching and Hate Crimes

It is believed that the practice of lynching came about during the Revolutionary War. During this period a Virginia planter, Charles Lynch, introduced the practice of holding court and trying individuals still loyal to the British and executing them; hence, Lynch's Law and lynching. Following in that vein, lawlessness in the Old Southwest (which included Tennessee in the late 1700s and early 1800s) was often dealt with via vigilante justice. Bank robbers and horse thieves were set upon by local posses without the sanctioned authority of a sheriff or marshal. Between the 1830s and 1850s the majority of those lynched in the United States were whites, but that would change in the years to come.

The term "lynch" is often erroneously used to imply illegal execution by hanging. In reality, it includes other, even more heinous methods of torture and death, and therefore has a much broader and more sinister meaning. According to Senator Mary Landrieu of Louisiana, quoted in *USA Today,* June 13, 2005, "Lynching was a form of terrorism practiced by Americans against other Americans." However, the frequent lynching of African Americans, in particular, was often an act of belligerence aimed at dehumanizing them. It was a way of physically and psychologically reminding them of their place in the social order. This ostensibly upheld the economic, social, and cultural superiority of whites, especially in the post-Reconstruction South. As the incidents of lynching increased, black men, women, and children, along with a smaller number of whites, were severely tortured, burned, strangled, beaten, shot, drowned, and dragged to death. Female black victims were frequently gang raped. Black men were often desexed and their various body parts severed, sometimes even before death.

Although such an overt act of racial murder would be met today with swift retribution for the perpetrators, in the past it was a crowd-gathering event. For example, at the lynching of Thomas Brooks, a black man from Fayette County, Tennessee, in 1915, "hundreds of Kodaks clicked all morning at the scene," wrote an observer in *Crisis,* the publication of the National Association for the Advancement of Colored People (NAACP). "People in automobiles and carriages came from miles around to view the corpse dangling from the end of a rope" (quoted in Apel, 37). Picture-card photographers even installed a portable printing press at the bridge, and lynching scenes became a burgeoning and profitable subventure of the postcard industry. By 1908 the trade had grown so large that the postmaster general banned the cards from the U.S. Mail. Today, these cards have become rare but grotesque collectibles.

Lynching and political massacres were heaviest in the mid- to late 1860s, with many such acts being perpetrated by the KKK. Lynchings rose in frequency until the enactment of the Klan Act of 1871, when they were curtailed for a short period. They finally peaked in the 1890s with the passage of Jim Crow laws. There were 214 confirmed lynchings in Tennessee between 1886 and 1930. It has been said that slavery was not abolished under the Thirteenth Amendment of the U.S. Constitution; rather, legislation simply changed the conditions under which it could exist. Historian Rayford W. Logan has referred to this period as the "Dark Ages of Recent American History" (xx).

The horrors of lynching inspired a poem by Abel Meerepol, a Jewish schoolteacher and union activist from New York. Titled "Strange Fruit," it was later set to music and performed by Billie Holiday, one of the most celebrated African American female jazz singers of all time. Holiday usually closed her concerts with this song, standing on a dark stage, a single spotlight dramatically illuminating her body. Containing such unsettling lines as "Black bodies swinging in the southern breeze / Strange fruit hanging in the poplar trees," the song evoked mixed emotions among those who performed it, as well as those who heard it. And in many places, the song was banned. Jack Schifrman, who booked Holiday at his famous Apollo Theater in New York, was familiar with the song and did not want her to sing it, afraid it might cause trouble. However, there was a clause in her contract specifying that she could sing the song whenever she wanted. At the end of her first performance of "Strange Fruit," according to Holiday biographer Donald Clarke, when the singer "wrenched the final words from her lips, there was not a soul in the audience, black or white, who did not feel half strangled. . . . A moment of oppressively heavy silence followed, and then a kind of rustling sound. . . . It was the sound of almost two thousand people sighing" (115).

Because of the large numbers of lynchings that took place in Tennessee, space does not allow a discussion or even a listing of all of them. Sad, too, is the fact that even the identities of some of the victims will never be known. Only a few of Tennessee's multiple lynchings, and two particularly heinous solitary events, are related herein. All of them demonstrate cruel and unusual punishments, and most were perpetrated under the guise of justice.

SOURCES: Dora Apel, *Imagery of Lynching: Black Men, White Women, and the Mob* (New Brunswick, NJ: Rutgers Univ. Press, 2004); Kathy Bennett, "Lynching," in *The Tennessee Encyclopedia of History and Culture,* ed. Carroll Van West, 560–61 (Nashville: Tennessee Historical Society and Rutledge Hill Press, 1998); Roger Bobley, ed., *Illustrated World Encyclopedia* (Woodbury, NY: Bobley Publishing, 1977); Donald Clarke, *Wishing on the Moon: The Life and Times of Billie Holiday* (New York: Viking, 1994); Meg Greene, *Billie Holiday: A Biography* (Westport, CT: Greenwood Press); Jessie P. Guzman, ed., *1952 Negro Yearbook* (New York: William H. Wise & Co., 1952); Rayford W. Logan, *The Betrayal of the Negro: From Rutherford Hayes to Woodrow Wilson* (New York: Collier Books, 1965); Walter White, *Rope and Faggot* (New York: Arno Press, 1969).

Gibson County Mass Lynching
TRENTON, AUGUST 27, 1874

Between 1:00 and 2:00 AM on August 27, 1874, a mob of some one hundred armed and masked vigilantes surrounded the Gibson County Jail in Trenton, demanding the release of sixteen black prisoners. According to witnesses, the leaders of the group were quoted as saying, "We have come for those niggers, and intend getting them; turn over the keys, or we will blow your brains out." Overpowered by the mob, the sheriff, jailer, and guards had no choice but to surrender the keys. The blacks were roped together in twos, taken from the jail, and quietly marched out of town.

After walking about half a mile south toward Huntingdon, six of the blacks were cut loose and told to run for their lives. As they ran, a volley of fire from the mob struck them down. Left for dead, the mob moved on with the other ten prisoners. Four of the six were killed outright, but two others were still alive, albeit mortally wounded when discovered. They were found by several Trenton citizens who had heard the shots and come to investigate.

The details of what happened next vary. Some witnesses insist that the ten remaining prisoners were taken two miles farther down the road, cut loose from their bonds, and told to run. This time all ten were killed by shots from the mob. Others accounts suggest that some of the remaining ten blacks escaped or were slaughtered in some other manner. After this the mob quickly dispersed into the night. Although John C. Brown, the governor of Tennessee, offered a $500 reward for information leading to the identification and apprehension of the vigilantes, no one was ever convicted or even arrested for the crime.

Shortly after the massacre, rumors spread quickly that 300 to 500 armed Negroes were marching toward Trenton to avenge their fallen neighbors and friends. Sentinels sent out to confirm the stories returned saying that they could find no such armed force. In spite of this, the whites began arming themselves against a possible retaliation. Panic gripped both the white and black communities of Gibson and surrounding counties for some time after the mass lynching. Armed men from nearby towns offered assistance to the citizens of Trenton to help put down the alleged "Negro uprising." Some people felt at the time that these vicious rumors of armed blacks, hell bent on retaliation, were spread by members of the mob to help cover their unlawful activities.

The whole affair began on August 22, when two white men, Monroe Morgan and James Warren, were fired upon by a group of some thirty or forty blacks just outside of Pickettsville. The two whites escaped, although one of their mules was struck by buckshot. Investigations into this incident lead to the uncovering of an alleged conspiracy by a number of blacks in Gibson and surrounding counties. Supposedly, members of the black community, tired of frequent attacks by the local Ku Klux Klan (KKK), were plotting to assassinate a number of whites in the area. They also planned to kill one or more blacks whom they feared would give away their plans. During an arraignment hearing by three local justices of the peace, one of the sixteen black prisoners, Jarrett Burrows, turned state's evidence. He related facts about the attempted murders of Morgan and Warren on August 22. He also confirmed that some blacks

were conspiring to rise up against the whites of Gibson County. His story was even corroborated by Nelson McGhee, another of the black lynch victims.

According to both witnesses, an extensive organization of Gibson County blacks were tired of the unrestrained actions of the local KKK. They also intended to overthrow and take control of the county. It was further alleged that President Grant himself had personally sanctioned these actions in response to persecution of innocent black men, women, and children by the KKK in the wake of the Civil War.

When word of the alleged conspiracy emerged, a mob of militant whites banded together to curtail the actions of the black militants. This apparently was the motivating factor for the mass lynching of August 27. Most of the vigilantes were believed to be Gibson County men, since the majority of the citizens of Trenton condemned the lynchings. In fact, a large group of whites later met with the blacks in Gibson County in mutual condemnation of such violent acts on the part of both whites and blacks.

SOURCES: *Atlanta Constitution,* Aug. 27, 28, 30, 1874; *Chicago Daily Tribune,* Aug. 27, 29, 31, 1874; Jessie P. Guzman, ed., *1952 Negro Yearbook* (New York: William H. Wise & Co., 1952); *Milan Exchange,* Sept. 3, 1874. White, Walter. *Rope and Faggot.* New York: Arno Press, 1969.

Mormon Massacre
LEWIS COUNTY, AUGUST 10, 1884

It was on the east fork of Cane Creek, in northwest Lewis County, that five members of the Mormon faith were attacked and murdered on August 10, 1884, by an angry mob of local masked men. The alleged assailants, dressed in outlandish colorful disguise, were determined to drive the "religious fanatics" from their county. This incident, later referred to by the church as "the Tennessee Massacre" and "the Cane Creek Killings," also resulted in the wounding of a Mormon woman and the death of the local vigilante leader.

Tennessee's Mormon massacre historical marker in Lewis County. Photograph by the author.

From the 1870s through the end of the century, Mormons brought their ministry to Tennessee and actively and faithfully sought converts. One group barely escaped mob violence in response to their teachings along the Tennessee and Georgia state line near Chattanooga. They eventually found their way into Lewis County. There they settled to raise their families and, to the dissatisfaction of many locals, to spread their radical gospel. Of particular distaste was what some viewed as the foul and despicable doctrine of polygamy (one husband with multiple wives). However, according to Mormon Church newspaper *Southern Star,* polygamy was not taught in this part of the country. Nevertheless, in a fun-

damentalist South, the dogma of the Latter-Day Saints was viewed with suspicion. Some even believed that the Mormons came here primarily to seduce and convert their wives and daughters. Many historians believe that the Mormons were one of the most persecuted religions in the Americas, at least in the early years. Tennessee was only one of the states that proved particularly inhospitable to the Mormon faith. This is one of the reasons so many of them eventually ended up in Utah: there they were allowed to practice their faith openly and without harassment.

A man named Church, after converting to Mormonism in Utah, returned to his native Hohenwald in Lewis

County with the intent of converting his friends and relatives to the new faith. John Clayborn Vandiver, a local Baptist minister, had different ideas. Vandiver's initial impression of the Mormon faith was based on personal observations mixed with hearsay, including stories about such things as nude baptisms, the seduction and defiling of young women, and other inaccuracies and half-truths. He was further influenced by what later proved to be a bogus published account of the Mormon doctrine by one "Bishop West," a man who may never really have existed. This account of an alleged sermon called "A Red Hot Address" stirred considerable anti-Mormon sentiment in claiming that Mormons were God's chosen people and otherwise prescribed doctrine unpalatable to the fundamentalist Tennessee Baptist minister. Although the credibility of this address, first published by an anti-Mormon newspaper, was refuted, the damage was already done.

It was in this climate of emotionalism and discrimination that the so-called Cane Creek Killings were perpetrated. When informed that a Mormon religious service was to be held on Sunday, August 10, at the home of James Conder, members of the faith made plans to attend. As one of the Mormon elders, William H. Jones, approached the Conder house on that Sunday, he was greeted by an angry mob of about a dozen masked men bearing pistols and shotguns and demanding his surrender. He was searched for weapons, but none were found, and the mob left him alone with a guard and proceeded to the Conder house.

Moments later, when shots rang out near the Conder house, the distraught guard allowed Jones to escape. In their assault on the home, the vigilantes killed one of James Conder's sons, his half-brother, and two Mormon elders, John H. Gibbs and William S. Berry, who were visiting the home. Conder's wife was wounded by a shotgun blast during the assault, and the leader of the mob, a prominent local farmer, was also killed. A fifth Mormon (who was not an elder), was later found dead near the home.

Questioned about the cause of the incident, a local woman, one of the more credible witnesses, explained what she had observed. She also said that the people of her otherwise peaceful community were "fed up with those Mormons and their attempts to convert neighbors to that faith."

Since the members of the mob had been well disguised, positive identifications were not possible. The official record, along with newspaper accounts, stated that the deaths had been at the hands of parties unknown. Persecutions of the local Mormons continued even after the massacre.

The Mormons' meetinghouse was burned down three times before the group decided to meet at the home of James Conder. Tennessee Governor William B. Bath was asked by Utah church officials to look further into the murders and to offer a reward for the arrest and prosecution of those responsible. Although a reward was finally offered, no one was accused, let alone tried, for the crime. One person was suspected, but he managed to escape before charges could be brought against him.

In the fall, when things appeared to have settled down, notices were posted demanding that the Mormons depart the county lest they suffer dire consequences. One such posting, illustrated with a coffin and cross, warned, "To all Latter Day Saints: You are hereby notified to leave this state within thirty days or you will go to meet Elders Gibbs and Berry" (quoted in Wingfield, 35). Eventually, most did move away, some returning years later to Lewis and Perry counties. Even some non-Mormon neighbors who had sympathized with and been kind to the elders moved away under duress.

SOURCES: *Southern Star*, no. 282, Oct. 1884; Lesley Talley, "'The Mormon Massacre': Glimpses of Hickman County History" (unpublished paper, Columbia State Community College, Columbia, TN, 1975); Marshall Wingfield, "Tennessee's Mormon Massacre," *Tennessee Historical Quarterly* 17 (Mar.–Dec. 1958): 19–37.

Eph Grizzard Lynching
NASHVILLE, APRIL 30, 1892

On the afternoon of April 30, 1892, Eph Grizzard, a black man, was taken from the Davidson County Jail and lynched for the alleged assault and murder of May (Mary) Bruce, a white woman from Goodlettsville, Sumner County. Three days earlier, his brother Henry had been lynched as an accomplice in the same crime.

After Grizzard was imprisoned for suspicion of murder, a mob of several hundred incensed city and county residents tried unsuccessfully to take him from the jail for their own brand of justice. As was their sworn duty, local authorities tried to restrain the mob and protect their prisoner, even trying in vain to disguise him in a so-called Mother Hubbard dress and secretly transfer him to the state prison. The first attempt to seize the prisoner failed, and two men were shot, one fatally, in the process. The second time, three men entered the jail, overpowered a guard, and finally dragged Grizzard out to an awaiting crowd, now estimated in the thousands. At the time of his abduction, he was still wearing the dress. According to the *Knoxville Journal,* as he was being dragged along,

> The back of this [dress] was literally cut to shreds by gleaming knives that dozens of men slashed the cringing prisoner's back with. He was dragged up Front Street to the square, the immense crowd followed and every moment giving vent to exultant cheers. Out on the [Cumberland River] bridge, he was dragged, a new hempen rope three-quarters of an inch thick had been prepared. The end was tied to the railing near the northern side. The noose was placed around the doomed man's neck and he was let over the railing. The mob did not throw him over, because they did not want him to die too quick. Grizzard's hands were not tied and he grasped the braces fifteen feet below

the bridge and was climbing up. Seeing this he was drawn up three feet and turned loose. His flesh had not ceased quivering when an aged man standing directly over him drew a revolver and fired five balls into his carcass. Instantly a hundred guns and revolvers were drawn and pointed at the body, and what was left of Eph Grizzard was riddled with bullets.

The hanging occurred just after 2:00 PM, only fifteen minutes after he had been taken from the jail. Shortly thereafter the body was pulled back onto the bridge, laid across a horse, and taken to Goodlettsville. After being displayed for the townspeople, the body was burned near the place where Eph Grizzard and his brother Henry were alleged to have raped and murdered the Goodlettsville woman. Evidence at their home seemed to support the fact that the Grizzard brothers had committed the crime, and it was rumored that their sister, Ann Grizzard, had said they were guilty. On the other hand, because the citizens of Davidson County did not want to wait for a fair trial, they took matters into their own hands, acting as judges, juries, and executioners.

An inquest was held, and the body was found to have sustained around 200 gunshots as well as a number of other wounds. The official ruling by the coroner's jury was that "Eph Grizzard came to his death at the hands of unknown parties from gunshot wounds and strangulation." According to the *Knoxville Journal,* these citizens, including many who were black, agreed that the lynching had been justified.

SOURCES: *Knoxville Journal,* May 1–3, 1892; *Nashville Banner,* Apr. 30, 1892.

Shelby County Lynching
AUGUST 31–SEPTEMBER 1, 1894

Shortly before midnight on the last day of August 1894, six black men, handcuffed and shackled together, were riding in a wagon en route to the Memphis-Shelby County Jail. They had been arrested that evening by a deputy sheriff and detective by the name of Richardson for suspicion of arson in Shelby County. The men had allegedly burned a large number of barns, residences, and other buildings in and around the communities of Kerrville, Lucy, Millington, and Bolton, north of Memphis. Richardson's assistant, a white man, was driving the wagon, and because it was dark and the road was difficult to negotiate, Richardson was walking ahead of the wagon to show the way. As he and the wagon approached a bridge, a voice from out of the darkness said, "You better not cross that bridge, it is defective." After checking the bridge and finding it sound, the deputy and the wagon crossed it and continued on. When he got to the second bridge he heard the voice again. "You better not cross that bridge either." After inspecting the second bridge, the sheriff found it in no condition to handle the weight of a wagon, and so he backed up the wagon and drove down to ford the stream. It was at this point that a large number of masked men surrounded the deputy and his wagon. They aimed several shotguns and other weapons at him and told him to raise his hands. The deputy asked what the men wanted, and the alleged leader said, "Never you mind."

The blacks instinctively knew what the men had come for, and one of them stood up in the wagon showing his shackled arms. Shots rang out in the night, and the black prisoner fell out of the wagon and was probably dead before he hit the ground. A second was shot through the stomach. The white driver was pulled from the wagon and told to join the deputy, and the men began shooting into the wagon, riddling the bodies of the last four black men with bullets from shotguns, rifles, and pistols. After the massacre, the leader ordered the others back into the woods, and they disappeared. Richardson stayed with the bodies, and his assistant rode a mule back to the town of Lucy to notify a local magistrate. Arriving back at the scene, the assistant and the magistrate found Richardson gone. He was eventually located at a

nearby home, where he had gone to rest after waiting for his assistant to return.

The magistrate swore in a jury of neighbors to view the scene of the lynching. The bodies had been so mutilated by bullets that it was nearly impossible to identify the individual remains. With no evidence except that of the sworn testimony of Richardson and his assistant, the inquest was completed with the jury officially concluding that the black men had been killed by parties unknown. Later testimony, however, was given that implicated several local men in the plot, and some believed that Richardson was in on the crime. Local sentiment seemed to be against those called the cowardly assassins.

SOURCES: *Knoxville Journal,* Sept. 2, 4, 1894; *Memphis Commercial Appeal,* Sept. 3, 1894.

Wild Bill Latura Assault
MEMPHIS, DECEMBER 10, 1908

> This thing of killing negroes without cause ought to be stopped. The first reason is, because it is wrong within itself, and the second is, that those white men who kill negroes, as a pastime, or in order to establish a reputation as bad men, usually end by killing white men.
>
> —*Memphis Commercial Appeal,* Dec. 12, 1908

Just before midnight on December 10, 1908, "Wild Bill" Latura, a white man of criminal record and bad reputation, walked into Hammet Ashford's saloon and pool hall at the corner of Beale Avenue and Fourth Street, a black section of Memphis. Before he entered the facility, he was said to have proclaimed, "I am going to turn the place into a funeral parlor." Speaking to the bartender as he entered, he said, "I'm just going back to the washroom for a minute." Seconds later, he entered a back room where half a dozen blacks were playing pool. Suddenly, and without apparent provocation, he opened his coat, took out a 38-caliber Colt automatic pistol, and started shooting. Then, he walked out of the establishment, where he pointed his gun at a seventh black man and told him not to move or that he would die too. Shortly thereafter, "Punch" Wilson, a friend and cohort of Latura, walked into Ashford's saloon, noted the carnage, and left.

Inside the pool room, three black men lay dead. Three others, including a black woman, lay wounded. The police responded immediately, and after being told what had happened, they started searching for Latura.

After leaving the scene of the murders, Latura walked straight down Beale Avenue to South Third. After disposing of his gun, he entered the Rose Bud Saloon, where he was soon arrested. He offered no resistance and, according to witnesses, showed absolutely no remorse. Latura was charged with three counts of murder and was quoted as saying, "I shot 'em, and that's all there is to it." He was placed in a cell along with "Punch" Wilson, who was charged as an accomplice after the fact.

Latura was a notorious Memphis criminal and had been in and out of trouble since his youth. An editorial in the *Commercial Appeal* stated that he should already have been in prison for a number of shootings, cuttings, clubbings, and killings that he had committed. Six years earlier, he had killed a white man with a baseball bat during a quarrel, for which he was acquitted on the grounds of self-defense. In 1903 he attempted to kill a black saloon keeper. On another occasion, he all but disemboweled another black man. In 1905 he shot and seriously wounded a black woman over a trivial matter. In 1907 he shot and wounded another black man over a disputed debt. Earlier in 1908 he had wounded another black man during a bar brawl. Most recently, he had pulled a gun on a gambler to recover money lost in a poker game.

Latura was bound over to the grand jury on the day after the melee and pleaded not guilty. He was held without bond and charged with the three murders. "Punch" Wilson, who had witnessed the saloon murders

"Wild Bill" Latura. Courtesy of Memphis News-Scimitar, Special Collections, University of Memphis Libraries.

but probably taken no part in them, was also charged as an accessory after the fact.

A coroner's inquest on December 11 found Latura guilty of killing three black men, Clarence "Candy" Allen, Charles "Long Boy" Miller, and Robert "Speck" Carter. Three others survived their injuries: Leslie Williams, who was shot in the hip; Richard Scot, who had a flesh wound on his left arm; and Birdie Hines, who was shot in the leg and hand.

Latura was eventually brought to trial for the three murders and three attempted murders. However, he once again made a mockery of the Memphis criminal justice system. In the minds of the all white jurors, the punishment for killing blacks was not considered the same as it would be for killing whites; and, as a result, Latura was found not guilty and set free. In 1912 he murdered another black man. He objected to being called "Will Bill" Latura, a fact that eventually led to his demise on the streets of Memphis. He called the editor of the *Commercial Appeal,* identified himself, and said that if the paper referred to him that way one more time he would kill their entire editorial staff. The editor, C.P.J. Mooney, took him seriously and ordered the reference to stop. However, in 1915 a young reporter mistakenly referred to "Wild Bill" as one of the city's principal tourist attractions. In a mad rage the following evening, he confronted the police, just outside his business establishment. He told them that he was going to get them and that reporter. As he turned to walk away, one of the officers fired five shots into his back.

SOURCES: *Memphis Commercial Appeal,* Dec. 11, 12, 1908; William D. Miller, *Memphis during the Progressive Era 1900–1917* (Memphis: Memphis State Univ. Press, 1957).

Eli Persons Lynching
Memphis, May 23, 1917

On April 2, 1917, a teenaged white girl was riding her bicycle to school when she was attacked and dragged into a thicket in the Macon Road community on the east side of Memphis. Her mutilated and decapitated body was found there two days later.

Eli C. Persons, a black man, was charged and allegedly confessed to the crime. Because of the heinous nature of the crime, he was placed in protective custody and his whereabouts kept quiet until he could be returned to Memphis for arraignment and to stand trial. It would be a difficult task to protect such a prisoner at a time when lynching was still commonplace in the South: any time a black man was accused of committing an injustice against a white, the situation was tense. In this case, the victim had been a teenaged white female, the crime abhorrent, and the public armed and determined to see retribution on behalf of a grieving, white parent. It was even difficult to convince the public defender appointed to the case to represent Persons.

Meanwhile, mobs of armed citizens, bent on vigilante justice, combed the countryside searching for Persons. He was eventually found in the custody of law enforcement officers at Holly Springs, Mississippi. There a party of armed citizens, in an orderly fashion, took Persons into their custody, mercifully without bloodshed. Word of his apprehension by the Tennessee vigilantes quickly spread. They intended to lynch him and to do it near the spot where he had allegedly killed and mutilated the teen victim. Furthermore, public opinion, although not unanimous, was clearly on their side. So strong and widespread was the support for the lynching that there was no official opposition to the action until after it occurred. Even then, opposition was inconsequential.

Soon after being taken into custody in Mississippi, Persons was transported via automobile back to the scene of the brutal crime. There, at the end of the bridge that crossed the Wolf River Bottoms in the little community of Macon Road, a crowd of 2,000 to 4,000 men, women, and children had already begun to assemble to await the arrival of the prisoner and his warranted execution. Word quickly spread about the approximate time and the exact place of the lynching. The crowd of onlookers that assembled for this event was not a typically impatient, bloodthirsty mob. For the most part they were orderly, sober, and simply eager to see the "fiend" punished for his despicable crime. So certain were those assembled that Persons would be brought to this spot that cars were already parked up and down the road for a mile along both sides of the bridge. According to the *Memphis Press Scimitar,* "Conspicuous among the mob were several venders of sandwiches and chewing gum." However, as the hours went by, some of the people became impatient and discouraged. Some left, others stayed, and still others keep coming.

In the words of the *Memphis Commercial Appeal:* "It was an execution probably without parallel in the history of the south. The approximate hour and place of the lynching were advertised widely, but the organized forces of the law and order, operating through the medium of the courts, dared not say nay to the outraged community in which Antoinette Rappel lived."

About 9:00 AM on May 22, two cars approached each other along the top of the levee. One car held Persons and his captors. In the other vehicle was the mother of the slain youth. The mother's statement to the crowd was simple and direct. "I want to thank all my friends who have worked so hard in my behalf," she cried. "Let the negro suffer as my little girl suffered, only 10 times worse."

When asked if he had any final words before he was put to death, he implicated two additional blacks in the crime. Although taken into custody and thoroughly interrogated, they presented air-tight alibis as to their presence at the time of the murder. They were also vouched for by reputable citizens and were later released.

There may have been an initial intention to hang Persons, but the decision was later made to burn him at the stake. A pyre of brush was prepared, but the post in the center, on which the prisoner was to be tied, could not be driven deeply enough into the ground to provide a sturdy stake. Therefore, Persons was simply chained to a large log. Gasoline was poured onto the brush, since it was still moist from a previous night's rain. Then, as the crowd watched, the brush was set ablaze. The victim, although obviously terrified, seemed calm through the ordeal. Perhaps he was in shock or just accepting of his fate, for he did not resist or even flinch when tied down on his funeral pyre. Neither did he cry out as the flames surged over his body. He writhed in agony, and he died quickly, taking a deep breath as the first flames surrounded his body. As the dark smoke from the brushfire, oil, and flesh rose into the morning air, the crowd cheered loudly. After the flames died down, one of the executioners cut out Persons's heart, two others cut off his ears, and a third severed his head. Such repugnant souvenir collecting was not uncommon after lynchings.

The mother and other relatives of the slain girl watched the drama from an automobile perched on a nearby levee, no doubt confident that justice had been served. Throughout the day, thousands continued to converge on the scene of the lynching. At one point the cars were backed up about two miles on either side of the bridge. Just after noon on May 23, the severed and charred head and a leg of Persons were thrown from a car onto the sidewalk at the corner of Beale Street and Rayburn Boulevard in a South Memphis neighborhood. This was undoubtedly a blatant warning to the black citizens of Memphis, and it almost caused a panic. The body parts were quickly picked up by police officers and taken to the county morgue. Another unspecified part of Person's burned body also was alleged to have been displayed for a short time at a Memphis barber shop.

The Shelby County attorney general convened a grand jury to investigate the lynching of Persons. This was in the wake of a coroner's inquest that concluded that Persons had come to his death from a cause unknown to the jury. On the morning of May 24, 1917, a meeting of Jewish, Catholic, and Protestant ministers convened in the Chamber of Commerce building in Memphis to discuss the lynching. It was formally condemned by them and by a number of other prominent Memphis citizens. The *Commercial Appeal* also published an editorial entitled "Lynching and Law" condemning the recent mob violence and the lack of action by law enforcement officers, the courts, and other public officials in the matter. They furthermore stated, "Men cannot give the law temporary paralysis and then expect it to resume vigor in protecting all of the rights of all of the people. Men cannot, at will, suspend the constitution of the United States and then expect that constitution to be the ark of the covenant of the liberties which our forefathers secured for us in their blood."

SOURCES: *Knoxville Journal and Tribune,* May 23, 1917; *Memphis Commercial Appeal,* May 22–24, 1917; *Memphis Press Scimitar,* May 22, 1917.

Bloody Family Feuds
and Political Conflicts

Blood feuds are not uncommon in history. Such conflict and turmoil often developed among extended family groups and, at times, became extremely violent, with events like the Hatfield-McCoy feud entering the pages of history and becoming a permanent part of American folklore. Occasionally, even insignificant events could rekindle old grudges and spark new bouts of retaliation, sometimes recurring over decades and causing numerous deaths. In Tennessee, the most significant conflict of this sort was the "Greene-Jones War," which took place in the late nineteenth century in Hancock and Hawkins counties.

Similarly, political differences have also ignited localized conflicts that result in violence. In the Volunteer State, the "Battle of Athens" in McMinn County, which pitted returning World War II veterans against a corrupt faction linked to Memphis political boss Edward H. Crump (a West Tennessee Democrat whose sphere of influence extended even to East Tennessee Republicans), is perhaps the most notable such clash.

Greene-Jones War
Hancock and Hawkins Counties, 1887–90

George Greene turned his head and looked back and a rifle ball went through his jaw knocking out one of his jaw teeth. When it hit the other side it had lost its velocity. He caught it in his mouth, spit it out in his hand, put it in his pocket, and rode on.

—*Rogersville Herald,* **June 9, 1888**

The Greene-Jones War was a family feud that took place in Hancock and Hawkins counties between 1887 and 1890. It was a battle between two rival families, second only to the infamous blood feud between the Hatfield and McCoy clans that took place in the Kentucky and West Virginia backcountry from 1878 to 1891. The Greene-Jones War is believed to have caused the deaths of some sixteen people, including at least one child. The feud was so intense that at one point the governor activated the state militia and declared martial law in the area.

A number of theories have been suggested as to what precipitated the feud, and for a time it was virtually unstoppable. For a couple of years the only law in the area was instituted by the Greene and Jones families themselves. The local sheriff avoided the conflict initially by simply staying out of that part of Hancock County. Eventually, however, the situation got so out of control that he had to request assistance through the governor. One account suggests that the Jones boys often teased Susan Greene, wife of Hampton (Hamp) Greene, about her nickname, "Sookie." They often called out her name in jest, as if she were a cow, "Here Sookie—here Sookie—Heeeere Sook, here Sook." This was particularly insulting to Hamp and his wife and was said to have caused the initial ill will between the two clans. This teasing certainly became a larger issue when Hamp eventually became the leader on the Greene side of the feud.

A second theory states that two of the Greene brothers came home after the Civil War and murdered two Jones men in revenge for the killing of their brother Alfred Greene in 1863.

A third theory involved Ace (or Asa) Jones, the patriarch of the Jones clan. He was said to be kind and compassionate but also capable of extreme anger and violence. Ace's son Jim, who had a drinking problem, was shot and killed when he got into an argument with Dick Greene. Incensed by this, Ace vowed to kill Dick. The other Joneses and Greenes were quickly drawn into the conflict, and the war was on.

A fourth theory, and the one most often cited, albeit embellished a bit through time, alleged that the feud arose over a hog. According to the *Rogersville Herald* of April 21, 1888,

> Apparently some of the Joneses who lived on or near the Greeneberry Greene's farm near Duck Creek were hauling logs down to the Clinch River to be floated to market in Chattanooga. Someone left the fence down after the Joneses crossed the property of one Richard Greene, and a hog belonging to Mr. Greene got through the fence and wandered up a hollow to a liquor still, ate and destroyed a considerable amount of mash; whereupon, a second Mr. Jones decided to keep the hog to pay for the damage incurred. Mr. Greene came to claim the hog. An argument ensued and hence, the Greene-Jones war.

Another slightly different version of the hog story says that when Richard Greene's hog crawled through a hole in Ace Jones's fence, Ace killed the hog and stuck it in the hole in revenge. Finding the dead hog, Richard went to Ace's home, and they argued. Richard then picked up an ax and broke a large iron kettle in Ace's yard. Several days later, Richard killed Ace's son Jim. As an aside, Ace Jones, leader of the Jones faction of the war, was the brother of Casey Jones, the legendary Illinois Central Railroad engineer who died in the wreck of the famous *Cannonball Express* in April 1900.

Whatever the cause or causes, the rivalry was severe enough for the deputy sheriff and Hancock County Court Clerk Robert Greene to raise a large posse and order a sizable shipment (some say a boxcar-load) of guns and ammunition in preparation for the battle.

The shootouts between the two clans continued to intensify over time. One battle was said to have lasted three days and nights all along War and Duck creeks. Both sides were said to have fought with great conviction.

> The Greenes and Jones of Hancock County got into another racket on last Sunday. It appears that while Richard, Lincoln and Tom Greene were out looking over their fields they were fired on by an ambushed party, supposed to be members of the Asa (Ace) Jones family, one of whom Richard killed a few months since. Tom Greene was badly wounded in one of his arms while his brothers received no further injury than to have their clothes torn by some of the bullets. (*Rogersville Herald,* Apr. 21, 1888)

Tom's arm eventually had to be amputated.

On June 9, 1888, the *Rogersville Herald* reported that "the Jones party, nine or ten in number, surrounded Mr. Hampton (Hamp) Greene's house. About the dawn of the day the Greene's discovered the Jones party and sending their wives and children out, both parties began firing at about the same time . . . supposed to have been about 3000 shots fired in succession on both sides." The son of Mary Greene was killed as he hid under his bed so as to stay in the house with the men.

Although the Hancock County sheriff and a posse of thirty-six men pursued the Jones clan for their attack on the Greene home, only one person was apprehended, arrested, and taken to the Sneedville jail. According to the *Rogersville Herald* on June 16, 1888:

The fuss between the Greenes and Jones is abating some. I have been informed that they stacked their arms. The Greene side went and gave up their arms last Monday and on Tuesday following a posse of about 60 men started in search of the other side. News came they had found one and arrested one. No other later reliable news at present, but it is thought that the Jones will relent and let civil law decide the trouble between them. The writer's opinion is that both sides will finally submit to whatever is right and live under the reign of the civil law instead of the hail of bullets.

SOURCES: "Greene Jones War," unpublished MS, vertical files, McClung Special Collections Library, Knoxville; Hancock County Historical and Genealogical Society, *Hancock County, Tennessee and Its People 1844–1989 and 1994,* vols. 1–2 (Waynesville, NC: Don Mills, 1994); Shane S. Rhyme, East Tennessee Historical Society, personal correspondence with author, Mar. 31, 1998; Gail Thompson Rindler, Hancock County, TN, personal correspondence with author, July 23, 2010; *Rogersville Herald,* Apr. 21, 1888–Sept. 24, 1890.

The Battle of Athens
McMinn County, August 1, 1946

Election Day saw Athens an armed camp. As the voters came to the polls, they found the Cantrell [political] machine in ominous demonstration of force. Almost two hundred armed deputies strutted about, pistols and blackjacks dangling from their belts, badges gleaming. The deputies were strangers.

—**Theodore H. White,**
"The Battle of Athens, Tennessee"

Common law states that citizens have a right to prevent a crime or felony, but it also says that law enforcement

People line the main thoroughfare in the aftermath of an Election Day melee known as the Battle of Athens, 1946. Photograph by Homer W. Anderson Sr. Courtesy of Andy Anderson.

agencies and courts have an obligation to put down insurrections. This was the dilemma that faced the town of Athens on August 1, 1946. It was Election Day, and two factions were vying for power. The incumbents were alleged to be a locally corrupt political machine with ties to equally corrupt politicians at the state level. The head of the state political organization was Memphis mayor Edward Hull "Boss" Crump, a powerful and long-standing politician who literally ran the state with a governor and other high-ranking political figures in his pocket. Until the election of August 1, 1946, no one had seriously challenged Crump or his Athens-McMinn County cronies. They stayed in power by fixing elections. One of their successful ploys to control votes was to assure that ballot boxes were controlled by local deputies bought and paid for by the incumbent politicians. The boxes were often stuffed ahead of time with the names of the local dead, those too young to vote, and so forth. They

Overturned vehicles after the Battle of Athens. Photograph by Homer W. Anderson Sr. Courtesy of McClung Historical Collection, Historical Photograph Copy Project, Knox County Public Library.

also made fortunes in illegal payoffs by turning a blind eye to bootlegging, gambling, and prostitution.

The challengers, called the Veteran's Party or GI ticket, consisted of young men who had recently returned to Tennessee from the battlefields of World War II. Even before they came home, many had heard horror stories about how their hometown had fallen into the hands of corrupt politicians. These political machines were refusing their citizens the very rights those soldiers had been fighting and dying for overseas. After returning home, some of the veterans met in secret and launched a reform campaign to return political control to the good, honest citizens of the town. This action erupted in a bloody and destructive confrontation that came to be called the Battle of Athens.

To assure a fair election, the GIs requested assistance from the governor, the U.S. attorney general, and the FBI. Unfortunately, all three turned them down. Boss Crump was powerful, indeed. But the veterans had made a promise to the citizens and intended to stand by it. They had assured all citizens that their votes would be counted as cast.

The Election Day turnout was big in 1946, but the presence that morning of some 200 armed deputies hired by the local political boss Paul Cantrell could only mean trouble. Because Tennessee law required that members of both political parties be represented at each voting precinct, the GIs posted their own poll watchers. When several of them attempted to examine the ballot boxes prior to the election, stop an underage girl from voting, and protest the failure of poll officials to allow a black man to vote, they were swiftly dragged away to jail.

By five o'clock, McMinn County Sheriff Pat Mansfield's deputies, true to form, removed the ballet boxes from two of the largest polling places and took them to the Athens Jail, allegedly for safekeeping and counting. Meanwhile, realizing that the ballot boxes could be tampered with, and that several of their fellow GIs were incarcerated, the remaining GIs met in the street to discuss their options and course of action.

When deputies showed up and demanded that they disband, a fight ensued, and five of the lawmen were disarmed, taken from town, stripped, and sent packing. By evening the GIs had broken into the local National Guard armory and secured weapons. Shortly thereafter they launched an attack on the local jail, demanding that the ballot boxes be surrendered and the GI prisoners released. According to a *Harper's Magazine* reporter, someone inside the jail yelled, "Are you the law?" To which someone outside answered, "There isn't any law in McMinn County."

At this point, the shooting began. The GIs outside were at an advantage: they had superior weapons, including machine guns, and fired volley after volley. Molotov cocktails were also hurled at the jail. After hours of almost continuous gunfire, it was apparent that this action alone was not going to work. Finally, under the direction of a GI specialist in demolition, they began dynamiting the jail. That worked.

The deputies surrendered and were paraded around the town by the GIs for all to see. In the turmoil that followed, the crowd continued to riot, breaking windows and randomly turning over and burning cars. Eventually, order was restored by the GI leaders, and the prisoners were escorted out of town. The next day the GI slate was certified and they took office.

No one was killed in the incident, but twenty were wounded, fourteen cars were burned, and twenty-five deputies were subsequently jailed. The story of how the GIs had defeated the local political machine and restored power to the citizens of Athens was carried nationwide by newspapers and magazines. It also launched similar movements elsewhere in the state. The numerous bullet holes in the walls of the jail are still visible today, reminders of the Battle of Athens.

SOURCES: Jennifer E. Brooks, "Battle of Athens," in *The Tennessee Encyclopedia of History and Culture,* ed. Carroll Van West, 35 (Nashville: Tennessee Historical Society and Rutledge Hill Press, 1998); C. Stephen Byrum, *McMinn County: Tennessee County History Series* (Memphis: Memphis State Univ. Press, 1984); James Ewing, *It Happened in Tennessee* (Nashville: Tennessee Historical Society and Rutledge Hill Press, 1986); Theodore H. White, "The Battle of Athens, Tennessee," *Harper's Magazine,* Jan. 1947, 54–61.

Appendix

Table 1. Palmer Drought Severity Index

Standard Precipitation Index Values

4.0 or more	extremely wet
3.0 to 3.99	very wet
2.0 to 2.99	moderately wet
1.0 to 1.99	slightly wet
0.5 to 0.99	incipient wet spell
0.49 to −0.49	near normal
−0.5 to −0.99	incipient dry spell
−1.0 to −1.99	mild drought
−2.0 to −2.99	moderate drought
−3.0 to −3.99	severe drought
−4.0 or less	extreme drought

Source: William Alley, "The Palmer Drought Severity Index: Limitations and Assumptions," *Journal of Climate and Applied Meteorology* 23 (July 1984): 1100–1109.

Note: The Palmer index is used in determining long-term drought (several months). It uses a 0 as normal, and drought is shown in terms of negative numbers; for example, –1 is a mild drought, –2 a moderate drought, etc. Excessive moisture is stated as positive numbers.

Table 2. Richter Scale of Earthquake Intensity

Richter scale number	Comparative strength	Effects
1–2	None to slight	Barely perceptible, if at all
3	Light	Felt only by people on top floors of buildings
4	Moderate	Windows, furniture rattle, cars rock
5	Strong	Trees sway, furniture moves, some damage
6	Destructive	Weak structures damaged, walls fall
7	Disastrous	Most masonry buildings, bridges destroyed
8	Catastrophic	Total destruction, shockwaves visible on ground

Note: There is no direct correlation between the modified Mercalli intensity (MMI) scale (table 3) and the Richter scale. However, an approximate comparison of the two can be made, as illustrated in table 4. The higher the Richter magnitude, the greater will be the MMI intensity, and vice versa. The MMI intensity decreases from the epicenter outward in irregular concentric rings depending upon the nature of the rock or soil through which the earthquake waves are emanating.

Table 3. Modified Mercalli Earthquake Intensity Scale

I	People cannot feel any earth movement. These are microquakes only discernable on seismographs.
II	A few people might notice movement if they are at rest and/or on the upper floors of tall buildings.
III	Many people indoors feel movement. Hanging objects swing back and forth. People outdoors might not realize that an earthquake is occurring.
IV	Most people indoors feel movement. Hanging objects swing. Dishes, windows, and doors rattle. The earthquake feels like a heavy truck hitting the walls. A few people outdoors may feel movement. Parked cars rock.
V	Almost everyone feels movement. Sleeping people are awakened. Doors swing open or close. Dishes are broken. Pictures on the wall move. Small objects move or are turned over. Trees might shake. Liquids might spill out of open containers.
VI	Everyone feels movement. People have trouble walking. Objects fall from shelves. Pictures fall off walls. Furniture moves. Plaster in walls might crack. Trees and bushes shake. Damage is slight in poorly constructed buildings. No structural damage.
VII	People have difficulty standing. Drivers feel their cars shaking. Some furniture breaks. Loose bricks fall from buildings. Damage is slight to moderate in well-built buildings and considerable in poorly built buildings.
VIII	Drivers have trouble steering. Houses that are not bolted down might shift on their foundations. Tall structures such as towers and chimneys might twist and fall. Well-built buildings suffer slight damage. Poorly built structures suffer severe damage. Tree branches break. Hillsides might crack and slide if the ground is wet. Water levels in wells might change.
IX	Well-built buildings suffer considerable damage. Houses that are not bolted down move off their foundations. Some underground pipes are broken. The ground cracks. Reservoirs suffer serious damage.
X	Most buildings and their foundations are destroyed. Some bridges are destroyed. Dams are seriously damaged. Large landslides occur. Water is thrown on the banks of canals, rivers, lakes. The ground cracks in large areas. Railroad tracks are bent slightly.
XI	Most buildings collapse. Some bridges are destroyed. Large cracks appear in the ground. Underground pipelines are destroyed. Railroad tracks are badly bent.
XII	Almost everything is destroyed. Objects are thrown into the air. The ground moves in waves or ripples. Large amounts of rock may move.

Source: U.S. Geological Survey, Earthquake Hazards Program, 2009.

Table 4. Approximate Comparison Between Earthquake Intensity and Magnitude

Mercalli intensity	Equivalent Richter magnitude	Witness observations
I. Instrumental	1.0–2.0	Felt by very few people; barely noticeable
II. Feeble	2.0–3.0	Felt by a few people, especially on upper floors
III. Slight	3.0–4.0	Noticeable indoors, especially on upper floors, but may not be recognized as an earthquake
IV. Moderate	4.0	Felt by many indoors, few outdoors; may feel like heavy truck passing by
V. Rather strong	4.0–5.0	Felt by almost everyone; some people awakened; small objects moved; trees and poles may shake
VI. Strong	5.0–6.0	Felt by everyone; difficult to stand; some heavy furniture moved; some plaster falls; chimneys may be slightly damaged
VII. Very strong	6.0	Slight to moderate damage in well-built, ordinary structures; considerable damage to poorly built structures; some walls may fall
VIII. Destructive	6.0–7.0	Little damage in specially built structures; considerable damage to ordinary buildings; severe damage to poorly built structures; some walls collapse
IX. Ruinous	7.0	Considerable damage to specially built structures; buildings shifted off foundations; ground cracked noticeably; wholesale destruction; landslides
X. Disastrous	7.0–8.0	Most masonry and frame structures and their foundations destroyed; ground badly cracked; landslides; wholesale destruction
XI. Very disastrous	8.0	Total damage; few, if any, structures standing; bridges destroyed; wide cracks in ground; waves seen on ground
XII. Catastrophic	8.0 or greater	Total damage; waves seen on ground; objects thrown up into air

Source: U.S. Geological Survey, Earthquake Hazards Program, 2009.

Table 5. Centers for Disease Control and Prevention Pandemic Severity Index

Category	Case fatality ratio (%)*	Example(s)
1	less than 0.1	Seasonal flu and H1N1 swine flu 2009
2	0.1–0.5	Asian flu of 1957 and Hong Kong flu of 1968
3	0.5–1.0	
4	1.0–2.0	
5	2.0 or higher	Spanish flu of 1918–19

*The case fatality ratio is the percentage of victims who die from the disease relative to the number who contract it.

Table 6. Rainfall Intensity Statistics for Tennessee

Location	Date	Amount (inches)	Duration (hours)	Rate (inches per hour)
Exact location unknown	June 2, 1937	5.5	0.33 (about 20 minutes)	16.7
Great Smoky Mountains National Park	Sept. 1, 1951	6.5	1.0	6.5
Nashville	Nov. 21, 1900	1.0	0.17 (about 10 minutes)	6
Exact location unknown	May 22, 1938	10.0	2.0	5.0
Exact location unknown	June 4, 1949	9.5	2.0	4.8
Spring City, Rhea County	Nov. 18, 1957	9.0	2.0	4.5
Pittman Center, Sevier County	Aug. 4–5, 1938	11.0	3.0–4.0	3.7–2.8
McMinnville, Warren County	June 13, 1952	10.5	3.0	3.5
Cardens Bluff, Carter County	June 13, 1924	15.0	8.0	1.9
Lewisburg, Marshall County	June 18, 1939	9.0	3.0	3.0
Dunlap, Sequatchie County	Aug. 8–9, 1954	10.0	4.0	2.5
Big Barren Creek, Claiborne County	Aug. 1–2, 1916	12.0–15.0	5.0	2.4–3.0
Tazewell, Claiborne County	Apr. 3, 1916	9.0	4.0	2.3
Morristown, Hamblen County	July 16, 1949	4.5	2.0	2.3
Cosby, Cocke County	June 28, 1947	6.5	3.0	2.2
Greeneville, Greene County	June 28, 1947	7.5	3.5	2.1
Tazewell, Claiborne County	Aug. 1–2, 1916	9.0	5.0	1.8
Central Cumberland Plateau	July 24–30, 1928	10.0	6.0	1.7
Rock Island, Warren County	Mar. 22–23, 1929	5.1	3.0	1.7
Clinchmore, Claiborne County	July 24, 1965	12.0	8.0	1.5
Middle and Lower Tennessee River Valley	Mar. 25, 1902	6.0	6.0	1.0
Lebanon, Wilson County	Aug. 2–3, 1939	14.0	16.0	0.9
Benton, Polk County	Apr. 2–3, 1920	10.0	12.0	0.8

Table 7. Fujita-Pearson Tornado Intensity Scale

Category	Descriptive title	Rotational wind speed	Degree of damage	Description of damage
F0	Gale tornado	40–72 mph	Light damage	Some damage to chimneys; trees branches broken; shallow-rooted trees pushed over; damage to sign boards
F1	Moderate tornado	73–112 mph	Moderate damage	The lower limit is the beginning of hurricane speed; surfaces peeled off roofs; mobile homes pushed off foundations or overturned; moving autos pushed off roads
F2	Significant tornado	113–57 mph	Considerable damage	Roofs torn off frame houses; mobile homes demolished; boxcars pushed over; large trees snapped or uprooted; light-object missiles generated
F3	Severe tornado	158–206 mph	Severe damage	Roofs and some walls torn off well-constructed houses; trains overturned; most trees in forest uprooted; heavy cars lifted off ground and thrown
F4	Devastating tornado	207–60 mph	Devastating damage	Well-constructed houses leveled; structures with weak foundations blown some distance; cars thrown; and large missiles generated
F5	Incredible tornado	261–318 mph	Incredible damage	Strong frame houses lifted off foundations, carried considerable distance, and disintegrated; automobile-sized missiles projected in excess of 100 yards; trees debarked; incredible phenomena will occur

Table 8. Human and Economic Losses in the West and Middle Tennessee Tornadoes of November 1900

Place	Date	Dead	Injured	Buildings lost
Columbia	Nov. 24	25–27	75	?
Nolensville	Nov. 24	J. D. Hampton	?	?
Unknown locale in Middle Tennessee	Nov. 23	Nannie Hampton	2	?
Tollgate	Nov. 20	3 Viles children	?	?
Thompson Station	Nov. 22	Child	?	?
Nolensville	Nov. 22	Nancy Brummitt	10	16 destroyed and 50 damaged
LaVergne	Nov. 22	George Robertson and George's child	61	?
Clovecroft	Nov. 22	3	?	?
Giles County	Nov. 24	1	Several	?
Williamson County	Nov. 22	7	20	?
La Grange	Nov. 22	3	6	Scores
Boxleys Store	Nov. 22	3	?	?

Table 9. Beaufort Wind Scale

Beaufort	Average mph	Knots	Effects on surroundings
0 (calm)	0	0–1	Smoke rises vertically
1 (light air)	1.2–3.0	1–3	Smoke moves slightly with breeze and shows direction of wind
2 (light breeze)	3.7–7.5	4–6	Wind can be felt on skin; leaves rustle
3 (gentle breeze)	8–12.5	7–10	Smoke moves horizontally; small branches sway; wind extends a light flag
4 (moderate breeze)	13–18.6	11–16	Loose dust or sand on the ground moves; larger branches sway; loose paper blows around
5 (fresh breeze)	19.3–25	17–21	Surface waves form on water; small trees sway
6 (strong breeze)	25.5–31	22–27	Trees bend; whistling in telephone wires
7 (moderate gale)	32–38	28–33	Large trees sway
8 (fresh gale)	39–46	34–40	Twigs break from trees
9 (strong gale)	47–55	41–47	Branches break from trees
10 (whole gale)	56–64	48–55	Trees are uprooted
11 (storm)	65–74	56–63	Widespread damage
12 (hurricane)	75+	64 +	Great structural damage on land

Source: NOAA/National Weather Service, "Beaufort Wind Scale," http://www.spc.noaa.gov/faq/tornado/beaufort.html.

CHRONOLOGY

Boldface type indicates an event discussed in detail earlier in the book.

Apr. 20, 1543	Flooding—A great flood occurred on the Mississippi River in the vicinity of modern-day Memphis, according to the chronicles of Hernando de Soto. At its peak, the flood extended twenty leagues (i.e., about seventy miles) on either side of the river, and only the tops of the tallest trees were visible above the water. According to an article in the October 1975 issue of the *West Tennessee Historical Papers,* the validity of this account is questionable.
Dec. 25, 1699	Earthquake—This earthquake occurred near modern-day Memphis. It is the earliest historical accounting of a Tennessee quake. Neither its magnitude nor intensity is known.
1738	**Epidemic, Smallpox** (see p. 20)—This scourge infected Cherokee Indians and was believed to have been transported with a shipment of trade goods brought by Guinea men (i.e., slaves) from Africa. The epidemic may have wiped out half of the Cherokee Nation that year.
Dec. 1779–Feb. 1780	Severe winter—The Cumberland River at the Cumberland Settlement (now Nashville) was frozen so solidly that a herd of thirty-eight cattle, as well as men and horses, were able to walk across it. The John Donelson party, then en route to the Cumberland Settlement from Fort Watauga in upper East Tennessee was forced to halt their expedition due to extremely cold weather statewide. In fact, they were marooned on the Upper Holston in Hawkins County from December to February.
Feb.–Mar. 1780	**Epidemic, Smallpox** (see p. 20)—This devastating epidemic occurred along the Tennessee River near Chattanooga. Chickamauga Indians contracted the disease when they attacked a flatboat of settlers traveling to the new Cumberland Settlement in Middle Tennessee. The number of Indians killed will never be known, but it is believed to have been one of the greatest epidemics, per capita, in what was to become Tennessee.
July 1780	Flooding—Disregarding the questionable Mississippi River flood account of 1543, this is the earliest known damaging flood in the history of the area. Called a freshet, it destroyed the crops in many early settlements along the Cumberland and Stones rivers of Middle Tennessee.
July 1781	Flash flood—This event occurred along the Caney Fork River near Flinns Creek (?) in Middle Tennessee. It destroyed crops and created many hardships for settlers of the area.
Winter 1784	Severe winter—Ice floes populated the Mississippi River. In fact, large blocks of ice floated past Memphis, past New Orleans, and into the Gulf of Mexico. This happened again in 1899.

Winter 1787–88	Severe winter—The winter was so cold that the Cumberland River at Nashville froze solid.
Apr. 1791	Flooding—One of earliest documented severe floods in the Tennessee Valley, it is referred to as a "great freshet" in historical records. Knoxville newspaper accounts describe the flood as being very high along the French Broad and upper reaches of the Tennessee River. David Crockett was said to have referred to this flood as "the second epistle to Noah's fresh."
1793	Flooding—Flooding was heavy on the Cumberland River. This was, at the time, either the second or third greatest flood in the recorded history of the Cumberland River at Nashville. It may have been exceeded by the December 1808 flood. The river is believed to have reached 58.5 feet on the flood gauge.
Winter 1795–96	Severe winter—This winter was so extremely cold that at Nashville the Cumberland River froze solid.
1797	Flooding—A heavy flood occurred at Knoxville. It is believed to be the flood of record on the Elk River.
1797	Drought—The earliest recorded drought in Tennessee, it was quite severe in the midstate area. According to a history of Wilson County, springs believed to be everlasting dried up in the droughts of 1797 and 1853–54.
1800	Epidemic—A severe and mysterious disease, some believe yellow fever, struck Knoxville, taking the lives of many citizens. One of the most prominent people killed was William Blount, then Speaker of the Tennessee Senate and former governor of the Territory South of the River Ohio. Hardly a family in the city escaped the baffling disease.
Feb. 1807	Severe winter—All of Tennessee was extremely cold, and the mercury dropped to –5°F at Nashville on February 6. Ice floes accumulated on the Mississippi River and along the West Tennessee River banks. This was disruptive to land and river life, and commerce.
May 24, 1807	Tornadoes—This was the earliest known Tennessee tornado for which there is a written record, and it apparently caused considerable damage in Cocke, Jefferson, Knox, Roane, and Sevier counties. As the twister passed over the Tennessee River in Knoxville it picked up a considerable amount of water, along with many fish. As it dissipated over the city, it literally "rained fish." At least two people—and many fish—are known to have died during the event.
Dec. 1808	Flooding—Heavy flooding was reported on the Tennessee River at Knoxville and on the Cumberland River at Nashville. The Cumberland reached fourteen feet above flood stage on Christmas Day, the same day that Newsom's Mill, now a prominent Davidson County heritage landmark, was washed away. This flood may have exceeded the Cumberland River flood of 1793, as recorded at Nashville. Therefore, it is either the second or third highest flood of record for the Cumberland River at Nashville.
Nov. 1811	Tornado—The exact date of this Davidson County twister has not been determined, but it was said to have occurred at 8:00 PM and to have caused an estimated $10,000 in damages.
Dec. 16, 1811	**Earthquake—New Madrid Earthquake** (see p. 9). This was the first in the series of three great New Madrid earthquakes to shake the Central Mississippi River Valley and West Tennessee in

just two months. It is believed to have been in the lower 7.0 range on the 10-point Richter scale, making it the second most severe of the three great events. Its intensity range was measured between VIII and IX.

1812	Structure fire—Fire destroyed all the buildings on both sides of Market Street from the St. Charles Hotel to the public square in Nashville.
Jan. 13, 1812	**Earthquake—New Madrid Earthquake** (see p. 9). This was the second of the series of three great quakes to strike the Central Mississippi River Valley along the New Madrid earthquake zone. It was also the least destructive of the series. It is believed to have registered somewhere just below 7.0 on the 10-point Richter scale, with an intensity of VIII.
Feb. 7, 1812	**Earthquake—New Madrid Earthquake** (see p. 9). This New Madrid, Missouri, quake was one of the worst ever to occur on the North American continent in recorded history. It is believed to have registered near 8.0 on the upper end of the 10-point Richter scale, with an intensity level of IX to X. The third in a series of three great quakes in a two-month period, it was felt over most of the continental United States and parts of Canada and Mexico.
1813	Epidemic—A so-called black tongue disease struck the state. Little more is known of this event, but many believe it was typhoid fever.
Sept. 4, 1813	Structure fire—Fire destroyed practically every building between College Street and Market Street on the public square in Nashville. The number of casualties, if any, and the economic impact is unknown.
Spring 1815	Flooding—Flooding was heavy on the Cumberland River. It was 11.5 feet above flood stage at Nashville, resulting in economic damages.
1815–21	Epidemic—"Cold plague." This mysterious disease was believed by some to have arisen in the aftermath of the great New Madrid earthquakes of 1811–12. "Cold plague," an archaic medical term, has been described as a severe form of congestive fever, prevalent in the South. It has also been referred to as a form of bilious pneumonia (i.e., an inflammation of the lungs, accompanied by gastric fever and exhibiting typhoid symptoms). Many people in Tennessee and elsewhere throughout the south may have experienced this malady during this time.
1816	**Severe winter—"Year without Summer"** (see p. 79). Temperatures were unusually cold across North America during this entire year. Water in cisterns was said to have been frozen in Tennessee on the Fourth of July. Crops failed, and the elderly and chronically ill suffered greatly. Birds that had flown north for the summer died from lack of food and low temperatures. This event was caused by sunlight being blocked by airborne dust and ash following the April 1815 volcanic eruption of Mount Tamboro, east of Java.
1819	Drought—During this drought a news article in the *Clarion and Tennessee Gazette* stated that no rain had fallen for two months, and the Cumberland River was at its lowest level since 1784. The woods were generally and uncommonly dry. For two weeks, the woods had been on fire, and the whole atmosphere was so darkened by smoke that a man could not see for 200 yards. It was said that the level of the Ohio River was the lowest it had ever been since European settlement. Crops failed, creating hardship for people and stock across the state.

1819	Economic crisis—The War of 1812 was followed by a speculative boom that eventually resulted in this economic panic. Prices fell rapidly, and many banks failed. Thousands lost their jobs, resulting in bank foreclosures on their homes and other possessions.
Mid-Feb. 1823	Severe winter—A severe cold front climaxed the winter of 1823, penetrating the Deep South and killing citrus and fig trees in Florida. The front passed through Tennessee on February 16.
July 28, 1823	Flash flood—Two people died while crossing a stream during this flash flood in White County. A third person drowned a few days later on a tributary of the Cumberland River.
Oct. 8, 1824	Flooding—According to the *Knoxville Register,* a great flood along the Nolichucky River washed away stream-side vegetation and mills. After the flood receded, the body of a man was found in a debris pile some distance below Jonesboro (Washington County). The river was said to be about fifteen feet higher than previously recorded to this date.
1825	**Epidemic, Smallpox** (see p. 20)—This epidemic was particularly severe in Nashville; however, few details of the incident are known.
Mar. 1826	Flooding—This flood rose to 53 feet 2 inches, or 12.1 feet above flood stage, on the Cumberland River at Nashville and 18 feet above flood stage on the Clinch River at Clinton (Anderson County). Celina (Clay County) was also heavily damaged. News accounts said that this flood was very costly, in terms of human life and property damage, particularly on the Clinch, Holston, and other tributaries of the Tennessee River. Flooding was severe at Knoxville and along nearby streams. A slaughterhouse was washed away on First Creek, as was a cooper shop belonging to Col. John White, founder of Knoxville. The *Knoxville Register* described the flood as the worst in thirty years in Knoxville. The Mississippi River was also at flood, and on June 2 it was probably higher than at any time in the previous forty years.
1828	**Epidemic, Yellow Fever** (see p. 22)—This was the first of eight great yellow fever epidemics in Tennessee. About 650 people contracted the disease and 150 died in Memphis.
Apr.– June 1828	Flooding—One of the greatest floods ever known in the lower Mississippi River swept the lowlands of West Tennessee and Memphis. Although little is known of the specifics of this event, it set the standards for destruction for years thereafter.
1829–31	Epidemic—A terrible fever struck the town of Fulton (Lauderdale County) only two years after its founding. The town was composed of shanties and was a port for numerous keelboats (e.g., small, cigar-shaped riverboats powered by long poles, oars, or sails and constructed to carry cargo). After 200 people died from the disease, most everyone else moved away, leaving a ghost town. The town was resettled in 1835.
1830	Tornado—A twister struck Carthage (Smith County), causing an unknown amount of damage.
1830	Drought—In May the *Nashville Banner* and *Nashville Whig* newspapers reported that the state, especially Nashville and Middle Tennessee, was suffering from excessive drought. It was thought at the time that no spring season had been as dry since settlement of the area. The water was so low during this drought period that no steamboats could operate on the Cumberland River. Crops failed throughout the area.

1830	Structure fire—A fire damaged or destroyed nearly half the business district of Chattanooga. Total economic losses are unknown.
Feb. 24, 1830	Riverboat accident—*Helen McGregor* Riverboat Disaster (see p. 175). The 400-ton paddle steamer *Helen McGregor,* built in 1823, exploded and sank on the Mississippi River at Memphis. The death toll is believed to have been somewhere between fifty and sixty.
May 30–31, 1830	Tornado—A strong twister struck Shelbyville (Bedford County) about 8:00 AM, causing great destruction. It damaged or destroyed fifty-three buildings, including the county courthouse, market house, and a number of homes. At least five people were killed and forty injured. Economic losses probably exceeded $100,000. Dickson and Maury counties also received tornado damages. This was the first officially recorded tornado episode in Middle Tennessee. A book was reported to have been blown seven miles from its point of origin during the event.
June 1, 1830	Tornado—A tornado in Charlotte (Dickson County) touched down around 10:30 PM, leaving the town in ruin. There were many injuries, some possibly fatal, but no official record of deaths can be found.
Dec.–Jan. 1831–32	Severe winter—A very long and hard freeze took place in Middle Tennessee. In fact, teams of horses with their wagons drove across the frozen Cumberland River at Nashville for a week. Snow was a foot deep in places, and on January 26 Nashville registered a temperature of –18°F This was a great period of hardship for the people of Middle Tennessee.
1832	Riverboat accident—A riverboat, name unknown, tied up at the Memphis wharf, suffered a boiler explosion that shattered the vessel and killed fifty or sixty people. Some of the victims were literally blown apart and some scalded to death. Some were said to have died immediately, and others lingered for hours.
1832–33	Epidemic, Cholera (see p. 15)—This was the first of seven great cholera epidemics in Tennessee.
Apr. 9, 1832	Riverboat accident—*Brandywine* Riverboat Disaster (see p. 176). The 483-ton steamboat *Brandywine,* built in 1829, caught fire when sparks from the smoke stack fell onto the hurricane deck. The fire spread to the entire boat within minutes. The number killed has been estimated at somewhere between 135 and 175, with the number of injured unknown.
Oct. 24, 1833	Riverboat accident—The riverboat *Thomas Yeatman* exploded on the Mississippi River at Memphis, killing seven. Further details are unknown.
Nov. 13–15, 1833	Meteor shower—General panic and hysteria occurred as the earth passed through an immense swarm of meteors estimated at somewhere between 100,000 and 200,000 per hour. This rare display of shooting stars occurred just after the comet Tempel-Tuttle reentered the inner solar system, as it does every thirty-three years. Many believed that the Day of Judgment was upon them and that the world was ending. Lesser but still spectacular meteor storms have occurred throughout history. Two of note occurred in 1866 and 1867.
1834	Epidemic, Cholera (see p. 15)—This outbreak occurred near Columbia (Maury County).

Jan. 4, 1834	Earthquake—An earthquake with an epicenter at New Madrid, Missouri, crumbled chimneys at Mills Point, near Arlington in Shelby County, and cracked walls, felled chimneys, and broke windows in Memphis. It had a MMI IX–X intensity range and was also felt in Nashville.
1835	**Epidemic, Smallpox** (see p. 20)—This epidemic was particularly severe in Nashville.
Feb. 1835	Severe winter—This was the outstanding winter event of the century with respect to severity, human suffering, and economic hardship. It was particularly severe in East Tennessee. Many cattle and hogs froze to death in –10°F weather on or around February 5, 1835. For many years thereafter, this date was referred to as "Cold Friday."
Mar. 21, 1835	Tornado—Eight were killed and many injured in one of the state's most destructive tornadoes up to that time. It occurred in the southern part of Tipton County.
May 25, 1835	Riverboat accident—As the riverboat *Majestic* was pulling out of the port of Memphis, a large number of passengers moved to the starboard side to view an object of interest on the riverbank, causing the boat to list considerably. As the passengers dispersed, the boat righted itself, and the larboard boiler (i.e., the one on the left side of the vessel) collapsed and exploded. The explosion resulted in a fire that killed thirty-eight to forty people and injured about fifty-six. (Refer also to entry on Dec. 5, 1837. This could be an error in names or a duplicate name.)
1836	Flooding—The Mississippi River was fifty-four feet above the high-water mark, creating havoc for those living along the stream, as well as for river boatmen and cargoes.
1836–37	**Epidemic, Yellow Fever** (see p. 22)—A high-mortality disease referred to as the "Black Death" was most likely yellow fever. If so, this would have been the second and third of eight great yellow fever epidemics in Tennessee.
1837–41	Economic crisis—Farm prices were depressed, many merchants were bankrupted, and some of the state's principal banks were near financial ruin following the boom of Andrew Jackson's second term as president.
Dec. 1837–Jan. 1838	Severe winter—Severe cold, snow, and ice occurred throughout the Cumberland River Basin. In the vicinity of Nashville, the Cumberland froze nine inches thick in places. On January 4 in Memphis, cattle had to be brought ashore, across the ice, from flatboats marooned on the open river.
Dec. 5, 1837	Riverboat accident—A flue collapsed on the steamboat *Majestic* about twenty miles above Memphis on the Mississippi River. Three people died in the incident. (Refer also to entry on May 25, 1835. This could be an error in names or duplicate names.)
1838	Native American exodus—Trail of Tears. The story of this infamous exodus of Native Americans, which began in East Tennessee, is one of the darkest pages in the nation's history. Between 16,000 and 17,000 Cherokee Indians, along with their black slaves and white spouses, were evicted from their aboriginal homeland in East Tennessee, Western North Carolina, North Alabama, and North Georgia and force-marched or otherwise transported to reservations in the Oklahoma Indian Territory. Some have estimated that as many as 4,000 to 5,000 may have perished during this event. Many were said to have died in stockades used to house the Cherokee

prior to the exodus. Others died en route during a bitter winter and were buried in unmarked graves along the way.

1838	**Epidemic, Cholera** (see p. 15)—This was the second of seven great cholera epidemics in Tennessee.
Summer 1838	Drought—Memphis newspapers refer to a seventy-two-day drought that ended on September 18 of this year.
June–Winter 1838	Epidemic, malarial fever—This incident, about which little is known, occurred in Knoxville.
May 29, 1839	Riverboat accident—The riverboat *Buckeye* exploded on the Mississippi River near Randolph (Tipton County) while allegedly in a race with the riverboat *General Brown*. The accident occurred around midnight when the *Buckeye*'s boilers overheated and exploded. Several passengers and crew members died, and several others were injured.
1840–75	**Pandemic, Cholera** (see p. 15)—This disease killed millions worldwide. However, it does not appear to have had as great an effect on Tennesseans as did some other outbreaks.
Jan. 13, 1840	Riverboat accident—The steamboat *Hermitage* collided with the *Hugh L. White* near Harpeth Shoals on the Cumberland River. The former sank in only ten feet of water. Although crowded with passengers, the only known fatality was the fireman, Hugh Pratt.
May 1840	Flooding—Early settlers tell of a great flood in the Little Tennessee River basin in May 1840. Four flood marks are found for this event on the Tuckasegee River, a tributary of the Little Tennessee in North Carolina. They indicate that most of the flooding probably occurred along that tributary of the Little Tennessee River into which it flows before entering the state. Some Cherokees were quoted as saying that this flood actually occurred in 1844. This is possible since there were disastrous floods on the Mississippi, Cumberland, and Tennessee rivers in 1844.
Jan. 1841	Flooding—According to a local newspaper account, the Cumberland River at Nashville was higher than it had been in several years, and steamboats could not get under the bridge. Some buildings along lower Broad Street had water up to their second stories, causing property damage and otherwise affecting the local economy.
Jan. 4, 1841	"Blood rain"—An area 40 to 60 yards wide and 600 to 800 yards long in Wilson County received a mysterious rain of blood and bits of flesh. It may have been caused by a tornado hitting a farm slaughterhouse or a flock of birds. Several theories were advanced by prominent scientists of the time, and there was a conspiracy theory that local slaves broadcasted the bits of blood and flesh over a local tobacco crop as a hoax on their masters.
Mar. 26, 1841	Severe winter—Four feet of snow in White and surrounding counties lingered for six weeks. It stalled transportation and caused economic impact to the area.
May 8, 1841	Hailstorm—Egg-sized hail in Memphis destroyed gardens and other vegetation, broke windows, killed chickens and other animals, and generally played havoc with the area.
Aug. 6, 1841	Riverboat accident—A 407-ton steam side-wheeler, the *Caroline,* built in 1841, snagged and sank at Plum Point (Lauderdale County). Thirty-seven people were killed. The number of injuries and the economic impact of the disaster are unknown.

Feb. 1842	Flooding—Heavy flooding along the Cumberland River, especially within a twenty-five-square-mile area of Jackson, Macon, and Smith counties, damaged many mills and farms, along with their stock and crops. At least six people lost their lives in this flood. The Collins River, at McMinnville (Warren County), was eight feet higher than previously known. There was also much destruction along Caney Fork at Rock Island (Warren County), where a dozen mills and many crops, valued at $50,000, were damaged or washed away. There is a flood-height mark chiseled into a rock bluff near the U.S. Hwy. 231 bridge at Fayetteville (Lincoln County). The words "John N--Water--1842" are inscribed beside the high-water mark. A flood on the Wolf River at Memphis on February 1 ripped thirty flatboats from their moorings and sank a steamboat.
May 1842	Tax dispute—Memphis levied a tax on flatboats and other commercial vessels, setting off what became known as "the Flatboat War." When some 500 boatmen protested and refused to pay the wharf, or dockage, fee, the militia, the town constable, and many citizens rallied against them. Shots were exchanged, and one boatman was killed. The city finally won, and the dockage fees were paid. Eventually, these wharf fees became the largest single revenue source for the city
1844	Flooding—Heavy flooding was reported along the Mississippi River in West Tennessee. This flooding also affected the Ohio River system, including the Cumberland River. An estimated 400 people perished along the Mississippi and Ohio rivers and their tributaries. The upper Tennessee River may also have been affected (see May 1840 flood).
Dec. 14, 1844	**Riverboat accident—*Belle of Clarksville* Riverboat Disaster** (see p. 177). The 250-ton steam side-wheeler *Belle of Clarksville,* built in 1843, collided with the riverboat *Louisiana* on the Mississippi River at Memphis. The *Belle* was demolished except for her cabin, which somehow managed to stay afloat. Thirty-six of the passengers and crew on the *Belle* were killed instantly or drowned. The *Louisiana* was relatively unscathed.
June 25, 1846	Hailstorm—A tremendous hailstorm nine miles east of Memphis created ten inches of hail, which ruined, among other things, the cotton crops of at least two farms.
Mar. 1847	Flooding—This was one of the worst floods on the Tennessee and Cumberland rivers known at the time. The Cumberland rose to fifty-five feet on the flood gauge, or almost fifteen feet above flood stage at Nashville. A steamboat was said to have crossed Gallatin Pike in East Nashville by going around the river bridge. The height of this flood was marked by the removal of a brick on the southwest side of a building at the foot of Broad Street. All but two of the roads leading into Nashville were submerged. The *Knoxville Register,* March 17, 1847, also told of great floods along the Clinch, Holston, and French Broad rivers in early March. The flood at Knoxville was three feet higher than the highest previously known flood in 1826. The flooding followed several days of almost uninterrupted rainfall.
Oct. 12, 1847	**Explosion—Sycamore Powder Mill Explosion** (see p. 93). This explosion occurred between 4:00 and 5:00 PM in a powder magazine at Sycamore Powder Mill (Cheatham County). Four workmen were killed, twenty were injured, and fifty homes were demolished when 500 kegs of gunpowder blew up during a violent thunderstorm.

Dec. 19, 1847	Flooding—Heavy floods occurred along the Tennessee and especially the Cumberland and Caney Fork rivers as the result of a severe storm. This very destructive storm caused damages as far away as Cincinnati. The Cumberland River at Nashville reached 54.9 feet on the flood gauge.
1848	**Epidemic, Smallpox** (see p. 20)—This disease struck Decatur and probably other counties in Tennessee.
1848	**Epidemic, Yellow Fever** (see p. 22)—This was the fourth of eight great yellow fever epidemics in Tennessee.
May 25, 1848	Flooding—Flooding was heavy on the Cumberland River, affecting at least 200 Nashville homes and other structures.
Nov. 21, 1848	Riverboat accident—The riverboat *Native* exploded on the Cumberland River at Dover (Stewart County), killing at least two people and likely injuring others.
1849	Structure fire—Most of the businesses in Macon (Fayette County) were destroyed by a great fire.
Jan. 22, 1849	Flooding—Flooding was heavy on the Cumberland River.
Feb. 26, 1849	Severe winter—The Mississippi River level dropped four feet in twenty-four hours due to an upstream ice jam. It rose rapidly when the ice jam eventually broke.
Mid–April 1849	Severe winter—Snow and freezing rain pounded the Deep South, damaging many crops and causing other hardships in Tennessee and other states.
June 11, 1849	Riverboat accident—The steamboat *Memphis* was struck by a tornado and allegedly sank, with appalling loss of life, a few miles upstream from Memphis.
July–Aug. 1849	**Epidemic, Cholera** (see p. 15)—This was the third of seven great cholera epidemics in the state. It also affected a large portion of North America.
Apr. 28–29, 1850	Flooding—There was heavy flood damage along the Tennessee River. Two boys were drowned at Woodbury (Cannon County) while trying to help a neighbor. At Nashville the river gauge measured 53.1 feet.
July 1850	**Epidemic, Cholera** (see p. 15)—This was the fourth of seven great cholera epidemics in Tennessee. Gainesboro (Jackson County) was particularly hard hit.
Feb. 24, 1851	Tornado—Half of the town of Fayetteville (Lincoln County), including sixty to seventy buildings, were damaged or destroyed by this twister. Three people were killed instantly when a chimney collapsed on them. An additional forty to fifty people were injured, and twenty-five families were left homeless.
Jan. 1852	Severe winter—Heavy floating ice and ice gorges formed on the Cumberland River. On January 21 the temperature in Nashville dropped to –18°F.
Jan. 25, 1852	Riverboat accident—En route between New Orleans and Pittsburg, the 265-ton steamboat *DeWitt Clinton,* built in 1847, became snagged on the Mississippi River at Dismal Point, opposite Presidents Island, eight miles below Memphis. Between thirty-six and forty people perished in the incident. She sank in only fifteen feet of water; only the fireman and officers survived.

Aug. 28–30, 1852	Flooding—Flood damage was particularly severe in the French Broad River Basin. The rains that prompted the flood commenced at 10:00 PM on August 28 and continued into the evening of the next day. Mills, bridges, and crops were washed away on the French Broad and Caney Fork rivers. There was also much destruction on many other tributaries of the Tennessee and Cumberland rivers. Damage was likewise severe along portions and other tributaries of the Ohio River.
1853–54	Drought—This incident was especially severe in Middle Tennessee during the period.
Mar. 26(?), 1853	Structure fire—A fire erupted in the town of Bolívar (Hardeman County), destroying many downtown businesses. Property losses were estimated at around $50,000. Damages to goods were estimated at around $25,000. Very little of the property and goods were insured. There were no known casualties.
1854	**Epidemic, Cholera** (see p. 15)—This was the fifth of eight great cholera epidemics in Tennessee.
Jan. 1854	Riverboat accident—The riverboat *General Bent* is reported to have been snagged below Memphis on the Mississippi River, sinking very quickly and drowning twenty-one deck passengers. Few details are known.
Jan. 28, 1854	Flooding—Flooding was great on the Cumberland River, which was almost seventeen feet above flood stage at Nashville.
1855	**Epidemic, Yellow Fever** (see p. 22)—This was the fifth of eight great yellow fever epidemics in Tennessee. Of 1,250 cases in Memphis, about 220 died.
Mar. 24, 1855	Riverboat accident—The riverboat *Huntsville No. 2* burned and caused destruction at Hamburg (Hardin County) on the Tennessee River.
Dec. 3–4, 1855	Riverboat accident—The Riverboat *George Collier* was just arriving at the lower landing of the Memphis docks when a fire broke out in a small closet under a flight of steps. Within five minutes, the fire had spread over the entire boat. The fire also ignited two other boats, *Mary Hunt* and the *Mayflower,* which lay on either side of her. Additionally, the fire spread to buildings along Howard Row, adjacent to the wharf. It is believed that ten to fifteen people died in this incident, and economic losses from the three boats and buildings on the wharf were estimated at around $250,000.
Jan.–Feb. 1856	Severe winter—The Cumberland River froze over, and ice gorges and floating ice were present for thirty days.
Mar. 16, 1856	Structure fire—Fires destroyed thirteen houses and eight other buildings, including the Masonic Hall, along the public square in Nashville.
Mar. 24–25, 1856	Structure fire—The town of Sevierville (Sevier County) was almost entirely destroyed by a conflagration on these two days. Forty-one houses and several shops were destroyed, along with a newly constructed courthouse and all its records. The jail also burned, killing one prisoner.
Apr. 13, 1856	Structure fire—A fire in downtown Nashville destroyed the county courthouse and half of the structures on the north side of the public square.
May 10, 1856	Flooding—This flood, referred to as the "May Fresh," brought destruction all along the Cumber-

land River. One house was swept away with four children in it. All drowned. At least four other people were killed in the deluge.

Sept. 13, 1856	Riverboat accident—The riverboat *James Laughlin* foundered on the Mississippi River at Memphis, killing six.
1857–58	**Economic crisis—Economic Panic of 1857–58** (see p. 190). Unemployment increased, breadlines formed, and social unrest was rampant. The affects of this depression were not as great in the southern states, where slave labor proved to be a positive economic factor. Nonetheless, adverse economic consequences did spread into Tennessee, other southern states, and eventually even South America, Europe, and Asia.
Jan. 1857	Severe winter—Floating ice and ice gorges formed along the Cumberland River.
Dec. 15, 1857	Flooding—Flooding was heavy on the Cumberland River, which was nine feet above flood stage at Nashville.
1858	Flooding—Flooding was heavy on the Mississippi River. On July 4, 5.7 inches of rain fell at Memphis, washing away all the bridges along Bayou Gayoso and destroying several houses.
May 12, 1858	Riverboat accident—The *City of Huntsville*, a 238-ton side-wheeler constructed in 1852 at Elizabeth, Pennsylvania, was snagged and sank. It went down at Palmyra Island (Montgomery County) on the Cumberland River. Eight were killed, but the number of injuries is unknown.
Sept. 1858	Riot—Memphis volunteer firefighters from Independent Company #1 and Washington Company # 6 rioted with guns, knives, and fists shortly after their two engines collided in the dark at the corner of Main and Poplar streets. Both firemen and citizen bystanders were injured by bricks thrown by rioters during the brawl. The incident was finally broken up by the Memphis Police Department and after a personal appeal by the mayor. In those days, volunteer fire departments were more like athletic teams. If two showed up at the same fire, at the same time, they would often fight to see who got to put out the fire.
Jan. 5, 1859	Structure fire—A Memphis conflagration took one life and destroyed more than twenty-five structures, all of them three to four stories high. Property damage was estimated at $200,000. Local volunteer firefighters were apparently unable to contain the blazes.
Dec. 12, 1859	Flooding—Flooding was heavy on the Cumberland River.
Jan. 27, 1860	Structure fire—This Memphis fire is believed to be the result of arson. It probably originated in some hay in the back section of the Stratton, McDavitt & Company Livery Stable. The stable adjoined the Post Office on Second Street in an area called the Post Office Block. Besides killing forty horses, several businesses were either destroyed or badly damaged. Total losses were estimated at over $75,000.
Apr. 26, 1860	Riverboat accident—The Tennessee steamboat *Alfred T. Lacy* caught fire and burned to the water line near the foot of Islands No. 16 and No. 17 on Linwood Bend. The wreck occurred just above the old river town of Boothpoint (Dyer County). Linwood Bend, located at mile 840.5, is named for another riverboat, the *Linwood,* which wrecked there in 1847. Interstate 155 now crosses the

	Mississippi River near the site of the wreck of the *Lacy*. Most passengers and officers were saved, but sixteen are known to have died. The boat and its cargo, along with its books and papers, the estimated value of which was over $180,000, were lost.
June 16, 1860	Tornado—A tornado in the community of Freedom, Washington County, on the Holston River, was said to have picked up animals and even bar iron, dropping them as much as a quarter mile away.
Aug.–Sept. 1860	Labor strike—Memphis's second firefighters' strike in two years protested slanderous accusations that the city's volunteer firemen displayed raucous behavior, as well as the city's attempt to develop a full-time paid fire department with an appointed chief.
Dec. 13, 1860	Riverboat accident—The riverboat *South Bend* collided with the *Goody Friends* at Fulton (Lauderdale County), killing at least two.
1862	**Epidemic, Yellow Fever** (see p. 22)—This episode was not as severe as other epidemics.
Nov. 1, 1862	Riverboat accident—*Eugene* was snagged and sank on the Mississippi River at Plum Point (Lauderdale County), killing fifteen.
Mar. 7, 1863	Tornado—A tornado touched down in Shelbyville (Bedford County), damaging many structures and causing at least one death. Economic losses are unknown.
Apr. 8, 1863	Riverboat accident—The *R.C.M. Lovell* caught fire and burned on the Cumberland River above Clarksville (Montgomery County), killing at least one person.
Aug. 21, 1863	Riverboat accident—The *Champion* caught fire and burned on the Mississippi River at Memphis, killing one person.
Sept. 29, 1863	**Structure failure—Maxwell House Stairway Collapse** (see p. 131). The Maxwell House Hotel at Nashville, under construction during the Civil War, was used to house Confederate war prisoners. Prisoners were descending a temporary wooden stairway when it suddenly collapsed. Somewhere between twenty and fifty men were killed instantly or died later of injuries sustained in the accident. Sympathetic townspeople tried to help rescue and provide medical assistance to the prisoners, but their efforts were prohibited by military officers at the scene.
Feb. 1, 1864	Riverboat accident—The riverboat *Belle Creole* was snagged and sank on the Mississippi River at Plum Point (Lauderdale County), killing at least one person.
Oct. 30, 1864	Riverboat accident—The *Universe* was snagged and sank on the Mississippi at Plum Point (Lauderdale County), killing seventeen.
Dec. 24, 1864	**Structure fire—Specht Bakery Fire** (see p. 104). A fire erupted in the basement of the Joseph Specht's Confectionery on Madison Street in Memphis around 3:00 AM. Sixteen people died either in the fire or from injuries sustained while attempting escape by jumping from the fourth floor to the ground below.
1865	Economic crisis—This economic depression hit the nation at the close of the Civil War, and southern states like Tennessee were particularly hard hit. The land had been neglected, and slave labor and capital investment in it had been lost. Homes, barns, and other structures had

been destroyed, and there was little money for feed, seed, laborers, and badly needed repairs. In short, the economy was in shambles.

Jan. 27, 1865   Riverboat accident—The *Eclipse,* a 223-ton steam-powered stern-wheeler built in 1862, exploded and sank on the Tennessee River near Johnsonville (Humphreys County), killing twenty-seven people.

Apr. 27, 1865   **Riverboat accident—*Sultana* Riverboat Disaster** (see p. 177). The *Sultana,* a 1,720 ton side-wheeler riverboat sank on the flood-swollen Mississippi River eight miles north of Memphis. This event remains the worst inland marine disaster in U.S. history. The boilers exploded on the overloaded vessel, ripping it apart, and the resulting fire burned it to the water line. Although licensed to carry only 376 passengers and crew, the vessel was transporting almost 2,700. Most were recently released Union Civil War prisoners bound for home. Estimates vary widely, but somewhere between 1,700 and 2,100 died in this tragedy.

May 26, 1865   Flooding—This flood put five to six feet of water in the public square at Lebanon (Wilson County). A two-inch layer of mud and silt covered the floors of every house and store in the central part of the town. Precise economic losses are not known.

June 9, 1865   Structure fire—Fire broke out at Taylor's Depot, a federal government warehouse, at the intersection of what is today Broadway and Fifth Avenue in Nashville. It destroyed about half of the facility and its quartermaster stores, valued at between $1 million and $4 million. The cause of the fire was never confirmed. Some believed it was a case of arson, while others attributed its ignition to sparks cause by a passing train.

Aug. 17, 1865   Earthquake—This quake occurred near Memphis and is said to have damaged masonry structures. It was felt as far away as Jackson, Mississippi; St. Louis, Missouri; and parts of Illinois. Its MMI intensity was around VII.

Aug. 25, 1865   **Railway accident—Reynolds Station Train Wreck** (see p. 158). A Louisville and Nashville train crashed when a Tennessee River trestle collapsed three-quarters of a mile south of what was then the town of Reynolds, or Reynolds Station (Giles County). This town was located where U.S. Highway 31 crosses the railroad tracks between Olivet and Milky Way, north of Pulaski. Details of the event are sketchy, but it is known that at least thirty-five people were killed and perhaps thirty others were injured, some possibly fatally. This was the fourth-worst train wreck in the state's history, based on injuries and loss of life.

1866–present   **Racial violence—KKK Insurrection and the Invisible Empire** (see p. 211). After the Civil War, Ku Klux Klan (KKK) extremist activity was strong in portions of West and Middle Tennessee and around Bristol in East Tennessee. To this day it continues to have some support, but little influence, throughout the country. Descriptions of its heinous atrocities have filled volumes.

Mar. 4, 1866   Riverboat accident—The steamboat *Lockwood* exploded, burned, and sank about eighteen miles downstream of the Memphis wharf. Twenty were killed instantly, and twenty-five were scalded or otherwise injured. The riverboat *Mephom* (or *Mepham*) was the first to arrive at the scene of the disaster to rescue the survivors.

May 1–3, 1866	**Racial Violence—Memphis Racial Massacre** (see p. 214). A race-motivated massacre in Memphis resulted in the deaths of sixty-eight people and the injury (including rapes and beatings) of seventy to eighty others. Although referred to as a race riot at the time, blacks were for the most part innocent victims of the incident, according to a detailed Congressional investigation.
May 31, 1866	Riverboat accident—The *City of Memphis,* a famous side-wheel packet, wrecked and sank when her three boilers exploded near the foot of Buck Island in Memphis. At least five people died in the incident.
June 11, 1866	Structure fire—A fire along Broad Street in Nashville consumed several businesses. Losses were estimated at $50,000.
Aug.–Sept. 1866	**Epidemic, Cholera** (see p. 15)—The sixth of seven great cholera epidemics in Tennessee occurred in the wake of the Civil War. Nashville lost 800 citizens and Memphis over 900. Other parts of the state were also severely affected.
Dec. 31, 1866	Tornado—A tornado struck the town of Pulaski (Giles County), killing at least five, injuring about a dozen, and causing considerable damage in and around the city. The twister destroyed a cotton factory and carried the structure and its contents some 200 feet away. Economic losses were estimated at $100,000.
1867	**Epidemic, Yellow Fever** (see p. 22)—This was the sixth of eight great yellow fever epidemics in Tennessee. The event lasted about seventy days. Of the approximately 2,500 people who contracted the disease in Memphis, the hardest hit city in the state, 550 died.
Mar. 1–13, 1867	**Flooding—Flood of March 1867** (see p. 32). This flood and the storm that spawned it were the worst known to date on the upper Tennessee, Little Tennessee, Holston, and French Broad rivers. Sixteen inches of rain, as well as snow, fell in only seven days. Downstream of Chattanooga, the water in the Tennessee River Gorge was as much as 100 feet above its normal level. Flooding was also heavy on the Mississippi and Cumberland rivers.
May 20, 1867	Flooding—There was considerable flood damage on the Holston River. The stream eventually reached twenty-seven feet above the low-water mark. Farmhouses, mills, and rich topsoil were washed away, along with already planted spring crops. The erosion was so great that it even exposed long-buried Native American artifacts in some areas.
July 6, 1867	**Racial violence—Franklin Race Riot** (see p. 217). Scores of blacks and whites were shot and four were killed during a political rally and march in Franklin (Williamson County). U.S. troops were eventually dispatched to the area, although order had already been restored and they were not needed.
Jan. 9, 1868	Racial violence—A small riot occurred in Pulaski (Giles County). Two blacks were killed and several wounded. The incident grew out of a longtime controversy between a black citizen and a white storekeeper.
May 6, 1868	Tornado—This twister touched down around 4:00 PM and cut a ten-mile-long path of destruction through Williamson and Davidson counties from fourteen miles southwest of Nashville to Brentwood. Five died and fifteen were injured in the incident.

July 15, 1868	Lynching—Three unidentified blacks were lynched in Maury County.
1869–71	Economic crisis—A sharp economic downturn started in New York City and spread across the nation, devastating the southern states, which were still in shambles following the Civil War. Money was in short supply and credit was limited. Skilled human resources, needed to reestablish a healthy economy, were seriously wanting.
1869	Riverboat accident—The *R. P. Converse* and *Last Chance* collided on a sharp bend of the Tennessee River near Dayton (Rhea County). They were moving in opposite directions at the time. The *R. P. Converse* sank and the other boat sustained major damage. There was no known loss of life on either vessel.
1869	Tornadic fire—A strange, so-called cylinder of fire was reported near Ashland City (Cheatham County) during this year. It was first spotted on the farm of Ed Sharp as it came across a wooded area, picking up tree branches and leaves, which were ignited to further fuel the twirling blaze. According to an account in *Simon's Monthly Meteorological Magazine* in 1869, some 200 people witnessed this bizarre event. As it moved at about five miles per hour, it seemed to grow larger. As the fiery twister passed over a house with wooden shingles, it set the building on fire. An adjacent wheat field with freshly cradled stacks of wheat was set ablaze. It even passed over a team of horses and singed their manes and tails. Finally, it moved straight toward the Cumberland River, where it picked up a column of water that quickly extinguished its flames. After that, only a steam cloud could be seen as it dissipated into the distance.
Jan. 29–30, 1869	Lynching and hate crimes—Five white men were lynched in Dyersburg (Dyer County) for horse thievery.
Aug. 1869	Lynching and hate crimes—Two unidentified black men were lynched in Rutherford County.
Aug. 1869	Lynching and hate crimes—Four unidentified black men were lynched at Hillsboro (Coffee County).
Dec. 1869	Lynching and hate crimes—Two unidentified black men were lynched in Obion County.
1870	Lynching and hate crimes—Three black men, accused of burning a Franklin County church, were taken from the local jail and hanged from a nearby bridge.
Mar. 7, 1870	Riverboat accident—The *Nettie Jones* foundered on the Mississippi River at Memphis, killing at least two people.
July 5, 1870	Riverboat accident—The *Mary Byrd,* while negotiating a torturous Tennessee River channel known as the "Suck," just downstream of Chattanooga, struck a submerged obstruction and sank with a large cargo. Fortunately, the crew and passengers escaped with their lives. Other details of the incident are sketchy.
Aug. 1, 1870	**Riverboat accident—*Silver Spray* Riverboat Disaster** (see p. 179). The stern-wheel steamboat *Silver Spray* exploded and caught fire about thirty miles up the Mississippi River from Memphis in the vicinity of Lauderdale County. Although all records were lost, it was estimated that twenty-six people either died in the flames or were drowned; others were injured as they were forced to jump into the Mississippi River.

1871	Structure fire—This conflagration destroyed twenty-one businesses along the west side of Market Street, between Seventh and Ninth streets in Chattanooga. Economic losses were estimated at $75,000 and led to the establishment of the city's first fire department. One building involved in the fire was Kirkpatrick's Wholesale Whiskey establishment on Market Street. There was no lack of volunteers to help save the several hundred barrels of spirits stored there. Of course, as a reward for doing so, many imbibed. Several people were injured in this fire from walls collapsing on them but there were no known deaths.
Jan. 3, 1871	Railway accident – At least five people were killed and others mortally injured when a trestle on the Mississippi and Tennessee Railroad gave way, causing two cars to derail and plunge into Nonconnah Creek. The final death toll was never recorded, but the wreck, which occurred about five miles south of Memphis, also resulted in injuries to other passengers and crew. The accident was believed to be caused by a broken axle on the baggage car. The crash occurred about 10:00 AM. One car was totally destroyed by flames and the others were smashed to pieces.
Jan. 2, 1872	Structure fire—Fire broke out along Market Street, now called Second Avenue, in Nashville, destroying or damaging a number of structures valued at around a quarter of a million dollars.
Mar. 14, 1872	Structure fire—Fire broke out in Nashville in the same general area as on January 2, 1872, again causing around a quarter of a million dollars in damages.
Fall of 1872	Epizootic incident—A so-called horse disease occurred across Tennessee and the nation, from Canada to Cuba, in the fall of this year. We now know that it was a form of equine influenza that affected almost 100 percent of the animals exposed to it. Since almost all commerce at that time was dependent upon horsepower it virtually paralyzed the nation's economy. Although trains and riverboats transported bulk cargo, it was horses that carried the coal to the trains and riverboats. It was horses that carried cargo from the boat or train to its marketplace. It was horses that carried crops from farms to markets. And it was horses that transported products from markets to homes. Where possible wagons were pulled by oxen until the disease subsided. The mortality rate for the disease ranged between 1 and 10 percent, but usually affected only about 1 to 2 percent of the animals. Within a few weeks, most of the horses and mules recovered from the illness, but not in time to avert the nationwide panic of 1873, for which they were at least partially responsible.
Sept. 16, 1872	Structure fire—A fire consumed a portion of the Memphis business district between Main and Second and Union and Monroe. A dozen businesses were involved, and damages were estimated at $266,000. Several firefighters were injured in the incident.
Oct. 3, 1872	Railway accident—Four or five people died and at least twenty-five were injured in a railway accident at Greeneville. The accident occurred on a downgrade curve as the engineer was attempting to make up time, since the train was already about an hour and fifteen minutes behind schedule. Some of the cars left the track and fell from a high trestle. It was miraculous that more people were not killed in such a horrific wreck.
1873–75	Economic crisis—This incident began in New York City and spread across the nation. It was the deepest and longest depression in the nation's history to that date. Nathan Bedford Forrest, a

Tennessee Confederate Civil War general, was said to have lost everything he had as a result of this panic, as did many other prosperous Tennesseans of the time.

1873	**Epidemic, Yellow Fever** (see p. 22)—This was the seventh of eight great yellow fever epidemics in Tennessee. Around 2,000 of some 5,000 cases in Memphis were fatal. Epidemics of cholera, smallpox, and yellow fever also were prevalent across the state during this year.
1873	Structure fire—This conflagration struck the town square of Paris (Henry County) and was similar in extent to the one that occurred on July 4, 1899.
1873	**Epidemic, Cholera** (see p. 15)—This was the worst outbreak of cholera in the state's history. Over a thousand cases occurred in Memphis in a four-month period, and over a quarter of them were fatal. Eighty died in one Memphis neighborhood. Nashville reported 647 deaths for the year. Chattanooga lost 141, a third of them in just two days. Murfreesboro (Rutherford County) was also hard hit. This was the last of seven great cholera epidemics in Tennessee.
Jan. 22, 1873	Severe winter—Middle Tennessee was struck by a blizzard so fierce that, "three score years later, old timers still shivered at the memory of it."
Mar. 28, 1873	Tornado—One person was killed and twenty injured when a tornado moved northeast across northwestern Memphis, damaging or destroying over fifty structures.
June 20, 1873	**Epidemic, Cholera** (see p. 15)—Called "Black Friday," seventy-two people died of cholera in Nashville. As early as 1866, the Nashville Board of Health had warned that the city's unsanitary condition was a disaster just waiting to happen. The disease was brought to the city by newly arrived inmates at the Tennessee State Prison.
Nov. 1–7, 1873	Labor strike—About 160 railroad employees walked off the job when they were informed by the East Tennessee, Virginia and Georgia Railroad that their wage rates were being cut. The company claimed that this was necessary due to falling passenger and freight rates brought about by the current depression (i.e., the economic panic of 1873). The workers felt that the wage rate reduction was not just an attempt to cut wages, but to devalue the worth of their labor. They favored a reduction in hours at the same rate of pay. Railroad traffic came to a virtual standstill at Knoxville during the strike, except for mail trains, which were allowed to operate through the city. There were threats of violence against the company and anyone attempting to operate the trains, but no physical assaults or vandalism was reported. In the end, the railroad brought an injunction against the strikers in chancery court preventing them from any further interference with the operation of the rail company. The strike ended, the employees lost their battle, and as a condition of being reemployed, they were also forced to abandon their union charter.
Apr. 1874	Flooding—This Mississippi River flood, the greatest known to this date, arose without warning and broke levees in many places. Tens of thousands of acres were inundated, destruction was immense, and hundreds of lives were believed lost in several states, including Tennessee. No attempt was made at the time to estimate the economic cost of this incident, and few specific details are known. Nonetheless, the losses surely amounted to many millions of dollars. Flooding was also heavy on the Cumberland River during this year.

May 24, 1874	**Riverboat accident—*Crescent City* Towboat Disaster** (see p. 180). The towboat *Crescent City,* pulling five barges and a tail boat, exploded and sank in the Mississippi River ten miles below Memphis. Between five and sixteen were killed and others were injured. Economic losses were estimated at $300,000.
Aug. 27, 1874	**Lynching and hate crimes—Gibson County Mass Lynching** (see p. 230). Sixteen black men charged with killing two whites were taken from Gibson County Jail at Trenton by a band of 100 or so hooded vigilantes. Six of the captives were shot, but the fate of the other ten is still in question. Actual details of the event are believed by some to have been suppressed by local, state, and even federal officials.
1875	Riverboat accident—*Emma (Emory City),* a 97-ton stern-wheeler from Chattanooga, exploded at Washington Landing, near its home port, on the Tennessee River. The number of casualties and the amount of economic loss is unknown.
Feb. 23–27, 1875	Flooding—According to many newspapers at the time, this episode consisted of two floods that occurred very close together. The floods resulted from fourteen to eighteen inches of rainfall that fell on frozen ground throughout the Tennessee River Basin. This greatly accelerated runoff and the overflow of streams throughout the region. The very rapid rise of this flood, in comparison to the flood of 1867, was due in part to snowmelt in the Appalachian Mountains, which inundated the eastern tributaries of the Tennessee River. This flood was at the time second only to the 1867 event on the French Broad River at Dandridge (Jefferson County) and on the main stream at Knoxville, Cleveland (Bradley County), Athens (McMinn County), and Sweetwater (Monroe County). There was also heavy flooding at Coal Creek [now Lake City (Anderson County)], Bristol (Sullivan County), and Pigeon Forge and Sevierville (Sevier County). This was the flood of record, or close to it, at the two Sevier County locations. There is some question as to whether the flood stage was approximately the same during the flood of April 1896. The French Broad railroad trestle at Leadvale (Jefferson County) was washed away, and according to the *Knoxville Chronicle,* the water was as high as in the flood of 1867 and still rising under the bridge. Very rich farmland was washed away at many locations. A local judge estimated the economic losses along the French Broad and Nolichucky rivers at a quarter of a million dollars. This was also the most severe flood ever recorded on the upper reaches of the Sequatchie River. To that date, it was considered the second greatest flood ever on the Tennessee River. The course of the Mississippi River, thirty miles north of Memphis, created a new two-mile cutoff from what was then a twenty-mile loop of the Devils Elbow (Chanal du Diable). A total of 73.87 inches of rain fell over Tennessee during 1875, almost one and a half times the state's average precipitation per year.
May 1875	Structure failure—Knoxville bridge collapse. A pontoon bridge constructed by the Union army during the Civil War at the present site of the Knoxville's Gay Street bridge was washed away in a flood in 1867. It was eventually replaced by another bridge that failed during a violent windstorm in this year. A new Gay Street bridge was constructed in 1880, and the present iron struc-

ture was erected in 1898. While these bridges were out, South Knoxville was often referred to as South America because of its physical remoteness to the rest of the city.

May 27, 1875	Structure fire—The east side of the square in Covington (Tipton County) was destroyed by fire.
Aug. 14, 1875	Riverboat accident—The *Hugh Martin* exploded and sank at Washington Landing on the Tennessee River, near Chattanooga. Four people, including the captain, were killed, and a number of passengers and deckhands were seriously injured. The captain was blown into the water, and his body was found fifty miles downstream several days after the accident. According to one theory, the boat had run far enough aground when it docked that the water level in the boilers dropped. When it backed off, cooler water flowed back into the hot, dry portion of the boilers with disastrous results.
Jan. 13, 1876	Structure fire—The Luck's block of Church Street in Nashville was destroyed by fire. The economic losses, although likely heavy, are unknown.
June 17, 1876	Flooding—The "June Freshet," as this event was called, was one of the greatest floods ever known in the upper reaches of the French Broad and Pigeon Rivers. However, as great as it was, information on the event is sketchy. On June 17, the *Knoxville Daily Chronicle* reported that "the water all came out of the French Broad [River] and the farms [including buildings crops and stock] were literally washed away."
Dec. 1876–Jan. 1877	Severe winter—Frigid weather covered the entire state, and it was the coldest December on record at Knoxville. Temperatures dropped to 29.2°F, and ice floes were observed on the Tennessee River. Fifteen inches of snow fell on the city on New Year's Day, and by the third of January the temperature had fallen to –25°F. Whiskey was said "to have frozen solid in barrels in Knoxville warehouses," likely an exaggeration to emphasize how cold it was. The adverse weather did not break for several days. The Cumberland River froze solid at Nashville by December 31, 1876. In Memphis the river's heavy ice jam froze over. Snow was three feet deep in places, and on January 3, 1877, the temperature dropped to –14°F.
1877–78	Drought—This event is believed to have affected the entire state and to have caused extensive crop damage.
Jan. 15, 1877	Snake storm—"The Great Memphis Snake Storm" occurred near the end of January as temperatures began to warm after a severe cold period. Shortly after a rainstorm developed over the city, thousands of snakes are said to have fallen from the sky or else become suddenly visible slithering along the ground. Although there were possible explanations for the phenomenon, it was never adequately explained. Some claim that the snakes, ranging from a foot to eighteen inches in length, must have been picked up by a tornadic funnel cloud and dropped as it dissipated over the city. Some say they were worms, not snakes. Strangely enough, no snakes or worms were reported to have been seen on the rooftops or other high places, only on the ground.
Apr. 18, 1877	Tornado—Touching down at 1:00 PM just north of Columbia (Maury County), a tornado traveled forty miles through Lewis, Maury, Williamson, Davidson, and Rutherford counties to LaVergne. An F4 tornado, it killed ten and injured fifty.

June 17, 1877	Tornado—A tornado struck Memphis around 7:00 PM, causing much damage. There is no record of the number killed or injured, nor is the amount of economic losses known.
Apr. 13, 1878	Structure fire—This Clarksville (Montgomery County) fire broke out around 11:30 PM in the back of a store on Franklin Street between First and Second streets. It was believed to have been intentionally set and racially motivated as the result of police shooting and killing a black man. The fire spread rapidly, eventually burning over fifteen acres, which was most of the downtown area. Economic losses, including the Montgomery County Court House, all of its records, and sixty-two other structures, were estimated at nearly half a million dollars. The town was rebuilt, but like many other Tennessee communities and cities, it suffered additional devastating fires, especially through the end of the century.
June–Nov. 1878	**Epidemic, Yellow Fever** (see p. 22)—This was the worst recorded yellow fever epidemic in the state's and nation's history, and Memphis was the hardest hit city in the country. By the height of the fever season, citizens who had the means to do so had fled the city, leaving over 20,000 primarily destitute blacks, whites, and merciful caregivers behind. Of those remaining, about 5,150 died. Among the dead were forty-two physicians. There were high death rates in other parts of the state as well. For example, 366 people died in Chattanooga from mid-September to November. This was about 3 percent of its population at that time. This was the last of eight great yellow fever epidemics in Tennessee. An estimated 14,000 died throughout the southern United States.
1879	**Epidemic, Yellow Fever** (see p. 22) and an economic crisis—Because of a mass publicity campaign aimed at stressing quarantine and other public health measures in Memphis, the yellow fever outbreak of 1879 was not as devastating as in some previous years. For example, of 3,000 reported cases of the dread disease, only 600 died. However, the fiscal and physical condition of the city by this time had become so severe that it was forced to surrender its municipal charter. The city charter was regained in 1891 as the result of a massive cleanup campaign and towering landmark local public health legislation and other initiatives. As a result of all this, a "New Memphis" arose to lead many other cities into a healthier twentieth century.
1880s–Present	Worldwide climate change—Some scientists by the turn of the twenty-first century began to speculate about the process of "global warming," which many believe began about this time. Between this decade and the decade of 2000, it is estimated that the average temperature of planet Earth has risen by 1.4°F. This does not sound like much, but its effects have become noticeable since the early 2000s. For example, on the whole, the last two decades of the twentieth century are alleged to have been the warmest in the last 400 years. The past 11 and 12 years appear to be the overall warmest since 1850. (See 2000.)
1880	Riverboat accident—During a heavy flood, the *Star* struck a railroad bridge at the former town of Johnsonville. Johnsonville was inundated in 1944 when the Tennessee Valley Authority finished construction of Kentucky Dam on the Tennessee River. The impact severely damaged the pilot house and a number of cabins. Several people were believed drowned as a result of this accident.

Jan. 6, 1880	Structure fire—The Henochsberg and Lange fire in Memphis was the first in which a city fireman was known to have died. Flames erupted sometime between 9:30 and 10:00 PM in a two-story brick building in the 300 block of Main Street. The fire was named for the two main buildings that burned: the M. Henochsberg Company and the Louis Lange Corset Factory. Three firemen fighting the flames in the front of the building did not notice that the wall above them was failing, and it buried them under rubble. One of the firemen died instantly, another died of injuries the following day, but the third survived. The cause of the fire is unknown.
Summer 1881	Epidemic, typhoid fever—Twenty-one people living at the Tabard Hotel in Rugby (Morgan County) were stricken by this disease the last week in July. Seven eventually died. A localized epidemic, its origin was traced to a single well near the hotel. According to Rugby's Dr. Kemp, the people of his community exhibited a remarkable immunity to the disease up until August 1. "The drouth, however, was preparing the way for the fever that subsequently became an epidemic," he said.
Summer 1881	Drought—This event effected a substantial part of the country, including Tennessee and much of the mid-South. Crops withered in the field, and the worst to suffer were the poor people living on farms. Little rain fell from early May through the end of September.
Jan.–Mar. 1882	**Flooding—Floods of 1882** (see p. 34). Flooding was prevalent along the Mississippi, Tennessee, and Cumberland rivers. Heavy snowfall and rain caused a general overflowing of the state's rivers. Deaths and damages were great; however, details of the flood were not widely known at the time due to communications difficulties, and follow-up studies were never initiated.
Mar. 30, 1882	**Riverboat accident—*Golden City* Riverboat Disaster** (see p. 181). The Cincinnati and New Orleans packet *Golden City,* carrying sixty deck and cabin passengers as well as a traveling circus with many animals, was docking on the Mississippi River at the foot of Beale Street in Memphis when it caught fire. Thirty-five people, mostly women and children, either drowned or died of burns. Most of the circus animals were burned to death in their cages.
June 1882	**Epidemic, Smallpox** (see p. 20)—A total of sixty-eight cases of smallpox was reported just outside the city limits of Chattanooga. Of that number, twenty-six died and the rest are believed to have recovered from the disease.
Dec. 7, 1882	Structure fire—The west and south sides of the square in Covington (Tipton County), as well as a number of buildings on South Main Street, were destroyed by this fire.
Winter 1882–83	**Epidemics, Smallpox** (see p. 20)—Some communities, like Chattanooga and Morristown (Hamblen County), were affected more than others. In these cities, few families escaped the dread disease. One hundred and three died in one month in Chattanooga. In some communities, houses where the disease struck were required by law to fly a yellow flag to signify quarantine. A yellow flag is still used by the U.S. Public Health Service to signify a quarantine.
Apr. 22, 1883	Tornado—A category F3 twister touched down in south Rutherford County around noon, killing one and injuring two.

Oct. 7, 1883	Structure fire—Fire broke out around 2:20 PM at the B. Lowenstein and Brothers retail store on Main Street in Memphis. The retail store was destroyed, and two adjacent structures on Main Street were severely damaged. The losses were estimated at around $227,100.
Oct. 8, 1883	Structure fire—Around 8:00 PM a fire was ignited in the Cole Manufacturing Company stores at 37 and 39 Union Street in Memphis. It soon spread west to 35 Union and the Greenlaw Opera House on Second Street. All four buildings were destroyed at an estimated cost of $137,000.
1884–86	Civil insurrection—Union City (Obion County) was under siege by an outlaw faction referred to variously as thugs, desperadoes, gangsters, and thieves operating between Jackson (Madison County), Tennessee, and Cairo, Illinois. They were said to be officially headquartered on West Main Street in Union City. They were engaged in burglaries and murders for about fifteen months, from December 1884 through the spring of 1886. Local law enforcement officials were too few to deal with the offenders. However, order was finally restored by local citizen vigilantes who methodically hanged the perpetrators as they were apprehended. During this episode of lawlessness, at least six blacks and two whites were executed.
Feb. 19, 1884	Tornadoes—Called the "Enigma Outbreak," the details of this tornadic incident are sketchy. At least sixty twisters, probably more, are believed to have struck eight southeastern states: Alabama, Georgia, Indiana, Kentucky, Mississippi, North Carolina, South Carolina, and Tennessee. It is estimated that as many as 10,000 structures were damaged or demolished. The number alleged to have been killed in the super outbreak range from 420 to 1,200, but eight hundred is the figure most often quoted. Some sources state that up to 2,500 may have been injured. This was undoubtedly the worst super outbreak of tornadoes to affect Tennessee prior to the April 3–4, 1974, incident. Tennessee-specific figures have not been found.
Mar. 1884	Flooding—Heavy flooding, referred to as the "March 1884 Freshet," occurred along the Mississippi, Tennessee, and Cumberland rivers. A two-to-six-inch rainfall in the Tennessee Valley above Chattanooga was preceded by a snowfall that ranged from two inches at Charleston (Bradley County) to twenty inches at Leadvale (Jefferson County). This resulted in a rapidly rising flood that crested at 42.9 feet at Chattanooga. The Mississippi River was forty miles wide at Memphis, and the gauge showed the flood level at 36.8 feet. Many levees failed below Memphis. The flood was aggravated by ice jams on the upper Mississippi River that sent an additional surge of water down the valley in the spring. This event caused great hardships and economic losses across the state.
Aug. 10, 1884	**Lynching and hate crimes—Mormon Massacre** (see p. 231). Five members of the Mormon faith were attacked and murdered by a mob of angry masked men in Lewis County. Many Mormons were persecuted for their beliefs here and elsewhere across the South. No one was ever prosecuted or even officially accused of this hate crime.
Sept. 7, 1885	Lynching and hate crimes—A black man, Charlie Williams, accused of murdering a former white policeman, Polk Mitchell, during an argument, was taken from his cell and hanged in the corridor of the Chattanooga Jail. The assailing mob used sledgehammers to enter the jail and

break into the cell of the accused. Two others were injured by gunfire during the incident, one mortally.

Sept. 16, 1885	Structure fire—A fire at the Southern Pulp Company in Nashville destroyed some six million board feet of lumber.
Nov. 6, 1885	Tornado—A twister touched down around 2:00 PM at Estill Springs (Franklin County), killing three and injuring eight.
Mar.–Apr. 1886	Flooding—A storm on March 25–31 resulted in a flood crest of 52.2 feet at Chattanooga. At that time, this was the third worst flood in the city's history. Water was backed up in the downtown area for days. Upstream, at Cleveland, creeks reached record flood heights, washing away businesses, homes, railroad works, bridges, and farms. There was considerable damage along the Tennessee River and all its tributaries in the vicinity of Knoxville. At Newport (Cocke County), the Scottish Caroline Timber and Land Company was heavily damaged. Loggers worked day and night to salvage what they could of the winter's timber harvest as log booms (jams) broke apart in the flood. Flooding was also heavy on the Cumberland River.
May 7, 1886	Structure fire—Henning (Lauderdale County), a small town in West Tennessee, was destroyed by fires. It was eventually rebuilt. This was the birthplace of Alex Haley, author of the classic book *Roots*.
July 20, 1886	Railway accident—Two trains collided on the L&N Railroad at Duck River Station. This whistle-stop town no longer exists but was located just north of Columbia (Maury County) where the railroad crosses the Duck River near the present town of Godwin. Several people were killed in the wreck, including the engineers and firemen on both trains. The accident occurred as one train entered a cut not far from the Rutherford Creek bridge. Most of the dead were scalded to the point that they were almost unrecognizable. It is believed that the accident occurred as the result of the engineer of the smaller of the two trains failing to consult his timecard or his watch. Had he done so, he would have pulled his train to a sidetrack to allow the larger train to pass.
Aug. 18, 1886	Lynching and hate crimes—An African American woman jailed in Jackson for allegedly poisoning her former employer was taken from her Madison County Jail cell, stripped naked, and hanged on the courthouse lawn. Her body was than riddled with bullets and left hanging until the next day.
Aug. 31, 1886	Earthquake—This Charleston, South Carolina, quake, the largest ever recorded in the southeastern United States, caused some damage to structures in East Tennessee. Three shocks were felt in Knoxville. They were in the MMI X intensity range.
Sept. 1, 1886	Earthquake—Over eighty aftershocks were associated with the previous day's Charleston, South Carolina, quake. The worst of the quakes were felt from Boston to New Orleans and west to Milwaukee. There was some damage to structures in East Tennessee in this MMI IX–X intensity quake.
Winter 1886	Severe winter—Twenty-five or more inches of snow fell in some areas of East Tennessee and the French Broad River, and other tributaries were frozen over north of Knoxville. Knoxville

received 22.5 inches of snow on December 4–6. Four feet of snow fell in Elizabethton (Carter County) and some other areas around the state. Many barns and other buildings collapsed under the weight of this snow. Greeneville (Greene County) recorded a temperature of –20°F in January. In February, Carthage (Smith County) recorded a temperature of –18°F. Nashville experienced the worst snowstorm in its history, closing turnpikes, railroads, and mail service for several days. The average depth of snow in Nashville around the first of February was twenty inches. This event resulted in great economic impact to the state.

1887   Flooding—West Tennessee was affected by a period of flooding that may have been twice as severe as the flood of 1927, at least in the Memphis area. Sections along the Mississippi River may have been 100 miles wide or more in 1887 as well. Although not as widespread along other river systems in the state and region, this could have made it comparable to the floods of 1937. Unfortunately, little comparative data is available on the event. What made the floods of 1937 greater is the fact that there were more built environments and more populated settlements along the river by then.

1887   Drought—This seasonal drought affected the entire state and had significant economic impacts, especially on farm crops and stock.

1887–90   **Family feud—Greene-Jones War** (see p. 240). This is believed to be the second greatest family feud ever fought in the United States. The worst was probably the Hatfield and McCoy feud fought in the West Virginia and Kentucky backcountry between 1878 and 1891. Several members of both the Greene and Jones families died in revenge slayings and counter-revenge slayings over a period of three years.

Feb. 19, 1887   Tornado—A tornado accompanied by fierce winds, along with hail, lightning, and torrential rain struck Lebanon (Wilson County). The roof of the Bank of Lebanon was torn off, and many other structures were damaged or demolished. There was also much flooding around the public square.

Apr. 3, 1887   Structure fire—A fire pushed by strong winds destroyed a large tobacco warehouse, several commercial buildings, and several homes in Clarksville (Montgomery County).

June 8–9, 1887   Structure fire—This fire erupted as a new gasoline-powered motor was being demonstrated in the Old Bee Hive Store at the corner of Market Street and Fourth Street in Chattanooga. It killed two firemen, severely injured another, and caused considerable property damage. It was said to be one of the most tragic fires in the city's history. Chattanooga's famous Fireman's Fountain statue, across from the Hamilton County Courthouse, was erected in commemoration of the two brave men who lost their lives in this conflagration.

Nov. 11, 1887   Structure fire—The Brooks and Neely and Company Cotton Warehouse, located on Main Street between Trezevant Street and Huling Street, caught fire. This Memphis fire, started by a careless employee around 2:45 PM, caused an estimated $225,000 in damages.

Nov. 17, 1887   **Structure fire—Memphis Navy Yard Fire** (see p. 105). What is believed to have been the greatest fire in Memphis history erupted sometime around 6:00 PM in the Memphis Navy Yard. A second fire broke out in the northwest corner of the site sometime after the first one was extinguished. Both fires were caused by arson, but the suspect was acquitted. Losses were estimated at over $800,000.

1888	Structure fire—A fire broke out in the Caldwell wholesale block of Chattanooga in the early morning hours. Damages were estimated at $100,000, and six people attempting to remove goods from the store were killed when a brick wall collapsed on them.
Aug. 9, 1888	Structure fire—This inferno started around 9:45 PM in the Bradt Printing Company in the Griffis-Caldwell block between 6th Street and 7th Street in Chattanooga. It destroyed or seriously damaged a four-block section of buildings before being brought under control. Several people were believed to have died or been seriously injured in the fire.
1889–90	**Pandemic, Influenza** (see p. 18)—This disease, called "Asian flu" or "Russian flu," was estimated to have affected as much as 40 percent of the earth's population. It was the first recognized worldwide influenza pandemic. Millions died. The official death toll for Tennessee is unknown.
Jan. 19, 1889	Lynching and hate crimes—Two men and one woman, all white, were taken from the Lake County Jail and lynched for robbery and murder.
Mar. 2, 1889	Tornado—Three were killed and a dozen others injured when a tornado touched down in Madisonville and other portions of Monroe County. A score of homes and outbuildings were damaged or destroyed by the storm. One victim, Jack Moser, was hurled some 700 yards from his home by the force of the wind. He was decapitated as he struck a wire fence.
Apr. 1889	Structure fire—The so-called Carlin fire took place in Chattanooga during this month. This business was involved in a fire for the second time in two years, but this time it was destroyed. The only casualty was Fire Capt. Charles Werner of Engine Company No. 3. He was electrocuted when his ladder came in contact with a power line at the scene.
Apr. 7, 1889	Lynching and hate crimes—Two white men accused of murder were taken from the Grainger County Jail and lynched.
Apr. 13, 1889	Structure fire—A fire that broke out around 12:30 AM raged between Railroad Street and Main Street in Dayton (Rhea County). A number of stores and other businesses were damaged or destroyed. Over 100 volunteers were said to have been involved in fighting this conflagration.
June 7, 1889	Lynching and hate crimes—Two white men accused of murder were taken from the Scott County Jail and lynched.
Aug. 22, 1889	**Railway accident—Flat Creek Train Wreck** (see p. 158). Six people were killed and over half the remaining forty-eight were injured as the rear coach of an excursion train left the tracks at the approach to a high trestle across Big Flat Creek. The ill-fated coach became uncoupled, turned over, plunged down a ravine, and landed upside down in the creek. The accident took place near Corryton (Knox County) on the Knoxville, Cumberland Gap, and Louisville line. The passengers were on a maiden promotional tour from Knoxville to Middlesboro, Kentucky.

Jan. 1890	Epidemic, meningitis—This incident struck Dayton (Rhea County), infecting scores of people, some fatally.
Mar. 27, 1890	Tornado—Three funnel clouds touched down in Middle Tennessee between 8:45 and 10:00 PM and moved across Lincoln, Rutherford, Sumner, and Macon counties. At least eight died, including two children; over 100 were injured, and economic losses were estimated at over $2 million in this category F3 tornadic incident.
Apr. 1890	Structure fire—In Memphis, the Hill, Fountain, and Company cotton shed in the old navy yard was struck by lightning and burned, causing great economic loss.
May 15 or 16, 1890	Railway accident—Two freight trains collided head-on just east of Chattanooga as a result of misunderstood orders on the part of one of the engineers. Five individuals were confirmed killed, one mangled almost beyond recognition and another literally cut in two. At least four transients stealing rides on the trains may also have been killed. Twenty-five or thirty cars were derailed, both engines were a total loss, and most of the freight was ruined.
Oct. 18, 1890	Structure fire—Fire broke out at the State Prison in Nashville. All the prisoners were evacuated safely by the state militia. Property damages, including destruction of approximately eight structures, amounted to a quarter of a million dollars. At that time, the prison was located on Church Street at Fifteenth Avenue.
Winter 1890–Spring 1891	Flooding—Over the Mississippi, Tennessee, and Cumberland River valleys. This was the Mississippi River's worst flood to date. Many levees broke in spite of enormous sandbagging and other reinforcement efforts. Levees gave way at two points between Arkansas City and Memphis, submerging many thousands of acres of farmland. In all, the Mississippi River inundated over 5,000 square miles of land, causing appalling economic losses, death to over a hundred people, and many injuries. February brought record flood damage to the Upper Cumberland River basin. On March 6 the Cumberland River was at 50.7 feet, or almost eleven feet above flood stage at Nashville.
1891–92	**Labor war—Coal Creek Miners Wars** (see p. 191). The miners at Coal Creek (now Lake City) and Briceville (Anderson County) were on strike for several bloody months as they battled with coal company owners over low wages, poor labor conditions, and the increasing use of state convicts as miners. This was the first major labor strike in Tennessee.
Mar. 14, 1891	**Structure fire—Nashville Insane Asylum Fire** (see p. 106). Fire broke out in the state asylum near Nashville around 10:15 PM Only the west wing of the structure was destroyed by the inferno. Seven died in the incident.
Apr. 9, 1891	Structure fire—The Hill Fountaine and Company Cotton Warehouse, owned by the MCP&S Company was struck by lightning and burned to the ground. The economic loss of this facility, located on the west corner of Auction and Promenade in the old Memphis Navy Yard, was estimated at $130,000. The fire erupted around 11:00 PM and spread rapidly. Fortunately firemen were successful in suppressing it before it ignited other structures.

Dec. 26, 1891	Structure fire—During this year a fire almost destroyed the Loveman and Van Deman blocks in Chattanooga. One person was killed while attempting to jump to safety from a third-story window. Several others were injured in the incident, and economic losses were estimated at over $150,000.
1892–96	**Civil insurrection—White Capping in Sevier County** (see p. 218). This was the so-called era of White Capping in and around the community of Pigeon Forge (Sevier County). The White Caps were a secret fraternity not unlike the Ku Klux Klan (KKK).
Jan. 1892–93	Riverboat accident—As the *J.C. Warner* was attempting to plow through ice on the Tennessee River near Chattanooga, the boiler flues collapsed, causing a horrendous explosion. Two deck hands were thrown into the river and drowned, and fifteen other people were severely injured. A large bull, tied up three feet from the boiler, was literally cooked to death in an instant.
Jan. 2, 1892	Structure fire—The entire 200 block of College Street between Market Street (now Second Avenue) and North College Street (now Third Avenue), including eleven structures, was destroyed by a fire that broke out around 5:30 PM. Fanned by heavy winds, it killed four firefighters. All four were crushed under a brick wall that fell on them. This was considered the most costly fire ever in Nashville's downtown business district, with damages estimated at over half a million dollars. The cause was arson.
Feb. 8, 1892	Structure fire—The so-called Main Street Business District fire was the most destructive ever in the heart of Memphis's downtown commercial quarter, and the most costly to this date. It is believed to have started as an electrical fire, either in a five-story auction house at 322 Main Street or in the Druz-Berne Hat factory at 230 Main Street. It eventually spread to, and destroyed, every building on the east side of Main from Union Street to Monroe Street. Buildings on the west side of Main were damaged by the heat but did not burn down. Eight large companies and an equal number of smaller firms and other businesses were destroyed by the conflagration, with an estimated economic loss of over $1 million. It took fifteen hours to extinguish the inferno. An estimated 10,000 spectators gathered to witness the event, which involved all six of the city's fire companies and sixty men.
Mar. 8, 1892	Lynching and hate crimes—Four black men accused of murdering four deputies were taken from the Memphis-Shelby County Jail and lynched by a mob of seventy-five masked white men.
Mar. 9, 1892	Racial violence—On the night of March 5, 1892, rocks were thrown and shots fired into an African American grocery store at the "Curve," the intersection of Mississippi Boulevard and Walker Avenue, where streetcar rails made a broad curve coming off one street onto the other. This store, owned by three prominent blacks, advertised lower prices in competition with a white-owned grocery across the street. Ill will arose as more whites began shopping at the black grocery. Two deputies responding to the scene on this day were fatally shot, allegedly by two of the owners of the black grocery. The accused were apprehended and taken to the Shelby County Jail along with a third black man. He was not involved but was a business partner. Around three the next morning a mob of masked whites broke into the jail, hauled the three blacks to a nearby rail

yard, and lynched them. They were shot at close range, and their heads were terribly disfigured and mutilated. The following day, rumors spread that a large group of blacks were assembled to seek revenge for the lynchings. The white community quickly armed itself in preparation for a confrontation that was not to come. The next day hundreds of members of the black community assembled in an orderly and peaceful manner to attend a triple funeral service at a local church. No revenge was ever sought by blacks, nor was punitive action ever taken against the vigilantes.

Mar. 17, 1892	Severe winter—A St. Patrick's Day snow paralyzed Memphis and other portions of West Tennessee. Snow was eighteen inches deep in the city, with drifts as high as several feet. Streets were blocked, streetcar service halted, roofs collapsed, and numerous injuries and considerable suffering were recorded. Nashville also measured a record-breaking snowfall of 17.0 inches in a twenty-four-hour period. Economic losses were also great as a result of this event.
Apr. 30, 1892	**Lynching and hate crimes—Eph Grizzard Lynching** (see p. 234). A mob stormed the Davidson County Jail and seized a black man by the name of Eph Grizzard. The prisoner had been arrested for the alleged rape and murder of a Goodlettsville (Sumner County) woman. His brother Henry, who was believed to have been an accomplice in the rape-murder, had also been lynched at Goodlettsville three days earlier.
July 29, 1892	Lynching and hate crimes—Two whites accused of rape were taken from the Campbell County Jail and lynched.
Aug. 13, 1892	Labor strike—Grundy County coal miners went on strike over wages, working conditions, and the use of state prisoners as miners. The strike eventually resulted in bloodshed and destruction of much coal company equipment. The National Guard had to be activated to quell the disturbances.
Dec. 7. 1892	Lynching and hate crimes—Two black men and possibly one white man accused of rape were taken from the Campbell County Jail and lynched at Jellico.
1893–94	Pandemic—Cholera killed millions worldwide; however, the number infected and the number who died in Tennessee is unknown.
1893	**Economic crisis—Economic Panic of 1893** (see p. 194). While in the throes of a four-year financial panic, numerous banks and financial institutions failed across the nation. It was also a turbulent period of labor strikes, bloody riots, and nationwide business failures.
Jan. 1893	Severe winter—Ice gorges formed, and the Cumberland River froze solid at Nashville. Temperatures dropped to –20°F in Greeneville (Greene County) and –18°F at Newport (Cocke County). Economic losses were undoubtedly heavy, but the exact cost is unknown.
Jan. 3, 1893	Structure fire—The three-story Matthews Hardware Company building at 35 Union Street in Memphis was destroyed by fire around 6:00 PM. Other structures, from 342 to 354 Main Street, and from 33 to 37 Union Street, were damaged. Losses were estimated at $130,000.
Feb. 18, 1893	Flooding—There was heavy flooding all along the Tennessee River. In fact, the *Knoxville Journal* reported that "the railroad from Coal Creek [now Lake City] to Briceville [Anderson County] was torn up from end to end [by the flooding]."

Apr. 22, 1893	Structure fire—A fire broke out just before noon and caused much destruction in the downtown business district of Kelso (Lincoln County). Although property damage was high, there was only one known injury.
Summer 1893	Tornado—A twister struck Bristol (Sullivan County) causing considerable damage. It destroyed the newly constructed market house and damaged or destroyed homes throughout the city.
July 1893	Structure fire—Ten structures in the Cook Block of Elizabethton (Carter County) were destroyed by fire. Losses were estimated at $25,000. The cause was never determined.
Nov. 8, 1893	Structure fire—A Memphis fire that began around midnight destroyed the five-story brick Amateur Athletic Association Club House, as well as the Lyceum Theater on the northwest corner of Third and Union streets. Adjoining property was also damaged, with losses estimated at $113,000. The cause of the fire was unknown.
Feb. 18, 1894	Cable car accident—Eight people were rescued after being suspended for several hours in a failed cable car over the Tennessee River at Cherokee bluffs in Knoxville. One seriously injured passenger died several hours after being rescued.
Apr. 8, 1894	Structure failure—Collapse of a Memphis tenement building. A dozen or more people were killed and others injured when a four-story brick tenement building collapsed near Belle and DeSoto streets in the early morning hours. Nine bodies were quickly recovered from the wreckage of the thirty-four-year-old structure. Others were found and removed later. Some of the bodies were impaled with splintered timbers, while others were crushed by bricks, mortar, and other falling debris. The rumble of the multiroom structure as it crashed to the ground was said to be heard up to a half mile away.
June 10, 1894	Lynching and hate crimes—A black man, James Perry, was taken from the Knox County Jail and lynched "for introducing smallpox into the community."
Aug. 1894	Labor war—A deputy warden and a convict were killed in Tracy City (Grundy County) during a prisoner/coal miner mutiny.
Aug. 21, 1894	Structure fire—A Memphis fire, ignited around midnight, destroyed the Mansfield Drug Company as well as adjacent buildings to the north and south. Losses were estimated at $110,000, and the cause of the fire was unknown.
Aug. 31–Sept. 1, 1894	**Lynching and hate crimes—Shelby County Lynching** (see p. 234). Six unidentified black men were being transported to the Memphis-Shelby County Jail when the wagon in which they were riding was stopped by a group of masked white men. As the white mob fired shots into the wagon, the bodies of the blacks were so mutilated by bullets that it was nearly impossible to identify their individual remains.
1894–96	Drought—This drought was severe statewide, as illustrated by the fact that on December 1, 1895, the Tennessee River at Knoxville (and also at other locations) fell to as low as one and a half feet below the zero gauge mark. Lower than normal rainfall continued in the area from March 1894 to June 1896. Agricultural losses were extensive.

Feb. 1895	Severe winter—Temperatures plummeted in Tennessee and sixteen other eastern and midwestern states. Transportation and commerce was disrupted, and the frigid conditions were particularly hard on the poor and impoverished.
July 19, 1895	Earthquake—Glassware and crockery fell from shelves during this quake, whose epicenter was near Memphis. Two of the quakes were even felt thirty-five miles away at Covington (Tipton County). There was much mass confusion as people panicked and ran from their homes. Its intensity was MMI V–VII.
Oct. 31, 1895	Earthquake—This Charleston, Missouri, quake was one of the two greatest earthquakes felt in the southeastern states, including Tennessee, since the 1811–12 episodes. It was of MM VIII–IX intensity.
Nov. 29, 1895	Lynching and hate crimes—Two unidentified black men accused of murder were taken from the Lincoln County Jail at Fayetteville and lynched.
Dec. 20, 1895	**Coal mine disaster—Nelson Mine Disaster** (see p. 117). A deadly coal mine explosion occurred in the Nelson Mine in Dayton (Rhea County) when open-flame lamps came in contact with deadly methane gas. Twenty-eight miners died in this incident, the first major coal mine disaster in Tennessee.
1896	Epidemic, typhoid fever—This epidemic occurred in Scott County, but little more is known about it.
Jan. 8, 1896	Lynching and hate crimes—Two men, probably black, were lynched at Lexington (Henderson County).
Apr. 1896	Flooding—Flooding was so great along the Mississippi River in the spring of this year that 6,000 victims had to be housed and fed in flood refugee camps in Memphis. Heavy floods also occurred along the Watauga and Doe rivers in the vicinity of Elizabethton (Carter County). It was the worst flood to date on the West Fork of the Little Pigeon River, but just barely exceeded a flood on this stream in August 1893. It was also a bad flood at Knoxville, believed to have been as high, or higher, than the flood of February 1875.
June 27, 1896	Explosion—Several kegs of blasting powder were ignited in the Joyner General Store near Petros (Morgan County). Three are believed to have been killed, including the grocer's son, who was alleged to have caused the accident. Several others were injured. The store was demolished. The powder was awaiting delivery to the nearby convict coal mines at Brushy Mountain State Prison.
1897	Structure fire—The entire downtown business section of Niota (McMinn County) burned.
Feb.–Mar. 1897	Flooding—Heavy precipitation March 3–19 resulted in record floods along the Cumberland and Tennessee rivers in East and Middle Tennessee. A storm around March 19 caused heavy flooding along streams in the western portion of the Tennessee River Valley. This was the flood of record on the Tennessee River downstream of Muscle Shoals, Alabama, with the exception of the lowest forty-eight miles, where it was exceeded by the backwater from the Ohio River flood of 1937. This may have been the flood of record for the Harpeth River, although even that may have been

exceeded by the flood of 1948. Some heavy flooding was also experienced along the Watauga and Doe rivers in upper East Tennessee. Total precipitation varied from 14.6 inches over a 10 square-mile area to 11.7 inches over a 43,500 square-mile area. Millions of dollars in damages occurred along the Mississippi, and five lives were known to be lost in the Memphis area. Bitter cold weather contributed to the flood.

Feb. 17, 1897	Lynching and hate crimes—Two black men accused of arson were taken from the Lawrence County Jail and lynched at Webb (Webber) City.
Feb. 24, 1897	**Highway accident—Harrison Pike Train and Wagon Wreck** (see p. 150). Southern Railway train No. 7 struck a horse-drawn farm wagon carrying ten people at the Harrison Pike crossing (Hamilton County) around 12:30 PM. A mother and six of her children were killed instantly, and two children, ages ten and eighteen, died shortly thereafter.
Mar. 1, 1897	Civil insurrection—A riot of sorts broke out as the Citizens Railway Company attempted to construct a new streetcar track along Depot Street. As Knoxville police, fire, and public officials responded to the site of the surprise construction, a crowd of some 2,000 citizens gathered to watch the action. Police began arresting laborers, but, as they did, other workers took their place. In desperation, firefighters were ordered to turn a hose on the workers. This effectively stopped the construction, but in the process a laborer by the name of William Arnold attacked the fire chief with a pick handle and was shot and mortally wounded. The shooting evoked an angry response from the mob, which obviously sided with the laborers, and began throwing bricks and rocks at policemen and firefighters. It took Knoxville Mayor Samuel G. Heiskell and Knoxville Citizens Railway Company president McAdoo to calm things down. As both men addressed the crowd, the sheriff arrived with an injunction allowing construction to continue. However, it was not long until he came back with a second injunction, this one again halting the work. By 10:30 AM the riot was over, and by the end of the year all of the city's streetcar lines were finally consolidated.
Apr. 8, 1897	**Structure fire—Knoxville's Million Dollar Fire** (see p. 106). This was by far the most memorable conflagration in the city's history, destroying a number of prominent businesses along the east side of Gay Street. Knoxvillians referred to it as their "Million Dollar Fire," almost as if bragging that their city had a million dollars worth of something to burn.
Apr. 20, 1897	Structure fire—The Woodruff Department Store fire burned out of control between Union Avenue and Wall Avenue in Knoxville. Economic losses were great, but the amount is unknown.
May 13, 1897	**Structure failure—Pinkney Mine Tipple Collapse** (see p. 132). A sixty-five-foot-high mine tipple collapsed at Pinkney (Lawrence County), killing thirteen and injuring several others, some fatally. Poor engineering and construction were allegedly the root cause of the incident.
May 31, 1897	Earthquake—A magnitude 5.9 earthquake had an epicenter at Giles County, Virginia, and was one of two great earthquakes felt in the Mississippi River Valley since 1811–12. Besides general panic, it caused chimneys to collapse, broke masonry structures, and cracked plaster walls in northeast Tennessee, including the Tri-Cities area. It even caused some masonry damage and

cracked plaster as far south as Knoxville. Its MM intensity was measured at VII–VIII. The quake was felt from Georgia to Pennsylvania and westward into Kentucky. Aftershocks continued through June.

July 6, 1897	**Explosion—Hartsville Threshing Machine Explosion** (see p. 93). A threshing machine boiler exploded in Hartsville (Trousdale County), killing nine and seriously injuring seven others. Five more were expected to die. All had just completed threshing wheat in a field and were leaving the scene when the explosion occurred. Its cause was never determined. Some of the victims were mangled and scalded beyond recognition, and the heads of two men were never found. Pieces of the boiler were blown 700 yards from the explosion.
Mar. 29, 1898	Explosion—Sycamore Powder Mill Explosion 1898. Four men were seriously injured, one critically, when the magazine and grinding assembly at Sycamore Powder Mill (Cheatham County) blew up. The explosion was said to have been heard sixty miles away.
Aug. 30, 1898	Structure fire—A fire broke out in the Nashville business district just after 2:00 AM, causing about half a million dollars in economic losses. The fire was believed to have erupted on the fifth floor of the Phillips-Butteroff Manufacturing Company on College Street. From there it spread to eight other facilities. There were no known causalities or injuries in this incident.
Sept. 8, 1898	Structure fire—A fire erupted just before 10:00 AM and destroyed the Memphis P&G Elevator Company, its grain elevator, and several adjacent railroad freight cars in Memphis. The Eagle Milling Company Flower Mill, south of the grain elevator, was also destroyed. Losses were estimated at $115,000, and the cause of the incident was unknown.
Winter 1899	**Severe winter—Severe Winter Storms of 1899** (see p. 80). The weather was so severe statewide that many birds froze to death. Cattle, horses, and other stock animals froze to death, and houses were said to "pop." Ice floes on the Mississippi River were said to have passed New Orleans and continued out into the Gulf of Mexico (see severe winter of 1784). Some record low temperature extremes occurred in nineteen towns and cities in the winter of 1899.
1899	Epidemic fever—The local newspaper referred to this disease as simply a "terrible fever," but it was probably typhoid. It struck the community of Taft (Lincoln County), killing many citizens during this year. A large number of local tombstones bear the date 1899, attesting to the high mortality during this epidemic.
Jan. 12–13, 1899	Structure fire—The Menken Company Emporium, located in the Jackson block of Main Street in Memphis was destroyed by fire. Damages to this historic landmark were estimated at $450,000.
Jan. 17, 1899	Lynching and hate crimes—Two black men were taken from the Moore County Jail in Lynchburg and lynched. It was said that both were killed for simply having a bad reputation and one also for an alleged rape.
Feb. 8, 1899	Riverboat accident—The wreck of the *P. D. Staggs,* a Tennessee River packet, occurred about midnight, when it struck a pier of the Nashville, Chattanooga & St. Louis Railway bridge at Johnsonville (Humphreys County). It was a windy, snowy, foggy, bitter cold night, and the accident

seems to have been unavoidable. The boat was disabled by the impact, losing its smokestacks, pilot house, and everything else above the boiler deck. It also lost all means of steerage. No lives are believed to have been lost among the eighty-five passengers and crew onboard. About 200 head of cattle and hogs, bales of cotton, lumber, and other cargo were lost. Everyone onboard either escaped or was rescued by other boats during its blind drift down the Tennessee River. The last three crewmen abandoned the *Staggs* at Paducah, Kentucky, just before she was lost to the daunting ice floes of the Ohio River.

Feb. 8, 1899	Railway accident—The Campbell County wreck on the Knoxville and Ohio branch of the Southern Railway killed five, seriously injured another, and resulted in economic losses exceeding $75,000. The head-on collision of freight train No. 68 and mixed passenger train No. 3 occurred two miles west of Elk Valley. It took place on a curve, in a ravine, and at the base of two steep grades. It was believed that the freight train engineer misread his orders, thinking that the other train was running fifteen minutes late when it was actually fifty minutes early. That would explain why he proceeded south and crashed head-on into the northbound train. The bodies of four of the dead were crushed and burned beneath the mangled locomotives. A tank car of turpentine burst into flames, encompassing the wreck and igniting a large quantity of coal. The fire was so intense within the burning refuge of the wreck that three of the bodies were never recovered. The engineer of the freight train and the fireman of the mixed train were pulled from the wreckage, but the fireman died an agonizing death from scalding ten hours later and, sadly, only twenty minutes before his wife reached his side.
July 4, 1899	Structure fire—A Paris (Henry County) Independence Day fire wiped out the west side of the square and was the most destructive in the city's history. A similar but not as destructive inferno struck the same area in 1873.
July 4, 1899	Structure fire—The Memphis Paper Company, located in the 300 block of South Front Street, burst into flames. One man was killed and several injured in the fire. Damages were estimated at between $300,000 and $500,000. The fire also spread to other structures, including the famous Memphis Gayoso Hotel.
Nov. 9, 1899	Structure fire—A 5:50 PM fire of unknown origin destroyed the Planters Warehouse, on the east side of Tennessee Boulevard, between Hulling and Talbot in Memphis. This fire also spread to the west side of Tennessee Boulevard, where it destroyed a Louisiana Refining Company building and damaged the DeSoto Oil Company Mill. Losses were estimated at $118,000.
1900–1940	Economic crisis—Extinction of the American chestnut (*Castanea dentata*) due to a fungus introduced from Asia had a profound economic impact on the state and the nation's economy. This was especially hard on the lumber industry and some small farmers, especially in the Appalachian states. The chestnut tree occupied perhaps 30 percent of the forests of the eastern United States, and its demise had wide-ranging consequences for wildlife as well. Chestnuts were gathered by the millions of bushels and sold in the city markets of Memphis, Nashville, Knoxville, Chattanooga, and smaller towns in between. Many poor farmers depended on the

fall crop of chestnuts to purchase shoes, clothes, school supplies, and Christmas presents for their families. The loss in the value of its timber, used for a great variety of purposes, from furniture to structures, was incalculable. Mountain people had also come to depend upon this free and abundant mass crop to fatten their hogs and turkeys in the fall. Within a mere three decades of the close of the nineteenth century, the chestnut was virtually extinct.

Winter 1900	Epidemic, typhoid—The spread of this infection in Nashville was traced to a single dairyman. More than twenty contracted the disease and two died. One to four members of each family who were supplied milk by this dairyman eventually contracted the disease. Those who did not drink the milk did not get sick.
May 4, 1900	Structure fire—The business district on the north side of the Hartsville (Trousdale County) square was destroyed by a fire. The cause of the fire was unknown. Losses were estimated at $100,000. Along with a number of businesses, the fire consumed the Bank of Hartsville, though its contents were saved. The courthouse and its records were a complete loss.
July 22, 1900	Civil insurrection—A riot occurred in the black work camp of the Cincinnati-Southern Railroad in Scott County. It resulted in the deaths of two black workers and the wounding of two deputies.
Dec. 1900–May 1901	**Epidemic, Smallpox** (see p. 20)—Between December 28, 1900, and May 13, 1901, Tennessee reported the greatest number of smallpox cases in the nation: 4,228 cases, as opposed to 592 cases the previous year. This resulted in ninety-eight deaths, as opposed to five the previous year. The high incidence of smallpox was attributed to lethargy on the part of the Board of Health, lawmakers, and the public, along with the ravings of antivaccination cranks.
Nov. 20, 1900	**Tornadoes—Tornadoes of 1900** (see p. 61). The first twister touched down at 9:30 PM and traveled twenty-five miles across Davidson, Williamson, and Robertson counties before dissipating. The second touched down in Columbia and traversed eight miles of Maury County. Together they killed over 50 and injured over 100. This was the most severe tornadic incident known to have occurred in the state up to this date.
May–Aug. 1901	**Flooding—Floods of 1901** (see p. 35). The storms that spawned this flooding were some of the most severe ever known in the upper reaches of the Tennessee River system. Local newspaper accounts described them as being "of unusual violence." A severe storm at Elizabethton (Carter County) was said to be the city's worst ever.
May 27, 1901	**Coal mine disaster—Richland Mine Disaster** (see p. 118). Twenty-one men were killed and nine injured in a double explosion inside the Richland Mine near Dayton (Rhea County).
May 31, 1901	Hailstorm—A very destructive hailstorm occurred along the Hiawassee River near Benton and Wetmore (Polk County). It was said to have caused considerable damage and to have accumulated in drifts as high as a horse's knee.
Summer 1901	Severe heat—Heat-related mortalities were the greatest ever recorded for the nation, with 9,508 deaths officially reported. A number of such fatalities are known to have occurred in Tennessee, but the exact number is unknown.

Oct. 5, 1901	**Civil Insurrection—White Capping in Marshall County** (see p. 219). On the evening of October 5, a group of some thirty-five blacks were returning from a meeting near Caney Springs (Marshall County). They were walking down the road between Caney Springs and Lewisburg when they were stopped by a group of some 100 hooded White Caps (see Civil insurrection 1892–96) stationed at a bridge. After violence erupted, twelve to fifteen blacks lay wounded and three or four lay dead or dying.
Oct. 6, 1901	Family feud—Around noon a blood feud erupted just outside of the Union Baptist Church at Big Springs (Claiborne County). Rush Morgan was at the spring near the church when Tip Chadwell approached and fired on him. Members of both families rushed out of the church or to the area and joined the battle. Half an hour later, the fighting ceased and the smoke cleared. Four, two from each family, lay dead, and five were wounded, two mortally. This family feud had been going on for some time, and this event was one of three that had occurred within the past year and a half in which several members of both families had died. According to the October 8, 1901, *Nashville American,* "both the Chadwells and Morgans are prosperous and influential and have large families and all their members are dead game. They will probably keep up the feud until all on each side are killed."
Nov. 7, 1901	Labor strike—Clashes between striking and nonstriking members of the Memphis Streetcar Union occurred near the streetcar powerhouse at Broadway and Davie. Shots were fired between factions and at least one black laborer was killed.
Feb.–July 1902	**Flooding—Floods of 1902** (see p. 36). Flooding and storms were sporadic yet severe at times throughout the Tennessee and Cumberland River valleys from late February into July of 1902. The storms that produced some of the worst flooding on the Tennessee and Upper Cumberland rivers dropped eleven inches of rain at McMinnville (Warren County), and a foot of rain fell in only 114 hours over other areas.
Mar. 1, 1902	Structure fire—This fire, the worst in Hartsville's (Trousdale County) history, broke out on Main Street shortly after midnight. Within an hour and a half it had burned several homes and businesses, along with many groceries and staples. Losses were estimated at $50,000.
Mar. 30, 1902	Flooding -- Heavy flooding occurred at Pulaski and in other areas of surrounding Giles County. Many structures and much infrastructure were washed away. A number of people died in the deluge, but only a dozen or so bodies were ever recovered.
Mar. 31, 1902	**Coal mine disaster—Nelson Mine Disaster 1902** (see p. 121). Twenty-five men and eighteen mules were killed in a methane or coal dust explosion inside the Nelson Mine near Dayton (Rhea County). The explosion was so intense it even killed and injured men standing outside of the mine entrance. This mine was reputed to be one of the most dangerous in the state.
May 19, 1902	**Coal mine disaster—Fraterville Mine Disaster** (see p. 119). The state's worst mining accident occurred at the Fraterville Mine at Coal Creek (now Lake City) in Anderson County. Between 200 and 214 men and boys were either killed by the initial methane gas explosion and flash fire or they slowly suffocated over the next several hours, in the far reaches of the mine, from the buildup of deadly gases.

June 19, 1902	Railway accident—An engineer misread his orders, leading to the collision of Train No. 98, the *Jasper Accommodation,* and Train No. 1, *Fast Mail,* from Nashville. The wreck occurred on the Nashville, Chattanooga & St. Louis line near Summit (Hamilton County) about twelve miles from Chattanooga. Three died instantly, and fifteen were injured. Two additional victims later died in the hospital.
July 5, 1902	Flooding—Heavy flooding in and around the Tennessee River basin resulted in the loss of at least twenty-five lives. Damages were estimated at $6 million.
Oct. 8, 1902	Lynching and hate crimes—Two black men, accused of murder, were taken from the Dyer County Jail at Newburn and lynched.
Feb. 28, 1903	Railway accident—A Southern Railway fast passenger train wrecked about 2:00 AM near Lenoir City (Loudon County). The wreck, which killed at least six and injured over twenty, was the result of a landslide that caused the train rails to spread apart on a steep slope. Four passenger coaches were telescoped into one another as they plummeted down an embankment. Three of the cars were completely consumed by flames. Other deaths and injuries were averted by a second locomotive that arrived at the scene in time to pull the two rear Pullman cars away from the rest of the wreckage.
Aug. 8, 1903	Lynching and hate crimes—Two blacks were taken from the Marshall County Jail and lynched for reasons unknown.
Sept. 3, 1903	Structure fire—An intense fire at the Oliver-Finnie Company in Memphis caused damages in excess of $391,000.
1904	Railway accident—A wreck in the Southern Railroad yard at Oneida (Scott County) killed a fireman and brakeman on the train and set fire to a John Carson's store, totally destroying it. The brakeman was a 300-pound man, who, according to written accounts, "was completely burned up except for his false teeth and his heart."
1904	Labor strike—Violent coal miner strikes took place at Coal Creek (now Lake City) in Anderson County.
1904	**Epidemic, Smallpox** (see p. 20)—About twenty people contracted smallpox in Putnam County.
1904–14	**Labor war—Black Patch War** (see p. 195). Tobacco farmers in north-central Tennessee (primarily Robertson and Montgomery counties) and southern Kentucky formed small vigilante groups of night riders. Their intent was to destroy warehouses and factories associated with the American Tobacco Company, which had a monopoly on sales and had begun paying rock-bottom prices to farmers for their dark leaf tobacco.
Feb. 2, 1904	Structure fire—A fire in the M. C. Ross Wholesale Grocery Store on South Gay Street in Knoxville killed two firemen.
July 11, 1904	Civil insurrection—A riot broke out on DeSoto Street in Memphis as a result of gambling raids in a black community. While a warrant was being served in a gambling establishment, shots were fired. As panicky patrons ran from the establishment, two white law officers lay dead. The proceedings ended in a mistrial, and no one was ever convicted of the murders.

Sept. 3, 1904	**Structure fire—Memphis Front Street Fire** (see p. 108). A fire along the city's Front Street destroyed around $1 million in structures and merchandise in the heart of the city's wholesale district.
Sept. 24, 1904	**Railway accident—New Market Train Wreck** (see p. 160). According to widely varying sources, between 63 and 114 people are estimated to have been killed and some 150–60 injured in the head-on collision of two Southern Railway passenger trains at Hodges, near New Market (Jefferson County). This is generally described as the second-worst railroad accident in the state's history. However, if 114 passengers were in fact killed, this would make it the worst such accident in U.S. history. The number killed in the Dutchmans Grade Train Wreck in Nashville (see entry of July 9, 1918) is alleged to have exceeded 100 and is usually described as the worst U.S. passenger rail accident.
Jan.– Feb. 1905	Severe winter—Frigid weather blanketed the state as the Tennessee and Cumberland rivers and their tributaries froze over. The average temperature for the state during January and February was 31.4°F, second only to the two-month period of December 1917 and January 1918. These extreme temperatures affected travel, commerce, and agriculture statewide. Some low-temperature extremes are included in the accompanying table.

Temperature extreme (°F)	Location
–28	Copperhill (Polk County)
–28	Benton (Polk County)
–23	Hohenwald (Lewis County)
–23	Tazewell (Claiborne County)
–22	Tullahoma (Coffee County)
–20	Decatur (Meigs County)
–20	McMinnville (Warren County)

June 20, 1905	Structure fire—Several businesses and homes were destroyed in a fire in Clinton (Anderson County).
July 6, 1905	Structure fire—The Louisville & Nashville railroad shops in Nashville were destroyed by fire.
Aug. 24–27, 1905	Labor strike—Tracy City coal miners' strike. Six companies of National Guardsmen were sent to quell disturbances by coal miners after two men were mortally wounded and another severely injured in labor strikes at Tracy City (Grundy County).
Sept. 10, 1905	Structure fire—Around 6:55 PM a watchman discovered flames erupting from the roof of the Cincinnati, New Orleans & Texas Pacific Railway Company in Chattanooga. Within minutes it spread to several freight cars along the railroad. Eventually the entire depot and forty-seven railroad cars, most loaded with mail, baggage, and other freight, were destroyed. Damages were estimated at half a million dollars. As the fire burned, thieves tried to rob other cars not yet involved in the inferno, and additional police officers were brought in to stop the looting.

1906	Flooding—Floods caused half a million dollars in damages in Memphis and Shelby County alone as homes, bridges, roads, property, and infrastructure were inundated or washed away. Even mail service and other such functions were disrupted by the tide. The worst flood ever known on the Ocoee River is believed to have occurred on November 19, 1906.
Apr. 9, 1906	Structure fire—A fire broke out at the Williams General Store between 7:30 and 8:00 PM. It damaged or destroyed every shop, store, and business in downtown Petros (Morgan County).
Sept. 21, 1906	**Explosion—Jellico Railroad Yard Explosion** (see p. 94). A freight car containing eleven tons of dynamite exploded in the Jellico (Campbell County) rail yard, killing twelve people, injuring 200, and leaving 500 homeless. The incident occurred on the Tennessee-Kentucky state line.
Oct. 11–12, 1906	Structure fire—A stockyard fire in Columbia (Maury County) killed 115 mules and ten horses.
Oct. 13, 1906	Mass murder/suicide—A man killed four of his children and seriously wounded his wife and another child before taking his own life. This heinous crime was thought to have been committed when the man learned from their doctor that his wife probably would not survive her pregnancy. However, she and her child did survive the pregnancy, in spite of ax wounds to her head.
Dec. 13, 1906	Structure fire—Twenty-one buildings, including the Bell Hotel, on the north side of Main Street, were destroyed by Alexandria's (DeKalb County) most disastrous fire.
1907	Economic crisis—A financial panic occurred after a severe drop in the stock market. Various factors contributed to the stock market crash and loss of confidence in banks, which led to runs on banks, initially in New York. After that city's third largest bank, the Knickerbocker Trust Company, failed, confidence waned even further, affecting markets nationwide. As usually happens in economic panics, fear trumped logic as depositors began simultaneously withdrawing even more funds. This was described as more of a banker's panic than anything else, and it eventually lead to the creation of the Federal Reserve System. Even the Tennessee Coal, Iron & Railroad Company almost failed before it was rescued by J. P. Morgan's U.S. Steel Corporation. Although this panic was short-lived, many people lost their jobs, several otherwise sound businesses failed, and many financial institutions across the nation barely survived.
Mar. 21, 1907	Structure fire—The Illinois Central freight house at the corner of Shelby and Calhoun streets in south Memphis was destroyed, along with twenty-five loaded and sixty unloaded freight cars. This fire could have been much worse, since it was situated in close proximity to the Union Passenger Depot and a number of warehouses and cotton sheds.
Mar. 25, 1907	Structure fire—A fire destroyed the Memphis Furniture Manufacturing Company; economic losses were estimated at $125,000.
Mar. 29, 1907	Structure fire—A fire at the Magnolia Stove Plant demolished that facility and an adjacent brick company. Economic losses were estimated at $80,000.
May 16, 1907	Railway accident—Five died and three others were seriously injured when a blast was set off prematurely at a construction site just below Lookout Mountain. The explosion, which was later found to involve 274 kegs of black powder, caused large pieces of rock to rain down, striking a railroad bridge over Chattanooga Creek. At that same moment, a freight train pulling eleven cars

was crossing the bridge. Three nearby homes and a pile driver working on a new Chattanooga Creek viaduct were also struck and crushed by heavy rocks hurled some 500 to 600 yards from the blast site.

July 1907	Epidemic, typhoid fever—A typhoid epidemic was recorded to have ravaged Nashville.
July 2, 1907	Structure fire—Most of the business section of the town of Whitwell (Marion County) was devastated by a fire that began in the Whitwell Mercantile Company.
July 22, 1907	Lynching and hate crimes—Two black men were taken from the Lake County Jail and lynched, allegedly for fighting with a white man.
Oct. 14, 1907	Railway accident—A train jumped the tracks and derailed three cars on a downhill grade at Monterey (Putnam County), killing two men and critically injuring several others.
Oct. 18, 1907	**Railway accident—Chattanooga Streetcar Wreck** (see p. 162). Six people were killed and approximately eighty injured, some seriously, when two streetcars collided head-on at a steep dip on Harrison Avenue in Chattanooga.
Nov. 11, 1907	Railway accident—Six were killed and scores injured when the Cincinnati-bound Ponce De Leon passenger train derailed near Oakdale (Morgan County). The wreck occurred about 1:30 AM on a curve at Glen Mary. The cause of the wreck was not immediately known.
Jan. 25, 1908	Structure fire—Clinton's (Anderson County) worst ever fire began at 10:00 PM. It destroyed thirty-one structures, both businesses and residences, along Market Street (then called Depot Street). Arson was suspected, and damages amounted to around $60,000.
May 1908	Flooding—Johnson City (Washington County) was inundated by floodwaters in latter May, resulting in considerable damage to homes, businesses, and infrastructure. The railroad station was flooded and a railroad bridge washed away.
Oct. 1908–Nov. 1909	**Civil insurrection—Night Riders of Reelfoot Lake** (see p. 197). This was a clandestine group banded together to assure continued fishing and hunting rights to an 18,000 acre natural lake in northwest Tennessee's Obion and Lake counties. When these rights were threatened by private ownership of the lake, violence broke out and the Tennessee militia was activated to restore order.
Oct. 19, 1908	Lynching and hate crimes—Two black men were taken from the Obion County Jail by night riders (see October 1908–November 1909) and lynched at Walnut Log for reasons unknown.
Nov. 24, 1908	Lynching and hate crimes—Three black men accused of murder, all members of the same family, were taken from the Lake County Jail and lynched. This incident was probably associated with night rider activity (see Oct. 1908–Nov. 1909).
Dec. 10, 1908	**Lynching and hate crimes—Wild Bill Latura Assault** (see p. 235). A white man, "Wild Bill" Latura walked into a black saloon and pool hall in Memphis and shot and killed three black men and wounded three others. The assault was without any apparent provocation, and the *Memphis Commercial Appeal* condemned it in a fiery editorial, claiming that it was typical of the lawlessness pervasive in Memphis in the first two decades of the twentieth century.

Spring 1909	Tornado—A twister struck the Shelton Grove community (Loudon County) near Erie and Blue Springs, killing a father and his two sons and injuring two other family members. One of the victims was reported to have had a board literally impale his skull. This tornado also produced considerable property damage.
Mar. 30, 1909	Structure fire—The C. C. Bell & Son Tobacco Factory in Springfield (Robertson County), along with its full inventory of tobacco, was destroyed by a fire of unknown origin. The factory was owned by the Imperial Tobacco Company; losses were estimated at $100,000.
Apr. 29–30, 1909	**Tornadoes—Tornadoes of April 1909** (see p. 62). This was by far the most costly tornadic period in Tennessee history in terms of number of deaths. The final death toll probably exceeded 100. At least six major tornadoes struck Dickson, Franklin, Giles, Hickman, Lincoln, Maury, Montgomery, Rutherford, Williamson, and Wilson counties. One reason for the high death toll was probably the fact that the storms formed suddenly and without warning.
Apr. 30, 1909	Railway accident—Three crewmen were killed when their coal and freight train struck and killed a horse on the North Carolina & St. Louis tracks about six miles south of Sparta, near Doyle Station (White County). The engine derailed and turned over.
May 27, 1909	**Railway accident—Runaway Mine Cars–Train Wreck** (see p. 163). Two runaway Dayton Coal and Iron Company mine cars careened down a steep track to collide with a train pulling four coal cars loaded with 250 miners at Richland Gulf in Rhea County. Six men were killed instantly, three died later, and twenty others were injured, some mortally.
May 29–31, 1909	Flooding—A localized cloudburst (also known as a "freshet") produced a record flood on Brush Creek at Johnson City (Washington County). Homes, businesses, roadways, and other infrastructure, including eight bridges and at least eight miles of railroad track, were damaged or destroyed. A small tornado associated with this storm also caused havoc. Moving up the side of a hill, it sucked up a barn. Moments later the barn crashed to the ground, breaking up like a giant eggshell but leaving a horse and calf inside unharmed.
May 31, 1909	Flooding—An intense storm, perhaps one of the most severe recorded in Tennessee history to this date, struck the Third Creek watershed in Knoxville. It caused extensive damage in that section of the city.
Oct. 14, 1909	Tornadoes—Category F2 and F3 twisters killed twenty-five and injured eighty-seven in Decatur, Hardin, McNairy, and Wayne counties, including six at Mt. Vinson and seven at Shiloh. Houses and other structures were also damaged or destroyed. Many large trees were blown down, historic monuments were severely damaged, and much debris was scattered about at the Shiloh Civil War Battlefield (Hardin County).
May 7, 1910	Structure fire—Just before 10:00 PM the Hamilton County Courthouse was struck by lightning and set ablaze. Although much of the building was destroyed, the vital records were saved.
July 4, 1910	Civil insurrection—A riot broke out in Chattanooga involving soldiers visiting from Mississippi. Two were arrested, and fights broke out in several sections of the city. There were a number of

injuries, as local law enforcement officers tried to quell the disturbances between soldiers and citizens.

Sept. 13, 1910 — Lynching and hate crimes—Two black men accused of attempted rape were taken from the Lake County Jail and lynched.

Jan. 10, 1911 — Structure fire—A fire of unknown origin erupted in the mail car of a Chattanooga-Nashville passenger train in Chattanooga. The entire train and shed of the Chattanooga & St. Louis Railroad station were quickly involved in the inferno. Several people were burned, some severely, but there was no loss of life. Damages were estimated at $125,000.

Feb. 19, 1911 — Lynching and hate crimes—Two black men were taken from the Bedford County jail and lynched.

June 26, 1911 — Structure fire—Fire broke out in Chattanooga's Loomis and Hart Manufacturing Company around 9:00 PM Damages were believed to have exceeded $100,000. Records are somewhat vague concerning the incident, and it is possible the fire occurred in 1912.

Dec. 6, 1911 — Lynching and hate crimes—Three blacks were taken from the Wayne County Jail and lynched for unknown reasons.

Dec. 9, 1911 — **Coal mine disaster—Cross Mountain Mine Disaster** (see p. 122). An explosion in the Cross Mountain Mine #1 at Briceville (Anderson County) killed eighty-four men out of a crew of eighty-nine who had entered the mine on the morning shift. Some died from the initial explosion and flash fire; others were trapped and died later from suffocation. Five moved deeper into the mine and barricaded themselves until rescue parties could reach them. This was the second deadliest mine disaster in the state's history.

Feb. 19, 1912 — Lynching and hate crimes—Three black men accused of murder were taken from the Bedford County Jail at Shelbyville and lynched by an angry mob.

Early Apr. 1912 — Flooding—Severe flooding along the Mississippi and Cumberland rivers caused about 250 deaths, left 30,000 homeless, and caused an estimated $10 million in damages. Flood levees broke at several locations along the mighty Mississippi both upstream and downstream of Memphis. Railroads were also inundated at several places along these streams. Flood refugee camps were established at the Memphis Fairgrounds. The Memphis water and sewerage systems were contaminated by the flood, which changed the course of the Mississippi River to create the now famous Mud Island at Memphis. The deluge was caused by a series of seven intense thunderstorms that tracked across the Mississippi and Ohio valleys in just a few days.

Nov. 5, 1912 — **Structure failure—Nashville Reservoir Failure** (see p. 133). A rupture in the twenty-two-foot-thick southeast wall of Nashville's Eighth Avenue reservoir sent a nine-foot-high wall of water plummeting downhill, causing considerable damage to buildings and roadways. No deaths or injuries were reported, but economic losses were severe.

1913–14 — Drought—This event occurred statewide during the two-year period. The worst part of the episode was from May 4 through August 2, 1914. Crops were very sparse throughout the mid-South.

Mar. 13, 1913	Tornado—At least four twisters touched down in Benton, Giles, Henderson, Lawrence, Marshall, Maury, Rutherford, and Stewart counties between 1:45 and 2:30 PM. They left seventeen dead, seventy-eight injured, and much destruction in their wake. One category F4 tornado left a trail of death and destruction from a point just east of Huron (Henderson County) through Lexington to Camden (Benton County). There was also much destruction, as well as deaths and injuries, reported in Indiana, Illinois, and Louisiana during this same period.
Apr. 9, 1913	Flooding—The Mississippi River rose to 46.5 feet at Memphis in one of the most severe floods in that section of the state. Since it occurred before flood walls and pumping stations were constructed along the Wolf River, the flood affected every low place in the city of Memphis. Economic losses were heavy.
July 23, 1913	Accidental deaths—Near the community of Townsend (Blount County), a mother sent three of her young children to collect chicken eggs. Encountering a nest of rattlesnakes, all three were fatally bitten and did not return. Concerned about their long absence, the mother left a fourth child, one and a half years old, by the stream, where she was washing clothes. She found the three children dead or dying, and while she was away the fourth child fell into the stream and drowned.
May 4, 1914	Tornado—A tornado touched down at 10:30 PM east of Delina in Lincoln County, killing one and injuring two.
June 9, 1914	Structure fire—A disastrous fire destroyed much of downtown Erin (Houston County). Among the buildings destroyed was the newspaper office.
1915	Epidemic typhoid—This incident occurred in Scott County and perhaps elsewhere in the state; little information on it is available.
Dec. 23, 1915	**Railway accident—Sherwood Train Wreck** (see p. 163). Malfunctioning signals caused a head-on collision of a southbound freight train (No. 55) and a northbound Chattanooga-to-Nashville local passenger train (No. 2) between Sherwood and Cowan (Franklin County). Fifteen were killed in the wreck, and twenty-two others were injured, some of whom died later.
1916	Epidemic, polio—Officially, 27,363 cases of polio were reported across the United States, and around 7,000 died. Many fled populated areas, which actually helped to spread the disease. This was the first, and worst, of four great polio epidemics in Tennessee; however, the actual number of affected Tennessee citizens is not known.
Sept. 13, 1916	Lynching of an elephant—The Sparks Brothers Circus was performing in Kingsport (Sullivan County) in the fall of 1916 when one of its elephants, a five-ton female, killed one of her handlers. Her name was Mary, and she was claimed to be the largest living animal on earth at the time. The details of the event have been distorted and embellished through time, but according to one eyewitness, it went something like this: While being led with other elephants to a watering hole, Mary veered momentarily to grab for a piece of watermelon on the side of the road. When her handler jerked her back into formation with a hook to the ear, she allegedly turned on him. "She threw him against [a] drink stand . . . and when he hit the ground she just walked over and

set her foot on his head . . . and blood and brains and stuff just squirted all over the street." This was too much for local spectators, who started yelling, "Kill the elephant!" The county sheriff took Mary into custody. It was difficult for the circus owner to give her up, but he knew he could never book another show once word of his "murderous" Mary got around. The manner of execution was debated. Shooting would have required a caliber of weapon unavailable. Electrocution was considered, but there wasn't enough electrical current in the town. Finally, it was decided that she would be hanged using a railroad derrick at the nearby town of Erwin (Unicoi County). A crowd of 2,500 gathered for the cruel spectacle. The first attempt failed as the chain around her neck broke. But the second time she was suspended for several minutes until she choked to death. A large grave was dug, and she was buried. Many Erwinites would prefer to forget the ordeal. Others celebrate being part of a town where an elephant was hanged, and they have the souvenir photos and trinkets to prove it.

Mar. 21, 1916	Structure fire—This fire, which destroyed downtown Knoxville's Imperial Hotel, was believed to have been ignited by lightning, since there was a severe thunderstorm in the area when the incident occurred. Two hundred guests were evacuated from the hotel, and damages were estimated at $200,000. The flames quickly spread to a five-story annex of the hotel and to the Tripure Water Company, setting off several chemical explosions. It damaged the nearby Royal Hotel on State Street, and its sparks also ignited several smaller fires in East Knoxville.
Mar. 22, 1916	**Structure fire—East Nashville Fire** (see p. 108). This was the worst conflagration in the state's history. Pushed along by a dry fifty mile per hour wind, this firestorm destroyed 700 dwellings in a thirty-two-block-area in less than five hours. One person was burned to death, many more were injured (several of whom later died), and 3,000 were left homeless. Damages were estimated at $2 million.
May 9, 1916	Structure fire—This Knoxville fire destroyed twenty-six homes, scores of other buildings, and left 125 people homeless. Believed to have started behind the Bridgeman Mattress Company, this fire was spread along a three-block area by strong southwesterly winds. It caused $50,000 in damage and burned the wheels off the city's first fire truck.
July 15–Aug. 6, 1916	Flooding—A storm spawned by a tropical hurricane in the Atlantic Ocean produced heavy precipitation and flooding within the upper watersheds of the French Broad and Nolichucky rivers, as well as many other streams flowing west into the Tennessee Valley from the Appalachian Mountains. Railroad tracks, bridges, and farms were washed away throughout the area. Some people, marooned on farms in the vicinity of Newport (Cocke County), had to climb trees to escape the floodwaters and await rescue. The worst damage, in respect to loss of life and property, was along the French Broad River. On August 6, 1916, rain fell in torrents during a severe thunderstorm in and around Jonesboro (Washington County). Buildings along a town stream were flooded, and waves lashed at all sides of the courthouse. Water was several feet deep in buildings along Main Street and area roads, and farmland was severely damaged. At the time, this was also the highest flood in Knoxville.

Aug. 1–2, 1916	**Structure failures—Barren Creek Dam Failures** (see p. 133). As a result of intense flooding within the Barren Creek Community (Claiborne County), five dams failed in succession. Twenty-four people were killed, and damages to crops, stock animals, roads, bridges, railroad tracks, homes, and other structures were estimated at around $750,000.
Sept. 28, 1916	Lynching and hate crimes—Two black men accused of murder were taken from the Lewis County Jail and lynched.
Oct. 28, 1916	Structure fire—A fire broke out at the Oliver-Finnie Company in Memphis. There was no known loss of life, but damages were estimated at $354,000.
Winter 1917–18	**Severe winter—Winter of 1917–18** (see p. 81). The average statewide temperature between December 1917 and January 1918 was 28.8°F, probably the lowest average in recorded history. Some thirty inches of snow lingered on the ground in many places. An ice gorge formed on the Mississippi River, and smaller ice jams were reported on the French Broad and Holston rivers above Knoxville. A freak winter storm created a snow, ice, and windblown-sand pack that, according to Scott County accounts, had razor-sharp edges, trapping, injuring, or killing many domestic and wild animals.
Mar. 1–7, 1917	Flooding—This flooding occurred in the northernmost part of the upper Tennessee River Valley March 1–5. It produced the sixth highest flood to date on the Clinch River at Clinton (Anderson County). About 6.7 inches of rain fell at Clinton, and 4–6 inches fell in surrounding areas. By March 7, there was flooding at the mouths of both the Clinch and Hiwassee rivers. At Chattanooga on March 7, the Tennessee River crested at 49.4 feet, the fourth highest flood record at the time. According to the *Knoxville News-Sentinel,* economic costs throughout the valley were estimated at $2 million.
Mar. 16, 1917	Tornado—One person was killed and eight injured when a category F2 tornado touched down near Pleasant Point and Dunn in Lawrence County between 4:00 and 5:00 PM.
Apr. 24, 1917	Structure fire—Fire broke out in the Mountain City Stove and Manufacturing Company (Johnson County) just before midnight. Other stores in the block were also damaged or destroyed.
May 23, 1917	**Lynching and hate crimes—Eli Persons Lynching** (see p. 237). One of the most violent and heinous, yet orderly, lynchings in the history of the South occurred in Memphis on this date. The accused, a black man, was burned to death before a crowd of 2,000–4,000 men, women, and children. The time and place of the lynching was actually publicized, and local authorities did not intervene.
May 26, 1917	Hailstorm—This violent storm, which began shortly after 4:00 AM, lasted fifteen to twenty minutes and was accompanied by severe lightning, brisk winds, and blinding rain. The hail, with some stones larger than hen eggs, fell in greatest abundance at Waverly Place, south and west Nashville, and elsewhere in Davidson County. Other episodes were also reported near Columbia (Maury County), Hendersonville (Sumner County), and Amqui (Davidson County). Other places got none at all. Perhaps the heaviest damage was in and around Flat Rock (Smith County), where the hailstones shattered windows and even penetrated the roofs of many homes and businesses.

Two Nashville streetcars were derailed by hail and other debris that covered their tracks. There was considerable damage to utility and communications lines, gardens, crops, fruit trees, and other woody vegetation as well. Some large trees were almost completely stripped of leaves.

May 27, 1917 — Tornadoes—Tornadoes ravaged a four-state area, killing 211 and causing considerable damage. In Tennessee, 25 were killed, 247 were injured, and economic losses were estimated at half a million dollars in Benton, Carroll, Davidson, Dyer, Gibson, Henderson, Henry, Hickman, Houston, Lake, McNairy, Perry, Stewart, Weakley, and Wilson counties. The tornado in Perry County was a category F4 event.

Sept. 6–24, 1917 — **Labor strike—Chattanooga Streetcar Strike** (see p. 200). During the Chattanooga streetcar strike motormen and conductors simply stepped off their cars, leaving the passengers abandoned. In the weeks that followed, many mobsters, some of them known streetcar workers, began systematically attacking and damaging the abandoned vehicles by turning them loose on hillsides to crash at the bottom in deference to public safety. One person was killed and several others seriously wounded during the conflict.

Oct. 29, 1917 — Tornado—One person was killed and another injured in a Hickman County and Dickson County category F2 tornado. It touched down at 12:30 PM, three miles west of Bon Aqua and traveled northeastward to Abiff.

Dec. 19, 1917 — **Coal mine disaster—Flat Rock Mine Disaster** (see p. 123). Eleven men were killed by an explosion inside Mine No. 3 at Catoosa (Cumberland County) at 4:00 PM. A blown-out shot (i.e., an improperly placed powder charge) was responsible for the tragedy.

Dec. 30, 1917 — Severe winter—The lowest temperature ever recorded in the state, –32°F, occurred at Mountain City (Johnson County). The entire mountain region of East Tennessee recorded subzero temperatures. Also see other record-breaking cold temperatures under winter 1917–18.

1918–19 — **Pandemic, Influenza** (see p. 18)—The so-called Spanish flu pandemic killed an estimated 50 million to 100 million people worldwide from 1917 through 1919. Of 20 million cases in the United States, about half a million died. Officially, Tennessee lost 7,721 to the dread disease. This event registered five on the Centers for Disease Control and Prevention Pandemic Severity Index (see table 5 in the appendix).

Jan. 1918 — Flooding—This flood on the Tennessee River was known as the "Ice Tide," since it occurred during a bitter cold winter when snow accumulations in the upper Clinch and Powell River basins were twenty to twenty-five inches deep. Near the Tennessee and Kentucky line, the Cumberland River rose 52.1 feet in only forty hours. The Mississippi River also froze at Memphis on January 19. It froze from bank to bank with no visible current at the surface. When the ice broke two days later, it swept four steamboats downstream, sinking one of them, the *de Soto*. Flooding took months to subside. At one point, the Mississippi River was forty miles wide at Memphis.

Feb. 10, 12, 1918 — Lynching and hate crimes—Two black men were lynched two days apart at Estill Springs (Franklin County). The first victim was a minister.

July 9, 1918	**Railway accident—Dutchmans Grade Train Wreck** (see p. 164). At 8:00 AM two Nashville, Chattanooga & St. Louis passenger trains collided head-on in west Nashville, killing 101 and injuring, by some accounts, almost 300. Many of the injured undoubtedly died later as a result of the accident, but no record of these additional fatalities appears to have been compiled. (See the Sept. 24, 1904, New Market Train Wreck of 1904 for comparison.) This was the worst passenger rail accident in U.S. history.
Aug. 30–31, 1919	**Racial violence—Knoxville Race Riot** (see p. 220). During a Knoxville race riot, a drunken mob of white men stormed the Knox County jail hoping to impose vigilante justice on a black man accused of killing a white woman. Finding that the prisoner had been moved to a different location for his own protection, they wrecked the jail and freed a number of prisoners.
Oct. 17–Nov. 5, 1919	**Labor strike—Knoxville Streetcar Strike** (see p. 201). A large number of Knoxville streetcar workers went on strike to demand higher wages and a better system of compensation. Riots broke out from time to time and many were injured.
1920	Labor strike—During the Memphis Firefighters Strike, firemen walked off their jobs and were replaced by volunteers. After four months of getting nowhere in negotiations, they asked for their jobs back, stating that they were no longer interested in unions.
Feb. 6, 1920	Railway accident—A passenger train derailed on the Illinois Central line at Pinson (Madison County), killing two people and causing considerable property damage.
Apr. 2–4, 1920	Flooding—Severe flooding occurred throughout the southeastern portion of the Tennessee Valley, resulting in the second highest flood ever west of Newport (Cocke County) and in the vicinity of the Little Pigeon River at Sevierville (Sevier County). On April 3, the *Knoxville News Sentinel* reported that scores of dead animals, buildings, and vast amounts of other debris were washed down the Pigeon River as a result of the flood. Knoxville-bound Southern Railway trains were marooned at Bridgeport, near Newport. Very heavy thunderstorms preceded the flood, and ten inches of rain fell during a twelve-hour period in an area centered near Benton (Polk County). This resulted in heavy flooding along Cane Creek.
Apr. 9, 1920	Structure fire—A fire at the York Lumber and Manufacturing Company was one of the most destructive in the history of Memphis. The blaze that broke out in the company's lumber shed at the corner of Bellevue and the North Carolina & St. Louis Railroad tracks destroyed fifteen structures and thirteen railroad cars. Damages were estimated at $350,000.
Apr. 20, 1920	Tornadoes—Three people were killed and ten injured by a Williamson County category F2 tornado that touched down seven miles south-southwest of Burwood and two miles north of Thompsons Station, at 10:30 AM. There was also tornado damage in Maury County around the same time.
Sept. 10, 1920	Tornado—An Obion County twister touched down at 5:00 PM, causing at least one death.
Jan. 24, 1921	**Explosion—Colyar Reese Oil Plant Explosion** (see p. 95). An 8,000-gallon railroad gasoline tank car exploded at a Sinclair Oil Company Plant in Memphis. The incident killed ten people and injured scores of others. Property damage was estimated at $200,000.

Mar. 24, 1921	Tornadoes—Four were killed and ten injured as category F3 twisters moved from east and southeast Maury County, and northwest Bedford County, into Murfreesboro (Rutherford County).
Apr. 16, 1921	Tornadoes—One twister touched down at 3:00 AM and traveled from Giles County into Marshall County, killing two and injuring fourteen others. A second tornado struck the Cornersville-Palmetto area of Marshall County at 4:15 AM and traveled into Bedford County, killing one and injuring eleven. A third touched down at 5:00 AM and traveled from Wheelerton to Delrose through Giles and Lincoln counties, killing one and injuring eight. Two additional twisters injured eight in Bedford, Lincoln, Marshall, and Rutherford counties. Over twenty-seven miles of combined tracks of destruction were associated with these events. None of the twisters were believed to have exceeded category F2 intensity.
Sept. 14, 1921	Racial violence—A race riot erupted at Montlake (Hamilton County) after an eight-year-old black girl shot four young white girls, one of which was mortally wounded. This followed an argument over the use of a spring. An estimated 30 to 50 blacks fled a white mob of 100 who pursued them with rifles, pistols, and even axes. Hundreds of shots were fired, but no one was known to be injured in the incident.
Dec. 24, 1921	Severe winter—This frigid weather episode killed 44 and injured another 100 in Arkansas, Louisiana, Mississippi, and Tennessee.
1922	Labor strike—A labor strike erupted in the Frisco Railroad Shops of the Yale Yards at East Parkway and Madison in Memphis. A foreman mistaken for another individual was shot and killed in the strike. Three men were jailed in the shooting, which resulted from disputes over wages and overall adverse working conditions.
June 7, 1922	Railway accident—A freight train was derailed due to a washout on the Southern Railway line at Middleton (Hardeman County), killing one person and causing considerable property damage.
June 27, 1922	**Quarry explosion—Strawberry Plains Quarry Explosion** (see p. 124). Twenty-four cases of dynamite exploded around 12:28 PM as charges were being set at the Houston Quarry Company near Strawberry Plains (Jefferson County). Nine workers were killed and others were injured, two seriously.
Oct. 20, 1922	Lynching and hate crimes—Two men, race unknown, were taken from the county jail by an angry mob of twenty-five and shot numerous times in a hollow near the Camden (Benton County) School.
1923	Epidemic, measles—A high incidence of this disease, 476 cases, was reported statewide during this year.
Feb. 6, 1923	Structure fire—A fire destroyed 250 automobiles at a Memphis dealership. Damages were estimated at half a million dollars.
Mar. 11, 1923	**Tornadoes—Tornadoes of 1923** (see p. 64). Twenty were killed and seventy injured in Chester and Madison counties when tornadoes touched down around 8:00 PM and created over seventy-five miles of combined tornadic tracks.

Jan. 25–Feb. 1924	Epidemic, typhoid—Fifty cases of typhoid fever were reported at Lincoln Memorial University, Harrogate (Claiborne County), and two of them were fatal. The carrier was found to be an infected food handler in the kitchen. There was also an outbreak of this disease at Dover (Stewart County).
Mar. 1924	**Epidemic, Smallpox** (see p. 20)—This outbreak of smallpox in Anderson County assumed such epidemic proportions that local officials telegraphed the Tennessee Department of Public Health asking for aid. This was the last known epidemic of smallpox in the state.
Mar. 29, 1924	Railway accident—The *Strawberry Special* freight train wrecked on the Southern Railway tracks near Emory Gap (Roane County), killing the engineer, flagman, and fireman. Economic damages were also heavy.
June 13, 1924	**Flash flood—Cardens Bluff Flash flood** (see p. 38). A severe storm dumped fifteen inches of rain in the vicinity of Cardens Bluff in eight hours, twelve inches of that in only three and a half hours. It created an eight- to ten-foot high wall of water that plummeted down a narrow valley, crushing two houses and killing a dozen people. The total economic cost of the disaster was estimated at over a million dollars.
Aug. 10, 1924	**Structure fire—Old Hickory Powder Plant Fire** (see p. 110). Approximately 22,500 tons of gunpowder and fifty buildings were lost in a fire at the Nashville Industrial Corporation Plant (formerly the Old Hickory Powder Plant) in Davidson County. Economic losses were estimated at between $2 million and $28 million. The discrepancy seems to be due to wartime-versus-peacetime values of the munitions. This has been rated as one of the most destructive munitions plant accidents in U.S. history.
Dec. 7, 1924	Tornado—An evening tornado struck Junction City (Carroll County), killing one and injuring three others.
1925–26	Drought—This event mainly affected the southeastern United States. Most crops, with the exception of those in low-lying areas along streams, failed during the period. It was probably Tennessee's fifth most severe drought. As farm and pasture lands dried up and springs and smaller streams ceased to flow, many towns and cities were forced to adopt stringent water conservation measures. Power shortages caused many factories to close or cut back to part-time operation. About 80 percent of the power during the drought came from steam plants. Wildland fires raged in the mountains, adding to the economic losses that grew into the millions of dollars. Many low-flow records were set on state streams during the drought. At Nashville, it was said that automobiles could be driven up and down the Cumberland River bed without getting wet.
1925	Wildland fires—Forest and brush fires were heavy statewide as a result of drought. Records indicate that 207,234 acres of fields and forests were burned in some 1,072 separate fires. Even sections of the so-called unburnable Great Smoky Mountains were ablaze.
Mar. 18, 1925	**Tornadoes—Tornadoes of 1925** (see p. 65). These twisters caused 689 deaths, 13,000 injuries, and $16–18 million in damages in five states within a three-hour period. Fifty-three of the deaths and 119 of the injuries occurred in Bedford, Rutherford, Sumner, and Williamson counties. Over

150 homes and other structures were either damaged or demolished in this incident. The tornadoes were F3 and F4 in intensity.

May 8, 1925 — **Riverboat accident—The *M.E. Norman* Riverboat Disaster** (see p. 183). This Memphis government stern-wheeler riverboat capsized and sank at Cow Island Bend, just south of Memphis. Twenty-three of the seventy-two passengers and crew onboard died in the incident. The passengers were all members of the American Society of Civil Engineers, on an inspection cruise as part of their annual meeting in Memphis.

July 23, 1925 — **Coal mine disaster—Roane Iron Company Mine Disaster 1925** (see p. 124). Ten men were killed while attempting to seal off a coal mine fire inside the Roane Iron Company Mine at Rockwood (Roane County). Either the fire or some other ignition source caused an initial explosion and then a second more violent blast, which killed and mutilated the victims.

Nov. 23, 1925 — Structure fire—A midnight fire destroyed an entire block of stores and other businesses on the north bank of the Tennessee River in Chattanooga. It extended along West Frazier Avenue from Woodlawn to North Market Street. Eight structures were destroyed, including two apartment buildings and a building under construction. Had it not been for the quick action and hard work of the Chattanooga Fire Department, the entire North Business District of Chattanooga would have been destroyed. Economic losses were estimated at $75,000.

Aug. 1926–June 1927 — **Flooding—Floods of 1926–27** (see p. 39). This was the second greatest flood episode in Tennessee history, and it followed the severe drought of 1925. Some areas received in excess of twenty-four inches of rain, the greatest amount of precipitation ever to fall over so wide an area of the state in a nine-day period. The Mississippi River is said to have spread 100 miles wide at some points as levees broke in 145 places. By some estimates, as many as 300 people may have died in the event.

Oct. 4, 1926 — **Coal mine disaster—Roane Iron Company Mine Disaster 1926** (see p. 126). Twenty-eight men were killed in a horrendous methane gas explosion three miles inside the Roane Iron Company coal mine at Rockwood (Roane County). The explosion was believed to be the result of an adjacent mineshaft fire that had been burning, perhaps unnoticed, for many years. The explosion occurred near the same locale as the Rockwood mine disaster of July 23, 1925.

Nov. 25–26, 1926 — Tornadoes—Fourteen tornadoes struck Arkansas, Alabama, Missouri, and Tennessee, killing seventy-eight and causing $1 million in economic losses.

Dec. 25, 1927 — **Civil insurrection—South Pittsburg Gunfight** (see p. 202). Six law enforcement officers were gunned down in South Pittsburg on Christmas Day. The deaths occurred during a labor dispute at a local stove company. Four others were wounded in the five-minute gun battle.

1928 — **Epidemic, Influenza** (see p. 18)—A heavy outbreak of influenza resulted in 2,752 deaths statewide.

1928 — Wildland fires—Forest and brush fires were very severe during this year. Some 1,127 separate wildland fires burned 148,381 acres. These events had a significant impact upon the environment as well as the economy.

Jan. 24, 1928	Tornadoes—A category F1 twister touched down around 2:00 PM in DeKalb County, six miles north of Smithville in Holmes Creek Hollow. Four were killed and six injured.
Feb. 29, 1928	Structure fire—A fire at the Tennessee Paper Mill in North Chattanooga took the life of one fireman and injured five others. This was said to be a particularly hot fire and extremely difficult to extinguish. Economic losses were estimated at $50,000.
Apr. 21, 1928	Tornadoes—A twister touched down at 2:22 AM near Tipton and traveled northeast toward Atoka (Tipton County), where it split and traveled toward the Mt. Carmel, Melrose, and Liberty Communities, all in Tipton County. In Atoka, fifteen homes and practically the entire town business district were destroyed. One person was killed and several injured. Several other homes were also damaged in the area.
June 28–29, 1928	Tornadoes—One person was killed and thirty-eight injured when tornadoes touched down between 1:00 and 2:15 PM in Davidson County, four miles north of Nashville. They wrought destruction from Nashville through Wilson County to Alexandria in DeKalb County. The most severe of the tornadoes reached category F4 intensity.
June 28–30, 1928	Flooding—The storm that caused this flooding in the Cumberland Plateau region struck so suddenly and in such widely separated areas that reliable data was difficult to obtain. Furthermore, there were no known follow-up studies. Seven to ten inches of rain fell near Cookeville (Putnam County) on June 28, from late evening into the early morning. Flash floods and slow-rise floods washed away or inundated homes, businesses, highways, railroads, and bridges, as well as crops and stock. This was the flood of record for the Falling Water River. Additional severe floods crested at Nashville on June 8, July 5, and November 24.
June 29, 1928	**Structure failure—Cookeville Power Dam Failure** (see p. 135). The hydroelectric dam at Burgess Falls (DeKalb County) failed at 5:30 PM, sending a wall of water thirty feet high plummeting down the Falling Water River to its confluence with the Caney Fork River near Dowelltown (DeKalb County). The breach, which occurred when a wing of the dam collapsed, also demolished the reservoir's downstream powerhouse.
Sept. 17, 1928	Structure fire—The Harahan River bridge, across the Mississippi, caught fire. It is believed that a locomotive ignited the wooden planks of the structure. The bridge carried both vehicular and train traffic, and its destruction created one of the worst traffic dilemmas in Memphis history. It took over four hours to bring the fire under control. Damages to the structure were estimated at some $200,000, and at least that much was also associated with other economic costs. At the time, it was the only vehicular bridge across the Mississippi River south of St. Louis. As a result, three temporary auto ferries were put into service, and trains had to be rerouted over hundreds of miles.
1929–40s	Economic crisis—Economic Crash of 1929 and the Great Depression. The collapse of the U.S. stock market and the onset of the Great Depression resulted in multiple bank failures across the nation. Losses approached $50 billion. Millions who had never known destitution were with-

out food, shelter, or any means of acquiring them. The entire economic fabric of the nation and eventually many other parts of the world was disrupted. This was the most severe economic crisis the nation had known before or since. The "hard times," as the old-timers called the Depression years, lasted from 1929 into the early 1940s.

Mar. 1929–Spring 1930	Labor strike—Elizabethton Rayon Workers Strike. An Elizabethton (Carter County) textile labor strike began in March and lasted through September. Some historians touted it as the beginning of the second phase of the industrial revolution in the South. It resulted in violence, picketing, disorder, kidnapping of company officials, and the dynamiting of the city's water supply.
Mar. 21–23, 1929	**Flooding—Floods of 1929** (see p. 41). One of the most severe floods ever experienced in the eastern United States in any area of comparable size occurred along the Emory River and in the Upper Cumberland River Basin during this period. It reached its highest intensities at Crossville (Cumberland County), Spencer (Van Buren County), Rock Island (Warren County), and Wartburg (Morgan County). Forty lives were lost, thirty-three of them in Tennessee; there were scores of injuries, and economic losses exceeded $10 million in Tennessee and Alabama.
Mar. 22, 1929	**Flash flood—Whites Creek Flash flood** (see p. 43). Seven Boy Scouts and their adult leader were drowned about five miles south of Rockwood, when a flash flood on Whites Creek struck the cabin in which they were spending the night. The Scout Master died trying to save one of his boys. Thirteen additional scouts survived the ordeal.
May 2, 1929	Tornadoes—Twisters touched down in Washington and Cocke counties around 2:00 PM, resulting in four deaths and four injuries.
Aug. 1929	Structure fire—A fire struck the 600 block of State Street in Bristol (Sullivan County). It damaged or destroyed several businesses.
Aug. 29, 1929	**Structure fire—Memphis Industrial Settlement Home Fire** (see p. 111). Eight children died in a fire in the Industrial Settlement Home on Driver Street in Memphis, a structure described as a firetrap. Around eighty other children survived the blaze. The bodies of the eight little victims, the oldest of which was six, were discovered in an upstairs bathroom as firefighters sifted through the remains of the building.
Nov. 11, 1929	**Railway accident—Glen Mary Train Wreck** (see p. 166). The Ponce de Leon Southern Limited en route to Florida derailed at Glenmary (Scott County) killing five and injuring another seventy-five. The locomotive left the main line with such force that upon impact it embedded itself some six feet into the ground.
1930–31	Epidemic, Meningitis—A high, statewide incidence of this disease killed 245 people in 1930 and 138 in 1931.
1930–31	Wildland fires—According to the state forester, Tennessee's severest fire seasons since the development of the Division of Forestry occurred in 1930 and 1931. During the spring of 1930, a prolonged period of dry windy weather made brush and forest fires easy to ignite but extremely difficult to extinguish. In fact, forest fires occurred without ceasing during every month of that

year. In 1930 alone, 435,203 acres of fields and forests burned in 2,828 separate fires. The year 1931 produced severe wildland fires, especially during the spring and fall.

1930–31   **Drought—Drought of 1930–31** (see p. 2). The nation's worst drought was compounded by a worldwide economic depression, the boll weevil's ravaging of southern cotton crops, the general collapse of the U.S. cotton market, and other related problems. In terms of statewide precipitation shortage, it was Tennessee's fourth most severe drought period, but economically it was much worse. The drought lasted from December 1930 through December 1931.

Apr. 27, 1930   **Airplane crash—Fayetteville Flying Circus Airplane Crash** (see p. 139). Eight people were killed and a score injured at a Fayetteville (Lincoln County) air show. The dead and injured were all standing along a railroad embankment that they had been warned to avoid. Four people were decapitated by the plane's propeller and the others crushed by its impact.

July 29, 1930   Severe heat—Highest temperature ever recorded in the state, 113°F, occurred, and again on August 9, 1930, at Perryville (Decatur County).

Aug. 9, 1930   Severe heat—The highest temperature ever recorded in the state, 113°F, was tied. The first event occurred on July 29, 1930 at Perryville (Decatur County).

1931   Epidemic, Diphtheria—This disease killed an estimated 17,000 individuals, mostly children, across the nation. The number who died in Tennessee is unknown.

1931   Structure fire—The Arcade Building Fire on Union Street in Knoxville devastated the city block bounded by Union and West Clinch avenues and Walnut and Market streets. It resulted in three deaths and $260,000 in damages. This was an arson fire, allegedly ignited by a German man who hoped to collect insurance on his business before leaving the country for his homeland. He was one of the victims.

Jan. 24, 1931   **Railway accident—Hellenwood Train Wreck** (see p. 167). Five were killed and forty injured, some seriously, as the tourist train *Suwannee Special* left the tracks along the Southern Railway Queen and Crescent route between New River and Hellenwood (Scott County).

Jan. 14, 1932   Tornadoes—Ten were killed and three injured when one or more tornadoes touched down at 5:30 PM and traveled an erratic eighty-mile path through Gibson County. The town of Eaton was particularly hard hit.

Mar. 1932   Structure fire—A fire broke out in a construction company plant on Wray Avenue in Knoxville. During that fire a large crude oil storage tank exploded, killing two firefighters, along with a third man who was helping fight the blaze.

Mar. 14, 1932   Tornado—A tornado ripped through Sullivan County, killing 11 and injuring another 200.

Mar. 21–22, 1932   Tornadoes—Tornadoes of category F2 to F4 intensity struck five states, killing 268, injuring 1,000, and leaving 8,500 homeless. Twenty-two deaths and 101 injuries occurred when a family of nine twisters struck Bedford, Bradley, Cannon, Davidson, DeKalb, Giles, Lawrence, Lewis, Marion, Marshall, Polk, Scott, Trousdale, Williamson, and Wilson counties in Tennessee. Damage was estimated at half a million dollars. A twister in Cleveland (Bradley County) was said to have snatched a baby from its mother's arms and dropped it to its death down a well.

Apr. 25, 1932	Tornadoes—Six people were killed and twenty-eight injured in twisters that touched down around 10:10 AM in north Shelby County. The combined length of the known tornado tracks was 160 miles.
July 9, 1932– Apr. 30, 1933	Labor strike—This labor strike occurred as a result of coal miners attempting to unionize. The dynamiting and burning of coal company property, including a major bridge and tipples at Wilder (Fentress County), resulted in several months of intense and sometimes bloody violence. The National Guard was eventually activated to restore order after many injuries, and a number of lives, including that of the union president, were lost. In the end, attempts to unionize failed.
July 20, 1932	Structure fire—Around 3:00 AM a fire erupted in the Southern Railway System's old Citoco Yards near Lincoln Park in Chattanooga. It eventually spread a half mile or more along the tracks, destroying some 287 boxcars. The cause of the fire was never determined.
Aug. 9, 1932	Highway accident—While transporting fifty-one Boy Scouts and their camping equipment, two trucks from Nashville went out of control on the Little River Road within the Great Smoky Mountains National Park. The lead truck turned into an uphill embankment and was stopped with no injuries. The second vehicle overturned on the road, pinning fifteen-year-old Cleo White under the vehicle, where he died instantly. Three others were seriously injured; one of these later died.
Nov. 11, 1932	Airplane crash—A small plane, en route from Chicago to Florida, crashed on the outskirts of Kempville (Smith County), killing five. All died on impact, except for a baby girl who lived for two hours. Bodies were strewn all about the site. Strong winds, drizzle, and possible engine trouble were blamed for the crash. This was the state's first major airplane crash (that is, involving more than four fatalities).
1933–34	Labor strike—East Tennessee textile industries labor strikes. Many strikes and labor disputes occurred, primarily in textile industries in and around Chattanooga, Knoxville, Harriman, Rockwood, and other East Tennessee communities. Violence erupted periodically.
Mar. 14, 1933	**Tornadoes—East Nashville Tornado 1933** (see p. 66). Six tornadoes, some as high as category F3 in intensity, struck Campbell, Claiborne, Davidson, Hancock, Smith, Sullivan, and Wilson counties. Fifty-two were killed, 556 were injured, and over 552 were left homeless. Economic losses were estimated at about $3 million. East Nashville, the hardest hit area, sustained fifteen of the deaths and forty-five of the injuries. In terms of lives lost, this was the third most severe tornadic incident in the state's history. In terms of injuries, it was the second worst. It was also the first major urban tornado in Tennessee history.
May 7, 1933	Tornado—Darkness, heavy rain, and hail preceded this twister, which touched down just south of Brighton and cut a fifteen-mile-long swath of destruction through the heart of Tipton County. Six people were killed and twenty injured. Between 75 and 100 homes were destroyed or severely damaged, and 400 people were left homeless.
May 9–10, 1933	Tornadoes—Tornadoes of May 1933. A number of tornadoes touched down in Overton, Pickett, and Wilson counties, killing 37 and injuring over 125. The storm that spawned these tornadoes

was unusually violent, and the rain turned the roads to bogs. In terms of lives lost, this was the seventh greatest tornadic episode in the state's history.

May 14, 1933   Tornado—A tornado struck the coal mining community of Pruden (Claiborne County), killing at least eight and injuring over fifty. Scores of homes, businesses, and other structures were either damaged or destroyed by hailstones, some as large as baseballs. Roads were impassible as ambulances from Middlesboro, Kentucky, attempted to reach the remote area. A tornado touched down at Harrogate (Claiborne County) killing two children and severely injuring their mother. It was estimated that buildings on the nearby Lincoln Memorial University campus sustained $10,000 in damages. Structures within the town of Harrogate were also damaged.

June 8, 1933   Lynching and hate crimes—Two Scott County Jail inmates, Jerome Boyett and Harvey Winchester, were shot and probably tortured by an angry mob of twenty-five hooded men.

1934   Drought—This statewide event was characterized by an unusually hot and dry spring and summer. Crop damages were severe.

1934   Epidemic, measles—Four hundred and fifty-one people died statewide from this disease.

Nov. 20–21, 1934   Severe storm—In the heaviest single rainfall ever to occur in Memphis, around ten and a half inches of rain fell almost without interruption. It was accompanied by a forty-eight-mile-per-hour wind that resulted in several deaths, injuries, and considerable damage along the Mississippi River. The flood halted streetcar traffic, covered roads, and washed out twenty bridges in Shelby County alone. It also played havoc with utility and phone services.

Dec. 3, 1934   Structure fire—Three firefighters lost their lives and several others were injured in a fire that broke out around 3:30 AM at the Johnson Motors Company in the 300 block of Monroe Street in Memphis. The deaths occurred when gasoline tanks in the basement of the structure exploded, causing a concrete block wall to collapse on them. This was the first time in the history of the Memphis Fire Department that more than one man was killed while fighting a fire.

1935–36   Wildland fires—Forest and brush fires were severe statewide. In December 1935, fires in Morgan County destroyed half of the town of Wartburg. Young men from the Civilian Conservation Corps Camp at Morgan State Forest, now Frozen Head State Park and Natural Area, heroically saved the town from total destruction.

1935–36   Epidemic, meningitis—A meningococcal meningitis epidemic killed 108 and 109 people respectively during these two years.

1935–37   Epidemic, pneumonia—Statewide there were 2,781, 3,429, and 2,761 cases reported respectively in the three years.

Spring 1935   Flooding—Heavy rains followed by four inches of snow fell over the Tennessee, Mississippi, and Obion River watersheds during this season. Nineteen died from drowning and exposure, and sixty-one suffered from frostbite as West Tennessee levees broke in many places. Property losses were in the hundreds of thousands of dollars. These floods were even worse than the events of

January 21, 1935, on the Big Sandy River at Bruceton (Carroll County) and on the South Fork of the Obion River near Greenfield (Weakley County).

Mar. 25, 1935	Tornadoes—Two were killed and fifteen injured as tornadoes touched down in Rutherford and Cannon counties at 7:00 PM and 7:20 PM respectively. Over twenty-two miles of combined tracks of destruction were identified in the two counties. This was a category F2 event.
Apr. 27, 1935	Structure fire—The most destructive conflagration in Grundy County's history was ignited around 10:00 PM by an arsonist in Tracy City. Eighty nearby Civilian Conservation Corps men finally brought the blazes under control, but not before over a dozen town businesses had been destroyed. Damage was estimated at $100,000. The arsonist, Clyde C. Newsom, was tried and convicted of the crime and was given a suspended sentence on the condition that he leave the state and never return.
Dec. 1935	Severe winter—An ice storm struck Arkansas, Georgia, and Tennessee, causing an estimated $2 million in damages and killing some 212 people.
Mar. 19, 1936	Structure fire—A fire that started in a private home spread through Whitwell (Marion County), destroying most of its south business district.
Apr. 5, 1936	Tornadoes—Twenty-two tornadoes struck six states, causing 421 deaths and $22 million in damages. Ten died and fifty-one were injured in Tennessee. One tornado touched down in east Hardin County and traveled to near Columbia (Maury County). Another entered Tennessee and traveled northeast through Lincoln County.
Summer–Fall 1936	Epidemic, polio—The largest number of cases of polio to date occurred. This was the second of four great statewide epidemics.
Sept. 15, 1936	Railway accident—Two people were killed and another injured when a freight train derailed on the Illinois Central line at Toone (Hardeman County). Property damage was also heavy.
Winter of 1936–37	**Epidemic, Influenza** (see p. 18) and pneumonia—This epidemic swept the nation during the time of the Great Mississippi-Ohio Valley floods. The floods and severe cold weather added greatly to the cause and spread of disease and suffering.
Dec. 1936–Jan. 1937	**Flooding—Floods of 1936–37** (see p. 45). This was the worst seasonal flooding in the state's history. Records indicated that 21.24 inches of rain fell over portions of the Mississippi, Tennessee, and Cumberland River valleys during the two months. It was nearly twice as severe as the flood of 1927, which had been the worst to date.
Dec. 1936–June 1937	Labor strike—Coal miners at the Fentress Coal and Coke Company's Zenith Coal Mine in Jamestown (Fentress County) went on strike to force recognition of the United Mine Workers Union. The company refused to recognize the union and fought back with evictions, injunctions, and imported strikebreakers. When Zenith reopened in March with non striking miners, violence erupted. On June 17 the general manager of the mine was ambushed and killed, at least two others were wounded and considerable property was destroyed. The National Guard eventually restored order.

Feb. 20, 1937	Structure fire—Three firemen died and seven were injured in a fire that flared up around 5:30 AM on the public square in Nashville. The Stephens Manufacturing Company and several adjacent buildings were affected. Fighting this intense blaze was exacerbated by high winds. Losses were estimated at $350,000.
May 18–June 8, 1937	**Labor strike—Aluminum Company of America Labor Strike** (see p. 202). Some 2,900 workers went on strike at the Alcoa Fabricating Plant in Blount County demanding higher wages. A confrontation between police and striking workers led to two men being killed and another twenty to forty-five injured, some seriously.
Nov. 5, 1937	Structure fire—A major fire in Moscow (Fayette County) began in an alley between Third and Fourth streets and quickly spread through forty-two buildings. It destroyed almost all the stores in the downtown area.
Aug. 4–5, 1938	**Flash flood—Pittman Center Flash Flood** (see p. 48). A torrential storm dropped eleven to fifteen inches of rain over a twenty-seven-square-mile area of Sevier County at Pittman Center (Sevier County) in a three- to four-hour period. Cabins, barns, stock, and crops were washed away. Eight people also lost their lives in what became known locally as the "Election Day Flood."
1939–40	Wildland fires—Forest and brush fires were particularly severe statewide.
1939	Epidemic, typhus fever—Seventy-seven cases of this rat-borne disease occurred in Nashville during this year. Epidemiological data indicated that the foci of the infection dated back to diagnosed cases in 1935. The U.S. Public Health Service dispatched a rat control specialist to coordinate a program to destroy the rat populations in the area by massive cleanup and by using gas and other poisons.
Jan. 4, 1939	Tornadoes—Four deaths and twenty injuries occurred as a result of tornadoes in Hardeman, Henderson, and White counties. One twister touched down near Silerton (Hardeman County) and traveled into Henderson County. Around 460 miles of combined tornado tracks were associated with this episode.
Mar. 1939	Flooding—Flooding was severe along First Creek in Knoxville.
Aug. 3, 1939	Flooding—Seven inches of rain fell in Wilson County between 10:00 PM and daylight, causing considerable soil erosion, crop, and other damages.
Sept. 4, 1939	Tornado—One person was killed and six injured by a category F2 tornado that touched down at 5:30 PM in White County and traveled from near Bear Cove north to Sparta.
1940–42	Drought—This was the second most severe drought in the state's history. An average of only 37.86 inches of rain fell across the state in 1941. The mean average is around 50 inches per year. Halls (Lauderdale County) recorded the lowest rainfall for the state at 25.23 inches. This led to widespread water supply shortages, water quality problems, wildland fires, crop failures, and other economic hardships.
Late Jan. 1940	**Severe winter—Severe Winter Storm of 1940** (see p. 83). Snowstorms reached almost to the Mississippi Gulf Coast. The mercury fell to –29°F just north of Crossville in Cumberland County

and –28°F at Oneida (Scott County). Many people were said to have frozen to death, and the event was also devastating for livestock. According to TVA records, January 1940 was the overall coldest month in Tennessee's recorded history.

Aug. 13–30, 1940	Flooding—The storms that caused this flooding were spawned by an Atlantic hurricane. As they moved along the Blue Ridge they dropped up to 17.0 inches and 16.8 inches in the French Broad and Pigeon River watersheds respectively. Fourteen inches of precipitation in the watersheds of the Watauga and Nolichucky river basins also resulted in the highest floods of record in that region. Newport (Cocke County) and Kingsport (Sullivan County) likewise received heavy flooding. Two and a half weeks after the mid-August storms of 1940, even heavier rain amounts began falling over the same general area. Ten inches of precipitation fell over the upper Tuckasegee River and its tributaries, causing record floods. This was the last flood to impact Knoxville before construction of TVA's Douglas and Cherokee dams, which tamed the river. Eventually Fort Loudoun Dam was also constructed below Knoxville. The flood of 1940 exceeded the flood of 1926–27 on the Cumberland River between mile 162 and the Tennessee state line. It was also the flood of record on the lower reaches of the Red River and the lower end of the Tennessee due to the backup of the Ohio River.
Dec. 21, 1940	Structure fire—Flames destroyed half of the business district of New Tazewell (Claiborne County).
1941–43	Epidemic, measles—Six thousand cases of measles were reported statewide during the first six months of 1941. More than 10,000 cases occurred during the three-year period.
1941	Epidemic, whooping cough—A high incidence of whooping cough killed 159 people across the state during this year.
Summer–Fall 1941	Epidemic, polio—The state's worst ever epidemic of acute polio spread panic and despair in its wake. Five hundred and fifty-two cases were reported, and the epidemic extended from the Hamilton County northwestward through Davidson and Sumner counties to the Kentucky Tennessee border. The highest concentration was in Davidson, Franklin, Hamilton, and Sumner counties, along the main highway from the southeast. This was the third of four great polio epidemics in Tennessee.
Sept. 18, 1941	Structure fire—Four buildings were destroyed or severely damaged and several others affected to a lesser degree in a fire on Nashville's Fourth Avenue N.
Oct. 10, 1941	**Highway accident—Eads Train–School Bus Wreck** (see p. 152). Eight were killed and another eight severely injured when a Memphis-bound North Carolina & St. Louis passenger train crashed into a county school bus as it crossed the tracks just east of the Eads (Shelby County) depot.
Jan. 1, 1942	Tornado—A category F2 tornado touched down four miles southeast of Clarksville (Montgomery County) around 12:30 PM and traveled eastward, killing one and injuring eight.
Feb. 5–6, 1942	Tornadoes—A series of sixteen tornadoes caused twenty-three deaths and over $2 million in economic losses in Alabama, Arkansas, Georgia, Mississippi, South Carolina, and Tennessee.

Feb. 7, 1942	**Structure fire—Southern Hotel Fire** (see p. 112). Five people were trapped, asphyxiated, and/or burned to death in a tragic fire in Chattanooga's Southern Hotel on Market Street.
Mar. 11, 1942	Tornado—A category F3 tornado touched down at 5:50 PM in Robertson County and traveled from Adams to Cedar Hill, killing two and injuring ten.
Mar. 15, 1942	**Railway accident—Waverly Train Wreck** (see p. 168). A head-on collision between a freight train and a fast passenger train occurred on the North Carolina & St. Louis tracks at a curve near the town of Denver, eight miles southwest of Waverly (Humphreys County). Four people were killed.
Mar. 16, 1942	Tornadoes—A family of five tornadoes that first touched down around 5:00 PM killed 25 people, injured 272, and caused almost $1 million in damages in Carroll, Cheatham, Chester, Decatur, Giles, Hardeman, Henderson, Henry, Humphreys, McNairy, Robertson, and Stewart counties.
1943	Epidemic, whooping cough—A high statewide incidence of whooping cough killed 179 people during this year.
Jan. 5, 1943	**Copper mine disaster—Burra Burra Copper Mine Disaster** (see p. 126). Nine men were killed in this mine as a result of a dynamite explosion. This was the worst disaster in the history of the Ducktown (Polk County) copper mines.
Feb. 14, 1943	Highway accident—Two firemen were killed and three seriously injured when their fire truck crashed into a house at the intersection of Rossville Boulevard and Thirty-seventh Street in Chattanooga. The accident occurred when the fire truck swerved to avoid colliding with a car. The three firemen who survived the tragic crash were injured so badly that all three retired on permanent disability. The fire truck was a total loss.
Mar. 27, 1943	**Airplane crash—Oliver Springs Airplane Crash** (see p. 140). Eleven soldiers were killed when their army plane exploded in midair near Oliver Springs (Roane and Morgan counties).
Apr. 29, 1943	Airplane crash—A twin-engine Army bomber crashed in a Memphis residential area, killing its three crewmen as well as four civilians on the ground. Two of the victims were women and one a twenty-month-old child. Five of the dead were burned almost beyond recognition as the aircraft's fuel tanks exploded. One home was demolished and two adjacent houses set on fire. No one else was injured in the incident.
May 5, 1943	**Coal mine disaster—Nu Rex Mine Disaster** (see p. 127). Twenty-eight men were involved in an explosion in the Nu Rex Mine, five miles north of LaFollette (Campbell County). Ten of the miners were killed by the initial explosion, flash fire, and deadly gases produced by the explosion.
June 5, 1943	**Highway accident—Nashville Army Truck Wreck** (see p. 152). A U.S. Army truck crashed through the guardrails of the Woodycrest Road bridge and plunged thirty feet down an embankment onto the Nashville, Chattanooga, & St. Louis Railroad tracks shortly before midnight. Nineteen of the soldiers were killed and seven others injured. This was the worst traffic accident in Tennessee history in terms of fatalities.
Oct. 15, 1943	**Airplane crash—Wrigley Airplane Crash** (see p. 141). An American Airlines passenger plane crashed at Wrigley (Hickman County), about forty-seven miles south of Nashville, killing four crew members and six passengers.

Feb. 10, 1944	**Airplane crash—Memphis Airplane Crash 1944** (see p. 141). An American Airlines twin-engine DC-3 transport plane crashed into the Mississippi River at Memphis, killing twenty-one passengers and a crew of three. At the time, this was the second worst commercial air crash in U.S. history. It is still ranked the second worst air crash in Tennessee history.
Mar. 26, 1944	Tornado—Five people were killed and two injured when this category F3 tornado touched down at 11:00 PM somewhere in or around Livingston in Giles County.
Mar. 26–27, 1944	Hailstorm—This storm, which lasted some twenty minutes, began around 8:15 PM in south and east Memphis. It was no doubt the city's worst such incident ever. Most of the hailstones were billiard ball to baseball size, but some were measured, unofficially, at between five and eleven inches in diameter. They dented automobiles, broke thousands of windows, and battered and even penetrated roofs. Over 100 planes were also damaged at the Memphis Airport. Some vegetation was severely damaged, as were crops, domestic stock, and wildlife.
Apr. 11, 1944	Tornado—An F2 category Wilson County twister struck the area in and around the Lebanon airport at 6:30 AM, causing one death and fourteen injuries.
Apr. 23, 1944	Tornado—A tornado touched down in Obion County at 4:23 AM, killing one and injuring nine others.
Apr. 29, 1944	Airplane crash—Three crewmen were killed when an Army B-25 crashed in the vicinity of Cleveland and Watkins, in the Crosstown area of Memphis. There were four additional casualties on the ground.
July 6, 1944	**Railway accident—High Cliff Train Wreck** (see p. 169). A Louisville and Nashville Special, transporting mostly new recruits, derailed at High Cliff (Campbell County) about seven miles south of Jellico at 9:00 AM. Thirty-four people were killed, and as many as 100 were injured, some of whom probably died later. It has been described as one of the nation's major troop train accidents and one of the top twenty-five U.S. railway accidents of all times.
Sept. 29–30, 1944	Flooding—The flood of record for First Creek in Knoxville occurred after seven to eleven inches of rain fell in a twenty-five-hour period. Two hundred and fifty acres of the city were involved. One hundred and fifty families, forty-five businesses, and several industries were directly affected. Numerous streets were inundated and streetcars put out of service. There was also heavy flooding on most of the streams in the vicinity of Jacksboro (Campbell County). This was the highest flood since 1929 in Lake City (Anderson County), where floodwaters were six to eighteen inches deep throughout the business district and three feet or more over the rest of the town. Fifty homes sustained flood damage.
Dec. 14, 1944	Structure fire—A fire erupted in the Memphis Owen Brothers Horse and Mule Commission Company on Stockyards Place around 2:30 AM. About twenty mules died in the flames and thirty-five to forty others were injured and had to be euthanatized. The fire began in a hay storage barn, and damages were estimated at around $100,000.
1945–46	Epidemic, polio—This disease struck 25,191 people, primarily children, in twenty-three states. This was the last of four great statewide epidemics prior to the development of the Salk and later the Sabin polio vaccines.

1945	Epidemic, diphtheria—One hundred and five Tennesseans died of diphtheria during this year.
1945	Poisoning—A serious outbreak of Salmonella food poisoning occurred in Weakley County. A tainted cheese was found to be the causative agent.
1945	Epidemic, typhoid fever—A severe outbreak of typhoid fever occurred at Lincoln Memorial University, Harrogate (Claiborne County).
Mar. 8, 1945	Structure fire—The Cumberland Hotel on the corner of Gay Street and Cumberland Avenue and the McNutt Battery Company on Highland Avenue were both destroyed by fire. The losses from these two Knoxville businesses were estimated at $225,000.
Mar. 23, 1945	Explosion—Two men died instantly in an explosion in the Atlas Power Company Plant press building at Ooltewah (Hamilton County). A third died on October 10 as a result of burns sustained in the incident.
Apr. 8, 1945	**Airplane crash—Whigs Mountain Airplane Crash** (see p. 143). A Flying Fortress (B-17) military aircraft crashed into the west slope of Whigs Mountain in Cherokee National Forest while on a training mission. The incident, originally reported as a forest fire, took the lives of ten soldiers.
Sept. 5, 1945	Railway accident—A train wreck on the Illinois Central line at Realto (Tipton County) caused thirty-three freight cars to leave the track, piling up three deep in places. Half of the cars were damaged beyond repair. The cause of the accident was a broken rail. The wreck produced no known fatalities or injuries, and the amount of economic losses is unknown.
Oct. 5, 1945	Airplane crash—An Army C-46 aircraft crashed on the south side of Mount Guyot in the Great Smoky Mountains National Park, killing six crewmen. The remote crash site was not located until October 14.
Jan. 5–9, 1946	Severe storms—Intense and destructive storms covered much of the south-central and southeastern United States. One of the most intense storm centers extended from Bolivar (Hardeman County) to Nashville, with the two areas receiving 9.3 and 10.4 inches of rainfall respectively during the five-day period. This was one of the worst storms ever recorded in the Cumberland River Basin of Middle Tennessee. A record of 6.2 inches of Nashville's total rainfall for the period fell in just twelve hours.
Feb. 25–28, 1946	**Racial violence—Columbia Race Riot** (see p. 222). This episode began when a black woman and her son, a World War II veteran, had an altercation with a white merchant. It quickly became a racial issue and eventually led to a riot in which the black community of Columbia was unjustly ransacked and its citizens harassed. Two black prisoners were killed in the fiasco.
June 12, 1946	**Airplane crash—Clingmans Dome Airplane Crash** (see p. 143). A B-29 bomber crashed in the Great Smoky Mountains National Park in the vicinity of Clingmans Dome, killing its entire crew of twelve. This was the fourth worst air crash in Tennessee history.
Aug. 1, 1946	**Political warring—Battle of Athens** (see p. 242). This famous Election Day riot erupted in Athens (McMinn County) as returning World War II veterans challenged the politically corrupt machine that was running their local government. Twenty people were wounded, fourteen cars were burned, and twenty-five deputies were incarcerated in their own jail after that facility came under siege with bullets and dynamite.

Jan. 15, 1947	Tornadoes—Tornadoes touched down at 3:01 AM in Henderson and Madison counties and traveled some seven miles before dissipating. Four people were killed in the incident at Pinson (Madison County).
Jan. 29, 1947	Tornadoes—Several twisters touched down in Haywood County at 11:15 PM, killing one and injuring five. A total of 110 miles of destructive tornado tracks were identified after the storm.
Feb. 16, 1947	Highway accident—Five people, described as prominent Nashvillians, were killed when their Chrysler sedan was struck by a train at the Old Harding Road crossing of the North Carolina & St. Louis Railroad tracks in the Belle Meade area near Nashville. It was described as a gruesome and totally unexpected crash. Since no one survived, and it was not witnessed by anyone else, its exact cause will never be known. Debris was scattered over a 150 foot stretch of Harding Road.
Feb. 27, 1947	**Explosion—Bristol Service Station Explosion** (see p. 97). Six people were killed and others were injured when a service station exploded at the corner of East State Street and Pennsylvania Avenue in Bristol (Sullivan County). The explosion was heard over a mile away, and economic losses were estimated at $100,000.
Dec. 11, 1947	**Airplane crash—Memphis Airplane Crash 1947** (see p. 144). Twenty-one soldiers en route home on Christmas furloughs were killed when their C-47 aircraft crashed about three miles short of the Memphis Airport. All twenty-one persons on board were killed instantly. This was the third worst air crash in Tennessee history.
1948–57	Labor dispute—Violence broke out during unionization attempts by 200 miners at the Meadow Creek Coal Company in Monterey (Putnam County). The strikers blocked the entrance to the mine, and during the demonstration one police officer was killed and another person injured. Property damage was extensive, and the turmoil did not end until September 1957, when a labor contract was finally negotiated.
Feb. 11–15, 1948	Flooding—Two-thirds of the Tennessee River Valley, including the west central and southwestern portions, received up to 10.4 inches of rain in a forty-eight-hour period. This was the flood of record to that date on the Duck River, between Columbia and its confluence with the Tennessee River and the Buffalo River. At Columbia (Maury County) both the water and power systems were disrupted for several days. One hundred and ten homes were damaged by floodwaters, as was much of the city's infrastructure. Damages exceeded $213,000 at Columbia. Flooding on the Elk River caused $172,000 in damages at Fayetteville (Lincoln County) and Pulaski (Giles County). Flooding on the Duck River and Spring Creek also caused an estimated $132,000 in damages at Shelbyville (Bedford County). This may also have been the flood of record for the Harpeth River, at least since its great flood of March 1897.
Dec. 31, 1948–Jan. 1, 1949	Tornadoes—Twisters struck Arkansas, Louisiana, Mississippi, and Tennessee, killing twenty-three, injuring others, and causing $2 million in damages.
1949	Epidemic polio—Of some 42,173 cases reported across the nation, 2,720 died. The number of Tennessee fatalities is unknown.

Jan. 1949	Flooding—Heavy flooding occurred along the Tennessee River and its tributaries. The Elk River, at Fayetteville (Lincoln County), rose to within inches of its 1842 and 1929 record flood levels. Damages in Fayetteville alone were estimated at $83,000.
Aug. 4, 1949	Structure fire—This was the worst fire in the history of Donelson (Davidson County). It damaged or destroyed several blocks of structures, including the U.S. Post Office.
1950	Labor strike—A strike occurred during this year at the American Snuff Company on North Main Street in Memphis. Company buses were pelted with rocks and bricks, vehicles were overturned, workers' homes were damaged, and at least two bombs were exploded. Many were jailed and/or fined.
Feb. 13, 1950	Tornado—A twister touched down at Ripley (Lauderdale County) at 2:00 AM. It traveled two miles, killing nine, injuring one, and causing considerable property damage.
Aug. 7, 1950	Structure fire—A fire erupted in an old wood-frame warehouse at 23 West Calhoun Avenue in Memphis. The building was owned by the Illinois Central Railroad but occupied by the Cudahy Packing Company. The fire was accidently ignited by workers using a blowtorch. They tried to extinguish the flames themselves but were unsuccessful. The Memphis Fire Department was called and arrived on the scene around 11:21 AM. While fighting the fire, the roof of the old structure collapsed, trapping fifteen firefighters. At that point, several hundred spectators rushed in and began lifting and cutting away at the collapsed roof in an attempt to rescue the trapped men. One fireman died within a few hours of the incident at a Memphis Hospital. A second died some days later from injuries sustained in the roof collapse. Ten others were injured, some severely. It took the firemen about an hour and a half to extinguish the blaze and the building was a total loss.
Sept. 16, 1950	Explosion—The explosion of a 15,000 gallon chemical tank at the Rohm and Haas Plexiglas Plant in Knoxville spread toxic fumes throughout the area, killing one, injuring sixty-one, and causing $100,000 in damages.
Nov. 23–28, 1950	Severe winter—An Appalachian storm dropped snow statewide during a cold wave, causing both physical and economic hardships. It was one of the worst snowstorms ever recorded in the western Appalachian states and other parts of the South.
Jan. 28–Feb. 4, 1951	**Severe winter—Blizzard of 1951** (see p. 83). This incident killed 25 people and resulted in $100 million in damages in Tennessee, Texas, and the New England states. This was one of the most destructive ice storms ever to occur in Tennessee.
Feb. 2, 1951	Structure fire—One man died in a fire that broke out in Kirk's Supermarket in Chattanooga. Twenty-nine people were rescued from the structure. A woman was carried from the fire over a fireman's shoulders. He also carried out her child at the same time, clutched in his teeth, like a dog carries her pups.
July 24, 1951	Structure fire—One of the most stubborn fires in the history of Chattanooga broke out in the Sears, Roebuck and Company on Market and Sixth streets around 6:45 PM. About a third of the 175 firefighters at the scene were overcome by smoke. A number of them were hospitalized.
Sept. 1, 1951	Flooding—Heavy precipitation resulted in flash flooding along tributaries of the Tennessee River, especially within the Great Smoky Mountains National Park. Four inches of rain fell in the

vicinity of Mt. LeConte and in the divide (that is, the valley) between Trout Branch and Alum Cave Creek within the park. This sent a wall of water sweeping down the valley of the Little Pigeon River through Gatlinburg and Pigeon Forge (Sevier County), causing considerable damage to homes, farms, motels, and other businesses.

1952	Epidemic, polio—This was Tennessee's worst polio epidemic since 1916. Of 57,626 cases reported throughout the United States, 3,300 died.
1952–53	Wildland fires—Forest and brush fires were severe statewide. This was probably the worst recorded fire season in the state's history up to that time.
1952–54	Drought—This was the third most severe drought in Tennessee history. Extremely dry conditions existed in practically every county in the state. According to one report, the longest drought and hottest weather to that date in the recorded history of Marshall and probably other Middle Tennessee counties occurred in 1954. Temperatures soared above 100°F on three separate occasions. Each period had three to eight consecutive days of high temperatures, resulting in thirty-eight known deaths.
Feb. 13, 1952	Tornadoes—Twelve people were killed and forty-eight injured when six tornadoes struck Benton, Davidson, Franklin, Giles, Grundy, Lincoln, and Moore counties. Damages were estimated at $1 million. The tornadoes in Franklin and Moore counties reached category F4 intensity.
Feb. 29, 1952	Tornadoes—Starting around 4:00 PM a family of four tornadoes caused five deaths and 316 injuries in Lincoln, Marshall, McMinn, and Warren counties. The Lincoln County tornado reached category F4 intensity. About 140 homes were destroyed, and over 300 were damaged. Economic losses were estimated at $43 million. Fayetteville was the most affected area, with over 575 structures damaged or destroyed.
Mar. 16, 1952	Highway Accident—Seven black youths died in a brutal single vehicle crash on Lebanon Road as their car skidded from the road in a deadly double-S curve. The car, headed for Nashville, was estimated to have been traveling in excess of ninety miles per hour. The crash was so violent that law enforcement officers and ambulance drivers literally picked up parts of mutilated bodies scattered throughout the accident scene. Ironically, the driver of the car was the only survivor. A local resident said that between sixty and seventy auto accidents had occurred along the same deadly stretch of highway, located about three miles from the Nashville city limits, over the past thirty years. According to the *Nashville Tennessean,* a patrolman radioed headquarters, "We'll need a couple of more ambulances out here. There's no hurry."
Mar. 21–22, 1952	**Tornadoes—Tornado Super Outbreak of 1952** (see p. 68). Thirty-one storms ravaged Tennessee and five other states. Damages were estimated at $15 million in the six-state area. In Tennessee, some of the tornadoes reached category F4 in intensity. Sixty-seven of 343 deaths and 282 of 1,400 injuries occurred in Tennessee as a result of ten separate tornadoes. In terms of number of lives lost, this was the most severe episode of tornadic activity in the state's history.
June–July 1952	Severe heat wave—During this statewide heat wave 100°F temperatures occurred for three to eight consecutive days on three occasions. Thirty-eight heat-related deaths were recorded during the period. Nashville experienced its hottest day on record, 107.3°F. During a five-day period, 160 deaths were recorded in sixteen Eastern states as temperatures hung at 100°F or above.

July 2, 1952	Structure fire—A barge burst into flames on the Tennessee River at Knoxville. This caused a massive traffic jam along area roads as drivers stopped to view the fire. It also involved every piece of firefighting equipment in the city.
May 2, 1953	Tornadoes—A swarm of tornadoes touched down in McMinn and Meigs counties around 3:00 AM, creating a total of twenty-three miles of tornado tracks before dissipating. Four people were killed and eight injured in the event. Tornadoes in both counties reached category F4 intensities.
June 15, 1953	Structure fire—A fire occurred at the Crisman Hardware Company and Valley Mills Store in the fiftieth block of Market Street in Chattanooga. Eight firemen were injured in the incident.
Feb. 1954	Wildland fire—Four youths were trapped and killed in a wildland fire on Jenkins Mountain in Carter County.
June 12, 1954	Airplane crash—Five were killed and eight injured, one seriously, in the crash of a Navy Cutlass, a twin-jet fighter plane at the Memphis Naval Air Station in Millington. The plane crashed into a small building, killing a sixth victim, who was working inside. The incident occurred just before the beginning of the 1954 Mid-South Festival, an event held to raise money for Memphis and Shelby County charities.
Aug. 9, 1954	Flooding—This may have been a record flood for South Mouse Creek, a tributary of the Tennessee River, at Cleveland (Bradley County). It resulted from an intense storm centered over the Sequatchie River Valley. Over ten inches of precipitation fell near the storm center. At Cleveland, heavy rain fell for nine hours and averaged five inches during the period. No deaths or injuries were reported, but several businesses, twenty-five homes, and much of the city's infrastructure were affected by the torrential rainfall.
Aug. 26, 1954	Labor strike—Five union members were wounded by gunfire at the Memphis Fairgrounds during a labor strike.
Oct. 2, 1954	Structure fire—An explosion occurred while gasoline was being offloaded from a barge. This ignited a fire at the ESSO Standard Oil Company Barge Plant located at 319 Wisconsin Avenue in Memphis. Ten barges, all loaded with gasoline, were eventually involved in the inferno. Several other explosions followed, and the wooden dock area was destroyed. The fire was difficult to approach from the shore, so firemen tried to fight it from a makeshift fireboat. This vessel, consisting of a high pressure truck and two pumpers, was maneuvered as close to the fire as possible. However, as a result of continuing explosions, they were unable to get close enough to be effective. As a result, the fire burned for two days. One worker was killed and several firemen were injured in the incident.
Mar. 20–21, 1955	Flooding—A severe storm caused heavy flooding in the western half of the Tennessee Valley. Rainfall amounts between 3 and 11 inches fell over a 170-mile-long by 650-mile-wide area. About 10.12 inches of precipitation was recorded at Iron City (Lawrence County) and flood levels equaled or exceeded previous ones at Lewisburg (Marshall County). This flood was the highest since 1902 on Richland Creek, the lower Elk River, and Shoal Creek. Only the floods of 1902 and 1948 exceeded the crest on the Duck River at Columbia (Maury County) and Centerville (Hickman County). The economic impact of this event, although extremely heavy, was never officially estimated.

Mar. 25, 1955	Tornadoes—Two tornadoes touched down around 5:30 PM, resulting in half a million dollars in damages but no known loss of life in Cocke, Hamblen, and Jefferson counties.
June 25, 1955	**Explosion—Texaco River Terminal Gasoline Explosion** (see p. 97). An explosion occurred on a gasoline barge, setting off other explosions and fires on adjacent fuel storage barges at the Texaco River Gasoline Storage Terminal on the Tennessee River in Chattanooga. Six people died in the incident and seven others were burned.
Aug. 22, 1955	**Highway Accident—Spring City Train–School Bus Wreck** (see p. 153). Eleven students were killed and thirty were injured when a Southern Railway freight train struck a school bus at the Main Street crossing in Spring City (Rhea County). This was the state's worst train-school bus accident and its fourth worst highway accident in terms of fatalities.
Oct. 17, 1955	Structure fire—About a third of Chattanooga's East Main Street business block was ravaged by an early morning fire. Three firemen were injured in the incident when a second-floor wall of the Bell's Garage on Main Street collapsed on them. The fire was discovered at six minutes past midnight on the day after the close of Fire Prevention Week in the city.
1956–58	**Clinton Racial Violence** (see p. 224). Racially motivated hostility erupted in Clinton (Anderson County). The National Guard had to be activated to restore order and institute federal integration mandates that local government was unable to enforce.
Apr. 3, 1956	Tornadoes—Three tornadoes caused three deaths, sixty injuries, and $1.3 million in damages in Henderson and Sumner counties. At least one of the tornadoes in Henderson County reached category F4 intensity.
Dec. 2, 1956	Structure fire—A fire at the Quaker Oaks Factory at 3324 Chelsea Avenue in Memphis erupted in the early morning hours, and firefighters arrived at 4:43 AM. It was ignited by spontaneous combustion within a 70,000 ton pile of corn cobs covering several acres of the plant area. The cobs were to be used in the manufacture of charcoal and alcohol. This was the longest lasting and most unusual fire to ever occur in Memphis, and it burned for several weeks. Firefighters pumped millions of gallons of water onto the smoldering mass before the fire was finally brought under control on Christmas Day. Damages were estimated at $420,000.
1957	Heavy precipitation—The heaviest annual rainfall ever officially recorded for the state was 114.88 inches at Haw Knob (Monroe County). The mean annual precipitation for Tennessee is about 50 inches.
1957	**Epidemic, Influenza** (see p. 18)—Of 180,164 cases of flu reported statewide, 104,524 occurred in November alone. The death rate for the period averaged about nine per 1,000 population. Called the "Asian flu," this pandemic killed around 70,000 nationwide and was twice as severe as the Hong Kong flu incident of 1968.
Jan. 22, 1957	Tornadoes—A family of four tornadoes touched down in Davidson, Coffee, Rutherford, Warren, and Wilson counties around 4:30 PM, causing $5 million in damages but no known deaths or injuries.
Jan. 30–31, 1957	Flooding—This event killed twenty-three people in Tennessee and other states.

Mar. 27, 1957   Tornadoes—Thirty-five were killed and 148 injured when a tornado touched down in Hardeman and Henderson counties.

Apr. 4, 1957   Tornadoes—Two tornadoes touched down around 1:00 AM in Henderson and McNairy counties, causing half a million dollars in damages but no known loss of life.

Nov. 18–19, 1957   Flash flood—From two to nine inches of rain fell within a two-hour period above the Piney River and Whites Creek watersheds, causing a flash flood at Spring City (Rhea County). Both the residential and business sections of the town suffered heavy damage. A dozen homes were swept away, downtown stores sustained mud and water damage, and the walls and front facades of six businesses toppled. Several stranded victims had to be rescued by National Guardsmen. The railroad bed acted as a dike, preventing even more flood damage to the western side of the town. One lady, interviewed the day after the flood, was quoted as saying, "I have heard of cloudbursts before, [but] this was the only time I ever heard a cloud burst." Another man described the rain storm as "not a toad strangler, but a duck drowner."

Feb. 26, 1958   Tornado—A tornado touched down in Hardin County, causing half a million dollars in damages but taking no lives.

Mar. 5, 1958   Flooding—Twenty businesses were flooded in downtown Jonesboro (Washington County). The water was five feet deep in some buildings, causing damages estimated in the tens of thousands of dollars. Jonesboro is the oldest city in Tennessee.

Oct. 5, 1958   Explosion—Clinton High School (Anderson County) was dynamited, presumably in reaction to federally mandated racial integration policies. This incident proved to be the last overt act of racial tension in the town (see 1956–58, Clinton Racial Violence).

Jan. 8, 1959   **Airplane crash—Tri-Cities Airplane Crash** (see p. 145). A Southeast Airlines DC-3 passenger plane crashed into a mountainside near Bristol (Sullivan County) on approach to the Tri-Cities Airport. The crash killed all ten passengers and crew on board.

Jan. 19, 1959   Structure failure—A railroad bridge collapsed while being constructed over U.S. Highway 70 at Arlington (Shelby County). No one was killed, but eleven construction workers were injured, some seriously.

Mar. 23, 1959   **Coal mine disaster—Phillips and West Mine Disaster** (see p. 128). An explosion ripped through the Phillips and West Coal Company Mine, ten miles east of Robbins, in Scott County, resulting in nine deaths.

Mar. 26, 1959   Tornado—A twister touched down in Coffee and Grundy counties around 6:10 PM, causing $500,000 in damages but no known loss of life.

Sept. 26, 1959   Tornado—A tornado touched down at 7:30 PM in Lauderdale County, causing $1 million in damages but no known loss of life.

1960–61   Epidemic, infectious hepatitis—There were 4,198 and 2,100 cases of this disease statewide during these two years respectively. Hickman, Knox, Sullivan, and Sumner counties were hardest hit.

1960–64   Labor dispute—Disputes between members of the United Mine Workers Union, the Southern Labor Union, and the consolidated and independent coal operators in Grundy and surrounding counties led to deaths, injuries, and extensive property damage as mines, buildings, and mining infrastructure were dynamited, burned, or otherwise destroyed. Violence erupted sporadically throughout this period.

Feb.–Mar. 1960 — **Severe winter—Ice Storm of 1960** (see p. 85). The most damaging ice storm in U.S. history, including a thirty-six-hour period of freezing rain, occurred in March. The accumulation of ice snapped trees, power lines, and even power poles like matchsticks. East Tennessee was particularly hard hit. This was the worst winter storm on record at that time. Winter storms in twelve states from Louisiana to New England killed several people and injured many others during the winter of 1960.

Apr. 17, 1960 — Structure fire—The largest and most damaging fire in Memphis history began in Russwood Ball Park shortly after an Easter Day major league exhibition game. Fortunately, the fire did not erupt until around 7:00 PM, after the game was over and the stadium was locked down. The park was located at 914 Madison Avenue, adjacent to the Baptist and John Gadiston hospitals. Within thirty minutes five fire companies had responded to the alarm, and soon after orders went out for every piece of equipment and every firefighter in the city to report to the scene. As the fire consumed the stadium, it also spread to dozens of surrounding buildings and even vehicles. Meanwhile, the hospitals began to evacuate hundreds of patients, visitors, and staff. The fire was so intense in the ballpark that the lobby of the multistory Baptist Hospital soon burst into flames. The fire continued to burn in the stadium and the surrounding medical center and other structures for three hours before the fire department was able to bring it under control. The stadium was a total loss and was never rebuilt. Several firefighters were injured in the incident, and the damage to the ballpark alone exceeded $1 million.

Oct. 4, 1960 — **Explosion—Tennessee Eastman Chemical Plant Explosion** (see p. 98). Fifteen people died and over 200 were injured as a result of an explosion at the Tennessee Eastman Plant, Kingsport (Sullivan County). Economic damages were estimated at $4.5 million.

Mar. 13, 1961 — Tornado—This tornado touched down in Warren County at 4:40 PM, causing $500,000 in damages but no known loss of life.

Aug. 31, 1961 — Highway-railway accident—A train collided with a truck, killing eight at Bethel Springs (McNairy County).

Dec. 25, 1961 — Structure fire—Fire broke out in the historic Maxwell House Hotel around 9:00 PM and burned for six hours, in spite of heroic efforts by the Nashville Fire Department to extinguish it. There was one fatality and a number of injuries associated with the event. Efforts to fight the fire were aggravated by icy temperatures. Construction of this historic structure began in August of 1859, and before it was completed it served for a time as a stockade for Confederate prisoners of war. (See reference to another tragedy that occurred here on September 29, 1863.)

July 3–4, 1962 — Flooding—An intense evening storm formed over a twenty-mile-long by ten-mile-wide area of the upper Tennessee River Basin. Two and a half inches of rain fell in this area in an hour and a half, causing major flooding along streams in Kingsport (Sullivan County) and Johnson City and Jonesboro (Washington County). Overall damages were estimated at $60,000.

1963	Wildland fires—About 5,000 fires burned 70,000 acres during this year. On average, they burned about 14 acres each. These events had a significant impact upon the environment as well as the economy.
Jan. 10, 1963	Tornado—A violent tornado touched down just before midnight in Maury County, causing $1 million in damages but no known loss of life.
Jan. 24, 1963	Severe winter—Arctic weather spread into the South with Nashville dropping to –15°F. At nearby Kingston Springs (Cheatham County), the temperature dropped to an all-time Middle Tennessee record of –30°F. This was just 2°F higher than the state's all-time record low at Mountain City (Washington County), which occurred on December 30, 1917. The community of Waverly (Humphreys County) also set a county record low of –26°F.
Mar. 4–19, 1963	**Flooding—Floods of 1963** (see p. 49). Three great storms struck the western slopes of the Appalachians, from Alabama to West Virginia, causing widespread flood damage along the Cumberland River and upper Tennessee River systems. Twenty-two people were killed, five of them in Tennessee, and 30,000 had to be evacuated in a fifty-county multistate area. Economic losses in the event exceeded $50 million.
Mar. 11, 1963	Tornadoes—A family of six tornadoes touched down at 9:00 PM in Cocke, Giles, Lawrence, Marion, Rutherford, Warren, and Wayne counties. Only one death was recorded (in Cocke County), but there were a number of injuries and an estimated $1.5 million in damages throughout the multicounty area.
Mar. 11, 1963	Labor strike—Kingsport Press Strike. This was a labor dispute between the Kingston Press and the local printing industry unions (e.g., International Brotherhood of Book Binders). The workers went on strike to protest the low wages paid to Kingsport employees in comparison to similar work elsewhere in the country. The company's view was that the cost of living was less in East Tennessee, and, hence, relatively speaking, their wages were not out of line with others. No one was killed during the incident, but there was widespread mob violence, mass demonstrations, use of teargas, bombings, and destruction of vehicles. There were also individual acts of violence, including rock and egg throwing and verbal and physical assaults. The economic impact of the incident is unknown.
Mar. 19, 1963	Tornadoes—Beginning at 12:40 PM a family of three tornadoes caused half a million dollars in damages in Bradley, McMinn Robertson, and Sumner counties. Fortunately, there was no known loss of life in these incidents.
Apr. 29, 1963	Tornadoes—Three people were killed and six injured when two tornadoes touched down just after 6:00 PM in Maury City (Crockett County). At least one reached category F3 intensity. Areas of Giles County were also affected, and damages were estimated at half a million dollars.
Oct. 5, 1963	Poisoning—A stock of improperly canned smoked white fish, sold at Kroger grocery stores, was found to be contaminated by type E botulism, a deadly food poisoning. Many people of the Jewish faith across the country ate and were poisoned by eating this product. Two are known to have died, and seven were hospitalized in Knoxville and three died and five were hospitalized in Nashville. Others may also have been affected.

Dec. 25, 1963	Severe winter—Lowest temperature ever recorded at Memphis, –13°F at 3:26 AM.
Feb. 1, 1964	Structure fire—One of the most memorable and largest fires in Memphis history occurred at the Nickey Brothers Lumber Company at 2700 Sumner Avenue. The thirty-seven-acre landmark plant, which once produced plywood and hardwood flooring, had been closed down for some time. Its fire sprinkler system, designed to protect the structures, had been turned off to prevent freezing, and there was no watchman on duty. Hence, the fire was well under way by the time it was noticed and reported. Between 3:00 and 3:30 PM twenty-seven fire companies and 100 fire-fighters had been dispatched to the scene. Six buildings were destroyed. However, the fact that the plant had been closed meant that economic losses were minimal. Thousands of spectators watched from a nearby railroad viaduct as determined firefighters contained the blazes before they could spread beyond the lumber company grounds. Fortunately, no one was hurt in this incident.
Mar. 4, 1964	Tornadoes—A family of three tornadoes touched down in Hardin, Shelby, Tipton, and Wayne counties, causing an estimated $5 million in damages. There was no known loss of life.
Mar. 21, 1964	Airplane crash—A Beechcraft E18S airplane crashed near Parsons Bald in the Great Smoky Mountains National Park, killing six. A seventh person on the ground died of a heart attack while responding to the incident.
Apr. 28, 1964	Flooding—An intense storm along the Tennessee River in the vicinity of Cleveland (Bradley County) produced between two and two and a half inches of precipitation in only one hour. Damages from this flood were estimated at $50,000 and occurred primarily along small branches in the commercial and industrial sections of the city. Some buildings were flooded to a depth of four feet.
July 9, 1964	**Airplane crash—Parrottsville Airplane Crash** (see p. 146). A United Airlines Viscount 745D turboprop airliner caught fire and crashed at Parrottsville, near Newport (Cocke County), at 6:15 PM. All thirty-five passengers and four crew members were killed. This was the worst airplane disaster in Tennessee history.
Dec. 25, 1964	Tornado—A tornado touched down in Davidson County, causing an estimated $1 million in damages. There was no known loss of life.
Dec. 30, 1964	Airplane crash—A Piper PA-22 airplane crashed near Pelham (Grundy County), killing five.
Mar. 21, 1965	Structure fire—A fire was reported in the Owen Graham Salvage and Sundry Store at 1332 Madison Avenue in Memphis, and the fire department responded quickly to bring it under control. Unfortunately, one fireman died at the scene and another was rendered unconscious and went into a coma from which he never recovered. He died fifteen years later in a nursing home. Both had succumbed to carbon monoxide poisoning. The fire caused little damage and was contained in the small shop in which it started. However, lessons learned from this incident brought innovative changes to the Memphis fire department, including better equipment, better training, and, for the first time, an ambulance service operated by the fire department.
Apr. 15, 1965	Tornadoes—One twister touched down at 1:15 PM at Allardt and moved northwest across Fentress County to near Jamestown. Others touched down at 4:13 and 6:30 PM, respectively, in

Cumberland, Knox, and Bradley counties, creating some sixty miles of combined tracks of destruction. Economic losses were estimated at $2 million, but miraculously only one person was killed. The death occurred in a category F3 intensity tornado in Cumberland County.

May 24, 1965   Coal mine disaster—Robbins Disaster. Five men were killed in this mine by a combination methane and coal dust explosion ignited by a single cigarette lighter. The methane seeped from crevices in the roof. The coal dust that helped propagate the explosion came from spillage along the mine's conveyor line. Had the mine been properly ventilated and the prohibition against smoking been enforced, this disaster would not have occurred.

July 24, 1965   **Flash flood—Clinchmore Flash Flood** (see p. 51). An intense rainstorm along the eastern escarpment of the Cumberland Plateau resulted in a disastrous flash flood at the mining community of Clinchmore in southern Campbell County. Five people, all members of the same family, were drowned and several others injured in this event. There was also much property damage in this community's worst-ever flood.

Sept. 20, 1965   **Structure fire—State Fairgrounds Fire** (see p. 112). A fire erupted at the State Fairgrounds in Nashville around 10:15 PM. Although hundreds of people panicked and began fleeing the area, no one was killed in the incident. In fact, only eighteen people were treated for injuries at local hospitals. Mass confusion ensued as many people running away from the fire collided with others trying to get into the area for a closer look. Damages were estimated at between $10,000 and $12,000.

1966–67   Drought—This event had significant effects on agricultural production all across the state.

Jan. 1966   Severe winter—Three people froze to death in Tennessee.

Mar. 16, 1966   Structure fire—The ten acres of Knoxville's Dean Planters Tobacco Warehouse, along with six homes on the east side of Preston Street, burned to the ground. Pushed by thirty mile per hour winds, the fire caused an estimated $1 million in damages and was fought by 200 firefighters in sixteen engine and two ladder companies. This was the largest fire, in total area burned, in the history of Knoxville.

Aug. 7, 1966   **Highway accident—National Guard Truck Wreck** (see p. 154). A five-ton National Guard truck sideswiped a passenger vehicle after losing its brakes on a rain-slick curve of U.S. Highway 11E near Chucky (Greene County). It then lunged off a twenty-foot embankment and flipped over on its top, pinning several dead and injured national guardsmen beneath. Eight were killed and twelve were injured, some seriously.

Nov. 8, 1966   Racial violence—One hundred black prisoners created chaos for about an hour inside the Shelby County Jail, breaking windows and setting mattresses and other objects on fire. The riots began about 4:00 PM and were allegedly caused by inmates complaining about their food. The fire department was brought in to extinguish fires as the riot was quelled.

Mar. 12, 1967   Tornadoes—A swarm of tornadoes with combined tracks in excess of ninety miles in length touched down around 5:30 AM in Greene County, causing one death and five injuries. At least one of the twisters was of category F2 intensity and damages were estimated at $250,000.

May 31, 1967	Tornado—This Tipton County category F1 tornado occurred around noon. It resulted in one death and at least one injury along a mile-long track. Damages were estimated at $25,000.
1968	**Pandemic, Influenza** (see p. 18)—The Hong Kong flu, a worldwide flu pandemic, was severe in Tennessee, causing tens of thousands of cases. Nationwide it killed 34,000.
Feb. 12–Apr. 16, 1968	**Labor strike—Memphis Sanitation Workers Strike** (see p. 203). This two-month strike resulted in one death, thirty-seven injuries, 329 arrests and 490 fire calls, only 49 of which were false alarms. The National Guard was activated on March 28 to curb further violence.
Apr. 3, 1968	Tornadoes—These twisters first touched down about 9:00 PM, causing a path of destruction from Millington in Shelby County to Covington in Tipton County. They resulted in four deaths, thirty-two injuries, and an estimated $2.5 million in damages.
Apr. 4, 1968	**Racial violence—Martin Luther King Assassination** (see p. 226). This event occurred at the Lorraine Motel in Memphis. It resulted in mob violence, scores of deaths, and hundreds of injuries across the state and nation.
Jan. 6, 1969	Airplane crash—A Piper PA-31 airplane crashed near Jamestown (Fentress County), killing six.
Mar. 29, 1969	Airplane crash—An Aero Commander 560-A airplane crashed just north of Crossville (Cumberland County), killing five.
June 23, 1969	**Flash flood—Red Boiling Springs Flash Flood** (see p. 53). Three people were killed by a flash flood at Red Boiling Springs (Macon County). Every business and several homes and trailers in this former health spa–mineral bath resort community was either damaged or destroyed. Forty to fifty families were left homeless. Damages to homes as well as vehicles and infrastructure were estimated at $2 million in Macon County alone.
1969–71	Drought—This statewide event caused economic hardships for many farmers and for agribusiness in general.
Apr. 24, 1970	Tornadoes—A family of three tornadoes touched down around 3:20 AM, causing an estimated $2 million in damages in Shelby County.
Apr. 27, 1970	Tornadoes—Tornadoes of category F4 intensity touched down in Robertson and Sumner counties, killing three, injuring eighty-five, and causing an estimated $5 million in damages. These tornadoes created a sixteen-mile-long, 250-yard-wide path, and a twenty-four-mile-wide, 250-yard-wide path respectively.
Feb. 21, 1971	Tornadoes—Between 110 and 120 people were killed and around 1,600 were injured in several tornadoes that touched down in Tennessee, Mississippi, Arkansas, and Louisiana. There were no deaths in Tennessee, but there were thirty-six injuries and damages exceeding $1 million. Overall, damages were estimated at somewhere between $8 million and $19 million in the four states.
Mar. 21, 1971	Tornado—This tornado touched down at 11:00 PM, killing one person and injuring eight along a mile-long path in Carroll County.
Apr. 20, 1971	Auto-train wreck—Seven people were killed as a train struck a carry-all van on U.S. Highway 11E at the entrance to the Morristown Industrial Park in Hamblen County, around 6:30 AM. The van, struck broadside, was dragged a half mile down the railroad track from the site of the impact.

Apr. 23, 1971	Wind storm—A violent storm struck the Memphis area, causing around $23 million in damages. Wind speeds exceeded hurricane force, gusting to a maximum of eighty-one miles per hour.
May 7, 1971	Tornadoes—Three deaths and 137 injuries resulted from a series of tornadoes in Benton, Carroll, Gibson, and Humphreys counties. The swarm of twisters began around 5:45 PM and caused damages in excess of $5.7 million. One of the tornadoes reached category F4 intensity.
May 24, 1971	Tornadoes—Twisters in Shelby, Madison, and Fayette counties caused no deaths, but they resulted in twenty-two injuries and caused a quarter of a million dollars' worth of damages.
Sept. 6, 1971	Severe lightning—Four men were killed by lightning in Lafayette (Macon County) while spiking tobacco on sticks and hanging it up to cure under a metal-roofed barn.
Oct. 20–23, 1971	Citywide violence—Bomb threats, fire bombings, and other random acts of violence occurred, mostly in the Johnson-Tillman area of Memphis. Entertainer Isaac Hayes, the mayor, the police chief, and other representatives of the black and white communities were involved in talks and negotiations. The issues, which revolved around alleged cases of police brutality, civil insurrection, vandalism, and personal injury, during threats of a citywide curfew, resulted in many police and fire calls, false alarms, bombings, and assaults. The incident was initiated by the death of a black teen, killed as he and two other youths tried to outrun police in a truck.
Jan. 2, 1972	Structure fire—An early-morning fire broke out in the East Gate Mall in Chattanooga. Eleven fire companies responded to the scene. Some twenty-two shops in the modern complex were damaged or destroyed. Economic losses were estimated at $2.5 million. The fire was caused by an arsonist who worked at a shoe store in the mall. He was convicted and sentenced to three to five years in prison for the crime.
Mar. 11, 1972	Structure fire—Fire destroyed the Monday Hotel Apartments in Knoxville, killing one person.
May 13, 1972	**Highway accident—U.S. Highway 11W Bus–Truck Wreck** (see p. 155). Fourteen people died and twelve were injured, twelve seriously, in a bus and truck collision on U.S. Highway 11W near Bean Station (Grainger County). This was the second worst highway accident in Tennessee history in terms of fatalities.
Aug. 7, 1972	Airplane crash—A Cessna 421 airplane crashed near Cleveland (Bradley County), killing five.
Sept. 25, 1972	Structure fire—The Southern Facilities Petroleum Terminal off Jersey Pike in Chattanooga burst into flames. The explosion occurred at 6:30 AM as the result of a large leak in one of the tanks. The fire sent nine people to the hospital. Three of the workers died from their burns. Economic losses were estimated in the millions of dollars.
Feb. 8–11, 1973	Severe winter—An ice storm paralyzed the Sunbelt states and took lives. No one was prepared for the snow, or for the ice that exacerbated the situation. Southeastern Tennessee was particularly hard hit, causing considerable damage to vegetation, utility lines, roadways, and other infrastructure. There were wide areas of extended power outages, numerous traffic accidents and personal injuries, as well as several fatalities.
Mid-Mar. 1973	Flooding—Some of the most damaging and disruptive flooding on the Tennessee River and its tributaries occurred during this period. There was little loss of life, but damages were conserva-

tively estimated at $50 million, and massive evacuations were necessary in many communities. There was also flooding along the Mississippi River in West Tennessee. After the widespread destruction wrought by the flood of 1927, Congress authorized a massive flood control project on the Mississippi River. When the floods of 1973 struck, about half of that project had been completed. Tennessee actually fared much better than other states in holding the waters of Old Man River at bay. The flooding was due, in part, to the fact that 1973 was the third wettest year ever recorded over the Tennessee River Basin. Rainfall averaged 63.11 inches. This was 11.24 inches higher than the eighty-five year (1890–1974) average mean rainfall of 51.87 inches. The 1972–75 period was also the wettest consecutive four years on record in Tennessee.

Mar. 15, 1973	Tornado—This category F2 tornado touched down at the town of Taft (White County) around 2:00 AM, causing destruction along a mile-long and 100-yard-wide path. One person was killed and at least three were injured. Economic losses were estimated at $250,000.
May 27, 1973	Dam failure—Renegade Mountain dam. A small dam on Renegade Mountain in Cumberland County failed at 2:30 PM, sending fifteen feet of water plummeting downslope into the community of Crab Orchard. Three houses were destroyed, and a section of U.S. Highway 70 was washed out. No deaths or injuries occurred.
July 27, 1973	**Highway accident—Silliman Evans Bridge Auto Wreck** (see p. 156). A 1971 Mercury crashed through a guardrail on the Silliman Evans bridge along a foggy stretch of I-65/I-24 in Nashville, plunging some ninety feet to the bank of the Cumberland River. Eight of the nine passengers in the vehicle were killed almost instantly, but a five-year-old child survived.
1974	Structure failure—Obion River bridge failure. The County Highway 229 bridge over the Obion River near the community of Lane in north Dyer County collapsed, killing two people.
Early Jan. 1974	Severe winter—The event was statewide, but Memphis and Clarksville were particularly hard hit. A number of deaths and injuries, as well as wide-scale damage resulted from this incident. Natchez Trace State Park and Forest and the West Tennessee counties of Benton, Carroll, Decatur, and Henderson were the most devastated areas in the state. Thousands of acres of pine forests, particularly within the park and forest, were severely damaged, closing roads and preventing access.
Mar.–Apr. 1974	Flooding—Heavy rainfall resulted in the most destructive floods ever on the Tennessee River and its tributaries. There was little loss of life and few injuries, but economic costs along the Tennessee, Cumberland, and Mississippi River systems were estimated at $1 billion. Some $50 million of that was in Tennessee.
Mar. 9, 1974	Highway accident—A seventeen-vehicle pileup occurred along the fog-shrouded northbound lane of I-75 just west of Calhoun (McMinn County) at the Hiwassee River bridge. This incident killed three and injured twenty, several seriously. This was the first of four major accidents to occur at this general location under similar fog conditions.
Apr. 1, 1974	Tornado—Two tornadoes struck Davidson and Wilson counties between 7 and 8:00 PM Two were killed and another twenty-two injured. The category F2 event left a path of destruction eleven miles long and 440 yards wide.

Apr. 3–4, 1974	**Tornadoes—Tornado Super Outbreak of 1974** (see p. 69). Forty-seven people were killed and over 774 injured in Bradley, Cannon, DeKalb, Fentress, Franklin, Knox, Lincoln, McMinn, Overton, Pickett, Polk, Putnam, Tipton, and Warren counties by a super outbreak of tornadoes. Some of the twisters reached category F4+ intensity. This was the highest number of tornadoes ever to touch down in Tennessee within a twenty-four-hour period. In terms of lives lost, it was the second most severe period of tornadic activity in Tennessee history. In terms of number injured, it was the worst.
May 9, 1974	Structure fire—This Knoxville City Hall fire killed a fireman when the roof of the burning structure collapsed on him.
June 7, 1974	Tornado—This category F1 tornado killed one person and injured at least one other. It touched down in Tipton County around 11:30 AM and left a three-mile-long, 100-yard-wide path of destruction. Damages were estimated at $25,000.
July 22, 1974	Structure fire—This fire, ignited by an arsonist just after midnight, destroyed three large businesses and damaged a third in the 300 block of Knoxville's Gay Street business district. Damages were estimated at $3 million. The structures were never rebuilt, which accounts for the large and prominent open space on the east side of the 300 block today.
Aug. 28, 1974	Structure fire—A violent explosion leveled half a block of the East Ninth Street district of Chattanooga around 3:00 AM. Sections of sidewalks, blocks, bricks, and timbers were blown across a four-lane road, damaging additional buildings and vehicles. Thirteen people were injured by the blast. An additional victim was found dead in the ruins nine hours later. Several buildings were destroyed or damaged in this unexplained explosion, with economic losses estimated at $300,000.
1975	Major riots occurred at the main Tennessee State Penitentiary in Nashville during this year, and lesser inmate insurrections continued through the mid-1980s. Overcrowding and other deficiencies resulted in violence and millions of dollars in damages. One inmate revolt, called the "pork chop riot," occurred at the main prison as a result of alleged deplorable living conditions. The situation was eased by the reopening of Brushy Mountain State Prison in Morgan County in 1976 and the construction of a new facility called the Lois M. DeBerry Institute for Special Needs Offenders a year later.
Feb. 24, 1975	Structure fire—This early evening apartment fire at the corner of Commerce and State in Knoxville killed one man and left 105 residents homeless.
Mar. 4, 1975	Structure fire—A fire in the Broadway Apartments at 2010 Broadway in Nashville killed four people, two from burns and two from smoke inhalation. Most of the thirty-five apartment units were destroyed in the inferno that ignited around 1:00 AM.
Mar. 11–15, 1975	Flooding—Severe floods along the Tennessee and Cumberland rivers were aggravated by freezing rain and snow. A large portion of the Opryland Theme Park in Nashville was inundated with damages estimated in the millions. A number of wild animals had to be set loose from the theme park to keep them from drowning.

Apr. 18, 1975	Tornado—This category F1 event resulted in one death, six injuries, and $2.5 million in property damage. It struck Madison County around 10:30 PM and left a seven-mile-long, 440-yard-wide path of devastation.
Apr. 24, 1975	Tornado—This category F-2 Cumberland County tornado caused one death, four injuries, and an estimated $250,000 in property damage. It touched down at 3:30 PM at Mayland and created a fifteen-mile-long path of destruction.
Apr. 25, 1975	Tornado—A Tipton County twister resulted in one death, four reported injuries, and $250,000 in property damage. It struck at 1:00 AM and created a 7.4-mile-long, 440-yard-wide path of destruction through the area. Its intensity was estimated in the category F1 range.
June 28, 1975	Structure fire—A fire broke out at the Commodore Yacht club off River Road in West Davidson County at about 2:00 PM. About $2 million in yachts and houseboats were lost in the inferno. The fire started as an engine on one of the boats burst into flames shortly after being fueled. Two people were injured and a dog was burned to death in the incident.
Sept. 6, 1975	Structure fire—A fire destroyed Knoxville's City Lumber Company and caused between half and three quarters of a million dollars in damages.
Oct. 1, 1975	Railway accident—An Amtrak passenger train derailed at Pulaski (Giles County), injuring thirty-one of the sixty-nine passengers onboard. This accident, which caused $1 million in property damage, resulted from the train hitting a defective rail at high speed.
Nov. 13, 1975	Airplane crash—A twin-engine turbojet exploded and burst into flames even before crashing into a field off Rock Town Road, in the Jefferson County community of Talbott, about five miles east of Jefferson City. The plane was reported to have crashed into the ground nose first before flipping over and killing all five people onboard. The private plane was en route from Memphis to the Tri-Cities area when the crash occurred.
Apr. 11, 1976	Airplane crash—A Cessna 210L airplane crashed north of Allardt (Fentress County), killing six.
May 23, 1976	Structure fire—Late in the evening a fire broke out and quickly spread through the Vol-State Chemical Warehouse on Hooker Road in Chattanooga. One after another, fifty-five-gallon drums of flammables began exploding and continued until firefighters were able to bring the incident under control. Damages to the building and products were estimated at $1 million.
1977	Wildland fires—About 6,700 fires burned 75,300 acres during this year. On average, they burned around eleven acres each. These events had a significant impact on the environment as well as the economy.
Feb. 2, 1977	Structure fire—A retail center and three clothing manufacturing companies were destroyed by this fire in Knoxville's Fort Sanders Industrial Area. The blaze put 1,500 people out of work, some permanently, and caused several million dollars in damages. This inferno was believed to have been caused by a small grass fire along the railroad track behind the structure. There was also some reason to believe that the grass fire was accidentally ignited by some children who had been smoking there.

Mar. 5, 1977	**Structure failure—Owl Creek Bridge Collapse** (see p. 136). The Owl Creek bridge, on State Highway 142, is located near Selmer (McNairy County). Sometime between 1:00 and 2:00 AM this bridge collapsed, allowing three cars to plummet into the stream below. Three people drowned in the incident.
Apr. 4–6, 1977	Flooding—Heavy flood damage, with economic impacts in the millions of dollars, occurred along the Clinch, Powell, and other tributaries of the Tennessee and Cumberland rivers.
Apr. 18, 1977	Structure fire—A massive explosion ripped through Chattanooga's landmark Siskin Building on the corner of Main and Market streets and then quickly spread to adjacent businesses. The Siskin Building was demolished and twenty other structures destroyed or damaged. Economic losses were estimated at over $2 million.
June 26, 1977	**Structure fire—Maury County Jail Fire** (see p. 113). A young inmate ignited a fire in the Maury County jail in Columbia, trapping and killing forty-two prisoners and visitors. The dead were not burned, but rather asphyxiated by toxic fumes from burning polyurethane mattresses that lined a padded cell.
Dec. 16, 1977	Highway accident—A fourteen vehicle pileup occurred along the fog shrouded south bound lane of I-75 just west of Calhoun (McMinn County), near the Hiwassee River bridge. The collisions, along with several fires and explosions, resulted in twenty-one injuries and sent eight to area hospitals. This was the second of four major accidents to occur at this general location under similar fog conditions.
Jan. 3, 1978	**Airplane crash—Parsons Bald Airplane Crash (#1)** (see p. 147). A Cessna 421B airplane crashed near Parsons Bald in the Great Smoky Mountains National Park, killing five.
Jan. 4, 1978	**Airplane crash—Parsons Bald Airplane Crash (#2)** (see p. 147). An Army helicopter crashed near Parsons Bald in the Great Smoky Mountains National Park, killing four, while searching for a downed Cessna 421B aircraft. (See Jan. 3, 1978.)
Feb. 24, 1978	**Explosion—Waverly Liquid Propane Gas Explosion** (see p. 99). Sixteen people were killed and ninety-seven injured in a devastating liquid propane gas railroad tank car explosion. The fatalities were primarily government officials and emergency workers. The event occurred at Waverly (Humphreys County). Damages were estimated at $1.8 million.
May 18, 1978	Airplane crash—Six people died in a fiery midair collision of two private planes just west of the Memphis International Airport. The event occurred around 12:25 PM near Winchester and Tulane. One of the planes was a Falcon Jet and the other a two-passenger Cessna 150. Debris was spread over a quarter-mile area.
May 21, 1978	Racial violence—Armed with a 30.06 caliber rifle, a deranged man fatally shot and killed four citizens and one police officer on a South Memphis Street around 2:40 PM. He also wounded four others. After what appeared to be random killings, the gunman ducked into a home on Kansas Avenue. The home was occupied by three children and their thirteen-year-old babysitter, who managed to hide from the assailant. They were all four rescued by neighbors, who were shot

at but not hit. After some 100 Memphis police officers surrounded the house and determined that all its residents except for the shooter were out of the premises, they fired teargas canisters into the structure. As the lone gunman exited the building, a volley of gunfire ended his life. The entire ordeal lasted less than thirty minutes. One neighbor stated that the gunman, who was an ex-convict and had long suffered from mental illness, did a strange little dance over one of the female victims before continuing on to the next.

June–Aug. 1978 **Labor strike—Memphis Firefighters Strike** (see p. 205). Beginning on July 1 and continuing for forty-eight hours, Memphis was ablaze as fires broke out in abandoned and condemned structures. Up to 95 percent of the fires were believed to have been intentionally set by members of the Memphis International Union of Firefighters Local 1784 or their sympathizers.

July 2, 1978 **Explosion—West Haven Home Explosion** (see p. 100). Three were killed and two injured as the result of an explosion that destroyed a private home in Knoxville's West Haven community. It was a black powder explosion triggered by a man reloading ammunition.

Nov. 5, 1978 Highway accident—Forty-one people were injured in a sixty-two vehicle chain reaction pileup along both lanes of I-75 just west of Calhoun (McMinn County), near the Hiwassee River bridge. This was the third of four such accidents to occur at this general location under similar fog conditions.

June 30, 1979 Tornado—Two deaths and one injury occurred in Jackson County when a category F1 tornado touched down at 1:30 AM in the Seven Knobs area near Freewill. The twister plowed a two-mile-long, 100-yard-wide path of destruction through the area, causing economic damages estimated at $25,000.

July 5, 1979 Explosion and fire—A Drexel Chemical Company accident, which occurred at 9:30 AM, sent over 500 people to area hospitals for treatment of minor injuries and illnesses. It also caused the evacuation of some 3,000 Memphis citizens. The area around the plant, including McKellar Lake and Nonconnah Creek, was contaminated by the incident. In fact, thousands of gallons of runoff water had to be diked and decontaminated. Had the winds not cooperated, as many as 500 people could have died and another 3,000 could have been seriously injured when a fireball from the plant explosion drifted west across the Mississippi River, rather than east over the city. The blast blew 55-gallon drums of chemicals hundreds of feet into the air. These exploded like skyrockets in the intense heat. Fire at the Pennsylvania Avenue chemical plant was ignited by the explosion of an 8,000 gallon tank of the toxic insecticide parathion. It took two and a half hours to bring the fire under control, and there was little property damage except within the plant itself.

Nov. 1, 1979 Airplane crash—A Mitsubishi MU-2F airplane crashed at Nashville, killing five.

Dec. 25, 1979 Structure fire—Five huge petroleum terminal tanks on the Jersey Pike in Chattanooga exploded into flames, killing three people on Christmas Day. The explosion and fire tore through areas along East Ninth, Main, and Market streets, damaging a large portion of Eastgate Mall and causing millions of dollars in damages.

1980	Wildland fires—Around 4,800 fires burned 60,700 acres during this year. On average, they burned about thirteen acres each. These events had a significant impact upon the environment as well as the economy.
1980–81	Drought—Statewide. This was the beginning of the drought that intensified in the mid and late 1980s.
July–Aug. 1980	**Severe heat—Severe Heat Wave of 1980** (see p. 4). One hundred and fifty-six heat-related deaths occurred in Tennessee during a thirty-three-day period when temperatures failed to drop below 100°F.
July 3, 1980	Airplane crash—A Piper PA-23 airplane crashed at Rockford (Blount County) near the Knoxville Airport, killing five.
1981	Wildland fires—About 5,500 fires burned 70,000 acres during this year. On average, they burned about thirteen acres each. These events had a significant impact on the environment as well as the economy.
June 29, 1981	Explosion—An explosion and fire destroyed the Owen Lumber and Mill Work Building on Summer Street in Memphis. Eight people were critically injured, and three eventually died. The explosion is believed to have been caused by a faulty gas line coupling.
Dec. 8, 1981	**Coal mine disaster—Whitwell Mine Disaster** (see p. 128). Thirteen were killed in a methane gas explosion inside Grundy County Mining Company's Coal Mine No. 21, at Whitwell (Marion County).
Dec. 28, 1981	Railway accident—One Louisville & Nashville freight train rear ended another, just north of New Johnsonville (Humphreys County). One person was killed, two injured, and damages amounted to almost $1 million.
1982–86	**Economic crisis—Tennessee Banking Empire Failure** (see p. 209). The corrupt financial empire of two Knoxville brothers and business partners, Jake and C. H. Butcher, came under investigation on November 1, 1982, as 180 federal banking agents converged on all the Butcher bank branches to begin simultaneous investigations. The first of the banks failed. Others soon followed, eventually leading to a total collapse and a $3 billion economic crisis for many east Tennesseans and southeast Kentuckians. This was the fourth and possibly the third worst cumulative bank failure in U.S. history.
Aug. 31, 1982	**Airplane crash—Cherokee National Forest Airplane Crash** (see p. 148). A C141B transport jet from Charleston Air Force Base crashed into the side of Johns Knob within Cherokee National Forest while on a low-level training flight. All nine crewmen were killed. The crash was so intense that it spread debris, bodies, and body parts over both sides of the mountain.
May 27, 1983	**Explosion—Benton Fireworks Factory Explosion** (see p. 100). Eleven people were killed, one seriously injured, and several buildings destroyed by explosions and fires at an illegal fireworks factory on the Webb Bait Farm near Benton (Polk County).
Aug. 6, 1983	Severe lightning—Three people were killed and ten others injured after lightning struck a maple tree under which they had gathered. This occurred at Decherd (Franklin County). The lightning discharge damaged the tree and produced a ten-foot-diameter circle of dead grass at its base.

1984–87	Wildland fires—Many woodland and brush fires occurred all across Tennessee. Many were arson-caused, and their effects were intensified by severe drought conditions.
1984–88	**Drought—Severe Drought 1984–88** (see p. 3). Economically speaking, this was the worst drought in the history of the state. It affected the entire southeastern United States. An estimated 5,000 to 10,000 died in the central and eastern United States from stress and other heat-related causes. Overall economic losses probably exceeded $40 billion.
Apr. 1, 1984	Airplane crash—Five were killed when a single-engine Piper Cherokee exploded in the air and crashed near Maynardville (Union County). The plane was said to have exploded in the air around 6:00 PM. Bodies and debris from the plane were scattered over a mile-long path. The flight had originated at Redstone Arsenal near Huntsville, Alabama, and was en route to Weyers Cave, Virginia.
Oct. 16, 1984	Tornado—This category F1 event caused one death, two injuries, and an estimated $2.5 million in property damage. The tornado touched down around 7:00 PM and cut a fifty-yard-wide, one-mile-long path of destruction through Carroll County.
Jan. 31, 1985	Severe winter—The temperature at Woodbury (Cannon County) fell to –28°F. This was the lowest temperature ever recorded in Middle Tennessee and only 4°F above the state's low temperature record of –32°F, which was reported at Mountain City (Johnson County) in 1917. Other low readings included –27°F at Allardt (Fentress County) and –25°F at both Crossville (Cumberland County) and Livingston (Overton County).
Summer 1985	A riot at the main Tennessee State Penitentiary in Nashville resulted in the death of one inmate and $11 million in damages. Lesser riots occurred at three other penal institutions. All four riots were exacerbated by overcrowding and other deficiencies and resulted in violence and millions of dollars in damages.
1986	Wildland fires—About 5,400 fires burned 60,000 acres during this year. On average, they burned about 25 acres each. These events had a significant impact on the environment as well as the economy.
1987	Wildland fires—About 5,500 fires burned 112,000 acres during this year. On average, they burned about 13 acres each. Many were believed to be the result of arson, and their effects were intensified by severe drought conditions. Like the fires the previous year, these events had a significant impact on the environment as well as the economy.
July 6, 1987	Poisoning—Eight people died of carbon monoxide poisoning at the Windcrest Apartment Complex in Memphis. The deaths were caused by the faulty venting of a furnace. The bodies were found at around 8:15 PM.
Late Dec. 1987	Flooding—Six hundred Tennessee homes were damaged or destroyed by torrential rains during the Christmas holidays. The entire state was involved, but West Tennessee was most affected, with some areas receiving in excess of fourteen inches of precipitation. A thousand people were forced to evacuate in Millington (Shelby County) and Memphis alone, as floodwaters inundated or washed away homes, bridges, roads, utility lines, and other infrastructure. The same storm system was responsible for three deaths in Williamson County and several others elsewhere.

| 1988 | Wildland fires—About 4,100 fires burned 51,000 acres during this year. On average, they burned about 13 acres each. These events had a significant impact upon the environment as well as the economy. |

Jan. 19, 1988   Tornadoes—Three severe tornadoes struck Fayette, Gibson, and Haywood counties, killing five, injuring thirty, and damaging or destroying over fifty buildings. The Fayette County tornado, which caused a majority of the deaths and injuries, reached category F2 or possibly F3 in intensity. Damages were estimated at $3 million.

Mar. 21, 1988   Structure fire—Three patients in the Oakville Health Care Center in Memphis died in a fire. It originated in one room of the facility when a patient dropped a cigarette onto his or her clothing. Eighteen other patients and staff were injured in the event.

Nov. 19, 1988   Highway accident—Thirty-one people were injured, fourteen seriously and two critcally, when a Greyhound bus swerved to avoid a car on rain-slicked I-65 in Nashville. The bus entered a drainage ditch, struck a tree, and rolled onto its left side before coming to rest. All the passengers were taken to area hospitals and ten were admitted.

Dec. 23, 1988   Highway accident—One person was killed and twenty injured in a twenty-eight-vehicle pileup on I-40, four miles west of Cookeville (Putnam County). The accident, which was fog related, occurred around 8:30 AM at mile marker 283.

Dec. 23, 1988   **Explosion—Memphis Liquid Propane Gas Tanker Truck Explosion** (see p. 101). Nine people were killed and twelve injured, two critically, as a 10,000-gallon, liquefied-propane gas tanker truck overturned and burst into flames on I-240 in Memphis. It was estimated that the fireball of the explosion was some 700 feet in diameter.

Dec. 24, 1988   Tornado—This tornado killed one, injured seven, destroyed thirty-one structures, and damaged thirty-nine others as it passed through Franklin and Brentwood in Williamson County. It also damaged several automobiles, small aircraft, and a radio station tower. Overall damages were estimated at $25 million. This tornado reached category F4 intensity.

Apr. 1, 1989   **Structure failure—Hatchie River Bridge Collapse** (see p. 136). A tractor-trailer truck and four automobiles plunged into the Hatchie River about 8:15 PM. The accident occurred when the eighty-four-foot-long section of the northbound lane of the U.S. Highway 51 bridge collapsed.

May 22, 1989   Tornado—A category F2 tornado touched down in Giles County at 7:37 PM at Minor Hill and traveled to a point three miles south-southeast of Pulaski. One was killed, two injured, and property damage was estimated at $250,000.

Dec. 24, 1989   **Structure fire—Johnson City Retirement Home Fire** (see p. 114). Sixteen people were killed, over 50 injured, and 145 elderly residents were left homeless in a Christmas Eve high-rise retirement home fire in Johnson City (Washington County).

Feb. 1990   Flooding—A number of deaths and injuries occurred and thousands of individuals were evacuated in southeast Tennessee, north Georgia, and northeast Alabama as a result of flooding along the Tennessee River and its tributaries. Copperhill (Polk County) and Chattanooga were particularly hard hit. Combined damages in the two cities were estimated at $14.3 million.

July 5, 1990	Highway accident—Four people died and fourteen were injured in a seven-vehicle pileup on Interstate 40 in Memphis. The incident took place just after 5:00 PM in the northeast section of the city at the Jackson exit near Raleigh. The accident occurred when a tractor trailer in the northbound lane swerved to avoid colliding with another car, flipped over, and crossed the median into the southbound lane. Most of the damage occurred in the southbound lane.
Dec. 1990	Flooding—Twenty-two counties were declared eligible for federal disaster assistance, and others were affected to varying degrees. Six deaths and several injuries were directly attributed to this incident, and damage estimates exceeded $4 million.
Dec. 11, 1990	**Highway accident—I-75 Multivehicle Wreck** (see p. 156). Twelve were killed and fifty-six injured in a ninety-nine-vehicle chain reaction pileup along both lanes of I-75 just after 9:00 AM. The incident took place near the Hiwassee River bridge just west of Calhoun (McMinn County). This was the state's worst highway traffic accident in terms of number of vehicles involved and property damage, but not in terms of number killed. It ranks third in terms of fatalities. It was also one of four such major multiple vehicle incidents to occur at this same general location under similar fog conditions.
Jan. 10, 1991	Flash flood—A flash flood occurred in Spring City (Rhea County) as water plummeted down Piney Creek from Grandview Mountain on the eastern escarpment of the Cumberland Plateau. It was the worst flood ever to hit Spring City, with damages estimated at $1 million.
Mar. 22, 1991	Tornado—Tornadoes struck Selmer (McNairy County) at 4:35 PM, killing four and injuring forty-five. A tornado also touched down in Lewis County at 6:05 PM, killing a baby girl and injuring fourteen other individuals. The combined storms resulted in an estimated $50 million in losses. The strongest of the tornadoes was in the category F3 range.
Aug. 17, 1991	A riot in the Shelby County Jail resulted in some $3.5 million in damages. During the eight-hour incident, 584 prisoners destroyed the fourth floor of the facility, breaking windows, vandalizing equipment, and throwing debris from the upper stories. Only two men were slightly injured. Several small fires were set and prisoners urinated on some of the guards. The situation was blamed on the overcrowding of the facility, dissatisfaction with the quality and quantity of food, and the recent firing of several guards believed to have been smuggling illegal drugs to inmates.
Nov. 22, 1992	Tornado—Forty-five tornadoes struck the Tennessee and Ohio valleys, killing 6 and injuring 144. One touched down in Hardeman County at 3:50 AM, killing 1 and injuring 3. Overall damages from this category F1 twister were estimated at $25,000.
Feb. 21, 1993	Tornadoes—Around 400 homes were damaged or destroyed and many people injured by seven tornadoes that ravaged Anderson, Blount, Cumberland, Knox, Loudon, McMinn, Monroe, Putnam, and Roane counties. Lenoir City (Loudon County) was the hardest hit area, with one death, eighty-four injuries, and 144 homes and eighteen businesses damaged or destroyed. One twister with estimated 200 mile per hour rotational winds cut a path of destruction a mile wide from a hilltop on the southwest to the intersection of U.S. highways 11 and 321. The community of Powell (Anderson County) incurred about $1.4 million in damages to homes and commercial buildings. Total damages during this storm were estimated at $5 million. One of the tornadoes was in

the category F3 range. One twister also touched down and caused some damage on the edge of the Y-12, Department of Energy National Security Complex at Oak Ridge (Anderson County).

Mar. 12–18, 1993   **Severe winter—Severe Winter of 1993** (see p. 86). The "Great Blizzard of '93" caused record-breaking snowstorm activity throughout East Tennessee. Costs statewide were estimated at $22 million. Called the "Storm of the Century" in the eastern United States, it took 270 lives and resulted in economic losses estimated at $3–6 billion.

Apr. 1, 1993   Airplane crash—Five were killed in the crash of a twin-engine Merlin Turboprop, six miles southeast of the Tri-Cities Airport. The accident occurred as the plane was making its final approach to the airport around 9:30 PM. Among the victims was NASCAR champion Alan Kulwicki.

Oct. 6, 1993   Structure fire—Around 10:30 PM fire broke out in a Wal-Mart store at 3950 Austin Peay Highway in Memphis. Forty fire companies and 200 firefighters responded to the scene. The fire was eventually contained, but not before destroying the 149,000 square-foot store. Federal, state, and local officials investigated the suspicious incident and determined it to be caused by an arsonist who was eventually apprehended and charged in the crime. Losses exceeded $12 million, making this the most expensive fire in the city's history.

Mid-Feb. 1994   **Severe winter—Severe Winter Storm of 1994** (see p. 87). The longest and costliest winter storm in the state's history closed schools, businesses, and government offices. Six fatalities and many injuries were blamed on the severe weather, which, in some places, was described as even more severe than the infamous Blizzard of 1951. Furthermore, this event occurred only a year after the Great Blizzard of 1993.

Apr. 11, 1994   Structure fire—Around 2:00 AM a fire broke out on the ninth floor of the Regis Towers apartment complex at 750 Adams Avenue in Memphis. An automatic alarm system alerted the fire department and they responded quickly to the scene. The building was familiar to them, since it was the twenty-ninth such alarm from this address in the past six months. Four people were killed in the fire, including two residents and two firefighters. Fourteen others were evacuated via raised aerial ladders. An investigation of the fire confirmed that it was caused by an arsonist who was eventually apprehended and later convicted of the crime.

Apr. 15, 1994   Tornado—A mile-wide tornado, along with severe storms, struck Bradley, Hamilton, McMinn, and Meigs counties, leaving one dead and scores injured and/or homeless. The worst damage occurred in the community of Birchwood (Hamilton County), northeast of Chattanooga. Here the tornado intensity was believed to have been in the category F3 range. A number of homes and other buildings were damaged or destroyed by the storm. Other communities affected included Athens, Englewood, and Riceville, all in McMinn County. Damages were estimated at $5 million.

June 9, 1994   Heavy rain—Nine and a half inches of rain fell in a four-hour period at Waynesboro (Wayne County). About sixteen homes were damaged, and thirty-one residents had to be evacuated. Losses were estimated at $500,000.

Nov. 27, 1994   Tornadoes—Tornadoes struck Crockett, Fayette, Shelby, Tipton, Wayne, and Weakley counties. Three were killed and twenty-five injured in Germantown (Shelby County). There was also one recorded death and some injuries in Crockett County. Twenty-eight homes were demolished and about 300 others damaged in the storm. Economic losses were estimated at $60 million. Some of these tornadoes reached category F3 intensity.

May 18, 1995   Tornadoes—Fifty-six tornadoes accompanied by severe thunderstorms struck forty-three Tennessee counties, killing three and injuring eighty-two. Twenty-six of the injuries were at the Rivergate Mall near Nashville. The three deaths and twenty-five of the injuries were in Ethridge (Lawrence County). Fifty-one structures were destroyed, and 212 buildings and nine miles of roadway were damaged by the twisters. Heavy rain and hailstones, some the size of baseballs, were reported in Anderson, Blount, Cumberland, Giles, Knox, Lawrence, Loudon, Morgan, and Roane counties of East and Middle Tennessee. The storm system moved east-northeast at forty-five to fifty miles per hour. Both the Lawrence County and Giles County tornadoes reached category F4 intensity. Many communities were affected. This severe event was caused by two primary super weather systems that tracked east across the state. Damages were estimated at $4.6 million. A canceled check from Etheridge was discovered some ninety miles away in Cannon County after the storm.

Jan. 29, 1996   Airplane crash—Five were killed when a Navy F-14A (Tom Cat) fighter jet crashed into a residential area shortly after takeoff. The incident occurred about two miles southeast of the Nashville International Airport. Two of the dead were Navy crewman, and the other three were in one of three homes demolished by the crash. The area was littered with debris from the jet up to a half mile from the point of impact. Smoke from the scene could be seen for miles.

Apr. 20, 1996   Tornadoes and severe weather—Tornadoes, straight-line winds, flash flooding, and deadly lightning caused an estimated $6 million in damages across the midstate region.

Aug. 11, 1996   Flooding—A seven- to nine-inch rainfall caused flooding and an estimated $4 million in damages along the Tennessee River and its tributaries in and around Chattanooga.

Jan. 4, 1997   Severe storms—Strong winds from a thunderstorm caused an estimated $500,000 in damages in the Rivergate Mall area of Madison (Davidson County). At Erin (Houston County) a 110-mile-per-hour straight-line wind picked up a mobile home and tossed it 100 feet, killing a man inside.

Jan. 24, 1997   Tornadoes—Thirteen tornadoes struck the midstate area, injuring thirty-one and damaging or destroying 240 structures. No one was killed in this event. About 70 percent of the damage was in Rutherford County, where a category F4 tornado touched down at Barfield near Murfreesboro. Other affected counties included Bedford, Cannon, DeKalb, Lincoln, Marshall, Putnam, Smith, and Wilson. Economic damages exceeded $9 million.

Mar. 1, 1997   Tornadoes—A category F4 tornado touched down at 7:00 PM in Dyer County, creating a fifteen-mile-long, 200-yard-wide path of destruction that ended in Gibson County. Almost 200 homes were destroyed between the communities of Chic and Churchton (Dyer County) and in a portion of Gibson County. A thirteen-year-old girl was the only fatality, but fifteen people were injured, and damages were estimated at around $2 million.

Mar. 1–2, 1997   Flooding and severe storms—Seven deaths, many injures, and considerable property damage occurred along streams in northern Middle Tennessee as a result of much higher than normal precipitation.

June 5, 1997	**Explosion—Pyro Shows Inc. Explosion** (see p. 102). An explosion at a multimedia fireworks display company, Pyro Shows Inc., in LaFollette (Campbell County), killed four and injured fourteen others around noon.
July 1, 1997	Flash flood—The Buffalo Springs and Tampico communities (Grainger County) sustained extensive flooding as a result of four to more than ten inches of rainfall in a twelve-hour period. One man died when his pickup truck was swept away by raging floodwaters.
July 4, 1997	Severe wind gusts—Straight-line winds alleged to have gusted up to 230 miles per hour were reported in sections of Hamilton County! Property and crop damages were estimated at $350,000. Wind gusts in excess of 100 miles per hour also caused extensive damage in parts of Blount County. The effects were felt in Maryville, Friendsville, and at the McGhee Tyson airport, where buildings, aircraft, and motor vehicles were involved. Utility lines were downed and other infrastructure damaged or destroyed. Economic losses in Blount County alone were estimated at around $1 million. Both storms produced up to golf ball–sized hail.
July 28, 1997	Explosion—Two construction workers were killed and fourteen other individuals injured in an 8:45 AM explosion at the I-440–Murfreesboro Road exit off Interstate 24 in Nashville. The event, believed to have been caused by construction machinery accidentally striking a detonation cord, occurred as explosive charges were being set during a ramp-widening project. Debris and the bodies of the two dead workers were scattered onto the roadway. The incident also caused a chain reaction motor vehicle pileup, injuring motorists and shattering glass in automobiles and nearby buildings. Eleven people were taken to an area hospital, and three were admitted.
Jan. 7–8, 1998	Flash flood—Seven people were killed in a flash flood. Six died in two separate vehicles while attempting to cross a flooded area, and a seventh, a rescue worker, drowned when his boat capsized during a rescue attempt. The worst of the flooding occurred along the Doe River in the communities of Roan Mountain, Hampton, and Valley Forge (Carter County). Over 200 trailers and fifteen houses were demolished. In addition, 193 other structures and businesses were damaged by the floodwaters. Losses were estimated at $20 million.
Feb. 3, 1998	Severe winter—Overall economic losses from this severe winter weather were estimated at $5 million. Traffic was stalled by snow and ice for eighteen hours along a section of I-40 on the Cumberland Plateau near Monterey (Putnam County).
Apr. 16, 1998	Tornadoes—Sixteen tornadoes killed 6 people, injured at least 123, and damaged or destroyed 1,600 homes and businesses in Middle and West Tennessee. Downtown Nashville was hard hit, with thirty-five of its structures red-tagged by local code and building inspectors. These structures required repair before they could be reoccupied. The storms that spawned the tornadoes in West and Middle Tennessee also caused flooding that killed a woman in East Tennessee. One of the tornadoes at Deerfield (Lawrence County) is now believed to have reached category F5 in intensity on the Fujita and Pearson scale. It is argued by scientists to have been the single most severe tornado (in terms of its potential for destruction) ever to occur in the state. Fortunately, it struck a rural area and resulted in no known deaths or injuries. It leveled many well-constructed buildings and wiped their foundations clean. It also debarked trees and moved a one-ton pickup

	truck over a hundred yards, all typical category F5 intensity phenomena. Economic losses from the tornadoes were estimated at $5.1 million.
Apr. 28, 1998	Tornadoes—A tornado that struck Manila, Arkansas, moved fifty miles east into Roellen (Dyer County) Tennessee, killing a man and his wife, whose bodies were flung about 200 feet from their home.
June 10, 1998	Hailstorm—A severe hailstorm occurred at Smithville (DeKalb County). Golf ball–sized hailstones damaged at least seventy cars, and the wind-driven projectiles broke windows and created holes in the siding of homes. Damages were estimated at $750,000.
July 15, 1998	Flash flood—Two were killed when their vehicles were washed downstream in a flash flood that occurred along Shoal Creek in Lawrenceburg (Laurence County). At least 30 were injured and about 200 people were temporarily evacuated from the area. Economic losses were estimated at $4 million.
Jan. 1, 1999	Tornado—A tornado killed one and injured five west of Camden and south of Faxon (Benton County).
Jan. 1, 1999	Wildland fires—Some 3,700 fires burned 45,000 acres during this year. On average, they burned about 12 acres each. These events caused both economic and environmental damage.
Jan. 17, 1999	Hailstorm and severe windstorms—Pulaski (Giles County) was pounded by some of the largest hailstones ever officially reported in Tennessee. Severe winds in Davidson and Maury counties also damaged hundreds of homes and businesses and uprooted mature trees.
Jan. 17, 1999	Tornadoes—Twisters, one as severe as a category F4, touched down in twenty-two counties of West Tennessee, with the city of Jackson (Madison County) sustaining the greatest damage. Trees and utility poles were uprooted or broken, and trailers and automobiles were tossed around like toys. The National Guard Armory, along with 500 other structures, were damaged or destroyed by the storm. Six people were killed in Jackson and three in other West Tennessee counties. Over 100 were taken to area hospitals with varying degrees of injuries, some serious and possibly resulting in additional casualties. Twelve counties were declared eligible for federal disaster assistance due to the tornadoes and accompanying straight-line winds that swept across the area at speeds exceeding 100 miles per hour. Economic losses were estimated at over $13 million.
Jan. 21–22, 1999	Tornadoes—A tornado struck a historic five-block area of Clarksville (Montgomery County) around 4:15 AM. The 121-year-old Montgomery County Courthouse and several nineteenth-century homes and churches were damaged or destroyed. There were a number of injuries in the Clarksville area, but, mercifully, no deaths. After plowing through the town, the tornado struck Austin Peay State University, damaging or destroying about half of the campus buildings. A dozen homes were demolished, and thirty-three homes and a number of businesses were heavily damaged. Economic losses were estimated at $4 million in Clarksville alone. Houston County also sustained damages, and an F3 tornado occurred in Benton County, killing one and injuring five. Many areas received hail; some hailstones were purported to be grapefruit-sized.

May 5, 1999	Tornado and severe storms—Severe thunderstorms with very high winds crossed Tennessee, killing three, injuring over fifty, and leaving many others homeless. Buildings and infrastructure were also damaged or destroyed. Thirty counties sustained damage, but it was greatest from the Cumberland Plateau east to the Appalachians. On the other hand, the worst affected area was the West Tennessee community of Linden (Perry County), where a category F4 tornado took the lives of three and caused six injuries. Nashville also incurred extreme damage from the storms.
2000	Worldwide climate change—Scientists by the turn of the twenty-first century began to speculate about the possibility of global warming, which many believe began around 1880. In the last 130 years, it is estimated that the average temperature of the planet has risen by 1.4°F. This does not sound like much, but its effects are presently being monitored by scientists around the world. On the whole, the last two decades of the twentieth century are alleged to have been the warmest in the last 400 years. The past 12 years appear to be the overall warmest since 1850. (See entry 1880s–Present.)
2000	Wildland fires—About 2,900 fires burned 84,000 acres. On average, they damaged about thirty acres each. These incidents had negative impacts on the environment as well as on the economy as a whole.
Apr. 20, 2000	Tornado—One person was killed by an F1 category tornado that touched down near Wartrace (Bedford County) at 6:14 PM. Economic damages were estimated at $30,000 along the twister's sixty-seven-yard-wide, two-mile-long path.
May 24–26, 2000	Tornadoes—Benton, Davidson, and Maury counties were affected by a number of tornadoes. A category F3 tornado also struck Houston County, causing property damages estimated at $1.3 million. There were no known fatalities as a result of these tornadoes, but three people were injured in Davidson County.
June 20, 2000	Severe storms—Severe thunderstorm winds downed utility lines and trees all across Lincoln County and killed one man in Vanntown.
June 21, 2000	Structure fire—Lightning struck the Saxony Apartments, one of the oldest apartment complexes in Cookeville (Putman County). Damages were estimated at $1 million. No one was hurt, but ten families were left homeless.
2001	Wildland fires—About 2,900 forest and brush fires ravaged 68,000 acres during this year. On average, the fires affected about twenty-five acres each. These events had a significant impact upon the environment as well as the economy.
May 31, 2001	Tornadoes—One person was killed and two injured in a category F2 tornado that struck Alburntown (Cannon County) around 8:10 PM. The man who was killed was swept from his home and carried a quarter mile before being slammed into a silo. Tornadoes also injured two in Lawrence County and caused damages in Hickman County around Bon Aqua. Economic losses were estimated at $80,000.
Oct. 24, 2001	Severe storm—Red Bank (Hamilton County) experienced an extreme thunderstorm that killed one person and injured another. Economic losses were estimated at $75,000.

Nov. 26, 2001	Tornadoes—Around 11:25 PM an F3 category tornado touched down at Paris (Henry County). It moved five miles to the northeast before dissipating near Oakland (Henry County) ten minutes later. Two were killed, a dozen injured, and economic losses were estimated at around $1.5 million. Ten buildings were destroyed and forty-six others damaged along the twister's 200-yard-wide path.
Jan. 25, 2002	Flooding—Flooding occurred in thirty-nine counties of Middle Tennessee, killing six and injuring at least eleven others. The Duck River at Columbia crested at more than thirteen feet above flood stage. Many homes and businesses were damaged by floodwaters. Losses were estimated at $2 million.
Mar. 18, 2002	Flooding—Heavy rainfall caused flooding in the midstate area, resulting in five deaths, all vehicle related.
May 17, 2002	Severe wind gusts—These straight-line winds, which gusted up to almost 100 miles per hour, caused extensive damage to structures, utility systems, and vegetation, particularly in the vicinity of the Shipps Bend (Hickman County) community. Damages were estimated at $120,000.
Oct. 10, 2002	Tornadoes—F1, F2, and F3 category tornadoes touched down in Cumberland, Coffee, and Montgomery counties, killing eight and injuring forty-two.
Nov. 9–10, 2002	**Tornadoes—Tornadoes of 2002** (see p. 71). Seventeen people died and eighty were injured when tornadoes, some as high as category F3 in intensity, struck Carroll, Coffee, Cumberland, Montgomery, and other Tennessee counties. Economic losses exceeded $100 million.
Nov. 13, 2002	**Tornadoes—Tornadoes of 2002** (see p. 71). Thirteen tornadoes touched down in sixteen Tennessee counties on the weekend of November 13. Seventeen people died and dozens were injured. Eight people were killed in the hardest-hit communities of Mossy Grove and Joyner (Morgan County).
Mar. 19, 2003	Tornado—A category F1 tornado struck Cookeville (Putnam County) causing a twelve-mile path of destruction, one fatality, one injury, and $100,000 in damages. It occurred around 11:15 AM and damaged or destroyed at least sixty-seven structures.
May, 2003	Flooding—Extreme precipitation across southeastern Tennessee and North Georgia resulted in heavy flooding along the Tennessee River and its tributaries in the vicinity of Chattanooga. Hundreds of people had to be evacuated. Damages were severe across many counties of southeast and central-east Tennessee. Economic damages were estimated at $20 million in Hamilton County alone.
May 4, 2003	**Tornadoes and severe wind gusts—Tornadoes of 2003** (see p. 72). Fifteen people were killed and one hundred injured in this category F4 tornado that touched down at 10:35 PM and plowed a path of destruction 880 yards wide and twenty-six miles long through Madison County.
May 5, 2003	Flash flood—A flash flood at Auburntown (Cannon County) killed three.
July 22, 2003	Severe storms, wind gusts, and heavy rain—One person was killed and three injured in Shelby County as a score of buildings collapsed and others were damaged by wind gusts of over 100 miles per hour. According to the *Memphis Commercial Appeal,* it was the proverbial perfect

storm: "with the frontal system, the jet stream and the high humidity, forecasters said all fuels were present for the storm to explode and produce the highest winds the city had seen in years." Power outages were extensive, affecting hundreds of thousands. Several other people were said to have died from carbon monoxide poisoning produced by improperly vented electric generators. Economic losses were estimated at $40,000.

Sept. 25, 2003	**Structure fire—Nashville Healthcare Center Fire** (see p. 115). Sixteen elderly residents died and twenty were injured in a nursing home fire. Eight women died at the scene, and another eight died later from injuries sustained in the fire. Over 100 patients, including the injured, were evacuated by firefighters and staff.
Jan. 20, 2004	Structure fire—Five people died as a result of a Maryville (Blount County) retirement home fire. Three residents were killed during or shortly after the fire, and two others later. About a dozen were injured.
May 30–31, 2004	Tornado and severe storms—A line of severe thunderstorms moved through Middle Tennessee on the evening and morning of May 30–31. Straight-line winds close to 100 mph and at least one F1-intensity tornado caused considerable damage in southeastern Bedford and southwestern Giles counties. A seven-year-old girl was killed at Minor Hill in Giles County, and economic losses were estimated at around $1 million.
May 26, 2005	Economic downfall—Seven state lawmakers and two other individuals were indicted on bribery charges, and three other county officials were subsequently charged. All were suspected of past criminal corruption or influence-peddling, which provided legal justification for a federal and state sting operation. This investigation was code named "Operation Tennessee Waltz," in honor of the famous state song. Both FBI and TBI (Tennessee Bureau of Investigation) agents launched the three-year-long undercover operation that led to the eventual arrest of all twelve individuals. All were charged with, and eventually convicted of, taking bribes from undercover agents in exchange for using their influence to support legislation in favor of a bogus corporation called E-Cycle. The bribes ranged from $2,500 to $55,000.
Nov. 6, 2005	Severe wind gusts—Straight-line winds that gusted up to 132 miles per hour caused extensive damage to an area north of Paris (Henry County). The path of the storm was about 300 yards wide and nearly nine miles long. Mobile homes, businesses, and residences, along with a church, were either destroyed or severely damaged. Other structures sustained minor damage. Many mature trees were either uprooted or snapped in two. Damages were estimated at $525,000.
Nov. 15, 2005	Tornadoes—A super outbreak consisting of nineteen tornadoes occurred in Middle Tennessee. This was the greatest number of tornadoes ever known to occur in the state on one day, with no deaths and only one injury. It occurred at Collinwood (Wayne County).
Mar. 11, 2006	Structure fire—A house fire in Evansville (Rhea County) killed nine members of a family, including six children. The fire started around 6:15 AM on the second floor of the two-story home occupied by an extended family. A nineteen-year-old man on the first floor was the only one who escaped the inferno.

Apr. 2, 2006	Tornadoes—A super outbreak of tornadoes, up to category F3 in intensity, killed over 30 and injured at least 240 in Benton, Carroll, Dyer, Fayette, Gibson, Haywood, McMinn, Sumner, Warren, and Weakley counties. Some surrounding states were also affected. Economic losses exceeded $95 million in Tennessee alone.
Apr. 7, 2006	Tornadoes—Ten people were killed and 147 injured by F1 to F3 category tornadoes in Cumberland, Davidson, Lewis, Sumner, and Warren counties. These storms occurred between 1:00 and 5:30 PM. Total economic losses were estimated at around $90 million.
Oct. 6, 2006	Structure fire—Flames destroyed the First United Methodist Church of Memphis at the corner of Second Street and Poplar Avenue and also partially destroyed three other downtown buildings. The fire erupted in the basement of the 182-year-old church sometime around 2:30 AM and quickly spread upward. Ashes and flaming embers from the inferno were quickly blown some three blocks to the west by a brisk wind, igniting the twenty-two-story Lincoln American Tower. Built in 1925, it was once the tallest building in Memphis. The fire then spread rapidly to the adjacent 121-year-old Lowenstein Building and the 109-year-old Court Annex. At the time, all three of these buildings were being renovated as part of the $45 million Court Square Center project in downtown Memphis. Three fire companies battled the blazes at both of these fire scenes. They also sprayed millions of gallons of water on vulnerable adjacent structures to prevent further spread of the conflagration. By 5:30 AM all four structures were still smoldering and smoking, but the danger had passed.
2007	Severe heat—One of the state's hottest years. By some accounts it was the second hottest year, and one of the driest on record, which had negative economic impacts on the state.
2007–2009	Economic crises—The onset of an economic recession began to occur in 2007, and by 2008 oil prices skyrocketed and the housing market took a nosedive. Businesses began to fail and jobs were lost as the stock market began a steep downturn. The federal government began bailing out large corporations, hoping to turn the economy around. At the writing of this book, the situation is too new and volatile to fully comprehend; however, there are indicators that the economy has either bottomed out or will soon do so. More federal funds are being authorized in hopes of shoring up the banking and financial system, and new jobs are being created. Fortunately, Tennessee seems to have fared better economically than many other states.
Sept. 2, 2007	Airplane crash—A single-engine Beech Bonanza aircraft crashed into Holston Mountain in Cherokee National Forest about 10:30 AM. The pilot and four passengers, all Jehovah's Witness ministers, were killed in the crash. The plane was en route to the Virginia Highlands Airport near Abingdon, Virginia, from the Elizabethton Municipal Airport in Hamblen County. Because the crash site was located in such rugged and remote terrain, it took rescuers several hours to reach it.
Feb. 5–6, 2008	**Tornadoes—Tornadoes of 2008** (see p. 75). Tornadoes, along with severe storms, straight-line winds, and flooding occurred. Thirty-three people were killed and dozens injured in twisters within Hardin, Hickman, Macon, Madison, Shelby, Stewart, Sumner, and Trousdale counties in Tennessee and Monroe County in Kentucky. Some of the tornadoes were of category F4 intensity. Economic losses were estimated at $73.2 million.

Dec. 22, 2008	**Structure failure—Kingston Coal Ash Reservoir Failure** (see p. 137). Approximately 5.4 million cubic yards of potentially toxic coal fly ash slurry spilled out of its eighty-four-acre detention pond at the Tennessee Valley Authority steam plant in Harriman (Roane County). It was one of the worst overall environmental disasters in U.S. history. The economic costs of this disaster were estimated to exceed $1 billion.
May 1–3, 2010	**Flooding—Floods of May 1–3, 2010** (see p. 54). Heavy precipitation over a forty-eight-hour period resulted in some of the worst flooding between Memphis and Nashville since the great floods of 1936–37. Twenty-four people died along the Cumberland River in both Tennessee and Kentucky, and economic losses were estimated in excess of $2 billion.
April 25–28, 2011	Tornadoes—One of the most violent and devastating tornadic episodes in U.S. history occurred during this period. Called the "2011 Super Outbreak," it affected many southern, northeastern, and midwestern states, resulting in as many as 350 deaths and thousands of injuries. Thirty-eight of the deaths and over 300 of the injuries occurred in two dozen Tennessee counties. Economic costs exceed $160 million. At least three of the forty-five Tennessee twisters were in the F4 and F3 intensity ranges. These storms produced heavy rainfall, extreme flooding, deadly lightning, and damaging hail. Some hailstones reached golf-ball size and caused extensive damage to vehicles, buildings, infrastructure, and vegetation. In terms of loss of life, it was only the seventh worst such incident in the state's history, but in terms of economic losses, it was number three.
April–May 2011	**Flooding—Floods of April–May 2011** (see p. 57). The Mississippi River floods of 2011 devastated portions of the state's western tier of counties, including the city of Memphis. Because the slow-rise flooding was still occurring as this book was in production, its full impact had not yet been ascertained. However, all indications were that it would become one of Tennessee's most catastrophic flood disasters since the Mississippi, Tennessee, and Cumberland rivers overflowed their banks in 1926–27, 1936–37, and 1973. This major late-spring deluge was the result of excessive snow melt in the upper Mississippi and Ohio river valleys and much higher than normal precipitation in the southern states.

Glossary

accident. An unintentional event that may result in bodily injury, death, and destruction of property and/or deliver environmental impacts.

acute disease. A disease characterized by relatively short duration, usually severe. Death may result suddenly as opposed to that from a chronic disease.

afterdamp. A mixture of mostly carbon monoxide, carbolic acid, nitrogen, and other toxic gases caused by a methane fire or coal dust explosion within a mine or other enclosed area. It has killed many coal miners who might otherwise have survived a mine explosion and flash fire. (Also called *blackdamp* and *choke damp*.)

aftershock. A quake, usually of lesser magnitude, that occurs after a major earthquake or one in a series of quakes within a given area. (Also see *foreshock*.)

agricultural drought. A period of crop failure or damage including widespread wildland fires as the result of prolonged drought.

backdraft. A situation that is initiated when a fire is starved of oxygen. Combustion ceases, but the fuel gases and smoke remain at high temperature. When oxygen is reintroduced to the fire (e.g., the door or window of a closed room is opened), combustion can erupt explosively as the gases reheat, expand, and ignite. (Also see *flashover*.)

barricading. A barrier erected inside a mine to prevent the inflow of toxic gases from a fire or explosion.

Beaufort wind scale. Devised by British Admiral Sir Francis Beaufort to assist sailors in handling ships, the scale ranges from 0 to 17 and indicates wind speeds for straight-line winds (as opposed to tornadoes). It is also applicable to winds on land. (See table 9 in appendix.)

blackdamp. See *afterdamp*. Also referred to as *lamp damp* and *choke damp*.

black vomit. A term used to describe the vomitus of yellow fever patients (and a symptom of that disease). It is said to have the look and consistency of coffee grounds.

BLEVE. A boiling liquid expanding vapor explosion (the acronym rhymes with "heavy"). An example is an explosion from an entire tank of flammable gas being ignited instantaneously.

blizzard. A very heavy snowstorm with high winds. A violent snowstorm with winds exceeding thirty-five miles per hour and with visibility of less than one-quarter of a mile for a minimum of three hours.

blown-out shot. When too much blasting agent is introduced into a shot-hole (a hole drilled into coal or hard rock to blast it loose), or if it is not properly tamped, the shot may blow outward (hence a blown-out shot). This action ignites any coal dust or flammable gas in the mine, causing an instantaneous secondary and more intense explosion.

brattice. A fire-resistant fabric or plastic partition or conduit used in mines to confine and force fresh air into the areas of a mine being worked.

breach. A failure of a solid structure such as a dam or levee. A dam break. A gap, tear, rupture, or rift in a structure causing it to weaken or fail.

built environment. Buildings, roads, or infrastructure and lifelines (e.g., electrical or communications wiring, or water, natural gas, and sewer pipes) constructed by humans and subject to damage or destruction during disasters.

casualty. One who is killed or injured in an accident or a disaster.

choke damp. See *afterdamp*.

cholera. An acute bacterial infection of the intestines contracted from water or food that has been contaminated by the feces of persons previously infected. It is characterized by severe diarrhea and vomiting, muscular cramps, and dehydration. Sometimes called Asiatic cholera.

chronic disease. A disease persisting over a long period of time as compared to the course of acute diseases. A chronic disease may result in partial or complete disability and eventual death.

coal dust. Very fine particles of coal that can become suspended in the atmosphere of a mine. Technically, they are small enough to pass through a No. 20 sieve.

coal famine. A term often used in the early days to describe a shortage of coal. It may have been the result of increased demand, insufficient quantities, adverse weather conditions (such as heavy snow or floods), labor strikes, or lack of labor that slowed or stopped the extraction or transportation of the resource.

cold plague. See *malaria*.

conflagration. A large and destructive fire, especially involving multiple structures in a city, town, community, business, or industrial area.

creeping disaster. A condition of insidious onset and slow progress, such as drought or a slowly developing epidemic, that may not be recognized or manifest until the danger has reached extensive proportions. (Also called a *slow disaster*.)

cross entry. A passage running at an angle to the main portal or passage of a mine.

deluge. A heavy downpour of rain, or a great flood, especially an overwhelming event. (Also see *freshet*.)

disaster. An incident that has killed or injured a number of individuals or caused extensive property damage. May produce fatalities but no property damage, as in the case of an epidemic, or may cause catastrophic property damage but few if any fatalities, as in the case of some floods. Disasters may be classified as natural (i.e., severe weather events), technological (i.e., human caused), or societal (i.e., riots, strikes, or lynchings). (Also see *emergency.*)

Dixie alley. An area of tornadic activity in the southern United States where late fall and early winter tornadoes can be prevalent. (Also see *tornado alley.*)

downburst. A phenomenon created by a column of rapidly sinking air that, after striking the ground, spreads out in all directions often producing destructive straight-line winds. (Also see *straight-line winds, wind shear,* and *microburst.*)

drought. A long period of deficit precipitation, especially one that adversely affects growing or living conditions. Also spelled *drouth.* (Also see *agricultural drought, hydrologic drought,* and *meteorologic drought.*)

dust devil. A strong, well-formed upward vortex or whirlwind resembling a small tornado in size and action. It generally forms under hot and sunny conditions and can cause minor injuries to people and damage to property, but rarely to the extent of a full-blown tornado. (Also see *waterspout.*)

earthquake. A sudden movement of the earth's crust caused by the release of stress accumulated along geologic faults or by volcanic activity. Also called a *quake* or *temblor.*

earthquake intensity. See *Modified Mercalli Intensity scale.*

earthquake magnitude. See *Richter scale.*

emergency. A serious situation that arises suddenly, and unexpectedly, threatening life or property. It is a crisis that demands immediate attention but can generally be dealt with by local authorities (e.g., police or fire department, rescue squad, or an ambulance service) as opposed to a more intense situation such as a disaster. (See *disaster.*)

epicenter. The point on the surface of the earth directly above the focus (origin) of an earthquake.

epidemic. An outbreak of a contagious disease that spreads very rapidly and widely. Examples of epidemics are smallpox, cholera, influenza, and yellow fever. (See *pandemic.*)

fatal injury. An injury that results in the death of an individual. Death may be instantaneous or may occur later (technically up to years later) as a result of the injury.

fatality. A death resulting from a disaster or accident or someone killed in such an incident.

Federal Emergency Management Agency (FEMA). A federal agency responsible for coordinating the response to disasters that overwhelm the capabilities or resources of local or state governments. They are also involved in disaster mitigation and coordinate the efforts of other federal agencies in times of crisis.

fire damp. A combustible gas called methane (CH) produced in some coal mines. A highly combustible mixture of methane (i.e., between 5 and 15 percent), other hydrocarbon gases, and air. (See *methane.*)

fireball. A brilliant, burning sphere of fire. A hot and luminous spherical cloud of gas, vapor, or a fire generated from an explosion. (See also *BLEVE.*)

firestorm. An extremely destructive conflagration or well-fueled wildland fire that can create and sustain its own wind system. Such fires are difficult to contain or extinguish.

flash flood. A sudden flood or rapid inundation of water as a result of heavy precipitation or the breaching of a dam or levee.

flashover. A nearly simultaneous ignition of combustible gases and solids within an enclosed area.

flood stage. An established gauge height for a given location on a given stream above which a rise in the water can create a hazard to lives, property, and commerce. It varies from stream to stream and within sections of streams.

focus. The point of origin of an earthquake beneath the earth's surface along a fault. (See *epicenter.*)

forecast. An estimate or prediction of the future occurrence of an event or conditions (e.g., weather, earthquakes, or floods.)

foreshock. A (usually) smaller tremor that precedes a larger earthquake in the same way that an aftershock follows one. (Also see *aftershock.*)

freshet. A once common term for a flood or sudden overflow of a stream as a result of heavy rainfall or thaw. (Also see *tide.*)

Fujita-Pearson (FPP) tornado scale. A numeric scale (from F0 to F5) that describes or ranks tornadoes based on the amount of damage or destruction they cause. Similar to the Saffir-Simpson scale of hurricane intensity. The FPP scale was developed and further modified by T. Theodore Fujita and Dr. Allen Pearson in the early 1970s. F0 causes slight damage and F5 causes incredible damage (e.g., strong frame houses lifted from their foundations and carried away, leaving few if any remnants behind, tree debarked, etc.). Some scientists suggest that an F6 tornado is theoretically possible. (See table 7 in the appendix.)

hazard. The potential for an accident. The chance of being injured or killed during an incident. A danger, peril, risk, or threat.

heat wave. A period of abnormally high temperatures, lasting for several days to several weeks. The intensity of the temperature of a heat wave is area dependent since some areas experience much higher temperatures than others. High humidity adds to the effects of high temperatures. Heat waves may also be associated with drought.

hydrologic drought. A period of water supply shortage within a region. (See *drought.*)

ice tide. See *tide.*

influenza. A highly contagious and infectious disease of the respiratory track that is contracted by breathing airborne droplets from the sneezes or coughs of other victims, or by touching surfaces on which the droplets have landed and then transferring them to one's nose or mouth. This disease is characterized by cough, fever, sore throat, muscular pains, and general weakness. Also called *flu, grip, grippe, la grippe,* and *Spanish influenza.* Two strains of influenza of present concern are H1N1 and H5N1.

infrastructure. Major lifelines including electrical and communications wires and cables, as well as water, natural gas, and sewer pipelines. Also includes roads, tunnels, bridges, viaducts, utility poles, communications towers, and rail lines.

insurrection. An open revolt against civil law or authority or a government. A rebellion. (Also see *riot, lynching, feud,* and *strike.*)

Ku Klux Klan (KKK). This is a secret society that was organized in the South after the Civil War to reassert white supremacy rule by means of terrorism. Some say the name is derived from the sound made by the cocking of a gun, with the word "klan" signifying a group. Other scholars attribute the name to the Greek word *kuklos,* meaning a circle or cycle. The latter is now considered the more feasible explanation. Some organized groups of very violent individuals engaged in hate crimes are still active today. Their hostilities have often extended beyond African Americans to Jews, Catholics, and other ethnic or minority groups, whom they consider inferior and not privy to the same rights and privileges as other white Americans.

Kukluxism. Generic term for acts of racial violence, hate crimes, or terrorism committed by KKK-type organizations. (See *Ku Klux Klan.*)

liquefied petroleum gas (LPG). An extremely flammable and explosive gas under pressure.

liquefaction. A phenomenon that may occur during an earthquake where there is a decrease of shearing resistance in soil materials, especially those saturated with water along streams and in swampy areas. This causes the soils to become quick, as in quicksand, allowing structures to settle, tip, or even collapse during an earthquake.

magnitude. The overall size, effect, or extent of a disaster. A measure of earthquake intensity expressed as the amount of energy released by elastic waves. (Also see *seismic* and *Richter scale.*)

malaria. An infectious disease characterized by recurring chills and fever. It is caused by a parasite (i.e., plasmodium) transmitted by the bite of an infected anopheles mosquito. Also called *marsh fever.*

meteorologic drought. A long period of precipitation deficiency over a region. (Also see table 1 in the appendix and *drought*).

methane. A colorless, odorless, volatile gas that often bleeds out of coal veins and enters the atmosphere of mines. It is highly flammable and has been the cause of (or has contributed to) many mine explosions. Also called *swamp gas* when it bubbles up from decaying organic matter from the bottom of a body of water. (See *fire damp.*)

miasma. Poisonous vapors or noxious atmosphere once thought to rise from swamps and putrid matter to cause diseases such as malaria.

microburst. A localized column of rapidly sinking air that can produce a damaging divergent and straight-line wind as opposed to the swirling effects of a tornado. (Also see *downburst, wind shear,* and *straight-line wind.*)

Modified Mercalli Intensity (MMI) scale. A scale of earthquake intensity as designated in Roman numerals from I to XII. This scale is descriptive of things that happen to people, buildings, and other structures during earthquakes, as opposed to the Richter scale, which describes the amount of energy released by an earthquake. Under this scale, I–III are earthquakes that are unfelt except under very favorable circumstances or recorded on seismographs. A reading of XII refers to total destruction of a landscape and everything on it. (Also see *Richter scale* and tables 2–4 in the appendix.)

morbidity. The rate at which an illness occurs. It is calculated by dividing the number of people in a group by the number in that group affected with the illness.

mortality. The death rate or number of deaths per unit of population in a specific region, age range, disease, or some other classification. It is usually expressed per 1,000, 10,000, or 100,000.

National Oceanic and Atmospheric Administration (NOAA). An agency of the U.S. Department of Commerce that collects, analyzes, and provides scientific data on the oceans, coasts, and atmosphere worldwide. Also see *National Weather Service.*)

National Transportation Safety Board (NTSB). An independent federal agency responsible for investigating the probable cause of airline, highway, marine, railroad, and pipeline accidents and hazardous materials incidents that are transportation related.

National Weather Service (NWS). One of several agencies of the National Oceanic and Atmospheric Administration responsible for providing weather, hydrologic, and climate information and advisories.

Night Riders. Hooded or masked groups of individuals who engage in tactics similar to the KKK to achieve vigilante justice. (Also see *Ku Klux Klan.*)

Palmer Drought Severity Index (PDSI). A meteorological drought index that measures weather conditions that have been abnormally dry or abnormally wet. It provides measurements of moisture conditions standardized so that comparisons can be made between locations and over periods of time. (Also see table 1 in the appendix.)

pandemic. A severe epidemic that covers a very broad geographic area. It may cover a state, a country, or even the entire globe, as in the case of the influenza pandemic of 1918–19. (See *epidemic.*)

peak ground acceleration (PGA). The rate of earthquake acceleration on the ground. Unlike the Richter scale, it is not a measure of the total size of an earthquake but rather how much the earth shakes within a given geographic area.

pest house. An old term for a hospital or quarantine area where patients with infectious diseases were housed or incarcerated. It usually provided food, water, and some manner of care. It is short for "pestilence house."

plague. An acute, highly infectious, and often fatal epidemic disease such as bubonic plague, cholera, smallpox, influenza, or yellow fever. The word is frequently used as a generic term for any epidemic or pandemic disease.

post-traumatic stress disorder (PTSD). Severe emotional stress caused by an anxiety disorder, characterized by some acute emotional response. Such a condition may result from exposure to a natural or technological disaster, from combat, or from physical or psychological torture. Also referred to as *post-traumatic stress syndrome, combat fatigue,* or *shell shock.*

Richter scale. A logarithmic scale of Arabic numbers from 1 to 10 used to express the total amount of energy released by an earthquake, as registered on an instrument called a seismograph. Each number on this scale indicates an earthquake magnitude about thirty times greater than the number below it. Under such a scale, an earthquake with a Richter reading of 8 would be almost a thousand (30 x 30) times greater than a 6 magnitude quake. Named for American seismologist Charles Francis Richter. (Also see *Modified Mercalli Intensity scale* and tables 2–4 in the appendix.)

risk. The danger, threat, or probability of loss. The possibility of suffering, harm, loss, injury, or death from a potential hazard. The mathematical or subjective probability that an incident will occur. (Also see *vulnerability*.)

sand blow. A sand blow forms as earthquake forces liquefy deep sands and violently push them to the earth's surface. Many were formed in West Tennessee during the great earthquakes of 1811 and 1812.

sawyer. An American navigational term for a large uprooted tree or log that has drifted down a stream and become stuck in the riverbed, where the current causes it to move up and down in a sawlike motion. Boats sometimes collided with such *snags* (as they were also called), damaging or penetrating their hulls or sinking them.

seismic. A term relating to an earthquake or earthquake vibrations.

seismic risk zone. Areas of earthquake potential on the surface of the earth ranging from low, or little risk (0), to very high, or extreme risk (3). (See map in the section on earthquakes.)

seismograph. An instrument used for detecting and recording the intensity, duration, and location of earthquakes.

seismologist. A scientist who studies earthquakes.

slow-rise flood. A prolonged or extended period of flooding or the swelling of a stream or reservoir over its banks and onto normally dry land.

smallpox. An acute, deadly, and highly contagious viral disease sometimes referred to as *variola*. It is characterized by high fever, body aches, and subsequent widespread eruption of blisters, or pustules, that erupt and cause scarring pockmarks. The causative agent is one of two viruses, *Variola major* or *Variola minor*.

snag. A rough, sharp, or jagged object such as a tree, limb, or log that protrudes above, or just below the surface, of a stream or other body of water. It may cause damage to or sink boats. Also called a *sawyer*.

straight-line winds. Very strong winds caused by a downburst of rapidly sinking air as it hits the ground and spreads out, producing damage similar to that of a tornado but without the rotational effects. Sometimes referred to as "thundergusts." (Also see *downburst, wind shear, microburst,* and table 9 in the appendix.)

structure failure. The collapse or destruction of a physical structure, such as a dam, storage reservoir, bridge, trestle, stairway, or building, as the result of factors other than fires or explosions. Also infrastructure failure (see *infrastructure*). The failure of structures as the result of fires and explosions is covered under those topics.

structure fire. A fire involving buildings, infrastructure, chemicals, or other build environments as opposed to wildland fires. See *fire*.

super-outbreak. A number of tornados occurring around the same time and in the same general area or over a wide region of a county, state, or nation. Also called a *family* or *swarm* of tornadoes. Such outbreaks occurred in Tennessee in 1952 and 1974.

technological emergency. Unplanned and unexpected occurrences, accidents, or failures of industrial systems or mechanisms resulting in potential or actual death or injury of humans or damage to property or the environment.

Tennessee Emergency Management Agency (TEMA). The state equivalent of FEMA, responsible for coordinating all state emergency response activities and resources. (See *Federal Emergency Management Agency.*)

Tennessee Valley Authority (TVA). A quasi-government-owned corporation established by Congress during the Great Depression to provide flood control, navigation, hydroelectric power, fertilizer, and economic development to the basin of the Tennessee River and its tributaries.

tide. As used in this book, a sudden flood or rise of water or ice on a stream, such as a spring tide or spring flood. Ice tides are heavy and destructive drifts of ice along streams. (Also see *freshet.*)

tipple. A section of elevated railroad track where mine cars are tipped to dump their load of raw ore for sizing, sorting, and washing before being processed onsite or transported to another furnace.

tornado alley. The area of spring and early summer tornadic activity primarily in the Great Plains of the United States but also extending eastward and northward in some seasons. (See *Dixie alley.*)

trauma. A physical injury caused by a violent or disruptive action or by the introduction of a toxic substance into the body. A psychic injury resulting from a severe emotional shock.

typhoid fever. A bacterial infection transmitted by contaminated water, milk, or other food. It is usually characterized by headache, high fever, delirium, cough, watery diarrhea, and a rash. Also called *bilious fever* and *swamp sickness.* The causative agent is the bacterium *Salmonella typhi.*

urban-wildland interface. The area or zone in which woodlands or grasslands and built environments overlap or intersect, where greenbelts extend into towns and cities, and where both are subject to hazards associated with each other (e.g., wildland fires in cities and structure fires in forests or wildland environments).

United States Army Corps of Engineers (USACE). A federal military agency composed of both civilian and military personnel responsible for the design, construction, and maintenance of dams, canals, flood protection, and other miscellaneous civil engineering projects.

WARNING, severe weather. A bulletin broadcasted by the National Weather Service advising that a severe storm or tornado is occurring or has been spotted in an area or is indicated by radar. Such advisories are given for specific areas for specific periods of time.

WATCH, severe weather. A bulletin broadcasted by the National Weather Service advising that conditions are favorable for the development of a severe storm or tornadoes in specific areas during a specific period of time.

waterspout. An intense vortex of air, often funnel-shaped like a small tornado that occurs over a body of water. It is connected to a cumulus (rain) cloud and sucks water upward. (Also see *dust devil.*)

white caps. Hooded or masked groups of individuals who engage in tactics similar to the KKK to achieve vigilante justice or terrorism. (Also see *Ku Klux Klan.*)

wildland fires. Woodland and grassland fires as opposed to those affecting populated areas and structures. (Also see *fire.*)

wind shear. A sudden down draft or a change in wind direction and speed between different altitudes. Also called *straight-line winds, downbursts,* and *microbursts.*

yellow fever. An acute viral infection transmitted by the *Aedes aegypti* mosquito. It is characterized by severe headaches, fever, jaundice, vomiting, and bleeding. A dark-colored vomit (black vomit), resulting from hemorrhaging in the digestive track, is characteristic of the disease. The causative agent is the yellow fever virus of the *Flaviviridae* family. Also called *strangers fever, yellow jack, yellow jacket, saffron scourge,* and *plague.*